Puerto Rico

9th Edition

by John Marino

787-888-7378
Antojitos
Puertorriqueños
Can 968 #160
Bo. Las Coles
Rio Grande,
PR
00745

Here's what the critics say about Frommer's:

"Amazingly easy to use. Very portable, very complete."

—*Booklist*

"Detailed, accurate, and easy-to-read information for all price ranges."
—*Glamour Magazine*

"Hotel information is close to encyclopedic."
—*Des Moines Sunday Register*

"Frommer's Guides have a way of giving you a real feel for a place."
—*Knight Ridder Newspapers*

WILEY

Wiley Publishing, Inc.

About the Author

John Marino is editor of the *The San Juan Star* and has written about Puerto Rico and the Caribbean for Reuters, *The Washington Post*, *The New York Times*, *Gourmet*, and other publications. He lives in San Juan, Puerto Rico with his wife Jova and son Juan Antonio, who both provided valuable research and insight for this book.

Published by:

Wiley Publishing, Inc.

111 River St.
Hoboken, NJ 07030-5774

ISBN 978-0-470-25711-1

Editor: Stephen Bassman
Production Editor: M. Faunette Johnston
Cartographer: Anton Crane
Photo Editor: Richard Fox
Production by Wiley Indianapolis Composition Services

Front cover photo: Colorful housing and doorways in Old San Juan
Back cover photo: Coastline of Cerromar Beach

For information on our other products and services or to obtain technical support, please contact our Customer Care Department within the U.S. at 800/762-2974, outside the U.S. at 317/572-3993 or fax 317/572-4002.

Wiley also publishes its books in a variety of electronic formats. Some content that appears in print may not be available in electronic formats.

Manufactured in the United States of America

5   4   3   2   1

Contents

What's New in Puerto Rico   1

1   The Best of Puerto Rico   3

1 The Best Beaches 4
2 The Best Hotel Beaches 6
3 The Best Scuba Diving 7
4 The Best Snorkeling 8
5 The Best Golf & Tennis 9
6 The Best Hikes 10
7 The Best Natural Wonders 11

8 The Best Family Resorts 12
9 The Best Honeymoon Resorts 12
10 The Best Big Resort Hotels 13
11 The Best Moderately Priced Hotels . . .14
12 The Best Attractions 15
13 The Best Restaurants 16
14 The Best Offbeat Travel
Experiences 18

2   Puerto Rico in Depth   20

1 Puerto Rico Today 20
2 History 101 22
   *Ponce de León: Man of Myth
   & Legend* 23
3 The Lay of the Land: Beaches,
Mountains, the Rainforest,
Off-Island Islands & More 34

4 The Population & Popular Culture . . .37
5 *Comida Criolla:* Puerto
Rican Cuisine 39
   Strange Fruit 41
6 Recommended Reading 44

3   Planning Your Trip to Puerto Rico   45

1 Visitor Information 45
2 Entry Requirements & Customs 45
3 Money 47
   What Things Cost in Puerto Rico 48
4 When to Go 49
   Puerto Rico Calendar of Events 51
5 The Active Vacation Planner 54
   *Take Me Out to the Beisbol
   Game* 57

6 Travel Insurance 62
7 Health & Safety 63
8 Specialized Travel Resources 65
9 Getting There & Getting Around 67
10 Package Deals & Group Tours 70
   *Great Discounts through the
   LeLoLai VIP Program* 71
11 For the Cruise-Ship Traveler 72
12 Tips on Accommodations 74

4 Suggested Puerto Rico Itineraries   78

1 The Regions in Brief 78   **4** Puerto Rico for Families 91
2 Puerto Rico in 1 Week 83   **5** Driving Tour: La Ruta Panorámica
3 Puerto Rico in 2 Weeks 88   in 2 Days .93

5 Getting to Know San Juan   96

1 Orientation 96   *Art on Wheels: Painted Taxis* 103
Neighborhoods in Brief 100   *Fast Facts: San Juan* 105
2 Getting Around 102

6 Where to Stay in San Juan   108

1 Old San Juan 109   **4** Miramar .121
Room with a Local's View: **5** Santurce & Ocean Park 122
Apartment Rentals 113   **6** Isla Verde 124
2 Puerta de Tierra 114   *Family-Friendly*
3 Condado .116   *Accommodations* 127

7 Where to Dine in San Juan   130

1 Best Bets .131   **6** Santurce & Ocean Park 149
2 Old San Juan 133   **7** Near Ocean Park 152
An Authentic Criolla Restaurant . . .138   **8** Isla Verde 152
3 Puerta de Tierra 142   *Two Family-Friendly Restaurants* . . .154
4 Condado .144   **9** Near Isla Verde 157
5 Miramar .148

8 Exploring San Juan   158

1 Seeing the Sights 158   **3** Shopping 179
The Best Places to See Puerto   *Grotesque Masks* 182
Rican Art .168   *Shopping for Santos* 185
The Cathedral of Rum 171   **4** San Juan After Dark 188
2 Diving, Fishing, Tennis &   *The Birth of the Piña Colada* 191
Other Outdoor Pursuits 172   *Barhopping* 194
La Criolla Chic 176

9 Near San Juan   197

1 El Yunque 198   **3** Dorado 205
2 Luquillo Beach 201   *World-Class Golf at the Former*
Hyatt Dorado 207

4 Arecibo & Camuy 209

5 Karst Country 211

6 Central Mountains 212

*Life After Death: Taíno Burial
& Ceremonial Sites* 213

10 Ponce & the Southwest   216

1 Ponce 216

Walking Tour: Ponce 221

2 The Southwest Coast 229

Puerto Rico's Secret Beaches 234

3 San Germán 239

4 Coamo 241

5 The Southern Mountains 242

11 Mayagüez & the Northwest   245

1 Mayagüez 245

*Mona Island: The Galápagos
of Puerto Rico* 251

2 Rincón 252

3 Aguadilla & the Northwest 260

4 The Western Mountains 264

12 Eastern Puerto Rico   267

1 Fajardo 267

*To the Lighthouse: Exploring
Las Cabezas de San Juan
Nature Reserve* 268

*Top Caribbean Spa: The Golden
Door* 272

2 Palmas del Mar 273

3 The Southeast 276

13 Vieques & Culebra   278

1 Vieques .278

2 Culebra 291

Appendix: Fast Facts, Toll-Free Numbers & Websites   296

1 Fast Facts: Puerto Rico 296

2 Toll-Free Numbers & Websites 299

Index   303

General Index 303

Accommodations Index 310

Restaurant Index 311

List of Maps

Puerto Rico   80

Suggested Puerto Rico Itineraries   86

San Juan Orientation   98

Old San Juan Accommodations &
   Dining   111

Puerta de Tierra, Miramar, Condado
   & Ocean Park Accommodations
   & Dining   115

Isla Verde Accommodations &
   Dining   125

Old San Juan Attractions   159

San Juan Attractions   162

Attractions Near San Juan   199

Walking Tour: Ponce   222

Mayagüez   247

Western Puerto Rico & the
   Northwest Coast   253

Eastern Puerto Rico   269

Vieques & Culebra   279

An Invitation to the Reader

In researching this book, we discovered many wonderful places—hotels, restaurants, shops, and more. We're sure you'll find others. Please tell us about them, so we can share the information with your fellow travelers in upcoming editions. If you were disappointed with a recommendation, we'd love to know that, too. Please write to:

Frommer's Puerto Rico, 9th Edition
Wiley Publishing, Inc. • 111 River St. • Hoboken, NJ 07030-5774

An Additional Note

Please be advised that travel information is subject to change at any time—and this is especially true of prices. We therefore suggest that you write or call ahead for confirmation when making your travel plans. The authors, editors, and publisher cannot be held responsible for the experiences of readers while traveling. Your safety is important to us, however, so we encourage you to stay alert and be aware of your surroundings. Keep a close eye on cameras, purses, and wallets, all favorite targets of thieves and pickpockets.

Other Great Guides for Your Trip:

Frommer's Caribbean

Frommer's Caribbean Ports of Call

Caribbean For Dummies

Frommer's Cruises & Ports of Call

The Unofficial Guide to Cruises

Cruise Vacations For Dummies

Frommer's Star Ratings, Icons & Abbreviations

Every hotel, restaurant, and attraction listing in this guide has been ranked for quality, value, service, amenities, and special features using a **star-rating system.** In country, state, and regional guides, we also rate towns and regions to help you narrow down your choices and budget your time accordingly. Hotels and restaurants are rated on a scale of zero (recommended) to three stars (exceptional). Attractions, shopping, nightlife, towns, and regions are rated according to the following scale: zero stars (recommended), one star (highly recommended), two stars (very highly recommended), and three stars (must-see).

In addition to the star-rating system, we also use **seven feature icons** that point you to the great deals, in-the-know advice, and unique experiences that separate travelers from tourists. Throughout the book, look for:

Finds	Special finds—those places only insiders know about
Fun Fact	Fun facts—details that make travelers more informed and their trips more fun
Kids	Best bets for kids and advice for the whole family
Moments	Special moments—those experiences that memories are made of
Overrated	Places or experiences not worth your time or money
Tips	Insider tips—great ways to save time and money
Value	Great values—where to get the best deals

The following **abbreviations** are used for credit cards:

AE	American Express	DISC	Discover	V	Visa
DC	Diners Club	MC	MasterCard		

Frommers.com

Now that you have this guidebook to help you plan a great trip, visit our website at **www.frommers.com** for additional travel information on more than 4,000 destinations. We update features regularly to give you instant access to the most current trip-planning information available. At Frommers.com, you'll find scoops on the best airfares, lodging rates, and car rental bargains. You can even book your travel online through our reliable travel booking partners. Other popular features include:

- Online updates of our most popular guidebooks
- Vacation sweepstakes and contest giveaways
- Newsletters highlighting the hottest travel trends
- Podcasts, interactive maps, and up-to-the-minute events listings
- Opinionated blog entries by Arthur Frommer himself
- Online travel message boards with featured travel discussions

What's New in Puerto Rico

In Puerto Rico, change is as constant as the trade winds. Even beaches come and go. Here are some of the latest developments.

WHERE TO STAY IN SAN JUAN At the heart of the Condado's redevelopment revival lies **Hotel La Concha: A Renaissance Resort** (© 977/524-7778 or 787/721-7500), which reopened in December 2007 on the 50th anniversary of its inauguration. A landmark of the island's Tropical Modernism movement, this hotel was saved from the wrecking ball by island architects and former governor Sila María Calderón. The building, by famed island architects Osvaldo Toro and Miguel Ferrer, with the seashell restaurant by Mario Savatori, has been beautifully restored and updated by architect José Marchand and interior designer Jorge Rosselló. Today, the lobby and pool areas combine a number of distinct locales in a world that is equal parts natural tropics and urban urbane. Everywhere one looks is water, from spraying fountains to serene infinity pools.

The property is adjacent to the Windows to the Sea oceanfront park and new luxury buildings, with designer boutiques, trendy restaurants and luxury residences as top tenants. Condado's main road, Avenida Ashford, is now lined with dining options and interesting shops from one end to the other, as well as spas, watersports outfitters and other services of interest.

WHERE TO DINE IN SAN JUAN You might think the view is the best thing at **Budatai** (© 787/725-6919), but that's only until you try the food. Roberto Trevino, who battled Mario Batali on TV's Iron Chef program, offers a phenomenal menu here and brings his Latino-Asian musings to new heights—literally. The second-floor space overlooks the oceanfront park adjacent to La Concha, and the terrace provides a palm-fringed view of the ocean. The people-watching is also spectacular, at the restaurant's bar or lounge.

A different temple to another superstar chef is **Delirio** (© 787/722-0444), the latest hit by the godfather of Nuevo Latino cuisine, Alfredo Ayala. The new digs are a slightly gothic renovation of a century-old Caribbean manor, a proper home to Ayala's experimentation with island culinary tradition (often delightfully combined with classic European culinary traditions). Check for occasional cooking classes with Ayala and other special events.

In the swanky **Ritz-Carlton San Juan Spa & Casino,** the most succulent steaks are being served at **BLT Steak 787** (© 787/253-1700), in deluxe surroundings. This is French chef Laurent Tourondel's take on the American steakhouse. His steaks are hailed as the Caribbean's finest.

Sadly, one of our favorite restaurants, **Zabó** (at Calle Candina 14), has closed. The place blended bucolic charm with the superb innovative food of Paul Carroll, who built it from a simple deli into one of the most sought-after restaurants in Condado. Look for what Carroll is now up to, and who or what is now occupying these charming premises (enter via the alleyway leading from Av. Ashford between aves. Washington and Cervantes).

SAN JUAN AFTER DARK A number of forces have converged to make San Juan the undisputed champion of nightlife in the Caribbean. The new **José Miguel Agrelot Puerto Rico Coliseum** (© 877/265-4736) gets the top world tours (Rolling Stones, Elton John, the Police, and so on), and it's a must-stop for Latin artists from Shakira to Maná. Meanwhile, the new **Puerto Rico Convention Center** (© 800/214-0420) hosts fabulous annual events like **CIRCO,** an international art fair, and the annual **Puerto Rico Tourism Company New Year's Eve,** which offers free entrance and the best in Latin musical talent. The event is broadcast live on Spanish language television across the states and Latin America.

The big new halls add to San Juan's existing entertainment options. For years, other city venues like the **Tito Puente Amphitheater,** a few art galleries, clubs, stadiums and gymnasiums have hosted first-class acts, from reggae to jazz bands, in more intimate settings. The annual **Puerto Rican Heineken Jazz Fest** is probably the genre's best annual showcase.

The new venues have also worked to put neighborhoods like **Miramar, Santurce,** and **Hato Rey** on the nightlife map, competing with well-worn tourist routes in Old San Juan, Condado, Ocean Park, and Isla Verde—so have new ventures like the recently opened **Fine Arts Cinema Café** (Popular Center, Hato Rey; © 787/765-2339), our favorite movie house ever, with plush seats, gourmet meals and snacks, and beer, wine, fruit drinks, and lattes.

The improved transportation provided by the **Tren Urbano** light rail system, and its special feeder bus lines, which conveniently stay open late for big shows and other events, has also brought more nighttime traffic to these New San Juan areas. Even if you have no particular place to go, taking a ride on the Urban Train is a fun experience that gives an interesting view of the city during the day or night, from the futuristic Hato Rey financial district to the wonderful backyards of the city's gilded suburbs.

WHERE TO STAY IN RIO GRANDE The **Sol Melia** property, a 582-room gem, ditched its all-inclusive concept and reopened as the **Gran Melia Puerto Rico** (© 866/436-3542 or 787/809-1770), with an emphasis on its luxurious first-rate spa, golf and watersports offerings (all squished in between the rainforest and gorgeous coastline).

The nearby Coco Beach golf course and country club was taken over by none other than The Donald himself, and renamed the **Trump International Golf Club Puerto Rico** (© 787/657-2000). Donald Trump announced a $600-million investment with a local partner to construct luxury vacation villas and make other improvements in 2008–9.

Meanwhile, a new Saint Regis resort of beachfront villas sprawling across the coast is being developed for a planned winter 2009 opening at the **Bahia Beach Plantation Resort and Golf Club** (© 787/857-5800). The golf course was renovated by Robert Trent Jones, Jr., with a breathtaking new design that was inaugurated in April 2008.

WHERE TO STAY ON VIEQUES It seemed like yesterday that the **Martineau Bay Resort & Spa** opened up on Vieques, its first "real" resort, just before the Navy pullout in 2003, but it's already closed for renovations. The 156-room property is getting a multi-million dollar makeover to reopen as a **W Resort & Spa** (a **Starwood** flagship property) for the 2009 tourism season.

The Best of Puerto Rico

It's only the size of Connecticut, but Puerto Rico pulsates with more life than any other island in the Caribbean. Whether it's the beat of *bomba y plena,* salsa, or reggaeton, there's a party going on here 24/7.

The 4 million people who live here have perfected the art of having fun on their dazzling island, and visitors are free to join right in. Puerto Ricans love their island and take pride in showing off its charms, which makes them among the world's great hosts. Especially on weekends, there seems to be something going on just about everywhere—whether it's an art fair in Old San Juan, a pig roast in the rural mountain area outside town, or a volleyball competition or free concert on the beach in Isla Verde. More so than on any other island, visitors are more likely to rub elbows with locals in Puerto Rico because so many of them are out enjoying themselves. For island hotels and restaurants, local residents are an important and loyal part of their clientele.

There's a reason that Puerto Rico has blossomed as a tourist destination ever since Fidel Castro scared the gringos out of Havana in the early 1960s. The island is blessed with towering mountains, rainforests, white sandy beaches along Caribbean shores, and a vibrant culture forged from a mix of Caribbean, Hispanic, African, and U.S. influences. History buffs will get more ancient buildings and monuments here than anywhere else in the Caribbean, many of them dating back some 500 years to the Spanish conquistadors. Add some of the best golf and tennis in the West Indies, posh beach resorts, tranquil and offbeat (though not luxurious) government paradores (country inns or guesthouses), and lots of Las Vegas–type gambling, glitter, and extravagant shows, and you've got a formidable attraction.

Good service, notoriously lacking in Puerto Rico for so many years, is actually on the rise. Gruff (or sometimes simply completely lacking) service has not been entirely eradicated, but frankly we find the majority of hotel and restaurant employees we encounter absolutely delightful these days.

Some visitors might be put off by the fact that Puerto Rico is one crowded island. Although there are country and coastal retreats where you can escape the masses, parts of San Juan are simply overcrowded, making for clogged roadways.

Tourists are generally safe, and a crime in a tourist district is rare. But homeless drug addicts and mentally ill beggars are a common sight in San Juan. There are also unfortunate problems with littering and treatment of animals—but great strides in these areas are being made. Most of Puerto Rico's crime and social problems remain largely invisible to tourists.

A clue to the Puerto Rican soul is reflected in the national anthem, "La Borinqueña." Forget the *machismo* of most national anthems, which sing of military muscle and battlefield triumphs. "La Borinqueña" evokes a gentle, maternal image of the island. It sings of "a flowering garden of exquisite magic . . . the daughter of the sea and the sun." Get to know this garden and the people who call it home.

1 The Best Beaches

White sandy beaches put Puerto Rico and its offshore islands on tourist maps in the first place. Many other Caribbean destinations have only jagged coral outcroppings or black volcanic-sand beaches that get very hot in the noonday sun. The best beaches are labeled on the "Puerto Rico" map on p. 80.

- **Best for Singles (Straight & Gay):** Sandwiched between the Condado and Isla Verde along San Juan's coast, **Ocean Park** beach attracts more adults and less of the family trade. The wide beach, lined with palm and sea grape trees, fronts a residential neighborhood of beautiful homes, free of the high-rise condos that line other San Juan beaches. A favorite for swimming, paddle tennis, and kite surfing, the beach is also a favorite spot for young and beautiful *sanjuaneros* to congregate, especially on weekends. Knowledgeable tourists also seek out Ocean Park, which has several guesthouses catering to young urban professionals from the East Coast, both gay and straight. So there is something of a South Beach–Río vibe here, with more than a fair share of well-stuffed bikinis and other beach outfits, but decidedly more low-key and Caribbean. It's a good spot for tourists and locals to mix. There are a few beachfront bar-restaurants housed in the guesthouses, good for a snack or lunch or cold drink. See "Diving, Fishing, Tennis & Other Outdoor Pursuits," in chapter 8.

- **Best Beach for Families: Luquillo Beach,** 30 miles (48km) east of San Juan, attracts both local families, mainly from San Juan, and visitors from Condado and Isla Verde beaches in San Juan. Beach buffs heading for Luquillo know they will get better sands and clearer waters there than in San Juan. The vast sandy beach opens onto a crescent-shaped bay edged by a coconut grove. Coral reefs protect the crystal-clear lagoon from the often rough Atlantic waters that can buffet the northern coast, making Luquillo a good place for young children to swim. Much photographed because of its white sands, Luquillo also has tent sites and other facilities, including picnic areas with changing rooms, lockers, and showers. See "Luquillo Beach" in chapter 9.

- **Best for Swimming: Pine Grove Beach,** which stretches between the Ritz-Carlton and the Marriott Courtyard at the end of Isla Verde near the airport, is a crescent, white-sand beach, whose tranquil, rich blue waters are protected by an offshore reef from the often rough Atlantic current. By the Ritz-Carlton and the Casa Cuba social club to the west, the water is completely sheltered, and a long sandbar means shallow water stretches way off shore. There's more of a surf to the east, which is a popular spot for surfing, boogie boarding, and body surfing. The waves are well formed but never too big, which makes it a perfect spot to learn to surf. Local surfers give lessons and rent boards from this beach, which is also a favorite for small sail boats and catamarans. There are no public facilities here, but it's a short walk to restaurants in the Isla Verde district. Both hotels on the beach have restaurants, bars and restroom facilities. The beach also connects to the **Carolina Public Beach,** which has lockers, outdoor showers and restrooms, and is immediately adjacent to the east. If you are driving here, parking at the public beach may be your best bet. It's right off Route 187 on the road to Piñones. Otherwise, enter the beach near the Ritz-Carlton or Marriott Courtyard hotel. Outside San Juan, the best beaches for swimming are probably Guánica's **Playa Santa** and **Caña Gorda** beaches in southwest Puerto Rico. The water is extremely warm and absolutely calm year round, and both spots boast wide, white-sand beaches with vistas of nothing but Caribbean Sea and hilly coastline.

- **Best for Scenery:** In the southwestern corner of Puerto Rico, **Boquerón Beach** and its neighboring area brings to mind a tropical Cape Cod. The beach town of Boquerón itself, filled with colorful scenery, stands along the coast just beside the beach running along a 3-mile (4.8km) bay, with palm-fringed white sand curving away on both sides. The water is always tranquil, making it perfect for families and swimming. There's fine snorkeling, sailing and fishing as well. The beach here is also one of the Puerto Rico's state-run public beaches, with lifeguards, lockers, bathrooms, showers, a cafeteria and sundries shop, and picnic tables and barbecue pits. The village is a ramshackle collection of open-air establishments along the coast selling seafood and drinks. Fresh oysters are shucked on the spot and doused with Tabasco. Try the fried fritters filled with freshly caught fish or Caribbean lobster. There are plenty of interesting photo ops at this beach and its adjacent town. See "The Southwest Coast" in chapter 10.

- **Best for Surfing:** The winter surf along Puerto Rico's northwest coast is the best in the region. Generally regarded as one of the best surf spots across the globe, it draws surfers from

around the world. **Rincón** is the center of the island surf scene, but it extends to neighboring **Isabela** and **Aguadilla.** Dubbed the "Caribbean Pipeline," winter waves here can approach 20 feet (6.1m) in height, equaling the force of the surf on Oahu's north shore. Rincón became a renowned surfing destination when it hosted the 1968 world surfing championships. Famed surfing beaches in town include **Puntas, Domes, Tres Palmas,** and **Steps.** In Aguadilla, surfers head to **Gas Chambers, Crash Boat,** or **Wilderness,** while in **Isabela** preferred spots include **Jobos** and **Middles.** The best time to surf is from November through April, but summer storms can also kick up the surf. In the summer season, however, when the waves diminish, these northwest beaches double as perfect spots for windsurfing and snorkeling, with calm waters filled with coral reefs and marine life. See "Rincón" in chapter 11.

- **Best for Windsurfing:** Puerto Rico is filled with places for windsurfing and, increasingly, kite surfing. San Juan itself is a windsurfer's haven, and you'll see them off the coast from **Pine Grove** beach near the airport all the way west to where **Ocean Park** runs into **Condado** at **Parque del Indio. Punta Las Marías,** in between Ocean Park and **Isla Verde,** is a center of activity. The **Condado Lagoon,** just behind the oceanfront strip of hotels, is also popular for windsurfing. (It's increasingly popular with kayakers too.) The northwest, from **Rincón** to **Isabela,** is another center for windsurfing, with strong winds throughout the year.

- **Best Beaches for Being Alone:** Puerto Rico is filled with isolated sandy coves and virgin white beaches accessible only by dirt roads that only the locals seem to know about. The best, all guaranteed to delight the escapist in you, stretch between Cabo Rojo (the southwesterly tip of Puerto Rico) all the way east to Ponce. **Guánica** has several, including **Las Paldas** and **La Jungla,** which are empty except during holiday weekends. In Fajardo, a 2-mile (3.2km) hike from the **Seven Seas Public Beach** will reward you with the breathtaking **El Convento Beach,** along the miles-long undeveloped coastline stretching between Fajardo and Luquillo. Besides the governor's official beach house, a rustic wooden cottage, there is nothing but white-sand beach and pristine aquamarine waters. The area is a nesting site for endangered sea turtles, and there is excellent snorkeling just offshore, where the water is rife with unspoiled coral reefs and marine life. Environmentalists hope to turn the area into a nature reserve, but two hotel projects are also planned for the area. The government has indicated it wants to develop small-scale, low impact tourism for the area. **Vieques** and **Culebra,** the **Spanish Virgin Islands,** also have their fair share of uncrowded, out of the way beaches. Because access to many of these is limited because of poor roads, it is necessary to bring supplies, including fresh drinking water. See the box, "Puerto Rico's Secret Beaches," in chapter 10.

- **Best for Snorkeling:** On the main island, the best spot for snorkeling is probably Fajardo's **El Convento Beach** (mentioned above). The southwest, from **Guánica** through **Boquerón,** also has excellent snorkeling with plenty of reefs and marine life right offshore. In the summer, once the big surf quiets down, several beaches in the northwest, from **Rincón** to **Isabela,** also boast good snorkeling. **Steps** is one of our favorite spots. The islands of **Vieques** and **Culebra** also have great snorkeling. On Vieques, try **Media Luna, Navio, Red,** and **Blue** beaches on the eastern side, and in the west, **Green Beach.**

- Culebra's most popular beach, **Flamenco** is picture perfect and has very good snorkeling, but a 20-minute hike from its parking leads to the **Playa Tamarindo** and **Playa Carlos Rosario,** beaches enveloped by a barrier reef. A quarter mile (.4km) to the south is a place called **"The Wall,"** which has 40-foot (12m) drop-offs, rainbow-hued fish, and other delights.

2 The Best Hotel Beaches

- **El San Juan Hotel & Casino** (San Juan; ✆ **787/791-1000**): This posh resort occupies the choicest beachfront real estate in San Juan at the heart of Isla Verde, a fat golden beach lined by luxury hotels and condominiums on one side and aquamarine waters on the other, evoking South Miami. The lush, multi-level pool area and outdoor restaurants form an oasis of cool right off the beach, which pulsates with beautiful crowds and activity every day of the week. You can do it all, from parasailing to taking a catamaran trip, but sunbathing and splashing in the surf are the main attractions here. The hotel has a full array of watersports and other activities and is home to some of the city's best restaurants and nightclubs. See p. 124.

- **Copamarina Beach Resort** (Caña Gorda; ✆ **787/821-0505**) lies west of Ponce, Puerto Rico's second-largest city, in the coastal town of Guánica. A laid-back retreat, the resort is located off a breathtaking country road that winds over a mountainside and back down toward the mangrove-lined coast. It sits on one of the prettiest and least crowded beaches in southwestern Puerto Rico, beside the Gúanica Dry Forest nature reserve and bird sanctuary. See p. 231.

- **The Ritz-Carlton San Juan Spa & Casino** (Isla Verde; © 787/ 253-1700): This elegant sandstone and azure blue resort blends effortlessly into its setting on one of San Juan's most pristine beaches at the secluded eastern end of Isla Verde. Majestic stone-lion fountains and towering rows of royal palm trees run through its pool area. A large gate opens to the white-sand beach, whose tranquil aquamarine waters are sheltered by a large coral reef offshore. See p. 126.

3 The Best Scuba Diving

With the continental shelf surrounding it on three sides, Puerto Rico has an abundance of coral reefs, caves, sea walls, and trenches for divers of all experience levels to explore. See "The Active Vacation Planner" in chapter 3.

- **Metropolitan San Juan:** This easy **beach dive off the Condado district** in San Juan is not as spectacular as other dives mentioned here, but it's certainly more convenient. Lava reefs sculptured with caverns, tunnels, and overhangs provide hiding areas for schools of snapper, grunts, and copper sweepers. In the active breeding grounds of the inner and outer reefs, divers of all levels can mingle with an impressive array of small tropical fish—French angels, jacks, bluehead wrasse, butterfly fish, sergeant majors, and more—along with sea horses, arrow crabs, coral shrimp, octopuses, batfish, and flying gunards. Visibility is about 10 to 20 feet (3–6m). The Condado reef is also ideal for resort courses, certification courses, and night dives. See "Diving, Fishing, Tennis & Other Outdoor Pursuits" in chapter 8.
- **Mona Island:** Mona Island, 40 miles (64km) west of the city of Mayagüez in western Puerto Rico, is the Caribbean version of the Galápagos

Islands. Renowned for its pirate tales, cave-pocked cliffs, 3-foot-long (.9m) iguanas, and other natural wonders, its waters are among the cleanest in Puerto Rico, with horizontal visibility at times exceeding 200 feet (61m). More than 270 species of fish have been found in Mona waters, including more than 60 reef-dwelling species. Larger marine animals, such as sea turtles, whales, dolphins, and marlins, visit the region during migrations. Various types of coral reefs, underwater caverns, drop-offs, and deep vertical walls ring the island. The most accessible reef dives are along the southern and western shores. There are a number of outfits operating trips from the west coast of Puerto Rico. The boat ride now takes about three hours through the often rough Mona Passage. See the box, "Mona Island: The Galápagos of Puerto Rico," in chapter 11.

- **Southern Puerto Rico:** The continental shelf drops off precipitously several miles off the southern coast, producing a dramatic wall 20 miles (32km) long and teeming with marine life. Compared favorably to the wall in the Cayman Islands, this Puerto Rican version has become the Caribbean's newest world-class dive destination. Paralleling the coast from the seaside village of La Parguera to the city of Ponce, the wall descends in slopes and sheer drops from 60 to 120 feet (18–37m) before disappearing into 1,500 feet (457m) of sea. Scored with valleys and deep trenches, it is cloaked in immense gardens of staghorn and elkhorn coral, deep-water gorgonians, and other exquisite coral formations. Visibility can exceed 100 feet (30m). There are more than 50 dive sites around Parguera alone. See "The Southwest Coast" in chapter 10.

- **Fajardo:** This coastal town in eastern Puerto Rico offers divers the opportunity to explore reefs, caverns, miniwalls, and channels near a string of palm-tufted islets. The reefs are decked in an array of corals ranging from delicate gorgonians to immense coral heads. Visibility usually exceeds 50 feet (15m). Divers can hand-feed many of the reef fish that inhabit the corals. Sand channels and a unique double-barrier reef surround Palomino Island, where bandtailed puffers

and parrotfish harems are frequently sighted. Cayo Diablo, farther to the east, provides a treasure box of corals and marine animals, from green moray eels and barracudas to octopuses and occasional manatees. See "Fajardo" in chapter 12.

- **Humacao Region:** South of Fajardo are some 24 dive sites in a 5-mile (8km) radius off the shore. Overhangs, caves, and tunnels perch in 60 feet (18m) of water along mile-long (1.6km) Basslet Reef, where dolphins visit in spring. The Cracks, a jigsaw of caves, alleyways, and boulders, hosts an abundance of goby-cleaning stations and a number of lobsters. With visibility often exceeding 100 feet (30m), the Reserve offers a clear look at corals. At the Drift, divers float along with nurse sharks and angelfish into a valley of swim-throughs and ledges. For the experienced diver, Red Hog is the newest site in the area, with a panoramic wall that drops from 80 to 1,160 feet (24–354m). See "Palmas del Mar" in chapter 12.

4 The Best Snorkeling

Puerto Rico offers top-notch snorkeling even though freshwater run-offs from tropical outbursts feeding into the sea can momentarily cloud the ocean's waters. In most places, when conditions are right, visibility extends from 50 to 75 feet (15–23m).

One of the best ways to experience this wonderful sport, even if you are staying in San Juan, is to take one of the day trips on one of the several luxury catamarans plying the waters off the coast of Fajardo, which make for some of the finest snorkeling in the Caribbean. They usually anchor on beach of a small cay for lunch and some sunbathing and swimming. Transportation from San Juan area hotels

is often provided. It's worth the trip even if you don't want to snorkel. There are a number of reputable operators (see "Watersports" in chapter 12).

- **Mona Island:** This remote island off the west coast of Puerto Rico (see "The Best Scuba Diving," above) also offers the best snorkeling possibilities. The reefs here, the most pristine in Puerto Rico, are home to a wide variety of rainbow-hued fish, turtles, octopuses, moray eels, rays, puffers, and clownfish: the single largest concentration of reef fish life in Puerto Rico. You must bring your snorkeling equipment to the island, however, as there are no rentals available once you are here. See the box, "Mona Island: The Galápagos of Puerto Rico," in chapter 11.

- **Caja de Muertos:** The best snorkeling off the coast of Ponce is on the uninhabited coast island of Caja de Muertos ("Coffin Island"). This isla got its name from an 18th-century French writer who noted that the island's shape resembled a cadaver in a coffin. Over the years there have been fanciful legends about the island, including tales of necrophilia, star-crossed lovers, and, of course, piracy. Several outfits will take you to this remote spot for a full day's outing, with plenty of snorkeling. See "Ponce" in chapter 10.

- **La Paguera:** The reefs surrounding the offshore cays just off La Paguera in southwest Puerto Rico are another fine spot for snorkeling. Several boat operators right in town will either rent you a boat with a guide or drop you off on one of the islands and return at a pre-arranged timed. See chapter 10.

- **Fajardo:** On the eastern coast of Puerto Rico, the clear waters along the beachfront are the best on mainland Puerto Rico for snorkeling. The best beaches here for snorkeling are walking distance from the Seven Seas public beach: **Playa Escondido** and **Playa Convento.** The snorkeling at Las Cabezas de San Juan nature refuge is also spectacular. See "The Best Beaches," earlier in this chapter and "Fajardo" in chapter 12.

- **Vieques & Culebra:** For a quick preview of the underwater possibilities, refer to "The Best Beaches," earlier in this chapter. For more information, see chapter 13.

5 The Best Golf & Tennis

- **Río Mar Beach Resort & Spa: A Wyndham Grand Resort** (Río Grande; ✆ **787/888-6000**): Two world-class golf courses are located here in the shadow of El Yunque rainforest along a dazzling stretch of coast. The entire 6,782 yards (6,201m) of Tom and George Fazio's Ocean Course has seaside panoramas and breezes, and fat iguanas scampering through the lush grounds. The other course, a 6,945-yard (6,351m) design by golf pro Greg Norman, follows the flow of the Mameyes River through mountain and coastal vistas. The resort is a 30-minute drive from San Juan on the northeast coast. Wind is often a challenge here. See p. 203.

- **Dorado Beach Resort & Club** (Dorado; ✆ **787/796-8961** or 787/626-1006): With 72 holes, Dorado has the highest concentration of golf on the island. The legendary Dorado Beach and Cerromar hotels run by Hyatt are now gone, but the four courses and other facilities—spectacular tennis courts, pools, and beaches—live on, and resort villa rentals are available. Of the courses, Dorado East is our favorite. Designed by Robert Trent Jones, Sr., it was the site of the Senior PGA Tournament of Champions throughout the 1990s. True tennis buffs head here, too. The Dorado courts are the best on the island.

- **El Conquistador Resort and Golden Door Spa** (Fajardo; ✆ **787/863-1000**): This sprawling resort on Puerto Rico's northeast corner is one of the island's finest tennis retreats, with seven Har-Tru courts and a pro on hand to offer guidance and advice. If you don't have a partner, the hotel will find one for you. There are also outstanding golf facilities as well. See p. 269.

- **Palmas del Mar Country Club** (Humacao; ☎ 787/285-2221): Lying on the east coast on the grounds of a former coconut plantation, the Palmas del Mar resort boasts the second-leading course in Puerto Rico—a par-72, 6,803-yard (6,221m) layout designed by Gary Player. Some crack golfers consider holes 11 through 15 the toughest five successive holes in the Caribbean. There's also an 18-hole championship-caliber course designed by Rees Jones. The Palmas del Mar Tennis Club meanwhile boasts the largest facilities in the Caribbean, and it has recently begun to host large-prize pro tournaments. See p. 272.

- **Trump International Golf Club** (Río Grande; ☎ 787/657-2000): Located on 1,200 acres (486 hectares) of glistening waterfront, this recently improved 36-hole golf course designed by Tom Kite allows you to play in the mountains, along the ocean, among the palms and in between the lakes. Its bunkers are carved from white silica sand. Real estate magnate Donald Trump announced plans in conjunction with local developer Empresas Díaz, Inc. to develop 500 luxury residences here. The first phase, announced in March 2008, consists of 56 villas, with starting prices of $1.4 million, which have access to private jet, yacht, and limousine service. See p. 202.

6 The Best Hikes

Take a hike. Puerto Rico's mountainous interior offers ample opportunity for hiking and climbing, with many trails presenting spectacular panoramas at the least-expected moments. There are also awesome beachfront and coastal trails around the island. See "The Active Vacation Planner" in chapter 3 for detailed information.

- **El Yunque** (☎ 787/888-1880 for information): Containing the only rainforest on U.S. soil, the El Yunque National Forest east of San Juan offers a number of walking and hiking trails. The rugged El Toro trail passes through four different forest systems en route to the 3,523-foot (1,074m) Pico El Toro, the highest peak in the forest. The El Yunque trail leads to three of the recreation area's most panoramic lookouts, and the Big Tree Trail is an easy walk to gorgeous, refreshing La Mina Falls, the perfect picnic stop. Just off the main road is La Coca Falls, a sheet of water cascading down mossy cliffs. See "El Yunque" in chapter 9.

- **Guánica State Forest** (☎ 787/724-3724 for information): At the opposite extreme of El Yunque's lush and wet rainforest, Guánica State Forest's climate is dry and arid, the Arizona-like landscape riddled with cacti. The area, cut off from the Cordillera Central mountain range, gets little rainfall. Yet it's home to some 50% of all the island's terrestrial bird species, including the rare Puerto Rican nightjar, once thought to be extinct. The forest has 36 miles (58km) of trails through four forest types. The petrified vegetation, tangling down hillsides to the brilliant coast, looks in places like a giant bonsai forest. See p. 230.

- **Mona Island:** Off the western coast of Puerto Rico, this fascinating island noted for its scuba-diving sites provides hiking opportunities found nowhere else in the Caribbean. Called the "Galápagos of Puerto Rico" because of its unique wildlife, Mona is home to giant iguanas and three species of endangered sea turtles.

Some 20 endangered animals also have been spotted here. Eco-tourists like to hike among Mona's mangrove forests, coral reefs, cliffs, and complex honeycomb of caves, ever on the alert for the diversity of both plant and animal life, including 417 plant and tree species, some of which are unique and 78 of which are rare or endangered. More than 100 bird species (two unique) have been documented. Hikers can camp at Mona for a modest fee, but they will also have to hire transportation to and from the island. See the box, "Mona Island: The Galápagos of Puerto Rico," in chapter 11.

7 The Best Natural Wonders

- **El Yunque** (✆ 787/888-1880): Thirty minutes by road east of San Juan in the Luquillo Mountains and protected by the U.S. Forest Service, El Yunque is Puerto Rico's greatest natural attraction, the only tropical rainforest in the United States National Forest System. It sprawls across 28,000 acres (1,133 hectares) of the rugged Sierra de Luquillo mountain range, covering areas of Canóvanas, Las Piedras, Luquillo, Fajardo, Ceiba, Naguabo, and Río Grande. The area is named after the Indian spirit Yuquiye, which means "Forest of Clouds," who local Taínos thought protected the island from disaster in times of storms. Originally established in 1876 by the Spanish Crown, it's one of the oldest reserves in the region. There are some 240 species (26 endemic) of trees and plants found here and 50 bird species, including the rare Puerto Rican Parrot (scientific name: *Amazona vitatta*), which is one of the ten most endangered species of birds in the world. The foot-long parrot is bright green, with red forehead, blue primary wing feathers, and flesh-colored bill and feet. Some 100 billion gallons of rain fall annually on this home to four forest types. Visitors and families can walk one of the dozens of trails that wind past waterfalls, dwarf vegetation, and miniature flowers, while the island's colorful parrots fly overhead. You can hear the song of Puerto Rico's *coquí*, a small tree frog, in many places. See "El Yunque" in chapter 9.
- **Río Camuy Caves** (✆ 787/898-3100): Some 2½ hours west of San Juan, visitors board a tram to descend into this forest-filled sinkhole at the mouth of the Clara Cave. They walk the footpaths of a 170-foot-high (52m) cave to a deeper sinkhole. Once they're inside, a 45-minute tour helps everyone, including kids, learn to differentiate stalactites from stalagmites. At the Pueblos sinkhole, a platform overlooks the Camuy River, passing through a network of cave tunnels. See "Arecibo & Camuy" in chapter 9.
- **Las Cabezas de San Juan Nature Reserve** (✆ 787/722-5882): This 316-acre (128-hectare) nature reserve about 45 minutes from San Juan encompasses seven different ecological systems, including forestland, mangroves, lagoons, beaches, cliffs, and offshore coral reefs. Reservations are necessary to enter, and the park is open five days a week (Wed–Sun). The park staff conducts tours in Spanish and English from 9am through 2pm. Each tour lasts 2½ hours and includes rides on trolleys and a walk along boardwalks through oceanfront mangrove forest. Tours end with a climb to the top of the still-working 19th-century lighthouse

for views over Puerto Rico's eastern coast and nearby Caribbean islands. Call to reserve space before going, as bookings are based on stringent restrictions as to the number of persons who can tour the park without damage to its landscape or ecology. One of the finest phosphorescent bays in the world is located here, and local tour operators take you in a kayak or electronic boat to experience the animals' glow firsthand during nighttime tours. See the box, "To the Lighthouse: Exploring Las Cabezas de San Juan Nature Reserve," in chapter 12.

8 The Best Family Resorts

Puerto Rico has a bounty of attractions, natural wonders, and resorts that welcome families who choose to play together. Here are some of the best.

- **Caribe Hilton** (San Juan; © 877/ **GO-Hilton,** or 787/721-0303): The Kidz Paradise center has games, toys, beach items and sports stuff for children free of charge available 9am to 5pm through a lending desk. There's a full recreational program with indoor and outdoor activities and a free welcome gift for children 12 and under. There are a video arcade, bicycle rentals, gym, tennis courts and watersports rentals. The hotel's family policy grants free stays to children under 18 and one free babysitting service, free meals to children under 5, and free breakfast and discounts on other meals for children 5 to 12. See p. 144.

- **Marriott Courtyard Aguadilla** (Aguadilla; © **787/658-8000**): The whole family will love this hotel with pool, aquatics playground, and spacious guest rooms. It's near some of the prettiest beaches on the island, and right around attractions like the Camuy Caves, Arecibo Observatory, local water park, and ice skating rink. Beautiful beaches ring the coast here from Isabela to the east and Rincón to the west. See p. 261.

- **El Conquistador Resort & Golden Door Spa** (Las Croabas; © **800/ 468-5228** or 787/863-1000): Located 31 miles (50km) east of San Juan, this resort offers Camp Coquí on Palomino Island for children 3 to 12 years of age. The hotel's free water taxi takes kids to the island for a half- or full day of watersports and nature hikes. The Coquí Waterpark also adds to the family appeal. Boasting several pools (including its main 8,500 sq.-ft. main pool, several slides, a rope bridge and a winding river attraction), this resort has some of the best facilities and restaurants in eastern Puerto Rico and all of the Caribbean. See p. 269.

9 The Best Honeymoon Resorts

- **El San Juan Hotel & Casino** (Isla Verde; © **787/791-1000**): Newlyweds will find themselves at the heart of San Juan's vibrant nightlife scene, yet they will be ensconced in luxury along a beautiful stretch of beachfront. In fact, the hotel boasts probably the best nightlife and entertainment, as well as fine dining, of any property in San Juan—and the competition is fierce. There's live music at the casino or adjacent nightclubs. Its elegant lobby, with wooden paneling and a sprawling, opulent chandelier, is a magnet for the young, beautiful, and moneyed visitors. Set on 12 lush acres (4.9 hectares) of prime beachfront, the rooms are as light and airy as the setting. Honey-mooners might want to try an Ocean Front Lanias room or one of the resort's villas. See p.124.

- **Hotel El Convento** (Old San Juan; ⓒ **800/468-2779** or 787/723-9020): Newlyweds can sleep in and spend their afternoons wandering the Old City or lolling around the rooftop splash pool, with its sweeping vistas of San Juan Bay and the bluff over-looking the Atlantic Ocean. There are bougainvillea and tropical flowers hanging from seemingly every win-dow and terrace, as well as colorful, restored Spanish colonial architecture everywhere you turn. You'll feel spoiled by your room's marble bath-room and elegant bed. Explore sq.-mile Old San Juan; it's chock-full of galleries and historic fortresses and churches, wonderful cafes and funky shops. The Romantic Memories of San Juan package will get you fresh flowers, champagne, and chocolates in your room, but all guests get a world-class wine and cheese tasting every early evening on one of the hotel's many spectacular terraces. There are also pre- and post-cruise packages. See p. 109.

- **Horned Dorset Primavera Hotel** (Rincón; ⓒ **800/633-1857** or 787/823-4030): The most romantic place for a honeymoon on the island (unless you stay in a private villa somewhere), this small, tranquil estate lies on the Mona Passage in western Puerto Rico, a pocket of posh where privacy is almost guaranteed. Accommodations are luxurious in the Spanish neocolo-nial style. The property opens onto a long, secluded beach of white sand. There are no phones, TVs, or radios in the rooms to interfere with the soft sounds of pillow talk. This is a retreat for adults only, with no facilities for children. Seven-night packages, with all meals included and round-trip transfers from the airport, are fea-tured. See p. 253.

- **Inn on the Blue Horizon** (Vieques; ⓒ **787/741-3318**): Celebrate your honeymoon in tropical splendor at this property on an oceanfront bluff overlooking the idyllic south coast of Vieques and the neighboring village of Esperanza. Relax with the sea breeze in the sumptuous furnishings of the main building's open-air atrium, or watch the sunset at the cir-cular Blue Moon Bar, which over-looks the striking coastline. The pool sprawls across the horizon with the beach and ocean beyond it, but the private rooms feel like home (some-body's extremely well-appointed home), with beautiful cotton linens, antique furniture, and art. Romantic packages suitable for honeymooners are available. Make sure to rent a jeep to explore secluded beaches or the hilly, forested interior of the island. See p. 282.

10 The Best Big Resort Hotels

- **Ritz-Carlton San Juan Spa & Casino** (San Juan; ⓒ **800/241-3333** or 787/253-1700): At last Puerto Rico has a Ritz-Carlton, and this truly deluxe, oceanfront property is one of the island's most spectacular resorts. Guests are pampered in a setting of elegance and beautifully furnished guest rooms. Hotel dining is second only to that at El San Juan, and a European-style spa features 11 treatments "for body and beauty." See p. 126.

- **Gran Melía Puerto Rico Golf Resort and Villas** (Río Grande; ⓒ **866/436-3542** or 787/809-1770): Twenty two-story villas are spread across a gorgeously landscaped property hugging the northeast coast in the shadow of the mountainous rainforest, El Yunque. The facilities are first rate; the stately lobby is a traditional mix of Puerto Rican and Spanish influences, flanked by an African-inspired mediation pond out front and Asian inspired lagoons behind, where most of the resort's top-notch restaurants are located. The rooms are spacious and have great views of the lushly landscaped walkways or the broad beachfront that runs the length of the property. The two adjacent Trump golf courses are world class, and the pool and beach area offer all major watersports activities. There's a full range of children's activities and organized fun for adults as well, from yoga lessons to beach volleyball games. The resort spa has first-class facilities and a wide range of treatments. See p. 203.

- **Rio Mar Beach Resort & Spa: A Wyndham Grand Resort** (Rio Grande; ✆ **800/4RIOMAR** [474-6627] or 787/888-6000): This $180-million 481-acre (195-hectare) resort, 19 miles (31km) east of the San Juan airport, is one of the largest hotels in Puerto Rico, but personal service and

style are hallmarks of the property. Eleven restaurants and multiple lounges boast an array of cuisines. It has two championship golf courses, two pools, a beach and watersports, horseback riding, fine tennis facilities, a full range of children's activities, entertainment and nightlife activity, and anything else you might need for your perfect Caribbean getaway. The resort is blissfully situated between the El Yunque rainforest and a beautiful stretch of north coast beach. See p. 203.

- **El Conquistador Resort & Golden Door Spa** (Las Croabas; ✆ **800/ 468-5228** or 787/863-1000): The finest resort in Puerto Rico, this is a world-class destination—a sybaritic haven for golfers, honeymooners, families, and anyone else. Three intimate "villages" combine with one grand hotel, draped along 300-foot (91m) bluffs overlooking both the Atlantic and the Caribbean at Puerto Rico's northeastern tip. The 500 landscaped acres (202 hectares) include tennis courts, an 18-hole Arthur Hills–designed championship golf course, and a marina filled with yachts and charter boats. There's a water park and an island beach just off shore for guests. See p. 269.

11 The Best Moderately Priced Hotels

- **Gallery Inn at Galería San Juan** (San Juan; ✆ **787/722-1808**): The most whimsically bohemian hotel in the Caribbean sits on a coastal bluff at the edge of the historic city. Once the home of an aristocratic Spanish family, it is today filled with verdant courtyards and adorned with sculptures, silk screens, and original paintings of artist Jan D'esopo, who along with husband Manuco Gandía owns the inn. Many of the rooms have

dramatic views of the coast, with two historic Spanish forts framing the view. Staying in one of the comfortable rooms here is like living in an art gallery. See p. 110.

- **At Wind Chimes Inn** (San Juan; ✆ **800/946-3244** or 787/727-4153): This renovated and restored Spanish manor house, a favorite with families, is one of the best guesthouses in the Condado district. The inn, which offers spacious rooms with kitchens, lies only a short block from one of San Juan's best beaches. There's also a pool and a nice restaurant/bar catering exclusively to guests. The nearby sister property **Acacia Sea Side Inn** is another good option, and guests at the Acacia can use the Wind Chimes' pool and get access to its bar/restaurant. See p. 120.

- **Copamarina Beach Resort** (Caña Gorda; ✆ 787/821-0505): In an undeveloped coastal area of Guánica, at the edge of the Guánica Dry Forest, this resort was once the private vacation retreat of local cement barons—the de Castro family. Today it's been converted into one of the best beach hotels along Puerto Rico's southern shore. In fact, its beach is one of the best in the area. Set in a palm grove, the resort is handsomely decorated and comfortably furnished, with a swimming pool and two tennis courts. See p. 231.

- **Casa Isleña Inn** (Rincón; ✆ 787/ 823-1525): Located on a beautiful beach in the Puntas sector of this west-coast surf capital, this casually elegant inn is a great value of surprising quality. A contemporary Ibero-Caribbean theme runs throughout its rooftop, beachfront and garden terraces, and inspires its colorfully painted architecture and the furnishing of its spacious, comfortable guest rooms. The only drawback is you might find it difficult to ever leave here, since it has one of the best pools in town in front of some of the nicest beach. But with a new tapas bar now open, you might not have to. The last time we visited was in the off season, in early summer, when the place was left blissfully to ourselves and a handful of other guests. See p. 254.

- **Crow's Nest** (Vieques; ✆ 787/741-0033 or 741-0993): Sixteen suites with kitchenettes and lounging/reading areas are spread out across this sprawling property in the lush Vieques countryside. The pool and its beautifully tiled terrace are surrounded by tropical plants and the green hillsides of this island paradise. The staff is extremely helpful, and the restaurant, Island Steakhouse, is top notch (with enough seafood and other non-steak fare to please everyone). Its country home setting off the beach is in fact a unique and charming part of the typical Vieques vacation experience. See p. 283.

12 The Best Attractions

- **The Historic District of Old San Juan:** There's nothing like it in the Caribbean. Partially enclosed by old walls dating from the 17th century, Old San Juan was designated a U.S. National Historic Zone in 1950. Some 400 massively restored buildings fill this district, which is chock-ablock with tree-shaded squares, monuments, and open-air cafes as well as shops, restaurants, and bars. If you're interested in history, there is no better stroll in the Caribbean. It continues to be a vibrant cultural center and enclave of the arts and entertainment, as well as one of the region's culinary capitals. See "Seeing the Sights" in chapter 8.

- **Castillo de San Felipe del Morro** (Old San Juan): In Old San Juan and nicknamed El Morro, this fort was originally built in 1540. It guards the bay from a rocky promontory on the northwestern tip of the old city. Rich in history and legend, the site covers enough territory to accommodate a 9-hole golf course. See p. 158.

- **The Historic District of Ponce:** Second only to Old San Juan in terms of historical significance, the central district of Ponce is a blend of Ponce Creole and Art Deco building styles, dating mainly from the 1890s to the 1930s. One street, Calle Isabel, offers an array of Ponceño architectural styles, which often incorporate neoclassical details. The city underwent a massive restoration preceding the celebration of its 300th anniversary in 1996. See "Ponce" in chapter 10.

- **Museo de Arte de Ponce** (Ponce): This museum has the finest collection of European and Latin American art in the Caribbean. Edward Durell Stone, the architect of the Museum of Modern Art in New York City, designed the building. Contemporary works by Puerto Ricans are displayed, as well as works by an array of old masters, including Renaissance and baroque pieces from Italy. See p. 219.

- **Tropical Agriculture Research Station:** These tropical gardens contain one of the largest collections of tropical species intended for practical use. These include cacao, fruit trees, spices, timbers, and ornamentals. Adjacent to the Mayagüez campus of the University of Puerto Rico, the site attracts botanists from around the world. See "Mayagüez" in chapter 11.

- **The City of San Germán:** In the southwestern corner of Puerto Rico and founded in 1512, this small town is Puerto Rico's second-oldest city. Thanks to a breadth of architectural styles, San Germán is also the second

Puerto Rican city (after San Juan) to be included in the National Register of Historic Places. Buildings, monuments, and plazas fill a 36-acre (15-hectare) historic zone. Today's residents descend from the smugglers, poets, priests, and politicians who once lived here in "the city of hills," so-called because of the mountainous location. See "San Germán" in chapter 10.

- **Iglesia Porta Coeli** (San Germán): The main attraction of this ancient town is the oldest church in the New World. It was originally built by Dominican friars in 1606. The church resembles a working chapel, although mass is held here only three times a year. Along the sides of the church are treasures gathered from all over the world. See "San Germán" in chapter 10.

- **Puerto Rico Museum of Art** (San Juan) features interesting traveling shows and a growing permanent collection emphasizing local artists in impressive surroundings—a restored 1920s classic in Santurce. There are beautiful botanical gardens outside, and a theater exhibits cutting-edge films and performances of all types. There are day workshops open to the public and children's activities held here nearly every weekend, and the museum is home to one of the island's top few restaurants, Pikayo, which takes Puerto Rican cuisine to artful new heights. See p. 162.

13 The Best Restaurants

- **Aquaviva** (San Juan; © 787/722-0665): This ultra modern, sleekly tropical restaurant looks as cutting edge as its "seaside Latino cuisine." Its buzzing, blue interior lightly evokes the shoreline and an aquarium all at once. Ceviche rules at the raw bar, and hot and cold seafood "towers"

group several of the inventive appetizers into a large portion for guests to share. The menu is expansive and full of wonders—grilled mahimahi with smoky shrimp salsa or seared halibut with crab and spinach fondue. The catch of the day is cooked with consummate skill. See p. 133.

- **Barú** (San Juan; ✆ **787/977-7107**): Fashionable and popular, this Old World styled restaurant is actually a creative culinary showcase for fusion Caribbean–Mediterranean cuisine and a popular nightspot. Craftsmanship marks the menu, which specializes in inventive risottos and carpaccios. See p. 134.

- **Parrot Club** (San Juan; ✆ **787/725-7370**): This place still sets the standard in style and service, and its Nuevo Latino cuisine beats any of the hotshot restaurants of its genre in New York and Miami that we've tried. The menu here is a thoughtful restyling of Puerto Rican and regional classics, drawing on the island's Spanish, African, Taíno, and American influences. There's a *criolla*-styled flank steak and a panseared tuna served with a dark rumorange sauce. See p. 135.

- **Ramiro's** (Condado; ✆ **787/721-9049**): Chef Jesús Ramiro has some of the most innovative dishes in San Juan, along with the city's best wine list. Ramiro's *"Nuevo Criolla"* cuisine reaches way back to its Spanish roots, and is as likely to mix in European as New World flourishes. His reputation rests on such dishes as quail stuffed with lamb in a port sauce and lamb loin in a tamarind coriander sauce, both equally delectable. His dessert menu is two pages long and includes the town's best soufflés. His death-by-chocolate mousse on a green grape leaf is equaled only by his caramelized fresh mango napoleon. See p. 144.

- **Budatai** (Condado; ✆ **787/725-6919**): Roberto Trevino's Asian–Latino cuisine has found its rightful home in this luxurious and stylish restaurant with an oceanfront view at the heart of Condado. With an emphasis on Puerto Rican herbs and seafood, the dishes rely on herbs and inspiration from the Far East without ever feeling too far away from home. There's a full sushi bar and lots of ceviche. On our last trip, we started with pork dumplings with shaved truffle and the fried calamari and sweet onion, while main courses were steamed halibut and seasoned potatoes and Spanish sausage and filet mignon with duck-fat potatoes and Asian mushrooms. See p. 144.

- **Mark's at the Meliá** (Ponce; ✆ **787/284-6275**): Mark French has elevated Puerto Rican dishes to a new height at this endearing restaurant that also serves an impeccable international cuisine. He brought haute cuisine to the Ponce dining scene, which had been a bit of a backwater and turned the place into an enclave of refined dining with such imaginative and good-tasting dishes as rack of lamb with goat cheese crust and tenderloin medallions with sautéed shrimp in a Hollandaise sauce. See p. 227.

- **Pikayo** (at the Puerto Rico Museum of Art, San Juan; ✆ **787/259-7676**): This dramatically beautiful restaurant has a menu as artful as its setting just off the main lobby over the art museum. The menu—with dishes like grilled shrimp and julienne chorizo in a soursop beurre blanc, and grilled sea bass in a pumpkin puree—fuses Caribbean, European, and Californian influences. For chef Wilo Bent, however, it's all about making high art out of his hometown cuisine. See p. 150.

- **bbh** (Vieques; ✆ **787/741-1128**): The best tapas in all of Puerto Rico are served at this restaurant at the elegant Bravo Beach Hotel. Tapas "by the sea" include everything from Jamaican jerk chicken to seared ahi tuna, grilled chorizo to marinated olives. See p. 286.

14 The Best Offbeat Travel Experiences

- **Attending a Cockfight:** Although a brutal sport that many find distasteful, cockfighting is legal in Puerto Rico and has its devotees. The most authentic cockfights are held in small central mountain towns, and it's popular along the south coast, such as in the town of Salinas. But it's not necessary to go that far to witness one of these bouts. Three fights a week are held at the **Coliseo Gallistico,** Isla Verde Avenue 6600 (© **787/791-6005**), in San Juan. Betting is heavy when these roosters take to the ring. See "San Juan After Dark" in chapter 8.

- **Diving off Mona Island** (Mayagüez): Surrounded by some of the most beautiful coral reefs in the Caribbean, Mona Island has the most pristine, extensive, and well-developed reefs in Puerto Rican waters. In fact, they have been nominated as a U.S. National Marine Sanctuary. The tropical marine ecosystem around Mona includes patch reefs, black coral, spore and groove systems, underwater caverns, deepwater sponges, fringing reefs, and algal reefs. The lush environment attracts octopuses, lobster, queen conch, rays, barracuda, snapper, jack, grunt, angelfish, trunkfish, filefish, butterfly fish, dolphin, parrotfish, tuna, flying fish, and more. The crystal waters afford exceptional horizontal vision from 150 to 200 feet (46–61m), as well as good views down to the shipwrecks that mark the site—including some Hispanic galleons. Five species of whales visit the island's offshore waters. See the box, "Mona Island: The Galápagos of Puerto Rico," in chapter 11.

- **Visiting Vieques & Culebra:** Puerto Rico's offshore islands—still relatively undiscovered by the modern world—remain an offbeat adventure, and they've got great beaches, too. The most developed is Vieques, which attracts visitors with its gorgeous stretches of sand with picnic facilities and shade trees. It is an ideal retreat for snorkelers and tranquillity seekers. The beaches are nearly always deserted, even though they are among the Caribbean's loveliest. Nearly three-quarters of the island is owned by the Fish & Wildlife Service. The even-less-developed Culebra has a wildlife refuge, coral reefs, and Playa Flamenco, another of the Caribbean's finest beaches. And is it ever sleepy here! See chapter 13.

- **Spending the Evening at Mosquito (Phosphorescent) Bay** (Vieques Island): At any time except when there's a full moon, you can swim in glowing waters lit by dinoflagellates called *pyrodiniums* (whirling fire). These creatures light up the waters like fireflies, and swimming among them is one of the most unusual things to do anywhere—truly a magical, almost psychedelic experience. It's estimated that a gallon of bay water might contain about three-quarters of a million of these little glowing creatures. See chapter 13.

- **Puerto Rican Road Food:** No other place offers as many road-side treats as Puerto Rico. There's something good to eat around virtually every turn in the road. Our favorites include barbecued chicken stands along Route 116 in Guánica, the pizzerias ringing northwest from Arecibo to Mayagüez, and the simple seafood restaurants fronting the quaint and picturesque harbor of Naguabo on the east coast. And you can't really forget Puerta de Tierra's oceanfront **El Hamburger,** or the taco joints along the old Caguas highway. Also try **Piñones,** east of Isla Verde (which has probably the largest concentration of *frituras,* fried beach snacks, near San Juan). Farther east, the cluster of food stands near the **Luquillo** public beach and Highway 3 are legendary for their seafood, as well as barbecued chicken. Make sure to try an *arepa,* a light flour pastry often filled with seafood ceviche but also made with coconut flavor and eaten plain with coffee for breakfast. For succulent roast pork, chicken, and turkey, head to a string of open air restaurants specializing in *criolla* barbecue in the mountain town of **Guavate,** about a half-hour south of San Juan. We've never eaten at a bad restaurant here in 15 years of trying.

2

Puerto Rico in Depth

One of the most popular tourist destinations south of Florida raises the rainbow flag to a diverse heritage. Modern Puerto Rico culture is a rich brew of Taíno Indian, Spanish, African, and American influences. Puerto Ricans maintain a strong and unique cultural identity, of which they are immensely proud, despite their home's century-old colonial ties to the United States. Those ties are not without their benefit, however, and most Puerto Ricans cherish their U.S. citizenship and want to maintain their political relationship, either through continued commonwealth status or statehood. A smaller percentage (the pro-independence party gubernatorial candidate usually gets 5% of the vote) favor outright separation from the United States to make Puerto Rico a sovereign nation.

Millions of Puerto Ricans have flocked stateside over the last six decades in search of economic and educational opportunities and an improved quality of life, and they continue to do so. In fact, Puerto Ricans living stateside now just about equal the number living on the island: roughly 4 million. But for most stateside *boricuas,* their heart's devotion still belongs to their island homeland, which means frequent trips during vacations and holidays. A sizeable number of Puerto Rican passengers are on most planes from the states arriving at Luis Muñoz Marín International Airport in San Juan. They will burst into applause upon touchdown on Puerto Rican soil. Many others return to Puerto Rico after retiring.

Puerto Rican writer René Marqués, who came of age in the 1940s and 1950s when Puerto Rico was modernizing into an industrial economy and getting a big dose of U.S. influence, spoke of the dual nature his island, which nevertheless contributed to its uniqueness. "Puerto Rico has two languages," he claimed, "and two citizenships, two basic philosophies of life, two flags, two anthems, two loyalties."

1 Puerto Rico Today

As the commonwealth moves more deeply into the new millennium, Puerto Rico continues to make headlines in mainland newspapers. Sometimes the news is good, other times troubling.

One result: People are visiting. Puerto Rico's tourism figures have been rising annually since the beginning of the 21st century; the island's aggressive hotel and marketing promotion seems to be paying off. Travelers from the United States are the major visitors, and their numbers rose steadily throughout the early 2000s. Tourism from Canada is also on the rise, and the greatest increase is in Latin American visitors.

A CHANGING ECONOMY

The island's 3.88 million people—1 million of whom live in the San Juan metropolitan area—have forged ahead economically and made rapid strides. Their annual income is the highest in Latin America, and their average life expectancy has risen to 73.8 years. The island's economy began evolving from its agricultural base in the 1950s when the Operation Bootstrap industrialization program began attracting stateside manufacturing plants. The sector, powered by Puerto Rico's unique political status that allows firms to escape federal taxation, grew to represent nearly half of the entire Puerto Rico. The demand for an educated workforce has resulted in at least 12 years of schooling for ordinary workers. More importantly, the solid manufacturing industry sparked the growth of a whole host of professional services on the island, including legal, financial, engineering, and accounting, so that today Puerto Rico remains a regional center for most professional services. The island has a number of universities, including the highly regarded University of Puerto Rico, with specialized programs in engineering, medicine, law, and increasingly research and development in a number of fields, including the life sciences.

Manufacturing, for so many years the workhorse of the island economy, has been hit by competition from low-cost destinations, as well as high local utility, shipping, and other fixed costs.

The sector's decline began in 1996, when a 10-year phaseout of U.S. industrial tax breaks began. This marked the end of 75 years of federal incentives that attracted stateside industries and helped make Puerto Rico the Caribbean's industrial powerhouse. It continues to produce about half the prescription drugs sold in the United States.

In response, the government is trying to entice its existing high-tech industry to stay through an increased focus on research and development. Another target is an island life-sciences research and manufacturing sector through joint private-industry and university ventures.

A big strategy is also to make up for the loss in manufacturing by increasing other economic drivers, from agriculture to shipping to increased professional services, which could be anything from health care to high finance.

THE TOURISM INDUSTRY

Tourism, which represents about 6% of the gross national product, is a small but important economic segment, and a good source of employment, especially for the island's well-educated, worldly, bilingual youths. The current administration, as with past administrations, wants to double the size of tourism to 12% of the economy.

At once both labor-intensive and environmentally friendly, tourism is seen as a partial answer to the slowdown in the manufacturing sector. Still, there are challenges: A Cuban reopening to the American tourism market could steal business from Puerto Rico, which saw its tourism industry's growth fueled enormously by the embargo imposed on Castro's communist government. Before Fidel Castro took over Cuba in 1959, Americans by the thousands flocked to Havana, and Puerto Rico was a mere dot on the tourist map.

Others say the island could still prosper with an open Cuba because the local tourism product is top of the line, aimed at the most wealthy and discriminating of travelers. They also predict Puerto Rico tourism industry players will have a role in an open Cuba.

Regardless, the tourism industry has been a perennially important part of the island's economic success, and it is poised to take on an even more significant role in the future—the industry will focus on ecotourism, smaller scale projects, and diversifying away from the oceanfront resort style tourism of Condado and Isla Verde, which still defines the experience of going to Puerto Rico for most visitors. The effort to diversify will result in more boutique properties, secluded beach getaways and mountain eco-lodges, which is good news for travelers here.

CRIME & UNEMPLOYMENT

Even with its advanced economy, Puerto Rico struggles with a 12.5% unemployment rate and a per capita income about half the level of the poorest U.S. state, Mississippi. Its bloated government bureaucracy is an increasing problem, responsible for deficit spending and high local taxation.

Mirroring the U.S. mainland, rising crime, drugs, AIDS, and other social problems plague Puerto Rico. Its association with the United States has made it a favorite transshipment point for drug smugglers entering the U.S. market (because once on the island, travelers don't have to pass through Customs inspectors again when traveling to the United States).

The drug problem is behind much of local violent crime, including killings that have pushed the local murder rate to among the highest in the United States.

Other violence and social ills associated with drugs have also beset the island.

Although the drug issue is of epidemic proportions, you can visit Puerto Rico and be completely unaware of any criminal activity. Tourist areas in San Juan (including Old San Juan, Condado, and Isla Verde) are generally free of violent crime and theft, and efforts in the past 20 years to resolve the drug and crime problem have helped make safer streets.

THE 51ST STATE?

The New Progressive Party wants to make Puerto Rico the 51st state, but the opposition is strong, both on the island and in Congress. A non-binding reference in 1998 resulted in a defeat of statehood.

The other major party, the Popular Democratic Party, backs the continued commonwealth status, while the Puerto Rican Independence Party typically achieves about 5% of popular support in gubernatorial elections. These three parties have dominated island politics of the last 4 decades.

See "Give Me Liberty or Give Me Statehood" on p. 32 for more.

2 History 101

IN THE BEGINNING

Although the Spanish occupation was the decisive factor defining Puerto Rico's current culture, the island was settled many thousands of years ago by Amerindians. The oldest archaeological remains yet discovered were unearthed in 1948. Found in a limestone cave a few miles east of San Juan, in Loíza Aldea, the artifacts consisted of conch shells, stone implements, and crude hatchets deposited by tribal peoples during the first century of the Christian Era. These people belonged to an archaic, semi-nomadic, cave-dwelling culture that had not developed either agriculture or pottery. Some ethnologists suggest that these early inhabitants originated in Florida, immigrated to Cuba, and from there began a steady migration along the West Indian archipelago.

Around A.D. 300, a different group of Amerindians, the Arawaks, migrated to Puerto Rico from the Orinoco Basin in what is now Venezuela. Known by ethnologists as the Saladoids, they were the first of Puerto Rico's inhabitants to make and use pottery, which they decorated with exotic geometric designs in red and white. Subsisting on fish, crab, and whatever else they could catch, they populated the big island as well as the offshore island of Vieques.

By about A.D. 600, this culture had disappeared, bringing to an end the island's historical era of pottery making. Ethnologists' opinions differ as to whether the tribes were eradicated by new invasions from South America, succumbed to starvation or plague, or simply evolved into

Ponce de León: Man of Myth & Legend

For an explorer of such myth and legend, Juan Ponce de León still remains an enigma to many historians, his exploits subject to as much myth as fact.

It is known that he was born around 1460 in San Tervas de Campos, a province of Valladolid in Spain, to a noble Castilian family. The red-haired youth grew into an active, aggressive, and perhaps impulsive young man, similar in some respects to Sir Francis Drake in England. After taking part in Spain's Moorish wars, Ponce de León sailed to America with Columbus on his second voyage, in 1493.

In the New World, Ponce de León served as a soldier in the Spanish settlement of Hispaniola, now the island home of Haiti and the Dominican Republic. From 1502 to 1504, he led Spanish forces against Indians in the eastern part of the island, finally defeating them.

In 1508 he explored Puerto Rico, discovering gold on the island and conquering the native tribes within a year. A year later, he was named governor of Puerto Rico and soon rose to become one of the most powerful Europeans in the Americas. From most accounts, Ponce de León was a good governor of Puerto Rico before his political rivals forced him from office in 1512.

At that time he received permission from King Ferdinand to colonize the island of Bimini in the Bahamas. In searching for Bimini, he came upon the northeast coast of Florida, which he at first thought was an island, in the spring of 1513. He named it La Florida because he discovered it at the time of Pascua Florida or "Flowery Easter." He was the first explorer to claim some of the North American mainland for Spain.

The following year he sailed back to Spain, carrying with him 5,000 gold pesos. King Ferdinand ordered him back to Puerto Rico with instructions to colonize both Bimini and Florida. Back in Puerto Rico, Ponce de León ordered the building of the city of San Juan. In 1521 he sailed to Florida with 200 men and supplies to start a colony. This was to be his downfall. Wounded by a poison arrow in his thigh, he was taken back to Cuba in June 1521 and died there from his wound.

Legend says Ponce de León searched in vain for the so-called Fountain of Youth, first in Bimini and later in Florida. He never once mentioned it in any of his private or official writings—at least those writings that still exist—and historians believe his goal was gold and other treasures (and perhaps to convert the natives to Catholicism).

His legacy lives on at the Casa Blanca in Old San Juan (p. 165). Casa Blanca is the oldest continuously occupied residence in the Western Hemisphere and the oldest of about 800 Spanish colonial buildings in Old San Juan's National Historic Zone. In 1968 it became a historic national monument. Today the building is the site of the Juan Ponce de León Museum. The conquistador's carved coat of arms greets visitors at the entrance.

the next culture that dominated Puerto Rico—the Ostionoids.

Much less skilled at making pottery than their predecessors but more accomplished at polishing and grinding stones for jewelry and tools, the Ostionoids were the ethnic predecessors of the tribe that became the Taínos. The Taínos inhabited Puerto Rico when it was explored and invaded by the Spanish beginning in 1493. The Taínos were spread throughout the West Indies but reached their greatest development in Puerto Rico and neighboring Hispaniola (the island shared by Haiti and the Dominican Republic).

Taíno culture impressed the colonial Spanish, and it continues to impress modern sociologists. This people's achievements included construction of ceremonial ballparks whose boundaries were marked by upright stone dolmens, development of a universal language, and creation of a complicated religious cosmology. They believed in a hierarchy of deities who inhabited the sky. The god Yocahu was the supreme creator. Another god, Juracán, was perpetually angry and ruled the power of the hurricane. Myths and traditions were perpetuated through ceremonial dances *(areytos),* drumbeats, oral traditions, and a ceremonial ballgame played between opposing teams (10 to 30 players per team) with a rubber ball; winning this game was thought to bring a good harvest and strong, healthy children. Skilled at agriculture and hunting, the Taínos were also good sailors, canoe makers, and navigators.

About 100 years before the Spanish invasion, the Taínos were challenged by an invading South American tribe—the Caribs. Fierce, warlike, sadistic, and adept at using poison-tipped arrows, the Caribs raided Taíno settlements for slaves (especially female) and bodies for the completion of their rites of cannibalism. Some ethnologists argue that the preeminence

of the Taínos, shaken by the attacks of the Caribs, was already jeopardized by the time of the Spanish occupation. In fact, it was the Caribs who fought most effectively against the Europeans; their behavior led the Europeans to unfairly attribute warlike tendencies to all of the island's tribes. A dynamic tension between the Taínos and the Caribs certainly existed when Christopher Columbus landed on Puerto Rico.

To understand Puerto Rico's prehistoric era, it is important to know that the Taínos, far more than the Caribs, contributed greatly to the everyday life and language that evolved during the Spanish occupation. Taíno place names are still used for such towns as Utuado, Mayagüez, Caguas, and Humacao. Many Taíno implements and techniques were copied directly by the Europeans, including the *bohío* (straw hut), the *hamaca* (hammock), the musical instrument known as the maracas, and the method of making bread from the starchy cassava root. Also, many Taíno superstitions and legends were adopted and adapted by the Spanish and still influence the Puerto Rican imagination.

SPAIN, SYPHILIS & SLAVERY

Christopher Columbus became the first European to land on the shores of Puerto Rico, on November 19, 1493, near what would become the town of Aguadilla, during his second voyage to the New World. Giving the island the name San Juan Bautista, he sailed on in search of shores with more obvious riches for the taking. A European foothold on the island was established in 1508, when Juan Ponce de León, the first governor of Puerto Rico, imported colonists from the nearby island of Hispaniola. They founded the town of Caparra, which lay close to the site of present-day San Juan. The town was almost immediately wracked with internal power struggles among the Spanish settlers, who pressed the native peoples into servitude, evangelized them, and frantically sought for gold, thus quickly changing the face of the island.

Meanwhile, the Amerindians began dying at an alarming rate, victims of imported diseases such as smallpox and whooping cough, against which they had no biological immunity. The natives paid the Spanish back, giving them diseases such as syphilis against which they had little immunity. Both communities reeled, disoriented from their contact with one another. In 1511 the Amerindians rebelled against attempts by the Spanish to enslave them. The rebellion was brutally suppressed by the Spanish forces of Ponce de León, whose muskets and firearms were vastly superior to the hatchets and arrows of the native peoples. In desperation, the Taínos joined forces with their traditional enemies, the Caribs, but even that union did little to check the growth of European power.

Because the Indians languished in slavery, sometimes preferring mass suicide to imprisonment, their work in the fields and mines of Puerto Rico was soon taken over by Africans who were imported by Spanish, Danish, Portuguese, British, and American slavers.

By 1521 the island had been renamed Puerto Rico ("Rich Port") and was one of the most strategic islands in the Caribbean, which was increasingly viewed as a Spanish sea. Officials of the Spanish Crown dubbed the island "the strongest foothold of Spain in America" and hastened to strengthen the already impressive bulwarks surrounding the city of San Juan.

PIRATES & PILLAGING ENGLISHMEN

Within a century, Puerto Rico's position at the easternmost edge of what would become Spanish America helped it play a major part in the Spanish expansion toward Florida, the South American coast, and Mexico. It was usually the first port of call for Spanish ships arriving in the Americas; recognizing that the island was a strategic keystone, the Spanish decided to strengthen its defenses. By 1540, La Fortaleza, the first of three massive fortresses built in San Juan, was completed. By 1600, San Juan was completely enclosed by some of the most formidable ramparts in the Caribbean, whereas, ironically, the remainder of Puerto Rico was almost defenseless. In 1565 the king of Spain ordered the governor of Puerto Rico to provide men and materials to strengthen the city of St. Augustine, Florida.

By this time, the English (and to a lesser extent, the French) were seriously harassing Spanish shipping in the Caribbean and north Atlantic. At least part of the French and English aggression was in retaliation for the 1493 Papal Bull dividing the New World between Portugal and Spain—an arrangement that eliminated all other nations from the spoils and colonization of the New World.

Queen Elizabeth I's most effective weapon against Spanish expansion in the Caribbean wasn't the Royal Navy; rather, it was buccaneers such as John Hawkins and Sir Francis Drake. Their victories included the destruction of St. Augustine in Florida, Cartagena in Colombia, and Santo Domingo in what is now the Dominican Republic, and the general harassment and pillaging of many Spanish ships and treasure convoys sailing from the New World to Europe with gold and silver from the Aztec and Inca empires. The Royal Navy did play an important role, however, as its 1588 defeat of the Spanish Armada marked the rise of the English as a major maritime power. The Spanish then began to aggressively fortify such islands as Puerto Rico.

In 1595, Drake and Hawkins persuaded Queen Elizabeth to embark on a bold and daring plan to invade and conquer Puerto Rico. An English general, the Earl of Cumberland, urged his men to bravery by "assuring your selves you have the maydenhead of Puerto Rico and so possesse the keyes of all the Indies."

Confident that the island was "the very key of the West Indies which locketh and shutteth all the gold and silver in the continent of America and Brasilia," he brought into battle an English force of 4,500 soldiers and eventually captured La Fortaleza.

Although the occupation lasted a full 65 days, the English eventually abandoned Puerto Rico when their armies were decimated by tropical diseases and the local population, which began to engage in a kind of guerrilla warfare against the English. After pillaging and destroying much of the Puerto Rican countryside, the English left. Their short but abortive victory compelled the Spanish king, Philip III, to continue construction of the island's defenses. Despite these efforts, Puerto Rico retained a less-than-invincible aspect as Spanish soldiers in the forts often deserted or succumbed to tropical diseases.

A DUTCH THREAT

In 1625 Puerto Rico was covetously eyed by Holland, whose traders and merchants desperately wanted a foothold in the West Indies. Spearheaded by the Dutch West India Company, which had received trading concessions from the Dutch Crown covering most of the West Indies, the Dutch armies besieged El Morro Fortress in San Juan in one of the bloodiest assaults the fortress ever sustained. When the commanding officer of El Morro refused to surrender, the Dutch burned San Juan to the ground, including all church and civil archives and the bishop's library, by then the most famous and

complete collection of books in America. Fueled by rage, the Spanish rallied and soon defeated the Dutch.

In response to the destruction of the strongest link in the chain of Spanish defenses, Spain threw itself wholeheartedly into improving and reinforcing the defenses around San Juan. King Philip IV justified his expenditures by declaring Puerto Rico the "front and vanguard of the Western Indies and, consequently, the most important of them and most coveted by the enemies of Spain."

Within 150 years, after extravagant expenditures of time and money, San Juan's walls were considered almost impregnable. Military sophistication was added during the 1760s, when two Irishmen, Tomas O'Daly and Alejandro O'Reilly, surrounded the city with some of Europe's most up-to-date defenses. Despite the thick walls, however, the island's defenses remained precarious because of the frequent tropical epidemics that devastated the ranks of the soldiers; the chronically late pay, which weakened the soldiers' morale; and the belated and often wrong-minded priorities of the Spanish monarchy.

A CATHOLIC CRUSADE

From the earliest days of Spanish colonization, an army of priests and missionaries embarked on a vigorous crusade to convert Puerto Rico's Taínos to Roman Catholicism. King Ferdinand himself paid for the construction of a Franciscan monastery and a series of chapels, and he required specific support of the church from the aristocrats who had been awarded land grants in the new territories. They were required to build churches, provide Christian burials, and grant religious instruction to both Taíno and African slaves.

Among the church's most important activities were the Franciscan monks' efforts to teach the island's children how to read, write, and count. In 1688 Bishop Francisco Padilla, who is now included among the legends of Puerto Rico, established one of the island's most famous schools. When it became clear that local parents were too poor to provide their children with appropriate clothing, he succeeded in persuading the king of Spain to pay for their clothes.

Puerto Rico was declared by the pope as the first *see* (ecclesiastical headquarters) in the New World. In 1519 it became the general headquarters of the Inquisition in the New World. (About 70 years later, the Inquisition's headquarters were transferred to the well-defended city of Cartagena, Colombia.)

FROM SMUGGLING TO SUGAR

The island's early development was shackled by Spain's insistence on a centrist economy. All goods exported from or imported to Puerto Rico had to pass through Spain itself, usually through Seville. In effect, this policy prohibited any official trade between Puerto Rico and its island neighbors.

In response, a flourishing black market developed. Cities such as Ponce became smuggling centers. This black market was especially prevalent after the Spanish colonization of Mexico and Peru, when many Spanish goods, which once would have been sent to Puerto Rico, ended up in those more immediately lucrative colonies instead. Although smugglers were punished if caught, nothing could curb this illegal (and untaxed) trade. Some historians estimate that almost everyone on the island—including priests, citizens, and military and civic authorities—was actively involved in smuggling.

By the mid-1500s, the several hundred settlers who had immigrated to Puerto Rico from Spain heard and sometimes believed rumors of the fortunes to be made in the gold mines of Peru. When

the island's population declined because of the ensuing mass exodus, the king enticed 500 families from the Canary Islands to settle on Puerto Rico between 1683 and 1691. Meanwhile, an active trade in slaves—imported as labor for fields that were increasingly used for sugar-cane and tobacco production—swelled the island's ranks. This happened despite the Crown's imposition of strict controls on the number of slaves that could be brought in. Sugar cane earned profits for many islanders, but Spanish mismanagement, fraud within the government bureaucracy, and a lack of both labor and ships to transport the finished product to market discouraged the fledgling industry. Later, fortunes were made and lost in the production of ginger, an industry that died as soon as the Spanish government raised taxes on ginger imports to exorbitant levels. Despite the arrival of immigrants to Puerto Rico from many countries, diseases such as spotted fever, yellow fever, malaria, smallpox, and measles wiped out the population almost as fast as it grew.

MORE SMUGGLING

As the philosophical and political movement known as the Enlightenment swept both Europe and North America during the late 1700s and the 1800s, Spain moved to improve Puerto Rico's economy through its local government. The island's defenses were beefed up, roads and bridges were built, and a public education program was launched. The island remained a major Spanish naval stronghold in the New World. Immigration from Europe and other places more than tripled the population. It was during this era that Puerto Rico began to develop a unique identity of its own, a native pride, and a consciousness of its importance within the Caribbean.

The heavily fortified city of San Juan, the island's civic centerpiece, remained under Spain's rigid control. Although it was the victim of an occasional pirate raid, or an attack by English or French forces, the outlying countryside was generally left alone to develop its own local power centers. The city of Ponce, for example, flourished under the Spanish Crown's lax supervision and grew wealthy from the tons of contraband and the high-quality sugar that passed through its port. This trend was also encouraged by the unrealistic law that declared San Juan the island's only legal port. Contemporary sources, in fact, cite the fledgling United States as among the most active of Ponce's early contraband trading partners.

RISING POWER

During the 18th century, the number of towns on the island grew rapidly. There were five settlements in Puerto Rico in 1700; 100 years later, there were almost 40 settlements, and the island's population had grown to more than 150,000.

Meanwhile, the waters of the Caribbean increasingly reflected the diplomatic wars unfolding in Europe. In 1797 the British, after easily capturing Trinidad (which was poorly defended by the Spanish), failed in a spectacular effort to conquer Puerto Rico. The *criollos,* or native Puerto Ricans, played a major role in the island's defense and later retained a growing sense of their cultural identity.

The islanders were becoming aware that Spain could not enforce the hundreds of laws it had previously imposed to support its centrist trade policies. Thousands of merchants, farmers, and civil authorities traded profitably with privateers from various nations, thereby deepening the tendency to evade or ignore the laws imposed by Spain and its colonial governors. The attacks by privateers on British shipping were especially severe because pirates based in Puerto Rico ranged as far south as Trinidad, bringing dozens of captured British ships into Puerto Rican harbors. (Several decades earlier, British privateers operating out of Jamaica had endlessly harassed Spanish shipping; the tradition of government-sanctioned piracy was well established.)

It was during this period that coffee—which would later play an essential role in the island's economy—was introduced to the Puerto Rican highlands from the nearby Dominican Republic.

Despite the power of San Juan and its Spanish institutions, 18th-century Puerto Rico was predominantly rural. The report of a special emissary of the Spanish king, Marshal Alejandro O'Reilly, remains a remarkably complete analysis of 18th-century Puerto Rican society. It helped promote a more progressive series of fiscal and administrative policies that reflected the Enlightenment ideals found in many European countries.

Puerto Rico began to be viewed as a potential source of income for the Spanish Empire rather than a drain on income. One of O'Reilly's most visible legacies was his recommendation that people live in towns rather than be scattered about the countryside. Shortly after this, seven new towns were established.

As the island prospered and its bourgeoisie became more numerous and affluent, life became more refined. New public buildings were erected; concerts were introduced; and everyday aspects of life—such as furniture and social ritual—grew more ornate. Insights into Puerto Rico's changing life can be seen in the works of its most famous 18th-century painter, José Campeche.

THE LAST BASTION

Much of the politics of 19th-century Latin America cannot be understood without a review of Spain's problems at that time. Up until 1850, there was political and military turmoil in Spain, a combination that eventually led to the collapse of its empire. Since 1796, Spain had been a military satellite of postrevolutionary France, an alliance that brought it into conflict with England. In 1804 Admiral Horatio Lord Nelson's definitive victory for England over French and Spanish ships during the Battle of Trafalgar left England in supreme control of the international sea lanes and interrupted trade and communications between Spain and its colonies in the New World.

These events led to changes for Spanish-speaking America. The revolutionary fervor of Simón Bolívar and his South American compatriots spilled over to the entire continent, embroiling Spain in a desperate attempt to hold on to the tattered remains of its empire. Recognizing that Puerto Rico and Cuba were probably the last bastions of Spanish Royalist sympathy in the Americas, Spain liberalized its trade policies, decreeing that goods no longer had to pass through Seville.

The sheer weight and volume of illegal Puerto Rican trade with such countries as Denmark, France, and—most importantly—the United States, forced Spain's hand in establishing a realistic set of trade reforms. A bloody revolution in Haiti, which had produced more sugar cane than almost any other West Indies island, spurred sugar-cane and coffee production in Puerto Rico. Also important was the introduction of a new and more prolific species of sugar cane, the Otahiti, which helped increase production even more.

By the 1820s the United States was providing ample supplies of such staples as lumber, salt, butter, fish, grain, and foodstuffs, and huge amounts of Puerto Rican sugar, molasses, coffee, and rum were consumed in the United States. Meanwhile, the United States was increasingly viewed as the keeper of the peace in the Caribbean, suppressing the piracy that flourished while Spain's navy was preoccupied with its European wars.

During Venezuela's separation from Spain, Venezuelans loyal to the Spanish Crown fled en masse to the remaining Royalist bastions in the Americas— Puerto Rico and, to a lesser extent, Cuba. Although many arrived penniless, having forfeited their properties in South America in exchange for their lives, their excellent understanding of agriculture and commerce probably catalyzed much of the era's economic development in Puerto Rico. Simultaneously, many historians argue, their unflinching loyalty to the Spanish Crown contributed to one of the most conservative and reactionary social structures anywhere in the Spanish-speaking Caribbean. In any event, dozens of Spanish naval expeditions that were intended to suppress the revolutions in Venezuela were outfitted in Puerto Rican harbors during this period.

A REVOLT SUPPRESSED & SLAVERY ABOLISHED

During the latter half of the 19th century, political divisions were drawn in Puerto Rico, reflecting both the political instability in Spain and the increasing demands of Puerto Ricans for some form of self-rule. As governments and regimes in Spain rose and fell, Spanish policies toward its colonies in the New World changed, too.

In 1865 representatives from Puerto Rico, Cuba, and the Philippines were invited to Madrid to air their grievances as part of a process of liberalizing Spanish colonial policy. Reforms, however, did not follow as promised, and a much-publicized and very visible minirevolt (during which the mountain city of Lares was occupied) was suppressed by the Spanish governors in 1868. Some of the funds and much of the publicity for this revolt came from expatriate Puerto Ricans living in Chile, St. Thomas, and New York.

Slavery was abolished in March 1873, about 40 years after it had been abolished throughout the British Empire. About 32,000 slaves were freed following years of liberal agitation. Abolition was viewed as a major victory for liberal forces throughout Puerto Rico, although cynics claim that slavery was much less entrenched in Puerto Rico than in neighboring Cuba, where the sugar economy was far more dependent on slave labor.

The 1895 revolution in Cuba increased the Puerto Rican demand for greater self-rule; during the ensuing intellectual ferment, many political parties emerged. The Cuban revolution provided part of the spark that led to the Spanish-American War, Cuban independence, and U.S. control of Puerto Rico, the Philippines, and the Pacific island of Guam.

THE YANKS ARE COMING, THE YANKS ARE COMING!

In 1897, faced with intense pressure from sources within Puerto Rico, a weakened Spain granted its colony a measure of autonomy, but it came too late. Other events were taking place between Spain and the United States that would forever change the future of Puerto Rico.

On February 15, 1898, the U.S. battleship *Maine* was blown up in the harbor of Havana, killing 266 men. The so-called yellow press in the United States, especially the papers owned by the tycoon William Randolph Hearst, aroused Americans' emotions into a fever pitch for war, with the rallying cry "Remember the *Maine*."

On April 20 of that year, President William McKinley signed a resolution demanding Spanish withdrawal from Cuba. The president ordered a blockade of Cuba's ports, and on April 24, Spain, in retaliation, declared a state of war with the United States. On April 25, the U.S. Congress declared war on Spain. In Cuba, the naval battle of Santiago was won by American forces, and in another part of the world, the Spanish colony of the Philippines was also captured by U.S. troops.

On July 25, after their victory at Santiago, U.S. troops landed at Guánica, Puerto Rico, and several days later they took over Ponce. U.S. Navy Capt. Alfred T. Mahan later wrote that the United States viewed Puerto Rico, Spain's remaining colonial outpost in the Caribbean, as vital to American interests in the area. Puerto Rico could be used as a military base to help the United States maintain control of the Isthmus of Panama and to keep communications and traffic flowing between the Atlantic and the Pacific.

Spain offered to trade other territory for Puerto Rico, but the United States refused and demanded Spain's ouster from the island. Left with little choice against superior U.S. forces, Spain capitulated. The Spanish-American War ended on August 31, 1898, with the surrender of Spain and the virtual collapse of the once-powerful Spanish Empire. Puerto Rico, in the words of McKinley, was to "become a territory of the United States."

Although the entire war lasted just over 4 months, the invasion of Puerto Rico took only 2 weeks. "It wasn't much of a war," remarked Theodore Roosevelt, who had led the Rough Riders cavalry outfit in their charge up San Juan Hill, "but it was all the war there was." The United States had suffered only four casualties while acquiring Puerto Rico, the Philippines, and the island of Guam. The Treaty of Paris, signed on December 10, 1898, settled the terms of Spain's surrender.

A DUBIOUS PRIZE

Some Americans looked on Puerto Rico as a "dubious prize." One-third of the population consisted of mulattoes and blacks, descended from slaves, who had no money or land. Only about 12% of the population could read or write. About 8% were enrolled in school. It is estimated that a powerful landed gentry—only about 2% of the population—owned more than two-thirds of the land.

Washington set up a military government in Puerto Rico, headed by the War Department. A series of governors-general were appointed to rule the island, with almost the authority of dictators. Although ruling over a rather unhappy populace, these governors-general brought about much-needed change, including tax and public health reforms. But most Puerto Ricans wanted autonomy, and many leaders, including Luís Muñoz Rivera, tried to persuade Washington to compromise. However, their protests generally fell on deaf ears.

Tensions mounted between Puerto Ricans and their new American governors. In 1900, U.S. Secretary of War Elihu Root decided that military rule of the island was inadequate; he advocated a program of autonomy that won the endorsement of President McKinley.

The island's beleaguered economy was further devastated by an 1899 hurricane that caused millions of dollars' worth of property damage, killed 3,000 people, and left one out of four people homeless. Belatedly, Congress allocated the sum of $200,000, but this did little to relieve the suffering.

Thus began a nearly 50-year colonial protectorate relationship, as Puerto Rico was recognized as an unincorporated territory with its governor named by the president of the United States. Only the president had the right to override the veto of the island's governors. The legislative branch was composed of an 11-member executive committee appointed by the president, plus a 35-member chamber of delegates elected by popular vote. A resident commissioner, it was agreed, would represent Puerto Rico in Congress, "with voice but no vote."

As the United States prepared to enter World War I in 1917, Puerto Ricans were granted U.S. citizenship and, thus, were subject to military service. The people of Puerto Rico were allowed to elect their legislature, which had been reorganized into a Senate and a House of Representatives. The president of the United States continued to appoint the governor of the island and retained the power to veto any of the governor's actions.

FROM HARVARD TO REVOLUTION

Many Puerto Ricans continued (at times rather violently) to agitate for independence. Requests for a plebiscite were constantly turned down. Meanwhile, economic conditions improved as the island's population began to grow dramatically. Government revenues increased as large corporations from the U.S. mainland found Puerto Rico a profitable place in which to do business. There was much labor unrest, and by 1909, a labor movement demanding better working conditions and higher wages was gaining momentum.

The emerging labor movement showed its strength by organizing a cigar workers' strike in 1914 and a sugar-cane workers' strike the following year. The 1930s proved to be disastrous for Puerto Rico, which suffered greatly from the worldwide depression. To make matters worse, two devastating hurricanes—one in 1928 and another in 1932—destroyed millions of dollars' worth of crops and property. There was also an outbreak of disease that demoralized the population. Some relief came in the form of food shipments authorized by Congress.

As tension between Puerto Rico and the United States intensified, there emerged Pedro Albizu Campos, a graduate of Harvard Law School and a former U.S. Army officer. Leading a group of militant anti-American revolutionaries, he held that America's claim to Puerto Rico was illegal, since the island had already been granted autonomy by Spain.

Terrorist acts by his followers, including assassinations, led to Albizu's imprisonment, but terrorist activities continued.

In 1935 President Franklin D. Roosevelt launched the Puerto Rican Reconstruction Administration, which provided for agricultural development, public works, and electrification. The following year, Sen. Millard E. Tidings of Maryland introduced a measure to grant independence to the island. His efforts were cheered by a local leader, Luís Muñoz Marín, son of the statesman Luís Muñoz Rivera. In 1938 the young Muñoz founded the Popular Democratic Party, which adopted the slogan "Bread, Land, and Liberty." By 1940 this party had gained control of more than 50% of the seats of both the upper and lower houses of government, and the young Muñoz was elected leader of the Senate.

Roosevelt appointed Rexford Guy Tugwell governor of Puerto Rico; Tugwell spoke Spanish and seemed to have genuine concern for the plight of the islanders. Muñoz met with Tugwell and convinced him that Puerto Rico was capable of electing its own governor. As a step in that direction, Roosevelt appointed Jesús Piñero as the first resident commissioner of the island. In 1944 the U.S. Congress approved a bill granting Puerto Rico the right to elect its own governor. This was the beginning of the famed Operation Bootstrap, a pump-priming fiscal and economic aid package designed to improve the island's standard of living.

SHOOTING AT HARRY

In 1946 President Harry S. Truman appointed native-born Jesús Piñero as governor of Puerto Rico, and the following year the U.S. Congress recognized the right of Puerto Ricans to elect their own governor. In 1948, Luís Muñoz Marín became the first elected governor and immediately recommended that Puerto

Rico be transformed into an "associated free state." Endorsement of his plan was delayed by Washington, but President Truman approved the Puerto Rican Commonwealth Bill in 1950, providing for a plebiscite in which voters would decide whether they would remain a colony or become a U.S. commonwealth. In June 1951, Puerto Ricans voted three to one for commonwealth status, and on July 25, 1952, the Commonwealth of Puerto Rico was born.

This event was marred when a group of nationalists marched on the Governor's Mansion in San Juan, resulting in 27 deaths and hundreds of casualties. A month later, two Puerto Rican nationalists made an unsuccessful attempt on Truman's life in Washington, killing a police officer in the process. And in March 1954, four Puerto Rican nationalists wounded five U.S. Congressmen when they fired down into the House of Representatives from the visitors' gallery.

Despite this violence, during the 1950s Puerto Rico began to take pride in its culture and traditions. In 1955 the Institute of Puerto Rican Culture was established, and 1957 saw the inauguration of the Pablo Casals Festival, which launched a renaissance of classical music and a celebration of the arts. In 1959 a wealthy industrialist, Luís A. Ferré, donated his personal art collection toward the establishment of the Museo de Arte de Ponce.

GIVE ME LIBERTY OR GIVE ME STATEHOOD

Luís Muñoz Marín resigned from office in 1964, but his party continued to win subsequent elections. The Independent Party, which demanded complete autonomy, gradually lost power. An election on July 23, 1967, reconfirmed the desire of most Puerto Ricans to maintain commonwealth status. In 1968 Luís A. Ferré won a close race for governor, spearheading a pro-statehood party, the Partido

Nuevo Progresista, or New Progressive Party. It staunchly advocated statehood as an alternative to the island's commonwealth status, but in 1972, the Partido Popular Democrático, or Popular Democratic Party, returned to power; by then, the island's economy was based largely on tourism, rum, and industry. Operation Bootstrap had been successful in creating thousands of new jobs, although more than 100,000 Puerto Ricans moved to the U.S. mainland during the 1950s, seeking a better life. The island's economy continued to improve, although perhaps not as quickly as anticipated by Operation Bootstrap.

Puerto Rico grabbed the world's attention in 1979 with the launching of the Pan-American Games. The island's culture received a boost in 1981 with the opening of the Center of the Performing Arts in San Juan, which attracted world-famous performers and virtuosos. The international spotlight again focused on Puerto Rico at the time of the first papal visit there in 1986. John Paul II (or Juan Pablo II, as he was called locally) kindled a renewed interest in religion, especially among the Catholic youth of the island.

In 1996, Puerto Rico lost its special tax-break status, which had originally lured U.S. industry to the island. Down the road, some dire consequences to the island's economy are predicted as a result of this loss.

A flare-up between the U.S. Navy and Puerto Ricans, especially the islanders of Vieques, burst into the headlines in 1999. Islanders vehemently protested the Navy's use of Vieques for the testing of bombardments.

In 2001, Sila M. Calderón was inaugurated as Puerto Rico's first female governor. The daughter of a rich entrepreneur whose holdings include ice-cream factories and hotels, she was raised to a life of privilege. As head of the Popular Democratic Party, she took office and immediately angered

Washington by advocating that the U.S. Navy halt bombing on Vieques. She also opposes statehood for Puerto Rico. "When I was a little girl everybody who had power were men," the new governor told the press. "Now girls know that it is very normal for power to be shared by men and women."

In 2003, the U.S. Navy closed its Roosevelt Roads Naval Station on the island of Vieques in the wake of massive protests. With the closing, more than 6,000 people lost their jobs and the island itself suffered a falloff of $300 million a year in income. Puerto Rican leaders are hoping to fill the economic gap with tourism.

The navy since 1947 had used parts of the island for test bombing. The former naval base has been turned over to the U.S. Fish and Wildlife Service for use as a nature refuge, as the landmass is the home to several endangered species.

In December 2005 the Bush administration asked Congress to set another vote to allow the citizens of the overpopulated island to decide on their future: to opt for statehood or else full independence. Statehood would bring the right to vote in U.S. elections, and full independence would require some islanders to relinquish their American citizenship.

Because of the possible disastrous economic consequences of full independence, only a small number of Puerto Ricans back full independence. As a state, Puerto Rico might alter the balance of power between Democrats and Republicans.

Of course, one option still remains on the table and that is for Puerto Rico to continue as a commonwealth of the U.S. At present, Puerto Rico has no voting representation in Congress. On the other hand, islanders pay no federal income taxes and benefit from billions in federal social programs.

In 2008, Gov. Aníbal Acevedo Vilá was indicted by federal authorities for crimes related to an alleged illegal campaign fundraising scheme. Ironically, he had squeaked into office in 2004 by around 3,500 votes largely because of a series of corruption cases involving the political associates of his opponent, former Gov. Pedro Rosselló, who served from 1993 through 2000.

Rosselló's two terms in office were marked by the construction of huge government works projects, including the Tren Urbano and a north coast water aqueduct, as well as a series of government reforms. Corruption cases involving Cabinet secretaries and other officials tarnished the image of his administration, however.

3 The Lay of the Land: Beaches, Mountains, the Rainforest, Off-Island Islands & More

Roughly half the size of New Jersey, this U.S. commonwealth with 272 miles (438km) of Atlantic and Caribbean coastline sits strategically some 1,000 miles (1,609km) southeast of Florida at the hub of the Caribbean chain of islands. You'll probably fly in and out of San Juan at least once if you're doing much touring in the region. And with a 2-year, $2.8-million project that restored its waterfront, this oldest capital city under the U.S. flag is also the world's second-largest home port for cruise-ship passengers.

Puerto Rico has experienced many political changes since the days of its first Spanish governor, Juan Ponce de León, the conquistador who sailed with Columbus and who allegedly tried in vain to find a fountain of youth in Florida. With nearly 500 years reflected in its restored Spanish colonial architecture, Old San Juan is the Caribbean's greatest historic center.

Puerto Rico is the most easterly and the smallest of the four major islands that form the Greater Antilles. The other three are Cuba, Jamaica, and Hispaniola (which is home to two nations, Haiti and the Dominican Republic). Surrounded by the Atlantic Ocean to the north and the Caribbean Sea to the south, Puerto Rico is flanked by a trio of smaller islands—Vieques and Culebra to the east and Mona to the west—which are its political and geologic satellites.

The island's terrain ranges from palm-lined beaches on four coastlines to rugged mountain ranges, gently rolling hills, and dry desert-like areas. There are 20 designated forest reserves in Puerto Rico.

BEACHES
The island has dozens of miles of sandy beaches, some long and straight, others broken into coves by headlands. On the northern coast, the Atlantic waters are often more turbulent than those along the more tranquil southern coast. (See "The Best Beaches" in chapter 1. For even more strips of sand, refer to the previews of beaches given in the individual chapters of this book.)

TOWERING MOUNTAINS
Besides the beaches, the island's most noteworthy geological feature is the Cordillera—the towering mountains that rise high above its central region. Geologists have identified the island's summits as the high parts of a chain of mountains whose mass is mostly submerged beneath the sea. These mountains are some of the oldest of the many landmasses in the West Indies.

What makes the mountain altitudes even more impressive is the existence, about 75 miles (121km) to the island's north, of one of the deepest depressions in the Atlantic, the Puerto Rico Trough. Running more or less parallel to the island's northern shoreline, it plunges to depths of up to 30,000 feet (9,000m). Although not as obvious as this trench, the sea floor a few miles from the island's southern coast also drops off, to nearly 17,000 feet (5,100m) below sea level. Geologists have calculated that if the base of this mountain chain were at sea level, it would be one of the highest landmasses in the world. Puerto Rico's highest summit—Cerro de Punta, at 4,389 feet (1,338m)—would exceed in altitude Mount Everest, the world's tallest peak.

Most of Puerto Rico's geology, especially its mountain peaks, resulted from volcanic activity that deposited lava and igneous rock in consecutive layers. To a lesser degree, the island is also composed of quartz, diamite, and, along some of its edges, coral limestone.

EL YUNQUE & THE OTHER FOREST PRESERVES

The mountains are home to the island's greatest natural attraction, El Yunque (© 787/888-1810 or 787/888-1880 for information), a 30-minute drive east of San Juan. Given national-park status by President Theodore Roosevelt, this 28,000-acre (11,331-hectare) preserve is the only tropical rainforest on U.S. soil and is protected by the U.S. Forest Service.

Today, El Yunque offers visitors close encounters of the natural kind, from picnics amid rare flora and fauna to hikes along scenic trails. Encompassing four distinct forest types, it is home to 240 species of tropical trees; flowers, including more than 20 kinds of orchids; and other wildlife, including millions of tiny tree frogs whose distinctive cry of *coquí* (pronounced "ko-*kee*") has given them their name. For details on touring this unique attraction, see chapter 9.

Puerto Rico also has 19 other forest preserves. Directly east of San Juan lies Piñones Forest, which contains the island's largest mangrove forest. West of

Ponce, Guánica Forest borders several white-sand beaches and the historic bay where U.S. troops first landed in 1898 during the Spanish-American War. Cambalache Forest, east of Arecibo, contains plantations of eucalyptus, teak, and mahoe trees. The driest vegetation and expansive views to the west coast are found in Maricao Forest. Few visitors will have time for a forest preserve other than El Yunque. If you do, make it Toro Negro Forest Reserve, which straddles the peaks of the Cordillera in the center of the island and boasts the island's tallest peak, with stunning drops to the Caribbean and the Atlantic. For more details on exploring Toro Negro, see the "Ponce" section of chapter 10. All of these forests are open to visitors, and several have picnic areas and campsites.

THE KARST COUNTRY & RIO CAMUY CAVES

One of the most mysterious areas of Puerto Rico is the Karst Country. One of the world's strangest rock formations, karst is formed by the process of water sinking into limestone. As time goes by, large basins are eroded, forming sinkholes. Mogotes, or karstic hillocks, are peaks of earth where the land didn't sink into the erosion pits. The Karst Country lies along the island's north coast, northeast of Mayagüez, in the foothills between Quebradillas and Manatí. The region is filled with an extensive network of caves. One sinkhole contains the 20-acre (8-hectare) dish of the world's largest radio/radar telescope at the Arecibo Observatory.

Reached by Route 446, the Guajataca Forest Reserve is found here, offering some 25 miles (40km) of trails that take you through some of the most rugged parts of this country.

Eons ago, one of the world's largest underground rivers carved the Río Camuy Caves in northwest Puerto Rico, which experts today consider to be among the most spectacular caves on earth. The Río Camuy Caves contain evidence of occupation long before the island was sighted by Columbus in 1493. The first professional explorers of the system were led to the site by local boys already familiar with some of the entrances.

For a journey through this foreboding landscape, see chapter 9.

OFF-ISLAND ISLANDS

Three offshore islands—Mona, Vieques, and Culebra—are well worth exploring.

Despite bad publicity generated by U.S. Naval bombing exercises, Vieques is the most developed of the offshore islands from a tourist perspective. Shaped like a long fish, its spine is a mountain range that separates it lengthwise from west to east. At 21 miles (34km) in length and 5 miles (8km) in width, Vieques is the largest landmass of the Spanish Virgin Islands.

Although the Spanish referred to both Vieques and Culebra as *las islas inútiles* (the useless islands) because there was no gold to be mined there, they are *islas bonitas* for the visitor. Offering the lazy life, Vieques has top-notch inns and excellent and relatively undiscovered dining. Most visitors come here to escape and to enjoy the gorgeous beaches.

Even sleepier than Vieques is the smaller and less developed island of Culebra. It's a place where you have to drive carefully to let Mother Hen cross the road. At a distance of some 17 miles (27km) east of the Puerto Rican port of Fajardo, Culebra, from the geologist's point of view, is closer to the U.S. Virgin Islands than "mainland" Puerto Rico. St. Thomas lies only 12 miles (19km) to the east.

With its rugged peaks, sandy beaches, and offshore caves, Culebra can quickly bring out the beach bum in you. Many visitors, in fact, have settled there. As two *culebrenses* (the name of the islanders) confided to us, "If you come here with gringo uptightness, you'll lose it in a few days."

Much of Culebra is a national wildlife refuge—so much so that in summer many of the beaches are closed by the U.S. Fish and Wildlife Service because they are nesting grounds for endangered sea turtles.

For touring details on Vieques and Culebra, see chapter 13.

A unique environment can be found on Mona Island, 50 miles (80km) west of Puerto Rico. Like the Galápagos Islands, this untouched island has species that are not found elsewhere. Mona is a protected island, under the management of the U.S. National Park Service and the Puerto Rico Department of Natural and Environmental Resources. Accessible by a sometimes difficult, long, boat ride, the island is available for sport diving to those who are willing to rough it. See p. 249.

The people of Puerto Rico represent a mix of races, cultures, languages, and religions. They draw their heritage from the original native population, from Spanish royalists who sought refuge here, from African slaves imported to work the sugar plantations, and from other Caribbean islanders who have come here seeking jobs. The Spanish they speak is a mix, too, with many words borrowed from the pre-Columbian Amerindian tongue as well as English. Even the Catholicism they practice incorporates some Taíno and African traditions.

4 The Population & Popular Culture

Nearly 4 million people inhabit the main island of Puerto Rico, making it one of the most densely populated islands in the world. It has an average of about 1,000 people per square mile, a ratio higher than that of any of the 50 states. There are nearly as many Puerto Ricans living stateside as there are on the island. If they were to all return home, the island would be so crowded that there would be virtually no room for them to live.

When the United States acquired the island in 1898, most Puerto Ricans worked in agriculture; today most jobs are industrial. One-third of Puerto Rico's population is concentrated in the San Juan metropolitan area.

When the Spanish forced the Taíno peoples into slavery, virtually the entire indigenous population was decimated, except for a few Amerindians who escaped into the remote mountains. Eventually they intermarried with the poor Spanish farmers and became known as *jíbaros*. Because of industrialization and migration to the cities, few *jíbaros* remain.

Besides the slaves imported from Africa to work on the plantations, other ethnic groups joined the island's racial mix. Fleeing Simón Bolívar's independence movements in South America, Spanish loyalists headed to Puerto Rico—a fiercely conservative Spanish colony during the early 1800s. French families also flocked here from both Louisiana and Haiti, as changing governments or violent revolutions turned their worlds upside down. As word of the rich sugar-cane economy reached economically depressed Scotland and Ireland, many farmers from those countries also journeyed to Puerto Rico in search of a better life.

During the mid–19th century, labor was needed to build roads. Initially, Chinese workers were imported for this task, followed by workers from countries such as Italy, France, Germany, and even Lebanon. American expatriates came to the island after 1898. Long after Spain had lost control of Puerto Rico, Spanish immigrants continued to arrive on the island. The most significant new immigrant population arrived in the 1960s, when thousands of Cubans fled from Fidel Castro's communist state. The latest arrivals in Puerto Rico have come from the Dominican Republic.

Islanders are most known for their contributions to popular music, and visitors here will no doubt see why. Sometimes, the whole island seems to be dancing. It's been that way since the Taínos, with music an important aspect of their religious and cultural ceremonies.

The latest musical craze born in Puerto Rico is reggaeton, an infectious blend of rap, reggae, and island rhythms, often accompanied by x-rated hip shaking. Daddy Yankee put the music on the world map with his hit "Gasolina"; other well-known island artists in the genre are the duo Wisin y Yandel and Don Omar. Vico C is a local rapper credited with being a pioneer for today's reggaeton stars.

Puerto Rico is still dominated by salsa, a mix of African, Caribbean, and North American rhythms. Salsa bands tend to be full orchestras, with brass sections and several percussionists. The beat is infectious and non-stop, but salsa dancing is all about smooth gyrations and style.

The late Tito Puente, a Latin Jazz master, was instrumental in the development of the music along with singer Ismael Miranda. Puerto Rican salsa won worldwide fame in the late 1970s and early 1980s through groups such as the Fania All Stars, which paired Héctor Lavoe, Rubén Blades and Willie Colón, and El Gran Combo, which still performs today after 40 years together. Famous contemporary practitioners are Gilberto Santa Rosa and Marc Anthony.

The most famous Puerto Rican singer, however, is pop star Ricky Martin, who continues to be a hometown favorite and sells out shows during his frequent island performances. Actress and singer Jennifer López, the wife of Anthony, is another of Puerto Rico's most famous descendants. Their pet project, the biopic "El Cantante," based on Lavoe's life, was filmed in Puerto Rico and New York in 2007.

A total of four Puerto Rican women have won the Miss Universe competition; most recently Zuleyka Rivera in 2006.

Puerto Ricans have also made their mark in professional sports, particularly baseball. The most famous, of course, was Roberto Clemente, who is still a local legend and a role model for young ball players. Current professional baseball players from Puerto Rico include Jorge Posada; Carlos Delgado; Carlos Beltrán; Iván Rodríguez; and the Molina brothers, Bengie and Yadier.

LANGUAGES

Spanish is the language of Puerto Rico, although English is widely spoken, especially in hotels, restaurants, shops, and nightclubs that attract tourists. In the hinterlands, however, Spanish prevails.

If you plan to travel extensively in Puerto Rico but don't speak Spanish, pick up a Spanish-language phrase book. The most popular is *Berlitz Spanish for Travelers,* published by Collier Macmillan. The University of Chicago's *Pocketbook Dictionary* is equally helpful. If you have a basic knowledge of Spanish and want to improve your word usage and your sentence structure, consider purchasing a copy of *Spanish Now,* published by Barron's.

Many Amerindian words from pre-Columbian times have been retained in the language. For example, the Puerto Rican national anthem, titled "La Borinqueña," refers to the Arawak name for the island Borinquén, and Mayagüez, Yauco, Caguas, Guaynabo, and Arecibo are all pre-Columbian place names.

Many Amerindian words were borrowed to describe the phenomena of the New World. The natives slept in *hamacas,* and today Puerto Ricans still lounge in hammocks. The god Juracán was feared by the Arawaks just as much as contemporaries fear autumn hurricanes. African words were also added to the linguistic mix, and Castilian Spanish was significantly modified.

With the American takeover in 1898, English became the first Germanic language to be introduced into Puerto Rico. This linguistic marriage led to what some scholars call Spanglish, a colloquial dialect blending English and Spanish into forms not considered classically correct in either linguistic tradition.

The bilingual confusion was also greatly accelerated by the mass migration to the U.S. mainland of thousands of Puerto Ricans, who quickly altered their speech patterns to conform to the language used in the urban Puerto Rican communities of cities such as New York.

RELIGIONS

The majority of Puerto Ricans are Roman Catholic, but religious freedom for all faiths is guaranteed by the Commonwealth Constitution. There is a Jewish Community Center in Miramar, and there's a Jewish Reformed Congregation in Santurce. There are Protestant services for Baptists, Episcopalians, Lutherans, and Presbyterians, and there are other interdenominational services.

Although it is predominantly Catholic, Puerto Rico does not follow Catholic dogma and rituals as assiduously as do the churches of Spain and Italy. Because the church supported slavery, there was a long-lasting resentment against the all-Spanish clergy of colonial days. Island-born men were excluded from the priesthood. When Puerto Ricans eventually took over the

Catholic churches on the island, they followed some guidelines from Spain and Italy but modified or ignored others.

Following the U.S. acquisition of the island in 1898, Protestantism grew in influence and popularity. There were Protestants on the island before the invasion, but their numbers increased after Puerto Rico became a U.S. colony. Many islanders liked the idea of separation of church and state, as provided for in the U.S. Constitution. In recent years, Pentecostal fundamentalism has swept across the island. There are some 1,500 Evangelical churches in Puerto Rico today.

As throughout Latin America, the practice of Catholicism in Puerto Rico blends native Taíno and African traditions with mainstream tenets of the faith. It has been said that the real religion of Puerto Rico is *espiritsmo* (spiritualism), a quasi-magical belief in occult forces. Spanish colonial rulers outlawed spiritualism, but under the U.S. occupation it flourished in dozens of isolated pockets of the island.

Students of religion trace spiritualism to the Taínos, and to their belief that *jípia* (the spirits of the dead—somewhat like the legendary vampire) slumbered by day and prowled the island by night. Instead of looking for bodies, the *jípia* were seeking wild fruit to eat. Thus arose the Puerto Rican tradition of putting out fruit on the kitchen table. Even in modern homes today, you'll often find a bowl of plastic, flamboyantly colored fruit resting atop a refrigerator.

Many islanders still believe in the "evil eye," or *mal de ojo.* To look on a person or a person's possessions covetously, according to believers, can lead to that individual's sickness or perhaps death. Children are given bead charm bracelets to guard against the evil eye. Spiritualism also extends into healing, folk medicine, and food. For example, some spiritualists believe that cold food should never be eaten with hot food. Some island plants, herbs, and oils are believed to have healing properties, and spiritualist literature is available throughout the island.

5 *Comida Criolla:* Puerto Rican Cuisine

Some of Puerto Rico's finest chefs—Wilo Benet and Alfredo Ayala—have based their supremely successful careers on paying gourmet homage to their mothers' and grandmothers' cooking. A whole new generation of rising culinary artists is following in their footsteps by putting Puerto Rico's *comida criolla* at the front and center of their Nuevo Latino experimentation.

Comida criolla, as Puerto Rican food is known, is flavorful but not hot. It can be traced back to the Arawaks and Taínos, the original inhabitants of the island, who thrived on a diet of corn, tropical fruit, and seafood. When Ponce de León arrived with Columbus in 1493, the Spanish added beef, pork, rice, wheat, and olive oil to the island's foodstuffs.

The Spanish soon began planting sugar cane and importing slaves from Africa, who brought with them okra and taro (known in Puerto Rico as *yautia*). The mingling of flavors and ingredients passed from generation to generation among the different ethnic groups that settled on the island, resulting in the exotic blend of today's Puerto Rican cuisine.

Its two essential ingredients are *sofrito,* a mix of garlic, sweet peppers, onion, and fresh green herbs, and *adobo,* a blend of dried spices like peppercorns, oregano, garlic, salt, olive oil, and lime juice or vinegar, rubbed on pork or chicken before it is slowly roasted. *Achiote* (annatto seeds) is often used as well, imparting an orange color to many common Puerto Rican dishes. Other seasonings and ingredients commonly used are coriander, papaya, cacao, *níspero* (a tropical fruit that's brown, juicy, and related to the kiwi), and *apio* (a small African-derived tuber that's sort of a more pungent type of turnip).

The rich and fertile fields of Puerto Rico produce a wide variety of **vegetables.** A favorite is the **chayote,** a pear-shaped vegetable called *christophine* throughout most of the English-speaking Caribbean. Its delicately flavored flesh is often compared to that of summer squash. Native root vegetables like yucca, breadfruit and plantain, called *viandas,* either accompany main meals or are used as ingredients in them.

APPETIZERS & SOUPS

Lunch and dinner generally begin with hot appetizers such as *bacalaitos,* crunchy cod fritters; *surullitos,* sweet and plump cornmeal fingers; and *empanadillas,* crescent-shaped turnovers filled with lobster, crab, conch, or beef. For starters, also look to *tostones* or *arepas,* baked flour casseroles, stuffed with seafood or meat. Fried cheeses in dipping sauces made with tropical fruit are another option.

Soups are also a popular beginning, with a traditional chicken soup *caldo gallego* being a local favorite. Imported from Spain's northwestern province of Galicia, it is prepared with salt pork, white beans, ham, and *berzas* (collard greens) or *grelos* (turnip greens), and the whole kettle is flavored with spicy *chorizos* (Spanish sausages). *Sopón de pescado* (fish soup), is prepared with the head and tail intact and relies on the catch of the day. Traditionally, it is made with garlic and spices plus onions and tomatoes with the flavor enhanced by a tiny dash of vinegar and varying amounts of sherry. Variations differ from restaurant to restaurant. Recently, thick comfort soups made with *viandas,* like plantain or pumpkin, have been taking a flavorful stand at many *nuevo criolla* restaurants.

There are also ever present accompaniments at every Puerto Rican meal. Yucca is often steamed then served in olive oil and vinegar with sweet roasted peppers and onions. Fried plantain disks called *tostones* accompany most meals. The plantains are also smashed with garlic and other seasonings and cooked into a casserole called *mofongo.* White rice and delicious stewed pink beans, called *arroz y habichuelas,* are also ever present side dishes to most main meals. Another is *arroz con gandules,* stewed rice with pigeon pieces.

MAIN COURSES

Stews loom large in the Puerto Rican diet, and none larger than **asopao,** a hearty gumbo made with either chicken or shellfish. Every Puerto Rican chef has his or her own recipe. *Asopao de pollo* (chicken stew) takes a whole chicken, which is then flavored with spices such as oregano, garlic, and paprika, along with salt pork, cured ham, green peppers, chile peppers, onions, cilantro, olives, tomatoes, chorizos, and pimientos. For a final touch, green peas might be added. Seafood lovers will adore versions using lobster or shrimp. The most basic version simply uses rice and pigeon peas, a healthy, more economical alternative that loses little on the flavor front. Stews are usually cooked in a *caldera* (heavy kettle). Another popular one is *carne guisada puertorriqueña* (Puerto Rican beef stew). The ingredients that flavor the chunks of beef vary according to the cook's whims or whatever happens to be in the larder. These might include green peppers, sweet chile peppers, onions, garlic, cilantro, potatoes, olives stuffed with pimientos, or capers. Seeded raisins may be added on occasion.

While *mofongo* is a dependable side dish, it also takes center stage at many meals when it is formed into a hollow casserole and stuffed with seafood (shrimp,

Fun Fact Strange Fruit

Reading of Capt. James Cook's explorations of the South Pacific in the late 1700s, West Indian planters were intrigued by his accounts of the **breadfruit tree,** which grew in abundance on Tahiti. Seeing it as a source of cheap food for their slaves, they beseeched King George III to sponsor an expedition to bring the trees to the Caribbean. In 1787 the king put Capt. William Bligh in command of HMS *Bounty* and sent him to do just that. One of Bligh's lieutenants was a former shipmate named Fletcher Christian. They became the leading actors in one of the great sea yarns when Christian overpowered Bligh, took over the *Bounty,* threw the breadfruit trees into the South Pacific Ocean, and disappeared into oblivion.

Bligh survived by sailing the ship's open longboat 3,000 miles (4,830km) to the East Indies, where he hitched a ride back to England on a Dutch vessel. Later he was given command of another ship and sent to Tahiti to get more breadfruit. Although he succeeded on this second attempt, the whole operation went for naught when the West Indies slaves refused to eat the strange fruit of the new tree, preferring instead their old, familiar rice.

Descendants of those trees still grow in the Caribbean, and the islanders prepare the head-size fruit in a number of ways. A thick green rind covers its starchy, sweet flesh whose flavor is evocative of a sweet potato. *Tostones*—fried green breadfruit slices—accompany most meat, fish, or poultry dishes served today in Puerto Rico.

lobster, or the catch of the day) or chicken in tomato sauce. It's called *mofongo relleno. Pastelones de carne,* or **meat pies,** are the staple of many Puerto Rican dinners. Salt pork and ham are often used for the filling and are cooked in a *caldero* (small cauldron). This medley of meats and spices is covered with a pastry top and baked.

Other typical main dishes include fried beefsteak with onions *(carne frita con cebolla), veal (ternera)* a la parmesana, and roast leg of pork, fresh ham, lamb, or veal *a la criolla.* These roasted meats are cooked in the Creole style, flavored with *adobo. Chicharrónes*—fried pork with the crunchy skin left on top for added flavor—is very popular, especially around Christmastime. Puerto Ricans also like such dishes as *sesos empanados* (breaded calves' brains), *riñones guisados* (calves' kidney stew), and *lengua rellena* (stuffed beef tongue). Other meats tend to be slowly grilled or sautéed until tender.

Both chicken and fish are important ingredients made dozens of different ways. Two common ways of serving them are *al ajillo,* in a garlic sauce, or *a la criolla,* in a tomato sauce with pepper, onions and Spanish olives. Puerto Ricans adore **chicken,** which they flavor with various spices and seasonings. *Arroz con pollo* (chicken with rice) is the most popular chicken dish on the island, and it was brought long ago to the U.S. mainland. Other favorite preparations include *pollo al kerez* (chicken in sherry), *pollo en agridulce* (sweet-and-sour chicken), and *pollitos asados a la parrilla* (broiled chicken).

A festive island dish is *lechón asado,* or **barbecued pig,** which is usually cooked for a party of 12 to 15. It is traditional for picnics and alfresco parties; one can sometimes catch the aroma of this dish wafting through the palm trees, a smell that must have been familiar to the Taíno peoples. The pig is often basted with *jugo de naranja agria* (sour orange juice) and *achiote* coloring and then rubbed with garlic and *adobe*. Slow roasted, *lechón* done right is juicy and just melts in the mouth. Green plantains are peeled and roasted over hot stones, then served with the barbecued pig. A sour garlic sauce called *aji-li-mojili,* made from garlic, whole black peppercorns, sweet peppers, lime, and olive oil, sometimes accompanies the pig. *Pasteles,* a kind of Puerto Rican turnover, are also popular at Christmas. A paste is formed from either plantain or yucca, which is then filled with seasoned beef or chicken. After it is shaped into a rectangle, it is wrapped in plantain leaves and tied up. They are then boiled and unwrapped, served steaming hot.

Local cuisine relies on seafood, with red snapper, or *chillo,* and dophinfish, or *dorado,* most likely to be offered as fresh catches of the day. Shellfish, especially conch, or *carrucho,* squid, and octopus are also frequently used in dishes. *Mojo isleno* is a delicious oil-and-vinegar-based sauce from the south-coast town of Patillas to pour on fresh grilled fish. The sauce is made with olives and olive oil, onions, pimientos, capers, tomato sauce, vinegar, garlic, and bay leaves. Caribbean lobster is usually the most expensive item on any menu, followed by shrimp. We find it lighter but just as sweet as the more common Maine lobster. Puerto Ricans often grill shrimp, *camarones,* and serve them in an infinite number of ways. Another popular shellfish dish is *jueyes,* crabs, which are either boiled or served inside fried turnovers.

Puerto Ricans love salted codfish, with codfish fritters being one of the more popular beach snacks, always available during festivals. A better way to experience this staple is *serenate de bacalao,* in which the cod is served in an olive oil–vinegar dressing with tomato, onion and avocado. It's a popular Easter dish.

Many tasty **egg dishes** are served, especially *tortilla española* (Spanish omelet), cooked with finely chopped onions, cubed potatoes, and olive oil.

THE AROMA OF COFFEE

Puerto Ricans usually end a meal with a small cup of the strong, aromatic coffee grown here, either black or with a dash of warm milk. Although the island is not as associated with coffee as Colombia or even the Dominican Republic, it has been producing some of the world's best for more than 300 years. It's been known as the "coffee of popes and kings" since it was exported to Europe's royal courts and the Vatican in the 19th century, and today Puerto Rico continues to produce some of the world's tastiest.

Coffee has several degrees of quality, of course, the lowest-ranking one being *café de primera,* which is typically served at the ordinary family table. The top category is called *café super premium.* Only a handful of three coffees in the world belong to super-premium class: With Puerto Rico's homegrown Alto Grande, coffee beans sought by coffee connoisseurs around the world, joining Blue Mountain coffee of Jamaica, and Kona coffee from Hawaii.

A wave of boutique high-quality local coffee brands have popped up more recently, including Yauco Selecto, with a new generation of farmers catering to the booming worldwide demand for gourmet coffee. Alto Grande Super Premium has been grown in Lares since 1839, in the central mountains known as one of the finest coffee growing areas in the world. Yacuo Selecto, grown in Yauco on the southern slope of the Cordillera Central, also traces its roots to this period when island coffee was courted by royalty. Other coffee-growing towns are Maricao, in the western mountains, and Adjuntas, at the island's heart.

You can ask for your brew *puya* (unsweetened), *negrito con azúcar* (black and sweetened), *cortao* (black with a drop of milk), or *con leche* (with milk).

RUM: KILL-DEVIL OR WHISKEY-BELLY VENGEANCE

Rum is the national drink of Puerto Rico, and you can buy it in almost any shade. Because the island is the world's leading rum producer, it's little wonder that every Puerto Rican bartender worthy of the profession likes to concoct his or her own favorite rum libation. You can call for Puerto Rican rum in many mixed drinks such as rum Collins, rum sour, and rum screwdriver. The classic sangria, which is prepared in Spain with dry red wine, sugar, orange juice, and other ingredients, is often given a Puerto Rican twist with a hefty dose of rum.

Today's version of rum bears little resemblance to the raw, grainy beverage consumed by the renegades and pirates of Spain. Christopher Columbus brought sugar cane, from which rum is distilled, to the Caribbean on his second voyage to the New World, and in almost no time rum became the regional drink.

It is believed that Ponce de León introduced rum to Puerto Rico during his governorship, which began in 1508. In time, there emerged large sugar-cane plantations. From Puerto Rico and other West Indian islands, rum was shipped to colonial America, where it lent itself to such popular and hair-raising 18th-century drinks as Kill-Devil and Whiskey-Belly Vengeance. After the United States became a nation, rum was largely displaced as the drink of choice by whiskey, distilled from grain grown on the American plains.

It took almost a century before Puerto Rico's rum industry regained its former vigor. This occurred during a severe whiskey shortage in the United States at the end of World War II. By the 1950s, sales of rum had fallen off again, as more and different kinds of liquor had become available on the American market.

The local brew had been a questionable drink because of inferior distillation methods and quality. Recognizing this problem, the Puerto Rican government drew up rigid standards for producing, blending, and aging rum. Rum factories were outfitted with the most modern and sanitary equipment, and sales figures (encouraged by aggressive marketing campaigns) began to climb.

No one will ever agree on what "the best" rum is in the Caribbean. There are just too many of them to sample. Some are so esoteric as to be unavailable in your local liquor store. But if popular tastes mean anything, then Puerto Rican rums, especially Bacardi, head the list. There are 24 different rums from Puerto Rico sold in the United States under 11 brand names—not only Bacardi, but also Ron Bocoy, Ronrico, Don Q, and many others. Locals tend to like Don Q the best.

Puerto Rican rums are generally light, gold, or dark. Usually white or silver in color, the biggest seller is light in body and dry in taste. Its subtle flavor and delicate aroma make it ideal for many mixed drinks, including the mojito, daiquiri, rum Collins, rum Mary, and rum and tonic or soda. It also goes with almost any fruit juice, or on the rocks with a slice of lemon or lime. Gold or amber rum is aromatic and full-bodied in taste. Aging in charred oak casks adds color to the rum.

Gold rums are usually aged longer for a deeper and mellower flavor than light rums. They are increasingly popular on the rocks, straight up, or in certain mixed drinks in which extra flavor is desired—certainly in the famous piña colada, rum and Coke, or eggnog.

Dark rum is full-bodied with a deep, velvety, smooth taste and a complex flavor. It can be aged for as long as 15 years. You can enjoy it on the rocks, with tonic or soda, or in mixed drinks when you want the taste of rum to stand out.

6 Recommended Reading

HISTORY

- *The Caribbean People,* by Reginald Honychurch. In three volumes, this is a well-balanced account written by one of the so-called new historians of the Caribbean.
- *Puerto Rico: A Political and Cultural History,* by Artura Morales Carrion This is one of the best major overviews of Puerto Rican history and culture.
- *A Short History of Puerto Rico,* by Morton Golding. This book suits those who want their history readable and condensed.
- *Sugar and Slavery in Puerto Rico: The Plantation Economy of Ponce, 1800–1850,* by Francisco A. Scarano. Scarano produces a scholarly study of an agrarian region of Puerto Rico far removed from the Spanish-controlled capital of San Juan.

POLITICS

- *Puerto Rico: A Colonial Experiment,* by Ramon Carr. Carr offers one of the most insightful views of island politics, which have been called the national religion of Puerto Rico.
- *Puerto Rico: Commonwealth or Colony?* by Roberta Johnson. This book attempts to answer the title's provocative question.
- *Puerto Rico: Commonwealth, State, or Nation?* by Byron Williams. This book offers a pointed discussion of the major Puerto Rican self-determination movements.
- *The United States and Puerto Rico: Breaking the Bonds of Economic Colonialism,* by Roland I. Perusse. This book traces the history of trade relations in Puerto Rico, the second-largest Western trading partner of the United States, after Canada. It is a cultural and economic survey with a strongly politicized point of view.

3

Planning Your Trip to Puerto Rico

This chapter discusses the where, when, and how of your trip to Puerto Rico—everything required to plan your trip and get it on the road. Here we've concentrated on what you need to do *before* you go.

1 Visitor Information

For information before you leave home, visit **www.gotopuertorico.com** or contact the **Puerto Rico Tourism Company** offices at La Princesa Building, Paseo La Princesa 2, Old San Juan, PR 00902 (© **800/866-7827** or 787/721-2400).

The advertising-driven **Caribbean-On-Line** (www.caribbean-on-line.com) has some useful information on deals at hotels, restaurants, and shops, along with information on sights and detailed maps of the islands. The site also includes links to travel agents and cruise lines that are up on the Web.

There are several tourism-related websites on Puerto Rico. The best, with the most accurate and current information, tend to be homegrown sites catering to local businesses in specific destinations like Rincón or Vieques.

These include: **The Tourism Association of Rincón** (www.rincon.org), **Insider's Guide to South Puerto Rico** (www.letsgotoponce.com), the Vieques website **Enchanted Isles** (www.enchanted-isle.com), **Discover Culebra** (www.culebra-island.com), and **Puerto Rico Travel Maps** (www.travelmaps.com).

You might also want to contact the U.S. State Department for background bulletins, which supply up-to-date information on crime, health concerns, import restrictions, and other travel matters. Write the **Superintendent of Documents, U.S. Government Printing Office,** Washington, DC 20402 (© **866/512-1800** or 202/512-1800).

A good travel agent can be a source of information. Make sure your agent is a member of the American Society of Travel Agents (ASTA). If you get poor service from an ASTA agent, you can write to the **ASTA—The American Society of Travel Agents**—at 1101 King St., Alexandria, VA 22314 (© **703/739-2782;** www.astanet. com).

2 Entry Requirements & Customs

ENTRY REQUIREMENTS

DOCUMENTS Because Puerto Rico is a commonwealth, **U.S. citizens** coming from mainland destinations do not need any documents to enter Puerto

Rico. It is the same as crossing from Georgia into Florida. They do not need to carry proof of citizenship or to produce documents. However, because of new airport security measures, it is necessary to produce a government-issued photo ID (federal, state, or local) to board a plane; this is most often a driver's license.

Be sure to carry plenty of documentation. You might need to show a government-issued photo ID (federal, state, or local) at various airport checkpoints. Be sure that your ID is *up-to-date:* An expired driver's license or passport, for example, might keep you from boarding a plane.

Visitors from other countries, including Canada, need a valid passport to land in Puerto Rico. For those from countries requiring a visa to enter the U.S., the same visa is necessary to enter Puerto Rico, unless these nationals are coming directly from the U.S. mainland and have already cleared U.S. Immigration and Customs there.

VACCINATIONS Vaccinations are not required for entry to Puerto Rico if you're coming from the United States or Canada.

Infectious hepatitis has been reported on other Caribbean islands but less frequently on Puerto Rico. Consult your doctor about the advisability of getting a gamma-globulin shot before you leave home.

Typhoid, poliomyelitis, and tetanus are not common diseases on the island, and inoculations against them are recommended mainly to visitors who plan to rough it in the wilds. If you're staying in a regular Puerto Rican hotel, such preventive measures are generally not needed, but your doctor can advise you based on your destination and travel plans.

CUSTOMS

U.S. citizens do not need to clear Puerto Rican Customs upon arrival by plane or ship from the U.S. mainland. All non–U.S. citizens must clear Customs and are permitted to bring in items intended for their personal use, including tobacco, cameras, film, and a limited supply of liquor (usually 40 oz.).

WHAT YOU CAN TAKE HOME

U.S. CUSTOMS On departure, U.S.-bound travelers must have their luggage inspected by the U.S. Agriculture Department because laws prohibit bringing fruits and plants to the U.S. mainland. Fruits and vegetables are not allowed, but otherwise, you can bring back as many purchased goods as you want without paying duty.

For specifics on what you can bring back, download the invaluable free pamphlet *Know Before You Go* online at **www.cbp.gov**. (Click on "Travel," and then click on "Know Before You Go! Online Brochure.") Or contact the **U.S. Customs & Border Protection (CBP)**, 1300 Pennsylvania Ave. NW, Washington, DC 20229 (© **877/287-8667**) and request the pamphlet.

For a clear summary of **Canadian** rules, write for the booklet *I Declare,* issued by the **Canada Border Services Agency** (© **800/461-9999** in Canada, or 204/983-3500; www.cbsa-asfc.gc.ca). Canada allows its citizens a C$750 exemption, and you're allowed to bring back duty-free one carton of cigarettes, one can of tobacco, 40 imperial ounces of liquor, and 50 cigars. In addition, you're allowed to mail gifts to Canada valued at less than C$60 a day, provided they're unsolicited and don't contain alcohol or tobacco (write on the package "Unsolicited gift, under $60 value"). All valuables should be declared on the Y-38 form before departure from Canada, including serial numbers of valuables you already own, such as expensive foreign cameras. *Note:* The C$750 exemption can only be used once a year and only after an absence of 7 days.

U.K. citizens returning from **a non-E.U. country** have a customs allowance of: 200 cigarettes; 50 cigars; 250 grams of smoking tobacco; 2 liters of still table wine; 1 liter of spirits or strong liqueurs (over 22% volume); 2 liters of fortified wine, sparkling wine or other liqueurs; 60cc (ml) of perfume; 250cc (ml) of toilet water; and £145 worth of all other goods, including gifts and souvenirs. People under 17 cannot have the tobacco or alcohol allowance. For more information, contact **HM Revenue & Customs** at ℂ **0845/010-9000** (from outside the U.K., 020/8929-0152), or consult their website at www.hmrc.gov.uk.

The duty-free allowance in **Australia** is A$900 or, for those under 18, A$450. Citizens can bring in 250 cigarettes or 250 grams of loose tobacco, and 2.25 liters of alcohol. If you're returning with valuables you already own, such as foreign-made cameras, you should file form B263. A helpful brochure available from Australian consulates or Customs offices is *Know Before You Go*. For more information, call the **Australian Customs Service** at ℂ **1300/363-263,** or log on to www.customs.gov.au.

The duty-free allowance for **New Zealand** is NZ$700. Citizens over 17 can bring in 200 cigarettes, 50 cigars, or 250 grams of tobacco (or a mixture of all three if their combined weight doesn't exceed 250g); plus 4.5 liters of wine and beer, or 1.125 liters of liquor. New Zealand currency does not carry import or export restrictions. Fill out a certificate of export, listing the valuables you are taking out of the country; that way, you can bring them back without paying duty. Most questions are answered in a free pamphlet available at New Zealand consulates and Customs offices: *New Zealand Customs Guide for Travellers, Notice no. 4*. For more information, contact **New Zealand Customs Service,** The Customhouse, 17–21 Whitmore St., Box 2218, Wellington (ℂ **04/473-6099** or 0800/428-786; www.customs. govt.nz).

3 Money

CURRENCY The U.S. dollar is the coin of the realm. Keep in mind that once you leave Ponce or San Juan, you might have difficulty finding a place to exchange foreign money (unless you're staying at a large resort), so it's wise to handle your exchange needs before you head off into rural parts of Puerto Rico.

ATMs ATMs are linked to a network that most likely includes your bank at home. Cirrus (ℂ **800/424-7787;** www. mastercard.com) and Plus (ℂ **800/843-7587;** www.visa.com) are the two most popular networks in the U.S.; call or check online for ATM locations at your destination. Be sure you know your four-digit PIN before you leave home and be sure to find out your daily withdrawal limit before you depart. You can also get cash advances on your credit card at an ATM. Keep in mind that credit card companies try to protect themselves from theft by limiting the funds someone can withdraw away from home; it's therefore best to call your credit card company before you leave and let them know where you're going and how much you plan to spend. You'll get the best exchange rate if you withdraw money from an ATM, but keep in mind that many banks impose a fee every time a card is used at an ATM in a different city or bank. On top of this, the bank from which you withdraw cash may charge its own fee.

CURRENCY EXCHANGE The currency exchange facilities at any large international bank within Puerto Rico's larger cities can exchange non–U.S. currencies for dollars. You can also exchange money at the Luis Muñoz Marín International Airport. Also, you'll find foreign-exchange facilities in large hotels and at the many banks in Old San Juan or Avenida Ashford in Condado. In Ponce, look for foreign-exchange facilities at

What Things Cost in Puerto Rico	US$	UK£	Euro€
Taxi from Airport to Condado	15.00	7.50	9.68
Average Taxi Fare within San Juan	12.00	6.00	7.74
Typical Bus Fare within San Juan	.75	.38	.49
Local Telephone Call	.50	.25	.32
Double Room at the Condado Plaza (very expensive)	650.00	325.00	505.00
Double Room at Numero Uno Guesthouse (moderate)	175.00	87.50	113.00
Double Room at El Canario Inn (inexpensive)	109.00	54.50	70.32
Lunch for One at Amadeus (moderate)	23.00	11.50	14.84
Lunch for One at Bebos (inexpensive)	12.00	6.00	7.74
Dinner for One at Ramiro's (very expensive)	50.00	25.00	32.26
Dinner for One at Ostra Cosa (moderate)	26.00	13.00	16.77
Dinner for One at La Bombonera (inexpensive)	15.00	7.50	9.68
Bottle of Beer in a Bar	3.50	1.75	2.26
Glass of Wine in a Restaurant	5.00	2.50	3.26
Roll of ASA 100 Color Film (36 exp.)	8.50	4.25	5.48
Movie Ticket	6.50	3.25	4.19
Theater Ticket	15.00–125.00	7.50–62.50	9.68–80.65

large resorts and at banks such as Banco Popular.

TRAVELER'S CHECKS Traveler's checks are something of an anachronism from the days before the ATM made cash accessible at any time. Even given the fees you'll pay for ATM use at banks other than your own, it is still probably a better bet than traveler's checks.

You can get traveler's checks at almost any bank. **American Express** offers denominations of $20, $50, $100, $500, and (for cardholders only) $1,000. You'll pay a service charge ranging from 1% to 4%. You can also get American Express traveler's checks over the phone by calling (© **800/221-7282;** Amex gold and platinum cardholders who use this number are exempt from the 1% fee.

Visa offers traveler's checks at Citibank locations nationwide, as well as at several other banks. The service charge ranges between 1.5% and 2%; checks come in denominations of $20, $50, $100, $500, and $1,000. Call (© **800/732-1322** for information. AAA members can obtain Visa checks for a $9.95 fee (for checks, minimum of $300 up to $1,500) at most AAA offices or by calling (© **866/339-3378. MasterCard** also offers traveler's checks. Call (© **800/223-9920** for a location near you.

CREDIT CARDS Credit cards are invaluable when you're traveling. They are a safe way to carry money and provide a convenient record of all your expenses. You can also withdraw cash advances from your credit cards at any bank (though you'll start paying hefty interest on the advance the moment you receive the cash). At most banks, you don't even need to go to a teller; you can get a cash advance at the ATM if you know your PIN. If you've forgotten yours, or didn't even know you had one, call the number on the back of your credit card and ask the card issuer to send it to you. It usually takes 5 to 7 business days, though some banks will provide the number over the phone if you tell them your mother's maiden name or pass some other security clearance.

In San Juan and at all the big resorts on the island, even some of the smaller inns, credit cards are commonly accepted. Moreover, an incredible array of establishments accepts payment with ATM cards. However, as you tour through rural areas and if you intend to patronize small, out-of-the-way establishments, it's still wise to carry sufficient amounts of the Yankee dollar for emergencies. Visa and MasterCard are accepted most widely throughout Puerto Rico.

For tips and telephone numbers to call if your wallet is stolen or lost, go to "Lost & Found" in the "Fast Facts: Puerto Rico" section, in the appendix.

4 When to Go

CLIMATE

Puerto Rico has one of the most unvarying climates in the world. Temperatures year-round range from 75° to 85°F (24°–29°C). The island is wettest and hottest in August, averaging 81°F (27°C) and 7 inches (18cm) of rain. San Juan and the northern coast seem to be cooler and wetter than Ponce and the southern coast. The coldest weather is in the high altitudes of the Cordillera, the site of Puerto Rico's lowest recorded temperature—39°F (4°C).

THE HURRICANE SEASON

The hurricane season, the curse of Puerto Rican weather, lasts—officially, at least—from June 1 to November 30. But there's no cause for panic. In general, satellite forecasts give adequate warnings so that precautions can be taken. The peak of the season, when historically the most damaging storms are formed and hit the island, is in August and December.

If you're heading to Puerto Rico during the hurricane season, you can call your local branch of the **National Weather Service** (listed in your phone directory under the U.S. Department of Commerce) for a weather forecast.

It'll cost 95¢ per query, but you can get information about the climate conditions in any city you plan to visit by calling © **800/WEATHER** (932-8437). When you're prompted, enter your Visa or MasterCard account number and then punch in the name of any of 1,000 cities worldwide whose weather is monitored by the **Weather Channel** (www.weather.com).

THE "SEASON"

In Puerto Rico, hotels charge their highest prices during the peak winter period from mid-December to mid-April, when visitors fleeing from cold northern climates flock to the islands. Winter is the driest season along the coasts but can be wet in mountainous areas.

If you plan to travel in the winter, make reservations 2 to 3 months in advance. At certain hotels it's almost impossible to book accommodations for Christmas and the month of February.

A second tourism high season, especially for hotels and destinations outside San Juan, does take place in July, when most islanders take vacation.

Average Temperatures in Puerto Rico

	Jan	Feb	Mar	Apr	May	June	July	Aug	Sept	Oct	Nov	Dec
Temp. (°F)	75	75	76	78	79	81	81	81	81	81	79	77
Temp. (°C)	24	24	25	26	26	27	27	27	27	27	26	25

SAVING MONEY IN THE OFF SEASON

Puerto Rico is a year-round destination. The island's "off season" runs from late spring to late fall, when temperatures in the mid-80s Fahrenheit (about 29°C) prevail throughout most of the region. Trade winds ensure comfortable days and nights, even in accommodations without air-conditioning. Although the noonday sun may raise the temperature to around 90°F (32°C), cool breezes usually make the morning, late afternoon, and evening more comfortable here than in many parts of the U.S. mainland.

Dollar for dollar, you'll spend less money by renting a summer house or fully equipped unit in Puerto Rico than you would on Cape Cod, Fire Island, Laguna Beach, or the coast of Maine.

The off season in Puerto Rico—roughly from May through November (rate schedules vary from hotel to hotel)—amounts to a summer sale. In most cases, hotel rates are slashed from 20% to a startling 60%. It's a bonanza for cost-conscious travelers, especially families who like to go on vacations together. In the chapters ahead, we'll spell out in dollars the specific amounts hotels charge during the off season.

But the off season has been shrinking of late. Many hotels, particularly outside of San Juan, will charge full price during the month of July and summer holiday weekends. Some properties, particularly guesthouses and small hotels in vacation towns like Vieques and Rincón, have dispensed with off-season pricing altogether.

In San Juan, a trend among smaller properties is to charge higher rates on weekends and holidays than during the week, rather than seasonal fluctuations in price.

OTHER OFF-SEASON ADVANTAGES

Although Puerto Rico may appear inviting in the winter to those who live in northern climates, there are many reasons your trip may be much more enjoyable if you go in the off season:

- After the winter hordes have left, a less-hurried way of life prevails. You'll have a better chance to appreciate the food, culture, and local customs.
- Swimming pools and beaches are less crowded—perhaps not crowded at all. Again, some areas will be extremely crowded in July and on summer holiday weekends.
- Year-round resort facilities are offered, often at reduced rates, which may include snorkeling, boating, and scuba diving.
- To survive, resort boutiques often feature summer sales, hoping to clear the merchandise they didn't sell in February to accommodate stock they've ordered for the coming winter.
- You can often appear without a reservation at a top restaurant and get a table for dinner, a table that in winter would have required a reservation far in advance. Also, when waiters are less hurried, you get better service.
- The endless waiting game is over: no waiting for a rental car (only to be told none is available), no long wait for a golf course tee time, and quicker access to tennis courts and watersports.
- Some package-tour fares are as much as 20% lower, and individual excursion fares are also reduced between 5% and 10%.
- All accommodations and flights are much easier to book.
- Summer is an excellent time for family travel, not usually possible during the winter season.
- The very best of Puerto Rican attractions remain undiminished in the off season—sea, sand, and surf, with lots of sunshine.

OFF-SEASON DISADVANTAGES

Let's not paint too rosy a picture. Although the advantages of off-season travel far outweigh the disadvantages, there are nevertheless drawbacks to traveling in summer:

- You might be staying at a construction site. Hoteliers save their serious repairs and their major renovations until the off season, when they have fewer clients. That means you might wake up early in the morning to the sound of a hammer.
- Single tourists find the cruising better in winter, when there are more clients, especially the unattached. Families predominate in summer, and there are fewer chances to meet fellow singles than in the winter months.
- Services are often reduced. In the peak of winter, everything is fully operational. But in summer, many of the programs such as watersports might be curtailed. Also, not all restaurants and bars are fully operational at all resorts. For example, for lack of business, certain gourmet or specialty dining rooms might be shut down until house count merits reopening them. In all, the general atmosphere is more laid-back when a hotel or resort might also be operating with a reduced staff. The summer staff will still be adequate to provide service for what's up and running.

HOLIDAYS

Puerto Rico has many public holidays when stores, offices, and schools are closed: New Year's Day, January 6 (Three Kings Day), Washington's Birthday, Good Friday, Memorial Day, July 4th, Labor Day, Thanksgiving, Veterans Day, and Christmas, plus such local holidays as Constitution Day (July 25) and Discovery Day (Nov 19). Remember, U.S. federal holidays are holidays in Puerto Rico, too.

PUERTO RICO CALENDAR OF EVENTS

January

Three Kings Day, islandwide. On this traditional gift-giving day in Puerto Rico, there are festivals with lively music, dancing, parades, puppet shows, caroling troubadours, and traditional feasts. January 6.

San Sebastián Street Festival, Calle San Sebastián in Old San Juan. Nightly celebrations with music, processions, crafts, and typical foods, as well as graphic arts and handicraft exhibitions. For more information, call © 787/721-2400. Mid-January.

February

San Blas de Illescas Half Marathon, Coamo. International and local runners compete in a challenging 13-mile (21km) half-marathon in the hilly south-central town of Coamo. Call **Delta Phi Delta Fraternity** (© 787/825-4077). Early February.

Coffee Harvest Festival, Maricao. Folk music, a parade of floats, typical foods, crafts, and demonstrations of coffee preparation in Maricao, a 1-hour drive east of Mayagüez. For more information, call © 787/838-2290 or 787/267-5536. Second week of February.

Carnival Ponceño, Ponce. The island's Carnival celebrations feature float parades, dancing, and street parties. One of the most vibrant festivities is held in Ponce, known for its masqueraders wearing brightly painted horned masks. For more information, call © 787/284-4141. Mid-February.

Casals Festival, Performing Arts Center in San Juan. *Sanjuaneros* and visitors alike eagerly look forward to the annual Casals Festival, the Caribbean's most celebrated cultural event. When renowned cellist Casals died in Puerto Rico in 1973 at the age of 97, the

Casals Festival was 16 years old and attracting the same class of performers who appeared at the Pablo Casals Festival in France, founded by Casals after World War II. When he moved to Puerto Rico in 1957 with his wife, Marta Casals Istomin (former artistic director of the John F. Kennedy Center for the Performing Arts), he founded not only this festival but also the Puerto Rico Symphony Orchestra to foster musical development on the island.

Ticket prices for the Casals Festival range from $30 to $40. A 50% discount is offered to students, people over 60, and persons with disabilities. Tickets are available through the **Puerto Rico Symphonic Orchestra** in San Juan (© **787/721-7727**), the **Luis A. Ferré Performing Arts Center** (© **787/620-4444**), or **Ticket Center** (© **787/792-5000**).

Information is also available from the **Casals Festival** (© **787/721-8370;** www.festcasalspr.gobierno.pr). The festivities take place from late February to early March.

March

Emancipation Day, islandwide. Commemoration of the emancipation of Puerto Rico's slaves in 1873, held at various venues. March 22.

April

Good Friday and Easter, islandwide. Celebrated with colorful ceremonies and processions. April 10 to April 12, 2009.

José de Diego Day, islandwide. Commemoration of the birthday of José de Diego, the patriot, lawyer, writer, orator, and political leader who was the first president of the Puerto Rico House of Representatives under U.S. rule. April 17.

Sugar Harvest Festival, San Germán. This festival marks the end of the island's sugar harvest, with live music, crafts, and typical foods, as well as exhibitions of sugar-cane plants and past and present harvesting techniques. Late April.

May

Puerto Rican Danza Week (*Semana de la "Danza" Puertorriqueña*), Convento de los Dominicos, Old San Juan. This week commemorates what is, perhaps, the most expressive art form in the Puerto Rican culture: danza music and dance. Throughout Danza Week, live performances and conferences are held at Convento de los Dominicos's indoor patio. The building is located on Old San Juan's Cristo Street. For information, call © **800/866-7827** or 787/721-2400. Second week of May.

Heineken JazzFest, San Juan. The annual jazz celebration is staged at Parque Sixto Escobar. Each year a different jazz theme is featured. The open-air pavilion is in a scenic oceanfront location in the Puerta de Tierra section of San Juan, near the Caribe Hilton. For more information, check out the website www.prheinekenjazz.com, which has schedules and links to buy tickets and package information. End of May through the beginning of June.

June

San Juan Bautista Day, islandwide. Puerto Rico's capital and other cities celebrate the island's patron saint with weeklong festivities. At midnight, *sanjuaneros* and others walk backward into the sea (or nearest body of water) three times to renew good luck for the coming year. June 24.

Aibonito Flower Festival, at Road 721 next to the City Hall Coliseum, in the central mountain town of Aibonito. This annual flower-competition festival features acres of lilies, anthuriums, carnations, roses, gardenias, and begonias. For more information, call ✆ 787/735-3871. Last week in June and first week in July.

July

Luis Muñoz Rivera's Birthday, islandwide. A birthday celebration commemorating Luis Muñoz Rivera (1829–1916), statesman, journalist, poet, and resident commissioner in Washington, D.C. July 15.

El Gigante Marathon, Adjuntas. This 9¼-mile (15km) race starts at Puerta Bernasal and finishes at Plaza Pública. For more information call ✆ 787/829-3310. Sunday before July 25.

Loíza Carnival. This annual folk and religious ceremony honors Loíza's patron saint, John (*Santiago*) the Apostle. Colorful processions take place, with costumes, masks, and *bomba* dancers (the *bomba* has a lively Afro-Caribbean dance rhythm). This jubilant celebration reflects the African and Spanish heritage of the region. For more information, call ✆ 787/876-1040. Late July through early August.

August

Cuadragésimo Cuarto Torneo de Pesca Interclub del Caribe, Cangrejos Yacht Club. This international blue-marlin fishing tournament features crafts, music, local delicacies, and other activities. For more information, call ✆ 787/791-1015. Mid-August.

International Billfish Tournament, at Club Náutico, San Juan. This is one of the premier game-fishing tournaments and the longest consecutively held billfish tournament in the world. Fishermen from many countries angle for blue marlin that can weigh up to 900 pounds (408 kilograms). For specific dates and information, call ✆ 787/722-0177. Late August to early September.

October

La Raza Day (Columbus Day), islandwide. This day commemorates Columbus's landing in the New World. October 12.

National Plantain Festival, Corozal. This annual festivity involves crafts, paintings, agricultural products, exhibition, and sale of plantain dishes; *neuva trova* music and folk ballet are performed. For more information, call ✆ 787/859-3060. Mid-October.

November

Start of Baseball Season, in Hiram Bithorn Park in San Juan and throughout the island. Six Puerto Rican professional clubs compete from November to January. Professionals from North America also play here. San Juan is also slated to host some of the games for the upcoming World Baseball Classic in 2009.

Festival of Puerto Rican Music, San Juan. An annual classical and folk music festival, one of its highlights is a *cuatro*-playing contest. (A *cuatro* is a guitar-like instrument with 10 strings.) For more information, call ✆ 787/721-5274. First week in November.

Jayuya Indian Festival, Jayuya. This fiesta features the culture and tradition of the island's original inhabitants, the Taíno Indians, and their music, food, and games. More than 100 artisans exhibit and sell their works. There is also a Miss Taíno Indian Pageant. For more information, call ✆ 787/828-2020. Second week of November.

Puerto Rico Discovery Day, islandwide. This day commemorates the "discovery" by Columbus in 1493 of the already inhabited island of Puerto Rico. Columbus is thought to have come ashore at the northwestern municipality of Aguadilla, although the exact location is unknown. November 19.

December

Old San Juan's White Christmas Festival, Old San Juan. Special musical and artistic presentations take place in stores, with window displays. December 1 through January 12.

Bacardi Artisans' Fair, San Juan. The best and largest artisans' fair on the island features more than 100 artisans who turn out to exhibit and sell their wares. The fair includes shows for adults and children, a Puerto Rican troubadour contest, rides, and typical food and drink—all sold by nonprofit organizations. It is held on the grounds of the world's largest rum-manufacturing plant in Cataño, an industrial suburb set on a peninsula jutting into San Juan Bay. For more information, call © 787/788-1500. First two Sundays in December.

Las Mañanitas, Ponce. A religious procession that starts out from Lolita Tizol Street and moves toward the city's Catholic church, led by mariachis singing songs to honor Our Lady of Guadalupe, the city's patron saint. The lead song is the traditional Mexican birthday song, *Las Mañanitas.* There's a 6am Mass. For more information, contact **Ponce City Hall** (© 787/284-4141). December 12.

Lighting of the Town of Bethlehem, between San Cristóbal Fort and Plaza San Juan Bautista in Old San Juan. This is the time that the most dazzling Christmas lights go on, and many islanders themselves drive into San Juan to see this dramatic lighting, the finest display of lights in the Caribbean at Christmas. During the Christmas season.

Hatillo Masks Festival, Hatillo. This tradition, celebrated since 1823, represents the biblical story of King Herod's ordering the death of all infant boys in an attempt to kill the baby Jesus. Men with colorful masks and costumes represent the soldiers, who run or ride through the town from early morning, looking for the children. There are food, music, and crafts exhibits in the town square. For more information, call © 787/898-4040. December 28.

YEAR-ROUND FESTIVALS

In addition to the individual events described above, Puerto Rico has two yearlong series of special events.

Many of Puerto Rico's most popular events are during the **Patron Saint Festivals** *(fiestas patronales)* in honor of the patron saint of each municipality. The festivities, held in each town's central plaza, include religious and costumed processions, games, local food, music, and dance.

At **Festival La Casita,** prominent Puerto Rican musicians, dance troupes, and orchestras perform; puppet shows are staged; and painters and sculptors display their works. It happens every Saturday at Puerto Rico Tourism's "La Casita" Tourism Information Center, Plaza Darsenas, across from Pier 1, Old San Juan.

For more information about all these events, contact the **Puerto Rico Tourism Company** (© 800/866-7827 or 787/721-2400) La Princesa Building, Paseo La Princesa 2, Old San Juan, PR 00902.

5 The Active Vacation Planner

There are watersports opportunities throughout Puerto Rico, from San Juan's waterfront hotels to eastern resorts and the offshore islands of Vieques and Culebra all the way to the Rincón on the west coast and Cabo Rojo in the south.

BOATING & SAILING

The waters off Puerto Rico provide excellent boating in all seasons. Winds average 10 to 15 knots virtually year-round. Marinas provide facilities and services on par with any others in the Caribbean, and

Beach Warning

In San Juan, don't go walking along the beaches at night, even as tempting as it may be to do with your lover. On unguarded beaches, you will have no way to protect yourself or your valuables should you be approached by a robber or mugger, which can happen. The exceptions may be the beaches in front of Barbosa Park in Ocean Park and Parque del Indio in Condado, which are lit up at night and draw many evening visitors. Beaches on the island, especially in vacation towns like Vieques and Culebra, Boquerón and Isabela, are genuinely safer, but it's still a good idea not to stray too far off the beaten path.

many have powerboats or sailboats for rent, either crewed or bareboat charter.

Puerto Rico is ringed by marinas. In San Juan alone, there are three large ones. The upscale **Club Nautico de San Juan** (© 787/722-0177) and neighboring **San Juan Bay Marina** (© 787/721-8062 are adjacent to the Condado bridge and the Convention Center district in Miramar. The other marina, the **Cangrejos Yacht Club** (Route 187, Piñones; © 787/791-1015), is near the airport, outside Isla Verde at the entrance to Piñones.

All three have several sailing charters and dive and fishing operators.

Fajardo, on Puerto Rico's northeast corner, boasts seven marinas, including the Caribbean's largest, the **Puerto del Rey Marina** (Rte. 3 Km 51.4; © 787/860-1000 or 787/801-3010), and the popular **Villa Marina Yacht Harbour** (Rte. 987 Km 1.3; © 787/863-5131 or 787/863-5011), offering the shortest ride to the best snorkeling grounds and offshore beaches. Other town marinas include **Puerto Chico** (Rte. 987 Km 2.4; © 787/863-0834) and **Puerto Real** (Playa Puerto Real; © 787/863-2188).

Along the south coast, one of the most established and charming marinas is the **Ponce Yacht & Fishing Club** (La Guancha, Ponce; © 787/842-9003).

But marinas, both small and large, can be found throughout island coasts. Check local listings for a "Club Nautico." Those with pleasure crafts, sailing and watersports offerings catering to tourists include **Club Nautico de Boquerón** (© 787/851-1336) and **Club Nautico de La Parguera** (© 787/899-5590), which are each located just outside their respective village centers.

Several sailing and ocean racing regattas are held in Puerto Rico annually. The east of Puerto Rico and the southwest are particularly attractive for sailors. Fajardo is the start of a series of ports, extending from Puerto Rico's own offshore islands through the U.S. and British Virgin Islands to the east, which is probably the Caribbean's top sailing destination.

The easiest way to experience the joys of sailing is to go out on a day trip leaving from one of the Fajardo marinas (with transportation from San Juan hotels often included). The trips usually take place on large luxury catamarans or sailing yachts, with a bar serving drinks and refreshments, a sound system, and other creature comforts. Typically, after a nice sail, the vessel weighs anchor at a good snorkeling spot, then makes a stop on one of the beautiful sand beaches on the small islands off the Fajardo coast. Operators include **Traveler Sailing Catamaran** (© 787/853-2821), **East Island Excursions** (© 787/860-3434), **Catamaran Spread Eagle** (© 787/887-8821), and **Erin Go Bragh Charters** (© 787/860-4401).

Also on the east coast is Karolette Charter, Palmas del Mar, AB-12 St., Route 3 Km 86.4, Humacao (© 787/850-7442), which offers snorkeling trips for $107 per person or charters for $680 for 4½ hours or $840 for 6 hours.

Out west, Katarina Sail Charters (© 787/823-SAIL [7245]) in Rincón gives daily sailing trips aboard a 32-foot (9.8m) catamaran; there are both a day sail and a sunset sail.

For the typical visitor interested in watersports—not the serious yachter—our favorite place for fun in the surf is the aptly named San Juan Water Fun on Isla Verde Beach in back of the Wyndham El San Juan Hotel and Casino, Avenida Isla Verde in Isla Verde, San Juan (© 787/ 644-2585). Here you can rent everything from a two-seater kayak for $30 per hour to a banana boat that holds eight passengers and costs $15 per person for a 20-minute ride.

If you're staying in eastern Puerto Rico, the best place for watersports rentals is Iguana Water Sports, Rio Mar Beach Resort, 6000 Rio Mar Blvd., Rio Grande (© 787/888-6000), which has the island's best selection of small boats. Waverunners cost $100 per hour, and two-seat kayaks go for $35 per hour.

In the southwest, Pino's Boat & Water Fun (© 787/821-6864 or 787/ 484-8083) at Guánica's Playa Santa has everything from paddle boats or kayaks to water scooters for rent.

CAMPING

Puerto Rico abounds in remote sandy beaches, lush tropical forests, and mountain lakesides that make for fine camping.

Although it has been technically illegal to camp on beaches (except in designated areas) for the last decade, it is commonly done in off-the-beaten path coastal areas, especially in Guánica, Isabela, Fajardo, and the offshore islands of Vieques and Culebra.

Also, there are more than enough campgrounds available in coastal areas, as well as in the mountains and local state forests and nature reserves.

Some of the nicest campgrounds, as well as the best equipped and safest, are those run by the government Compañia de Parques Nacionales (Av. Fernández Juncos 1611, Santurce; © 787/622-5200).

Six of the eight campsites it operates are located on the coast—at Luquillo, Fajardo, Vieques, Arroyo, Añasco, and Vega Baja. It also runs two fine campgrounds in the mountain town of Maricao and in Camuy's Cave Park.

Some of these are simple places where you erect your own tent, although they are outfitted with electricity and running water; some are simple cabins, sometimes with fireplaces. Showers and bathrooms are communal. To stay at a campsite costs between $15 and $25 per night per tent.

Many sites offer very basic cabins for rent. Each cabin is equipped with a full bathroom, a stove, a refrigerator, two beds, and a table and chairs. However, most of your cooking will probably be tastier if you do it outside at one of the on-site barbecues. In nearly all cases, you must provide your own sheets and towels.

The agency, the National Parks Company in English, also operates more upscale "vacation centers," which feature rustic cabins and more tourist-ready "villas," on par with many island inns.

State forests run by the Departamento de Recursos Naturales y Ambientales also allow camping with permits. Except for cabins at Monte Guilarte State Forest, which cost $20 per night, camping sites are available at $5 per person. For further information about permits, contact the DRNA at (Rte. 8838, Km 6.3, Sector El Cinco, Río Piedras; © 787/999-2200).

There are seven major on-island camping sites in the following state forests: Cambalache State Forest, near Barceloneta; Carite State Forest, near Patillas; Guajataca State Forest, near Quebradillas; Monte Guilarte State Forest, near Adjuntas; Susua State Forest, near Yauco; Río Abajo State Forest, near Arecibo;

Take Me Out to the *Beisbol* Game

Baseball has a long, illustrious history in Puerto Rico. Imported around the turn of the 20th century by plantation owners as a leisure activity for workers, *beisbol* quickly caught fire, and local leagues have produced such major-league stars as Roberto Alomar, Bernie Williams, and the late great Roberto Clemente. Current stars include Carlos Delgado, Jorge Posada, Iván Rodríguez, Carlos Beltrán, and the Molina brothers. A top-notch league of six teams—featuring many rising professionals honing their skills during the winter months—holds its season November through January and plays in ballparks throughout Puerto Rico. This is a chance to see good baseball in a more intimate setting than is afforded in the U.S. major leagues.

Puerto Rico will host some of the games in the 2009 World Baseball Classic, just at it did in the international baseball tournament's inaugural run in 2006. Top-notch regional teams from the Dominican Republic, Venezuela, and Cuba will play against the hometown favorite Puerto Rico team.

and our favorite, **Toro Negro Forest Reserve,** near Villaba, where you can camp in the shadow of Puerto Rico's highest peaks.

It's also possible to camp at either of two wildlife refuges, **Isla de Mona Wildlife Refuge,** lying some 50 miles (80km) off the west coast of Puerto Rico surrounded by the rough seas of Mona Passage, and at **Lago Lucchetti Wildlife Refuge,** a beautiful mountain reservoir between Yauco and Ponce.

Meanwhile, visitors can also camp at **El Yunque National Forest (© 787/ 888-1810),** which is under the jurisdiction of the U.S. Forest Service. There is no cost, but permits are required. They can be obtained in person at the Catalina Service Center (Rte. 191 Km 4.3) daily from 8am to 4:30pm and weekends at the Palo Colorado Visitor Center (Rte. 191 Km 11.9) on weekends from 9:30am to 4pm. It's primitive camping within the rainforest.

DEEP-SEA FISHING

While fishing is good year round, the winter season from October to early March is among the best. Blue marlin can

be caught all summer and into the fall, and renowned big game fish tournaments take place in August and September.

Charters are available at marinas in major cities and tourism areas. Most boats range between 32 and 50 feet; fit six passengers; can be chartered for half- or full-day; and usually include bait, crew, and equipment.

Big game fish are found close to shore across Puerto Rico, so you won't waste time traveling to fishing spots. A mile off the San Juan coast, the ocean floor drops 600 feet (183m), and the awesome Puerto Rico Trench, a 500-mile-long (805km) fault that plunges to a depth of 28,000 feet (8354m), lies about 75 miles (121km) directly north. It's a 20-minute ride to where the big game fish are biting, so it's possible to leave in the morning, make the catch of the day, and be back at the marina in the early afternoon.

Deep-sea fishing is top-notch throughout the island. Allison tuna, white and blue marlin, sailfish, wahoo, dolphin (mahimahi), mackerel, and tarpon are some of the fish that can be caught in Puerto Rican waters, where 30 world records have been broken. Charter arrangements can be made through most major hotels and resorts and at most marinas. The big game fishing grounds are very close offshore from San Juan, making the capital an excellent place to hire a charter. A half-day of deep-sea fishing (4 hours) starts at around $550, while full-day charters begin at around $900. Most charters hold six passengers in addition to the crew.

In San Juan, experienced operators include Capt. Mike Benítez at **Benítez Fishing Charters** (© 787/723-2292), as well as **Castillo Fishing Charters** (© 787/726-5752), which has been running charters out of the **Caribbean Outfitters** (© 787/396-8346).

Rincón also has a number of deep-sea fishing charters, like **Makaira Fishing Charters** (© 787/823-4391 or 787/299-7374) and **Moondog Charters** (© 787/823-3059).

In Palmas del Mar, which has some of the best year-round fishing in the Caribbean, you'll find **Capt. Bill Burleson** (see "Palmas del Mar" in chapter 12).

GOLF

With nearly 30 golf courses, including several championship links, Puerto Rico is rightly called the "Scotland," or the "golf capital" of the Caribbean, especially since they have been designed by the likes of Robert Trent Jones, his son Rees Jones, Greg Norman, George and Tom Fazio, Jack Nicklaus, Arthur Hills, and Puerto Rico's own Chi Chi Rodriguez.

Many of the courses are jewels of landscape architecture, running through verdant tropical forest and former coconut groves, or winding in dramatic switchbacks aside a breathtaking stretch of coast. Year-round summer weather and mostly gentle breezes add to the joy of playing here.

The bad news is it's often quite expensive to tee off in Puerto Rico, with prices starting at $120 and ranging up to nearly $200.

There are some bargains, however, particularly the **Berwind Country Club** (© 787/876-5380) in **Loiza** (the closet course to San Juan) and the **Punta Borinquén Golf Club,** Route 107 (© 787/890-2987), 2 miles (3.2km) north of Aquadilla's center. Berwind is the closest to San Juan, in a breathtaking setting on a former coconut plantation, while the Aguadilla course struts across a beautiful patch of coast.

The legendary Dorado courses are 35 minutes west of San Juan at the **Dorado Beach Resort & Club** (© 787/796-8961), the scene of world championships and legendarily difficult holes, making it among the most challenging in the Caribbean still. Jack Nicklaus rates the challenging 13th hole at the Dorado as one of the top 10 in the world. See chapter 9 for more details.

Río Grande, however, is becoming as important a center for golf as Dorado. The **Wyndham Río Mar Beach Resort** golf offerings (© 787/888-7060) have world-class rainforest and coastal courses, designed, respectively, by Greg Norman and Tom and George Fazio. **The Trump International Golf Club** (© 787/657-2000) is actually four different nine-hole courses sprawled out across 1,200 acres (486 hectares) of coast. Each course is named after its surrounding environment: the Ocean, the Palms, the Mountains, and the Lakes. Also in town is the **Bahia Beach** course (© 787/957-5800), recently renovated as part of a new St. Regis resort development.

Also, on the east coast, crack golfers consider holes 11 through 15 at the **Golf Club at Palmas del Mar** (p. 272) to be the toughest five successive holes in the Caribbean. At **El Conquistador Resort & Golden Door Spa** (p. 269), the spectacular $250-million resort at Las Croabas east of San Juan, you play along

200-foot (61m) changes in elevation that provide panoramic vistas.

There are now golf courses along the south coast, in Coamo and Ponce, as well as the southwest in Cabo Rojo. These are a needed complement to the north-coast courses. The **Costa Caribe Golf & Country Club** (© **787/848-1000** or 787/812-2650), on the site of the Ponce Hilton & Casino (see below), commands views of the ocean and mountains, while the **Club Deportivo del Oeste,** Hwy. 102 Km 15.4, Barrio Jogudas, Cabo Rojo (© **787/851-8880** or 787/254-3748) is more no-frills.

HIKING

The mountainous interior of Puerto Rico provides ample opportunities for hill climbing and nature treks. These are especially appealing because panoramas open at the least-expected moments, often revealing spectacular views of the distant sea.

The most popular, most beautiful, and most spectacular trekking spot is **El Yunque,** the sprawling "jungle" maintained by the U.S. Forest Service and the only rainforest on U.S. soil.

El Yunque is part of the **Caribbean National Forest,** which lies a 45-minute drive east of San Juan. More than 250 species of trees and some 200 types of ferns have been identified here. Some 60 species of birds inhabit El Yunque, including the increasingly rare Puerto Rican parrot. Such rare birds as the elfin woods warbler, the green mango hummingbird, and the Puerto Rican lizard-cuckoo live here.

Park rangers have clearly marked the trails that are ideal for walking. See "El Yunque" in chapter 9 for more details.

A lesser forest, but one that is still intriguing to visit, is the **Maricao State Forest,** near the coffee town of Maricao. This forest is in western Puerto Rico, east of the town of Mayagüez. For more details, see "Mayagüez" in chapter 11.

Ponce is the best center for exploring some of the greatest forest reserves in the Caribbean Basin, notably **Toro Negro Forest Reserve** with its **Lake Guineo** (the lake at the highest elevation on the island), the **Guánica State Forest,** ideal for hiking and bird-watching, and the **Carite Forest Reserve,** a 6,000-acre (2,428-hectare) park known for its dwarf forest. For more details, see "Ponce" in chapter 10.

Equally suitable for hiking are the protected lands (especially the **Río Camuy Cave Park**) whose topography is characterized as "karst"—that is, limestone riddled with caves, underground rivers, and natural crevasses and fissures. Although these regions pose additional risks and technical problems for trekkers, some people prefer the opportunities they provide for exploring the territory both above and below its surface. See "Arecibo & Camuy" in chapter 9 for details about the Río Camuy Caves.

Aventuras Tierra Adentro (© **787/ 766-0470;** www.aventuraspr.com) offers the best island adventure tours, focusing on hiking through virgin forests, rock climbing, or cliff jumping. Four different adventures are offered, costing $150 per person, which includes transportation from San Juan. Most of the jaunts take place on weekends.

SCUBA DIVING & SNORKELING

SCUBA DIVING The continental shelf, which surrounds Puerto Rico on three sides, is responsible for an abundance of coral reefs, caves, sea walls, and trenches for scuba diving and snorkeling.

Open-water reefs off the southeastern coast near **Humacao** are visited by migrating whales and manatees. Many caves are located near Isabela on the west coast. A large canyon, off the island's south coast, is ideal for experienced open-water divers. Caves and the sea wall at **La Parguera** are also favorites. **Vieques** and **Culebra islands** have coral formations.

Mona Island offers unspoiled reefs at depths averaging 80 feet (24m), with an amazing array of sealife. Uninhabited islands, such as **Icacos,** off the northeastern coast near Fajardo, are also popular with both snorkelers and divers.

These sites are now within reach because many of Puerto Rico's dive operators and resorts offer packages that include daily or twice-daily dives, scuba equipment, instruction, and excursions to Puerto Rico's popular attractions.

Introductory courses for beginners range are between $90 and $130, and two-tank dives for experienced divers run up to $150.

In San Juan, try **Caribe Aquatic Adventures,** Normandie Hotel San Juan, Calle 19 1062, Villa Nevarez (© **787/281-8858**), or **Ocean Sports** (Av. Isla Verde 77; © **787/268-2329**).

We recommend diving off the east, west or south coasts, however.

In Rincón, there's **Taíno Divers,** Black Eagle Marina at Rincón (© **787/823-6429**), which offers trips to the waters surrounding Desecheo island natural reserve.

The ocean wall in the southwest is famous, with visibility ranging from 100 to 120 feet (30–37m) and reefs filled with abundant sea life. **Paradise Scuba Center,** Hotel Casa Blanca Building, at La Parguera (© **787/899-7611**), and **Mona Aquatics,** Calle José de Diego, Boquerón (© **787/851-2185**), are two good operators in the area.

In Guánica, there's **Sea Venture Dive Copamarina** (© **787/821-0505,** ext. 729), part of the Copamarina Beach Resort.

The Dive Center at the Wyndham Rio Mar Beach Resort (© **787/888-6000**) is one of the largest in Puerto Rico.

(See "Diving, Fishing, Tennis & Other Outdoor Pursuits" in chapter 8 for more details).

Elsewhere on the island, several other companies offer scuba and snorkeling instruction. We provide details in each chapter.

SNORKELING   Because of its overpopulation, the waters around San Juan aren't the most ideal for snorkeling. In fact, the entire north shore of Puerto Rico fronts the Atlantic, where the waters are often turbulent.

Yet there are some protected areas along the north coast that make for fine snorkeling, even in surf capitals like Rincón and Aguadilla. Many of the best surfing beaches in winter turn into a snorkeler's paradise in summer when the waves calm down.

The most ideal conditions for snorkeling in Puerto Rico are along the shores of the remote islands of **Vieques** and **Culebra** (see chapter 13).

The best snorkeling on the main island is found near the town of **Fajardo,** to the east of San Juan and along the tranquil eastern coast (see chapter 12).

The calm, glasslike quality of the clear Caribbean along the south shore is also ideal for snorkeling. The most developed tourist mecca here is the city of Ponce. Few rivers empty their muddy waters into the sea along the south coast, resulting in gin-clear waters offshore. You can snorkel off the coast without having to go on a boat trip. One good place is at **Playa La Parguera,** where you can rent snorkeling equipment from kiosks along the beach. This beach lies east of the town of Guánica, to the east of Ponce. Here tropical fish add to the brightness of the water, which is generally turquoise. The addition of mangrove cays in the area also makes La Parguera more alluring for snorkelers. Another good spot for snorkelers is **Caja de Muertos** off the coast of Ponce. Here a lagoon coral reef boasts a large number of fish species (see chapter 10).

Even if you are staying in San Juan and want to go snorkeling, you are better off taking a day trip to Fajardo, where you'll get a real Caribbean snorkeling experience, with tranquil, clear water and stunning reefs teaming with tropical fish. Several operators offer day trips (from 10am to 3:30pm) leaving from Fajardo marinas, but transportation to and from your San Juan hotel can also be arranged. Prices start at around $99 (see "Boating & Sailing, earlier in this chapter.)

SURFING

Puerto Rico's northwest beaches attract surfers from around the world. Called the "Hawaii of the East," Puerto Rico has hosted a number of international competitions. October through February are the best surfing months, but the sport is enjoyed in Puerto Rico from August through April. The most popular areas are from Isabela to Rincón—at beaches such as Wilderness, Middles, Jobos, Crashboat, Las Marías, and the Spanish Wall.

There are surf spots across the entire north coast from San Juan to the northwest, including Los Tubos in Vega Baja.

San Juan itself has great surfing spots, including La 8, just outside of Old San Juan in Puerta de Tierra, near Escambrón Beach, which has some of the largest waves. Pine Grove in Isla Verde is a great spot to learn, because of the small, steady, well formed waves there.

International competitions held in Puerto Rico have included the 1968 and 1988 World Amateur Surfing Championships and the annual Caribbean Cup Surfing Championship. Currently, Corona sponsors an annual competition circuit taking place in Isabela and Rincón.

If you want to learn to surf, or perfect your technique while in Puerto Rico, it's quite easy.

Operating right near the Ritz-Carlton and Courtyard Marriott hotels in Isla Verde, the best surf lessons are given by professional surfer William Sue-A-Quan at his **Walking on Water Surfing School** (© 787/955-6059; www.gosurfpr.com). He and a few associates work right on the beach at Pine Grove and also offer lessons through the Ritz-Carlton. He's a great teacher, and takes on students as young as 5 and as old as 75.

Rincón also has many surf schools, some of which book packages including lodgings.

The Rincón Surf School (PO Box 1333, Rincón; © 787/823-0610) offers beginners lessons and week-long packages. **Puntas Surf School** (PO Box 4319, HC-01 Calle Vista del Mar; © 787/823-3618 or 207/251-1154) is another good option run by Melissa Taylor and Bill Woodward.

Lessons start at around $50 per hour.

Board rentals are available at many island surf shops, with prices starting at $25 a day. We list them in subsequent chapters.

TENNIS

Puerto Rico has approximately 100 major tennis courts. Many are at hotels and resorts; others are in public parks throughout the island. Several paradores also have courts. A number of courts are lighted for nighttime play.

In San Juan, the **Caribe Hilton** and the **Condado Plaza Hotel & Casino** have tennis courts. Also in the area are the **public courts** at the San Juan Central Municipal Park. The **Hyatt Dorado Beach Resort & Country Club** maintains a total of 21 courts. (**Note:** The property is closing as we go to print, but the golf courses and tennis courts will remain open.) See chapter 8.

WINDSURFING

The best windsurfing is found at Punta Las Marias in the Greater San Juan metropolitan area. Other spots on the island for windsurfing include Santa Isabel,

Guánica, and La Parguera in the south; Jobos and Shacks in the northwest; and the island of Culebra off the eastern coast.

Kite-boarding is becoming increasingly popular as well. Watch them flying through the choppy waters off Ocean Park in San Juan.

Lessons, advice, and equipment rental is available at **Velauno,** Calle Loíza 2430, Punta Las Marias in San Juan (© **787/ 728-8716**).

6 Travel Insurance

If you're buying travel insurance, expect to pay between 5% and 8% of the vacation itself. You can get estimates from various providers through **InsureMyTrip. com.** Enter your trip cost and dates, your age, and other information for prices from more than a dozen companies.

TRIP-CANCELLATION INSURANCE

Trip-cancellation insurance will help retrieve your money if you have to back out of a trip or depart early, or if your travel supplier goes bankrupt. Permissible reasons for trip cancellation can range from sickness to natural disasters. In this unstable world, trip-cancellation insurance is a good buy if you're purchasing tickets well in advance—who knows what the state of the world, or of your airline, will be in 9 months? Insurance policy details vary, so read the fine print and make sure that your airline or cruise line is on the list of carriers covered in case of bankruptcy. A good resource is "Travel Guard Alerts," a list of companies considered high-risk by Travel Guard International (see website below). Protect yourself further by paying for the insurance with a credit card—by law, consumers can get their money back on goods and services not received if they report the loss within 60 days after the charge is listed on their credit card statement.

Note: Many tour operators, particularly those offering trips to remote or high-risk areas, include insurance in the total trip cost or can arrange insurance policies through a partnering provider,

which is a convenient and often cost-effective way for the traveler to obtain insurance. Make sure the tour company is a reputable one, however, and be aware that some experts suggest you avoid buying insurance from the tour or cruise company you're traveling with. They contend it's more secure to buy from a "third party" than to put all your money in one place.

For more information, contact one of the following recommended insurers: **Access America** (© 866/807-3982; www. accessamerica.com); **Travel Guard International** (© 800/826-4919; www.travel guard.com); **Travel Insured International** (© 800/243-3174; www.travel insured.com); and **Travelex Insurance Services** (© 888/457-4602; www.travelex-insurance.com).

MEDICAL INSURANCE

Most health insurance policies cover you if you get sick away from home, but they are not likely to provide for medical evacuation in case of life-threatening injury or illness. It's a good idea to buy a travel insurance policy that provides for **emergency medical evacuation.** If you have to buy a one-way same-day ticket home and forfeit your nonrefundable round-trip ticket, you might be out big bucks. And the cost of a flying ambulance could wipe out your life's savings.

Check with your insurer, particularly if you're insured by an HMO, about the extent of its coverage while you're overseas. With the exception of certain HMOs and Medicare/Medicaid, your medical insurance should cover medical treatment—even hospital care—overseas. However, most out-of-country hospitals make you pay your bills upfront, and they send you a refund after you've returned home and filed the necessary paperwork.

If you require additional insurance, try one of the following companies:

- **MEDEX International** (© 888/ **MEDEX-00** [633-3900] or 410/ 453-6300; fax 410/453-6301; www. medexassist.com)
- **Travel Assistance International** (© 800/821-2828; www.travel assistance.com); for general information on services, call the company's Worldwide Assistance Services, Inc. at © **800/777-8710.**
- **The Divers Alert Network (DAN;** © **800/446-2671** or 919/684-2948; www.diversalertnetwork.org)

LOST-LUGGAGE INSURANCE
On domestic flights, checked baggage is covered up to $2,500 per ticketed passenger. On international flights (including U.S. portions of international trips), baggage coverage is limited to approximately $9.07 per pound, up to approximately $635 per checked bag. If you plan to check items more valuable than what's covered by the standard liability, see if your homeowner's policy covers your valuables, or get baggage insurance as part of your comprehensive travel-insurance package. Don't buy insurance at the airport, where it's usually overpriced. Be sure to take any valuables or irreplaceable items with you in your carry-on luggage, because many valuables (including books, money, and electronics) aren't covered by airline policies.

If your luggage is lost, immediately file a lost-luggage claim at the airport, detailing the luggage contents. Most airlines require that you report delayed, damaged, or lost baggage within 4 hours of arrival. The airlines are required to deliver luggage, once found, directly to your house or destination free.

7 Health & Safety

STAYING HEALTHY
Puerto Rico poses no major health problem for most travelers. If you have a chronic condition, however, you should check with your doctor before visiting the islands. For conditions such as epilepsy, diabetes, or heart problems, wear a **MedicAlert Identification Tag** (© 800/825-3785; www.medicalert.org), which will immediately alert doctors to your condition and give them access to your records through MedicAlert's 24-hour hot line.

Finding a good doctor in Puerto Rico is easy, and most speak English. See "Fast Facts: Puerto Rico" in the appendix for the locations of hospitals.

If you worry about getting sick away from home, consider purchasing **medical travel insurance** and carry your ID card in your purse or wallet. In most cases, your existing health plan will provide the coverage you need. See "Travel Insurance," above, for more information.

Pack **prescription medications** in your carry-on luggage, and carry prescription medications in their original containers. Also bring along copies of your prescriptions in case you lose your medication or run out. Carry the generic name of prescription medicines, in case a local pharmacist is unfamiliar with the brand name.

And don't forget **sunglasses** and an extra pair of **contact lenses** or **prescription glasses.**

Contact the **International Association for Medical Assistance to Travelers (IAMAT;** © 716/754-4883 or, in Canada, 416/652-0137; www.iamat.org) for tips on travel and health concerns in the countries you're visiting, and for lists of local, English-speaking doctors. The United States **Centers for Disease Control and Prevention** (© 800/311-3435; www.cdc.gov) provides up-to-date information on health hazards by region or country and offers tips on food safety. The website **www.tripprep.com**, sponsored by a consortium of travel medicine practitioners, may also offer helpful advice on traveling abroad. You can find listings of reliable clinics overseas at the **International Society of Travel Medicine** (www.istm.org).

It's best to stick to **bottled mineral water** here. Although tap water is said to be safe to drink, many visitors experience diarrhea, even if they follow the usual precautions. The illness usually passes quickly without medication if you eat simply prepared food and drink only mineral water until you recover. If symptoms persist, consult a doctor.

The **sun** can be brutal, especially if you haven't been exposed to it in some time. Experts advise that you limit your time on the beach the first day. If you do overexpose yourself, stay out of the sun until you recover. If your exposure is followed by fever or chills, a headache, or a feeling of nausea or dizziness, see a doctor.

Sandflies (or "no-see-ums") can still be a problem in Puerto Rico but are not the menace they are in other Caribbean destinations. They appear mainly in the early evening, and even if you can't see these tiny bugs, you sure can "feel-um."

Your favorite insect repellent will protect you from them should they become a problem.

Although **mosquitoes** are a nuisance, they do not carry malaria in Puerto Rico. However, after a long absence, the dreaded dengue fever has returned to Puerto Rico. The disease is transmitted by the Aede mosquito, and its symptoms include fever, headaches, pain in the muscles and joints,

skin blisters, and hemorrhaging. Most of its victims lack any defense against it.

Hookworm and other **intestinal parasites** are relatively common in the Caribbean, though you are less likely to be affected in Puerto Rico than on other islands. Hookworm can be contracted by just walking barefoot on an infected beach. *Schistosomiasis* (also called *bilharzia*), caused by a parasitic fluke, can be contracted by submerging your feet in rivers and lakes infested with a certain species of snail.

Puerto Rico has been especially hard hit by **AIDS.** Exercise *at least* the same caution in choosing your sexual partners, and in practicing safe sex, as you would at home.

STAYING SAFE

The U.S. State Department issues no special travel advisories for the Commonwealth of Puerto Rico, the way it might for, say, the more troubled island of Jamaica. However, there are problems in Puerto Rico, especially muggings along San Juan's Condado and Isla Verde beaches. Auto theft and cars getting broken into are other major problems. Do not leave valuables in cars, even when the doors are locked.

Take precautions about leaving valuables on the beach, and exercise extreme care if you're searching for a remote beach where there's no one in sight. The only person lurking nearby might be someone not interested in surf and sand but a robber waiting to make off with your possessions.

Avoid wandering around the darkened and relatively deserted alleys and small streets of San Juan's Old City at night, especially a section called El Callejón, near the intersection of calles San Sebastián and Tanca. Be especially careful along the narrow alley that connects this intersection with Calle Norzagaray. The district attracts more drug dealers than any other spot in Puerto Rico.

But the Old City and other tourist areas are generally safe. Avoid the seaside ghetto known as La Perla and the Cementerio de San Juan at night.

8 Specialized Travel Resources

TRAVELERS WITH DISABILITIES

Most disabilities shouldn't stop anyone from traveling. There are more options and resources out there today than ever before.

The Americans with Disabilities Act is enforced as strictly in Puerto Rico as it is on the U.S. mainland—in fact, a telling example of the act's enforcement can be found in Ponce, where the sightseeing trolleys are equipped with ramps and extra balustrades to accommodate travelers with disabilities. Unfortunately, hotels rarely give much publicity to the facilities they offer persons with disabilities, so it's always wise to contact the hotel directly, in advance, if you need special facilities. Tourist offices usually have little data about such matters.

You can obtain a free copy of *Air Transportation of Handicapped Persons,* published by the U.S. Department of Transportation. Write for *Free Advisory Circular No. AC12032,* Distribution Unit, U.S. Department of Transportation, Publications Division, 3341Q 75 Ave., Landover, MD 20785. No phone requests are accepted, but you can write for a copy of the publication or download it for free at http://isddc.dot.gov.

The U.S. National Park Service offers a Golden Access Passport that gives free lifetime entrance to U.S. national parks, including those in Puerto Rico, for persons who are blind or permanently disabled, regardless of age. You can pick up a Golden Access Passport at any NPS entrance fee area by showing proof of medically determined disability and eligibility for receiving benefits under federal law. Besides free entry, the Golden Access Passport also offers a 50% discount on federal-use fees charged for such facilities as camping, swimming, parking, boat launching, and tours. For more information, go to www.nps.gov/fees_passes.htm or call © **888/467-2757.**

Many travel agencies offer customized tours and itineraries for travelers with disabilities. **Flying Wheels Travel** (© **507/451-5005;** www.flyingwheelstravel.com) offers escorted tours and cruises that emphasize sports and private tours in minivans with lifts. **Access-Able Travel Source** (© 303/232-2979; www.accessable.com) offers extensive access information and advice for traveling around the world with disabilities. **Accessible Journeys** (© 800/846-4537 or 610/521-0339; www.disabilitytravel.com) caters specifically to slow walkers and wheelchair travelers and their families and friends.

Organizations that offer assistance to travelers with disabilities include **Moss-Rehab** (800/CALL-MOSS; www.moss resourcenet.org), which provides a library of accessible-travel resources online; the **American Foundation for the Blind** (**AFB;** © 800/232-5463 or 212/502-7600; www.afb.org), a referral resource for the blind or visually impaired that includes information on traveling with Seeing Eye dogs; and **SATH** (Society for Accessible Travel & Hospitality; © 212/447-7284; www.sath.org; annual membership fees: $45 adults, $30 seniors and students), which offers a wealth of travel resources for all types of disabilities and informed recommendations on destinations, access guides, travel agents, tour operators, vehicle rentals, and companion services. **AirAmbulanceCard.com** is now partnered with SATH and allows you to pre-select top-notch hospitals in case of an emergency for $195 a year ($295 per family), among other benefits.

For more information specifically targeted to travelers with disabilities, the community website **iCan** (www.ican online.net) has destination guides and several regular columns on accessible travel. Also check out the quarterly magazine *Emerging Horizons* (www.emerging horizons.com; $14.95 per year, $19.95 outside the U.S.); and *Open World* magazine, published by SATH (see above; subscription: $13 per year, $21 outside the U.S.).

A tip for British travelers: The **Royal Association for Disability and Rehabilitation (RADAR),** Unit 12, City Forum, 250 City Rd., London, EC1V 8AF (© **020/7250-3222;** fax 020/7250-0212; www.radar.org.uk), publishes information for travelers with disabilities.

GAY & LESBIAN TRAVELERS

Puerto Rico is the most gay-friendly destination in the Caribbean, with lots of accommodations, restaurants, clubs, and bars that actively cater to a gay clientele. A free monthly paper, *Puerto Rico Breeze,* lists items of interest to the island's gay community. It's distributed at the Atlantic Beach Hotel (p. 120) and many of the gay-friendly clubs mentioned in this book.

The **International Gay & Lesbian Travel Association (IGLTA;** © **800/448-8550** or 954/776-2626; www.iglta.org) links travelers up with gay-friendly hoteliers, tour operators, and airline and cruise-line representatives. It offers monthly newsletters, marketing mailings, and a membership directory that's updated once a year. Membership is $225 yearly, plus a $100 administration fee for new members.

Above and Beyond Tours (© **800/ 397-2681;** www.abovebeyondtours.com) offers gay and lesbian tours worldwide and is the exclusive gay and lesbian tour operator for United Airlines.

Now, Voyager (© **800/255-6951;** www.nowvoyager.com) is a San Francisco–based gay-owned and -operated travel service.

Olivia Cruises & Resorts (© **800/ 631-6277;** www.olivia.com) charters entire resorts and ships for exclusive lesbian vacations and offers smaller group experiences for both gay and lesbian travelers. (In 2005, tennis great Martina Navratilova was named Olivia's official spokesperson.)

Gay.com Travel (© **800/929-2268** or 415/644-8044; www.gay.com/travel or www.outandabout.com), is an excellent online successor to the popular *Out & About* print magazine. It provides regularly updated information about gay-owned, gay-oriented, and gay-friendly lodging, dining, sightseeing, nightlife, and shopping establishments in every important destination worldwide. It also offers trip-planning information for gay and lesbian travelers for more than 50 destinations, along various themes, ranging from Sex & Travel to Vacations for Couples.

The following travel guides are available at many bookstores, or you can order them from any online bookseller: *Spartacus International Gay Guide* (Bruno Gmünder Verlag; www.spartacusworld. com/gayguide) and *Odysseus: The International Gay Travel Planner* (Odysseus Enterprises Ltd.), both good, annual, English-language guidebooks focused on gay men; and the *Damron* guides (www. damron.com), with separate, annual books for gay men and lesbians.

SENIOR TRAVEL

Mention the fact that you're a senior when you first make your travel reservations. All major airlines and many Puerto Rican hotels offer discounts for seniors.

Though much of the island's sporting and nightlife activity is geared toward youthful travelers, Puerto Rico also has much to offer the senior. The best source of information for seniors is the Puerto Rico Tourism Company (see "Visitor Information," earlier in this chapter), or, if you're staying in a large resort hotel, talk to the activities director or the concierge.

Members of **AARP,** 601 E St. NW, Washington, DC 20049 (© **888/687-2277** or 202/434-2277; www.aarp.org), get discounts on hotels, airfares, and car rentals. AARP offers members a wide range of benefits, including *AARP The Magazine* and a monthly newsletter. Anyone over 50 can join.

The **U.S. National Park Service** offers a **Golden Age Passport** that gives seniors 62 years or older lifetime entrance to U.S. national parks for a one-time processing fee of $10. The pass must be purchased in person at any NPS facility that charges an entrance fee. Besides free entry, a Golden Age Passport also offers a 50% discount on federal-use fees charged for such facilities as camping, swimming, parking, boat launching, and tours. For more information, click onto www.nps.gov or call © **888/467-2757.**

Grand Circle Travel (© **800/221-2610** or 617/350-7500; fax 617/346-6700; www.gct.com) offers package deals for the 50-plus market, mostly of the tour-bus variety, with free trips thrown in for those who organize groups of 10 or more.

SAGA Holidays (© **800/343-0273**) offers tours and cruises for those 50 and older. SAGA also offers a number of single-traveler tours.

Recommended publications offering travel resources and discounts for seniors include: the quarterly magazine *Travel 50 & Beyond* (www.travel50andbeyond .com); *Travel Unlimited: Uncommon Adventures for the Mature Traveler* (Avalon); *101 Tips for Mature Travelers,* available from Grand Circle Travel (© **800/221-2610** or 800/959-0405; www.gct.com); and *Unbelievably Good Deals and Great Adventures That You Absolutely Can't Get Unless You're Over 50* (McGraw-Hill), by Joann Rattner Heilman.

9 Getting There & Getting Around

Puerto Rico is by far the most accessible of the Caribbean islands, with frequent airline service. It's also the major airline hub of the Caribbean Basin.

For airline and car rental contact information, see "Appendix: Fast Facts, Toll-Free Numbers & Websites."

GETTING THERE
BY PLANE

With San Juan as its hub for the entire Caribbean, **American Airlines** offers nonstop daily flights to San Juan from Baltimore, Boston, Chicago, Dallas–Fort Worth, Hartford, Los Angeles, Miami, Newark, New York (JFK), Orlando, Philadelphia, Tampa, Fort Lauderdale, and Washington (Dulles), plus flights to San Juan from both Montreal and Toronto with changes in Chicago or Miami.

Delta has three daily nonstop flights from Atlanta Monday to Friday, six nonstop on Saturday, and six nonstop on Sunday. Flights into Atlanta from around the world are frequent, with excellent connections from points throughout Delta's network in the South and Southwest.

United Airlines and **American Airlines** offer daily nonstop flights from Chicago to San Juan. **KLM Royal Dutch Airways** and **Northwest Airlines** offer three nonstop flights weekly to San Juan from Detroit, while **Continental** offers one weekly flight. United also offers flights to San Juan from both Memphis and Minneapolis, with a schedule that varies according to the season and the day of the week.

US Airways has several daily direct flights between Charlotte, NC, and San Juan. The airline also offers three daily nonstop flights to San Juan from Philadelphia, and one daily nonstop Saturday and Sunday flight to San Juan from Pittsburgh.

Continental Airlines flies nonstop daily from Newark, Houston, and Cleveland. The airline also flies from Newark direct to the northwestern airport outside Aguadilla should you wish to begin your tour of Puerto Rico in the west. In winter, service is increased to daily flights. **JetBlue** flies two times a day from New York's JFK airport to San Juan. The airline also serves 20 other U.S. cities, including Boston, Las Vegas, San Diego, and Seattle. **Spirit Air** offers two daily nonstop flights from Orlando, and one from Fort Lauderdale to San Juan.

Canadians can fly **Air Canada** from either Montreal or Toronto to San Juan.

Puerto Rico is the major transportation hub of the Caribbean, with the best connections for getting anywhere in the island. In addition to American Eagle (see below), **Cape Air** links two of the major islands of the U.S. Virgin Islands, St. Thomas and St. Croix, as well as Tortola in the B.V.I., with San Juan.

Seaborne Airlines offers daily links between St. Croix and St. Thomas with San Juan. The one-way cost from the U.S. Virgin Islands to Puerto Rico is $146 per person. The planes are small and frequent, carrying 15 to 19 passengers. Often there are more than 50 flights a day.

LIAT provides an air link to the Lesser Antilles islands.

British travelers can take a **British Airways** weekly flight direct from London to San Juan on Sunday. **Lufthansa** passengers can fly on Saturday (one weekly flight) from Frankfurt to San Juan via

USAir from Philadelphia. And **Iberia** has two weekly flights from Madrid to San Juan, leaving on Thursday and Saturday.

GETTING AROUND
BY PLANE

Cape Air flies from Luis Muñoz Marín International Airport to Mayagüez, Ponce, and Vieques several times a day. They also offer many flights daily to St. Thomas, St. Croix, and Tortola. **American Eagle** is the leader of the short-haul carriers, offering service to 37 destinations in the Caribbean and The Bahamas.

BY RENTAL CAR

There is good news and bad news about driving in Puerto Rico. First, the good news. Puerto Rico offers some of the most scenic drives in all the Caribbean. Driving around and discovering its little hidden beaches, coastal towns, mountain villages, vast forests, and national parks is reason enough to visit the island. In fact, if you want to explore the island in any depth, driving a private car is about the only way, as public transportation is woefully inadequate.

Of course, if you want to stay only in San Juan, having a car is not necessary. You can get around San Juan on foot or by bus, taxi, and in some cases, hotel minivan.

Now the bad news. Renting a car and driving in Puerto Rico, depending on the routes you take, can lead to a number of frustrating experiences, as our readers relate to us year after year. These readers point out that local drivers are often dangerous, as evidenced by the number of fenders with bashed-in sides. The older coastal highways provide the most scenic routes but are often congested. Some of the roads, especially in the mountainous interior, are just too narrow for automobiles. If you do rent a car, proceed with caution along these poorly paved and maintained roads, which most often follow circuitous routes. Cliffslides or landslides are not uncommon.

Some local agencies may tempt you with special reduced prices. But if you're planning to tour the island by car, you won't find any local branches that will help you if you experience trouble. And some of the agencies widely advertising low-cost deals won't take credit cards and want cash in advance. Also, watch out for "hidden" extra costs, which sometimes proliferate among the smaller and not very well-known firms, and difficulties connected with resolving insurance claims.

If you do rent a vehicle, it's best to stick with the old reliables: **Avis, Budget,** or **Hertz.** Each of these companies offers minivan transport to its office and car depot. Be alert to the minimum-age requirements for car rentals in Puerto Rico. Both Avis and Hertz require that renters be 25 or older; at Budget, renters must be 21 or older, but those between the ages of 21 and 24 pay a $10 to $25 daily surcharge to the agreed-upon rental fee.

Added security comes from an antitheft double-locking mechanism that has been installed in most of the rental cars available in Puerto Rico. Car theft is common in Puerto Rico, so extra precautions are always needed.

Distances are often posted in kilometers rather than miles (1km = 0.62 mile), but speed limits are displayed in miles per hour.

INSURANCE   Each company offers an optional collision-damage waiver priced at around $15 to $40 a day. Purchasing the waiver eliminates most or all of the financial responsibility you would face in case of an accident. With it, you can simply go home, leaving the rental company to sort it all out. Without it, you would be liable for up to the full value of the car in case it was damaged. Paying for the rental with certain credit or charge cards sometimes eliminates the need to buy this extra insurance. Also, your own automobile insurance policy might cover some or all of the damages. You should check with both your own insurer and your credit card issuers before leaving home.

GASOLINE   There is usually an abundant supply of gasoline in Puerto Rico, especially on the outskirts of San Juan, where you'll see all the familiar signs, such as Texaco and Shell. Gasoline stations are also plentiful along the main arteries traversing the island. However, if you're going to remote areas of the island, especially on Sunday, it's advisable to start out with a full tank. *Note:* In Puerto Rico, gasoline is sold by the liter, not by the gallon. The cost of gasoline is often somewhat cheaper than in the United States. A liter in the summer of 2008 sold for a bit above $1 a liter (3.78 of which make up a gallon—or about $4 per gallon).

DRIVING RULES   Driving rules can be a source of some confusion. Speed limits are often not posted on the island, but when they are, they're given in miles per hour. For example, the limit on the San Juan–Ponce *autopista* (expressway) is 70 mph (113kmph). Speed limits elsewhere, notably in heavily populated residential areas, are much lower. Because you're not likely to know what the actual speed limit is in some of these areas, it's best to confine your speed to no more than 30 mph (48kmph). The highway department places *lomas* (speed bumps) at strategic points to deter speeders. Sometimes these are called "sleeping policemen."

Like U.S. and Canadian motorists, Puerto Ricans drive on the right side of the road.

ROAD MAPS   One of the best and most detailed road maps of Puerto Rico is published by International Travel Maps and distributed in the United States by Rand McNally. It's available in some bookstores and is a good investment at $9.95. The *Gousha Puerto Rico Road*

Map, available in the United States and Canada, has a good street map of San Juan but lacks detailed information about minor highways on the island and is very similar to the map of Puerto Rico distributed free at tourist offices.

BREAKDOWNS & ASSISTANCE   All the major towns and cities have garages that will come to your assistance and tow your vehicle for repairs if necessary. There's no national emergency number to call in the event of a mechanical breakdown. If you have a rental car, call the rental company first. Usually, someone there will bring motor assistance to you. If your car requires extensive repairs because of a mechanical failure, a new one will be sent to replace it.

BY PUBLIC TRANSPORTATION

Cars and minibuses known as *públicos* provide low-cost transportation around the island. Their license plates have the letters "P" or "PD" following the numbers. They serve all the main towns of Puerto Rico; passengers are let off and picked up along the way, both at designated stops and when someone flags them down. Rates are set by the Public Service Commission. *Públicos* usually operate during daylight hours, departing from the main plaza (central square) of a town.

Information about *público* routes between San Juan and Mayagüez is available at **Lineas Sultana,** Calle Esteban González 898, Urbanización Santa Rita, Río Piedras (© 787/765-9377). Information about *público* routes between San Juan and Ponce is available from **Choferes Unidos de Ponce,** Terminal de Carros Públicos, Calle Vive in Ponce (© 787/764-0540). There are several operators listed under Lineas de Carros in the local Yellow Pages.

Fares vary according to whether the *público* will make a detour to pick up or drop off a passenger at a specific locale. (If you want to deviate from the predetermined routes, you'll pay more than if you wait for a *público* beside the main highway.) Fares from San Juan to Mayagüez range from $20 to $40; from San Juan to Ponce, from $20 to $40. Be warned that although prices of *públicos* are low, the routes are slow, with frequent stops, often erratic routing, and lots of inconvenience.

10 Package Deals & Group Tours

PACKAGE DEALS FOR THE INDEPENDENT TRAVELER

Before you start your search for the lowest airfare, you might want to consider booking your flight as part of a travel package such as an escorted tour or a package tour. What you lose in adventure, you'll gain in time and money saved when you book accommodations, and maybe even food and entertainment, along with your flight.

Package tours are not the same thing as escorted tours. With a package tour, you travel independently but pay a group rate. Packages usually include airfare, a choice of hotels, and car rentals, and packagers often offer several options at different prices. In many cases, a package that includes airfare, hotel, and transportation to and from the airport will cost you less than just the hotel alone would have, had you booked it yourself. That's because packages are sold in bulk to tour operators—who resell them to the public at a cost that drastically undercuts standard rates.

One good source of package deals is the airlines themselves. Most major airlines offer air/land packages, including **American Airlines Vacations** (© 800/321-2121; www.aavacations.com), **Delta Vacations** (© 800/221-6666; www.deltavacations.com), **US Airways Vacations** (© 800/455-0123; www.usairways

(Value) Great Discounts through the LeLoLai VIP Program

With San Juan's **LeLoLai VIPs** (Value in Puerto Rico) free program, you can enjoy the equivalent of up to $250 in travel benefits. You'll get discounts on admission to folklore shows, guided tours of historic sites and natural attractions, lodgings, meals, shopping, activities, and more. Of course, most of the experiences linked to LeLoLai are of the rather touristy type, but it can still be worth joining the program.

With membership, the *paradores puertorriqueños,* the island's modestly priced network of country inns, give cardholders 10% to 20% lower room rates Monday through Thursday. Discounts of 10% to 20% are offered at many restaurants, from San Juan's toniest hotels to several *mesones gastronómicos,* government-sanctioned restaurants that serve Puerto Rican fare. Shopping discounts are offered at many stores and boutiques, and, best yet, cardholders get 10% to 20% discounts at many island attractions.

The card also entitles you to free admission to some of the island's folklore shows. For more information about this card, call ✆ 787/722-1709 or go to the Centro de Información Turística, Plaza Darsenas, Old San Juan. Although you can call for details before you leave home, you can only sign up for this program once you reach Puerto Rico. Many hotel packages include participation in this program as part of their offerings.

---

vacations.com), **Continental Airlines Vacations** (✆ 800/301-3800; www.co vacations.com), and **United Vacations** (✆ 888/854-3899; www.unitedvacations. com).

Vacation Together (✆ 877/444-4547; www.vacationtogether.com) allows you to search for and book packages offered by a number of tour operators and airlines. The **United States Tour Operators Association**'s website (www. ustoa.com) has a search engine that allows you to look for operators that offer packages to a specific destination. Travel packages are also listed in the travel section of your local Sunday newspaper. **Liberty Travel** (✆ 888/271-1584; www. libertytravel.com), one of the biggest packagers in the Northeast, often runs full-page ads in Sunday papers. Or check ads in the national travel magazines such as *Arthur Frommer's Budget Travel Magazine, Travel & Leisure, National Geographic Traveler,* and *Condé Nast Traveler.*

To save time comparing the price and value of all the package tours out there, consider calling **TourScan Inc.** (✆ 800/962-2080; www.tourscan.com). Every season the company gathers and computerizes the contents of about 200 brochures containing 10,000 different vacations in the Caribbean. Write to TourScan for their catalogs, costing $4 each, the price of which is credited to any TourScan vacation.

Other options for general independent packages include:

Just-A-Vacation (✆ 800/683-6313 or 301/559-0510; www.justavacation.com) specializes in all-inclusive upscale resorts in Puerto Rico.

AAA Island Tours, 1759 Pinero Ave., Summit Hills, San Juan (✆ 787/793-3688; www.aaaislandtours.com), offers some good packages ranging from 2 days to 2 weeks.

ESCORTED GENERAL-INTEREST TOURS

An escorted tour is a structured group tour with a group leader. The price usually includes everything from airfare to hotel, meals, tours, admission costs, and local transportation.

Puerto Rico Tours, Condo Inter-Suite, Suite 5M, on Isla Verde in San Juan (© 787/306-1540 or 787/791-5479; www.puertorico-tours.com), offers specially conducted private sightseeing tours of Puerto Rico, including trips to the rainforest, Luquillo Beach, the caves of Camuy, and other attractions, such as a restored Taíno Indian village.

Backstage Partners (© 787/791-0099; www.backstagepartners.com) offers customized tours that take in a wide range of island attractions, including eco-tours, deep-sea fishing, scuba diving and snorkeling, safaris, and golf packages.

Other leading escorted tour operators include **Atlantic San Juan Tours** (© 787/644-9841; www.puertoricoexcursions.com), which helps you take in all the major sights of the island from Ponce to El Yunque; and **Sunshine Tours** (© 866/785-3636; www.puerto-rico-sunshine tours.com), which covers much the same ground as the others. **Legends of Puerto Rico** (© 787/605-9060; www.legends ofpr.com) hosts personalized tours, specializing in entertaining cultural and nature adventure tours.

11 For the Cruise-Ship Traveler

Miami is the cruise capital of the world, but San Juan is second. Unless you have never visited Miami and would like to include it as part of your extended Caribbean itinerary, there is justification in flying directly to San Juan by plane and beginning your cruise here. It puts you immediately in the Caribbean, which means you save a 2-day ocean voyage just to get here. Instead of sailing from Florida, you can spend the time getting to know Puerto Rico.

Consult a good travel agent for the latest offerings. Some of the most likely contenders include the following: **Ambassador Tours,** 50 First St., Suite 610, San Francisco, CA 94104 (© 800/989-9000 or 415/357-9876; www.ambassadortours.com); **Cruises One,** 1415 NW 62 St., Suite 205, Fort Lauderdale, FL 33309 (© 800/832-3592 or 954/958-3700; www.cruiseone.com); **Cruises of Distinction,** 4557 Woodward Ave., Bloomfield Hills, MI 48304 (© 800/634-3445); **Cruises Only,** 1011 E. Colonial Dr., Orlando, FL 32808 (© 800/242-9000 or 407/898-5353; www.cruises only.com); **Kelly Cruises,** 1315 W. 22nd St., Suite 105, Oak Brook, IL 60521 (© 800/837-7447 or 630/990-1111; www.kellycruises.com); and **Hartford Holidays Travel,** 129 Hillside Ave., Williston Park, NY 11596 (© 800/828-4813 or 516/746-6670; www.hartford holidays.com). Any of these providers stay tuned to last-minute price wars brewing among such megacarriers as Carnival, Princess, Royal Caribbean, and Holland America, as well as such low-budget contenders as Premier.

Vacations to Go, 1502 Augusta Dr., Suite 415, Houston, TX 77057 (© 800/338-4962 or 713/974-2121; www.vacationstogo.com), provides catalogs and information on discount cruises through the Caribbean, as well as the Atlantic and Mediterranean.

THE CRUISE LINES

Here's a brief rundown of some of the cruise lines that serve San Juan and the Caribbean. For detailed information, pick up a copy of one of our companion guides in this series, *Frommer's Caribbean Cruises and Ports of Call, Frommer's Caribbean Ports of Call,* or *Unofficial Guide to Cruises.*

- **Carnival Cruise Lines** (© 888/ CARNIVAL, or 305/599-2200; www. carnival.com), a specialist in the maintenance of some of the biggest and most brightly decorated ships afloat, is the richest, boldest, brashest, and most successful mass-market cruise line in the world. Many of its vessels depart from Florida area or Caribbean ports—including San Juan, Galveston, Miami, and Tampa— as well as New York. If you prefer to depart from one of the ports of Florida (especially Miami), know in advance that many of the company's cruises make San Juan a focal point of their stopovers. Most of the company's Caribbean cruises offer good value, last between 4 and 8 days, and feature nonstop activities, lots of glitter, and the hustle and bustle of armies of clients and crew members embarking and disembarking at every port.
- **Celebrity Cruises** (© 800/647-2251 or 800/722-5941; www.celebrity. com) maintains eight medium-to-large ships offering cruises of between 7 and 10 nights to such ports as Key West; Grand Cayman; St. Thomas; Aruba, St. Lucia; and Cozumel, Mexico, among others. Passengers interested in maximum exposure to Puerto Rico usually opt to cruise aboard *Galaxy*, a 77,713-ton megaship that's based (Dec–Mar) in San Juan, and which embarks every week throughout the year for tours to such southern Caribbean islands as Barbados, St. Kitts, and Aruba.

  Despite a merger of Celebrity with the larger and better-financed Royal Caribbean International, Celebrity maintains its own identity and corporate structure within the larger framework. The niche this line has created is unpretentious but classy, several notches above mass market, but with pricing that's nonetheless relatively competitive.
- **Costa Cruise Lines** (© 800/462-6782 or 954/266-5600; www.costa cruises.com), the U.S.-based branch of an Italian cruise line that has thrived for about a century, maintains hefty-to-megasize vessels that are newer than those of many other lines afloat. Two of these offer virtually identical jaunts through the western and eastern Caribbean on alternate weeks, each of them departing from Fort Lauderdale, Florida. Ports of call during the eastern Caribbean itineraries of both vessels include a stopover in San Juan, followed by visits to St. Thomas, Catalina Island (a private island off the coast of the Dominican Republic known for its beaches), and Cozumel. There is an Italian flavor and lots of Italian design onboard here, and an atmosphere of relaxed indulgence.
- **Princess Cruises** (© 800/PRINCESS; www.princess.com) has a large and far-flung fleet that totals 12 megavessels. The ships cruise at various times of the year through Caribbean and Bahamian waters, sometimes with stops at San Juan as part of the itinerary. The *Sun Princess* sails from Fort Lauderdale on round-trip 10-night cruises that variously cover the eastern and the south Caribbean. Princess is one of the very few lines in the world to offer luxury accommodations and upscale service as a standard feature aboard its megaships. These usually carry a smaller number of passengers than similarly sized vessels on less elegant lines. The company's clientele is upscale, with an average passenger age of 55 or over. A respectable percentage of the staff is British.
- **Radisson Seven Seas Cruises** (© 800/ 285-1835 or 954/776-6123; www.

rssc.com) is noted for the level of glamour and prestige that permeates its cruises. It sends all three of its ships—the *Seven Seas Mariner, Seven Seas Voyager,* and *Seven Seas Navigator*—into the Caribbean on a regular basis. The *Mariner,* carrying 700 passengers, is an all-suite vessel, and the *Navigator* carries 490 passengers on luxe cruises. The *Voyager* is a newer version of the all-suite *Mariner.* Cruises are relatively expensive compared to those offered by less prestigious lines, and roam freely, with less allegiance to a fixed home port than many other vessels.

• **Royal Caribbean International** (© **800/327-6700** or 305/539-6000; www.royalcaribbean.com) leads the industry in the development of megaships. Marketed as a mainstream mass-market cruise line whose components have been fine-tuned through endless repetition, the line encourages a restrained house-party theme that's somehow a bit less frenetic than that found aboard the more raucous megaships of other cruise lines, including Carnival. Using either Florida ports or San Juan as their home port, RCI ships call regularly at such oft-visited ports as St. Thomas, Ocho Rios, Sint Maarten, Grand Cayman, St. Croix, and Curaçao. Most of the company's cruises last for 4 to 7 days. If Puerto Rico is the focal point of your itinerary, your best bet is *Adventure of the Seas* or *Serenade of the Seas,* offering 7-night cruises through the southern and eastern Caribbean regions, using San Juan as a base. Royal Caribbean is the only cruise line in the business that owns, outright, two tropical beaches (one in The Bahamas, the other along an isolated peninsula in northern Haiti), whose sands and watersports facilities are the focus of many of the company's Caribbean cruises.

12 Tips on Accommodations

HOTELS & RESORTS

There is no rigid classification of Puerto Rican hotels. The word "deluxe" is often used—or misused—when "first class" might be a more appropriate term. We've presented fairly detailed descriptions of the hotels in this book, so you'll get an idea of what to expect once you're there.

Puerto Rico has had a bum rap for bad service, but our experience is that service in hotels and restaurants has been on a dramatic upswing over the last decade. There is still the slow tropical pace, what folks mean when they talk about "island time," however.

Ask detailed questions when booking a room. Entertainment in Puerto Rico is often alfresco, so light sleepers obviously won't want a room directly over a band. In general, back rooms cost less than oceanfront rooms, and lower rooms cost less than upper-floor units. Always ascertain whether transfers (which can be expensive) are included. And make sure that you know exactly what is free and what costs money. Some resorts seem to charge every time you breathe and might end up costing more than a deluxe hotel that includes most everything in the price.

Also factor in transportation costs, which can mount quickly if you stay 5 days to a week. If you want to go to the beach every day, it might be wise to book a hotel on the Condado and not stay in romantic Old San Juan, from which you'll spend a lot of time and money transferring back and forth between your hotel and the beach.

Most hotels in Puerto Rico are on the windward side of the island, with lots of waves, undertow, and surf. If a glasslike smooth sea is imperative for your stay, you can book on the leeward (eastern shore) or Caribbean (southeast coast) sides, which are better for snorkeling. The major centers in these areas are the resort complex of Palmas del Mar and the "second city" of Ponce.

MAP VS. AP, OR DO YOU WANT CP OR EP?

All resorts offer a **European Plan (EP)** rate, which means you pay for the price of a room. That leaves you free to dine around at night at various other resorts or restaurants without restriction. Another plan preferred by many is the **Continental Plan (CP)**, which means you get your room and a continental breakfast of juice, coffee, bread, jam, and so on, included in a set price. This plan is preferred by many because most guests don't like to "dine around" at breakfast time.

Another major option is the **Modified American Plan (MAP)**, which includes breakfast and one main meal of the day, either lunch or dinner. The final choice is the **American Plan (AP)**, which includes breakfast, lunch, and dinner.

At certain resorts you will save money by booking either the MAP or AP because discounts are granted. If you dine a la carte for lunch and dinner at various restaurants, your final dining bill will no doubt be much higher than if you stayed on the MAP or AP.

These plans might save you money, but if as part of your holiday you like to eat in various places, you might be disappointed. You face the same dining room every night, unless the resort you're staying at has many different restaurants on the dining plan. Often they don't. Many resorts have a lot of specialty restaurants, serving, say, Japanese cuisine, but these more expensive restaurants are not included in MAP or AP; rather, they charge a la carte prices.

One option is to ask if your hotel has a dine-around plan. You might still keep costs in check, but you can avoid a culinary rut by taking your meals in some other restaurants if your hotel has such a plan. Such plans are rare in Puerto Rico, which does not specialize in all-inclusive resorts the way that Jamaica and some other islands do.

Before booking a room, check with a good travel agent or investigate on your own what you are likely to save by booking in on a dining plan. Under certain circumstances in winter, you might not have a choice if MAP is dictated as a requirement for staying there. It pays to investigate, of course.

PUERTO RICAN GUESTHOUSES

A unique type of accommodations is the guesthouse, where Puerto Ricans themselves usually stay when they travel. Ranging in size from 7 to 25 rooms, they offer a familial atmosphere. Many are on or near the beach; some have pools or sun decks, and a number serve meals.

In Puerto Rico, however, the term "guesthouse" has many meanings. Some guesthouses are like simple motels built around pools. Others have small individual cottages with their own kitchenettes, constructed around a main building in which you'll often find a bar and a restaurant serving local food. Some are surprisingly comfortable, often with private bathrooms and swimming pools. You may or may not have air-conditioning. The rooms are sometimes cooled by ceiling fans or by the trade winds blowing through open windows at night.

For value, the guesthouse can't be topped. If you stay at a guesthouse, you can journey over to a big beach resort and use its seaside facilities for only a small fee. Although bereft of frills, the guesthouses we've recommended are clean and safe for families or single women. However, the cheapest ones are not places where you'd want to spend a lot of time because of their modest furnishings.

For further information on guest-houses, contact the **Puerto Rico Tourism Company** (© 800/866-7827 or 787/721-2400), La Princesa Building, Paseo La Princesa 2, Old San Juan, PR 00902.

PARADORES

In an effort to lure travelers beyond the hotels and casinos of San Juan's historic district to the tranquil natural beauty of the island's countryside, the Puerto Rico Tourism Company offers *paradores puertorriqueños* (charming country inns), which are comfortable bases for exploring the island's varied attractions. Vacationers seeking a peaceful idyll can also choose from several privately owned and operated guesthouses.

Using Spain's parador system as a model, the Puerto Rico Tourism Company established the paradores in 1973 to encourage tourism across the island. Each of the paradores is situated in a historic place or site of unusual scenic beauty and must meet high standards of service and cleanliness.

Some of the paradores are located in the mountains and others by the sea. Most have pools, and all offer excellent Puerto Rican cuisine. Many are within easy driving distance of San Juan.

Properties must meet certain bench-mark standards of quality to be admitted to the program, so tourists feel comfort-able staying at the property. One com-plaint about the program is that variances in quality still range widely from one property to the next. For more informa-tion call © 800/866-7827 or check out www.gotoparadores.com.

Our favorite paradores are all in west-ern Puerto Rico (see chapter 11). **Parador Posada Porlamar** in La Par-guera gives you a taste of the good life in a simple fishing village. For a plantation ambience and an evocation of the Puerto Rico of colonial times, there is the **Parador Hacienda Gripiñas** at Jayuya,

some 30 miles (48km) southwest of San Juan; it was a former coffee plantation. **Parador Vistamar,** at Quebradillas, one of the largest paradores in Puerto Rico, is located on a coastal bluff with beautiful gardens of tropical flowers.

The Tourism Company also operates a similar program which promotes local restaurants called **Mesones Gastronómi-cos** (© 800/981-7575). Restaurants in this program also have to pass muster with the Tourism Company for inclusion.

VILLAS & VACATION HOMES

You can often secure good deals in Puerto Rico by renting privately owned villas and vacation homes.

Almost every villa has a staff, or at least a maid who comes in a few days a week. Villas also provide the essentials of home life, including bed linens and cooking paraphernalia. Condos usually come with a reception desk and are often comparable to life in a suite at a big resort hotel. Nearly every condo complex has a swim-ming pool, and some have more than one.

Private apartments are rented either with or without maid service. This is more of a no-frills option than the villas and condos. An apartment might not be in a building with a swimming pool, and it might not have a front desk to help you. Among the major categories of vaca-tion homes, cottages offer the most free-wheeling way to live. Most cottages are fairly simple, many opening in an ideal fashion onto a beach, whereas others may be clustered around a communal pool. Many contain no more than a simple bedroom together with a small kitchen and bathroom. For the peak winter sea-son, reservations should be made at least 5 or 6 months in advance.

Dozens of agents throughout the United States and Canada offer these types of rentals (see "Rental Agencies," below, for some recommendations). You can also write to local tourist-information offices, which can advise you on vacation-home rentals.

Travel experts agree that savings, especially for a family of three to six people, or two or three couples, can range from 50% to 60% over what a hotel would cost. If there are only two in your party, these savings probably don't apply.

RENTAL AGENCIES
Agencies specializing in renting properties in Puerto Rico include:

• **VHR, Worldwide,** 235 Kensington Ave., Norwood, NJ 07648 (© **800/ 633-3284** or 201/767-9393; www. vhrww.com), offers the most comprehensive portfolio of luxury villas, condominiums, resort suites, and apartments for rent in the Caribbean, including complete packages for airfare and car rentals.

• **Hideaways Aficionado,** 767 Islington St., Portsmouth, NH 03801 (© **800/843-4433** or 603/430-4433; www.hideaways.com), provides a 144-page guide with illustrations of its accommodations so that you can get an idea of what you're renting. Most villas come with maid service. You can also ask this travel club about discounts on plane fares and car rentals.

4

Suggested Puerto Rico Itineraries

It would be fun to get "lost" on the island of Puerto Rico, wandering about at your leisure, discovering unspoiled villages and remote mountain hamlets off the beaten path. But few of us have such a generous amount of time in the speeded-up 21st century. Vacations are getting shorter, and you'll need a "lean-and-mean" schedule if you want to experience the best of any destination—even a small one like Puerto Rico—in a ridiculously short amount of time.

Try our "Puerto Rico in 1 Week" tour, or our "Puerto Rico in 2 Weeks" if you have more time. If you've been to Puerto Rico before and have already visited San Juan and El Yunque, you may want to take a more esoteric drive, following the trail of the Panoramic Route.

Puerto Rico has some good highways along the coast but as you venture deeper into the heartland, driving conditions become more difficult. Take along a detailed road map, and remember to blow your horn as you turn dangerous curves in the mountains.

The itineraries that follow take you to some major attractions with some surprise discoveries. The pace may be a bit breathless, so skip a town or sight occasionally for some chill-out time—after all, you're on vacation. Of course, you can use any of these itineraries as a jumping-off point for your own custom-made trip that more closely matches your interests.

One thing to keep in mind, you can base yourself out of San Juan for longer time periods, seeing much of the island in separate day trips from the capital. See chapter 1, "The Best of Puerto Rico," for some ideas.

1 The Regions in Brief

For a small island, Puerto Rico is a big place, with astounding geographic diversity squeezed into its 110×35-mile (177×56km) landmass. Beautiful beaches ring nearly its entire coast, which fronts both the rough Atlantic, making for among the biggest waves in the Caribbean, and the tranquil waters of the Caribbean Sea, a sailor's and diver's paradise.

Puerto Ricans are great hosts, eager to entertain and intensely proud of their island's natural beauty, their culture, and their achievements as a people.

SAN JUAN

The largest and best-preserved complex of Spanish colonial architecture in the Caribbean, Old San Juan (founded in 1521) is the oldest capital city under the U.S. flag. Once a lynchpin of Spanish dominance in the Caribbean, it has three major fortresses, miles of solidly built stone ramparts, a charming collection of antique buildings, and a modern business center. The city's economy is the most stable and solid in all of Latin America.

San Juan is the site of the official home and office of the governor of Puerto Rico (La Fortaleza), the 16th-century residence of Ponce de León's family, and several of the oldest places of Christian worship in the Western Hemisphere. Its bars, restaurants, shops, and nightclubs attract an animated group of fans. In recent years, the old city has become surrounded by densely populated modern buildings, including an ultramodern airport, which makes San Juan one of the most dynamic cities in the West Indies.

THE NORTHWEST: ARECIBO, RIO CAMUY, RINCON & MORE

A fertile area with many rivers bringing valuable water for irrigation from the high mountains of the Cordillera, the northwest also offers abundant opportunities for sightseeing. The region's districts include the following:

AGUADILLA Christopher Columbus landed near Aguadilla during his second voyage to the New World in 1493. Today the town has a busy airport, fine beaches, and a growing tourism-based infrastructure. It is also the center of Puerto Rico's lace-making industry, a craft imported here many centuries ago by immigrants from Spain, Holland, and Belgium.

ARECIBO Located on the northern coastline a 2-hour drive west of San Juan, Arecibo was originally founded in 1556. Although little remains of its original architecture, the town is well known to physicists and astronomers around the world because of the radar/radio-telescope that fills a concave depression between six of the region's hills. Equal in size to 13 football fields and operated jointly by the National Science Foundation and Cornell University, it studies the shape and formation of the galaxies by deciphering radio waves from space.

RINCON Named after the 16th-century landowner Don Gonzalo Rincón, who donated its site to the poor of his district, the tiny town of Rincón is famous throughout Puerto Rico for its world-class surfing and beautiful beaches. The lighthouse that warns ships and boats away from dangerous offshore reefs is one of the most powerful on Puerto Rico.

RIO CAMUY CAVE PARK Located near Arecibo, this park's greatest attraction is underground, where a network of rivers and caves provides some of the most enjoyable spelunking in the world. At its heart lies one of the largest known underground rivers. Aboveground, the park covers 300 acres (121 hectares).

UTUADO Small and nestled amid the hills of the interior, Utuado is famous as the center of the hillbilly culture of Puerto Rico. Some of Puerto Rico's finest mountain musicians have come from Utuado and mention the town in many of their ballads. The surrounding landscape is sculpted with caves and lushly covered with a variety of tropical plants and trees.

DORADO & THE NORTH COAST

Dorado, directly east of San Juan, is actually a term for a total of six white-sand beaches along the northern coast, reached by a series of winding roads. Dorado is the island's oldest resort town, the center of golf, casinos, and a once-major Hyatt resort that has closed. (p. 205). Luckily, the Hyatt's golf courses remain open: 72 holes of golf, the greatest concentration in the Caribbean—all designed by Robert Trent Jones, Sr. The former Dorado Beach has a number of beachside villas available, and the old resort's facilities are available through its club, while there's a vacation club at the former Cerromar. Plans are afoot for a new resort.

Puerto Rico

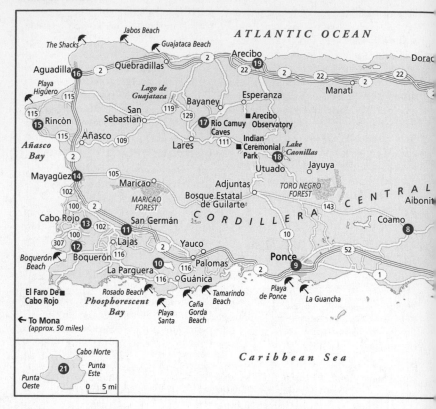

Meanwhile, the Embassy Suites Dorado is another jewel in this town, with its own Chi Chi Rodríguez–designed oceanfront golf course.

Another big resort that has gained from the closing of the Hyatt Dorado is El Conquistador Resort & Country Club in Fajardo near Las Croabas, a fishing village on the northeastern tip of Puerto Rico's north coast. The resort has a commanding perch overlooking the place where the Atlantic and Caribbean meet.

It has a water park and private island paradise with sandy beaches and recreational facilities. Challenging El Conquistador are the Rio Mar and Gran Melía properties in Río Grande, which are also top-of-the-line resorts.

THE NORTHEAST: EL YUNQUE, A NATURE RESERVE & FAJARDO

The capital city of San Juan (see above) dominates Puerto Rico's northeast. Despite the region's congestion, there are still many remote areas, including some of the island's most important nature reserves. Among the region's most popular towns, parks, and attractions are the following:

EL YUNQUE The rainforest in the Luquillo Mountains, 25 miles (40km) east of San Juan, El Yunque is a favorite escape from the capital. Teeming with plant and animal life, it is a sprawling tropical forest (actually a national forest)

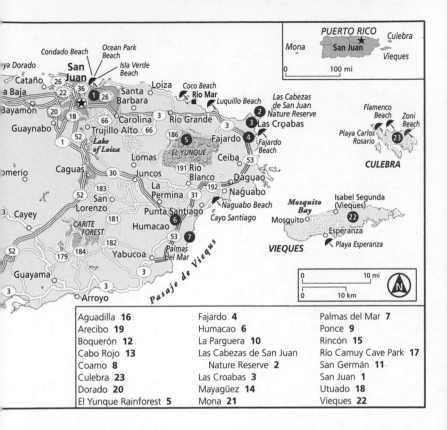

Aguadilla **16**	Fajardo **4**	Palmas del Mar **7**
Arecibo **19**	Humacao **6**	Ponce **9**
Boquerón **12**	La Parguera **10**	Rincón **15**
Cabo Rojo **13**	Las Cabezas de San Juan	Río Camuy Cave Park **17**
Coamo **8**	Nature Reserve **2**	San Germán **11**
Culebra **23**	Las Croabas **3**	San Juan **1**
Dorado **20**	Mayagüez **14**	Utuado **18**
El Yunque Rainforest **5**	Mona **21**	Vieques **22**

whose ecosystems are strictly protected. Some 100 billion gallons of rainwater fall here each year, allowing about 250 species of trees and flowers to flourish.

FAJARDO Small and sleepy, this town was originally established as a supply depot for the many pirates who plied the nearby waters. Today, a host of private yachts bob at anchor at one of its many marinas, and the many offshore cays provide visitors with secluded beaches. From Fajardo, ferryboats make choppy but frequent runs to the offshore islands of Vieques and Culebra.

LAS CABEZAS DE SAN JUAN NATURE RESERVE About an hour's drive from San Juan, this is one of the island's newest ecological refuges. It was established in 1991 on 316 acres (128 hectares) of forest, mangrove swamp, offshore cays, coral reefs, and freshwater lagoons—a representative sampling of virtually every ecosystem on Puerto Rico. There are a visitor center, a 19th-century lighthouse (El Faro) that still works, and ample opportunity to forget the pressures of urban life.

THE SOUTHWEST: PONCE, MAYAGÜEZ, SAN GERMAN & MORE

One of Puerto Rico's most beautiful regions, the southwest is rich in local lore, civic pride, and natural wonders.

BOQUERÓN   Famous for the beauty of its beach and the abundant birds and wildlife in a nearby forest reserve, this sleepy village is now ripe for large-scale tourism-related development. During the early 19th century, the island's most-feared pirate, Roberto Cofresí, terrorized the Puerto Rican coastline from a secret lair in a cave nearby.

CABO ROJO   Established in 1772, Cabo Rojo reached the peak of its prosperity during the 19th century, when immigrants from around the Mediterranean, fleeing revolutions in their own countries, arrived to establish sugar-cane plantations. Today, cattle graze peacefully on land originally devoted almost exclusively to sugar cane, and the area's many varieties of exotic birds draw bird-watchers from throughout North America. Even the offshore waters are fertile; it's estimated that nearly half of all the fish consumed on Puerto Rico are caught in waters near Cabo Rojo.

LA PARGUERA   Named after a breed of snapper *(pargos)* that abounds in the waters nearby, La Parguera is a quiet coastal town best known for the phosphorescent waters of *La Bahía Fosforescente* (Phosphorescent Bay). Here, sheltered from the waves of the sea, billions of plankton (luminescent dinoflagellates) glow dimly when they are disturbed by movements of the water. The town comes alive on weekends, when crowds of young people from San Juan arrive to party the nights away. Filling modest rooming houses, they temporarily change the texture of the town as bands produce loud sessions of salsa music.

MAYAGÜEZ   The third-largest city on Puerto Rico, Mayagüez is named after the *majagua,* the Amerindian word for a tree that grows abundantly in the area. Because of an earthquake that destroyed almost everything in town in 1917, few old buildings remain. The town is known as the commercial and industrial capital of Puerto Rico's western sector. Its botanical garden is among the finest on the island.

PONCE   Puerto Rico's second-largest city, Ponce has always prided itself on its independence from the Spanish-derived laws and taxes that governed San Juan and the rest of the island. Long-ago home of some of the island's shrewdest traders, merchants, and smugglers, it is enjoying a renaissance as citizens and visitors rediscover its unique cultural and architectural charms. Located on Puerto Rico's southern coast, about 90 minutes by car from the capital, Ponce contains a handful of superb museums, one of the most charming main squares in the Caribbean, an ancient cathedral, dozens of authentically restored colonial-era buildings, and a number of outlying mansions and villas that, at the time of their construction, were among the most opulent on the island.

SAN GERMÁN   Located on the island's southwestern corner, small, sleepy, and historic San Germán was named after the second wife of Ferdinand of Spain, Germaine de Foix, whom he married in 1503. San Germán's central church, Iglesia Porta Coeli, was built in 1606. At one time, much of the populace was engaged in piracy, pillaging the ships that sailed off the nearby coastline. The central area of this village is still sought out for its many reminders of the island's Spanish heritage and colonial charm.

THE SOUTHEAST: PALMAS DEL MAR & MORE

The southeastern quadrant of Puerto Rico has some of the most heavily developed, as well as some of the least developed, sections of the island.

COAMO   Although today Coamo is a bedroom community for San Juan, originally it was the site of two different Taíno communities. Founded in 1579, it now has a main square draped with bougainvillea and one of the best-known Catholic churches on Puerto Rico. Even more famous, however, are the mineral springs whose therapeutic warm waters helped President Franklin D. Roosevelt during his recovery from polio. (Some historians claim that these springs inspired the legend of the Fountain of Youth, which in turn set Ponce de León off on his vain search of Florida.)

HUMACAO   Because of its easy access to San Juan, this small, verdant inland town has increasingly become one of the capital's residential suburbs.

PALMAS DEL MAR   This sprawling vacation and residential resort community is located near Humacao. A splendid golf course covers some of the grounds. Palmas del Mar is at the center of what has been called the "New American Riviera"—3 miles (4.8km) of white-sand beaches on the eastern coast of the island. Palmas del Mar is the largest resort in Puerto Rico, lying to the south of Humacao on 2,800 acres (1,133 hectares) of a former coconut plantation—now devoted to luxury living and the sporting life.

The Equestrian Center at Palmas is the finest riding headquarters in Puerto Rico, with trails cutting through an old plantation and jungle along the beach. The resort is ideal for families and has a supervised summer activities program for children ages 5 to 12.

THE OFFSHORE ISLANDS: CULEBRA, VIEQUES & MORE

Few *norteamericanos* realize that Puerto Rico has at least four well-known islands and a multitude of tiny cays lying offshore. The most famous of these are:

CAYO SANTIAGO   Lying off the southeastern coast is the small island of Cayo Santiago. Home to a group of about two dozen scientists and a community of rhesus monkeys originally imported from India, the island is a medical experimentation center run by the U.S. Public Health Service. Monkeys are studied in a "wild" but controlled environment both for insights into the behavioral sciences and for possible cures for such maladies as diabetes and arthritis. Casual visitors are not permitted on Cayo Santiago, but they can cruise along the shore and watch the monkeys.

CULEBRA & VIEQUES   Located off the eastern coast, these two islands are among the most unsullied and untrammeled areas in the West Indies, even though Vieques is being belatedly discovered. Come here for sun, almost no scheduled activities, fresh seafood, clear waters, sandy beaches, and teeming coral reefs. Vieques is especially proud of its phosphorescent bay, Mosquito Bay.

MONA   Remote, uninhabited, and teeming with bird life, this barren island off the western coast is ringed by soaring cliffs and finely textured white-sand beaches. The island has almost no facilities, so visitors seldom stay for more than a day of swimming and picnicking. The surrounding waters are legendary for their dangerous eddies, undertows, and sharks.

2 Puerto Rico in 1 Week

If you budget your time carefully, you can see some of the major highlights of Puerto Rico in just 1 week. Naturally, most of your time will be spent in **San Juan,** the capital, but you'll also have time to visit **El Yunque** (a rainforest) and the most famous beach in Puerto Rico, **Luquillo.** There also will be time for days spent in **Ponce,** Puerto

Rico's second city, the beautiful beaches of the southwest, the historic town of **San Germán,** and a side trip to an offshore island or the northwest coast. *Start:* San Juan.

Days ❶ & ❷: San Juan ✦✦✦
Take a flight that arrives in San Juan as early as possible on **Day 1.** Check into your hotel and if it's sunny, head for the pool or beach directly, stopping only for maybe a pick-me-up coffee and a pastry to go. As surely as there will be hours of sunshine most likely every day on your trip here, at certain times of the year, it also clouds up frequently for a few hours, so we always recommend enjoying the sun while it's shining (even if it's for an hour or so).

After a quick swim and some sunshine, you can still spend the afternoon in Old San Juan, enjoying some sightseeing and shopping. A 2-hour walking tour covers the important churches, forts, and other highlights. Add another hour or so because you'll want to shop while you explore, and probably stop for refreshment, a rum drink or fresh fruit frappe, at one of the Old City's famous watering holes. The city is also one of the shopping meccas of the Caribbean, with bargains galore, lots of local arts and crafts, and high-profile retail shops.

Visit one of the area's many fine cafes and restaurants for an early dinner. Then return to your hotel for an early evening and a well-deserved rest.

On **Day 2,** with shopping and sightseeing behind you, prepare for a full day in the sun. Most hotel and resort pools are great, and the beaches in San Juan are glorious white-sand, turquoise-water affairs. For many visitors, that's why they came to San Juan in the first place. Depending on the location of your hotel, the finest beaches are **Condado Beach** (p. 172), **Isla Verde Beach** (p. 173), and **Ocean Park Beach** (p. 172). Enjoy the watersports activities along the beaches of the Greater San Juan area. See the "Diving, Fishing, Tennis & Other Pursuits"

section beginning on p. 172. Of course, there's nothing wrong with spending a day at the beach.

Make it a point tonight to enjoy some of the nightlife of the capital, either bar-hopping, taking in the club or music scene, or going casino gambling. San Juan is one of the nightlife capitals of the Caribbean. There's likely a lot going on right around your hotel; Old San Juan, Condado, and Isla Verde are centers of activity. See the "San Juan After Dark" section, beginning on p. 188.

Day ❸: El Yunque ✦✦✦ **& Luquillo Beach** ✦✦✦
While still based in San Juan, drive east for 25 miles (40km) to **El Yunque** for a morning visit. This 28,000-acre (11,331-hectare) attraction is the only tropical rainforest in the U.S. National Forest Service system. Stop first at **El Portal Tropical Forest Center** (p. 200) for maps and guidance. You're faced with a choice of hiking trails or else driving through. Unless you engage in extensive hiking, you can see some of the forest's greatest beauty in time for lunch.

After a visit to the rainforest, head north toward the town of Rio Grande and follow the signs to **Luquillo Beach** in the east. There are many roadside signs and kiosks where you can enjoy a tasty but inexpensive lunch. Shaded by tall coconut palms, the beach is crowded on weekends. Surfing, kayaking, diving, and snorkeling are just some of the activities you can enjoy here, along with the golden sands of the beach itself. There are also refreshment stands and a bathhouse as well as toilets. Return west to San Juan for a final night.

Days ❹ & ❺: Ponce & the Southwest Coast ✦✦
Leave San Juan on the morning of **Day 4** and drive 75 miles (121km) southwest to

the city of **Ponce,** the island's "second city." Take Route 1 south to Highway 52, then continue south and west to Ponce, following the road signs. Allow at least 1½ hours for the drive. Once in Ponce, check into a hotel for 2 nights.

For orientation and to see the historic city, see "Walking Tour: Ponce," on p. 221, which includes a stopover at **Parque de Bombas,** the famous firehouse, on the city's gorgeous central plaza. Another chief attraction of Ponce, which can easily absorb 2 hours of your time, is the **Museo de Arte de Ponce** (p. 219).

After some shopping and a local lunch in the old town, we recommend continuing on to one of the beach towns to the west, along Route 116: **Guánica, La Parguera** or **Boquerón.** Heading to the coast today will mean more time for fun in the sun the next day because Ponce has no real beach. The only reason to stay in Ponce is to go out for a great meal and enjoy the entertainment at the **Ponce Hilton,** maybe squeezing in a round of golf or some pool time in the afternoon before dinner. (If it's a weekend, there could be a concert at the nearby **La Guancha,** a public marina and boardwalk where harborfront restaurants serve up local treats and drinks.)

Guánica's three lodging options—**Copamarina Beach Resort, Mary Lee's By the Sea** and **Hotel 1812**—are among the best in their class for the region, and the town has seven spectacular beaches. La Parguera and Boquerón are considered the "Cape Cod of Puerto Rico," with ample simple, clean lodging options, from small hotels to guesthouses.

If you head out of Ponce on Day 4, you will also be able to spend two hours in the afternoon exploring the **Guánica State Forest,** the best-preserved subtropical ecosystem on the planet. There are 750 plants and rare tree species that grow here, and many trails descend to the beautiful coastline. Grab a fresh seafood meal at a local restaurant by your hotel. Hopefully, there's live music.

On **Day 5,** you'll want to head to the beach because among the finest on the island are all around you. In Guánica, go to **Caña Gorda** or **Playa Santa;** your best bet in La Parguera is to take a boat to **Mata La Gata** islet offshore, while the public beach at Boquerón has tranquil waters, white sand, and a healthy grove of palm trees running behind the beach.

In the afternoon, take a drive to the historic city of San Germán or farther on to Mayagüez. Make sure to drive by **El Faro de Cabo Rojo,** a lighthouse at Puerto Rico's southernmost corner, for a look. It's on a dramatic, blissfully isolated coastal perch.

In San Germán, the town's major attractions, including **Iglesia Porta Coeli** and **San Germán de Auxerre,** are in its historic downtown, a beautiful array of Spanish colonial and turn-of-the-20th-century buildings. If you go to Mayagüez, visit its beautiful downtown plaza, and then either its zoo or botanical gardens. Have dinner before heading back to your hotel.

Day ⑥: Mountain Retreat 🐟🐟

It's time to head up to the mountains because you can't spend a week in Puerto Rico without spending a night at one of its country mountain retreats.

You can visit the **Toro Negro Forest Reserve** (p. 242), a 7,200-acre (2,914-hectare) park straddling the highest peak of the Cordillera Central, north of Ponce. Visit Lake Guineo or take a hike to the beautiful Juanita waterfalls. You should also have time to visit the other area forest reserve, **Monte Estado State Forest** in Maricao. There are fine country inns near both reserves. Most also offer traditional Puerto Rican fare. Have a restful night in the clean mountain air.

Suggested Puerto Rico Itineraries

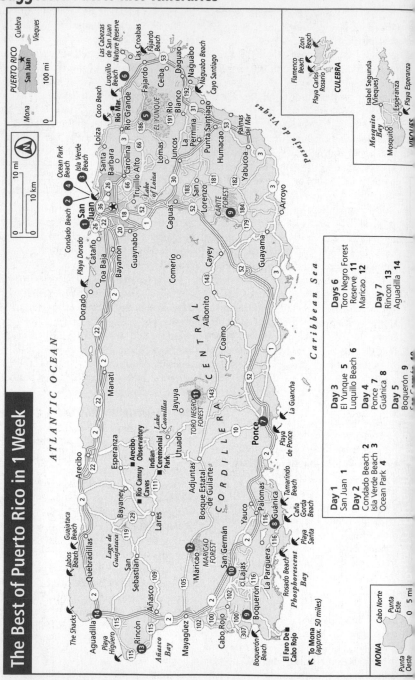

The Best of Puerto Rico in 1 Week

Day 1
San Juan **1**

Day 2
Condado Beach **2**
Isla Verde Beach **3**
Ocean Park **4**

Day 3
El Yunque **5**
Luquillo Beach **6**

Day 4
Ponce **7**
Guánica **8**

Day 5
Boquerón **9**
San Germán **10**

Days 6
Toro Negro Forest
Reserve **11**
Maricao **12**

Day 7
Rincón **13**
Aguadilla **14**

The Best of Puerto Rico in 2 Weeks

Day 1
San Juan 1

Day 2
Condado Beach 2
Isla Verde Beach 3
Ocean Park 4

Day 3
El Yunque 5
Luquillo Beach 6

Day 4
Las Croabas 7
Palmas del Mar 8
Fajardo 9

Days 5 & 6
Vieques 10

Day 7
Culebra 11

Day 8
San Juan 1

Day 9
Ponce 12
Guánica 13

Day 10
Boquerón 14
San Germán 15

Day 11
Rincon 16

Day 12
Isla Mona 17

Day 13
Aguadilla 18
Isabela 19

Day 14
Arecibo Observatory 20
Indian CeremonialPark 21
Rio Camuy Caves 22

ATLANTIC OCEAN

Caribbean Sea

Pasaje de Vieques

Mona Passage

CORDILLERA CENTRAL

CARITE FOREST

TORO NEGRO FOREST

MARICAO FOREST

Lake of Loíza

Lake Caonillas

Lago de Guajataca

Phosphorescent Bay

Añasco Bay

CULEBRA
Flamenco Beach
Playa Carlos Rosario
Zoni Beach
11

VIEQUES
Isabel Segunda (Vieques)
Esperanza
Playa Esperanza
Mosquito Bay
Mosquito
10

MONA
Cabo Norte
Punta Este
Punta Oeste
17

San Juan
Mona
Vieques
Culebra

Condado Beach 2
San Juan 1
Ocean Park Beach 4
Isla Verde Beach 3
Santa Loíza
Santa Barbara
Carolina
Trujillo Alto
Lomas
Juncos
La Permina
Punta-Santiago
Humacao
Palmas del Mar 8
Yabucoa
Arroyo
Guayama

Coco Beach
Río Mar
Luquillo Beach 6
Las Cabezas de San Juan Nature Reserve
Las Croabas 7
Fajardo Beach
Fajardo 9
Ceiba
Daguao
Blanco
Naguabo
Naguabo Beach
Cayo Santiago

EL YUNQUE 5
Río Grande

Cataño
Bayamón
Guaynabo
Toa Baja
Playa Dorado
Dorado
Toa Baja
Comerío
Caguas
San Lorenzo
Cayey
Aibonito
Coamo

Manati
Arecibo
Esperanza
Bayaney
Lares
Adjuntas
Utuado
Jayuya
Bosque Estatal de Guilarte
Ponce 12
Playa de Ponce
La Guancha
Guayanilla

Arecibo Observatory 20
Rio Camuy Caves 22
Indian Ceremonial Park 21

Quebradillas
Aguadilla 18
The Shacks 19
Jabos Beach
Guajataca Beach
San Sebastián
Añasco
Mayagüez
Playa Higüero
Rincon 16
Boquerón 14
Cabo Rojo
El Faro De Cabo Rojo
To Mona (approx. 50 miles)

Isabela 19
Guánica 13
Caña Gorda Beach
Tamarindo Beach
San Germán 15
Yauco
Lajas
Palomas
La Parguera
Rosado Beach
Playa Santa

0 100 mi
0 10 km
0 5 mi

Day ⑦: Rincón & the Northwest ⭐⭐⭐

Get up early and begin driving up the west coast north of Mayagüez to **Rincón.** After checking in at a hotel, hit one of the town's famous beaches. If you surf or windsurf, today's the day for it because you are in the surfing capital of the Caribbean. If it's summer, and the surf is down, then the snorkeling is great. Most hotels and guesthouses have fine pools as well.

If it's winter, consider spending some time whale-watching, as it's the season they breach right offshore. It's also possible to rent a boat to take you to **Desecheo Island** (just off shore) or the much longer trek to **Mona Island,** some 40 miles off the coast. Called "the Galápagos of Caribbean," the island is inhabited by giant iguanas and three species of endangered sea turtles, among other rare plant, animal, and marine life. (If you want to squeeze this in on a one-week trip, it would be best to eliminate the mountain retreat or the second day in the southwest.)

Rincón has a number of fine bars and restaurants, with great food and live entertainment. So make sure you have a great meal and some fun on your final night. And you'll want to be sure to watch the sun go down, which is a beautiful thing on the west coast of Puerto Rico.

The following morning, you'll find that it's only a 98-mile (158km) drive northeast back to San Juan, the hub of all the island's major transportation. The nearby Aguadilla airport, however, also has international flight service, so you could squeeze in some more beach time or another attraction (say the **Camuy Caves** or the **Arecibo Observatory**) if you did not have to return to San Juan before flying out.

3 Puerto Rico in 2 Weeks

This tour, the longest in this chapter, is also the most recommended. It encapsulates the very essence of the island—it's "Puerto Rico in a Nutshell." Because of the island's small size, you can visit not only its three major cities (**San Juan, Ponce,** and **Mayagüez**) but also its greatest attraction, the **El Yunque** rainforest; its finest beach (**Luquillo**); its offshore islands (**Mona, Vieques,** and **Culebra**); and even its most intriguing man-made attractions, such as the alien-hunting **Arecibo Observatory.** To start, follow the first 3 days of the "Puerto Rico in 1 Week" itinerary above (San Juan on Days 1 and 2, El Yunque and Luquillo Beach on Day 3), then head to Las Croabas to begin Day 4. *Start:* San Juan.

Days ①, ② & ③: San Juan, El Yunque ⭐⭐⭐ & Luquillo Beach ⭐⭐⭐

Follow the first 3 days of the "Puerto Rico in 1 Week" itinerary above.

Day ④: Las Croabas & Palmas del Mar

The northeast corner of Puerto Rico is filled with sports and attractions and is deserving of at least a day of your time, especially if you like outdoor pursuits. We'd recommend that you check into **El** **Conquistador Resort & Golden Door Spa** (p. 269) for the day, taking advantage of its vast array of facilities and restaurants, as well as its water park, health club, spa, children's programs, and watersports equipment.

Using the resort as a base, you can explore **Las Cabezas de San Juan Nature Reserve** (p. 266), with its famous lighthouse, "El Faro" and untrammeled tropical forest and beaches. Boaters are attracted to **Puerto del Rey** (the

Caribbean's largest and most modern marina), and beach buffs flock to such strips of white sand as **Playa Seven Seas** or **Playa Escondido ("Hidden Beach").** See p. 268 for more coverage of these sandy strips.

The resort has several fine restaurants, and the village of Los Croabas, a quaint fishing port, has several simple but high-quality seafood restaurants. You could also drive into downtown Fajardo to eat.

Another option would be to continue driving south along the east coast to **Humacao** and the nearby resort of **Palmas del Mar** where you can participate in the best-organized sporting activities in eastern Puerto Rico, ranging from vast tennis courts to scuba diving and golf, along with deep-sea fishing (see coverage beginning on p. 271). Palmas also has 3 miles (4.8km) of exceptional white sandy beaches, all open to the public. There are also a large number of places for lunch and dinner at the resort and a good, affordable seafood restaurant serving freshly caught fish.

If you can't afford the prices of these large resorts, there are several smaller inns throughout this area, from Luquillo to Naguabo. See "Paradores" in chapter 3.

Days ❺ & ❻: Vieques ☆

Regardless of where you based for the night, arrive early at the port of Fajardo on Puerto Rico's eastern coast for a 1-hour ferryboat ride to the island of **Vieques,** the largest of the so-called Spanish Virgin Islands (it is, in fact, a U.S. territory). Check into a hotel here for 2 nights. Resorts and small inns come in all price ranges (coverage of hotels begins on p. 276).

A stopover in Vieques might be the most idyllic spot in your vacation, as the island offers 40 beautiful, white, sandy beaches, all open to the public. See **"The Best Beaches,"** with coverage beginning on p. 279. Lazy days in the sun aren't the only activities on the island. You can tour

the luminous waters of **Phosphorescent Bay,** join mountain-bike excursions, go fishing from a kayak, take snorkeling trips, or go scuba diving. **Fort Conde de Mirasol Museum** (p. 281) is an interesting museum housed in an historic fort, and federal authorities operate two wildlife refuges on former military lands. At night Vieques offers a wide range of bars and good restaurants, the best available on any of Puerto Rico's offshore islands.

Day ❼: Culebra ☆

Should you have come down with island fever, you can return to the port of Fajardo and take another ferry for an overnight stopover on the island of Culebra, which is far more offbeat and undiscovered than Vieques. Though still undeveloped, Culebra facilities have seen substantial upgrades in recent years, and there are many more rooms available and many more quality rooms over the last few years.

Like Vieques, Culebra is chock-full of white sandy beaches, and you can explore the **Culebra Wildlife Refuge** (p. 289). Also snorkel here, or kayak, fish, sail, or hike. *Tip:* The best way to explore the island is to rent and drive a jeep—though most visitors prefer to hang out for the day on one of Culebra's beaches. Our preferred beach for the day? It's the mile-long (1.6km) **Flamenco Beach.** The next morning return by ferry to the port of Fajardo for a continuation of the tour.

Day ❽: San Juan ☆☆☆

On the morning of **Day 8,** leave Culebra by taking a ferryboat back to the port of Fajardo. From here, drive west to San Juan for an overnight stopover. Since the city is so vast and so filled with amusements, try to use the time to mop up all the shopping, attractions, and nightlife options you missed on your first visit. Review chapter 8 for all the possible options, including outdoor pursuits, awaiting you.

Day ➒: Ponce & the Southwest 𝒢𝒢

On the morning of **Day 9,** leave San Juan and drive south to Ponce, the chief city on the southern coast. Follow the suggestions as outlined in Day 4 and Day 5 of "Puerto Rico in 1 Week" (above).

Day ➓: Mountain Retreat 𝒢𝒢

Follow the suggestions for Day 6 of "Puerto Rico in 1 Week," above.

Day ⓫: Rincón & the Northwest 𝒢

For suggestions, refer to Day 7 in "Puerto Rico in 1 Week," above. However, save a separate day for Isla Mona (see below), which richly deserves it.

Day ⓬: Isla Mona 𝒢𝒢𝒢

Boat excursions over to this island are not as organized as they should be, but it's worth the trouble to get to Mona, even enduring a difficult sea crossing across Pasaje de la Mona. Coverage begins on p. 249. Most visitors use Mayagüez (see above) as their base for exploring Mona Island, returning to the mainland for the night. Other more adventurous travelers camp out on the island. Lying some 50 miles (80km) off the Puerto Rican mainland, Mona has been called the Jurassic Park of the Caribbean.

A nature reserve since 1919, Mona has been uninhabited for the past half-century except for day-trippers. Living here is every species from fish-eating bats to wild goats and pigs, and especially giant iguanas. The environment is beautiful, but potentially hostile because of its wildness. Department of Natural and Environmental Resources rangers are on hand to offer advice and guidance. There are toilets and saltwater showers at Playa Sardinera, but visitors need to bring fresh water. You can go camping, but the itinerary assumes you'd rather return to the comfort of a hotel room in Mayagüez.

Day ⓭: Mayagüez & the Northwest

Squeeze in some chill time by the pool in this west-coast suburban city. Go explore the beautifully restored downtown area. Highlights include the elegant central **Plaza Colón,** dominated by a monument of Christopher Columbus, surrounded by 16 bronze statues of courtly ladies, and the historic **Yaguez Theater, City Hall,** and **Post Office.** Two huge fires and an earthquake at the turn of the 20th century destroyed much of the city three different times, but there's much fine architecture from the 1920s and later.

You'll also want to visit the city's zoo, **Puerto Rico National Parks Zoo** (p. 247), or its **Tropical Agriculture Research Station** (p. 247), next to the Mayagüez Campus of the University of Puerto Rico. Anyone can walk through this site for botanical research, whose grounds feature towering bamboo, wildfruit trees, and the various plant species grown here.

After lunch, as you head north out of the city, drive by its historic harbor and warehouse district with a restored Customs House from the 1920s.

You'll be going to the beautiful towns of the northwest coast, most probably **Isabela** (p. 259) with abundant affordable lodging options right near the coast, about 30 miles (48km) north. It's so close, you'll have time for a quick swim at whatever beach is right outside your hotel or at its pool. There is no bad beach here. (p. 259).

A kind of alternative-culture vibe accompanies the town's surf culture, so the young and young at heart will find great entertainment and live music at area bars.

Day ⓮: Arecibo 𝒢, Indian Ceremonial Park & Rio Camuy Caves 𝒢𝒢𝒢

As you head east for your return to San Juan, you can take in three wonders of Puerto Rico. The **Observatorio de Arecibo** (p. 209) is the world's largest and most sensitive radar/radio-telescope, searching for extraterrestrial life in the universe beyond. In Karst Country, the **Caguaña Indian Ceremonial Park** in

Utuado (p. 213) was built by the Taíno Indians a thousand years ago. The grandest attraction of all, the **Rio Camuy Caves** (p. 210), contains the third-largest underground river in the world. With proper timing, all three of these attractions can be explored in 1 day, with time still left for the final drive back into San Juan. Arm yourself with a good map and explore our coverage of these attractions in chapter 9 before heading here.

Following your visits, continue to San Juan, at a distance of some 68 miles (109km) to the west. But remember, it's probably also possible to book a flight into San Juan and out of Aguadilla, especially during the winter high tourism season. Again, this would buy you another afternoon on the beach at Isabela.

4 Puerto Rico for Families

Puerto Ricans love their **niños,** and places all over the island are kid-friendly. The nature of the island itself, with its parks, beach-studded seaside resorts, and amusement centers, virtually invites you for a family outing. Because of islanders' welcoming attitude toward children, you will meet a lot more Puerto Ricans on your trip if you are traveling with children. And remember, don't forget that picnic lunch. *Start:* San Juan.

Days ❶ & ❷: San Juan ⭐⭐⭐

Old San Juan has more to offer children than any other Caribbean capital. The massive wall of the sq.-mile Spanish colonial enclave joins the two historic fortresses that were built at the land and sea entrances to the city. Children will enjoy exploring the tunnels, vaults, lookout points, dungeons, and ramps of **Castillo de San Felipe del Morro** (the must-visit of the two) and **Fort San Cristóbal** (p. 160). And the grassy fields surrounding El Morro are a favorite spot for kite-flying. You can buy a kite at the streetside refreshment carts outside the park's entrance. You'll also want to visit **Museo del Niño (Children's Museum,** p. 171), with interactive exhibits, a rooftop nature center, play areas, and a theater. It's right in the middle of major sites, next to **Hotel El Convento** (p. 109) and **Catedral de San Juan** (p. 161). The historic city's plazas are also a playground for kids, who love feeding the pigeons in **Plaza de Las Armas** (p. 166) and running through the shooting fountains at **Plaza del Quinto Centenario** (p. 166). Skateboarding is also popular at some.

There's a free trolley to ride, a dirt-cheap ferry that goes across the bay and back in about a half-hour, and even horse and buggies to rent. Abundant high-quality Puerto Rican, Mediterranean, Asian, and European cuisines are available at Old City restaurants, so a nice lunch is in order. Follow our recommendations for flavorful food at good prices (see chapter 7). Make sure to take a break at **Ben and Jerry's,** with free Internet, DJ music, books, magazines, big tables and chairs, and, oh yes, those baked goods and that ice cream (p. 170).

Afterwards, walk off lunch by doing some shopping and maybe taking in a few more sights. Another option is to take a cab back to the hotel for some sunshine and a swim before sunset.

The next day, you'll want to take your kids to the beach. Depending on where you are staying, that will likely be Condado, Ocean Park, or Isla Verde. And of course, kids prefer some of the resort pools, many of which cater to them with slides, tunnels, and spray and play areas.

If you don't want the little ones in the sun too long, take a cab to **Plaza las**

Américas (p. 188), the largest mall in the Caribbean. There's **Time Out** (p. 171), which has top-of-the-line video games, and **Galaxy Lanes,** a state-of-the-art bowling alley with pool tables, two restaurants, two bars, a DJ booth, a stage for live performances, and a dance floor. It caters to the family and kids during the day and their older siblings on weekend evenings. There's also a multiplex cinema, lots of great shops for kids (Discovery, a Border's with a reading room), a food court, and countless restaurants.

Day ❸: El Yunque 👍👍👍 & Luquillo Beach 👍👍👍

While still based in San Juan, journey east for a day to two of the island's biggest attractions: **El Yunque** rainforest and the island's most famous and best beach, **Luquillo.** For suggestions, refer to Day 3 of "Puerto Rico in 1 Week," earlier in this chapter.

Days ❹ & ❺: Ponce & the Southwest Coast 👍👍

On the morning of **Day 4,** leave San Juan early in the morning for a scenic drive southwest to the second city of Ponce, a distance of 75 miles (121km). Stop at the historic downtown area, concentrating on the ring of sites surrounding Plaza las Delicias, the central plaza dominated by a huge lion statue. Kids will enjoy the 1883 **Parque de Bombas,** a strangely shaped, black and red, wooden firehouse. (See p. 220 for directions.) After stretching the legs, it's time for lunch.

If your kids are just as happy at a hotel pool as a beach, then you can stay the night in Ponce, which lacks a good swimming beach. After some fun in the sun and dinner, you can take a stroll on the boardwalk along a public harbor called **La Guancha** (p. 224). This is like a more wholesome version of New York's Coney Island and is often mobbed with families. Food stands sell local delicacies and snacks, and there are often free concerts and other events with family appeal. It's particularly lively on weekends and holidays.

But unless there is some event or other compelling reason to stay in Ponce, we'd recommend heading out straight after lunch to **Guánica,** the first of a string of beach towns 21 miles (34km) west of Ponce that makes a good base to explore the southwest regardless of your budget.

En route, you can drive the family through parts of the **Guánica Dry Forest,** an internationally protected biosphere home to 100 rare bird species and unique vegetation that gives it its distinctive stunted forest look. There's still plenty of time for the beach after checking in. You might consider taking a 15-minute boat ride to **Gilligan's Island** (yes, the same name as that old TV sitcom). Part of the forest reserve, the island is one of a series of mangrove and sandy cays off the Caña Gorda peninsula. Kids have a blast in the shallow water surrounding it and the saltwater canals that cut through the island.

Have dinner at your hotel or head down to the main harbor in downtown Guánica. The **Blue Marlin** and several other simple seafood restaurants front the water, serving up freshly caught fish *criollo* style.

The next day, take a scenic drive west along the green Lajas Valley, with the towering Cordillera Center looming dramatically over it in the distance. Your destination is the palm-fringed public beach at **Boquerón** (p. 229), whose calm, warm waters are perfect for families. A big, wide beach, Boquerón offers plenty of room for all sorts of beach play as well as picnic tables, barbecue pits, and roofed shelters. The facilities also include showers and changing rooms, as well as restrooms. There are numerous hotel rooms for all budgets here, or you could stay a second night in Guánica.

After showering up and changing from the beach, take a short drive to the nearby fishing village of La Parguera. Restaurants in town cater to families with freshly caught seafood and local Puerto Rican food. There are also food stands selling everything from pizza and fried chicken to fresh seafood salads and turnovers made with lobster and conch. There are video game arcades and other activities for kids. After dinner and a stroll, take a 90-minute boat trip through the glowing waters of the Bioluminescent Bay. Boats leave frequently from the docks in town.

Day ❻: Aguadilla

On the morning of **Day 6,** head to the northwest coastal town of **Aguadilla** (p. 258), which has an enormous number

of reasonably priced hotels perfect for families. You'll have time to visit picture-perfect **Crash Boat Beach** (p. 259). The town is also popular with kids since it has **Las Cascadas Water Park** (p. 260), and **Aguadilla Ice Skating Rink** (p. 260), undoubtedly the only rink of its kind in Aguadilla.

Day ❼: Arecibo ⒼＸ, Indian Ceremonial Park & Rio Camuy Caves ⒼＸⒼＸⒼＸ

For your final day, you can take in three major island attractions before your drive east back to San Juan and its transportation hub. If you choose to fly directly out of Aguadilla, you will buy an extra afternoon in the region.

For details, refer to Day 14 under "Puerto Rico in Two Weeks."

---

5 Driving Tour: La Ruta Panorámica in 2 Days

"The Panoramic Route"—called *La Ruta Panorámica* by Puerto Ricans—winds its way through the Central Mountains in the heart of the island for some 100 miles (161km). This is the most scenic drive in the Caribbean. The mountains are the home of the *jíbaro,* the country farmer whose way of life is fast disappearing in modern Puerto Rico. The agricultural life and ways of the *jíbaro,* which have inspired some of the most important works of literature and a whole genre of country music, still live on in the central mountain towns, however, and this route is the most comprehensive way of seeing them. Expect winding, twisting roads, and don't forget to blow your horn as you turn blind curves. After rainstorms, there are frequent washouts. Although locals speed by you as if in a race car, it's advisable for newcomers to go no more than 25 mph (40kmph). In spite of some difficulties, it's worth the effort to cross through the Cordillera Central's dramatic peaks and valleys. The Cordillera mountains rise more than 4,000 feet (1,219m) in some places. You'll pass by **Cerro de Punta,** which at 4,389 feet (1,338m) is the highest in Puerto Rico. These mountains have helped define Puerto Rico. *Start:* Drive from San Juan.

Day ❶: From Carite Forest ⒼＸ to Jayuya

Leave San Juan early in the morning for the drive south, taking Highway 52 to exit 32, which will take you to Route 184, also heading south. Stay on 184 as it cuts right through the most scenic parts of the **Carite Forest Reserve.** Roadside grills tempt with the succulent *lechón* (roasted pig) sold at the area's famous *lechoneras. Sanjuaneros* flock here on

weekends to enjoy the cool mountain breezes, the grills, and even dance halls that line 184. There are also cool swimming holes throughout the forest and recreation areas. For more information, refer to Carite Forest Reserve (p. 215).

Highway 184 leads into Route 179, which you can follow out of the forest reserve (signposts lead to **Lago Carite,** the largest lake in the forest). To continue west along the route, follow the signs northwest to the town of Cayey. The surrounding area is called the "Switzerland of Puerto Rico," and many *sanjuaneros* use it as their vacation homes.

Once at Cayey, follow Route 1 south to Route 7722. On Route 7722, turn right onto Route 722 which leads directly into **Aibonito.**

You'll feel you've wandered back in time, especially in the Aibonito town center with its main plaza and historic church. Only the most adventurous hike the **Cañon de San Cristóbal,** a canyon lying between Aibonito and Barranquitas. Scenically, it's beautiful but can be dangerous without a guide (visitors have been killed here). With its waterfalls and forbidding cliffs, it's a thrill but risky. San Cristóbal is cut 500 feet (152m) into the Cordillera Central and lies some 5 miles (8km) north of Aibonito.

In Aibonito, there are many cafeterias around the main plaza, but the best restaurant in town is **La Piedra Restaurant** (p. 215; ℂ 787/735-1034), offering gourmet *comida criolla* using mountain-grown herbs.

Leave Aibonito and follow the signs toward your next stopover, **Toro Negro Forest Reserve** and **Lake Guineo** (p. 242). The forest reserve lies to the west and is reached by heading west on Route 723, which becomes Route 143 as it winds its way to the reserve.

The route winds through lush tropical forest then ascends to panoramic views reaching from the north to the south coasts. Stop inside the forest at the Recreativa Doña Juana, a picnic area beside a swimming pool fed by mountain streams. The restaurant here serves good Puerto Rican barbecue. The nearby **Visitors Center,** at Route 143 Km 32.4 (ℂ 787/867-3040), offers you a trail map; it's open daily from 8am to 4pm. There are no supplies in the park, so bring mosquito repellent and bottled water.

In the eastern side of the forest is the famous **Doña Juana Waterfall** (Rte. 149 Km 41.5), cascading 120 feet (37m) over a rock-strewn cliff.

Head for the remote mountain town of **Jayuya,** surrounded by big green mountains, to the country inn **Parador Hacienda Gripiñas** (p. 243). From Route 143 cut north along Route 149 and then turn west at the junction of Route 144 signposted into Jayuya.

Day ❷: Utuado, Adjuntas & Maricao

Leave Jayuya in the morning, cutting south on Route 44, then northwest along Route 140 (which becomes Rte. 111), following the signs into the town of **Utuado,** site of another well-known parador, **Casa Grande Mountain Retreat** (p. 212), which could have made another stopover for you if you had chosen not to spend the night at Jayuya. For more details on the town, see p. 242.

With its Spanish-styled central plaza, Utuado still reflects its colonial roots, although it was once inhabited by the Taíno Indians. Most visitors arrive here to explore the **Indian Ceremonial Park** at Caguaña (p. 213). This is the largest site of Taíno ruins in Puerto Rico.

After wandering around the town for an hour or two, head for our next stopover, the coffee-exporting town of **Adjuntas.** Follow the curvy Route 10 south, a grand panoramic ride but tricky. Once again, you confront a colonial-inspired central plaza and can spend another hour or two exploring the narrow streets. This town has an **Oficina de Turismo** at the Town Hall (Acaldía) on a corner of the main square (ℂ 787/829-5000), open Monday to Friday 8am to 4:30pm. Adjuntas is known as "the town of the sleeping giant" because of its silhouette created by the enveloping mountains. In addition to coffee, it is also an important producer of oranges.

Ruta Panorámica winds south (follow the signs) to **Bosque Estatal de Guilarte,** another beautiful spot. Composed of 3,600 acres (1,457 hectares), most of Guilarte is rainforest (hardly El Yunque, however). Sierra palms dot the forest, and **Lago Garzas,** a lake, is popular with fishermen. If you purchased the makings of a picnic lunch in Adjuntas, you can enjoy it in a sheltered area at the junction of Route 518 and Route 131, complete with cooking grills and toilets. You can climb a trail that takes you to the peak of **Monte Guilarte** at 3,950 feet (1,204m).

After a visit, head north again along Route 518, traveling west to our final stopover at **Maricao.** This winding road changes its number so many times you'll lose track; follow the signposts to Maricao and not the route numbers and you won't go wrong.

For details on Maricao's **Monte del Estado Forest,** see p. 262. This is the largest state forest on the island, and you can spend all day exploring it. The coffee-producing town is the smallest municipality in Puerto Rico. It lies at the far western end of Ruta Panorámica, and is an idyllic retreat for exploring, as it's surrounded by mountain gorges, old bridges, terraced houses, rushing streams of cold water, and enough switchback roads to challenge the most skilled of alpine drivers.

Since there are picnic areas in the forest, we suggest you take lunch here surrounded by mountain peaks. You can pick up food at **El Buen Café** (© 787/ 838-4198), on the main plaza of Maricao, ordering sandwiches and drinks or else plates of *comida criolla,* local island dishes. You'll find home-cooked Puerto Rican food for big flavor and few bucks. It's open most all the time, closing for Monday evenings.

There is a **Visitor Center** at Route 120 Km 16.2 (© 787/838-1040), which will provide maps of the forest and even hook you up with a private guide if you want to do more extensive exploring. Hours are Monday to Friday 7am to 3:30pm and Saturday and Sunday 8am to 3:30pm. If you climb **Torre de Observación,** you can take in a panoramic sweep of the entire western half of Puerto Rico. It is open daily from 8am to 4pm (free admission).

The best place for overnighting in the area is **Parador Hacienda Juanita** (p. 263), a converted, 160-year-old former coffee plantation lodge in a beautiful setting. There's a wonderful restaurant on site, and meals are served in a dining room and a back porch overlooking a lush forest. Another option is to barrel on west down to Mayagüez, and then go on to the beach towns to the northwest or to the southwest. It's a two-hour drive from Mayagüez to San Juan, a distance of 98 miles (158km) up the west coast and across the north coast.

5

Getting to Know San Juan

All but a handful of visitors arrive in San Juan, the capital city. It is the political base, economic powerhouse, and cultural center of the island, and it's home to about one-third of all Puerto Rico residents.

The second-oldest city in the Americas (behind Santo Domingo in the Dominican Republic), this metropolis presents two different faces. On the one hand, the charming historic district, Old San Juan, has some of the best examples of Spanish colonial architecture in the hemisphere, as well as stunning Art Deco and other buildings from the early part of the 20th century. From La Fortaleza (the governor's mansion) to the two old Spanish forts to the Catedral de San Juan, the wonders of the city are a short walk from each other.

New San Juan has its charms as well, particularly evident in its more storied residential architecture in Santurce, Miramar, and Río Piedras. The coastal areas are more modern, but there are several beautiful areas—particularly Ocean Park and Punta Las Marías. Condado and parts of Isla Verde resemble Miami Beach, with their luxury hotels and condominiums and fat golden beaches.

Much of San Juan, however, is a planning disaster, with urban sprawl eliminating or stressing green areas and ugly condo towers blotting out the view and access to the coast.

Improvements are ongoing all the time, however. San Juan has quietly been transforming over the past decade, with a light rail train system, a new coliseum, and a state-of-the-art convention center now on line.

Old San Juan is a 7-square-block area that was once completely enclosed by a wall erected by the Spanish with slave labor. The most powerful fortress in the Caribbean, this fortified city repeatedly held off would-be attackers. By the 19th century, however, it had become one of the Caribbean's most charming residential and commercial districts. Today, it's a setting for restaurants and shops, a large concentration of art galleries and museums. Most of the major resort hotels are located nearby, along the Condado beachfront and at Isla Verde (see chapter 6).

1 Orientation

ARRIVING BY PLANE

Visitors from overseas arrive at **Luis Muñoz Marín International Airport,** the major transportation center of the Caribbean. The airport is on the easternmost side of the city, conveniently located near the Isla Verde, Condado, and Old San Juan tourist districts.

The airport offers services such as a tourist-information center, restaurants, hair stylists, coin lockers for storing luggage, bookstores, banks, currency-exchange kiosks, and bars. There are also a number of shops selling souvenirs and local rums and coffees for last-minute shopping for gifts for folks back home.

GETTING FROM THE AIRPORT TO THE CITY

BY TAXI   Some of the larger hotels send vans to pick up airport passengers and transport them to various properties along the beachfront. It's wise to find out if your hotel offers this service when making a reservation. If your hotel doesn't have shuttle service between the airport and its precincts, you'll have to get there on your own steam—most likely by taxi. Dozens of taxis line up outside the airport to meet arriving flights, so you rarely have to wait. There are set fares for destinations within San Juan; for other destinations, the cost of the trip should be determined by the taxi meter. Fares and travel time can vary widely, depending on traffic conditions, with late-afternoon and early-morning traffic jams common during commuter hours Monday through Friday. With no traffic delays, Condado is only a 15-minute drive from the airport, but if you get stuck in a one of the island's legendary *tapones,* as traffic jams are called here, it could take up to an hour.

There are flat rates from the airport to different areas in San Juan, which eliminates the usual negotiations with island cab drivers and buffers you from paying too much if you have the misfortune of getting caught in a traffic jam. The island's **Puerto Rico Tourism Company (Transportation Division) (© 787/999-2100** or 787/253-0418) establishes the flat rates between the Luis Muñoz Marín International Airport and major tourist zones: From the airport to any hotel in Isla Verde, the fee is $10; to any hotel in the Condado district, the charge is $15; and to any hotel in Old San Juan, the cost is $19. Taxi service from the airport is quite well regulated, with a dispatcher handing you a ticket detailing your costs. These also include baggage costs (50 cents for each of the first three bags, then $1 per bag) and a 10% to 15% tip is expected.

BY LIMOUSINE   There are more than enough reputable limousine rental companies to choose from, but arrangements must be made beforehand. Limousines don't sit at the airport like taxis. You must arrange pickup in advance or call once you get in. A simple pickup from the airport to your hotel ranges in cost from $100 to $125. Most vehicles fit six passengers comfortably. Your driver will meet you outside the baggage-claim area.

BY PUBLIC CAR   Public cars, called *públicos,* are either vans or large sedans that are shared by passengers. The ride can sometimes be crowded and take longer, the more passengers there are. They are a bargain for budget travelers who have to travel a distance from the airport and do not want to rent a car. It will cost you $20 to get to Ponce and $10 to Caguas, plus baggage fee.

BY CAR   All the major car-rental companies have kiosks at the airport. Although it's possible to rent a car once you arrive, your best bet is to reserve one before you leave home. See the "Getting Around" section of chapter 3 for details.

To drive into the city, head west along Route 26 or the Baldorioty de Castro Expressway, which cuts just south of San Juan's Atlantic coastline. Immediately to your right you will see an Isla Verde exit, and soon the towering oceanfront condominiums of Isla Verde are visible to the right. The road cuts through the Santurce section at the heart of San Juan, and then you will see exits for Condado. All hotels have parking lots open to the public, and several lots are visible from the main roads in the area—Ashford Avenue in the Condado and Isla Verde Avenue in Condado. The road then passes by the Condado Lagoon and crosses into Puerta de Tierra near the Caribe Hilton. The road at this point becomes Avenida Muñoz Rivera, as it passes a beautifully landscaped park of the same name on one side and the El Escambrón public

San Juan Orientation

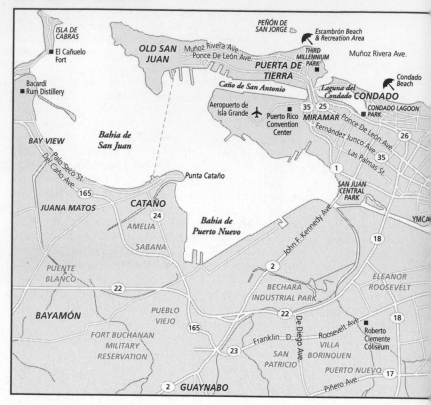

beach and adjacent Third Millennium Park on the other side. The road then climbs a bluff overlooking the Atlantic coastline, offering a dramatic view of waves crashing against the rocky coastline.

Here, you will pass the capitol building on your left, and then the historic Spanish fortress Fort San Cristóbal at the entrance of Old San Juan. If you continue straight down into the city along Calle San Sebastián, the northern border of Plaza Colón, you will find parking at **La Cochera** near Plaza de Armas, which is the closest to the center of the historic district. Another option is to turn right and take the northern coastal road to **Ballaja,** where there is parking. If you plan on visiting the San Sebastian Street area or El Convento hotel, these two options work best.

If you plan on hanging around the jumping SoFo section near La Fortaleza, you may want to head straight at the stop sign in front of Plaza Colón, taking the street that passes beside the Tapia Theater. Right behind the theater, where the road intersects with Calle Recinto Sur, is the large **Paseo Portuario** parking garage (© 787/722-2233). Bear right for the entrance. Farther down the one-way street is the city-run **Doña Fela** parking garage (no phone). Another option at Plaza Colón is to turn left at Plaza Colón as if exiting the city. Take your first two rights, which will turn you around again past the Treasury Building, and park your car in another **Covadonga Parking Garage** (© 787/721-6911) on the left. Operating hours vary, but they are

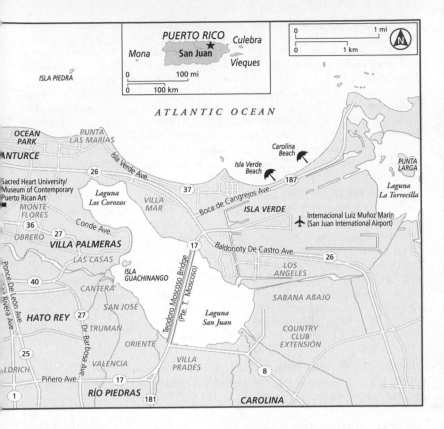

open at least until midnight during weekdays and 3am weekends. Prices vary, with municipal-run lots cheaper than private lots, but figure on paying $1 per hour.

BY BUS   Those with little luggage can take a bus at a cost of 75¢. You need to hop on the B-40 or the C-45, taking it one stop to Isla Verde. From there, you can take the A-5, which runs through Isla Verde, swings to Condado near Avenida de Diego, and then heads into Old San Juan. To go farther into the Condado, you can then transfer to another bus.

VISITOR INFORMATION

Tourist information is available at the **Luís Muñoz Marín Airport** (© 787/791-1014) daily from 9am to 10pm. Another office is at **La Casita,** Pier 1, Old San Juan (© 787/722-1709), open Saturday to Wednesday 9am to 8pm, Thursday and Friday 8:30am to 6:30pm.

CITY LAYOUT

Metropolitan San Juan includes the walled Old San Juan at the end of a long peninsula, Puerta de Tierra, the narrow bridge of land between San Juan Bay and the Atlantic Ocean that connects the Old City with the rest of San Juan. You can take a bridge into Condado, a narrow strip of land between the ocean and a lagoon, or continue on to the Miramar neighborhood, a neighborhood of beautiful residential homes whose once seedy waterfront section is being revamped into a world-class leisure development. The city also includes Santurce, its traditional downtown area, which has also been experiencing a revitalization in recent years, with large theaters and old apartment buildings being polished up so that the sector is starting to shine again like it did in its 1940s heyday. The Hato Rey financial district has taken on an almost futuristic look with its elevated Tren Urbano and distinctive Puerto Rico Coliseum, which has something exciting going on just about every week. Río Piedras is the site of the University of Puerto Rico and one of the best street markets in the Caribbean.

The Condado strip of beachfront hotels, restaurants, casinos, and nightclubs is separated from Miramar by a lagoon. Isla Verde, another resort area, is near the airport, which is separated from the rest of San Juan by an isthmus.

FINDING AN ADDRESS   Finding an address in San Juan isn't always easy. You'll have to contend not only with missing street signs and numbers but also with street addresses that appear sometimes in English and at other times in Spanish. The most common Spanish terms for thoroughfares are *calle* (street) and *avenida* (avenue). When it is used, the street number follows the street name; for example, the El Convento hotel is located at Calle del Cristo 100, in Old San Juan. Locating a building in Old San Juan is relatively easy. The area is only 7 square blocks, so by walking around, it's possible to locate most addresses. Also, *sanjuaneros,* for reasons we have yet to determine, still use the stop numbers, or *paradas,* from a trolley that stopped running back in the 1950s as a reference point for directions. For example, *parada* 18 is at the heart of Santurce. In general, the higher the stop number, the farther its distance from Old San Juan.

STREET MAPS   *¡Qué Pasa!,* the monthly tourist magazine distributed free by the tourist office, contains accurate, easy-to-read maps of San Juan and the Condado that pinpoint the major attractions.

NEIGHBORHOODS IN BRIEF

OLD SAN JUAN This is the most historic area in the West Indies. Filled with Spanish colonial architecture and under constant restoration, it lies on the western end of an islet. It's encircled by water; on the north is the Atlantic Ocean and on the south and west is the tranquil San Juan Bay. The historic Spanish wall built to hold off attacks still circles the city, which is filled with beautiful churches, shady plazas, majestic promenades, and wonderful residences and gardens. It's a robust cultural and commercial district with theaters, galleries, clubs, bars and restaurants, and some of the most interesting shops in the region.

PUERTA DE TIERRA Translated as "land gateway," Puerta de Tierra lies just east of the old city walls of San Juan. It is split by Avenida Ponce de León and interconnects Old San Juan with the Puerto Rican "mainland." Founded by freed black slaves, the settlement today functions as the island's administrative center and is the site of military and government buildings, including the capitol and various U.S. naval reserves. It is dominated by the green **Luis Muñoz Rivera Park** and the oceanfront **Third Millennium Park** and adjacent **El Escambrón public beach.**

MIRAMAR Miramar is an upscale residential neighborhood, with a small business district and a large port across San Juan Bay. It has two marinas where fishing boats and yachts lie at anchor. The whole harbor-side area is being redeveloped, spearheaded by the state-of-the-art **Puerto Rico Convention Center.** A new hotel is under construction, and luxury retail, office, and residential units are being planned, as is a huge bayside promenade to connect the area to Old San Juan. It's also the site of **Isla Grande Airport,** where you can board flights to the islands of Vieques and Culebra.

CONDADO Linked to Puerta de Tierra and Old San Juan by a bridge built in 1910, the Condado was once known as the "Riviera of the Caribbean," enjoying a voguish reputation in the 1920s. This beach-bordering district is wedged between the Atlantic Ocean and the Condado Lagoon. After several years of decline, when prostitution and drug dealing became more prevalent and crime became a problem, the area has been undergoing a frenzy of redevelopment, and is again one of the most coveted neighborhoods in Puerto Rico.

The beautiful oceanfront **Window of the Sea Park** is at the center of the area, which is now surrounded by designer fashion stores like Gucci and Salvatore Ferragamo, luxury condos and Budatai, one of the island's best restaurants. The former La Concha has opened next door after a 10-year renovation, and luxury condos are being built in the former Vanderbilt hotel nearby. Luxury hotels and more modest guesthouses fill the sector, as do wonderful restaurants of all types.

One central road, **Avenida Ashford,** runs through Condado, which, at night especially, still evokes something of Miami Beach, with its restored Art Deco properties and modern luxury condos and hotels. The area is popular

with the gay community, but straights flock here, too.

OCEAN PARK Dividing the competitive beach resort areas of the Condado and Isla Verde, Ocean Park is a beachfront residential neighborhood with probably the prettiest and most low-key beach in San Juan. The beaches are wide here, and the sun beats down on the beach longer because there are few large condominiums. The tree-covered streets are filled with beautiful suburban homes, a charming mix of Malibu, Spanish, and Caribbean influences.

The white, arching **Ultimate Trolley Beach** delineates the border between Ocean Park and Punta Las Marias, with the area surrounding **Barbosa Park** being a border neighborhood of equally nice homes called **Santa Teresita.**

The park is usually filled with soccer and basketball players, and there are tennis courts, a baseball field, and a track that are always a beehive of activity.

The beach disappears into a rock formation at **Punta Las Marías,** which is a gated community open to pedestrian visitors during the day. But unless you're a windsurfer using one of the neighborhood's famed launching points, your experience of the area will likely be confined to the **string of fine restaurants along Calle Loíza,** right before it turns into Avenida Isla Verde. The neighborhood is also popular with the gay and lesbian community, both residents and visitors.

ISLA VERDE East of the Condado, en route to the airport, Isla Verde—technically a part of the municipality of Carolina but in spirit more a part of San Juan—is the chief rival of the Condado. It's another row of luxury condos and hotels along a main oceanfront boulevard. But where Condado may score higher with its restaurants and shops, and its older and more artful architecture, Isla Verde wins hands down in the beach department—you'll find a wide, clean, white-sand beach running the full length of the neighborhood just off its main strip. The main road here is called **Isla Verde Avenue. Pine Grove Beach,** a favorite with sailors and surfers, is located east of where the main beach ends. After Isla Verde is a municipal public beach and then the undeveloped area of **Piñones,** with its rural coastal charms.

Don't come here for history or romance. Two features put Isla Verde on the tourist map: some of San Juan's best beaches and its most deluxe hotels. This district appeals to travelers who like a hotel to be a virtual theme park, with everything under one roof: entertainment, vast selections of dining, convenient shopping, pools, and an array of planned activities.

HATO REY The city's financial district is the Wall Street of the West Indies, filled many high-rises, a large federal complex, and many business and banking offices.

The sector has been transformed by the **Puerto Rico Coliseum** and the **Tren Urbano,** which snakes through the towers of capitalism on elevated tracks. The new arena gets top acts (it got the Rolling Stones). There's also the **Fine Arts Cinema,** with art and foreign films, luxury seats, gourmet food, and yes, beer and wine.

The sector does contain the huge **Luis Muñoz Marín Park,** with miles of bicycle and jogging paths, picnic areas and fields, interrupted by scores

of small ponds and islands of tropical vegetation. The park also features a top-notch amphitheater and a cable car ride.

RIO PIEDRAS South of Hato Rey and Santurce, this is the site of the **University of Puerto Rico,** which could be an Ivy League school except for the tropical vegetation. It's dominated by the landmark **Roosevelt Bell Tower,** named for Theodore Roosevelt, who donated the money for its construction. The grounds are beautiful, and it's a top-notch institution.

There's also a large shopping area surrounding the **Río Piedras Marketplace** (selling fresh fruit and vegetables) and the pedestrian walkway Paseo de Diego with bargains galore. The shops attract travelers from across the Caribbean.

The **UPR Botanical Gardens** are located here as well, with a beautifully arranged array of tropical trees and plants.

SUBURBAN SAN JUAN The San Juan sprawl has enveloped surrounding towns, reaching all the way down south into Caguas. Neighboring Bayamón, Guaynabo, and Carolina are practically considered part of the city, however. Guaynabo and Caguas have fine arts centers with top-name acts and full cultural performances, while Bayamón has such family activities as a bicycle linear park and the **Luis A. Ferré Science Technology Park.** Visitors will also likely go to Cataño to visit the **Bacardi Rum Plant.** It's a modest community built right across the bay from Old San Juan.

2 Getting Around

BY TAXI There is a flat-rate system for most destinations within San Juan, which is effective, and if you're caught in impenetrable traffic, it might actually work to your advantage. The island's **Puerto Rico Tourism Company (Transportation Division)** (© **787/999-2100** or 787/253-0418) establishes flat rates between well-traveled areas

Art on Wheels: Painted Taxis

Take a picture of yourself riding smooth inside one of **San Juan's fleet of painted taxis,** ranging in style from classic figurative to graffiti-inspired to abstract expressionistic works. Dozens of artists painted 40 taxis as part of the "Taxi Galería" project, which started in 2005. Local artists, including Alexander Rosado, Wichie Torres, Roberto Pérez, Celso González, and Eric French, used the entire taxi body as their canvas, completing fully realized paintings on the vehicles. The artists clearly loved the project. "It's not the same as painting on a flat plain. It gives a certain volume to your work. You have to keep going around and around it," Torres told a local newspaper. And participating taxi drivers say driving in a work of art instead of an ordinary taxi has increased demand for services. You'll see these painted taxis darting around the city. All you have to do is hail one.

On one of our rides in a painted taxi (it could have been one of Joan Miró's vibrant and fun pieces), the driver enthused about how his painted car had improved his existence. "People standing in the street just stare at my taxi," he said. "Most cars go down in value with age, but this one is going up."

within San Juan. From Luis Muñoz Marín International Airport to Isla Verde, $10; to Condado, $15; and to Old San Juan, $19.

There are also set fees from the cruise-ship piers outside of Old San Juan to set destinations: Isla Verde, $19; Condado, $12; and Old San Juan, $7. You will also be charged 50¢ per bag for your first three bags and $1 per bag thereafter. Metered fares start off with an initial charge of $1.75, plus $1.90 per mile, and a 10¢ charge for each 25 seconds of waiting time. Tolls are not included in either fare. Normal tipping supplements of between 10% and 15% of these fares are appreciated.

But while meters are supposed to be used, on most trips outside the zoned rates, drivers will probably offer you a flat rate of their own devising. San Juan cabbies are loath to use the meter. We've always suspected it had more to do with ripping off the house or the taxman than the customer because more often than not, the quoted price is fair. But feel free to refer to the established flat rate (if it applies) or ask him to turn on the meter. Drivers normally comply immediately. If they refuse, we would get out and refer the driver to the Tourism Company Transportation Division numbers cited above. But if the quoted price seems fair (use the $19 flat rate for the airport to Old San Juan as a guide), it's probably easier to go ahead and pay it.

Taxis are invariably lined up outside the entrance to most of the island's hotels, and if they're not, a staff member can almost always call one for you. But if you want to arrange a taxi on your own, some reliable operators in San Juan are: **Metro Taxis** (© 787/7725-2870), the **Rochdale Cab Company** (© 787/721-1900), and the **Major Cab Company** (© 787/723-2460).

You'll have to negotiate a fare with the driver, usually at a flat rate, for trips to far-flung destinations within Puerto Rico.

BY BUS   The **Metropolitan Bus Authority** (© 787/767-7979 for route information) operates buses in the greater San Juan area. Bus stops are marked by upright

San Juan Mass-Transit: Tren Urbano

Tren Urbano, the first mass-transit project in the history of Puerto Rico, opened in 2005, linking San Juan to its suburbs such as Santurce, Bayamón, and Guaynabo. Costing about $2 billion, the system provides an easy mode of transportation to the most congested areas of metropolitan San Juan. During rush hour (5–9am and 3–6pm), the train operates every 8 minutes; otherwise, it runs every 12 minutes. There is no service daily from 11:20 pm to 5:30 am. The fare is $1.50 one-way and includes a transfer to buses. It's a beautiful ride and gives tourists a different experience of the city; the train passes on an elevated track through the modern, Hato Rey financial district, plunges way underground in Río Piedras, and then snakes through upscale suburban neighborhoods, with tropical foliage and pools in many backyards. The fare includes a transfer because a special class of buses has been created to link up with particular Tren Urbano routes. The train and accompanying buses keep special expanded schedules during big events, like a festival in Old San Juan, and also for when big acts play at the Puerto Rico Coliseum, or the Tourism Company throws a New Year's Eve party at the Convention Center. For more information, call ℂ **866/900-1284** or log onto www.ati.gobierno.pr.

metal signs or yellow posts that say PARADA. The bus terminal is the dock area in the same building as the Covadanga parking lot next to the Treasury Department. Fares are 75¢.

This section of Old San Juan is the starting point for many of the city's metropolitan bus routes. One useful route is the A-5, which hits downtown Santurce, Avenida de Diego near Condado, then goes along Loíza Street and down Isla Verde's oceanfront drive where all the hotels are located. You can switch to the B-21 at De Diego Street if you want to go down Condado's main drive, Avenida Ashford.

The B-21 runs from Old San Juan to Condado, while also servicing Plaza Las Americas. The privately run MetroBus runs express buses between Old San Juan and Río Piedras, with stops in Hato Rey and Santurce.

Any bus marked ATI hooks up with the Tren Urbano, probably at its Sagrado Corazón Station, which is its last stop into the city. The ticket costs $1.50 but includes a transfer to take a trip on the train.

ON FOOT   This is the only way to explore Old San Juan. All the major attractions can easily be covered in a day. If you're going from Old San Juan to Isla Verde, however, you'll need to rely on public transportation.

BY TROLLEY   When you tire of walking around Old San Juan, you can board one of the free trolleys that run through the historic area. Departure points include the Covadonga, La Puntilla, Plaza de Armas, and the two forts, but you can board along the route by flagging the trolley down (wave at it and signal for it to stop) or by waiting at any of the clearly designated stopping points. Relax and enjoy the sights as the trolleys rumble through the old and narrow streets. The city has also begun operating a trolley along Loiza Street near Ocean Park.

BY LIMOUSINE   San Juan has nearly two dozen limousine rental companies, so there are more than enough reputable companies to choose from. There is a wide range of luxury vehicle rentals, called *limosinas* (their Spanish name), available, from

Lincoln Town Car limousines to deluxe stretch Hummers. A simple pickup from the airport to your hotel ranges in cost from $100 to $125. Rentals for other standard trips range from about $70 to $125 per hour, with most cars seating six passengers comfortably. Many firms use drivers who hold tour-guide permits, and limousine operators often give tours of Old San Juan, El Yunque, or other sites to small groups or families. If the driver or another guide leaves the vehicle to tour a specific place by foot, it will cost another $15 to $25 hourly.

BY RENTAL CAR   See "Getting Around" in chapter 3 for details—including some reasons you should avoid driving in Puerto Rico.

BY FERRY   The **Acua Expreso** (© 787/729-8714) connects Old San Juan with the industrial and residential community of Cataño, across the bay. Ferries depart daily every 30 minutes from 6am to 9pm. The one-way fare to Cataño is 50¢. Departures are from the San Juan Terminal at pier number 2 in Old San Juan. However, it's best to avoid rush hours because hundreds of locals who work in town use this ferry. The ride lasts 6 minutes.

BY PUBLIC CAR   Public cars, called *públicos,* are either vans or large sedans that are shared by passengers. Though they can be crowded and uncomfortable, more often than not they are quite comfortable and spacious. And they are a bargain for budget travelers who have to travel a distance from the airport and do not want to rent a car. Most public cars travel set routes at prices far below what taxis would charge. You should consider taking one from the airport if traveling on a budget to areas outside of San Juan.

In San Juan, *público* departure and arrival points include the airport, right outside Old San Juan near Plaza Colón, and by the Río Piedras public marketplace. Every town on the island has at least one area where *públicos* congregate.

If you are traveling out on the island, you also can look them up in the telephone book and Yellow Pages under *la linea,* which are public cars that will pick you up where you are staying and bring you to a specific destination at an agreed-upon price. A two-hour drive from San Juan to Guánica costs $25 one-way. Since you travel with other passengers, you may have to wait until the driver takes them to their destinations first. He will pick up and drop off passengers according to what is best for his route and schedule.

BY BIKE   Rentals are available at **Hot Dog Cycling,** Av. Isla Verde 5916, La Plazoleta Shopping Center (© 787/721-0776), open Monday to Saturday 9am to 6pm. Charges for rentals are $15 per half-day, $25 for a full day.

FAST FACTS: San Juan

Airport   See "Arriving by Plane" and "Getting from the Airport to the City," earlier in this chapter.

American Express   Call the company's local toll-free customer service line: © 800/327-1267.

Banks   Local banks have branches with ATMs in San Juan that function on U.S. networks. Branches are open Monday to Friday 8:30am to 4pm. Bank branches in malls are open Saturday 8:30am to 6pm and Sunday 9am to 3pm.

Bus Information See "Getting Around," earlier in this chapter. For information about bus routes in San Juan, call ℂ 787/767-7979.

Camera & Film **Foto One** (ℂ 787/722-1949), located at Calle Fortaleza 259 in Old San Juan, offers a wide variety of photographic supplies. The shop is open Monday through Saturday from 9am to 6pm.

Car Rentals See "Getting Around" in chapter 3. If you want to reserve after you've arrived in Puerto Rico, try **Avis, Budget,** or **Hertz.**

Consulates Many countries maintain honorary consulates here, mostly to try to drum up mutually beneficial trade on the island, but they can be of assistance to travelers. **Britain** has a consulate at Av. Chardón 350 (ℂ 787/758-9828) at Hato Rey, open Monday to Friday 9am to 1pm and 2 to 5pm. The consulate for **Canada** is at Av. Ponce de León 268 (ℂ 787/759-6629), also at Hato Rey and open only by appointment.

Currency Exchange The unit of currency is the U.S. dollar. Most banks provide currency exchange, and you can also exchange money at the **Luis Muñoz Marín International Airport.** See "Money" in chapter 3.

Drugstores One of the most centrally located pharmacies is **Puerto Rican Drug Co.,** Calle San Francisco 157 (ℂ 787/725-2202), in Old San Juan. It's open Monday to Friday from 7:30am to 9:30pm, Saturday 8am to 9:30pm, and Sunday 8:30am to 7:30pm. **Walgreens,** Av. Ashford 1130, Condado (ℂ 787/725-1510), is open 24 hours. There are also other Walgreens throughout the city, one in practically every neighborhood. There are other locations in Old San Juan, Miramar, Isla Verde, and on Calle Loíza near Ocean Park.

Emergencies In an emergency, dial ℂ 911. Or call the local police (ℂ 787/343-2020), fire department (ℂ 787/343-2020), ambulance (ℂ 787/766-2222), or medical assistance (ℂ 787/754-2550).

Eyeglasses Services are available at **Pearle Vision Express,** Plaza Las Americas Shopping Mall (ℂ 787/753-1033). Hours are Monday to Saturday from 9am to 9pm and Sunday from 11am to 5pm. **Tropical Vision,** La Fortaleza St. 308, (ℂ 787/723-5488) is located in Old San Juan.

Hospitals **Ashford Presbyterian Community Hospital,** Av. Ashford 1451 (ℂ 787/721-2160), maintains a 24-hour emergency room.

Internet Access Try **CyberNet Café,** Av. Ashford 1128 (ℂ 787/724-4033) on the Condado; it charges $5 for 35 minutes or $7 for 50 minutes. Open Monday to Saturday 9am to 11pm, Sunday 10am to 11pm. There is another branch in Isla Verde. If you have a laptop or other wireless device, there are Internet hotspots throughout the city at food courts in malls, Starbucks, Burger King and McDonalds, and historic plazas in Old San Juan.

Police Call ℂ 787/726-7020 for the local police.

Post Office In San Juan, the **General Post Office** is at Av. F.D. Roosevelt 585 (ℂ 787/622-1758). If you don't know your address in San Juan, you can ask that your mail be sent here "c/o General Delivery." This main branch is open Monday to Friday from 5:30am to 6pm, Saturday from 6am to 2pm. A letter from Puerto Rico to the U.S. mainland will arrive in about 4 days. See "Fast Facts: Puerto Rico," in the appendix, for more information.

Restrooms Restrooms are not public facilities accessible from the street. It's necessary to enter a hotel lobby, cafe, or restaurant to gain access to a toilet. Fortunately, large-scale hotels are familiar with this situation, and someone looking for a restroom usually isn't challenged during his or her pursuit.

Safety At night, exercise extreme caution when walking along the back streets of San Juan, and don't venture onto the unguarded public stretches of the Condado and Isla Verde beaches at night. All these areas are favorite targets for muggings.

Salons Most of San Juan's large resort hotels, including the Condado Plaza, the Marriott, and the Sheraton Old San Juan Hotel, maintain hair salons. **Los Muchachos** in Old San Juan has an army of stylists cutting and sprucing walk-in traffic as well as appointments.

Taxis See "Getting Around," earlier in this chapter.

Telephone & Fax There are many public telephone centers for international callers around the cruise-ship docks (catering mostly to crew). Most have fax and Internet service as well. Long distance calling cards are widely available in drugstores and variety shops. For more information, see "Appendix: Fast Facts, Toll-Free Numbers & Websites."

6

Where to Stay in San Juan

Whatever your preferences in accommodations—a beachfront resort or a place in historic Old San Juan, sumptuous luxury or an inexpensive base from which to see the sights—you can find a perfect fit in San Juan.

In addition to checking the recommendations listed here, you might want to contact a travel agent; there are package deals galore that can save you money and match you with an establishment that meets your requirements. See "Package Deals for the Independent Traveler," in chapter 3.

Before talking to a travel agent, you should refer to our comments about how to select a room in Puerto Rico. See "Tips on Accommodations" in chapter 3. You should also refer to "Package Deals for the Independent Traveler" in the same chapter, particularly if you're planning to book a deal with all your meals included.

Not all hotels here have air-conditioned rooms. We've pointed them out in the recommendations below. If air-conditioning is important to you, make sure "A/C" appears after *"In room"* at the end of the listing.

If you prefer shopping and historic sights to the beach, then Old San Juan might be your preferred nest. The high-rise resort hotels lie primarily along the Condado beach strip and the equally good sands of Isla Verde. The hotels along Condado and Isla Verde attract the cruise-ship and casino crowds. The hotels away from the beach in San Juan, in such sections as Santurce, are primarily for business clients.

The guesthouses of Ocean Park, free from the high rises elsewhere but with an equally beautiful beach, attract a young urban crowd and those looking for a more low-key ambience.

TAXES & SERVICE CHARGES

All hotel rooms in Puerto Rico are subject to a tax that is not included in the rates given in this book. At casino hotels, the tax is 12%; at non-casino hotels, it's 9%. At government-sponsored country inns called *paradores puertorriqueños,* you pay a 7% tax. San Juan also began charging a head tax on hotel guests ranging from $3 to $5 nightly. Some hotels add a 10% service charge; if not, you're expected to tip for services rendered. Many large hotels also charge resort fees, ostensibly to offset the costs of facilities like a pool or health club, which can add substantially to your bill. Fees range from 12% to 22% of the cost of your room per night. When you're booking a room, it's a good idea to ask about these charges.

MAKING RESERVATIONS

You can make accommodations reservations via telephone, mail, fax, and, in most cases, the Internet. If you're booking into a chain hotel, such as a Hilton, you can easily make your reservations by calling the chain's toll-free numbers in many countries. We provide the North American toll-free numbers in this book.

You can usually cancel a room reservation 1 week ahead of time and get a full refund. A few places will return your money on cancellations up to 3 days before the reservation date; others won't return any of your deposit, even if you cancel far in advance. It's best to clarify this issue when you make your reservation. If booking by mail, include a stamped, self-addressed envelope with your payment so that the hotel can easily send you a receipt and confirmation.

If you arrive without a reservation, you need to begin your search for a room as early in the day as possible. If you arrive late at night and without a reservation, you might have to take what you can get, often in a price range much higher than you'd like. Finding an available room in San Juan on weekends is particularly difficult. San Juan has become a year-round destination, and summers are no longer as tranquil as they used to be. Nonetheless, hotels still have lower occupancy from mid-April to mid-December. Off-season discounts, especially at large resorts outside San Juan, can still be found during this slower period.

1 Old San Juan

Old San Juan is 1½ miles (2.4km) from the beach. You should choose a hotel here if you're more interested in shopping and attractions than you are in watersports. The closest beach is Escambrón public beach in Puerta de Tierra, about a half-hour walk from the center of the Old San Juan. For most visitors, a cab ride (15 min.) or bus ride (45 min.) to Condado, Ocean Park, or Isla Verde is a better option. For the locations of hotels in Old San Juan, see the map on p. 111.

EXPENSIVE

Chateau Cervantes ★★ This 12-unit boutique hotel seamlessly blends the colonial charm of its 16th-century quarters with ultra modern interiors by local designer Nono Maldonado. While we prefer the Old World charm of the El Convento (below), this is an impressive upscale alternative. The hotel's high ceilings, arched doorways, windows, and wrought iron balcony railings are quintessential Old San Juan, but Maldonado, working from a gold and muted gemstone palette, has remade the guest rooms into a plush world of velvet and silk. Paintings by island artist Carlos Dávila add to the decor, and the small bathrooms are lined with marble. We were impressed by the comfort of the beds and the furnishings, but a 200 square-foot (19 sq.-m) room (standard) may be too small for most travelers; we recommend at least a junior suite. Only the presidential suite has a full bathtub. The hotel is located on one of Old City's busiest streets in the midst of many bars and restaurants, so weekend noise levels may bother some guests. Rates include continental breakfast at Panza restaurant on its ground floor, which serves creative international cuisine in a chic setting.

Calle Recinto Sur 307, Old San Juan, PR 00901. ✆ 787/724-7722. Fax 787/289-8909. www.cervantespr.com. 12 units. $225 double; $285 junior suites; $425 Cervantes suites; $925 penthouse for 4. Rates include continental breakfast. AE, MC, V. Bus: Old Town Trolley. **Amenities:** Restaurant; nonsmoking rooms. *In room:* A/C, TV/CD/DVD, dataport (in some), Wi-Fi Internet access, hair dryer, ironing board, safe.

Hotel El Convento ★★ Puerto Rico's most famous hotel came back to life after a 1997 restoration, and it remains one of the most charming historic hotels in the Caribbean and a quintessential Old San Juan experience. The core of the building was constructed in 1651 as the New World's first Carmelite convent, but over the years it played many roles, from a dance hall to a flophouse to a parking lot for garbage trucks. It first opened as a hotel in 1962. The restoration has returned the property to its past glory, while injecting it with an urban, up-to-date feel, very much like Old San Juan itself. Its 4th floor rooftop has a small pool, adjacent Jacuzzi, and a big sun terrace with blessed views of the nearby Catedral de San Juan, as well as views of the bay and the Atlantic. The lower two floors feature a collection of shops, bars, and restaurants, all worth staying for a while. A late-afternoon wine and cheese offering is served on a beautiful mid-floor dining area spilling onto an outdoor terrace overlooking Calle Cristo. The midsize accommodations include Spanish-style furnishings, throw rugs, beamed ceilings, paneling, and Andalusian terra-cotta floor tiles. Each unit contains king-size, queen-size, or two double or twin beds, fitted with fine linens. The small bathrooms, with tub/shower combinations, contain scales and second phones. For the ultimate in luxury, there are two specialty suites: Gloria Vanderbilt's restored suite and the Pablo Casals suite, which run, respectively, $1,700 and $850 nightly. Room no. 508 is a corner room with panoramic views.

Calle del Cristo 100, San Juan, PR 00901. © 800/468-2779 or 787/723-9020. Fax 787/721-2877. www.elconvento. com. 68 units. Winter $355–$410 double, from $650 suite; off season $225–$285 double. Rates include afternoon wine and cheese reception and free Wi-Fi Internet service. AE, DC, DISC, MC, V. Parking $20. Bus: Old Town Trolley. **Amenities:** 4 restaurants; 3 bars; small rooftop plunge pool; fitness center; Jacuzzi; massage; laundry service; dry cleaning; rooms for those w/limited mobility. In room: A/C, TV, dataport, coffeemaker, hair dryer, iron, safe.

Sheraton Old San Juan Hotel & Casino 🄲   This may be convenient for cruise-ship passengers wanting to spend a few nights in San Juan before or after a cruise, but don't expect Old City charm. Opened in 1997, this dignified, nine-story, waterfront hotel was part of a $100-million renovation of San Juan's cruise-port facilities. With an unusual and desirable position between buildings erected by the Spanish monarchs in the 19th century and the city's busiest and most modern cruise-ship terminals, it remains a good option for cruise travelers wanting to extend their trip with a stay in San Juan. Most of the major cruise ships dock nearby. On days when cruise ships pull into port, the hotel's lobby and bars are likely to be jammed with passengers stretching their legs after a few days at sea.

The modern, pastel building has iron railings and exterior detailing that convey a sense of colonial San Juan. The triangular shape of the building encircles an inner courtyard that floods light into comfortable bedrooms that otherwise lack character, feeling more like a place for business travelers, devoid of Old City character. Most of the lobby level here is devoted to a mammoth casino. Take a pass on the hotel restaurants; you are steps from SoFo (South Fortaleza street near Plaza Colón), which has some of the finest eateries in the city.

Calle Brumbaugh 100, San Juan, PR 00902. © 800/325-3535 or 787/721-5100. Fax 787/721-1111. www.sheraton. com. 240 units. Winter $255–$345 double, $395–$595 suite; off season $209–$345 double, $339–$475 suite. AE, DC, DISC, MC, V. Valet parking $21. Bus: A7. **Amenities:** 2 restaurants; 3 bars; outdoor pool; fitness center; Jacuzzi; car-rental desk; business center; room service (6:30am–11:30pm); nonsmoking rooms; casino; rooms for those w/limited mobility. In room: A/C, TV, dataport, minibar, coffeemaker, hair dryer, iron, safe.

MODERATE

Gallery Inn at Galería San Juan 🄲 Finds   This unique hotel's location and ambience are unbeatable. The inn rambles through a 300-year-old building overlooking Old San Juan's northern sea wall. There are sweeping sea views as well as the vista across the colonial city rooftops, extending all the way down to San Juan Bay. Verdant courtyards, interior gardens, and patios and terraces appear around every bend one takes in the inn. The chatter of tropical birds and the murmur of fountains complete the atmosphere in the Caribbean's most whimsically bohemian hotel. In the 1700s it

Old San Juan Accommodations & Dining

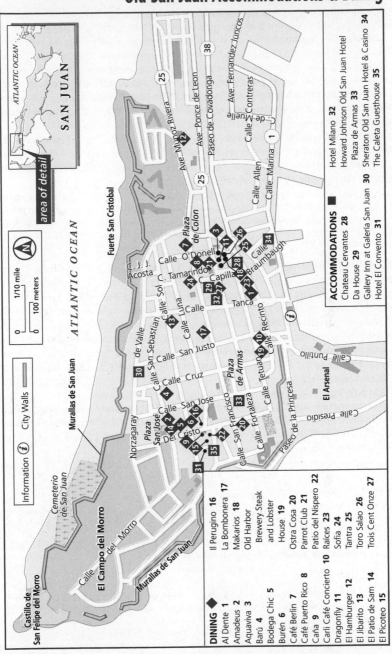

DINING ◆
Al Dente **1**
Amadeus **2**
Aquaviva **3**
Barú **4**
Bodega Chic **5**
Burén **6**
Café Berlín **7**
Café Puerto Rico **8**
Caña **9**
Carli Café Concierto **10**
Dragonfly **11**
El Hamburger **12**
El Jibarito **13**
El Patio de Sam **14**
El Picoteo **15**
Il Perugino **16**
La Bombonera **17**
Makarios **18**
Old Harbor Brewery Steak and Lobster House **19**
Ostra Cosa **20**
Parrot Club **21**
Patio del Nispero **22**
Raíces **23**
Sofía **24**
Tantra **25**
Toro Salao **26**
Trois Cent Onze **27**

ACCOMMODATIONS ■
Chateau Cervantes **28**
Da House **29**
Gallery Inn at Galería San Juan **30**
Hotel El Convento **31**
Hotel Milano **32**
Howard Johnson Old San Juan Hotel Plaza de Armas **33**
Sheraton Old San Juan Hotel & Casino **34**
The Caleta Guesthouse **35**

was the home of an aristocratic Spanish family, but today Jan D'Esopo and Manuco Gandia created this inn out of their home and Jan's art studio. The entire inn is covered with clay and bronze figures as well as other original art by Jan, and each guest room also functions as gallery space, with Jan's original silk screens, paintings and prints on display. We suggest booking one of the least expensive doubles; even the cheapest units are fairly roomy and attractively furnished, with good beds. The rooftop Wine Deck has the best view in Old San Juan. Classical music concerts are often held in the Music Room and are free for guests. A small pool has also been added to the property.

Note to lovers: The honeymoon suite has a Jacuzzi on a private balcony with a panoramic view of El Morro. From the rooftop terrace, there is a 360-degree view of the historic Old Town and the port. This is the highest point in San Juan and the most idyllic place to enjoy a breeze at twilight and a glass of wine.

Calle Norzagaray 204–206, San Juan, PR 00901. ✆ 866/572-ARTE (2783) or 787/722-1808. Fax 787/977-3929. www.thegalleryinn.com. 22 units (some with shower only). Year-round $225–$325 double; $410 suite. Off-season specials available. Rates include continental breakfast and 6pm wine and cheese reception. AE, DC, MC, V. 6 free parking spaces, plus parking on the street. Bus: Old Town trolley. **Amenities:** Breakfast room. *In room:* A/C, dataport, hair dryer.

Hotel Milano
There's not much remarkable about this hotel built from a 1920s warehouse, except clean, modern facilities at a good price in a great location, right near all the restaurants and bars along South Fortaleza Street. You enter a wood-sheathed lobby at end of Calle Fortaleza before ascending to one of the clean, well-lit bedrooms. The simple, modern rooms have cruise-ship-style decor and unremarkable views, and there's excellent Wi-Fi Internet access. The rooftop terrace has outstanding views, and is a great spot to relax or enjoy the $5 continental breakfast. The best rooms are on the upper floors overlooking the street. You're in SoFo, home to some of Puerto Rico's best restaurants.

Calle Fortaleza 307, San Juan, PR 00901. ✆ 877/729-9050 or 787/729-9050. Fax 787/722-3379. www.hotelmilano pr.com. 30 units. Winter $95–$185 double; off season $85–$145 double. $5 continental breakfast. AE, MC, V. Bus: Old Town trolley. **Amenities:** Rooftop terrace cafe; nonsmoking rooms; rooms for those w/limited mobility; Wi-Fi. *In room:* A/C, TV, fridge, hair dryer.

INEXPENSIVE

Da House
This has the feel of a European hostel, with bright, sunny, affordable rooms and a young and creative clientele, all on top of the legendary Nuyorican Café. The rooftop sun deck is a great place to chill out with lounge chairs, a tikki bar, great views, a hot tub, and showers. The downstairs cafe is a great venue for theater and music (it can be quite loud, so if you don't want to be in the middle of a nightlife scene, this is not your place). The Wi-Fi Internet cafe in the lobby is a good spot to pick up insider tourist tips. Great art adorns the guesthouse, and the staff is friendly and helpful. Rooms are clean and comfortable.

Calle San Francisco 312, entrance down Callejon de la Capilla, San Juan, PR 00901. ✆ 787/366-5074 or 787/977-1180. Fax 787/722-3379. www.dahousehotelpr.com. 30 units. Winter $80–$120 double. AE, MC, V. Bus: Old Town trolley. **Amenities:** Music and theater nightclub; pizza restaurant; bar. *In room:* A/C, high-speed Internet.

Howard Johnson Old San Juan Hotel Plaza de Armas
This renovated apartment building at the center of Old San Juan gives you a sense of how *sanjuaneros* live in the historic quarter, with rooms wrapped around a prominent interior courtyard. It's right on Old San Juan's central Plaza de Armas, also home to San Juan City Hall

Room with a Local's View: Apartment Rentals

Despite the explosion of Old City hotel and guesthouse rooms over the past few years, one of the best ways to experience the city remains getting a furnished apartment for a short-term rental. Many are restored, historic quarters with beautiful rooftop terraces or verdant interior courtyards, or both. All have high ceilings, with large windows and the classic double wooden doors, and many open up onto balconies. The interiors often boast original artwork and beautiful furnishings. In short, you'll get a great sense during your vacation of what it feels like to live in this enchanted city, and you'll normally save money (especially if you're a large group). Many of the rentals cater to discriminating travelers, offering first-rate creature comforts like Swedish mattresses and plush bathrobes, as well as upscale kitchens and bathrooms.

Prices range from $500 weekly for a basic studio to $2,500 weekly for a three-bedroom, restored colonial beauty with rooftop terrace and ocean views. Short-term rentals are assessed a 7% tax, and many require a minimum 3-day or 4-day stay. Cleaning fees are also assessed, which can range from $50 to $75.

The expert in Old City short-term rentals is **Vida Urbana,** Calle Cruz 255, Old San Juan, PR 00901 (© **787/587-3031;** www.vidaurbanapr.com), a spin-off of Caleta Realty, a veteran in this field. Years ago, we found a three-bedroom apartment through Caleta, a place near Catedral de San Juan with huge adjoining living and dining rooms and a rooftop terrace running the length of the apartment. We loved it. We had a reception there, and a group of about eight friends stayed there for the week. A comparable apartment would cost around $1,500 for the week today. There are two lovely apartments for rent above the gallery and gift shop **Bóveda,** Calle Cristo 209, Old San Juan, PR 00901 (© **787/725-0263;** www.boveda.info), with artful, bright decor in a restored colonial building, complete with interior garden courtyard and balconies with double-door entrances. A cool tropical vibe flows through the duplex ($950 weekly) and studio suite ($500 weekly). **The Caleta Guesthouse,** Caleta de las Monjas 11, Old San Juan, PR 00901 (© **787/725-5347;** www.thecaleta.com), has affordable studios and one-bedroom furnished apartments. It's located on one of Old San Juan's most charming streets, across from a lookout over San Juan Bay, but the accommodations are fairly basic.

Likewise, **Condado** and **Isla Verde** also have an ample supply of short-term rentals for visitors wanting to spend the bulk of their time at the beach. Most of the beachfront condos in both areas have some apartments up for short-term lease. In addition to their prime location, many of the condos have first-class pools and other facilities like tennis courts, health clubs, and beautiful common areas for picnics or gatherings. And at rates ranging from $525 a week for a studio to $2,250 a week for a deluxe, modern, three-bedroom condo, it's a great deal for groups. **San Juan Vacations,** Cond. Marbella del Caribe, Suite S-5, Isla Verde 00979 (© **800/266-3639** or 787/727-1591; www.sanjuanvacations.com), is the biggest name in the business. We've also worked through **Ronnie's Properties,** Calle Marseilles 14, Ritz Condominium, Suite 11-F, San Juan, PR 00907 (www.ronniesproperties.com), which has an extensive and growing list of properties in Condado and Isla Verde.

and the Puerto Rico State Department. Like those at Hotel Milano (above), these are clean, comfortable rooms in the heart of the city. Visitors here know what to expect, and they leave satisfied. There are several spots for a meal, including an open-air cafe on the plaza serving tasty local coffee, as well as two drugstores, a supermarket, and Marshall's Department store—plus this is conveniently near all Old San Juan attractions. The entire plaza has Wi-Fi Internet access. Continental breakfast is served in the lobby.

Calle San José 202, San Juan, PR 00901. ⓒ **877/722-9191**. Fax 787/725-3091. www.hojo.com. 30 units. Winter $179–$199 double, $109 single; off season $115–$175 double, $95 single. Includes continental breakfast. AE, MC, V. Bus: Old Town Trolley. **Amenities:** Nonsmoking rooms; rooms for those w/limited mobility. *In room:* A/C, TV, high-speed Internet, hair dryer.

2 Puerta de Tierra

Stay in Puerta de Tierra only if you have a desire to be at either the Caribe Hilton or the Normandie Hotel. When you stay in Puerta de Tierra, you're sandwiched halfway between Old San Juan and the Condado, but you're not getting the advantages of staying right in the heart of either. At night, you must travel by taxi or stay in your hotel. The area is not safe to walk around at night, largely because there is nowhere to walk to except the mammoth Luis Muñoz Rivera Park and the Third Millennium Park, which are mostly deserted at night. For the location of hotels in Puerta de Tierra, see the map on p. 115.

Caribe Hilton 🌀🌀🌀 A pioneering hotel (it was considered Puerto Rico's first big luxury hotel and was the first Hilton built outside the continental U.S.), this has been an integral part of Puerto Rico's tourism industry since 1949 and remains one of the most up-to-date luxury properties in San Juan. Because of an unusual configuration of natural barriers and legal precedents, the hotel has the only private beach on the island. The property abuts the historic Fort San Gerónimo, and a residential and commercial development is taking place on a portion of the Caribe's plot (which totaled 17 acres/6.9 hectares before the sale) but its sprawling facilities, with parks, gardens, and an exhibition center, is still a hit with conventions and tour groups. Only the Condado Plaza and the El San Juan rival it for nonstop activity.

Rooms have larger-than-expected bathrooms with tub/shower combos as well as comfortable, tropical-inspired furniture. In the Caribe Terrace Bar, you can order the bartender's celebrated piña colada, which was once enjoyed by movie legends Joan Crawford and Errol Flynn. Caribe lore has it that a bartender here invented the drink, but other places take credit as well. The bar looks out over the infinity pool area, and the palm-fringed beach beyond it, yet there's always a whirl of activity in the Terrace Bar area, with good tropical music that says "party time." There's no questioning it's one of the best places to enjoy a piña colada. An oceanfront spa and fitness center features such tantalizing delights as couples massages, body wraps, hydrotherapy tub treatments, and soothing cucumber sun therapies. The casino is closed, but there are great restaurants here.

The best place to stay here is in one of the 158 luxury villas with more than 1,500 square feet (139 sq. m) of space, all part of the Condado Lagoon Villas. Up for grabs are studios or one- or two-bedroom luxury accommodations, each with spectacular views of the Condado Lagoon and the Atlantic Ocean. Each comes with a kitchen, private balcony, and a marble bathroom with Jacuzzi. All the services of the Caribe

Puerta de Tierra, Miramar, Condado & Ocean Park Accommodations & Dining

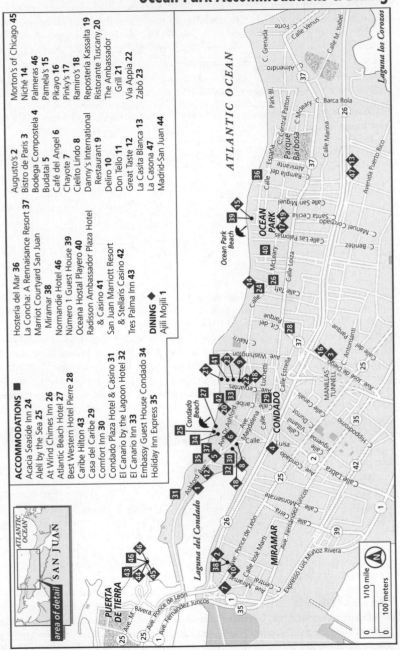

ACCOMMODATIONS ■

Acacia Seaside Inn **24**
Aleli by the Sea **25**
At Wind Chimes Inn **26**
Atlantic Beach Hotel **27**
Best Western Hotel Pierre **28**
Caribe Hilton **43**
Casa del Caribe **29**
Comfort Inn **30**
Condado Plaza Hotel & Casino **31**
El Canario by the Lagoon Hotel **32**
El Canario Inn **33**
Embassy Guest House Condado **34**
Holiday Inn Express **35**

Hostería del Mar **36**
La Concha: A Rennaisance Resort **37**
Marriot Courtyard San Juan
  Miramar **38**
Normandie Hotel **46**
Número 1 Guest House **39**
Oceana Hostal Playero **40**
Radisson Ambassador Plaza Hotel
  & Casino **41**
San Juan Marriott Resort
  & Stellaris Casino **42**
Tres Palma Inn **43**

DINING ◆

Ajili Mojili **1**

Augusto's **2**
Bistro de Paris **3**
Bodega Compostela **4**
Budatai **5**
Café del Angel **6**
Chayote **7**
Cielito Lindo **8**
Danny's International
  Restaurant **9**
Deliro **10**
Don Tello **11**
Great Taste **12**
La Casita Blanca **13**
La Casona **47**
Madrid-San Juan **44**

Morton's of Chicago **45**
Niché **14**
Palmeras **46**
Pamela's **15**
Pikayo **16**
Pinky's **17**
Ramiro's **18**
Repostería Kassalta **19**
Ristorante Tuscany **20**
The Ambassador
  Grill **21**
Via Appia **22**
Zabó **23**

115

Hilton's main hotel are provided to guests of the villas. This is a great spot for families, with one of the most extensive children's programs.

Calle Los Rosales, San Juan, PR 00901. © 800/HILTONS (445-8667) or 787/721-0303. Fax 787/725-8849. www. caribe.hilton.com. 646 units. Winter $320–$640 double; off season $159–$325 double; year-round $750–$1,600 villas and suites. Children 16 and under stay free in parent's room (maximum 4 people per room). AE, DC, DISC, MC, V. Valet parking $25; self-parking $15. Bus: B21. **Amenities:** 5 restaurants; 2 bars; Starbucks; outdoor pool; health club; spa; children's activities and playground; business center (7am–7pm weekdays, 8am–5pm weekends); limited room service; babysitting; laundry service; dry cleaning; nonsmoking rooms; rooms for those w/limited mobility. *In room:* A/C, TV, Wi-Fi Internet, minibar, hair dryer, iron, safe.

Normandie Hotel *Overrated*   A recent upgrade has buffed up this architectural gem, but its location still dooms it, and unlike its recommended neighbor, the property does not have the facilities and services to overcome that weakness. We include it here only because it first opened in 1942 and remains one of the purest examples of Art Deco architecture in Puerto Rico. Originally built for a Parisian cancan dancer by her tycoon husband, the building has a curve-sided design that was inspired by the famous French ocean liner, *Le Normandie.* The gardens are not particularly extensive, and the beach and pool area are unexceptional. Bedrooms are tastefully outfitted, each with a neatly tiled tub-and-shower bathroom. The lobby retains its original Art Deco zest, and soars upward into an atrium. A new Latin fusion restaurant and lounge have made hanging around a bit more appealing, but you'll still feel trapped here at night. Better to come by for a drink or perhaps dinner, soak up some of the ambience, and stay elsewhere. The location is our major complaint. Besides the Hilton next door, the sector (dominated by two lovely parks in the day) is a ghost town in evenings. You're likely to get a better rate here than at other hotels in Condado or Isla Verde, but it's worth it to pay more elsewhere. In Condado or Isla Verde, you'll get a better beach and a nicer pool area. The two sectors are also bustling tourist zones and centers of nightlife and entertainment, so dozens of restaurants and nightclubs are a short walk away from where you'll stay.

Av. Muñoz-Rivera 499, San Juan, PR 00919. © 877/987-2929 or 787/729-2929. Fax 787/729-3083. www.normandie pr.com. 175 units. Winter $190–$220 double; off season $160–$175 double. AE, DC, DISC, MC, V. Parking $10. Bus: A5 or B21. **Amenities:** Restaurant; bar; pool; health club; 24-hr. room service; babysitting; laundry service; dry cleaning; rooms for those w/limited mobility. *In room:* A/C, TV, dataport, coffeemaker, hair dryer, iron, safe.

3 Condado

The Condado has undergone a revitalization in recent years. Right at its heart, the Windows to the Sea Park has risen from the ashes of an old convention center, and La Concha, a landmark of the island's Tropical Modernism movement, has been beautifully redeveloped. Designer boutiques and trendy restaurants have been mounted on the ruins of tacky souvenir shops and cheap eateries. From one end of Ashford Avenue to the other, there are great dining options for every budget, all sorts of stores from book shops to upscale jewelers, plus spas, watersports outfitters, and anything else you might think of. The area around Magdalena Avenue has an extraordinary number of boutiques. There are good bus connections into Old San Juan, and taxis are plentiful. For the locations of hotels in Condado, see the map on p. 115.

VERY EXPENSIVE

Condado Plaza Hotel & Casino *©*   This is one of the busiest hotels on Puerto Rico, with enough facilities and restaurants to keep a visitor occupied for weeks. It's a favorite of business travelers, tour groups, and conventions, but it also attracts independent travelers. A $65-million renovation spiffed up guest rooms and the multiple lobby areas. The pool area, with salt and fresh water pools, overlooks a pretty beach at the entrance to Condado Lagoon, but there are both nicer beaches and hotels elsewhere in Condado and Isla Verde. The rooms, however, all have private terraces and are spacious, bright, and airy, fitted with deluxe beds and mattresses, either king-size or doubles, but most often twins. The good-size bathrooms contain tub/shower combinations. Only Hotel El San Juan has a larger choice of dining options. This place is known for creating restaurants with culinary diversity. Fine restaurants include Gusta de Italia, a casual delicious classic Italian eatery and the Strip House, which serves up delectable steaks in a boudoir-red interior with art that pays erotic homage to female beauty. The Eight Noodle Bar, outside its 24-hour casino, has become one of the favorite late-night snacking spots for San Juan's party set, with its kitchen open from noon to 4am daily. The casino remains one of the island's best.

Av. Ashford 999, San Juan, PR 00907. © 800/468-8588 or 787/721-1000. Fax 787/721-1968. www.luxuryresorts. com. 570 units. Winter $259–$499 double, $585–$1,500 suite; off season $150–$400 double, $450–$1,400 suite. AE, DC, DISC, MC, V. Valet parking $15; self-parking $10. Bus: C10 or B21. **Amenities:** 5 restaurants; 3 bars; 3 outdoor pools; 2 tennis courts; health club; spa; 3 Jacuzzis; watersports equipment; children's activities; car-rental desk; business center; salon; 24-hr. room service; laundry service; dry cleaning; nonsmoking rooms; casino; rooms for those w/limited mobility. *In room:* A/C, TV, minibar, coffeemaker, hair dryer, iron, safe.

La Concha: A Renaissance Resort ⊙⊙

The reopening of this hotel—50 years to the day from when it first opened to rave reviews in December 1958—took 7 years and carried a $220-million price tag, but it was well worth it. Thank former San Juan mayor and governor, Sila Calderón, and the Puerto Rico Architects Association for stopping the wrecking ball on this one. This renovation completes the comeback of Condado, with oceanfront rooms that feel as if they are part of the horizon, and multilevel infinity pool area and adjoining beaches that form a dreamscape in which guests willfully lose themselves. The water motif extends to the cascading fountain at its entrance, the fountains surrounding an open-air deck, and views of the sea from every vantage point. The lobby's Italian marble, white furniture, and huge window to sea also pull the resort's exteriors and interiors together. The signature shell structure, which sits on the beach surrounded by water, is home to Perla restaurant, a seafood restaurant run by prominent local chef Dayn Smith. The hotel's lobby bar is a great spot for tapas and wine, and the casino sits just off it. Surrounded by designer boutiques and trendy restaurants, La Concha has been a local hot spot since it reopened, and its lobby area always has the sound of Latin rhythms.

Guest rooms have the latest high-tech gadgets; understated natural wood and beige interiors form a canvas for the beautiful views and tropical prints on the walls.

Av. Ashford 1077, San Juan, PR 00907. © 877/524-7778 or 787/721-7500. Fax 787/724-7929. www.laconcha resort.com. 248 units. Winter $369–$439 double, $522–$549 suite; off season $199–$258 double, $438–$459 suite. AE, DC, DISC, MC, V. Valet parking $25; self-parking $18. Bus: B21. **Amenities:** 6 restaurant; 2 bars; pools; full-service business center; room service; high-speed Wi-Fi; rooms for those w/limited mobility. *In room:* A/C, flatscreen TV, music players for any format, hair dryer, iron, coffeemaker, tea service, safe, full desk.

San Juan Marriott Resort & Stellaris Casino ⊙

This centrally located hotel is on one of the Condado's nicest beaches, and within walking distance of two parks and the best restaurants in the sector. The tallest building on the Condado, this 21-story landmark packs lots of postmodern style and has an open, comfortable lobby area. A hit with families and kids, it has extensive children's activities and a pool with two water slides. It also has a jumping casino and lobby area, the scene of big band and Latin jazz performances. Even the sports bar by the pool is active with sports fans from up and down the East Coast. The guest rooms are generally spacious, with good views of the water, and each comes with a tiled bathroom with a tub/shower combination. The pastel tones of the comfortable bedrooms are a bit too washed out for our taste, but that's the only legitimate gripe about this property. Junior suites have a living area with a sofa bed. We can't say enough about its great location in the best part of Condado, which is not immediately apparent to visitors. It's an easy walk to anywhere you want to go. And the staff is among the friendliest in town.

Av. Ashford 1309, San Juan, PR 00907. ⓒ 800/228-9290 or 787/722-7000. Fax 787/722-6800. www.marriottpr.com. 525 units. Winter $295–$410 double, $510 junior suite; summer $219–$309 double, $410 junior suite, $1,500 vice-presidential suite, $2,000 presidential suite. Suite rate includes breakfast. AE, DC, DISC, MC, V. Valet parking $20; self-parking $16. Bus: B21. **Amenities:** 3 restaurants; 3 bars; 2 pools; 2 tennis courts; health club; Jacuzzi; sauna; tour desk; car-rental desk; business center; 24-hr. room service; babysitting; laundry service; dry cleaning; casino; business center w/computers; rooms for those w/limited mobility. *In room:* A/C, TV, Wi-Fi Internet, minibar, coffeemaker, hair dryer, iron, safe.

EXPENSIVE

Radisson Ambassador Plaza Hotel & Casino *Overrated*   This property is not a big enough bargain to get you to stay here. There are better bargains to be had, or you could pay a bit more and get a whole lot more. It lacks the resort amenities associated with the Hilton, the Condado Plaza, the Ritz-Carlton, and the Hotel El San Juan, as well as a sense of whimsy and fun. Accommodations are in a pair of towers, one of which is devoted to suites. Each unit has a balcony with outdoor furniture. The beds (twins or doubles) are fitted with fine linens, and each bathroom has generous shelf space and a tub/shower combination.

Av. Ashford 1369, San Juan, PR 00907. ⓒ 800/333-3333 or 787/721-7300. Fax 787/723-6151. www.radisson.com. 233 units. Winter $190–$265 double, $200–$305 suite; off-season $149–$230 double, $185–$205 suite. AE, DISC, MC, V. $189–$260 suite. Self-parking $8. Bus: B21 or C10. **Amenities:** 2 restaurants; 2 bars; rooftop pool; health club; limited room service; babysitting; laundry service; dry cleaning; casino; rooms for those w/limited mobility. *In room:* A/C, TV, coffeemaker, hair dryer, iron, safe (in suites).

MODERATE

Best Western Hotel Pierre *Value*   The seven-floor "Lucky Pierre" is one of San Juan's major bargains. It's 4 blocks from the beach and an easy drive to most major San Juan attractions if you rent a car. It's a small resort, with a large pool and deck in a setting of palm trees. The bedrooms, although hardly grand, have been remodeled. Each has a tiled bathroom with tub and shower. Its two restaurants are moderately priced and serve respectable cuisine. The luxury Gallery Plaza residential condo and retailer boutiques surround the hotel, and it's a short walk to the Puerto Rico Museum of Art. The main drawback is you're a good 15-minute walk from the beach.

Av. José De Diego 105, Condado, San Juan, PR 00914. ⓒ 787/721-1200 or 787/625-3121. Fax 787/721-3118 (reservations). Fax 787/721-3118. www.hotelpierresanjuan.com. 184 units. Winter $209–$309 double; off season $130–$199 double. Continental breakfast included. AE, DC, DISC, MC, V. Children 11 and under stay free in parent's room. Bus: A5 or B21. **Amenities:** Restaurant; bar; outdoor pool; small health club; Jacuzzi; room service; babysitting; laundry service; dry cleaning; rooms for those w/limited mobility. *In room:* A/C, TV, dataport, coffeemaker, hair dryer, iron, safe.

Comfort Inn *Kids*   This family-oriented hotel rises seven stories above a residential neighborhood across the street from Condado Beach. The accommodations are small and not particularly imaginative in their decor. Each room has either one or two queen-size beds, and each has a tub-and-shower bathroom. Some rooms have sofas that convert into beds for children. There's a small swimming pool on the premises. The bars, restaurants, and facilities of the Condado neighborhood are within walking

distance. Computers with Internet access are available for guests. It's near the area's best beach right behind the newly renovated La Concha hotel, as well as a newly renovated oceanfront plaza with open-air restaurants and lots of nice spots to hang out on one of the benches. The rules (no bicycles, no ball games, no pets, no fun) will likely freak out your kids if you have them. Don't worry; they should. The beach beside it, however, is wide and partially shaded by a palm grove. The waters are partially protected by a set of breakers. A good spot for families with vendors selling ice cream, cold drinks and snacks is right here on the spot.

Calle Clemenceau 6, Condado, San Juan, PR 00907. © **800/858-7407** or 787/721-0170. www.comfortinn.com. 50 units. Winter $130 double, $200 suite; summer $110 double, $180 suite. AE, DC, DISC, MC, V. Parking $11. Bus: B21 or C10. **Amenities:** Outdoor pool; laundry service; dry cleaning; rooms for those w/limited mobility. *In room:* A/C, TV, dataport, hair dryer, iron/ironing board, safe.

El Canario by the Lagoon Hotel

A relaxing, informal, European-style hotel, El Canario is in a quiet residential neighborhood just a short block from Condado Beach. This is one of the better B&Bs in the area. The hotel is very much in the Condado style, which evokes Miami Beach in the 1960s. The bedrooms are generous in size and have balconies. Most units have twin beds and sleek and contemporary bathrooms, with shower stalls and enough space to spread out your stuff. If the hotel doesn't have room for you, it can book you into its sibling properties, either El Canario Inn or El Canario by the Sea.

Calle Clemenceau 4, Condado, San Juan, PR 00907. © **800/533-2649** or 787/722-5058. Fax 787/723-8590. www.canariohotels.com. 44 units. Winter $120–$135 double; off season $90–$100 double. $3 energy surcharge. Rates include continental breakfast. AE, DC, DISC, MC, V. Bus: B21 or C10. **Amenities:** Tour desk; coin-operated laundry; nonsmoking rooms. *In room:* A/C, TV, Wi-Fi Internet, safe.

INEXPENSIVE

Acacia Seaside Inn (Value)

This inn, originally built as a private home in 1943 and transformed into a simple hotel in 1948, didn't become well known until the late 1960s, when its reasonable rates began to attract families with children and college students traveling in groups. It's a stucco-covered building with vaguely Spanish-colonial detailing on a residential street lined with similar structures. For the past four years, it has been a sister property of the At Wind Chimes Inn, and the inn has been steadily being made over since then. The lobby and the fabulous restaurant Niché have granite walls, tiled floors with mood lighting, and are connected by an interior tropical garden. The guest rooms are bright and cheery, and there are great areas to hang out, including a rooftop terrace. The beach, among the city's finest, is at the end of the block, and guests can hang out at the Wind Chimes pool and cafe bar. Each unit has simple furniture and a small shower-only bathroom. There's a whirlpool and sun deck. You are literally steps from the beach here.

Calle Taft 8, Condado, San Juan, PR 00911. © **787/725-0668.** Fax 787/728-0671. www.acaciaseasideinn.com. 15 units (shower only). Winter $120–$210 double; summer $105–$185 double. AE, DISC, MC, V. Bus: A5 or B21. *In room:* A/C, TV, fridge (in some).

Aleli by the Sea (Value)

This is a lone budget holdout in a sea of expensive hotel options. Right on the Condado, it's a charming little guesthouse that opens onto the beach 1 block off Ashford Avenue. Most of the bedrooms, which are small to midsize, overlook the ocean, and all of them have rattan furnishings and compact, tiled, shower-only bathrooms. A pleasant touch is the second-floor Sun Deck overlooking the Atlantic, where guests gather to watch the sunsets.

Calle Seaview 1125, Condado, San Juan, PR 00907. © 787/725-5313. Fax 787/721-4744. 9 units (shower only). Winter (including taxes) $76–$119 double; off season (including taxes) $69–$108 double. AE, DISC, MC, V. Bus: B21 or C10. **Amenities:** Self-service laundry; communal kitchen. *In room:* A/C, TV, ceiling fan, no phone.

Atlantic Beach Hotel This is the most famous gay hotel in Puerto Rico. Housed in a five-story building with vaguely Art Deco styling, the hotel is best known for its ground-floor indoor/outdoor bar—the most visibly gay bar in Puerto Rico. It extends from the hotel lobby onto a wooden deck about 15 feet (4.6m) above the sands of Condado Beach. The units are simple cubicles, all nonsmoking, with stripped-down but serviceable and clean decor. Some of the rooms are smaller than others, but few of the short-term guests seem to mind—maybe because the place can have the spirit of a house party. Each unit has a small, shower-only bathroom with plumbing that might not always be in prime condition.

Management insists it does not have a restrictive policy of not allowing a guest to take a visitor back to the room. But the front desk acknowledges that "hustlers" are not allowed on the property or in the guest rooms.

Calle Vendig 1, Condado, San Juan, PR 00907. © 787/721-6900. Fax 787/721-6917. www.atlanticbeachhotel.net. 36 units (shower only). Winter $130–$170 double; off season $89–$115 double. AE, DISC, MC, V. Bus: B21. **Amenities:** Restaurant; bar; laundry service; dry cleaning; rooms for those w/limited mobility. *In room:* A/C, TV, safe.

At Wind Chimes Inn 🦋 *Kids*   This restored and renovated Spanish manor, 1 short block from the beach and 3½ miles (5.6km) from the airport, is one of the best guesthouses on the Condado. Upon entering a tropical patio, you'll find tiled tables surrounded by palm trees and bougainvillea. There's plenty of space on the deck and a covered lounge for relaxing, socializing, and eating breakfast. Dozens of decorative wind chimes add melody to the daily breezes. The good-size rooms offer a choice of size, beds, and kitchens; all contain ceiling fans and air-conditioning. Beds are comfortable and come in four sizes, ranging from twin to king-size. The shower-only bathrooms, though small, are efficiently laid out. Families like this place not only because of the accommodations and the affordable prices but because they can also prepare light meals here, cutting down on food costs.

Av. McLeary 1750, Condado, San Juan, PR 00911. © 800/946-3244 or 787/727-4153. Fax 787/728-0671. www.at windchimesinn.com. 22 units (shower only). Winter $80–$155 double; off season $65–$125 double. AE, DISC, MC, V. Parking $10. Bus: B21 or A5. **Amenities:** Bar; outdoor pool; limited room service; rooms for those w/limited mobility. *In room:* A/C, TV, wireless Internet, kitchen (in some).

Casa del Caribe *Value*   Don't expect the Ritz, but if you're looking for a bargain on the Condado, this is it. This renovated guesthouse was built in the 1940s, later expanded, and then totally refurbished with tropical decor. A very Puerto Rican ambience has been created, with emphasis on Latin hospitality and comfort. On a shady side street just off Ashford Avenue, behind a wall and garden, you'll discover Casa del Caribe's wraparound veranda. The small but cozy guest rooms have ceiling fans and air conditioners, and most feature original Puerto Rican art. The bedrooms are inviting, with comfortable furnishings and efficiently organized bathrooms. The front porch is a social center for guests, and you can also cook out at a barbecue area. The beach is a 2-minute walk away, and the hotel is also within walking distance of some megaresorts, with their glittering casinos.

Calle Caribe 57, El Condado, San Juan, PR 00907. © 787/722-7139. Fax 787/723-2575. www.casadelcaribe.net. 13 units. Winter $85–$125 double; off season $65–$99 double. Rates include continental breakfast. AE, DISC, MC, V. Parking $5. Bus: B21. **Amenities:** Nonsmoking rooms; 1 room for those w/limited mobility. *In room:* A/C, TV, kitchen (in some).

El Canario Inn *Value*   Affiliated with El Canario by the Lagoon Hotel (see above), this little bed-and-breakfast, originally built as a private home, is one of the best values along the high-priced Condado strip. The location is just 1 block from the beach (you can walk there in your bathing suit). This well-established hotel lies directly on the landmark Ashford Avenue, center of Condado action, and is close to casinos, nightclubs, and many restaurants in all price ranges. Although surrounded by megaresorts, it is a simple inn, with rather small but comfortable rooms and good maintenance by a helpful staff. All units are nonsmoking and have small, tiled, shower-only bathrooms. You can relax on the hotel's patios or in the whirlpool area, which is surrounded by tropical foliage. There is no elevator. This is the most charming of the three El Canario properties. El Canario by the Sea is right around the block.

Av. Ashford 1317, Condado, San Juan, PR 00907. *(C)* **800/533-2649** or 787/722-3861. Fax 787/722-0391. www. canariohotels.com. 25 units (shower only). Winter $119–$134 double; off season $90–$100 double. $3 energy fee. Rates include a continental breakfast. AE, DC, MC, V. Bus: B21 or C10. *In room:* A/C, TV, safe.

Embassy Guest House Condado   Located near the Atlantic Beach Hotel (above), this guesthouse is under the same management and also caters to gay vacationers. The staff here is helpful and friendly, and while this is far from the luxury of Ritz-Carlton, it offers a relaxed atmosphere—you could live in a swimsuit or shorts for your entire stay. The small bedrooms are simply furnished, and the small shower-only bathrooms are tiled. Each unit has a kitchenette or access to one. The rooftop sun deck has a view directly over the beach, and there's a pool and whirlpool.

Calle Seaview 1126, Condado, San Juan, PR 00907. *(C)* **787/725-8284** or 787/724-7440. Fax 787/725-2400. www. embassyguesthouse.com. 22 units (shower only). Winter $95–$170 double; off season $65–$115 double. AE, MC, V. Bus: B21. **Amenities:** Pool; whirlpool. *In room:* A/C, TV, kitchenette, coffeemaker, safe, ceiling fan.

Holiday Inn Express   This seven-story, white-painted structure, expanded in 2003, offers a desirable Condado location but without the towering prices of the grand resorts along the beach. The hotel is about a 2-minute walk from Condado Beach and is convenient to Old San Juan (a 15-min. drive) and the airport (a 20-min. drive). Most accommodations have two double beds (ideal for families) and ceiling fans, and each has a small bathroom with tub and shower. Many open onto balconies with water views. There's a small pool with a nice shaded area as well. It's close to the renovated La Concha and the Window of the Sea Park beside it. For years, we avoided this area beside the Condado Lagoon that suffered from the closure of La Concha and neighboring hotels. Compounding problems were the severe sewage backups that would occur in area streets after heavy rains. This problem has abated, and with the new hotel now opened, this area of Avenida Ashford is now home to top-name designer boutiques and great restaurants of all price ranges. So we're hot on this hood again, making this one of your better budget options.

Calle Marinao Ramirez Bages 1, Condado, San Juan, PR 00907. *(C)* **888/465-4329** or 787/724-4160. Fax 787/721-2436. www.ichotels.com. 115 units. Winter $149 (daily), $189 (weekend) double; off season $119 (daily), $139 (weekend) double. Children 18 and under stay free in parent's room. Rates include continental breakfast. AE, DC, DISC, MC, V. Parking $10. Bus: B21. **Amenities:** Pool; whirlpool, health club; business center w/computers; laundry service; dry cleaning. *In room:* A/C, TV, dataport, hair dryer, iron, safe.

4 Miramar

Miramar, a residential neighborhood, is very much a part of metropolitan San Juan, and a brisk 30-minute walk will take you where the action is. Regrettably, the beach is at least half a mile (.8km) away. For the location of hotels in Miramar, see the map on p. 115.

Marriot Courtyard San Juan Miramar *(Value)*   This handsome, budget-friendly, family-owned hotel only makes sense if you plan to rent a car and drive to a different destination everyday—or if you're tied to the nearby Convention Center, this is a viable budget alternative. Otherwise, if your main priority is the beach, this hotel is probably too far. Because the Condado Lagoon and the Baldorioty De Castro Expressway are between the hotel and the beach, you'll walk about an hour to many of our recommended spots. The hotel is in upscale Miramar, with great restaurants, fun shops, and an art-film movie house. The two excellent restaurants here attract area doctors, lawyers, and politicians for lunch, and a broader cross section of *sanjuaneros* for dinner. The pool area is small but sunny, and the public areas have wireless Internet access. The guest rooms are of good quality, if uninspired. Both the Bar Association and the Justice Department are nearby.

Av. Ponce de León 801, San Juan, PR 00907. (*C*) **800/289-4274** or 787/721-7400. Fax 787/722-1787. excelsior@ caribe.net. 140 units. Winter $205 double, $230 suite; off season $149 double, $174 suite. Children 12 and under stay free in parent's room; cribs free. Valet parking $15 daily. AE, DC, DISC, MC, V. Bus: 1, 2, A3, or A5. **Amenities:** 2 restaurants; outdoor pool; health club; limited room service; babysitting; laundry service; dry cleaning; rooms for those w/limited mobility. *In room:* A/C, TV, DVD and video rentals, dataport, hair dryer, safe.

5 Santurce & Ocean Park

Less fashionable (and a bit less expensive) than their nearest neighbors, Condado (to the west) and Isla Verde (to the east), Santurce and Ocean Park are wedged into a modern, not particularly beautiful neighborhood that's bisected with lots of roaring traffic arteries and commercial enterprises. Lots of *sanjuaneros* come here to work in the district's many offices and to eat in its many restaurants. The coastal subdivision of Ocean Park is a bit more fashionable than landlocked Santurce, but with the beach never more than a 20-minute walk away, few of Santurce's residents seem to mind. For the location of hotels in Santurce and Ocean Park, see the map "Puerta de Tierra, Miramar, Condado & Ocean Park Accommodations & Dining" on p. 115.

MODERATE

Hosteria del Mar *(A)*   Lying a few blocks from the Condado casinos and right on the beach are the white walls of this distinctive landmark. It's in a residential seaside community that's popular with locals looking for beach action on weekends. The hotel boasts medium-size, oceanview rooms. Those on the second floor have balconies; those on the first floor open onto patios. The decor is invitingly tropical, with wicker furniture, good beds, pastel prints, and ceiling fans. The bathrooms are small but efficient, some with shower, some with tub only. There are standard and oceanview rooms, suites with kitchenettes, and apartments with full kitchens and living rooms. Our favorite unit is 201, with a king-size bed, private balcony, kitchenette, and a view of the beach; it's idyllic for a honeymoon.

There's no pool, but you are right on the beach. Uvva is one of the hardest working restaurants in town, open from 8am to 10pm, and it doesn't just serve food, it upscales basic breakfast and lunch choices, and also throws in some cutting-edge, creative world cuisine. On a beachfront street completely enveloped by a canopy of trees, this is one of San Juan's most charming spots. Given the setting, the place is simple, but puts out its own elegance and warm hospitality.

Calle Tapía 1, Ocean Park, San Juan, PR 00911. (*C*) **877/727-3302** or 787/727-3302. Fax 787/268-3302. hosteria@ caribe.net. 27 units. High season $89–$239 double, $244–$264 apt; off season $69–$179 double, $199–$209 apt.

Children 11 and under stay free in parent's room. AE, DC, DISC, MC, V. Bus: A5. **Amenities:** Restaurant; limited room service. *In room:* A/C, TV, dataport, Wi-Fi Internet, kitchenette (in 3 units), coffeemaker (in some).

Número 1 Guest House ★★ *finds*   As a translation of its name implies, this is the best of the small-scale, low-rise guesthouses in Ocean Park. It was originally built in the 1950s as a private beach house in a prestigious residential neighborhood adjacent to the wide sands of Ocean Park Beach. A massive renovation transformed the place into the closest thing in Ocean Park to the kind of stylish boutique hotel you might find in an upscale California neighborhood. Much of this is thanks to the hardworking owner, Esther Feliciano, who cultivates within her walled compound a verdant garden replete with splashing fountains, a small swimming pool, and manicured shrubbery and palms. Stylish-looking bedrooms (all of which are nonsmoking) contain tile floors, wicker or rattan furniture, comfortable beds, and tiled, shower-only bathrooms. Some repeat clients, many of whom are gay, refer to it as their fantasy version of a private villa beside a superb and usually convivial beach. The staff can direct you to watersports emporiums nearby for virtually any tropical watersport. Although it lacks the staggering diversity of the big hotels of the nearby Condado or Isla Verde, some guests value its sense of intimacy and small-scale charm.

Calle Santa Ana 1, Ocean Park, San Juan, PR 00911. ℂ 866/726-5010 or 787/726-5010. Fax 787/727-5482. www. numero1guesthouse.com. 13 units (shower only). High season (Dec 15–Apr 30) $139–$279 double, $269–$279 apt, $249 suite; low season (Aug 1–Oct 31) $89–$179 double, $169–$179 apt, $159 suite; mid-season (May 1–July 31, Nov) $75–$115 double, $165 apt, $145 junior suite. $20 each additional occupant of a double room. Rates include continental breakfast. AE, MC, V. Bus: A5. **Amenities:** Restaurant; bar; outdoor pool; limited room service; rooms for those w/limited mobility. *In room:* A/C, TV, dataport, Wi-Fi Internet, minibar, hair dryer, iron, safe, ceiling fan.

INEXPENSIVE

Oceana Hostal Playero *finds*   Yeah, it's a block from the beach, but it's the best beach in the city—so you might say that's better than beachfront at another beach. In any case, this B&B deserves to be better known, and probably will be once the beloved L'Habitation closes nearby (it's up for sale as we go to press), making Oceana the best bargain in Ocean Park. It's a comfortable, snug nest with helpful, friendly staff and clean, newly renovated rooms. All units have small refrigerators and a tiled bathroom with either a tub or a shower. The entire property is a Wi-Fi Internet zone. You can enjoy the complimentary breakfast outdoors on the patio if you wish, and the pool area is a big plus. The PuraVida restaurant lounge serves good local and vegetarian cuisine. The most recent renovations have greatly improved this guesthouse since the days of the Beach Buoy Inn, but the price can still be nice.

Av. McLeary 1853, Ocean Park, San Juan, PR 00911. ℂ 787/728-8119 or 787/728-8119. Fax 787/268-0037. 17 units (some shower only, some tub only). Winter $90–$357 double, $381 efficiency; off season $79–$267 double, $318 efficiency. Children 11 and under stay free in parent's room. Rates include continental breakfast. MC, V. Free parking. Bus: A5 or A7. **Amenities:** Restaurant; 1 room for those w/limited mobility. *In room:* A/C, TV, Wi-Fi, fridge, no phone.

Tres Palmas Inn *Value*   Across the street from the ocean, this apartment-style guesthouse overlooks a windswept stretch of beach at the eastern end of Ocean Park, right before it disappears into the rocky coastline along Punta Las Marías. The beautiful beach at Ultimo Trolley is a block west, and the hotel's pool is located in a secluded courtyard. You can also relax on the rooftop sun deck while soaking in the whirlpool. The medium-size bedrooms are simply but comfortably furnished, with rather standard motel items. Each guest room has a private entrance and a ceiling fan, and most have small refrigerators. Larger rooms also have small kitchens, and each unit has a small, tiled bathroom with either a tub or a shower. We have friends who love this place and stay here for annual visits to the island.

Ocean Park Blvd. 2212, San Juan, PR 00913. © **888/290-2076** or 787/727-4617. Fax 787/727-5434. www.trespalmas inn.com. 18 units (some with shower only, some with tub only). Winter $87–$175 double; off season $81–$146 double. Rates include continental breakfast. AE, MC, V. Bus: A5 or A7. **Amenities:** Pool; 2 whirlpools; sun deck; Internet access; 1 room for those w/limited mobility. *In room:* A/C, TV, dataport, kitchen, fridge (in some), hair dryer, safe.

6 Isla Verde

Beach-bordered Isla Verde is closer to the airport than the Condado and Old San Juan. The hotels here are farther from Old San Juan than those in Miramar, Condado, and Ocean Park. It's a good choice if you don't mind the isolation and want to be near fairly good beaches. For the location of hotels in Isla Verde, see the map "Isla Verde Accommodations & Dining" on p. 125.

VERY EXPENSIVE

El San Juan Hotel & Casino ℛ *Kids*   Despite formidable competition by the Ritz-Carlton and the Water Club for elite and sophisticated travelers, this posh resort still has the power to dazzle. The beachfront hotel is surrounded by 350 palms, century-old banyans, and gardens. It lies on a 2-mile-long (3.2km) golden sandy beach with aquamarine water that is the finest in San Juan. Lined with luxury hotels and condominiums, the beach is always full of activity and has great watersports activities.

The lobby is the most opulent and memorable in the Caribbean. Entirely sheathed in red marble and hand-carved mahogany paneling, the public rooms stretch on almost endlessly. No other hotel in the Caribbean offers such a rich diversity of dining options and such high-quality food. Oriental, Italian, Caribbean, and the world famous the Palm Restaurant steakhouse are just a few of the options. And with live music and DJs playing at nightclubs nearly every night, and a beautiful casino, El San Juan is still the place to be seen in the city.

The large, well-decorated rooms are outfitted with the latest in high tech, with Wi-Fi Internet access, flatscreen TVs with movie service, and iPod docking stations. The Vista guest rooms are bright and tropical, while the Lanai rooms are imbued with honey-hued woods and rattans, with darker wooden doors, windows and other furnishing. Bathrooms have all the amenities and tub/shower combos; a few feature Jacuzzis. The oceanfront Lanai rooms overlook the fern-lined paths of the resort's tropical garden. There are also suites and one- and two-bedroom accommodations. While the larger units make sense for families, the hotel has cut down recently on organized activities for children, although there are still board games, pool toys, and a summer camp for children. It's still a great place for families, however.

Av. Isla Verde 6063, San Juan, PR 00979. © **787/791-1000.** Fax 787/791-0390. www.luxuryresorts.com. 382 units. Winter $279–$1150 double, from $1,700–$2,200 suite; off season $192–$509 double, from $599–$799 suite. AE, DC, DISC, MC, V. Valet parking $15; self-parking $10. Bus: A5. **Amenities:** 7 restaurants; 4 bars; 2 outdoor pools; tennis courts; health club; spa; sauna and steam room; watersports equipment/rentals; children's programs; business center; 24-hr. room service; massage; babysitting; laundry service; dry cleaning; casino; rooms for those w/limited mobility. *In room:* A/C, TV w/in-house movies, Wi-Fi Internet, iPod docking station, minibar, coffeemaker, hair dryer, iron, safe.

Inter-Continental San Juan Resort & Casino   We love the pool area and the cafe overlooking the beach, but this is a regimented resort where service often proves too rigid or flops. On the plus side, the comfortable, medium-size rooms, which underwent a needed renovation in 2007, have balconies and terraces and tastefully conservative furnishings. Executive Club–level rooms carry additional features such as

Isla Verde Accommodations & Dining

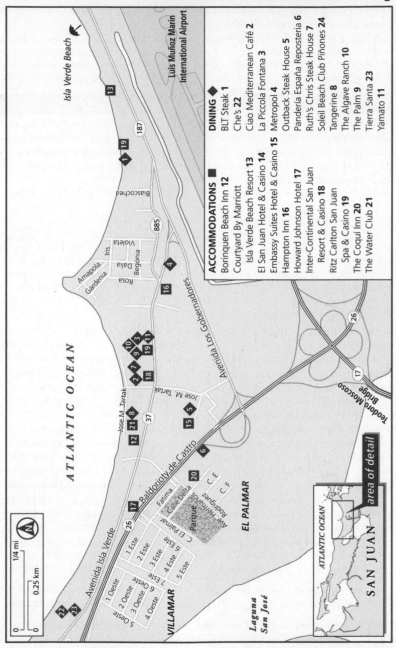

ACCOMMODATIONS ■

Borinquen Beach Inn **12**
Courtyard By Marriott
Isla Verde Beach Resort **13**
El San Juan Hotel & Casino **14**
Embassy Suites Hotel & Casino **15**
Hampton Inn **16**
Howard Johnson Hotel **17**
Inter-Continental San Juan
Resort & Casino **18**
Ritz Carlton San Juan
Spa & Casino **19**
The Coquí Inn **20**
The Water Club **21**

DINING ◆

BLT Steak **1**
Che's **22**
Ciao Mediterranean Café **2**
La Piccola Fontana **3**
Metropol **4**
Outback Steak House **5**
Panderia España Reposteria **6**
Ruth's Chris Steak House **7**
Soleil Beach Club Piñones **24**
Tangerine **8**
The Algave Ranch **10**
The Palm **9**
Tierra Santa **23**
Yamato **11**

125

complimentary meals and drinks. However, neither the casino nor the lobby entertainment can compete with those at the El San Juan next door.

There are some fine restaurants here. **Ciao Mediterranean Café** ✯✯ (p. 155) is the
best beachfront restaurant perhaps in the city, with tables stretched out along a long
boardwalk, in the shade of the palms, where you can enjoy a brick-oven pizza and
watch the frolicking in the water. There's also **Ruth's Chris Steak House,** and an
excellent sushi teppanyaki place, **Momoyama,** where the tableside chefs put on quite
a show.

Warning: We've been frustrated by the staff's inability to resolve a variety of situa-
tions (ranging from an air conditioner problem to changes to a bill). If it's not in the
book of rules, they are clueless. We were particularly annoyed by the aggressive
enforcement of a guest-only policy at the pool by security personnel—that is, don't
enter the pool area without your room key and or your day-glo wristband, or you'll be
asked to leave (and not too politely). And if you want visitors to sit with you by the
pool, the hotel will charge you a steep per-person fee for the privilege. Since many
travelers going to Puerto Rico are visiting friends or family, this can be an issue.

Av. Isla Verde 5961, Isla Verde, PR 00979. ℂ 800/468-9076 or 787/791-6100. Fax 787/253-2510. www.ichotels
group.com. 402 units. Winter $329–$545 double, $579–$1,090 suite; off season $212–$312 double, $300–$979
suite. Children 15 and under stay free in parent's room. AE, DC, DISC, MC, V. Valet parking; $22; self-parking $16. Bus:
A7, M7, or T1. **Amenities:** 3 restaurants; lounge; the Caribbean's largest free-form pool; whirlpool; health club;
sauna; scuba diving; limo service; business center; 24-hr. room service; massage; babysitting; laundry service; dry
cleaning; Wi-Fi Internet, rooms for those w/limited mobility. *In room:* A/C, TV, dataport, minibar, coffeemaker, hair
dryer, iron, safe.

Ritz-Carlton San Juan Spa & Casino ✯✯✯

The Ritz-Carlton is one of the most
spectacular deluxe hotels in the Caribbean. Set on 8 acres (3.2 hectares) of prime
beachfront, within a 5-minute drive from the airport, it appeals to both business travelers and vacationers. The hotel decor reflects Caribbean flavor and the Hispanic culture of the island, with artwork by prominent local artists. More visible, however, is
an emphasis on Continental elegance. Some of the most opulent public areas feature
wrought-iron balustrades and crystal chandeliers.

Beautifully furnished guest rooms open onto ocean views or the gardens of nearby
condos. Rooms are very large, with excellent furnishings, fine linens, and dataports.
The marble bathrooms are exceptionally plush, with tub/shower combinations, scales,
bathrobes, and deluxe toiletries. Preferred accommodations are in the ninth-floor
Ritz-Carlton Club, which has a private lounge and personal concierge staff.

The scope and diversity of dining here is second only to that at the El San Juan
Hotel & Casino (see above), and as for top-shelf dining venues, the Ritz-Carlton has
no equal. Renowned gourmet chains BLT Steak and Il Mulino of New York are both
located here. The hotel also houses one of Puerto Rico's largest casinos, and it's most
stylishly elegant. This is a great spot for families with a full range of children's activities and a great beach for kids, with lots of watersports options for active families.

Av. de los Gobernadores (State Rd.) 6961, no. 187, Isla Verde, PR 00979. ℂ 800/241-3333 or 787/253-1700. Fax
787/253-1777. www.ritzcarlton.com. 416 units. Winter $399–$769 double; off season $285–$599 double; year-round
from $1,109–$1,529 suite. AE, DC, DISC, MC, V. Valet parking $22; self-parking $17. Bus: A5, B40, or C45. **Amenities:** 5 restaurants; 3 bars; nightclub; large pool; 2 tennis courts; health club; spa; children's program; salon; 24-hr.
room service; babysitting; laundry service; dry cleaning; Caribbean's largest casino; rooms for those w/limited mobility. *In room:* A/C, TV, dataport, minibar, hair dryer, safe.

Family-Friendly Accommodations

At Wind Chimes Inn (p. 120)   Families like this hotel not only because of the accommodations and the affordable prices, but also because they can prepare meals here, cutting down on food costs.

Caribe Hilton (p. 114)   This hotel, although expensive, offers more programs for children than any other hotel in Puerto Rico. Its supervised Kids' Klub provides daily activities—ranging from face painting to swimming lessons—for children 5 to 12 years of age.

Courtyard by Marriott Isla Verde Beach Resort (see below)   This is an affordable option, and the kids will enjoy the Bananas Ice Cream Parlour, the game room, and Kids' Club activities for ages 3 through 11. Summer family packages can save you money and usually include coupons for pizza and banana sundaes.

Hampton Inn (p. 128)   For families seeking the kind of lodging values found on the mainland, this new hotel is highly desirable, as many of its rooms have two double beds. There's also a beautiful swimming pool in a tropical setting. Suites have microwaves and refrigerators.

Ritz-Carlton (p. 126)   For the family seeking an upmarket resort with lots of facilities, this is among the top choices. There's a full range of children's activities: arts and crafts, bowling, sand castle sculpting, sports, board games, and Spanish lessons. It's also a great place for active families, with plenty of watersports opportunities. Lessons and rentals are available for surfing, windsurfing, kite surfing, and sailing.

The Water Club 🐬🐬   A refreshing change from the megachain resorts of San Juan, this ultrachic hotel is hip and contemporary. It's the city's only "boutique hotel" on a beach. We find much to praise at this small and exclusive hotel because of its highly personalized and well-trained staff. Although avant-garde, the design is never off-putting. The illuminated lobby might recall *2001: A Space Odyssey,* but it's still warm and friendly. Behind glass are "waterfalls," even on the elevators, and inventive theatrical-style lighting is used to bring the outdoors inside. The one-of-a-kind glass art doors are from Murano, the famed center of glassmaking outside Venice. Overlooking Isla Verde's best beach area, all the bedrooms are spacious and contain custom-designed beds positioned to face the ocean. Bathrooms are tiled and elegant, with tub/shower combinations. Unique features are the open-air 11th-floor exotic bar with the Caribbean's only rooftop fireplace. The pool is a level above; it's like swimming in an ocean in the sky. This hotel is super pet friendly; it offers four-legged friends complimentary doggie bags and their owners welcome drinks. Grooming, walking, and massage services are available.

Calle José M. Tartak 2, Isla Verde, Puerto Rico 00979. ℭ **888/265-6699** or 787/253-3666. Fax 787/728-3610. www.waterclubsanjuan.com. 84 units. Winter $275–$450 double; off season $209–$399 double. AE, DC, DISC, MC, V. Bus: T1 or A5. **Amenities:** Restaurant; 2 bars; outdoor rooftop pool; fitness center; Jacuzzi; limited room service; dry cleaning; nonsmoking rooms; rooms for those w/limited mobility. *In room:* A/C, TV, dataport, high-speed Internet, minibar, hair dryer, safe.

EXPENSIVE

Embassy Suites Hotel & Casino 🏄   The location is 2 blocks from the beach, and the hotel has its own water world, with waterfalls and reflecting ponds set against a backdrop of palms. As you enter, you're greeted with an aquarium, giving a tropical-resort aura to the place. The excellent accommodations are all suites, and they're comfortably furnished and roomy, with bedrooms separated from the living rooms. Each has a wet bar, a tub/shower combination bathroom, two phones, a safe, and a dining table. The most spacious suites are those with two double beds; each of the smaller suites is furnished with a king-size bed. The best view of the water is from units above the third floor. Two restaurants are on the premises, including the Embassy Grill, a low-key indoor/outdoor affair, and an independently managed Outback Steakhouse branch. There's also a small-scale casino on the property.

Calle José M. Tartak 8000, Isla Verde, San Juan, PR 00979. © **800/362-2779** or 787/791-0505. Fax 787/991-7776. www.embassysuites.com. 299 suites. Winter $200–$420 one-bedroom suite, $400–$520 2-bedroom suite; off season $179–$215 one-bedroom suite, $350 2-bedroom suite. Rates include breakfast and free drinks 5:30–7:30pm. AE, DC, DISC, MC, V. Valet parking $16; self-parking $10. Bus: A5 or B21. **Amenities:** 2 restaurants; 3 bars; pool; health club; car-rental desk; business center; limited room service; laundry service; coin-operated laundry; dry cleaning; small casino; rooms for those w/limited mobility. *In room:* A/C, TV, wet bar (in suites), fridge, coffeemaker, hair dryer, iron, safe, microwave.

MODERATE

Courtyard by Marriott Isla Verde Beach Resort 🏄 *Kids*   This is affordable Caribbean at its best. It's on a beautiful beach at the end of Isla Verde, with the public beach just to the east and Pine Grove beach, popular with surfers and sailors, just to the west. Close to the airport, the refurbished hotel serves meals on a wraparound veranda, and there are comfortable hammocks and beach chairs beside the pool and the beach in front. Updated comfort makes it suitable for business travelers, families, or the random vacationer. The 12-floor hotel rises on the site of the old Crowne Plaza. It's a big, bustling place with many amenities and midsize and well-furnished bedrooms. Art Deco furnishings dominate, and there is plenty of comfort. The casino and lobby restaurants are filled with the sounds of Latin rhythms at night. The pool and beach are great for kids. They can get surf lessons down the beach on foam boards designed for beginners.

Boca de Cangrejos Avenida 7012, Isla Verde, PR 00979. © **800/791-2553** or 787/791-0404. Fax 787/791-1460. www.sjcourtyard.com. 293 units. Winter $189–$385 double, $485 suite; off season $160–$320 double, $395 suite. AE, DC, DISC, MC, V. Bus: M7. **Amenities:** 3 restaurants; ice-cream parlor; bar; pool; fitness center; kids' club; business center; limited room service; laundry service; dry cleaning; casino; high-speed Internet. *In room:* A/C, TV, dataport, minibar, hair dryer, iron, safe.

Hampton Inn *Kids*   Opened in 1997, this chain hotel is set across the busy avenue from Isla Verde's sandy beachfront, far enough away to keep costs down but within a leisurely 10-minute walk of the casinos and nightlife. Two towers, with four and five floors, hold the well-maintained, well-furnished, and comfortable bedrooms. There's no restaurant on the premises and no real garden; other than a whirlpool and a swimming pool with a swim-up bar, there are very few facilities or amenities. Because of its reasonable prices and location, however, this Isla Verde newcomer could be a good choice. Families are especially fond of staying here despite the fact that there are no special children's programs; many of the rooms have two double beds, and suites have microwaves and refrigerators.

Av. Isla Verde 6530, Isla Verde, PR 00979. © 800/HAMPTON (426-7866) or 787/791-8777. Fax 787/791-8757. 201 units. Winter $199–219 double, $229 suite; off season $169–$199 double, $209 suite. Rates include breakfast bar. AE, DC, DISC, MC, V. Parking $5. Bus: A5 or C45. **Amenities:** Bar; pool; health club; whirlpool; babysitting; laundry service; dry cleaning; high-speed Internet, rooms for those w/limited mobility. *In room:* A/C, TV, fridge (in suites), coffeemaker, hair dryer, iron, microwave (in suites).

Howard Johnson Hotel   Rising eight stories above the busy traffic of Isla Verde, this chain hotel offers comfortable but small bedrooms, furnished simply with bland, modern furniture. They're done in typical motel style, with small but serviceable tub-and-shower bathrooms. Many guests carry a tote bag to the beach across the street, and then hit the bars and restaurants of the expensive hotels nearby. There's a restaurant and a pool. Though it's simple and not very personal, this is a good choice for the money. The Fontana di Roma Italian restaurant is excellent.

Av. Isla Verde 4820, Isla Verde, PR 00979. © 787/728-1300. Fax 787/727-7150. www.hojo.com. 115 units. $150 double; $185 suite. AE, MC, V. Parking $6.50. Bus: A5. **Amenities:** 2 restaurants; pool; health club; laundry service; dry cleaning; rooms for those w/limited mobility. *In room:* A/C, TV, fridge, coffeemaker, hair dryer, iron.

INEXPENSIVE

Borinquen Beach Inn *Value*   Lying just 1 block from the beach and a 5-minute drive from the airport, this is a good deal. This modest, one-story guesthouse has been popular with islanders and visitors for more than 2 decades. The unassuming white facade is in keeping with the plain interior decor, with its pastel-painted walls, communal lounge and kitchen, and small serving area where guests can order coffee. The rooms are small and plain, but they're clean and comfortable enough, and each has a small bathroom with a shower stall. The overall aura here is very laid-back, but the low prices and convenient location keep the place booked with holidaymakers year-round.

Av. Isla Verde 5451, Isla Verde, San Juan, PR 00979. © 866/728-8400 or 787/728-8400. Fax 787/268-2411. www. borinquenbeachinn.com. 12 units. High season $90 double; low season $72 double. AE, DC, DISC, MC, V. Free parking. Bus: A5. **Amenities:** Communal kitchen; 1 room for those w/limited mobility. *In room:* A/C, TV, no phone.

The Coquí Inn *Value*   This property incorporates three former guesthouses in the area (the Mango Inn, Green Isle Inn, and Casa Mathiesen). The beach is about a 10-minute walk, and you have to cross Baldority de Castro Expressway to get to Isla Verde's main drag and the beach (via pedestrian bridge)—but it's a real deal, and it's the nicest part of Isla Verde. Guests get access to three pools, each with terraces with lounge chairs and umbrellas. The three connected properties also offer an Asian restaurant and American–Puerto Rico cafe. You'll find free Wi-Fi Internet and public computers and movie rentals. Management is moving toward a green approach. Bedroom furnishings are summery, simple, and comfortable. Each has a tiled tub-and-shower bathroom.

Calle Uno 36, Villamar, Isla Verde, PR 00979. © 800/677-8860 or 787/726-8662. Fax 787/268-2415. www.coqui-inn.com. 54 units. Weekdays $89–$109 double; weekends $99–$119 double. AE, DISC, MC, V. Free parking. Bus: A5. **Amenities:** Restaurant; bar; 2 small pools; laundry service; shared areas w/microwaves and fridges; rooms for those w/limited mobility. *In room:* A/C, TV, kitchenette (in some), safe.

7

Where to Dine in San Juan

San Juan's fine dining scene is the most varied and developed in the Caribbean. City restaurants serve up excellent Spanish, French, American, Italian, Chinese, Mexican, and Asian cuisines.

While tasty Puerto Rican food has always been widely available on the island, in recent years it has moved front and center at many of the city's finer restaurants. Several of the island's most talented chefs are striving to bring their hometown cuisine to new heights at some of its trendier eating establishments.

San Juan literally has some of the best steakhouses in the world (BLT Steak, the Palm, Ruth's Chris Steak House, Moron's of Chicago, plus a number of superb local Latino steakhouses specializing in grilled meats). And the island has long delivered expert renditions of Spanish cuisine, as well as traditional French and other Continental cookery.

Of special note are the Italian restaurants (and local pizzerias), which take their inspiration directly from the New York City area and are competitive with the best in the genre stateside. Many others are Argentinean kitchens, which serve up a lighter Italian fair and delectable grilled skirt steak.

There also are several seafood restaurants in the city. Seafood also plays a big role in many other local restaurants as well. Local seafood is generally in plentiful supply. Many of the finer San Juan restaurants also import fresh seafood from off island, especially for non-native species like Maine lobster and salmon. Red snapper and dolphinfish (known as *chillo* and *dorado,* respectively) are two local favorites, with fresh catch of each being widely available.

What may surprise the visitor is the quality and variety of Asian restaurants in the city, which include several gourmet eateries specializing in regional cuisines of China and top-notch Japanese steakhouses and sushi emporiums. There are about a dozen Lebanese and Arabian restaurants offering great food at modest prices. Many transport diners to the Middle East with Arabian music, belly-dancing, and a sheik's tent decor.

San Juan also has unexpected surprises: gourmet Indian, German baked goods, a Peruvian ceviche house, and an Irish bar and grill plucked out of midtown Manhattan.

The resort hotels along Condado and Isla Verde house excellent restaurants, among them, some of the island's finest. But you will miss out on some of the more unique and memorable dining experiences if you don't search beyond the hotel establishments.

There has been a restaurant explosion in San Juan in the past few years, first in Old San Juan, and now more recently in Miramar, Condado, and surrounding areas. Isla Verde and Hato Rey also have a large number of restaurants.

There is a string of traditional restaurants that have been established for more than 30 years. Most of these specialize in Spanish or Continental cuisine, with a Puerto Rican flair.

Of course, the pleasures of eating in San Juan go beyond formal dining in restaurants. A fixture in the city is the presence of Spanish *panaderías,* or bakeries, an excellent choice for breakfast or lunch but an option for dinner as well. They have fresh baked goods, fat deli sandwiches, and traditional Spanish entrees like *caldo gallego* and *arroz con pollo.* You get strong and tasty Puerto Rican coffee, fresh juices, and frappes as well.

Also be on the look out for *fondas,* which are basic restaurants, often with just a counter or a few tables, that serve tasty local food at rock bottom prices. There are a number of these around Avenida Ponce de León in downtown Santurce, which cater to office workers and students. Look to a *fonda* for an authentic island meal and a chance to brush up on your Spanish and rub elbows with Puerto Rican workers.

The city is one of the fast food capitals of the world, with all the familiar American brands, but also more obscure regional favorites, like **Pollo Tropical.** U.S. casual chain-style restaurants also have a big presence on the island, with everything from **Chili's** to **Marcano's Macaroni Grill** to **Applebee's** here.

Street-food aficionados will also find solace in San Juan. There are many stand-up only cafes throughout the city serving barbecued kabobs, fried codfish fritters and turnovers stuffed with fish, spiced chicken, or beef. The **Piñones** area, east of Isla Verde, has oceanfront wooden stands where the *frituras,* or fried beach snacks, and kebabs are cooked over open fires.

The restaurants listed in this chapter are classified first by area and then by price, using the following categories: **Very Expensive,** dinner from $50 per person; **Expensive,** dinner from $35 per person; **Moderate,** dinner from $25 per person; and **Inexpensive,** dinner under $25 per person. These categories reflect prices for an appetizer, a main course, a dessert, and a glass of wine.

For much more on Puerto Rico's food scene, see chapter 2.

1 Best Bets

- **Best Classic Dining:** Out in Miramar, **Augusto's Cuisine,** in the Marriott Courtyard San Juan Miramar Hotel, Av. Ponce de León 801 (© **787/725-7700**), combines impeccable service and an elegant dining room while delivering one of the best French and international cuisines in the Caribbean, backed up by an extensive wine list.
- **Best Steakhouse:** In the swanky Ritz-Carlton San Juan Hotel, **BLT Steak,** De los Gobernadores 6961 (© **787/253-1700**), serves the most succulent steaks in Puerto Rico. French chef Laurent Tourondel reinvents the American steakhouse with the classic cooking techniques of his homeland, serving up aged beefs, other meats, and fresh seafood. Sauces, sides, and desserts are all heavenly remakes of your father's favorite food, and it still tastes good today.
- **Best Food Value: Bebo's Cafe,** Calle Loiza 1600 (© **787/726-1008**), has good *comida criolla,* plus steaks, sandwiches, and fruit frappes at incredibly low prices. That's why it draws crowds despite its rather slow, if well intentioned, service. It's open all the time, nearly.
- **Best Italian Restaurant:** Across the street from Hotel El Covento, **Il Perugino,** Cristo St. 105 (© **787/722-5481**), takes you on a culinary tour of sunny Italy. Plate after plate of delectable northern Italian food is presented nightly—everything from grilled filets of fresh fish to succulent pastas. Service is first-rate, and the welcome warm.

- **Best French Restaurant:** Housed in a beautifully renovated building across the street from the Museo de Arte de Puerto Rico, **Bistro de Paris,** Plaza de Diego, Av. De Diego 310 (© 787/998-8929), takes elements of a classic Parisian bistro and kicks up the comfort level several notches. This is classic French cuisine with innovative flourishes, prepared and served with love and precision by talented chefs and a near perfect wait staff.

- **Best for a Romantic Dinner:** It's erotic meeting your lover outside the bathroom in the dimly lit, breathtaking lobby of the Museum of Art of Puerto Rico when it is closed. And you'll still have opportunities for appreciation of the arts at **Pikayo,** Av. José de Diego 299 (© 787/721-6194), where the walls of the dining room serve as a rotating gallery, and chef Wilo Benet delivers food every bit as artful as the surroundings. Taste the masterpiece of reinvented *comida criolla* together.

- **Best Nuevo Latino Cuisine: Parrot Club,** Calle Fortaleza 363 (© 787/725-7370), wows taste buds with its modern interpretation of Puerto Rican specialties. Even San Juan's mayor and the governor have made it their favorite. Husband-and-wife team Emilio Figueroa and Gigi Zafero borrow from a repertoire of Puerto Rican and Spanish recipes, and they also use Taíno and African influences in their cuisine. The seared tuna is the best in town, and their Creole-style flank steak is worth the trek from Condado Beach.

- **Best Burgers:** Patrons freely admit that **El Patio de Sam,** Calle San Sebastián 102 (© 787/723-1149), is not always on target with its main dishes. But they agree on one thing: The hamburgers are the juiciest and most delectable in San Juan. The Old City atmosphere is also intriguing—with an airy courtyard and lots of local artwork.

- **Best *Asopao*:** Soul food to Puerto Ricans, *asopao* is the regional gumbo, made in as many different ways as there are chefs on the island. Most versions are too thick to be called soup; stew is more fitting. Try the seafood variety at **La Bombonera,** Calle San Francisco 259 (© 787/722-0658), in the Old City. The most basic version is a delicious mix of pigeon peas and rice.

- **Best Spanish Cuisine:** You'd have to go all the way to Madrid to find Spanish food as well prepared as it is at **Ramiro's,** Av. Magdalena 1106 (© 787/721-9049). The chefs take full advantage of fresh island produce to create an innovative cuisine. In fact, the style is New Creole, although its roots are firmly planted in Spain. Their fresh fish and chargrilled meats are succulent, and any dessert with the strawberry-and-guava sauce is a sure palate pleaser.

- **Best Local Cuisine:** Devoted to *comida criolla,* **Ajili Mójili,** Av. Ashford 1006 (© 787/725-9195), features food that islanders might have enjoyed in their mamas' kitchens. Try such specialties as *mofongos* (green plantains stuffed with veal, chicken, shrimp, or pork) or the most classic *arroz con pollo* (juicy chicken baked right in the middle of the pot of saffron rice).

- **Best Hotel Restaurant:** In the San Juan Marriott Resort, Av. Ashford 1309 (© 787/722-7000), **Ristorante Tuscany** has consistently maintained high standards over the last decade in delivering some of the best northern cuisine on the island. We've found it even better in the early 21st century than it was in the 1990s.

- **Best Late-Night Dining:** This is where your waitress and bartender go when they get off of work. With an after-hours menu that's available until dawn, **Tantra,** Calle Fortaleza 356 in Old San Juan (© 787/977-8141), is the place to go when midnight munchies strike. Try some tandoori chicken kebabs, coconut sesame shrimp in a mango peach salsa, or fried calamari in tomato masala sauce. There are plenty of tasty choices from the Indian–Latin fusion menu. Although the kitchen officially closes at 2am, it stays open until the crowd stops asking for more. It's a good place to find out what's going on around town as well.

- **Best Family Meals:** In the Inter-Continental San Juan Resort & Casino, Av. Isla Verde 5961 (ℂ **787/791-6100**), **Ciao Mediterranean Café** offers an excellent and reasonably priced menu. Many tables are placed on a private boardwalk adjacent to the beach. Pizza and pasta are favorite dishes, and you can also choose from a large selection of other Mediterranean fare.

- **Best Pizza:** For pizza pies like the ones from the boardwalk stands on the Jersey shore, try **Mike & Charlie's,** Av. Ashford 1024 (ℂ **787/725-8711**). As much about the tomato as the cheese, the slices are huge, but the crust is so light, they are never overfilling. We can't say the same about the huge and delicious submarines, calzones, and pasta dishes also served here.

- **Best Sunday Brunch:** Both locals and American visitors flock to **Palmeras** at the Caribe Hilton, Calle Los Rosales (ℂ **787/721-0303**), for its delectable all-you-can-eat Sunday brunch. Good food, glamour, and live music are combined here. The freshly prepared seafood alone is worth the set price, which includes champagne.

- **Best Aphrodisiac Cuisine:** Take someone special to **Ostra Cosa,** Calle del Cristo 154 (ℂ **787/722-2672**), for a night of romance. Even if you aren't in the mood, the owner promises that you will be after consuming his dishes, which are "chockfull of aphrodisiacs." It's not just the prawns and oysters; the romantic setting in a Spanish colonial courtyard does not hurt either.

- **Best Ice Cream:** On a cobble-covered street in Old San Juan, **Ben & Jerry's,** Calle del Cristo 61 (ℂ **787/977-6882**), is a block from the landmark cathedral, Catedral de San Juan, across from the entrance to Hotel El Convento. This North American chain offers the best ice cream in San Juan. Any of the 32 flavors—10 of them low-fat—tastes particularly good on hot, steamy days, when their names, such as Chubby Hubby and Phish Food, seem ironic and flavorful, depending on your point of view.

- **Best Drinks:** We get thirsty just thinking about the **San Juan Water & Beach Club,** Tartek St. 2 (ℂ **787/728-3666**), the ultra chic Isla Verde boutique hotel, where water gushes through the translucent walls of the lobby and elevator, which you take to **Wet.** You can have sushi under the stars at this rooftop bar, and any drink you want. The elegant African, world-beat decor, which matches the music, is perfect with the ocean breeze and the view that goes all the way down the coast. Grab a seat at the long bar or one of the comfortable lounge seats.

2 Old San Juan

For the locations of Old San Juan restaurants, see the map "Old San Juan Accommodations & Dining" on p. 111.

VERY EXPENSIVE

Aquaviva 𝕲𝕲 LATINO/SEAFOOD   Located on Calle Fortaleza near Plaza Colón at the entrance of Old San Juan, this cool, turquoise-colored restaurant features sometimes as frenetic action as the three large replicas of three *aquaviva* (jellyfish), quivering with illumination, each painstakingly manufactured from stained glass specifically for this site. Bioluminescent drinks are served at the bar, and the hip raw bar here features sushi and a host of ceviches, including one made with *dorado* and mango and lemon juices and another with marlin and garlic. The hot and cold appetizer towers are great for small groups (fried oysters, coco-flavored shrimp, fried octopus, and calamari). The best main courses include grilled fresh mahimahi with smoky shrimp, salsa, and coconut-poached yucca; seared medallions of halibut with a fondue of spinach and crabmeat; and a succulent version of paella garnished with seafood and pork sausage.

Calle Fortaleza 364. ℰ 787/722-0665. Reservations not accepted. Main courses $16–$45. AE, MC, V. Lunch daily 11am–4pm; dinner Mon–Wed 6–11pm, Thurs–Sat 6pm–midnight, Sun 4–11pm. Bus: Old Town Trolley.

Il Perugino ℰℰ ITALIAN   Located across from Hotel El Convento, this is Puerto Rico's finest Italian restaurant, serving an inspired cuisine that chef and owner Franco Seccarelli says he hopes is authentic to his homeland of Umbria. Our favorite home-made pastas include black fettuccine with a shellfish ragout or ricotta and spinach gnocchetti with fresh tomatoes. For a starter, opt for the shrimp salad with grilled zucchini, a sublime dish, as is another salad made with scallops and porcini mushrooms. Seccarelli shines with his pheasant breast alla Cacciatora and his pork filets flavored with an unusual combination of thyme and blueberries. We also raved about the rack of lamb with fresh herbs and a rich red-wine sauce. Homemade desserts are also succulent, and wine comes from a cellar in a converted dry well in the center of the restaurant. Service is impeccable and friendly.

Cristo St. 105. ℰ 787/722-5481. Reservations recommended. Main courses $29–$41. AE, DISC, MC, V. Thurs–Sat 11:30am–2:30pm; Tues–Sun 6:30–11pm. Bus: Old San Juan Trolley.

EXPENSIVE

Barú ℰ CARIBBEAN/MEDITERRANEAN   This is one of the most fashionable and popular of a wave of imaginative new restaurants in Old San Juan, with an attractive and hard-playing clientele, some of whom look like they walked out of one of those Hispanic soap operas. Named after an unspoiled island off the north coast of Colombia, a personal favorite of its Colombian-born owner, it occupies a stately look-ing, high-ceilinged space capped with massive timbers, fronted with a hyper-convivial mahogany bar, and decorated with paintings by such Colombia-born artistic luminaries as Botéro.

Many dishes are deliberately conceived as something midway between an appetizer and a main-course platter, so it's hard to know how much, or how many courses, to order. If unsure, ask your waitperson to guide you. Menu items include an unusual choice of five different kinds of carpaccio (tuna, halibut, salmon, beef, or Serrano ham). Ceviche of mahimahi is appropriately tart, appealingly permeated with citrus; and the marinated lamb chops with a paprika and pineapple mojo sauce are flavorful. Other culinary creations include almond-encrusted goat cheese with Jamaican jerk mango dip and yucca chips, and sliced filet mignon. Regrettably, the place is not cheap, and service is well intentioned but disorganized as the youthful staff maneuvers as best it can through the packed-in crowd.

Calle San Sebastián 150. ℰ 787/977-7107. Reservations recommended. Main courses $15–$28. AE, MC, V. Mon–Sat 6pm–3am; Sun 6pm–midnight. Bus: Old Town Trolley.

Carli Café Concierto ℰ INTERNATIONAL   This stylish restaurant is owned by Carli Muñoz. The gold disc hanging on the wall attests to Carli's success in his previous role as a pianist for the Beach Boys. Nowadays, Carli entertains his dinner guests nightly with a combination of standards, romantic jazz, and original material on his grand piano. Diners can sit outside on the Plazoleta, where they can enjoy a panoramic view of the bay, or they can eat inside against a backdrop of a tasteful decor of terra-cotta walls and black marble tables. The chef tempts visitors with an imaginative international menu, including such delights as plantain-crusted sea scallops with a coconut curry sauce. The filet of salmon and a mouthwatering rack of lamb are among the finest main dishes. The bar, with its mahogany and brass fittings, is an ideal spot to chill out. The concert starts every night at 8pm.

Edificio Banco Popular, Calle Tetuán 206, off Plazoleta Rafael Carrión. ✆ 787/725-4927. Reservations recommended. Main courses $16–$36. AE, V. Mon–Fri 3:30–11pm; Sat 4–11:30pm. Bus: M2 or M3.

Parrot Club ✿✿ NUEVO LATINO/CARIBBEAN   This bistro and bar, owned by husband-and-wife team Emilio Figueroa and Gigi Zafero, is one of the most sought-after restaurants in Old San Juan. The Nuevo Latino cuisine blends traditional Puerto Rican cookery with Spanish, Taíno, and African influences. The restaurant is set in a stately 1902 building that was originally a hair-tonic factory. Today you'll find a cheerful-looking dining room, where San Juan's mayor and the governor of Puerto Rico can sometimes be spotted, and a verdantly landscaped courtyard, where tables for at least 200 diners are scattered amid potted ferns, palms, and orchids. Live music (either Brazilian, salsa, or Latino jazz) is offered nightly as well as during the popular Sunday brunches.

Menu items are updated interpretations of old Puerto Rican specialties. They include an excellent ceviche of halibut, salmon, tuna, and mahimahi; delicious crab cakes; *criolla*-style flank steak; and pan-seared tuna served with a sauce made from dark rum and essence of oranges. Everybody's favorite drink is a "Parrot Passion," made from lemon-flavored rum, triple sec, oranges, and passion fruit.

Calle Fortaleza 363. ✆ 787/725-7370. Reservations not accepted. Main courses $18–$36 at dinner; $12–$20 at lunch. AE, DC, MC, V. Daily 11am–4pm and 6–11pm. Closed 2 weeks in Sept. Bus: Old Town Trolley.

Sofia ✿ ITALIAN   Although our favorite Italian restaurant in Old Town San Juan remains Il Perugino, this challenger also serves a finely honed cuisine, though it's a bit pricey, especially if you opt for the fresh seafood. Its interior, with its columns and arched doorways, evokes a trattoria deep in the heart of Rome. Red colors and exposed brick, as well as an interior courtyard, aid in the impression. Service is first-rate, as are the market-fresh ingredients, and many of the specialties are quintessentially Italian. The chef is justifiably proud of his chopino Sofia, served for two people. It's like a paella, but linguini is used instead of rice. The seared blackened tuna is also a perfect choice, and the classic saltimbocca alla romana (with veal and prosciutto flavored with sage and served in a buttery wine sauce) is another specialty. The beef dishes are good and tender, and are especially delectable when served in a chianti sauce. The pasta dishes are savory, and the pizza oven turns out lush, tasty pies.

Calle San Francisco 355. ✆ 787/721-0396. Reservations recommended at night. Main courses $20–$42; pizzas $12–$14. AE, DC, MC, V. Mon–Fri 11am–2:30pm and 5–9pm (until 10pm Fri); Sat 5–10pm.

Toro Salao ✿✿ SPANISH TAPAS   With dark wood interior and a Spanish colonial facade, bullfighting posters and splashes of red, this is the kind of place Ernest Hemingway would have written home about. Toro Salao, "the salty bull" in Spanish, is another restaurant by Emilio Figueroa and Gigi Zaferos (owners of the Parrot Club and Aguaviva, among others) that seamlessly matches the cuisine with the restaurant ambience. We gorged on a Spanish flatbread pizza with artichokes and Mediterranean olives; a papas bravas (spicy potatoes) redux that wasn't overly spicy; and seared

---

Tips Take a Strong Coffee Break

A coffee break in Old San Juan might last an afternoon. *Taza* (cup) after *taza* of Puerto Rico's rich brew might make you desert Jamaican Blue Mountain coffee or Hawaiian Kona forever. By law, Puerto Rican coffeehouses must serve coffee made from homegrown beans, most often from the mountains in the center of the island. For years we've taken our espresso—from early morning until our final "nightcap"—at **Cuatro Estaciones** (no phone), a rather shady kiosk in bustling Plaza de Armas. You'll get a quick jolt from this tasty brew, which attracts local java heads day and night.

---

octopus with sundried tomato vinaigrette. We also loved the crisp and clean mussels in a chunky green salsa and the sweet veal meatballs with romesco sauce and plantains. Full meals include paella seafood with chicken and sausage, seared pork with coriander *mojo*, and classic *churrasco*. Order a pitcher of sangria, among San Juan's finest. There are several inventive varieties, including a tropical fruit version, which add flavor without ever losing the essence of this Spanish tavern standard.

Calle Tetuan 367. © 787/722-3330. Reservations not accepted. Tapas $12–$25; main courses $22–$35. AE, MC, V. Mon–Sat 6pm–midnight. Bus: A5.

Trois Cent Onze (311) ✷✷ FRENCH   When the French and Puerto Rican owners of this place renovated this building in 1999, they discovered some of the most beautiful Moorish–Andalusian tilework in San Juan's Old Town buried beneath layers of later coverings. Because of those tiles, and because of the delicate Andalusian-style iron rosette above the door, they wisely decided to retain the area's Moorish embellishments during the reconfiguration of their restaurant's decor. What you'll get today is the premier French restaurant of San Juan, replete with a zinc bar near the entrance, a soaring and richly beamed ceiling, and decor in the Casbah of old Tangiers. The building was used as the photography studio that developed many of Puerto Rico's earliest movies. Colors, textures, and flavors combine here to produce an irresistible array of dishes. Menu items include a carpaccio of salmon marinated in citrus; sautéed sea scallops served with an almond-flavored butter sauce; mango and crabmeat salad; magret of duckling roasted with honey; and pork medallions served with caramelized onions, stewed white beans, and spicy *merguez* sausage.

Calle Fortaleza 311. © 787/725-7959. Reservations recommended. Main courses $19–$35. AE, MC, V. Tues–Thurs noon–2:30pm and 6:30–10pm; Fri–Sat noon–2:30pm and 6–11pm; Sun 5–10pm. Bus: Old Town Trolley, T2, or 2.

MODERATE

Al Dente SICILIAN/ITALIAN   Since the closing of some of its competitors in 2003, this is now the oldest continuously operated Italian restaurant in Puerto Rico, with a clientele that includes an awe-inspiring number of high-pressure lawyers, politicians, and judges every day at lunch, and a more leisurely crowd of friends and romantics every night at dinner. The venue includes a friendly and accommodating bar area near the entrance, a warm-toned color scheme of scarlets and blues, and a replica of a brightly painted Sicilian fishing boat—personally crafted by the owner—hanging on one of the walls. Sicily-born Giancarlo Amenta and his Puerto Rican wife Margie are the owners, fusing with skill the aesthetics of their respective countries. The relatively short list of culinary staples is enhanced with a changing array of daily specials, leading to a choice of dishes that's more varied than the relatively abbreviated menu might suggest. Your meal might include *osso buco,* house-made ravioli, rib-eye steak, several kinds of risotto (including versions with crayfish, Portobello mushrooms, or Parmesan cheese), calamari with polenta, and *arancini di spinachi fritti* (an old Sicilian specialty and one of the restaurant's bestsellers—spinach balls with rice, ricotta cheese, and pink sauce). Note the large-scale paintings that decorate the dining room. Executed by Margie Alcaraz Amenta herself, who will likely be on hand to greet you when you arrive, they're for sale, selling briskly at prices that range from between $2,000 and $4,500 each.

Calle Recinto Sur 309. (© 787/723-7303. Reservations recommended. Main courses $16–$23. AE, MC, V. Mon–Fri noon–10:30pm; Sat noon–11pm. Bus: Old Town Trolley.

Amadeus ☞ CARIBBEAN   Housed in a brick-and-stone building that was constructed in the 18th century by a wealthy merchant, Amadeus offers Caribbean ingredients with a nouvelle twist. The appetizers alone are worth the trip here, especially the Amadeus dumplings with guava sauce and arrowroot fritters. And try the smoked-salmon-and-caviar pizza. One zesty specialty is pork scaloppine with sweet-and-sour sauce.

Calle San Sebastián 106 (across from the Iglesia de San José). (© 787/722-8635. Reservations recommended. Main courses $8–$25. AE, DISC, MC, V. Mon 6pm–midnight; Tues–Sun 11am–midnight. Bus: Old Town Trolley, M2, M3, or A5.

Bodega Chic ☞ *Finds* FRENCH BISTRO   This small French/Algerian bistro blends delicious Mediterranean and Caribbean herbs and flavors, reasonable prices, and unpretentious friendly service. Chef and partner Christophe Gourdain trained with chef Jean-Georges Vonegerichten, and he learned well, apparently. Start out with the baked goat cheese croustillant with eggplant caviar and the grilled calamari. The hangar steak with sautéed potatoes and string beans is as close to perfection as the fresh mussels Provençal. The braised lamb shank is also worthy, and the roasted chicken breast in curry banana sauce is much better than it sounds. The high-ceilinged dining room and small adjacent bar room open out onto Calle Cristo just around the corner from the popular Calle San Sebastián. Desserts include a fantastic crème brûlée and warm chocolate cake.

Calle Cristo 51. (© 787/722-0124. Reservations recommended. Main courses $15–$26. AE, MC, V. Tues–Fri 6pm–midnight; Sun 11:30am–4pm; closed Mon. Bus: Old Town Trolley.

Burén ☞ *Value* INTERNATIONAL   This friendly, funky little place serves up unique, flavorful pizza, plus pastas and Latino grilled steaks—and inventive entrees are surprisingly sophisticated as well. The main bar and adjoining lounge area are brightly colored, while the back courtyard is all about earth tones. The *plátano* soup and *tostones* stuffed with shrimp in tomato sauce are excellent starters, as are the classic Greek salad and the spinach salad served with mozzarella cheese and passion fruit dressing. Pizza lovers will be happy with the usual ingredients, or some creative combinations: The Tamarindo combines proscuitto, sundried tomatoes, and manchego cheese, while the Las Monjas has feta cheese, black olives, tomatoes, and peppers. If you can resist the pizza, try the veal osso buco in a basil-rosemary emulsion served with fettuccini. Juicy pork medallions are served in a peppercorn pineapple sauce.

Calle Cristo 103. (© 787/977-5023. Reservations recommended Sat–Sun. Main courses $16–$26. AE, DC, DISC, MC, V. Daily 6–11pm. Bus: Old Town Trolley.

An Authentic *Criolla* Restaurant

When you've had too many hotel meals or patronized too many first-class restaurants and want something authentic, head for **El Jibarito**, Calle del Sol 280 (© **787/725-8375**), where locals flock for food like their mamas used to make.

Set within a residential section of Old San Juan that's a few blocks removed from the showcase-style tourist haunts, this is a bustling local restaurant that's known to virtually everyone in the Old City for its avid loyalty to the kind of cuisine that many *sanjuaneros* remember from their childhoods. Established as a testimonial to their rustic (*jíbaro*) backgrounds by Pedro and Aida Ruiz, it's a high-ceilinged, decent, and very clean enclave of brightly painted walls (mostly pinks and tones of green), paper napkins, solid porcelain, and completely unpretentious *criolla* cuisine. Menu items focus on rich, sometimes starchy, food that kept Puerto Rico alive throughout the early 20th century. Examples include fritters studded with pieces of seasoned pork, cube steak with onions, conch salad, oven-baked grouper, fried red snapper, chicken filets with garlic, and shrimp in garlic. A whopping portion of *mofongo* (chopped plantains with butter and seasonings) can be ordered as a folkloric side dish, and salad comes with every main course. Dessert might include a genuinely excellent wedge of coconut flan. Service is attentive, unpretentious, and extremely polite. Main courses cost $8 to $18 and are served daily from 10am to 9pm. American Express, Diners Club, MasterCard, and Visa are accepted.

Café Berlin INTERNATIONAL   Other than the hardworking staff, there's very little about this place that's particularly Hispanic. What you'll get is a corner of central Europe, identified by a *Jugendstil*-inspired sign, serving coffee, pastries, and a limited array of light platters such as pasta, on tiny marble-top tables like what you'd expect in Vienna. Paintings, all of them for sale, are displayed on scarlet-colored walls, and lavishly caloric pastries are arranged behind glass display cases. More substantial, rib-sticking fare includes salmon in orange- and garlic-flavored herb broth, scallops in pesto sauce, and turkey breast Stroganoff.

Plaza de Colón 407. © 787/722-5205. Main courses $8–$19. AE, MC, V. Mon–Fri 10am–10pm; Sat–Sun 8am–10pm. Bus: Old Town Trolley.

Caña PUERTO RICAN   Set close to the landmark Hotel El Convento, this cafe presents the kind of irreverent aura you'd expect within a hip and arts-conscious cafe in Madrid. There are tables set up on an outdoor terrace, a welcome separation from the congested sidewalk and street outside, a rectangular and granite-topped bar area, and a dining area tucked between the massive columns of the El Convento's 400-year-old masonry. The menu has recently refocused (with the cafe undergoing a renaming as well) on Puerto Rican cuisine, but its spirit and ownership remain. We loved the tropical roast pork loin, the whole red snapper in coconut sauce, and the chicken in white wine–garlic sauce. They make a yucca *mofongo*, called yuccafongo, that can be had as a side or stuffed with chicken or seafood in a *criolla* tomato sauce as an entree.

There are also sandwiches, sushi, and shrimp Creole, among other dishes. Despite the tasty food, many clients come here strictly for drinks. Tuesday nights attract a largely gay clientele.

Calle Cristo 100. © **787/723-9200.** Reservations recommended. Main courses $17–$26. AE, MC, V. Daily 11am–2am. Bus: Old Town Trolley.

Dragonfly ✶✶ LATIN/ASIAN FUSION   One of San Juan's hottest restaurants, the place has been compared to both an Old San Francisco bordello and a Shanghai opium den, descriptions that evoke as much the lusty appeal and addictive power of its cuisine as the red-walled interior, a world of fringed lamps and gilded mirrors behind beaded curtains. It's good for a late meal, as the portion sizes, called *platos* or plates, are somewhere between appetizers and entrees. We always order the marinated churrasco and the pork and plantain dumplings with orange dipping sauce. Other standouts: seared tuna in green peppercorn sauce, tempura rock shrimp tacos with chunky salsa, and the Chino Latino lo-mein. This is the island's first Latin–Asian menu, and it remains one of the best anywhere. An expansion has added a lounge and full sushi bar to the original dining room, but the crowds keep filling the place, one of the city's trendiest places for a night out.

Calle Fortaleza 364. © **787/977-3886.** Reservations not accepted. Main courses $8–$30. AE, MC, V. Mon–Wed 6–11pm; Thurs–Sat 6pm–midnight. Bus: A5 or T1.

El Patio de Sam AMERICAN/PUERTO RICAN   Established in 1953, this joint has survived several generations of clients, who came here for booze, fantastic juicy burgers, Puerto Rican food, and dialogue. There is the unmistakable aura of pop, youth culture, Margaritaville, and college-age drinking ethos. The setting includes an exterior space with tables that overlook a historic statue of Ponce de León and a well-known church, and a labyrinth of dark, smoked-stained inner rooms with high-beamed ceilings and lots of potted plants. Dining usually occurs in a skylit garden-style courtyard in back where there is no view but a welcome sense of calm. In addition to those burgers, you can also order more sophisticated dishes such as Puerto Rican–style fried pork, ceviche, shellfish paella, chicken and rice, and *churrasco* (Argentine-style grilled meats).

Calle San Sebastián 102 (across from the Iglesia de San José). © **787/723-1149.** Sandwiches, burgers, and salads $9–$11; platters $13–$35. AE, DISC, MC, V. Daily noon–1am. Bus: Old Town Trolley.

El Picoteo ✶✶ *Moments* SPANISH   Spilling across a front and interior terrace overlooking the courtyard of the historic El Convento Hotel, this is the best place in the Old City to savor some drinks and tapas, while watching the action near Calle San Sebastián. On most nights, there's a parade of people walking up and down Calle Cristo in front of the restaurant, as they go back and forth to the bars and restaurants just up the hill. We love the spicy potatoes *(papas bravas),* shrimp in garlic sauce, and the brick oven pizza, but there are also full meals like seafood paella. With 80 tapas to choose from, there's also real Spanish flavor here, in such dishes as garbanzo salad, sausages, various ceviches, fresh octopus, and the best selection of cheese in the city. The setting amidst Spanish colonial facades and wildly blooming bougainvillea is one of the Old City's most charmed. It's equally inviting for a weekend lunch. Try the champagne-laced sangria. Dinner is festive, accompanied by salsa and lights in the courtyard.

In El Convento hotel, Calle del Cristo 100. © **787/723-9202.** Reservations recommended. Main courses $6–$17; paella $20–$35. AE, MC, V. Tues–Sun noon–midnight. Bus: Old Town Trolley.

La Mallorquina ⚜ PUERTO RICAN   Founded in 1848, this old favorite has been run by the Rojos family since 1900. If you look carefully at the floor adjacent to the old-fashioned mahogany bar, you'll see the building's original gray-and-white marble flooring, which the owners are laboriously restoring, square foot by square foot, to its original condition. Lunches here tend to attract local office workers; dinners are more cosmopolitan and more leisurely, with many residents of the Condado and other modern neighborhoods selecting this place specifically because of its old-fashioned, old-world charm. The food has changed little here over the decades, with special emphasis on *asopao* made with rice and chicken, shrimp, or lobster and shrimp. *Arroz con pollo* is almost as popular. Begin with either garlic soup or gazpacho, end with flan, and you'll have eaten a meal that's authentically Puerto Rican.

Calle San Justo 207. ✆ 787/722-3261. Reservations not accepted at lunch, recommended at dinner. Dinner main courses $15–$36 (lobster is priciest). Lunch starts at $7.95. AE, MC, V. Mon–Sat 12:30–10pm. Closed Sept. Bus: Old Town Trolley.

Makarios GREEK/LEBANESE   Set above a sometimes raucous cafe-bar, a few steps from Piers 1, 2, and 3 in Old San Juan, this is the only restaurant in Old San Juan that serves Lebanese and, to a lesser degree, Greek food. To reach it, you'll climb a flight of stairs immediately adjacent to the entrance to reach the second-floor dining room. Here, beneath a gracefully arched ceiling of a dining room trimmed in varnished wood, you can order good-tasting dishes that include baba ghanouj, hummus, falafel, baked halibut, salmon with honey-mustard dressing, grilled shrimp, grilled snapper, shish kebab, and couscous. On Friday and Saturday there is belly dancing from 9 to 11pm. The high-energy cafe is on the establishment's street level, where blaring music combines traditional Greek and Arabic rhythms with a danceable house and garage beat. It also serves from a menu that includes simple selections from the dinner menu (kebabs, hummus, falafel, etc.) as well as tasty brick oven pizza. There's a definite Middle Eastern vibe at work: An Arabian MTV-like station blares on the video screens and there's fast communications among the mostly Jerusalem-born staff. Diners can eat inside at the bar or an adjacent lounge area, or on the much quieter but far from serene outside terrace.

Calle Tetuán 361. ✆ 787/723-8653. Reservations not necessary. Main courses $15–$24. AE, DISC, MC, V. Daily noon–midnight (till 3am Fri–Sat). Bus: M2 or M3.

Old Harbor Brewery Steak and Lobster House ⚜ AMERICAN   San Juan's only microbrewery also has top-drawer tavern fare in an upscale mariner setting. Brewmaster Brad Mortensen handcrafts five distinct house beers, as well as seven seasonal beers, on the premises in state-of-the-art brewing facilities. The restaurant specializes in top-quality steaks and fresh Puerto Rican spiny lobster. The cuts are served steakhouse-style with a choice of sauces (we recommend the mushroom and chimichurri) and a la carte sides (our favorites are the Lyonnise potatoes and asparagus with béarnaise). The hanging tender steak was as promised, and the New York Strip was flavorful and cooked to perfection. We've grown used to the taste of Caribbean lobster, which is lighter than Maine lobster, and the ones here are among the best we tried. Go with the citrus beurre blanc sauce rather than the coconut, almond-spiced rum. We always start with the rich French onion or lobster bisque soup, probably because both are so hard to find here. The crisp Santo Viejo pilsner and the flavorful Old Harbor pale ale are our favorites. The restaurant dates to the 1920s, when it housed the New York Federal Bank, and it was beautifully restored before opening in 2005. A classic tavern setup surrounds the elegant brew vats, but the place is formal, with fully dressed tables, classic black and white tiles, and metal and wooden finishings.

Calle Tizol 202 (near Recinto Sur). ✆ **787/721-2100**. Reservations recommended. Platters and main courses $13–$38. AE, MC, V. Daily 8am–7pm. Bus: Old Town Trolley.

Ostra Cosa ⭐ *Finds* ECLECTIC/SEAFOOD   This artfully promoted restaurant has an ambience that is one of the most sensual and romantic in Old San Juan. Former advertising executive Alberto Nazario, a lifestyle guru who mingles New Age thinking with culinary techniques to promote love, devotion, and a heightened sexuality, created Ostra Cosa. Couples dine beneath a massive quenepe tree—waiters will tell you to hug the tree and make a wish—in a colonial courtyard surrounded by a 16th-century building that was once the home of the colony's governor. The atmosphere, enhanced by domesticated quail and chirping tree frogs, will make you feel far removed from the cares of the city. Featured foods are high in phosphorus, zinc, and flavor, designed to promote an "eat-up, dress-down experience." The ceviche is superb; the small grilled (still-shelled) prawns were tasty but difficult (and a bit messy). But it is the conch, known as Caribbean Viagra, that rates "Wow!" or "Ay Ay Ay!"

Calle del Cristo 154. ✆ **787/722-2672**. Reservations recommended. Main courses $18–$29. AE, MC, V. Sun–Wed noon–10pm; Fri–Sat noon–11pm. Bus: Old Town Trolley.

Tantra ⭐ *Value* INDO-LATINO   Set in the heart of "restaurant row" on Calle Fortaleza, it has become famous for a sophisticated fusion of Latino with South Indian cuisine. Its chef and owner, Indian-born Ramesh Pillai, oversees a blend of slow-cooked tandoori cuisine from South India with Puerto Rico–derived spices, flavors, and ingredients. All of this occurs within a warm, candlelit environment that focuses on Indian handicrafts and Hindu and Buddhist symbols.

An appropriate way to begin a meal here is to order one of the best martinis we've ever had—a concoction flavored with cinnamon and cloves. Menu highlights include sesame masala-crusted sushi tuna with peanut sauce, fried coconut sesame jumbo shrimp with Indian noodles, chicken tikka masala with nan (flatbread), and rice and chicken rolls with passion-fruit sauce. One of the establishment's bestsellers is an absolutely brilliant version of tandoori chicken that combines the traditional Indian recipe with manchego and mozzarella cheese, guyaba fruit, guava-flavored dip, and nan. There's also belly-dancing shows on many nights and huge water pipes in a lounge area where you can buy legal weed to puff.

Calle Fortaleza 356. ✆ **787/977-8141**. Reservations only for groups. Main courses $13–$19. AE, MC, V. Mon 3pm–3am; Tues–Sat noon–3pm; Sun noon–midnight. Bus: T1 or 2.

INEXPENSIVE

Café Puerto Rico CREOLE/PUERTO RICAN   On the Plaza de Colón, this restaurant offers balconies overlooking one of the most charming of Old Town squares. The setting is colonial, with beamed ceilings and tile floors, and with ceiling fans whirling overhead. The menu features hearty regional fare. Tasty options include fried fish filet, paella, and lobster cooked as you like it. Eggplant parmigiana is an excellent vegetarian option, and you might also order eye round stuffed with ham in Creole sauce. Of course, if you're getting hungry during a day of strolling Old San Juan's windy streets, don't wait for dinner—you'll enjoy a lunch break here, too.

Calle O'Donnell 208. ✆ **787/724-2281**. Main courses $9–$20. AE, MC, V. Mon–Sat 11am–11pm; Sun 11m–9pm. Bus: Old Town Trolley.

La Bombonera ★ *Value* PUERTO RICAN   This place offers exceptional value in its homemade pastries, well-stuffed sandwiches, and endless cups of coffee—and it has done so since 1902. Its atmosphere evokes turn-of-the-20th-century Castille transplanted to the New World. The food is authentically Puerto Rican, homemade, and inexpensive, with regional dishes such as rice with squid, roast leg of pork, and seafood *asopao* (a thick rice soup). For dessert, you might select an apple, pineapple, or prune pie, or one of many types of flan. Service is polite, if a bit rushed, and the place fills up quickly at lunchtime.

Calle San Francisco 259. © **787/722-0658.** Reservations recommended. American breakfast $4.50–$6.45; main courses $6–$18. AE, MC, V. Daily 7:30am–8pm. Bus: Old Town Trolley.

Patio del Nispero INTERNATIONAL   Surrounded by the soaring atrium of Old San Juan's most historic hotel, this restaurant provides a charming oasis of calm and quiet. Pots of verdant plants thrive under the direct sunlight of the open sky, and big canvas umbrellas shield diners from the rain. No one will mind if you order just a drink (the daiquiris are excellent) or a cup of coffee while resting after a tour of the Old Town or the cathedral next door. But if you want food, consider filet of red snapper with Creole sauce, chicken breast with chestnuts and mushrooms in cognac sauce, broiled veal chop with Marsala sauce, and one of a wide selection of desserts. Live music is featured 2 evenings a week.

In the El Convento hotel, Calle del Cristo 100. © **787/723-9020.** Reservations not necessary. Sandwiches $9.50–$12; platters $14–$24. AE, DC, MC, V. Daily 11:30am–3:30pm. Bus: Old Town Trolley.

Raíces ★ PUERTO RICAN   Don't let the apparent touristy trappings fool you; it's not the cheapest meal in town, but it's among the tastiest and most authentic, and we recommend it for a big taste of Puerto Rican cuisine. These are Caguas boys in the kitchen, so enjoy the rustic Puerto Rican setting—beautifully outfitted with local arts and crafts—and the waitresses and waiters decked out in the beautiful folkloric dress. It's a perfect fit for its location near the cruise ship docks, but the first location was in Caguas, which is decidedly untouristy. The "typical festival" combines a number of classic island treats, like meat turnovers, stuffed fried plantain fritters, codfish fritters, and mashed cassava, but you'll also want to try the delicious plantain soup. The stuffed *mofongo* entrees are the real specialty here; along with the typical stuffed chicken or shrimp, the options range to breaded pork, skirt steak, and Creole-style mahimahi. If you want hearty fare, the chicken or shrimp *asopao* is another option. The coconut flan and guava cheesecake do not disappoint. Traditional Puerto Rican music, with occasional live entertainment, further compliments the experience.

Calle Recinto Sur 315. © **787/289-2121.** Reservations not necessary. Main courses $10–$26. AE, MC, V. Mon–Fri 11am–4pm, 6–10pm; Sat 11am–11pm; Sun noon–11pm. Bus: Old Town Trolley.

3 Puerta de Tierra

For the locations of restaurants in Puerta de Tierra, see the map "Puerta de Tierra, Miramar, Condado & Ocean Park Accommodations & Dining" on p. 115.

EXPENSIVE

Morton's of Chicago ★★ STEAKHOUSE   When it comes to steaks, Ruth's Chris Steak House in Isla Verde enjoys a slight edge, but otherwise Morton's is king of the steaks and other choice meats. The chain of gourmet steakhouses was founded in 1978 by Arnie Morton, former executive vice president of the *Playboy* empire. Beef lovers, from Al Gore to Liza Minnelli, know they'll get quality meats perfectly cooked at Morton's. Carts laden with everything from prime Midwestern beefsteaks to succulent lamb or veal chops are wheeled around for your selection. And Morton's has the island's best prime rib. This is a place where the bartenders make stiff drinks, and the waiters tempt you with their fresh fish, lobster, and chicken dishes. The vegetables here are among the freshest in the area. The house specialty is a 24-oz. porterhouse. Appetizers include perfectly cooked jumbo shrimp with cocktail sauce and smoked Pacific salmon. For dessert, we always gravitate to one of the soufflés, such as raspberry or Grand Marnier.

In the Caribe Hilton, Calle Los Rosales. (✆ 787/977-6262. Reservations required. Main courses $20–$40. AE, DC, DISC, MC, V. Daily 5–11pm. Bus: B21.

MODERATE

Madrid-San Juan SPANISH   This restaurant is the newest eatery within the mega-compound known as the Caribe Hilton (p. 114). Its decor, especially that of its baronial-looking dining room in back, emulates that of a gracious and rather formal tasca in Spain, replete with Serrano hams hanging above the bar, a roster of oil paintings (many of which are for sale), a scarlet-covered dining room which you might have imagined as a *tableaux* within a still-life by Goya, and rack upon rack of wine. There's something big, generous, and well-mannered about this place, as a quick perusal of the list of tapas (both hot and cold) and the conventional lunch or dinner menu will quickly show. Highlights include piquillo peppers stuffed with pulverized codfish; fried plantain with smoked salmon; codfish fritters; *fabada asturianas* (a well-seasoned and soupy version of stew that combines fava beans, sausages, and ham); fried fresh anchovies; and chorizo sausages in red-wine sauce. Main courses include breast of chicken in garlic sauce; filet mignon with manchego cheese and Serrano ham; thin-sliced filets of beef with onions; *asopao de mariscos; mofongo* stuffed with shrimp; and halibut steak garnished with shrimp, mushrooms, and raisin sauce.

In the Caribe Hilton, Calle Los Rosales. (✆ 787/721-0303. Reservations recommended. Tapas $6.50–$15; main courses $21–$35. AE, DC, DISC, MC, V. Mon–Thurs 11:30am–midnight; Fri–Sun 11:30am–1am. Bus: B21.

Palmeras 🍴 🧒 INTERNATIONAL   Every Sunday the Hilton's brunch captivates the imagination of island residents and U.S. visitors with its combination of excellently prepared food, glamour, and entertainment. There's a clown to keep the children amused, as well as live music on the bandstand for anyone who cares to dance. Champagne is included in the price. Food is arranged at several different stations: Puerto Rican dishes, seafood, paella, ribs, cold cuts, steaks, pastas, and salads. Although Sunday is the most festive time to visit, Palmeras prides itself on serving the biggest and most elaborate breakfast buffet in Puerto Rico on any morning. Another lavish buffet is the Friday-night seafood fiesta. On other nights dinner is a la carte. Specialties include pastas, paellas, chicken, and cheese quesadillas, along with an array of other international food.

In the Caribe Hilton, Calle Los Rosales. (✆ 787/721-0303. Reservations recommended for Sun brunch and Fri night. Breakfast buffet $18 daily, $30 Sun; lunch buffet $21 daily; main courses $12–$26. AE, DC, DISC, MC, V. Daily 6–11am, 12:30–3:30pm, and 5–11pm (until midnight Fri–Sat). Bus: 21.

INEXPENSIVE

El Hamburger 🍴 BURGERS   This no-frills burger stand offers tasty grilled burgers and hot dogs, cold beer, and perfectly golden french fries and onion rings. From its perch overlooking the Atlantic on the oceanfront drive into San Juan, the grill has become a late-night local favorite for those leaving the bars of Old San Juan, and is also popular for a bite during work or after the beach. A really good, cheap opportunity to soak up some real local atmosphere, the ramshackle wooden establishment is the kind of burger joint that has disappeared throughout much of the United States with the advent of the modern fast-food restaurant. One of its joys lives on here with a selection of condiments, from onions to relish to thick tomatoes to pickles, which is brought to your table with your burger. There's a patch of palm trees on the undeveloped coastal bluff across the street, and the ocean breeze flows all through the white wooden building. It's always packed, but service is still super fast and the conversation animated.

Muñoz Rivera 402. ⓒ 787/721-4269. Reservations not accepted. Burgers from $3.50. No credit cards. Sun–Thurs 11am–11pm; Fri–Sat 11am–1am. Bus: A-5, M-1.

4 Condado

For the locations of Condado restaurants, see the map "Puerta de Tierra, Miramar, Condado & Ocean Park Accommodations & Dining" on p. 115.

VERY EXPENSIVE

Budatai 𝒦𝒦𝒦 LATIN/ASIAN   The new home of Puerto Rico's "Iron Chef" mixes local flavors with Asian ingredients to deliver one of San Juan's finest dining experiences. Scrumptiously situated in an Art Deco town house overlooking an oceanfront park at the heart of Condado's redevelopment revival, Budatai's muted brown interior is as stylish as the designer boutiques surrounding it. With wall-sized windows inside and a rooftop terrace, diners have great views and are pampered with oversized tables and leather chairs. Chef Roberto Trevino, who fell just short against Mario Batali on the Food Network's "Iron Chef America" (the secret ingredient was catfish), reworks the Nuevo Latino and Asian fusion concepts he developed at Old San Juan's Parrot Club, Dragonfly, and Aguaviva restaurants and kicks up the portion sizes. Get started with the sesame crusted pork-wrapped asparagus with a soy mayonnaise, an explosion of flavor and texture, or if sushi's your thing, the geisha roll—lobster, cream cheese, jicama, and meringue kisses. The soy-glazed salmon with coconut hash main course artfully balances the salty and sweet, while the veal sirloin with lobster mashed Asian potatoes is as rich as it sounds. Skip the lo mein with chicharon de pollo and the Karate pork chop, which are not bad, just ordinary. The waitstaff is friendly, efficient, and knowledgeable about the menu and extensive wine list. The second floor bar and lounge is a hotspot for the city's young and beautiful, especially on weekends.

Av. Ashford 1056, Condado. ⓒ 787/725-6919. Main courses $24–$35. AE MC, V. Mon–Sat 6am–6pm; Sun 11:30am–10 p.m.; Mon–Weds 11:30am–11pm; Thurs–Sat 11:30am–midnight. Bus: Old Town Trolley.

Ramiro's 𝒦 SPANISH/INTERNATIONAL   This restaurant boasts the most imaginative menu on the Condado. You might begin with breadfruit *mille-feuille* with local crabmeat and avocado. For your main course, any fresh fish or meat can be charcoal-grilled for you on request. Some of the latest specialties include grilled salmon on a bed of black rice and a Spanish prawn sauce, and a tantalizing roast duckling with a kumquat sauce. Among the many homemade desserts are caramelized mango on puff pastry with strawberry-and-guava sauce, and "four seasons" chocolate.

Av. Magdalena 1106. ⓒ 787/721-9049. Reservations recommended off season, required in winter. Main courses $27–$39. AE, MC, V. Sun–Fri noon–3pm and 6:30–11pm; Sat 6–10pm. Bus: A7, T1, or M2.

EXPENSIVE

Ajili Mójili *☞* PUERTO RICAN/CREOLE   This restaurant serves *comida criolla,* the starchy, down-home cuisine that developed on the island a century ago. It's housed in a huge two-story building on the Condado Lagoon. Locals come here for a taste of the food they enjoyed at their mother's knee, like *mofongo* (green plantain casserole stuffed with veal, chicken, shrimp, or pork), *arroz con pollo* (chicken and rice), *medallones de cerdo encebollado* (pork loin sautéed with onions), *carne mechada* (beef rib-eye stuffed with ham), and *lechon asado con maposteado* (roast pork with rice and beans). Wash it all down with an ice-cold bottle of local beer. The staff will eagerly describe menu items in colloquial English.

Av. Ashford 1006. ℂ 787/725-9195. Reservations recommended. Main courses $18–$39; lunch $13–$26. AE, DISC, MC, V. Mon–Thurs 11:45am–3pm and 6–10pm; Fri noon–3pm and 6–11pm; Sat 11:45am–3:30pm and 6–11pm; Sun 12:30–4pm and 6–10pm. Bus: B21.

Bodega Compostela *☞☞* TAPAS/WINE CELLAR   This established Galician restaurant, which for years has served the finest Spanish food in the capital, was reborn this year as a chic wine and *tapas* bar without losing anything in the transition. Diners walk through an accompanying wine cellar, with a translucent floor over corks, to a long bar area, or retreat back to the dining room. There are over 50 *tapas,* or appetizers, served here, ranging from crispy goat cheese–mesclun salad to lentil stew with chorizo and pancetta to octopus carpaccio with sundried tomatoes. Seafood selections are plentiful, but we also gorged on the red pepper stuffed with barbecued Spanish sausage and potato stuffed with lamb shank confit. For those wanting more traditional meals, Compostela still offers the outstanding dishes grounded in Spanish traditions that garnered it such a strong reputation over the years, like seared tuna with apple julienne and couscous, or a large platter of rice with veal, pork, sausage, rabbit, and chicken for two. There's a daily dessert special. The wine cellar, comprising some 10,000 bottles, is one of the most impressive in San Juan.

Av. Condado 106. ℂ 787/724-6099. Reservations required. Tapas $3–$26; main courses $34–$45. AE, DC, MC, V. Mon–Fri noon–3pm; Mon–Sat 6:30–10:30pm. Bus: M2.

Niché *☞☞ Finds* LATIN FUSION   Just inside an Asian garden, this small restaurant makes a big impression, wowing guests with its boldly modern, yet natural design, and a menu as awesome in taste as audacity. The single-room restaurant is outfitted with a small bar and tables with seating for 20 or so diners. Its spare design, employing natural wood, glass, and metal, makes it feel much bigger than it is. Strolling through the lobby of the quiet guesthouse on a residential block to get here, we at first felt as if we stumbled onto a fabulous party just steps from the choicest beach in Condado. Chef Juan Camacho delivers dishes as awe-inspiring as the surroundings, preparing world cuisine heavy on rare meats and seafood with down-home Puerto Rican flavor. We stayed away from the rabbit, ostrich, and boar that our friend Thelma swears by. The meat we tried, liked the trio of Latin sausages appetizer, was excellent, however. If you like octopus, the appetizer with smoked paprika olive oil is excellent, as are the lobster-pumpkin saffron tarts. For the main event (what entrees are called here) we recommend From East to West Pasta, the filet mignon cinnamon kebab, and a shrimp sugar cane kebab on a bed of island pesto linguini. We also loved that Puerto Rican classic, the red snapper served with *mofongo.* The ostrich, if you dare, is rosewater marinated and served with risotto with green grapes and prosciutto. The Kobe churrasco is among the best in town, done straight up, with chef-special chimichurri sauce and fries.

At the Acacia Boutique Hotel, Calle Taft 8. © 787/725-0669. Reservations recommended. Main courses $20–$40. AE, MC, V. Sun–Sat 6–11pm. Bus: A5.

Ristorante Tuscany ⊛⊛ NORTHERN ITALIAN   This is the showcase restaurant of one of the most elaborate hotel reconstructions in the history of Puerto Rico, and the kitchen continues to rack up culinary awards. Notable entrees include grilled veal chops with shallots and glaze of Madeira, and grilled chicken breast in cream sauce with chestnuts, asparagus, and brandy, surrounded with fried artichokes. The seafood selections are excellent, especially the fresh red snapper sautéed in olive oil, garlic, parsley, and lemon juice. The risottos prepared al dente in the traditional northern Italian style are the finest on the island, especially the one made with seafood and herbs. The cold and hot appetizers are virtual meals unto themselves, with such favorites as grilled polenta with sausages or fresh clams and mussels simmered in herb-flavored tomato broth.

In the San Juan Marriott Resort, Av. Ashford 1309. © 787/722-7000. Reservations recommended. Main courses $20–$34. AE, DC, DISC, MC, V. Daily 6–11pm. Bus: B21.

Zabó ⊛ AMERICAN/PUERTO RICAN/INTERNATIONAL   This restaurant enjoys citywide fame, thanks to its blend of bucolic charm and superb innovative food. It's set in a dignified villa that provides some low-rise dignity in a sea of skyscraping condos. The creative force here is owner and chef/culinary director Paul Carroll, who built the place from its origins as a simple deli into one of the most sought-after restaurants on the Condado. Menu items fuse the cuisines of the Mediterranean, the Pacific Rim, and the Caribbean into a collection that includes dishes such as blini stuffed with medallions of lobster with ginger, thyme, and beurre blanc; carpaccio of salmon with mesclun salad and balsamic vinegar; and baked chorizo stuffed with mushrooms, sherry, paprika, and cheddar. The black-bean soup is among the very best in Puerto Rico, served with parboiled cloves of garlic marinated in olive oil that melt in your mouth like candy. The restaurant also often has special events such as weekend barbecues, which it serves in the villa's charming side yard.

Calle Candina 14 (entrance via alleyway leading from Av. Ashford between aves. Washington and Cervantes). © 787/725-9494. Reservations recommended. Snacks $6; main courses $15–$35. AE, MC, V. Tues–Thurs 6–10pm; Fri–Sat 7–11pm. Bus: B21.

MODERATE

Most main courses in the restaurants below are at the low end of the price scale. These restaurants each have only two or three dishes that are expensive, almost invariably involving shellfish.

The Ambassador Grill PUERTO RICAN/ECLECTIC   This comfortable and cozy eatery for many years was the most famous Howard Johnson's in the Caribbean. It attracts prestigious politicians and financiers (many luminaries live nearby and consider it their neighborhood diner). Depending on the time of day, you can be served pancakes, omelets, muffins, hash browns, and sausages; or you can order lunch and dinner foods like fish fries, teriyaki steaks, clam platters, and an array of sandwiches and burgers, as well as typical Puerto Rican dishes.

In the Radisson Ambassador Plaza Hotel, Av. Ashford 1369. © 787/721-7300. Reservations not necessary. Breakfast $7–$11; main courses $8–$21. AE, MC, V. Mon–Thurs 6:30am–2pm and 5–11pm; Fri–Sun 6:30am–11pm. Bus: B21 or C10.

Great Taste 🍴🍴CHINESE   This is the place where the island's Chinese community goes to eat dim sum, and with good reason, as this restaurant has been serving up among the best Chinese food on the island for decades. About five years ago, it also installed a sushi bar and added a few menu items. Set in a 1970s condominium with a tattered facade, the dining room is spacious, comfortable, and bright, with Japanese prints, huge lobster tanks, and an enviable view over the Condado lagoon. We come here for the Chinese, and everything we've tried from the cashew chicken to the Peking duck to the shrimp in lobster sauce is excellent, but we really come for the dim sum: the sticky rice in lotus leaf, skewered beef, and steamed vegetable dumplings. Sunday specials attract droves of diners from the local Chinese community and elsewhere with a refined sense of what good dim sum is all about.

Av. Ashford 1018 ✆ 787/721-8111. Reservations recommended. Main courses $8–$45. AE, MC, V. Daily 11 am–midnight. Bus: B21.

INEXPENSIVE

Café del AngelCREOLE/PUERTO RICAN   Don't come here for the decor. The juice bar up front looks like it was transported from Miami's Flagler Street in 1950, and the terrace furniture won't compel you to get *Architectural Digest* on the phone. If indeed there is an "angel," as the cafe's name suggests, it is in the kitchen. The chef serves remarkably good food at affordable prices. The place has been in operation for more than a decade. Paintings and figures of its namesake angels decorate the dining room. Some 100 hungry diners can be fed here at one time, in a relaxed atmosphere that is welcoming and friendly. The service is also efficient. Prepare for some real island flavor, as in the traditional *mofongo relleno con camarones,* which is sautéed, mashed plantain with shrimp. You can order a generous helping of tender beefsteak sautéed with onions and peppers or a perfectly grilled chicken. *Pastel,* a kind of creamy polenta of cornmeal, is served with many dishes, and the fresh garlic bread is complimentary.

Av. Ashford 1106. ✆ 787/643-7594. Reservations not necessary. Main courses $7–$20. AE, DC, MC, V. Wed–Mon 11am–10pm. Bus: B21.

Cielito Lindo *Value* MEXICAN   One of the most likable things about this restaurant is the way it retains low prices and an utter lack of pretension, despite the expensive Condado real estate that surrounds it. Something about it might remind you of a low-slung house in Puebla, Mexico, home of owner Jaime Pandal, who maintains a vigilant position from a perch at the cash register. Walls are outfitted with an intriguing mix of Mexican arts and crafts and ads for popular tequilas and beer. None of the selections has changed since the restaurant was founded, a policy that long-term clients find reassuring. The place is mobbed, especially on weekends, with those looking for heaping portions of well-prepared, standardized Mexican food. Examples include fajitas of steak or chicken; strips of filet steak sautéed with green peppers and onions, covered with tomatoes and spicy gravy; enchiladas of chicken or cheese, covered with cheese and served with sour cream; and several kinds of tacos.

Av. Magdalena 1108. ✆ 787/723-5597. Reservations recommended for dinner. Main courses $5–$20. AE, MC, V. Mon–Fri 11am–11pm; Sat–Sun 5–11pm. Bus: B21 or C10.

Danny's International RestaurantPIZZA CAFÉ   Don't expect atmosphere, but you can sit at the tables out on the front terrace and watch the street parade down Condado's main drag. The pizzas are thick and tasty, and there's an extensive selection, including the "mariscos," which has mussels, calamari, shrimp, octopus and a special sauce, and the *bomba,* with local sausage, olives, hot peppers, and blue cheese. There's also a complete menu of hot Italian subs and cold subs, a variety of cheese steaks, and burgers and club sandwiches. Skip the few Italian entree selections, which compare to the offerings right across the street. The pizza is excellent, however. The place is also one of the better restaurants serving American-style breakfasts near major area lodgings like the Marriott and the Ambassador and guesthouses like El Canario. Tables are spread throughout a single dining room, and there's a round bar filled with newspapers and outfitted with televisions you can eat at from morning to night.

Av. Ashford 1351. ℂ **787/724-0501** or 724-2734. Reservations not accepted. Main courses $7–$15. AE, MC, V. Daily 7am–1am. Bus: B21 or C10.

Via Appia ℛ PIZZA/ITALIAN   A favorite of *sanjuaneros* with a craving for Italian, Via Appia offers praiseworthy food at affordable prices. Its pizzas are among the best on the island, and basic pasta dishes like baked ziti, lasagna, and spaghetti taste like somebody's Italian grandmother prepared them. However, the restaurant really shows its stuff with dishes like clams posillipo, veal and peppers, broiled sirloin with redwine mushroom sauce, and the delectable chicken francaise. The house sangria is tasty and packs a punch, and the house wine is tasty and helps keep a meal here in the budget category. A wine bar and more formal dining room have been added to the original deli-like main building, but the place to sit is on one of the two terraces fronting the establishment.

Av. Ashford 1350. ℂ **787/725-8711**. Pizza and main courses $9–$16. AE, MC, V. Mon–Fri 11am–11pm; Sat–Sun 11am–midnight. Bus: B21 or C10.

5 Miramar

For the locations of restaurants in Miramar, see the map "Puerta de Tierra, Miramar, Condado & Ocean Park Accommodations & Dining" on p. 115.

EXPENSIVE

Augusto's Cuisine ℛℛℛ FRENCH/INTERNATIONAL   With its European flair, this is one of the most elegant and glamorous restaurants in Puerto Rico. It is set on the lobby level of a 15-story hotel in Miramar. Menu items are concocted from strictly fresh ingredients, including such dishes as lobster risotto; rack of lamb with aromatic herbs and fresh garlic; an oft-changing cream-based soup of the day (one of the best is corn and fresh oyster soup); and a succulent version of medallions of veal Rossini style, prepared with foie gras and Madeira sauce. The wine list is one of the most extensive on the island.

In the Hotel Excelsior, Av. Ponce de León 801. ℂ **787/725-7700**. Reservations recommended. Main courses $24–$38. AE, MC, V. Tues–Fri noon–3pm; Tues–Sat 7–9:30pm. Bus: A5.

Chayote ℛ PUERTO RICAN/INTERNATIONAL   The cuisine of this restaurant is among the most innovative in San Juan. It draws local business leaders, government officials, and visiting celebs like Sylvester Stallone and Melanie Griffith. It's an artsy, modern, basement-level bistro in a surprisingly obscure hotel (the Olimpo). The restaurant changes its menu every 3 months, but you might find appetizers like a yucca turnover stuffed with crabmeat and served with mango and papaya chutney, or ripe plantain stuffed with chicken and served with fresh tomato sauce. For a main dish, you might try red-snapper filet with citrus vinaigrette made of passion fruit, orange, and lemon. An exotic touch appears in the pork filet seasoned with dried fruits and spices in tamarind sauce and served with green banana and taro-root timbale. To finish off your meal, there's nothing better than the mango flan served with macerated strawberries.

In the Olimpo Hotel, Av. Miramar 603. © 787/722-9385. Reservations recommended. Main courses $21–$28. AE, MC, V. Tues–Fri noon–2:30pm; Tues–Sat 7–10:30pm. Bus: A5.

Deliro ✺✺✺ *Finds* NUEVO LATINO   The latest venture by the godfather of Nuevo Latino cuisine is his boldest and tastiest yet—and one of the prettiest restaurants in San Juan. The restaurant rambles through three rooms of a wooden, century-old manor house made modern with boudoir red and flat gray interiors, steel bead curtains and other metallic decor—yet, like Ayala's cuisine, the design manages to remain true to the building's traditional, classic roots. Ayala calls his food Puerto Rican cuisine influenced by flavors of the world and inspired by his life experiences in South America, Africa, Asia, and Europe. The menu changes seasonally to enable the use of the freshest ingredients. We started with grouper ceviche salad with New World sweet potatoes and corn and avocado in a pomegranate honey dressing, plus duck meatballs in a Moroccan sauce with balsamic and passion fruit extract with Spanish almonds. The roasted cod filet was served in a Puerto Rican celeriac puree, with leeks and sweet pea cream, while the beef tenderloin was bathed in a mushroom Provençal sauce. The signature dish is probably the pan-seared tuna with bacon crust, served with lime risotto in a parmesan broth. Ayala is a serious mixologist as well; two recent creations are the Delirium Tremens (beet-infused white rum, yuzu lime, and rosemary) and the Caribbean Breeze (white rum, ginger juice, cream of tartar, and lime juice). We can't wait to return. Deliro occasionally hosts cooking workshops and other special events.

Av. Ponce de León 762. © 787/722-0444 or 722-6042. Reservations recommended. Main courses $20–$40. AE, MC, V. Daily 6–11:30pm. Tues–Fri noon–2:30pm; Tues–Thurs 6–10:30pm; Fri–Sat 6–11:30pm; closed Sun–Mon. Bus: M1, A5.

6 Santurce & Ocean Park

For the locations of restaurants in Santurce and Ocean Park, see the map "Puerta de Tierra, Miramar, Condado & Ocean Park Accommodations & Dining" on p. 115.

VERY EXPENSIVE

Bistro de Paris ✺✺ FRENCH   This elegant version of a classic Paris bistro has moved to freshly restored quarters across from Puerto Rico's beautiful art museum, but the growing legend of its classic French cuisine continues to attract a huge local following. The restrained beige and green bistro has a front terrace under shaded awnings and a dining room with huge glass windows and doors all around. Roomy and comfortable chairs and tables are the only things not authentic about the place. Basic genre dishes like French onion soup, Nicoise salad, and mussels Provençal are executed with perfection. The boneless whole trout in "Meuniere" sauce was the best fish one member of our party ever tried, and the shrimp blazed with Pastis liquor, ratatouille, and sundried tomatoes also knocked some socks off. A big question each night is whether to go for the strip loin with tomatoes Provençal or the steak au poivre. The crème brûlée is fantastic, but the warm apple tart also reins supreme.

Plaza de Diego, Av. José de Diego 310. © 787/998-8929. Reservations recommended. Main courses $25–$37; weekend brunch $17. AE, MC, V. Sun, Tues–Thurs noon–10pm; Fri–Sat noon–midnight; closed Sun. Bus: A5.

La Casona *SPANISH/INTERNATIONAL* In a turn-of-the-20th-century mansion surrounded by gardens, La Casona offers the kind of dining usually found in Madrid, complete with a strolling guitarist. The much-renovated but still charming place draws some of the most fashionable diners in Puerto Rico. Paella marinara, prepared for two or more, is a specialty, as is *zarzuela de mariscos* (seafood medley). Or you might select filet of grouper in Basque sauce, octopus vinaigrette, *osso buco,* or rack of lamb. Grilled red snapper is a specialty, and you can order it with almost any sauce you want, although the chef recommends one made from olive oil, herbs, lemon, and toasted garlic. The cuisine here has both flair and flavor.

Calle San Jorge 609 (at the corner of Av. Fernández Juncos). ℂ **787/727-2717.** Reservations required. Main courses $25–$35. AE, DC, MC, V. Mon–Fri noon–3pm; Mon–Sat 6–11:30pm. Bus: M1, A5.

Pikayo *Moments* PUERTO RICAN FUSION This is an ideal place to go for the next generation of Puerto Rican fusion cuisine. Pikayo not only keeps up with the latest culinary trends, but it also often sets them, thanks to the inspired guidance of owner and celebrity chef Wilo Benet. Formal but not stuffy, and winner of more culinary awards than virtually any other restaurant in Puerto Rico, Pikayo is a specialist in the *criolla* cuisine of the colonial age, emphasizing the Spanish, Indian, and African elements in its unusual recipes. Appetizers include a dazzling array of taste explosions: Try shrimp spring rolls with peanut *sofrito* sauce; crab cake with aioli; or perhaps a ripe plantain, goat-cheese, and onion tart. Main-course delights feature charred rare yellowfin tuna with onion *escabeche* and red-snapper filet with sweet-potato purée served with foie gras butter. Our favorite remains the grilled shrimp with polenta and barbecue sauce made with guava.

In the Museum of Art of Puerto Rico, Av. José de Diego 299. ℂ **787/721-6194.** Reservations recommended. Main courses $28–$40; fixed-price menus $65. AE, DC, MC, V. Tues–Fri noon–3pm; Mon–Sat 6–11pm. Bus: M2, A7, or T1.

EXPENSIVE

Pamela's *Finds* CARIBBEAN FUSION One of San Juan's new oceanfront restaurants, the food here matches its impressive setting on a white-sand beach free of the high-rises that dominate much of the city's coast. The menu takes flavors from distinct Caribbean cuisines and wraps them around classic continental fare. The result is appetizers like green lip mussels served in *sofrito* (a Puerto Rican blend of onion, garlic, sweet peppers, and herbs) and spicy tomato sauce and plantain-crusted calamari with toasted African peanut and chili vinaigrette. Main courses include roasted chicken over caramelized ripe plantain in a coriander au jus and grilled lamb chops with dark rum and star anise sauce. Diners can eat in a courtyard, marked by hand-painted tiles and stone fountains, or take a table under a palm tree outside and listen to the rumble of the ocean. Tasty snacks—like club sandwiches stuffed with barbecued shrimp and cilantro-flavored mayonnaise or Jamaican jerk chicken—and a full-service bar make this a great spot for a beach break, too. Service is friendly but a bit laid back during the day; it improves for dinner. Actor Benicio del Toro has said this is one of his favorite restaurants when visiting his hometown.

In the Número 1 Guest House, Calle Santa Ana 1, Ocean Park. ℂ **787/726-5010.** Reservations recommended. Lunch $8–$24; main course $15–$35. AE, MC, V. Daily noon–3pm and 7–10:30pm. Tapas daily 3–7pm. Bus: A5.

INEXPENSIVE

Don Tello *Finds* PUERTO RICAN Right at the Santurce Market Square (Plaza del Mercado), this is a family-run restaurant serving an authentic *criolla* cuisine. In a

casual atmosphere, diners dress informally, eat well, and don't pay a lot of money for
the privilege. The service is excellent, and the ingredients are fresh and well prepared.
The fish tastes among the freshest in San Juan. We've enjoyed the filet of sea bass in a
plantain sauce, or a well-seasoned whole roasted sea bass. Grilled filet of mahimahi
is another one of our favorites, as is the grilled filet of hake. You can also enjoy the
traditional *asopao* of Puerto Rico, made with chicken, shrimp, lobster, or shellfish.
A savory chicken stew is also served, as is a tender filet of steak roasted with onions.

Dos Hermanos 180, Santurce. © 787/724-5752. Reservations recommended. Main courses $6–$13. AE, MC, V. Mon
11am–4pm; Tues–Sat 11am–10pm. Bus: 1.

Pinky's CAFE/DELI   This tiny spot just in front of the main entrance to the Ocean
Park beach serves up some of San Juan's finest wraps and fruit frappes, and breakfasts
are also tasty and filling. For a small place, the sandwich and wrap menu is pretty long,
but you can catch up on the owner's love life while deciding between the Pink Sub
(turkey, salami, mozzarella, basil, olive, tomato, onion); a pork and sweet plantain
wrap; or the upscale sashimi-grade tuna with wasabi mayo and salad combo. The filet
mignon and grilled onion sandwich tastes even better with a cold beer, with alcoholic
beverages now available. The stream-of-consciousness menu ramblings are just part of
this place's charm; there's also the cheerful staff, funky ambiance, magazine and newspaper library, and good music. The best part, however, is you don't even have to come
here to enjoy the food and frappes. They deliver, "even to the beach, your hotel to your
bed." Just look for the guy on the scooter with the "eat me" T-shirt.

51 María Moczo (off Calle McLeary). © 787/727-3347. Wraps and specialty sandwiches $5.50–$13. MC, V.
Mon–Sat 7am–8:30pm; Sun 7am–8pm. Bus A5, M-1.

Repostería Kasalta *Value* SPANISH/PUERTO RICAN   This is the most widely
known of San Juan's cafeterias/bakeries/delicatessens. You'll enter a cavernous room
flanked with sun-flooded windows and a long row of display cases filled with meats,
sausages, and pastries appropriate to the season. Patrons line up to place their orders
at a cash register, then carry their selections to one of the many tables. Knowledge of
Spanish is helpful but not essential. Among the selections are steaming bowls of
Puerto Rico's best *caldo gallego,* a hearty soup laden with collard greens, potatoes, and
sausage slices, served in thick earthenware bowls with hunks of bread. Also popular are
Cuban sandwiches (sliced pork, cheese, and fried bread); steak sandwiches; a savory
octopus salad; and an assortment of perfectly cooked omelets. Paella Valenciano is a
Sunday favorite.

Av. McLeary 1966. © **787/727-7340.** Reservations not accepted. Full American breakfast $3.50–$5; soups $3–$6;
sandwiches $4.50–$6; platters $4–$22. AE, DC, MC, V. Daily 6am–10pm. Bus: A5.

7 Near Ocean Park

For the locations of these restaurants, see the map "Puerta de Tierra, Miramar, Condado & Ocean Park Accommodations & Dining" on p. 115.

EXPENSIVE

Che's ARGENTINE   This established Argentine steakhouse re-creates some of the color and drama of the Argentine pampas in a relaxed, informal atmosphere. You'll get one of the best *churassacos,* grilled flank steak, in the city. If you're not in the mood for beef, your options run toward pasta, seafood, and chicken dishes. These, along with the standard sides and desserts, are perfectly prepared. There's nothing fancy here, but the quality is top drawer and its unpretentiousness is refreshing. The meats here are very tender and well flavored, and the chimmichuri sauce is the city's best.

Calle Caoba 35. (✆ **787/726-7202.** Reservations recommended for dinner. Main courses $15–$30. AE, DC, DISC, MC, V. Sun–Thurs 11:30am–10:45pm; Fri–Sat noon–midnight. Bus: A5.

Tierra Santa Restaurant *finds* MIDDLE EASTERN   Housed in fanciful quarters, with glass mosaics etched into the facade and the main dining room adorned with Arabian fabric and scenic oil paintings, this is one of the better of the city's many fine Middle Eastern restaurants. We always start out with the hummus and falafel, and get the baba ganouch if there are more than two of us. The succulent, perfectly seasoned grilled chicken, beef, and shrimp kebabs are what draw us here, but we have also enjoyed the grilled lamb shank, curry chicken, and the stuffed grape leaves. The entrees are served with a tasty cucumber and tomato salad and Arabian rice pilaf with almonds. Don't leave without trying the baklava; there's a reason it's the oldest dessert in the world. On Thursday, Friday, and Saturday nights, a belly-dancing show starts at 9pm. It's a great show.

Calle Loíza 2440. (✆ **787/726-6491.** Reservations not necessary. Main courses $11–$30. AE, MC, V. Sun–Sat 11am–midnight. Bus: A5.

MODERATE

La Casita Blanca *finds* CREOLE/PUERTO RICAN   Island politicians are said to have the best noses for good home cooking. We don't know if that is true or not, but one of their favorite places is this eatery. Governor wannabes (What politician doesn't want to be?) come here to order excellent regional fare, and enjoy an ambiance that oozes the culture of the Puerto Rican countryside. This is a converted family home that opened its door to diners in the mid-1980s, and it's been a favorite of locals from all walks of Puerto Rican society ever since. Off the tourist trail and best reached by taxi, the restaurant does down home island fare like *guisado y arroz con gandule* (beef stew with rice and small beans), or *bacalao* (salt codfish with yucca). Guaranteed to put hair on your chest is *patita* (pigs' trotters in a Creole sauce). Veal with sautéed onions is popular, as is grilled red snapper or chicken fricassee. A typical chicken *asopao,* a soupy rice stew, is also served. If you ever wanted to try stewed rabbit or goat, this is the place.

Calle Tapía 351. (✆ **787/726-5501.** Main courses $8–$16; Sun buffet $12–$13. MC, V. Mon–Thurs 11:30am–6:45pm; Fri–Sat 11:30am–9:30pm; Sun noon–4:30pm. Bus: C10 or C11.

8 Isla Verde

For the locations of restaurants in Isla Verde, see the map "Isla Verde Accommodations & Dining" on p. 125.

VERY EXPENSIVE

BLT Steak 🏶🏶 STEAKHOUSE   French chef Laurent Tourondel takes the American steakhouse to new highs with an awesome selection of Black Angus, Prime and Kobe beef, as well as chicken, lamb, veal, and fresh fish. There's nothing fancy here—just the best steakhouse fare you can imagine prepared by a chef with the talent to match the quality of the ingredients. We started with some littleneck clams from the raw bar and the crab cakes. The signature steak is a bone-in sirloin for two, which was among the finest cuts we've had on the island. The sautéed Dover sole is an old-school classic that hits its mark. We loved the potato gratin and parmesan gnocchi, as well as the roasted tomatoes and poached green beans. Steaks are served with a selection of sauces including chimichuri, béarnaise, peppercorn, and horseradish. The blueberry lemon pie makes for a refreshing finale. There's also peanut butter chocolate mousse with banana ice cream and warm coconut bread pudding with rum ice cream if you dare.

In the Ritz-Carlton San Juan Hotel, Spa & Casino, Av. de los Gobernadores (State Rd.) 6961, no. 187, Isla Verde. ℂ 787/253-1700. Reservations required. Main courses $22–$88; fixed-price menus $45–$75. AE, DC, DISC, MC, V. Sun–Thurs 6–10:30pm; Fri–Sat 6–11pm. Bus: A5.

The Palm 🏶🏶 STEAK/SEAFOOD   The management of San Juan's most elegant hotel invited the Palm, a legendary New York steakhouse, to open a branch on the premises. The setting includes a stylish, masculine-looking saloon, where drinks are stiff, and a dining room with artfully simple linen-covered tables and caricatures of local personalities. If you've hit it big at the nearby casino, maybe you'll want to celebrate with the Palm's famous and famously pricey lobster. Otherwise, there's a tempting number of options, all served in gargantuan portions: jumbo lump crabmeat cocktail; Caesar salad; lamb chops with mint sauce; grilled halibut steak; prime porterhouse steak; and steak "a la stone," which finishes cooking on a sizzling platter directly atop your table. One thing is certain—you'll never go hungry here.

In El San Juan Hotel & Casino, Av. Isla Verde 6063. ℂ 787/791-1000. Reservations recommended. Main courses $18–$40, except lobster, which is priced by the pound and can easily cost $22 per lb. or more. AE, DC, MC, V. Daily 5–11pm. Bus: A5.

Ruth's Chris Steak House 🏶🏶 STEAK   This Puerto Rican branch of one of the most famous steakhouse chains in the world presents macho food, especially steaks that are among the best beef dishes in San Juan. It obsessively focuses on big drinks and big steaks, grilled in the simplest possible way—usually just with salt, pepper, and a brush-over of butter. These are served within two dark blue, mahogany-trimmed dining rooms, separated by a saloon-style bar.

You might begin with barbecued shrimp, mushrooms stuffed with crabmeat, or seared ahi tuna. Or you might opt for a salad as an appetizer. Portions are large and very filling. Steaks are the finest from the U.S. cattle country. Examples include rib-eyes, veal chops, porterhouse, New York strips, and filet mignons. There's also roasted chicken, lobster, and a fresh catch of the day.

In the Inter-Continental San Juan Resort & Casino, Av. Isla Verde 187. ℂ 787/253-1717. Reservations recommended. Main courses $32–$83. AE, DC, MC, V. Sun–Thurs 6–10pm; Fri–Sat 6–11pm. Bus: A5.

Kids **Two Family-Friendly Restaurants**

Ciao Mediterranean Café (p. 155)   Right on the beach, this is a family favorite that offers some of the best pizzas and pastas at Isla Verde. Prices are affordable, too.

Palmera (p. 143)   Located in the Caribe Hilton (p. 114), this place has a Sunday brunch—which is half-price for children—with an all-you-can-eat buffet. There's even a clown on hand to keep the kids entertained.

EXPENSIVE

La Piccola Fontana ⭑ NORTHERN ITALIAN   Just off a luxurious wing of El San Juan Hotel, this restaurant delivers plate after plate of delectable food nightly. From its white linens to its classically formal service, it enjoys a fine reputation. The food is straightforward, generous, and extremely well prepared. You'll dine in one of two neo-Palladian rooms whose wall frescoes depict Italy's ruins and landscapes. Menu items range from the appealingly simple (grilled filets of fish or grilled veal chops) to more elaborate dishes such as *tortellini San Daniele*, made with veal, prosciutto, cream, and sage; or *linguine scogliere*, with shrimp, clams, and seafood. Grilled medallions of filet mignon are served with braised arugula, Parmesan cheese, and balsamic vinegar.

In El San Juan Hotel & Casino, Av. Isla Verde 6063. ⓒ 787/791-0966. Reservations required. Main courses $18–$30. AE, MC, V. Daily 6–11pm. Bus: A5.

Tangerine ⭑ EURO-ASIAN   This is the ultimate in chic Isla Verde dining, and it just happens to lie adjacent to the street-level reception area of the Water Club (see chapter 6). Hailed by many international food critics, it glows in its much-deserved praise. A world of gurgling water, where even the solid furniture sometimes appears to be flowing, the prominent bar area has bubbling waterfalls, big-windowed views of the tropical landscapes outside, and an occasional and rather whimsical reference to the orange-colored fruit that gave the place its name. Lighting radiates gently outward from the kind of ultraglam fixtures that makes ordinary-looking people look good and beautiful people look fabulous. We the loved caprese salad with pesto vinaigrette and roasted eggplant and lobster roll with seaweed salad and spicy mango sauce. The most basic entree might be its version of a diner meal (tarragon chicken with stir-fried vegetables and spiced mash potatoes). Baby back ribs are perfectly suited to the house honey guava glaze, while a juicy duck breast in apple teriyaki sauce is served with equally amazing saffron risotto. The house *churrasco* and *chillo* are among the city's best–and that's stiff competition. All the desserts sound good, but we have yet to get beyond the chocolate crème brûlée.

Tartak St. 2. ⓒ 787/728-3666. Reservations required. Main courses $21–$29. AE, DC, MC, V. Tues–Sat 6:30–11pm. Bus: A5.

Yamato ⭑ JAPANESE   The artfully simple decor at Yamato shows the kind of modern urban minimalism that you might expect in an upscale California restaurant. Separate sections offer conventional seating at tables; at a countertop within view of a sushi display; or at seats around a hot grill where chefs shake, rattle, and sizzle their way through a fast but elaborate cooking ritual. Many visitors include at least some sushi with an entree such as beef sashimi with tataki sauce, shrimp tempura with noodle soup, filet mignon or chicken with shrimp or scallops, or several kinds of rice and noodle dishes.

In Wyndham El San Juan Hotel & Casino, Av. Isla Verde 6063. © 787/791-1000. Reservations recommended. Sushi $2.50–$3 per piece; sushi and teppanyaki dinners $25–$43. AE, MC, V. Daily 6pm–midnight. Bus: A5.

MODERATE

The Algave Ranch *Kids* AMERICAN/STEAK   When the very posh El San Juan Hotel carved out a space for this irreverent, tongue-in-cheek eatery on its top (10th) floor, it was viewed as a radical departure from an otherwise grand collection of in-house restaurants. The result is likely to make you smile, especially if you have roots anywhere west of Ohio. You'll be greeted with a hearty "Howdy, partner" and the jangling of spurs from a crew of denim-clad cowboys as you enter a replica of a corral in the North American West. Banquettes and barstools are upholstered in faux cowhide; the decor is appropriately macho and rough-textured, and even the cowgirls on duty are likely to lasso anyone they find particularly appealing. The cowboys sing as they serve your steaks, barbecued ribs, country-fried steaks, Tex-Mex fajitas, and enchiladas. Food that's a bit less beefy includes seared red snapper with a cilantro-laced *pico de gallo* sauce and a slowly roasted succulent chicken. And if you want to buy a souvenir pair of cowboy spurs, you'll find an intriguing collection of Western accessories and uniforms for sale outside. Consider beginning your meal with any of 20 kinds of tequila cocktails at the Tequila Bar, which lies a few steps away, on the same floor.

In El San Juan Hotel & Casino, Av. Isla Verde 6063. © 787/791-1000. Reservations recommended at dinner Fri–Sat; otherwise, not necessary. Main courses $16–$38. AE, DC, DISC, MC, V. Tues–Thurs 5:30–11pm; Fri–Sat 5:30pm–midnight. Bus: A5.

Outback Steakhouse *Value* STEAK   This Puerto Rican branch of the two-fisted, Australian-themed restaurant chain occupies a dark-paneled room with booths positioned around a prominent bar area. Here you can study memorabilia devoted to the Land Down Under while ordering such drinks as a genuinely delicious Wallabee Darn. There's a simple steak-and-potato-with-salad special priced at $14, a cost-conscious meal in itself. But more appealing are some of the chain's signature dishes, such as a Bloomin' Onion (a batter-dipped deep-fried onion that fans out from its platter like a demented lotus and tastes delicious with beer); at least four kinds of steaks, including filet mignon; fish, including mahimahi and salmon; and our favorite of the lot, Alice Springs chicken, a breast of chicken layered with bacon, mushrooms, and cheese, and served with honey-mustard sauce and french fries.

In the Embassy Suites Hotel & Casino, Calle José M. Tartak 8000. © 787/791-4679. Reservations not accepted. Main courses $14–$23. AE, MC, V. Mon–Thurs 5:30–10:30pm; Fri–Sat 5:30pm–midnight; Sun 3–10pm. Bus: A5, M7.

INEXPENSIVE

Ciao Mediterranean Café *Kids* MEDITERRANEAN   This is the most charming restaurant in Isla Verde, and it is one of our enduring favorites. It's draped with bougainvillea and set directly on the sands, attracting both hotel guests and locals wandering in barefoot from the beach for delicious tropical drinks. The visual centerpiece is an open-air kitchen set within an oval-shaped bar. A crew of cheerfully animated chefs mingles good culinary technique with Latino theatricality.

Tips **Eating Like a *Sanjuanero***

To become a true *sanjuanero,* you've got to learn to love *bacalaitos* (codfish fritters) and *alcapurrias* (meat-stuffed plantain fritters). The best of these are found at little fast-food stands on the **beaches of Piñones and Loiza,** east of the resorts of Isla Verde and the airport. Here you'll find rows of ramshackle shacks where women cook up these delicacies in time-blackened cauldrons over open fires.

Pizzas and pastas are popular here, and even more appealing are such dishes as seafood salad, wherein shrimp, scallops, calamari, peppers, onions, and lime juice create something you might expect in the south of Italy. *Kalamarakia tiganita* (Greek-style squid), consisting of battered and deep-fried squid served with ratatouille and spicy marinara sauce; rack of lamb with ratatouille, polenta, and Provençal herbs; and a mixed grill of seafood are evocative of what you'd expect in Marseilles, thanks to the roe-enhanced aioli and couscous. Compared to most of the restaurants around here, this cafe serves lighter fare that kids go for, especially in its selection of pizzas and pastas. The desserts are also some of the most luscious at Isla Verde, especially the ice cream.

In the Inter-Continental San Juan Resort & Casino, Av. Isla Verde 5961. ② **787/791-6100.** Reservations recommended for dinner. Pizzas and salads $8–$20; main courses $14–$30. AE, MC, V. Daily 11:30am–11pm. Bus: A5.

Metropol CUBAN/PUERTO RICAN/INTERNATIONAL This is part of a restaurant chain known for serving the island's best Cuban food, although the chefs prepare a much wider range of dishes. Metropol is the happiest blend of Cuban and Puerto Rican cuisine we've ever had. The black-bean soup is among the island's finest, served in the classic Havana style with a side dish of rice and chopped onions. Endless garlic bread accompanies most dinners, including Cornish game hen stuffed with Cuban rice and beans or perhaps marinated steak topped with a fried egg (reportedly Castro's favorite). Smoked chicken and chicken-fried steak are also heartily recommended; portions are huge. Plantains, yucca, and all that good stuff accompany most dishes. Finish with a choice of thin or firm custard. Most dishes are at the low end of the price scale.

Club Gallistico, Av. Isla Verde. ② **787/791-4046.** Main courses $10–$30. AE, MC, V. Daily 11:30am–11:30pm. Bus: C41, B42, or A5.

Panadería España Repostería SANDWICHES The Panadería España makes San Juan's definitive Cuban sandwich—a cheap meal all on its own. The biggest sandwich weighs 3 pounds. Drinks and coffee are dispensed from behind a much-used bar. You can purchase an assortment of gourmet items from Spain, arranged as punctuation marks on shelves set against an otherwise all-white decor. The place has been serving simple breakfasts, drinks, coffee, and Cuban sandwiches virtually every day since it opened around 1970.

Centro Comercial Villamar, Marginal Baldoriti de Castro. ② **787/727-3860.** Reservations not necessary. Soups and tapas $4–$6; sandwiches $5–$8. AE, DISC, MC, V. Daily 6am–10pm. Bus: A5.

9 Near Isla Verde

For the location of this restaurant, see the map "Puerta de Tierra, Miramar, Condado & Ocean Park Accommodations & Dining" on p. 115.

Soleil Beach Club Piñones *(Finds* CARIBBEAN   When it opened in 1997, Soleil was a pioneer in operating a fine dining establishment among the barbecues, wooden shacks, and open-air bars of the Piñones dining scene. More than a decade later, Soleil still rules from its roost amidst the sand dunes and palm trees of the undeveloped beach it fronts. Soak in that breeze and listen to those waves from a table or the bar on the oceanfront terrace and have a drink as the sun goes down before dinner. The food here's as good as its rustic beachfront surroundings. For starters, we like the fish skewers with mango sauce and the coconut breaded shrimp in aioli sauce. The surf and turf pairs Argentinean style skirt steak with shrimp, baby octopus, mahimahi, and scallops. The halibut is served in an oriental beurre blanc sauce and cassava *mofongo,* the tuna is grilled, topped with a tropical fruit salsa, and served with cilantro jasmine rice. This is the best oceanfront dining in San Juan, and one of the best in Puerto Rico. Today, the restaurant hosts corporate dinners and special events, with facilities for concerts and live shows, a dance floor, and DJ area. There's also Wi-Fi Internet service.

Soleil Beach Club, Carretera 187 Km.4.6, Piñones. © **787/253-1033.** Reservations recommended. Lunch and dinner main courses $13–$39; lunch specials $7–$10; lunch and dinner main courses $18–$38. AE, DISC, MC, V. Sun–Thurs 11am–11pm; Fri–Sat 11am–2am. Bus: Call ahead to arrange free transportation to and from your hotel in the Soleil Beach Club van.

8

Exploring San Juan

The Spanish began to settle in the area now known as Old San Juan around 1521. At the outset, the city was called Puerto Rico ("Rich Port"), and the whole island was known as San Juan.

The streets are narrow and teeming with traffic, but a walk through Old San Juan—in Spanish, *El Viejo San Juan*—makes for a good stroll. Some visitors have likened it to a "Disney park with an Old World theme." Even fast food restaurants and junk stores are housed in historic buildings. It's the biggest and best collection of historic buildings, stretching back 5 centuries, in all the Caribbean. You can do it in less than a day. In this historic 7-square-block area of the western side of the city, you can see many of Puerto Rico's chief sightseeing attractions and do some shopping along the way.

On the other hand, you might want to plop down on the sand with a drink or get outside and play. "Diving, Fishing, Tennis & Other Outdoor Pursuits," later in this chapter, describes the beaches and sports in the San Juan area.

1 Seeing the Sights

FORTS

Castillo de San Felipe del Morro ⊀ *Kids*   Called "El Morro," this fort stands on a rocky promontory dominating the entrance to San Juan Bay. Constructed in 1540, the original fort was a round tower, which can still be seen deep inside the lower levels of the castle. More walls and cannon-firing positions were added, and by 1787, the fortification attained the complex design you see today. This fortress was attacked repeatedly by both the English and the Dutch.

The U.S. National Park Service protects the fortifications of Old San Juan, which have been declared a World Heritage Site by the United Nations. With some of the most dramatic views in the Caribbean, you'll find El Morro an intriguing labyrinth of dungeons, barracks, vaults, lookouts, and ramps. Historical and background information is provided in a video in English and Spanish. The nearest parking is the underground facility beneath the Quincentennial Plaza at the Ballajá barracks (Cuartel de Ballajá) on Calle Norzagaray. Sometimes park rangers lead hour-long tours for free, although you can also visit on your own.

The park, along with Fort San Cristóbal (see below), form the **San Juan National Historic Site.** The forts are connected by ancient underground tunnels, but today two modern trolleys ferry visitors back and forth. The walk, however, is beautiful along the oceanfront Calle Norzagary. A museum at El Morro provides a history of the fort through exhibits of historic photographs and artifacts, written orientations, and a video presentation. A guided tour is offered hourly, but informational brochures allow you to walk around on your own while learning the story. There's also a gift shop. Make sure to walk out on the northernmost point, a narrow wedge overlooking the

Old San Juan Attractions

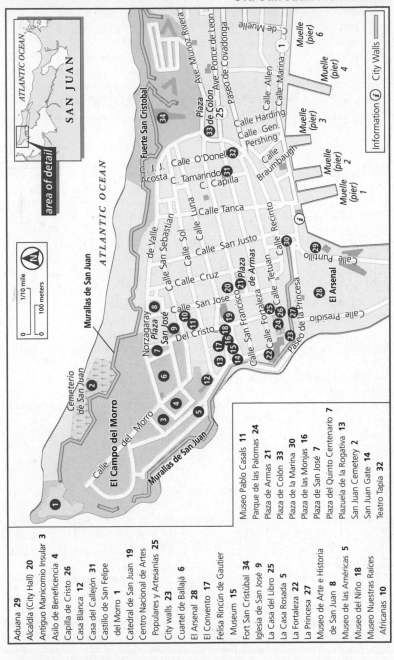

Moments **Joggers' Trail or Romantic Walk**

El Morro Trail, a jogger's paradise, provides the Old City's most scenic views along San Juan Bay. The first part of the trail extends to the San Juan Gate. The walk then goes by El Morro and eventually reaches a scenic area known as Bastion de Santa Barbara. The walk passes El Morro's well-preserved walls, and the trail ends at the entrance to the fortress. The walkway is designed to follow the undulating movement of the ocean, and sea grapes and tropical vegetation surround benches. The trail is romantic at night, when the walls of the fortress are illuminated. Stop at the tourist office for a map, and then set off on the adventure.

waves crashing into the rocky coast. The promenade circling the base of the fort is also worth exploring. The grounds of El Morro are a great spot to fly a kite, and families and children are out every weekend doing so. An annual festival is in March. You can buy a kite at stands right in front of the fort, or at Puerto Rico Drug or Walgreen's on Plaza Colón.

At the end of Calle Norzagaray. © **787/729-6960.** Admission $3 adults (16 and older) for one fort, $5 for both, $2 for seniors, free for children 15 and under. Daily 9am–5pm. Bus: A5, B21, or B40.

Fort San Cristóbal ✦   This huge fortress, begun in 1634 and reengineered in the 1770s, is one of the largest ever built in the Americas by Spain. Its walls rise more than 150 feet (46m) above the sea—a marvel of military engineering. San Cristóbal protected San Juan against attackers coming by land as a partner to El Morro, to which it is linked by a half-mile (.8km) of monumental walls and bastions filled with cannon-firing positions. A complex system of tunnels and dry moats connects the center of San Cristóbal to its "outworks," defensive elements arranged layer after layer over a 27-acre (11-hectare) site. You'll get the idea if you look at the scale model on display. Like El Morro, the fort is administered and maintained by the U.S. National Park Service. Be sure to see the Garita del Diablo (the Devil's Sentry Box), one of the oldest parts of San Cristóbal's defenses, and famous in Puerto Rican legend. The devil himself, it is said, would snatch away sentinels at this lonely post at the edge of the sea. In 1898 the first shots of the Spanish-American War in Puerto Rico were fired by cannons on top of San Cristóbal during an artillery duel with a U.S. Navy fleet. Park rangers lead hour-long tours for free here too, but wandering on your own is fun.

In the northeast corner of Old San Juan (uphill from Plaza de Colón on Calle Norzagaray). © **787/729-6960.** Admission $3 adults (16 and older) one fort, $5 both forts, free for children 15 and under. Daily 9am–5pm. Bus: A5, B21, or B40; then the free trolley from Covadonga station to the top of the hill.

CHURCHES

Capilla de Cristo   Cristo Chapel was built to commemorate what legend says was a miracle. In 1753 a young rider lost control of his horse in a race down this very street during the fiesta of St. John's Day and plunged over the precipice. Moved by the accident, the secretary of the city, Don Mateo Pratts, invoked Christ to save the youth, and he had the chapel built when his prayers were answered. Today it's a landmark in the old city and one of its best-known historical monuments. The chapel's gold and silver altar can be seen through its glass doors. Because the chapel is open only 1 day a week, most visitors have to settle for a view of its exterior.

Calle del Cristo (directly west of Paseo de la Princesa). (C) **787/722-0861.** Free admission. Tues 8am–5pm. Bus: Old Town Trolley.

Catedral de San Juan   This, the spiritual and architectural centerpiece of Old San Juan, as you see it in its present form, was begun in 1540 as a replacement for a thatch-roofed chapel that was blown apart by a hurricane in 1529. Chronically hampered by a lack of funds and a recurring series of military and weather-derived disasters, it slowly evolved into the gracefully vaulted, Gothic-inspired structure you see today. Among the many disasters to hit this cathedral are the following: In 1598 the Earl of Cumberland led the British navy in a looting spree, and in 1615 a hurricane blew away its roof. In 1908 the body of Ponce de León was disinterred from the nearby Iglesia de San José and placed in a marble tomb near the transept, where it remains today (see the box "Ponce de León: Man of Myth & Legend" in chapter 2 for more about Ponce de León). The cathedral also contains the wax-covered mummy of St. Pio, a Roman martyr persecuted and killed for his Christian faith. The mummy has been encased in a glass box ever since it was placed here in 1862. To the right of the mummy is a bizarre wooden replica of Mary with four swords stuck in her bosom. After all the looting and destruction over the centuries, the cathedral's great treasures, including gold and silver, are long gone, although many beautiful stained-glass windows remain. The cathedral faces Plaza de las Monjas (the Nuns' Square), a shady spot where you can rest in front of Hotel El Convento.

Calle del Cristo 153 (at Caleta San Juan). (C) **787/722-0861.** Free admission. Mon–Sat 8am–4pm; Sun 8am–2pm. Bus: Old Town Trolley.

MUSEUMS

Many of the museums in Old San Juan close for lunch between 11:45am and 2pm, so schedule your activities accordingly if you intend to museum-hop.

Felisa Rincón de Gautier Museum   The most heralded woman of modern Puerto Rico served as the mayor of San Juan for 22 consecutive years, between 1946 and 1968. The museum that commemorates her memory is in a 300-year-old building a few blocks downhill from San Juan's cathedral, near one of the medieval gates (La Puerta San Juan) that pierces the walls of the Old City. The interior is devoted to the life and accomplishments of Felisa Rincón de Gautier, and proudly displays some of her personal furniture and artifacts, as well as 212 plaques, 308 certificates of merit, 11 honorary doctorates, and 113 symbolic keys to other cities, such as Gary, Indiana, and Perth Amboy, New Jersey. Her particular areas of influence included child welfare and elementary education. Photographs show her with luminaries from Eleanor Roosevelt to the pope. The oldest of nine children, and the daughter of a local lawyer and a schoolteacher, she shouldered the responsibilities of rearing her younger siblings after the death of her mother when she was 12. Today the museum illuminates Doña Felisa's life as well as the reverence in which Puerto Ricans hold their most celebrated political matriarch. As such, it's a quirky, intensely personalized monument that combines a strong sense of feminism with Puerto Rican national pride.

Caleta de San Juan 51, at Recinto Oeste. (C) **787/723-1897.** Free admission. Mon–Fri 9am–4pm. Bus: Old Town Trolley.

Luis Muñoz Marín Foundation   A 30-minute drive south of San Juan, this museum offers a chance to visit the former home of the island's most famous governor, Luis Muñoz Marín. As the first elected governor of Puerto Rico, Marín enjoys somewhat the same position in Puerto Rican history that George Washington does for

San Juan Attractions

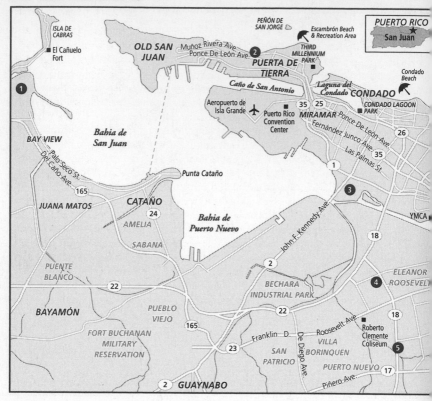

the mainland United States. A documentary acquaints you with the governor's life and achievements. You can walk through Marín's study and library and view his extensive art collection, and later you can relax in his tropical garden and gazebo. There's also an on-site antique automobile exhibition.

Marginal Rd. 877 Km 0.4, Trujillo Alto Expwy. ✆ 787/755-7979. Admission $2 adults, $1 children. Tours Mon–Fri (reservations required) 10am and 2pm. Bus: C-31 or public car from Plaza Colón (easier).

Museo de Arte de Puerto Rico 𝒢𝒢   Puerto Rico's most important art museum since opening in 2000, it was constructed at a cost of $55 million and is a state-of-the-art showcase for the island nation's rich cultural heritage, as reflected mainly through its painters. Housed in a former city hospital in Santurce, the museum features both a permanent collection and temporary exhibitions. Prominent local artists are the stars—for example, Francisco Oller (1833–1917), who brought a touch of Cézanne or Camille Pissarro to Puerto Rico (Oller actually studied in France with both of these Impressionists). Another leading star of the permanent collection is José Campeche, a late-18th-century classical painter. The museum is like a living textbook of Puerto Rico, beginning with its early development and going on to showcase camp aspects, such as the poster art created here in the mid–20th century. All the important modern island artists are also presented, including the late Rafael Tufiño and Angel

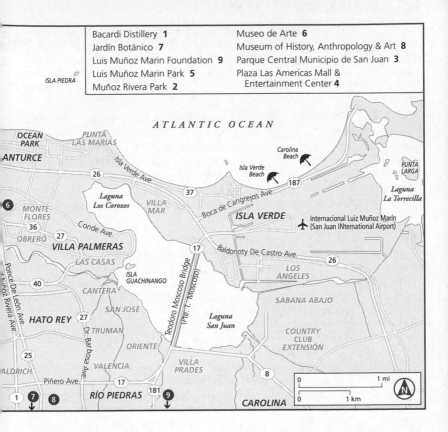

Bacardi Distillery **1**	Museo de Arte **6**
Jardín Botánico **7**	Museum of History, Anthropology & Art **8**
Luis Muñoz Marin Foundation **9**	Parque Central Municipio de San Juan **3**
Luis Muñoz Marin Park **5**	Plaza Las Americas Mall &
Muñoz Rivera Park **2**	Entertainment Center **4**

Botello, Arnaldo Roche Rabelle, and Antonio Martorell. The building itself is a gem, and you have to stroll through the relaxing botanical gardens behind.

Av. José de Diego 299, Santurce. ℂ 787/977-6277. www.mapr.org. Admission $6 adults; $3 students, seniors, and children; free for children 4 and under and seniors over 75. Tues and Thurs–Sat 10am–5pm; Wed 10am–8pm; Sun 11am–6pm. Bus: A5 or B21.

Museo de Arte e Historia de San Juan   Located in a Spanish colonial building at the corner of Calle MacArthur, this cultural center was the city's main marketplace in the mid–19th century. Local art is displayed in the east and west galleries, and audiovisual materials reveal the history of the city. Sometimes major cultural events are staged in the museum's large courtyard. English- and Spanish-language audiovisual shows are presented Tuesday to Friday every hour on the hour from 9am to 4pm. Some of the city's finest young artists show here.

Calle Norzagaray 150. ℂ 787/724-1875. Free admission, but donations accepted. Tues–Fri 9am–4pm; Sat–Sun 10am–4pm. Bus: To Old San Juan terminal; then a trolley.

Museo de las Américas 𝒻   This museum showcases the artisans of North, South, and Central America, featuring everything from carved figureheads from New England whaling ships to dugout canoes carved by Carib Indians in Dominica. It is unique in Puerto Rico and well worth a visit. Also on display is a changing collection of paintings by artists from throughout the Spanish-speaking world, some of which are for sale, and a permanent collection called "Puerto Rican *Santos,*" donated by Dr. Ricardo Alegría.

Sala Cuartel de Ballajá, at Calle Norzagaray and Calle del Morro. © **787/724-5052.** Free admission, except the Indigenous Peoples of the Americas exhibition is $2, which is a must-see. Tues–Sun 10am–4pm. Bus: Old Town Trolley.

Museo de Pablo Casals   This museum is devoted to the memorabilia left to the people of Puerto Rico by the musician Pablo Casals. The maestro's cello is here, along with a library of videotapes (which can be played upon request) of some of his festival concerts. This small 18th-century house also contains manuscripts and photographs of Casals. The annual Casals Festival draws worldwide interest and internationally known performing artists; it's held from the end of February through early March.

Plaza San José, Calle San Sebastián 101. © **787/723-9185.** Admission $1 adults, 50¢ students and children. Tues–Sat 9:30am–4:30pm. Bus: Old Town Trolley.

HISTORIC SIGHTS

In addition to the forts and churches listed above, you might want to see the sites described below.

San Juan Gate, Calle San Francisco and Calle Recinto Oeste, built around 1635, just north of La Fortaleza, several blocks downhill from the cathedral, was the main point of entry into San Juan if you arrived by ship in the 17th and 18th centuries. The gate is the only one remaining of the several that once pierced the fortifications of the old walled city. For centuries it was closed at sundown to cut off access to the historic old town. Bus: Old Town Trolley.

Plazuela de la Rogativa, Caleta de las Monjas, is a little plaza with a statue of a bishop and three women, commemorating one of Puerto Rico's most famous legends. In 1797, from across San Juan Bay at Santurce, the British held Old Town under siege. That same year they mysteriously sailed away. Later, the commander claimed he feared that the enemy was well prepared behind those walls; he apparently saw many lights and believed them to be reinforcements. Some people believe that those lights were torches carried by women in a *rogativa,* or religious procession, as they followed their bishop. Bus: T1.

The **city walls** around San Juan were built in 1630 to protect the town against both European invaders and Caribbean pirates. The city walls that remain today were once part of one of the most impregnable fortresses in the New World and even today are an engineering marvel. Their thickness averages 20 feet (6m) at the base and 12 feet (3.7m) at the top, with an average height of 40 feet (12m). At their top, notice the balconied buildings that served for centuries as hospitals and also residences of the island's various governors. Between Fort San Cristóbal and El Morro, bastions were erected at frequent intervals. The walls come into view as you approach from San Cristóbal on your way to El Morro. Bus: Old Town Trolley.

San Juan Cemetery, on Calle Norzagaray, officially opened in 1814 and has since been the final resting place for many prominent Puerto Rican families. The circular chapel, dedicated to Saint Magdalene of Pazzis, was built in the 1860s. Aficionados of old graveyards can wander among marble monuments, mausoleums, and statues, marvelous examples of Victorian funereal statuary. Because there are no trees, or any other form of shade here, it would be best not to go exploring in the noonday sun. In any case, be careful—the cemetery is often a venue for illegal drug deals and can be dangerous. Bus: Old Town Trolley.

Alcaldía (City Hall)   The City Hall, with its double arcade flanked by two towers resembling Madrid's City Hall, was constructed in stages from 1604 to 1789. Still in use, this building today contains a tourist-information center downstairs plus a small art gallery on the first floor.

Calle San Francisco. *✆* **787/724-7171.** Free admission. Mon–Fri 8am–5pm. Closed holidays. Bus: Old Town Trolley.

Casa Blanca   Ponce de León never lived here, although construction of the house— built in 1521, 2 years after his death—is sometimes attributed to him. The work was ordered by his son-in-law, Juan García Troche. The parcel of land was given to Ponce de León as a reward for services rendered to the Crown. Descendants of the explorer lived in the house for about 2½ centuries, until the Spanish government took it over in 1779 for use as a residence for military commanders. The U.S. government also used it as a home for army commanders. On the first floor, the **Juan Ponce de León Museum** is furnished with antiques, paintings, and artifacts from the 16th through the 18th centuries. In back is a garden with spraying fountains, offering an intimate and verdant respite.

Calle San Sebastián 1. *✆* **787/725-1454.** Admission $3. Tues–Sat 9am–noon and 1–4:30pm. Bus: Old Town Trolley.

El Arsenal   The Spaniards used a shallow craft to patrol the lagoons and mangroves in and around San Juan. Needing a base for these vessels, they constructed El Arsenal in the 19th century. It was at this base that they staged their last stand, flying the Spanish colors until the final Spaniard was removed in 1898, at the end of the Spanish-American War. Changing art exhibitions are held in the building's three galleries.

La Puntilla. *✆* **787/723-3068.** Free admission. Wed–Sun 8:30am–4:30pm. Bus: Old Town Trolley.

La Casa del Libro   This restored 19th-century house shelters a library and museum devoted to the arts of printing and bookmaking, with examples of fine printing, which date back 5 centuries, and some illuminated medieval manuscripts.

Calle del Cristo 255. *✆* **787/723-0354.** Free admission. Tues–Sat 11am–4:30pm. Bus: Old Town Trolley.

La Fortaleza   The office and residence of the governor of Puerto Rico is the oldest executive mansion in continuous use in the Western Hemisphere, and it has served as the island's seat of government for more than 3 centuries. Its history goes back even further than that to 1533, when construction began on a fortress to protect San Juan's Spanish settlers during raids by Carib tribesmen and pirates. The original medieval towers remain, but as the edifice was subsequently enlarged into a palace, other modes of architecture and ornamentation were also incorporated, including baroque, Gothic, neoclassical, and Arabian. La Fortaleza has been designated a national historic site by the U.S. government. Proper attire is required (informal okay).

Calle Fortaleza, overlooking San Juan Harbor. *✆* **787/721-7000,** ext. 2211. Free admission. 30-min. tours of the gardens and building (conducted in English and Spanish) given every half-hour. Mon–Fri 9am–3:30pm. Bus: Old Town Trolley.

Museo Nuestras Raíces Africanas   Set within the Casa del Contrefueras, this museum documents the African contribution to the sociology of Puerto Rico. You'll find a series of tastefully arranged art objects, including musical instruments, intricately carved African masks, drums, graphics, and maps that show the migratory patterns, usually through the slave trade, from Africa into Puerto Rico. There are graphic depictions of the horrendous disruptions to families and individuals caused by the slave trade during the plantation era.

Plaza San José, Calle San Sebastián. © 787/724-4294. Admission $2 adults; $1 seniors, children, and students; free for ages 12 and under. Tues–Sat 8:30am–4:30pm. Bus: Old Town Trolley.

Teatro Tapía Standing across from the Plaza de Colón, this is one of the oldest theaters in the Western Hemisphere, built about 1832. In 1976 a restoration returned the theater to its original appearance. Much of Puerto Rican theater history is connected with the Tapía, named after the island's first prominent playwright, Alejandro Tapía y Rivera (1826–82). Various productions—some musical—are staged here throughout the year, representing a repertoire of drama, dance, and cultural events.

Av. Ponce de León. © 787/721-0180. Prices vary. Access limited to ticket holders at performances (see "San Juan After Dark," later in this chapter). Bus: A5, B21, any other to Old San Juan Station.

HISTORIC SQUARES

In Old San Juan, **Plaza del Quinto Centenario (Quincentennial Plaza)** overlooks the Atlantic from atop the highest point in the city. A striking and symbolic feature of the plaza, which was constructed as part of the 1992–93 celebration of the 500th anniversary of the discovery of the New World, is a sculpture that rises 40 feet (12m) from the plaza's top level. The monumental sculpture in black granite and ceramics symbolizes the earthen and clay roots of American history and is the work of Jaime Suarez, one of Puerto Rico's foremost artists. From its southern end, two needle-shaped columns point skyward to the North Star, the guiding light of explorers. Placed around the plaza are fountains, other columns, and sculpted steps that represent various historic periods in Puerto Rico's 500-year heritage.

Sweeping views extend from the plaza to El Morro Fortress at the headland of San Juan Bay and to the Dominican Convent and San José Church, a rare New World example of Gothic architecture. Asilo de Beneficencia, a former indigents' hospital dating from 1832, occupies a corner of El Morro's entrance and is now the home of the Institute of Puerto Rican Culture. Adjacent to the plaza is the Cuartel de Ballajá, built in the mid–19th century as the Spanish army headquarters and still the largest edifice in the Americas constructed by Spanish engineers; it houses the Museum of the Americas.

Centrally located, Quincentennial Plaza is one of modern Puerto Rico's respectful gestures to its colorful and lively history. It is a perfect introduction for visitors seeking to discover the many rich links with the past in Old San Juan.

Once named St. James Square, or Plaza Santiago, **Plaza de Colón** at the main entrance to Old San Juan is at times bustling and busy, but also has a shady, tranquil section. Right off Calle Fortaleza, the square was renamed Plaza de Colón to honor the 400th anniversary of Christopher Columbus' so-called discovery of Puerto Rico, which occurred during his second voyage. Of course, it is more politically correct today to say that Columbus explored or came upon an already inhabited island. He certainly didn't discover it. But when a statue here, perhaps the most famous on the island, was erected atop a high pedestal, it was clearly to honor Columbus, not to decry his legacy. There are some benches beside a newspaper stand in a shady part of the plaza that make a great place to sit. You can grab something cool to drink from a corner store.

Plaza de Las Armas is located at the heart of Old San Juan. The main square is home to San Juan City Hall, built in 1789 as a replica of the Madrid City Hall, and the Puerto Rico State Department, in a beautiful colonial building from the 18th century. The plaza also has a fountain (which unfortunately is usually not working) with four statues representing the four seasons and some gazebos and a cafe. The

Cuatro Estaciones, or Four Seasons, cafe is a nice spot for a strong cup of coffee or a cold drink. In a recent renovation, large trees were planted in the plaza, which provides blissful shade in several spots.

The **Paseo la Princesa** is a wide bayside promenade with outstanding views. The walkway runs along the bay beneath the imposing Spanish colonial wall that surrounds the Old City. It takes its name from a prominent building along it, La Princesa, a former prison in the 1800s that has been blissfully restored and now houses the Puerto Rico Tourism Company Headquarters. The sexy fountain at its center, "Raíces," or "Races," shoots powerful streams of water over the bronze naked Adonises and Amazon warrior goddesses riding huge horses and fish, so you'll get wet if you get too close. Spanish artist Luis Sanguino undertook the work as part of the 500th anniversary of San Juan's founding. The statue is meant to show the Taíno, African, and Spanish roots of Puerto Rico and its people. Farther along, the promenade bends around the bay and passes a shaded area before heading down to San Juan Gate. The new El Morro trail, which goes around the base of the fortress, is actually an extension of this promenade. There are food and drink vendors and often artisans selling their crafts, especially at the start of the route near the cruise ship docks. Enter near the cruise ship docks at the corner of Recinto Sur and Calle La Puntilla or via the San Juan Gate (Calle San Francisco and Calle Recinto Oeste).

PARKS & GARDENS

Jardín Botánico   Administered by the University of Puerto Rico, Jardín Botánico is a lush tropical garden with some 200 species of vegetation. You can pack a picnic lunch and bring it here if you choose. The orchid garden is exceptional, and the palm garden is said to contain some 125 species. Footpaths blaze a trail through heavy forests opening onto a lotus lagoon.

Barrio Venezuela (at the intersection of routes 1 and 847), Río Piedras. ✆ 787/765-1845. Free admission. Daily 6am–6pm. Bus: 19.

Luis Muñoz Marín Park ✸ *Kids*   This 140-acre (57-hectare) park is the best-known, most frequently visited children's playground in Puerto Rico—although it has equal appeal to adults. Conceived as a verdant oasis in an otherwise crowded urban neighborhood, it's a fenced-in repository of swings, jungle gyms, and slides set amid several small lakes and rolling green fields. Here you'll also find an incomparable view of San Juan. A small-scale cable car carries passengers aloft at 10-minute intervals for panoramic views of the surrounding landscape ($2 per person).

Av. Piñero, at Hato Rey. ✆ 787/763-0787. Free admission for pedestrians; parking $2 or $3. Wed–Sun 8am–6pm. Bus: A1 to Río Piedras, then switch to bus 52.

Luis Muñoz Rivera Park   This 27-acre (11-hectare) park, frequently confused with Luis Muñoz Marín Park (see above), is a green rectangle in the middle of Puerta de Tierra. You'll drive by the seaward-facing park on your way to San Juan. It was built 50 years ago to honor Luis Muñoz Rivera, the Puerto Rican statesman, journalist, and poet. It's filled with picnic areas, wide walks, shady trees, landscaped grounds, and recreational areas. There's a new children's playground that's filled with fun on weekends. Its centerpiece, El Pabellon de la Paz, is sometimes used for cultural events and expositions of handicrafts. A new pedestrian and bicycle path connects the park with the oceanfront Tercer Milenio, or Third Millennium Park, across Avenida Muñoz Rivera. The Commonwealth Supreme Court is located at the eastern side of the park.

Between aves. Muñoz Rivera and Ponce de León. ✆ 787/721-6133. Free admission. Daily 24 hrs. Bus: A5.

The Best Places to See Puerto Rican Art

With its dozen or so museums and even more art galleries, Old San Juan is the greatest repository of Puerto Rican arts and crafts. Galleries sell everything from pre-Columbian artifacts to paintings by well-known artists such as Angel Botello, who died in 1986, and Rafael Tufiño, who died in 2008. There's also contemporary traditional crafts, like *santos,* the hand-carved wooden saints the island is known for. Galleries also show a large cast of talented established and up-and-coming contemporary artists.

Noches de galleria, or Gallery Nights, take place the first Tuesday of each month and offer visitors an excellent opportunity to experience the island's vibrant art scene. Most galleries have openings or special exhibits, as well as wine and cheese receptions, and occasionally live music or theatrical performances. Bars and restaurants get into the act and hold art shows or performances. Around about midnight, it all mixes into a terrific party along Calle San Sebastián. If you'd rather visit during the day, a cluster of galleries is spread along Calle Cristo and Calle San José, which is one block east. For specific galleries, see "Art," later in this chapter. The **Galería Nacional,** or National Gallery, located inside Old San Juan's Antiguo Convento de los Dominicos, a restored former convent, has exhibits from the Institute of Puerto Rican Culture's vast holdings. It displays many of the most important works by Puerto Rican painters, from José Campeche and Francisco Oller to Rafael Tufiño and the generation of painters from the 1950s (© **787/977-2700**). Another good place to see Puerto Rican art is the **Museum of History, Anthropology & Art** (© **787/763-3939**). Because of space limitations, the museum's galleries can exhibit only a fifth of their vast collection at one time, but the work is always top-notch. The collection ranges from pre-Columbian artifacts to works by today's major painters.

Parque Central Municipio de San Juan   This mangrove-bordered park was inaugurated in 1979 for the Pan-American Games. It covers 35 acres (14 hectares) and lies southeast of Miramar. Joggers appreciate its labyrinth of trails, and a long boardwalk runs along mangrove canals. Recently renovated, it boasts 20 tennis courts, four racquetball courts, a full track and field area with stadium bleachers, a cafe, and children's play area (just look for the huge jacks sculpture). A golf course is being developed on an adjacent former landfill and a brand-new Olympic standard diving and swimming arena was completed in 2006. Fat, huge iguanas slither from the mangrove-choked channels and into the park's pathways.

Calle Cerra. © **787/722-1646.** Free admission for pedestrians; parking $1. Mon–Thurs 6am–10pm; Fri 6am–9pm; Sat–Sun 6am–7pm. Bus: A1.

SIGHTSEEING TOURS

If you want to see more of the island but you don't want to rent a car or manage the inconveniences of public transportation, perhaps an organized tour is for you.

Santurce, however, is equally important as the Old City, now that it has some of the island's top museums. The grandest repository of art in San Juan is at the **Museo de Arte de Puerto Rico** (p. 162), which is a virtual textbook on all the big names in the art world who rose from Puerto Rico, often to international acclaim. The gorgeously restored building is also part of the appeal, as are the adjoining botanical gardens. The **Museo de Arte Contemporáneo** (© 787/977-4030; aves. Ponce de León and Robert H. Todd) is also an exceptional museum in a restored brick schoolhouse, showing contemporary art from Puerto Rico, but also throughout Latin America and the Caribbean.

Outside San Juan, the greatest art on the island can usually be seen at the **Museo de Arte de Ponce** (p. 219). In addition to such European masters as Reubens, Van Dyck, and Murillo, the museum features works by Latin American artists, including Diego Rivera. Puerto Rican artists who are represented include José Campeche and Francisco Oller. **CIRCO,** an international art fair held at the new Puerto Rico Convention Center annually in April, is growing in stature and quality each year, and many local art venues plan special shows for the occasion.

Unfortunately, the museum is closed for major renovations until 2010—but it continues to be a force in the island's art scene through an exhibition space at the San Juan's **Plaza Las Américas,** the largest mall in the Caribbean, where it will hold shows until its south-coast home is renovated. The inaugural show at the temporary space during the summer of 2008 was a pop art exhibition featuring such giants as Roy Lichtenstein, Andy Warhol, Jasper Johns, and Cindy Sherman. The new space is known as **MAPR at Plaza** (Av. Roosevelt 525, 3rd floor, Plaza Las Américas; © 787/200-7090 or 787/848-0505).

Castillo Sightseeing Tours & Travel Services, 2413 Calle Laurel, Punta La Marias, Santurce (© 787/791-6195), maintains offices at some of the capital's best-known hotels, including the Caribe Hilton and San Juan Marriott Resort. Using six of their own air-conditioned buses, with access to others if demand warrants it, the company's tours include pickups and drop-offs at hotels as an added convenience. Other reputable operators include **Sunshine Tours** (© 787/647-4545), **Rico Suntours** (© 800/844-2080), and **AAA Island Tours** (© 787/793-3678).

All their offerings are pretty similar. One of the most popular half-day tours departs most days of the week between 8:30 and 9am, lasts 4 to 5 hours, and costs about $50 per person, $68 if you take one of the more extensive hiking tours. Leaving from San Juan, it tours along the northeastern part of the island to El Yunque. Another favorite is a city tour of San Juan that departs daily around 1pm. The 4-hour trip costs around $50 per person and includes a stop at the Bacardi Rum Factory. Other trips include the Arecibo Observatory and the Camuy Caves, as well as snorkeling and offshore beach excursions on plush catamarans.

Few cities of the Caribbean lend themselves so gracefully to walking tours. You can embark on these on your own, stopping and shopping en route.

Captain's Duck Tours (© 787/725-0077) offers amphibious excursions in and around Old San Juan in a nifty "boat-bus"—a rubber-ducky yellow vehicle that takes passengers from the streets of Old San Juan to the bay that surrounds it. The 90-minute tours are half land and half water and cost $24 for adults, $17 for children ages 2 to 13. The Duckmobile departs at 11am and 1pm from outside the Covadonga Bus Station in Old San Juan near the cruise ship docks, Thursday through Monday. If you have a short amount of time here, it's a fun way to get a quick overview of the city.

ESPECIALLY FOR KIDS

Puerto Rico is one of the most family-friendly islands in the Caribbean, and many hotels offer family discounts. Programs for children are also offered at a number of hotels, including day and night camp activities and babysitting services. Trained counselors at these camps supervise children as young as 3 in activities ranging from nature hikes to tennis lessons, coconut carving, and sand-sculpture contests.

Teenagers can learn to hip-hop dance Latino-style with special salsa and merengue lessons, learn conversational Spanish, indulge in watersports, take jeep excursions, or scuba-dive in some of the best diving locations in the world. All the major hotels have full children's programs, so it might depend on what you are looking for. Top city hotels like **El San Juan Hotel & Casino** (p. 124), the **Ritz-Carlton San Juan** (p. 126), the **San Juan Marriott & Stellaris Casino** (p. 117), and the **Caribe Hilton** (p. 114) have great pool facilities for kids, day camp activities, watersports and other sports equipment, play areas for little kids, and video arcades for older ones. The **Holiday Inn San Juan** (p. 121) in Isla Verde has a "spray park" that is great for young kids and toddlers.

Children love **El Morro Fortress** (see "Forts," earlier in this chapter) because it looks just like the castles they have seen on TV and at the movies. On a rocky promontory, El Morro is filled with dungeons and dank places and also has lofty lookout points for viewing San Juan Harbor. And the grounds make for great kite flying. The city's historic plazas offer their own possibilities, such as running through the gushing fountains of Quincentennial Plaza or feeding the pigeons at Plaza de Armas.

Luis Muñoz Marín Park (see "Parks & Gardens," above) has the most popular children's playground in Puerto Rico. It's filled with landscaped grounds and recreational areas—lots of room for fun in the sun. And kids love the short cable car ride.

Ben & Jerry's Café Galería Puerto Rico *Kids*   You can't go to Old San Juan with a kid without stopping here. It's the perfect ending to an afternoon of exploring the ancient oceanfront forts and flying kites afterwards, something a kid will always remember. The full 32 flavors—10 of them low-fat—taste particularly good on hot, steamy days. We still love Cherry García, the Chocolate Fudge Brownie, and the Chunky Monkey. But the place also has homemade goodies, pita pizzas, sandwiches, burgers, salads, and snacks. They also have DJ music, art exhibits, Internet access, books, magazines, and more. A great place.

Calle del Cristo 61. © 787/977-6882. Daily 11am–11pm. Bus: Old Town Trolley.

Galaxy Lanes *Kids*   This is a state-of-the-art bowling alley, disco, restaurant, and bar complex located on the third floor just off the food court of the Caribbean's largest mall. The 32-lane alley has huge video screens and a great sound system. It's the place for pre-teen birthday parties, and the place for university kids to spend a night out.

The Cathedral of Rum

Called "the Cathedral of Rum," the **Bacardi Distillery** at Route 888 Km 2.6 at Cataño (② **787/788-1500**), is the largest of its kind in the world. Reached by taking a 20-minute ferry ride across San Juan Bay (50¢ each way), the distillery produces 100,000 gallons of rum daily. At the site, you can go to the **Casa Bacardi Visitor Center**, Carretera 165, Cataño (② **787/788-8400**), for free 90-minute tours Monday to Saturday from 9am to 4:30pm, Sunday 10am to 3:30pm. You are taken on a visit of seven historical displays, including the Bat Theatre, and the Golden Age of the Cocktail Art Deco bar.

Upon entering the first floor, you'll get a glimpse of what rum production was like a century ago, including oak barrels used in the aging process and an old sugar-cane wagon. On the fifth floor you'll enter the Hall of Rum, with a collection of beverages made by the corporation over a period of years. You'll then witness "the birth of rum"—the fermentation processes of molasses (it takes 100 gal. of molasses to produce one barrel of rum).

You'll visit the Bacardi Family Museum, documenting the family's history, and you can watch a short video about the bottling process. At the end of the tour you're taken on a trolley ride to the Hospitality Pavilion, where you can pick up a souvenir and have one for the road.

Great food complements the modern Americana ambiance. Get ready to swing into the beat of reggaeton or some sweet Spanish pop. Lanes cost between $18 and $35 per hour depending on time, and shoe rental is $3.

Plaza de las Américas, Las Américas Expwy. at Av. Roosevelt, Hato Rey. ② 787/777-5016. Free admission (lanes, $18–$35 hourly, shoe rental $3). Sun–Thurs 8am–1pm; Fri–Sat 8am–3am. Bus: B21 from Old San Juan.

Museo del Niño (Children's Museum) *Kids*   In the late 1990s, the city of San Juan turned over one of the most desirable buildings in the colonial zone—a 300-year-old villa directly across from the city's cathedral—to a group of sociologists and student volunteers. Jointly, they created the only children's museum in Puerto Rico. Through interactive exhibits, children learn simple lessons, such as the benefits of brushing teeth or recycling aluminum cans, or the value of caring properly for pets. Staff members include lots of student volunteers who play either one-on-one or with small groups of children. Nothing here is terribly cerebral, and nothing will necessarily compel you to return. But it does provide a play experience that some children will remember for several weeks.

Calle del Cristo 150. ② 787/722-3791. Admission $5 adults, $4 children 14 and younger. Tues–Thurs 9am–3:30pm; Fri 9am–5pm; Sat–Sun 12:30–5pm. Bus: Old Town Trolley.

Time Out Family Amusement Center *Kids*   This is the most popular venue for family outings on Puerto Rico. On weekends, seemingly half the families in the city show up. It has a large variety of electronic games for children and adults alike, but there are no rides.

Plaza de las Américas, Las Américas Expwy. at Av. Roosevelt, Hato Rey. ② 787/753-0606. Free admission (prices of activities vary). Mon–Thurs 9:30am–10pm; Fri–Sun 9am–11pm. Bus: B21 from Old San Juan.

2 Diving, Fishing, Tennis & Other Outdoor Pursuits

Active vacationers have a wide choice of things to do in San Juan, from beaching to windsurfing. The beachside hotels, of course, offer lots of watersports activities (see chapter 6).

THE BEACHES

Some public stretches of shoreline around San Juan are overcrowded, especially on Saturday and Sunday; others are practically deserted. If you find that secluded, hidden beach of your dreams, proceed with caution. On unguarded beaches you'll have no way to protect yourself or your valuables should you be approached by a robber or mugger, which has been known to happen. Thefts on beaches are actually rare, however.

All beaches on Puerto Rico, even those fronting the top hotels, are open to the public. Public bathing beaches are called **balnearios** and charge for parking and for use of facilities, such as lockers and showers. Beach hours in general are 9am to 5pm in winter, to 6pm off season. Most **balnearios** are operated by the Puerto Rico National Parks Company, with others operated by island municipalities. There are two public beaches in the San Juan area with lifeguards, bath and changing rooms, and showers. **El Escambrón public beach** (Ave. Muñoz Rivera, Puerta de Tierra; ℰ 787/721-5185; Wed–Sun and holidays 8:30am–5pm; parking $3) is right next to the Caribe Hilton and surrounded by two sprawling parks. There's a great swimming beach protected by reefs and rock formations jutting out of the water. The famed El 8 surf spot is just to the west, however. There's good snorkeling around the rocks with lots of fish. There's a snack bar and a full-scale restaurant located here. The other public beach is **Isla Verde public beach** (Av. Los Gobernadores, Carolina; ℰ 787/791-8084; daily 8am–6pm; parking $2), a huge expanse of white sand and tranquil waters between Isla Verde and Piñones. There are lifeguards; changing rooms, bathrooms and showers; and picnic areas and barbecue grills.

Famous with beach buffs since the 1920s, **Condado Beach** 𝒦𝒦 put San Juan on the map as a tourist resort. Backed up against high-rise hotels, it seems more like Miami Beach than any other beach in the Caribbean. All sorts of watersports can be booked at the activities desk of the hotels. A small beach near the Condado Plaza hotel is the only one with lifeguards, which are on duty from 8:30am to 5pm. There are also outdoor showers. The beaches in the rest of the Condado are much nicer, but as there are no lifeguards and the surf can get rough, particularly by the San Juan Marriott; swimmers should exercise caution. There are powerful rip tides here that have been responsible for past drownings. Public toilets are rare along the Condado. People-watching is a favorite sport along these golden strands, which stretch from the Ventana del Mar park to beyond the Marriott. The best stretch of beach in the Condado runs from the Ashford Presbyterian hospital to Ocean Park. The area behind the Atlantic Beach Hotel is popular with the gay crowd.

One of the most attractive beaches in the Greater San Juan area is **Ocean Park Beach** 𝒦𝒦, a mile (1.6km) of fine gold sand in a neighborhood east of Condado. This beach attracts young people, travelers looking for a guesthouse rather than the large hotel experience, and those looking for a big gay crowd. The beach runs from Parque del Indio in Condado all the way to the Barbosa Park in the area known as El Ultimo Trolley and offers paddle tennis, kite-boarding, and beach volleyball. You can grab lunch and refreshments from several area guesthouses, and vendors walk up and down the beach, selling cold beer, water and soft drinks, and even snacks like fried seafood turnovers. Farther east, there's no real beach at **Punta Las Marias,** but it's one of the favorite launch points for windsurfers.

Isla Verde Beach 🏖🏖 is the longest and widest in San Juan. It is ideal for swimming, and it, too, is lined with high-rise resorts a la Miami Beach. Many luxury condos are on this beachfront. Isla Verde is good for watersports, including parasailing and snorkeling, because of its calm, clear waters, and many kiosks will rent you equipment, especially by the El San Juan. There are also cafes and restaurants at hotels and more reasonably priced individual restaurants nearby.

Isla Verde Beach extends from the end of Ocean Park to the beginning of a section called Boca Cangrejos. The most popular beach is probably behind the Hotel El San Juan and the Intercontinental San Juan hotels. But Pine Grove beach, behind the Ritz-Carlton, is a great swimming beach and very popular as well, particularly with surfers and sailors.

SPORTS & OTHER OUTDOOR PURSUITS

BIKE RENTALS   The best places to bicycle are in city parks like Luis Muñoz Marín (Hato Rey) and Luis Muñoz Rivera (Puerta de Tierra). You can make it from Condado to Old San Juan driving mostly through the latter park. There are also bicycle trails; we recommend the coastal boardwalk running along Piñones, which is beautiful and safe, especially on the weekends. There are bike rentals available in the area during weekends, although most San Juan streets are too crowded for bicycle riding. **Hot Dog Cycling,** Av. Isla Verde 5916, La Plazoleta Shopping Center (✆ 787/721-0776), open Monday to Saturday 9am to 6pm, charges $5 per hour for rentals, $25 for a full day.

CRUISES   For the best cruises of San Juan Bay, go to **Caribe Aquatic Adventures** (see "Scuba Diving," below). Bay cruises start at $25 per person.

DEEP-SEA FISHING 🎣   Deep-sea fishing is top-notch here. Allison tuna, white and blue marlin, sailfish, wahoo, dolphin (mahimahi), mackerel, and tarpon are some of the fish that can be caught in Puerto Rican waters, where 30 world records have been broken. Charter arrangements can be made through most major hotels and resorts. The big game fishing grounds are very close offshore from San Juan, making the capital an excellent place to hire a charter. A half-day of deep-sea fishing (4 hours) starts at around $550, while full-day charters begin at around $900. Most charters hold six passengers in addition to the crew.

There are three marinas in the San Juan metropolitan area, with fishing charters and boat rentals available at all three. The **Cangrejos Yacht Club** (Route 187, Piñones; ✆ 787/791-1015) is right near the airport on Route 187, the road from Isla Verde to Piñones, while the two other marinas are next to each other near the Condado bridge and the Convention Center in Miramar: **San Juan Bay Marina** (✆ 787/721-8062) and **Club Nautico de San Juan** (✆ 787/722-0177).

Capt. Mike Benítez, of **Benítez Fishing Charters** (✆ 787/723-2292), is the most experienced operator in San Juan sailing out of Club Nautico. His crew is knowledgeable and informative, and the 45-foot air-conditioned deluxe Hatteras called the *Sea Born* is plush and comfortable. We also recommend another veteran outfit, **Castillo Fishing Charters** (✆ 787/726-5752), that has been running charters out of the San Juan Bay Marina since 1975. Capt. Joe Castillo runs the company with his son José Iván and daughter Vanessa and they also know their stuff. *The Legend*, a 48-foot

Hatteras, is also an excellent vessel built for fishing and comfort. Capt. Omar Orracar of **Caribbean Outfitters** (℅ **787/396-8346**) runs deep-sea fishing charters but also runs fly-fishing trips in San Juan lagoons for snook and tarpon. The boat is docked at Cangrejos Yacht Club.

GOLF   The island's best golf courses are within a short drive of San Juan. The legendary Dorado courses are 45 minutes west at the **Dorado Beach Resort & Club** (℅ **787/796-8961**). Designed by Robert Trent Jones, Sr., these courses have hosted professional tournaments, including the World Cup of Golf (see the "World-Class Golf at the Former Hyatt Dorado" box on p. 207). Fees for guests are $160.

Driving east for 45 minutes will get you to the world-class golf courses of Río Grande and Fajardo. The **Wyndham Río Mar Beach Resort** golf offerings (℅ **787/ 888-7060**) include two world-class courses, stretching out in the shadow of El Yunque rainforest along a dazzling stretch of coast. There is a 6,782-yard (6,201m) ocean course by Tom and George Fazio, and a 6,945-yard (6,354m) course by Greg Norman that cuts through jungle and mountain areas. Greens fees for guests are $175, for walk-ins $200. **The Trump International Golf Club** (℅ **787/657-2000**), also in Río Grande, is actually four different nine-hole courses sprawled out across 1,200 acres (486 hectares) of coast. Each course is named after its surrounding environment: the Ocean, the Palms, the Mountains, and the Lakes. Fees range from $140 to $160 for visitors.

Berwind Country Club (℅ **787/876-5380**) in **Loiza** is the nearest full-size course to the city. Built on a former coconut plantation, it's a beautiful place with ocean views, towering palms, and frenzied tropical foliage. Experts say the course is quite challenging, with plenty of water hazards and three of the toughest holes to finish on the island. And with greens fees of $65, it's a bargain. On weekend mornings, the course is reserved for members. The 9-hole **Río Bayamón Golf Course** (℅ **787/ 740-1419**) is a municipal course in the San Juan suburb Bayamón. Greens fees are $30 and rentals just $15.

HORSE RACING   Great thoroughbreds and outstanding jockeys compete year-round at **Camarero Racetrack,** Calle 65 de Infantería, Route 3 Km 15.3, at Canovanas (℅ **787/641-6060**), Puerto Rico's only racetrack, a 20-minute drive east of the center of San Juan. Races begin at 3pm Monday, Wednesday, Friday, Saturday, Sunday, and holidays. The clubhouse has a fine dining restaurant, the Terrace Room, that serves good local food, and there's Winner's Sports Bar with pub fare. The grandstand has free admission.

RUNNING   The cool, quiet, morning hours before 8am are a good time to jog through the streets of Old San Juan. Head for the wide thoroughfares adjacent to El Morro and then San Cristóbal, whose walls jut upward from the flat ground. The seafront Paseo de la Princesa, at the base of the governor's mansion La Fortaleza, is another fine site. **San Juan Central Park** (Calle Cerra; exit from Av. Muñoz Rivera or Rte. 2; ℅ **787/722-1646**) has an excellent professional track in an outdoor track and field stadium with bleachers. There is a similar setup at **Parque Barbosa** right off the beach in Ocean Park. A renovation of the park is slated to be completed by 2009.

Condado's Avenida Ashford and the hardpacked sands of Isla Verde are busy sites for morning runners as well.

SCUBA DIVING   In San Juan, the best outfitter is **Caribe Aquatic Adventures,** Normandie Hotel San Juan, Calle 19 1062, Villa Nevarez (℅ **787/281-8858;**

Tips **Swimmers, Beware**

You have to pick your spots carefully if you want to swim along Condado Beach. The waters at the beach beside the Condado Plaza Hotel are calmer than in other areas because of a coral breakwater. The beach near the Marriott is not good for swimming because of rocks, a strong undertow, and occasional rip tides. There are no lifeguards except at public beaches. Ocean Park is better to swim, but can still be hazardous when the tides kick up. Isla Verde beach is generally much calmer, especially at its eastern end.

---

www.diveguide.com/p2046.htm). Its dive shop is open daily from 9am to 9pm. This outfitter will take you to the best local dive sites in the Greater San Juan area. Dives begin at $125 per person and a resort course for first-time divers also costs $125. Escorted dive and snorkeling jaunts to the eastern shore are also offered. Snorkeling lessons or tours lasting 1 hour and including basic equipment go for $50. Another good outfitter is **Ocean Sports.** Its main office is Av. Isla Verde 77 (© **787/268-2329**), but it also has other offices at the Isla Verde Mall, near the Ritz-Carlton at the other end of the avenue; and right on Avenida Ashford in Condado near the big hotels. It offers diving courses and scuba diving, as well as snorkeling trips in San Juan and also to the east coast. Kayak rentals are also available.

SNORKELING   Snorkeling is better in the outlying portions of the island than in overcrowded San Juan. But if you don't have time to explore greater Puerto Rico, you'll find that most of the popular beaches, such as Luquillo and Isla Verde, have pretty good visibility and kiosks that rent equipment. Snorkeling equipment generally rents for $15. If you're on your own in the San Juan area, one of the best places is the San Juan Bay marina near the Caribe Hilton.

Watersports desks at the big San Juan hotels at Isla Verde and Condado can generally make arrangements for instruction and equipment rental and can also lead you to the best places for snorkeling, depending on where you are in the sprawling metropolis. If your hotel doesn't offer such services, you can contact **Caribe Aquatic Adventures** (see "Scuba Diving," above), which caters to both snorkelers and scuba divers.

Still, even if you are staying in San Juan and want to go snorkeling, you are better off taking a day trip to Fajardo, where you'll get a real Caribbean snorkeling experience, with tranquil, clear water, and stunning reefs teaming with tropical fish. Several operators offer day trips (from 10am–3:30pm) leaving from Fajardo marinas, but transportation to and from your San Juan hotel can also be arranged. Prices start at around $69 per person, or $99 including transportation to and from San Juan. Even if you don't particularly want to snorkel, the trips are still worth it for a day of fun in the sun. The trips usually take place on large luxury catamarans, holding about 20 passengers or more. Most have a cash bar serving drinks and refreshments, a sound system, and other creature comforts. Typically, after a nice sail, the cat will weigh anchor at different snorkeling spots and then in sheltered waters near one of the scores of small islands lying off Fajardo's coast, the perfect spot for a swim or sunbathing. Most trips include lunch, which usually is served on a beach. The boats know the best reefs and hot spots for bigger fish, and will plan the trip according to weather conditions and other variables. A huge reef extending east to Culebra protects the ocean off Fajardo's coast, which makes for calm seas with great visibility.

(Finds) **La *Criolla* Chic**

San Juan has Latino chic to rival South Beach. Puerto Rican royalty (from Benicio del Toro to Marc Anthony and J-Lo to Ricky Martin) are regularly jetting in, and so are other interesting people. The city has been transformed by the opening of the **Puerto Rico Miguel José Miguel Agrelot Coliseum** (500 Arterial B Street Hato Rey; (C) **877/265-4736;** box office open Mon–Fri 10am–5pm) and the **Puerto Rico Convention Center** (100 Convention Blvd., San Juan; (C) **800/214-0420**). Since the opening of "the Choliseo," as the coliseum is known locally, performers like the Rolling Stones, Elton John, the Police, and Billy Joel have played there, and it regularly gets top-name Latino acts, like Shakira and Juanes. The Convention Center is attracting all sorts of national groups as well as other entertainment events. CIRCO, an annual art fair, is getting serious attention, and the center is also the host of an annual fashion week with shows by local and international designers. The Puerto Rico Tourism Company's annual New Year's Eve party, broadcast live on Spanish language television and featuring some of the top names in Latino music, is also held here. Even when there are no stars, both venues have cafe-bars that have become hangouts for young urban professionals to let loose after work, especially on Thursday and Friday nights.

There is no trendier place in San Juan today than the new temple of island art, **Museo de Arte** (p. 162). It took $55 million to turn this 1920s city hospital in Santurce, an eyesore for decades, into this new home for art. The new museum has become a way of life for some Puerto Ricans, many of whom go here at least once a week—perhaps to see a production in the 400-seat theater, named for Raúl Juliá, the late Puerto Rican actor, or perhaps to go for a romantic stroll through the museum's 5-acre (2-hectare) garden. There may also be no better place to go at night for a *nuevo criolla* meal than the restaurant here, **Pikayo** (p. 150).

San Juan even has **SoFo,** a once abandoned sector of La Fortaleza Street that is now buzzing with activity, home to some of Old San Juan's best restaurants, bars, and clubs. A play on the name of New York City's SoHo, SoFo purportedly refers to South Fortaleza Street. The name has stuck, even though it's geographically inaccurate, as the area is actually East Fortaleza Street. The **Parrot Club** (p. 135) is the original hot spot of the neighborhood, opening more than a decade ago with its brash and flavorful Nuevo Latino cuisine in a land of crusty Chinese restaurants and delis, run-down tourist

Inquire at your hotel desk about operators providing service there. There are many reputable companies. We and friends have all been satisfied with **Traveler Sailing Catamaran** ((C) 787/853-2821), **East Island Excursions** ((C) 787/860-3434), and **Catamaran Spread Eagle** ((C) 787/887-8821). **Erin Go Bragh Charters** ((C) 787/860-4401) offers similar day trips aboard a 50-foot sailing ketch, which is an equally pleasurable experience.

shops, and dusty fabric stores. Today, these run-down businesses have been renovated. The area is a center for world cuisine, where you can get everything from French **Trois Cent Onze** (p. 136) to Indian **Tantra** (p. 141) to Asian Fusian **Dragonfly** (p. 139).

And we would put the beach at Ocean Park against that at South Beach. It's just naturally far more beautiful, and its guesthouses and restaurants attract an eclectic set of trendsetters: students, surfers, gay people, and urban creatives from the East Coast who prefer its low-lying skyline and laid-back ambience over the big resorts and condos of Condado and Isla Verde.

And there's perhaps no place as timelessly chic as the **Plaza de Mercado de Santurce** (near Calle Canals and Av. Ponce de León). The traditional food market is a great place to buy tropical fruits and vegetables, and there's a bunch more oddities like old Puerto Rican music recordings, herbs, and religious artifacts involving *santería*. There are several good restaurants in the surrounding neighborhood (**Don Tello** and **La Tasca del Pscador**) and several bars. The neighborhood is a swirl of activity from early in the day through late evening. On Thursday and Friday nights, large crowds gather as the streets are blocked off from traffic. Several spots have live music. It's a favorite after-work spot for locals and a lot of fun. Just join the crowd and meander from one spot to the next. Seafood fritters, chicken kebabs, and meat turnovers are sold from street vendors, and there is music everywhere.

The city also has several beautiful green parks with loads of activities during weekends. A plan to connect them via bicycle and pedestrian pathways is underway. It will build on the **Parque Lineal Marti Coli,** which stretches for nearly 2 miles (3.2km) along Caño de Martín Peña, from Hato Rey to Parque Central. Eventually this boardwalk will reach a distance of nearly 12 miles (19km), linking the Old City with Río Piedras. Biking, hiking, and jogging pathways are planned; one day bikers will be able to go along the breadth of San Juan without having to encounter traffic. In the meantime, enough trails have been completed for a memorable stroll.

Later you can head to Old San Juan for some island music, either to **Rumba** (p. 190) or the **Nuyorican Café** (p. 190) to dance the night away to the sounds of salsa and Latin rhythms with an African beat.

SPAS & FITNESS CENTERS   If a spa figures into your holiday plans, the grandest and largest such facility in San Juan is found at **Ritz-Carlton San Juan Hotel, Spa & Casino** ✿, Avenida de los Gobernadores 6961, no. 187, Isla Verde (© **787/253-1700**). You get it all here: the luxury life, with state-of-the-art massages, body wraps and scrubs, facials, manicures, pedicures, and a salon guaranteed to make you look like a movie star.

In an elegant marble-and-stone setting, there are 11 rooms for pampering, including hydrotherapy and treatments custom-tailored for individual needs. The spa also features a 7,200-square-foot outdoor swimming pool.

The Ritz-Carlton facility offers the exotic and ritualistic treatments known to spa lovers around the world as the Balinese Massage and the Javanese Lulur. The fragrant Balinese Massage uses compression, skin-rolling, wringing, and percussion and thumb-walking to "de-stress" the most uptight guests. The Lulur originated centuries ago in the royal palaces of Central Java as part of a ritual for royal brides-to-be. The Lulur was performed daily to beautify, soften, and "sweeten" the bride's skin. Today women and men alike enjoy it.

The newly launched Olas Spa at the **Carib Hilton,** Calle Los Rosales (© 787/721-0303) offers everything from traditional massages to more exotic body and water therapies, using such products as honey, cucumber, sea salts, seaweed, or mud baths. You can choose your delight among the massages, including one called "Rising Sun," a traditional Japanese form of massage called shiatsu that uses pressure applied with hands, elbows, and knees on specific body points. Among body wraps is one known as Firm Away, a super-firming, brown and green algae body cocoon therapy for a soft, toned, and smooth skin.

The Hilton Spa has the town's best program for hair treatments, including thinning hair and "tired perm." It also has a state-of-the-art fitness center with Universal and Nautilus weight machines, aerobics and yoga classes, treadmills, aerobicycles, loofah body polishes, and facials.

After the extravaganza of these two spas, it's a bit of a comedown at the other leading resorts. The Plaza Spa at the **Condado Plaza Hotel & Casino,** Av. Ashford 999 (© 787/721-1000), features Universal weight-training machines, video exercycles, a sauna, whirlpools, and a spa program of facials and massage. We'd recommend this mainly for people who want only minor spa or fitness-center facilities during their stay, and not for those who want to make a spa the number-one goal of their sojourn in San Juan.

El San Juan Hotel & Casino Resort, Av. Isla Verde 6063 (© 787/791-1000), offers a stunning panoramic view of San Juan that almost competes with the facilities. You'll find full amenities, including fitness evaluations, supervised weight-loss programs, aerobics classes, a sauna, a steam room, and luxury massages. A daily fee for individual services is assessed if you want special treatment or care.

Another option is **Zen Spa,** Av. Ashford 1054, Condado (© 787/722-8433), which has a full range of massages, facial treatments, body wraps and therapeutic services. It's open 8am to 7pm weekdays, 9am to 6pm weekends.

Most hotels have quality gyms. If your hotel doesn't have a gym or health club of its own, consider working the kinks out of your muscles at **International Fitness** ⨍, Av. Ashford 1131, Condado (© 787/721-0717). It's air-conditioned, well equipped, and popular with residents of the surrounding high-rent district. Entrance costs $15 per visit, $50 for 5 days, or $55 for a week. Hours are Monday to Thursday 5am to 10pm, Friday 5am to 9pm, Saturday 9am to 7pm, and Sunday 10am to 3pm.

TENNIS   Most of the big resorts have their own tennis courts for their guests. There are 20 public courts, lit at night, at **San Juan Central Park,** at Calle Cerra (exit on Rte. 2; © 787/722-1646), open daily. Fees are $3 per hour from 6am to 5pm, and $4 per hour from 6 to 10pm. There are also four racquetball courts here. The **Isla Verde Tennis Club** (© 787/727-6490) is open all week, weekdays from 8am to

10pm, Saturdays from 8am to 7pm, and Sundays from 8am to 6pm. Courts cost from $15 to $20 hourly.

WINDSURFING/KITE SURFING   The most savvy windsurfing and kite surfing advice and equipment sales and rental are available at **Velauno,** Calle Loíza 2430, Punta Las Marías in San Juan (© **787/982-0543**). A beginner's class with equipment rental in either kite or windsurfing is $150; private lessons with gear included are $50 hourly. One-day rental cost for windsurfing gear is $75, 3 days $150, and 1 week $225; for kite-surfing gear 1 day is $40, 3 days $90, and 1 week $130. The staff here will guide you to the best windsurfing, right near the store in Punta Las Marías and Ocean Park. Office hours are Monday to Friday 10am to 7pm, Saturday 11am to 7pm. There is a summer windsurfing camp for kids.

3 Shopping

Because Puerto Rico is a U.S. commonwealth, U.S. citizens don't pay duty on items brought back to the mainland. And you can still find great bargains on Puerto Rico, where the competition among shopkeepers is fierce. Even though the U.S. Virgin Islands are duty-free, you can often find far lower prices on many items in San Juan than on St. Thomas. Since November 2006, a local 7% sales and use tax has been instituted on most goods and services.

The streets of the Old City, such as Calle San Francisco and Calle del Cristo, are the major venues for shopping. Malls in San Juan are generally open Monday to Saturday 9am to 9pm, Sunday 11am to 5pm. Regular stores in town are **usually open Monday to Saturday 9am to 6pm**. In Old San Juan most stores are open on **Sunday, too, from about 11am to 5pm**.

Native handicrafts can be good buys, including needlework, straw work, ceramics, hammocks, and papier-mâché fruits and vegetables, as well as paintings and sculptures by Puerto Rican artists. Among these, the carved wooden religious idols known as *santos* (saints) have been called Puerto Rico's greatest contribution to the plastic arts and are sought by collectors. For the best selection of *santos,* head for Galería Botello (see "Art," below), Olé, or Puerto Rican Arts & Crafts (see "Gifts & Handicrafts," later in this chapter).

Puerto Rico's biggest and most up-to-date shopping mall is **Plaza Las Américas,** in the financial district of Hato Rey, right off the Las Américas Expressway. This complex, with its fountains and modern architecture, has more than 200 mostly upscale shops. The variety of goods and prices is roughly comparable to that of large stateside malls. There are also several top-notch restaurants, a full Cineplex, a fabulous bowling alley and entertainment center, plus art galleries and food stores. If you want a break from the sun (or if it's raining), there are entertainment options here for all.

Unless otherwise specified, the following stores can be reached via the Old Town Trolley.

ANTIQUES

El Alcazar *Finds*   Established in 1986 by retired career officers with the U.S. Army and the U.S. State Department, this is the largest emporium of antique furniture, silver, and art objects in the Caribbean. The best way to sift through the massive inventory is to begin at the address listed below, on Calle San José between Calle Luna and Calle Sol, and ask the owners, Sharon and Robert Bartos, to guide you to the other three buildings that are literally stuffed with important art and antiques. Each

---

Tips Know When the Price Is Right

The only way to determine if you're paying less for an item in San Juan than you would at home is to find out what the going rate is in your hometown. Obviously, if you can find items in San Juan cheaper than back home, go for it. But know the prices before you go. Otherwise, you could end up lugging merchandise back on an airplane when the same item was available at about the same price, or less, where you live.

---

shop lies within a half-block of the organization's headquarters, and each is within a historic building of architectural or historical importance (public areas of several large Puerto Rican hotels contain furnishings acquired here). For antique silver, crystal, delicate porcelain, glittering chandeliers, Russian icons, and objects of religious devotion such as *santos,* look first at the organization's headquarters. Some of the objects, especially the 1930s-era dining-room sets, whose chair backs are composed of wood medallions held in place by woven canes or wicker, derive from Puerto Rico. The majority of the objects, however, are culled from estates and galleries throughout Europe. Calle San José 103. ✆ 787/723-1229.

ART

Butterfly People   Butterfly People is a gallery in a handsomely restored building in Old San Juan. Butterflies, sold here in artfully arranged boxes, range from $35 for a single mounting to thousands of dollars for whole-wall murals. The butterflies are preserved and will last forever. The dimensional artwork is sold in limited editions and can be shipped worldwide. Most of these butterflies come from farms around the world, some of the most beautiful hailing from Indonesia, Malaysia, and New Guinea. It's open Saturday and Sunday from 10am to 6pm. Calle Cruz 257. ✆ 787/723-2432.

Galería Botello   A contemporary Latin American art gallery, Galería Botello is a living tribute to the late Angel Botello, one of Puerto Rico's most outstanding artists. Born after the Spanish Civil War in a small village in Galicia, Spain, he fled to the Caribbean and spent 12 years in Haiti. His paintings and bronze sculptures, evocative of his colorful background, are done in a style uniquely his own. This galería is his former colonial mansion home, which he restored himself. Today it displays his paintings and sculptures, showcases the works of many outstanding local artists, and offers a large collection of Puerto Rican antique *santos,* hand-carved wooden statues of the saints. Calle del Cristo 208. ✆ 787/723-9987.

Galería Exodo   This exciting gallery shows work from young contemporary island and regional artists, many of whom are not afraid to engage in bold experimentation. The work ranges from Radamés Rivera's limestone and coral art pieces that could have existed at the time of the dinosaurs to Yolanda Velasquez's vibrant abstract paintings. Over 40 artists, from Cuba to Mexico, showcase work here. Calle Cristo 200B. ✆ 787/725-4252.

Galería Sánchez   This new gallery represents a collection of talented international artists with different styles, including: Patrick McGrath, contemporary realism; Moisés Castillo, expressionist; Erick Sánchez, neo-impressionist; and Claus Costa, mixed media pop. New shows are held monthly, in conjunction with Noches de

Galería, and it publishes a monthly cyber-newsletter. Open Monday through Wednesday from 1 to 6pm, Thursday through Saturday from 1 to 9pm. In SoFo. Calle Fortaleza 320. ℂ 787/829-4663 or 466-5494.

Galería San Juan This shop, located at the Gallery Inn, specializes in the sculpture and paintings of Jan D'Esopo, a Connecticut-born artist who has spent a great deal of time in Puerto Rico. Many of her fine pieces are in bronze. In the Gallery Inn, Calle Norzagaray 204. ℂ 787/722-1808.

Haitian Gallery This is the best store, now with two locations, in San Juan for Haitian art and artifacts. Its walls are covered with framed versions of primitive Haitian landscapes, portraits, crowd scenes, and whimsical visions of jungles where lions, tigers, parrots, and herons take on quasi-human personalities and forms. Most paintings range from $20 to $350, although you can usually bargain them down a bit. Look for the brightly painted wall hangings crafted from sheets of metal. Also look for satirical metal wall hangings, brightly painted, representing the *tap-taps* (battered public minivans and buses) of Port-au-Prince. They make amusing and whimsical souvenirs of a trip to the Caribbean. Open daily from 10am to 6pm. Calle Fortaleza 206. ℂ 787/721-4362. The other location is at Calle Fortaleza 367. ℂ 787/725-0986.

Obra Galería Alegría A bit off the well worn gallery route along Calle Cristo and Calle San José, this gallery is worth searching out for its representation of such important masters as Lorenzo Homar; Domingo García; Julio Rosado del Valle; and younger, accomplished, contemporary artists like Nick Quijano, Jorge Zeno, and Magda Santiago. The gallery was started by José Alegría, with the assistance of his uncle Ricardo Alegría, the founder of the Institute of Puerto Rican Culture. It's open Tuesday through Saturday from 10am to 6pm. Calle Cruz 301 (corner Recinto Sur). ℂ 787/723-3206.

BOOKS
La Tertulia A bookstore with a wide selection of books and music in a large, beautiful setting, La Tertulia carries the latest hits in Spanish and English, plus non-fiction, fiction, and classics in both Spanish and English. It's open Monday through Saturday from 9am to 10pm and Sunday from 10am to 8pm. Recinto Sur 305, Old San Juan. ℂ 787/724-8200. Bus: A5.

Librería Cronopios This is the leading choice in the Old Town, with the largest selection of titles. It sells a number of books on Puerto Rican culture as well as good maps of the island. Calle San José 255. ℂ 787/724-1815.

CARNIVAL MASKS
La Calle Every Puerto Rican knows that the best, and cheapest, place to buy brightly painted carnival masks *(caretas)* is in Ponce, where the tradition of making them from papier-mâché originated. But if you can't spare the time for a side excursion to Ponce, this store in Old San Juan stocks one of the most varied inventories of *vegigantes* in the Puerto Rican capital. Depending on their size and composition (some include coconut shells, gourds, and flashy metal trim), they range from $10 to $2,500 each. Side-by-side with the pagan-inspired masks, you'll find a well-chosen selection of paintings by talented local artists, priced from $25 to $2,800 each. Calle Fortaleza 105. ℂ 787/725-1306.

Fun Fact **Grotesque Masks**

The most popular of all Puerto Rican crafts are the frightening *caretas*—papier-mâché masks worn at island carnivals. Tangles of menacing horns, fang-toothed leering expressions, and bulging eyes of these half-demon, half-animal creations send children running and screaming to their parents. At carnival time, they are worn by costumed revelers called *vegigantes*. *Vegigantes* often wear bat-winged jumpsuits and roam the streets either individually or in groups.

The origins of these masks and carnivals may go back to medieval Spain and/or tribal Africa. A processional tradition in Spain, dating from the early 17th century, was intended to terrify sinners with marching devils in the hope that they would return to church. Cervantes described it briefly in *Don Quijote*. Puerto Rico blended this Spanish procession with the masked tradition brought by slaves from Africa. Some historians believe that the Taínos were also accomplished mask makers, which would make this a very ancient tradition indeed.

The predominant traditional mask colors were black, red, and yellow, all symbols of hellfire and damnation. Today, pastels are more likely to be used. Each *vegigante* sports at least two or three horns, although some masks have hundreds of horns, in all shapes and sizes. Mask making in Ponce, the major center for this craft, and in Loíza Aldea, a palm-fringed town on the island's northeastern coast, has since led to a renaissance of Puerto Rican folk art.

The premier store selling these masks is **La Calle** (p. 181). Masks can be seen in action at the three big masquerade carnivals on the island: the Ponce Festival in February, the Festival of Loíza Aldea in July, and the Día de las Máscaras at Hatillo in December.

CIGARS

The Cigar House This is retail outlet has a great selection of cigars, including Puerto Rican–based *jibarito* cigars, but it sells quality Dominican brands as well. It's a no-frills cigar shop with a nice selection. At The Doll House (which sells souvenirs now, "no dolls" the owner will shriek at you). Calle Fortaleza 255. ℂ **787/723-7797**or 725-0652.

Don Collin's Cigars This is the main store of this locally produced brand of cigars, hand rolled on the island from locally grown tobacco and wraps, and sometimes mixed with fine tobacco from the Dominican Republic and elsewhere. There are nine varieties, and 5-count and 9-count variety packs are available. Open daily from 9am to 8pm. Calle Cristo 59. ℂ **787/977-2983**.

CLOTHING & BEACHWEAR

Costazul This surf shop stocks major brands of beachwear, surfwear, sunglasses, and bathing suits for men, women, and children. The prices are not bad, and the merchandise is top rate. Worth a stop if you really need something for the beach. Calle San Francisco 264. ℂ **787/722-0991**.

Hecho a Mano Beautiful locally made ethnic clothing for women, using island fabric but also those from Guatemala, Indonesia, India, and Africa. Styles range from willowy dresses and wraps in tribal patterns, to more modern, tropical-fashion party dresses. It has gorgeous clothes, plus handmade jewelry and other interesting finds. The ambience in the store is wonderful, complete with incense, world music, and the beautiful sales staff outfitted in the store's fashion. Founded in 1993, the company prides itself on its dealings with its artisans and its efforts to undertake practices and designs in harmony with nature. Now with 12 locations, including Condado and Plaza Las Américas. Main location open Monday through Saturday from 10am to 7pm, Sunday from 11am to 5pm. Calle San Francisco 260, Viejo San Juan. ℂ 787/722-5322.

Mrs. and Miss Boutique The home of the "the magic dress," which is crafted in Morocco of a silky-looking blend of rayon and cotton, in 10 different colors or patterns, each of which can be worn 11 different ways. There are much better deals on the sarongs and long dresses, sometimes from Indonesia. Calle Fortaleza 154. ℂ 787/724-8571.

Nono Maldonado Named after its owner, a Puerto Rico–born designer who worked for many years as the fashion editor of *Esquire* magazine, this is one of the most fashionable and upscale haberdashers in the Caribbean. Selling both men's and women's clothing, it contains everything from socks to dinner jackets, as well as ready-to-wear versions of Maldonado's twice-a-year collections. Both ready-to-wear and couture are available here. Av. Ashford 1051. ℂ 787/721-0456. Bus: A7.

Polo Ralph Lauren Factory Store *(Value* It's as stylish and carefully orchestrated as anything you'd expect from one of North America's leading clothiers. Even better, its prices are often 35% to 40% less than in retail stores on the U.S. mainland. You can find even greater discounts on irregular or slightly damaged garments, but inspect them carefully before buying. The store occupies two floors of a pair of colonial buildings, with one upstairs room devoted to home furnishings. Calle del Cristo 201. ℂ 787/722-2136.

Wet Boutique The ever chic Erika has been selling the sexiest swimsuits in town for decades. There's a wide selection of the top-name bikini and one-piece designs, plus upscale beach accessories. Calle Cruz 150, Old San Juan. ℂ 787/722-2052.

COFFEE & SPICES

Casa Galesa With "style and harmony" as its motto, this shop has beautiful stuff for home and gourmet items. From soap and candles to kitchen utensils, there's some beautiful stuff here for homebodies, or those who want to get a gift for one. Calle Cristo. ℂ 787/977-0400.

Corné Port-Royal Chocolatier A purveyor of the finest chocolate in the world: Belgian chocolates, pralines, truffles. They also sell cookies and jellies. Open Monday through Saturday 10am to 6pm. Calle San Justo 204, Old San Juan. ℂ 787/725-7744.

Spicy Caribbee This shop has the best selection of Puerto Rican coffee, which is gaining an increasingly good reputation among aficionados. Alto Grande is the grandest brand, but other specialty brands, like Yauco Selecto, are also quite wonderful. Other favorite brands of Puerto Rican coffee are Café Crema, Café Rico, Rioja, and Yaucono—in that order. The shop also has Old City's best array of hot spicy and sweet sauces of the Caribbean. Calle Cristo 154. ℂ 787/725-4690.

The Coffee of Kings & Popes

Of all the coffees of Puerto Rico, our favorite is **Alto Grande,** which has been a tradition in Puerto Rican households since 1839. Over the years, this super premium coffee has earned a reputation for being the "Coffee of Popes and Kings," and is hailed as one of the top three coffees in the world. A magnificently balanced coffee, Alto Grande is a rare and exotic coffee with a sweet, pointed aroma and a bright sparkling flavor. The bean is grown in the highest mountains of the Lares range. This coffee is served at leading hotels and restaurants in Puerto Rico. Should you develop a taste for it, it is also available at various specialty stores throughout the United States.

DEPARTMENT STORES

Marshalls   This store, part of the U.S. discount chain, is one of our favorite department stores in the whole Caribbean. Thousands of *sanjuaneros* also consider it their favorite shopping destination as well. A few dedicated born-to-shop advocates pop in virtually every day to see what new items have gone on sale. At Plaza de Armas, across from the City Hall, expect to see a massive array—at cut-rate prices—of designer clothes, housewares, home furnishings, and shoes, plus a variety of other merchandise. There's also an incredible amount of quality stuff at good prices for the traveler: from bathing suits to shorts to sandals to luggage to sunglasses. In fact, this is probably your best bet for an affordable bathing suit. Calle Rafael Cordero 154, Old San Juan. © 787/722-3020.

GIFTS & HANDICRAFTS

Bared & Sons *Value*   Now in its fourth decade, this is the main outlet of a chain of at least 20 upper-bracket jewelry stores on Puerto Rico. It has a worthy inventory of gemstones, gold, diamonds, and wristwatches on the street level, which does a thriving business with cruise-ship passengers. But the real value of this store lies one floor up, where a monumental collection of porcelain and crystal is on display in claustrophobic proximity. It's a great source for hard-to-get and discontinued patterns (priced at around 20% less than at equivalent stateside outlets) from Christofle, Royal Doulton, Wedgwood, Limoges, Royal Copenhagen, Lalique, Lladró, Herend, Baccarat, and Daum. San Justo 206 (at the corner of Calle Fortaleza). © 787/724-4811.

Bóveda   This long, narrow space is crammed with exotic jewelry, clothing, greeting cards with images of life in Puerto Rico, some 100 handmade lamps, antiques, Mexican punched tin and glass, and Art Nouveau reproductions, among other items. Calle del Cristo 209. © 787/725-0263.

DMR Designs   Located at La Cochera parking garage in the heart of the historic zone, this gallery of fine art furniture and furnishings is a cool respite and well worth a look. The designs by Diana M. Ramos are reproductions and originals of classic Caribbean plantation furniture, more traditional Spanish colonial work, and spare, modern pieces. Their common traits are the artistic standards brought to them through their organic form and creativity. Calle Luna 204, Old San Juan. © 787/722-4181.

Olé   Browsing this store is a learning experience. Even the standard Panama hat takes on new dimensions. Woven from fine-textured *paja* grass and priced from $20 to

Tips Shopping for *Santos*

The most impressive of the island's crafts are the *santos,* carved religious figures that have been produced since the 1500s. Craftspeople who make these are called *santeros;* using clay, gold, stone, or cedar wood, they carve figurines representing saints, usually from 8 to 20 inches (20–51 cm) tall. Before the Spanish colonization, small statues called *zemi* stood in native tribal villages and camps as objects of veneration, and Puerto Rico's *santos* may derive from that pre-Columbian tradition. Every town has its patron saint, and every home has its *santos* to protect the family. For some families, worshipping the *santos* replaces a traditional Mass.

Art historians view the carving of *santos* as Puerto Rico's greatest contribution to the plastic arts. The earliest figures were richly baroque, indicating a strong Spanish influence, but as the islanders began to assert their own identity, the carved figures often became simpler.

In carving *santos,* craftspeople often used handmade tools. Sometimes such natural materials as vegetable dyes and even human hair were used. The saints represented by most *santos* can be identified by their accompanying symbols; for example, Saint Anthony is usually depicted with the infant Jesus and a book. The most popular group of *santos* is the Three Kings. The Trinity and the Nativity are also depicted frequently.

Art experts claim that *santos*-making approached its zenith at the turn of the 20th century, although hundreds of *santeros* still practice their craft throughout the island. Serious *santos* collectors view the former craftsmen of old as the true artists in the field. The best collection of *santos* is found at Puerto Rican Arts & Crafts (p. 185).

Some of the best *santos* on the island can be seen at the Capilla de Cristo in Old San Juan. Perhaps at some future date, a museum devoted entirely to *santos* will open in Puerto Rico.

$1,000, depending on the density of the weave, the hats are all created the same size, then blocked—by an employee on-site—to fit the shape of your head. Dig into this store's diverse inventory to discover a wealth of treasures—hand-beaten Chilean silver, Peruvian Christmas ornaments, Puerto Rican *santos*—almost all from Puerto Rico or Latin America. Calle Fortaleza 105. (C) 787/724-2445.

Puerto Rican Arts & Crafts Set in a 200-year-old colonial building, this unique store is one of the premier outlets on the island for authentic artifacts. Of particular interest are papier-mâché carnival masks from Ponce, whose grotesque and colorful features were originally conceived to chase away evil spirits. Taíno designs inspired by ancient petroglyphs are incorporated into most of the sterling silver jewelry sold here. There's an art gallery in back, with silk-screened serigraphs by local artists. The outlet has a gourmet Puerto Rican–food section with items like coffee, rum, and hot sauces for sale. A related specialty of this well-respected store involves the exhibition and sale of modern replicas of the Spanish colonial tradition of *santos,* which are carved and sometimes polychromed representations of the Catholic saints and the infant Jesus.

Priced from $50 to $1,100 each, and laboriously carved by artisans in private studios around the island, they're easy to pack in a suitcase because the largest one measures only 12 inches (31cm) from halo to toe. Open Monday through Saturday 9:30am to 6pm and Sunday 11am to 5pm. Calle Fortaleza 204. ✆ **787/725-5596.**

Tienda del Instituto de Cultura Puertorriqueño   The official store of the Institute of Puerto Rican Culture sells books and other publications, audio and video productions, arts and crafts, typical foods, and other items related to Puerto Rico culture. You'll find high-quality work by artisans who practice time-treasured crafts with considerable skill. Closed Sunday. Plaza San José, beside the San José Church. ✆ **787/721-6866.**

Vaughn's Gifts & Crafts   This store offers crafts from Puerto Rico and elsewhere, but specializes in straw and Panamanian hats. It's quite a large collection for the tropical hat collector, plus other colorful crafts from the island and elsewhere in the region. Calle Fortaleza 262. ✆ **787/721-8221.**

Xian Imports   Set within a jumbled, slightly claustrophobic setting, you'll discover porcelain, sculptures, paintings, and Chinese furniture, much of it antiques. Island decorators favor this spot as a source for unusual art objects. Calle de la Cruz 153. ✆ **787/ 723-2214.**

JEWELRY

Barrachina   The birthplace, in 1963, of the piña colada (an honor co-claimed by the staff at the Caribe Hilton), Barrachina's is a favorite of cruise-ship passengers. It offers one of the largest selections of jewelry, perfume, cigars, and gifts in San Juan. There's a patio for drinks where you can order (what else?) a piña colada. There is also a Bacardi rum outlet (bottles cost less than stateside but cost the same as at the Bacardi distillery), a costume jewelry department, a gift shop, and a section for authentic silver jewelry, plus a restaurant. Calle Fortaleza 104 (between Calle del Cristo and Calle San José). ✆ **787/725-7912.**

Eduardo Barquet   Known as a leading cost-conscious place to buy fine jewelry in Old San Juan, this shop has 14-karat Italian gold chains and bracelets that are measured, fitted, and sold by weight. You can purchase watches or beautiful gems in modern settings in both 14- and 18-karat gold. The store's collection also includes emerald, ruby, diamond, and pearl jewelry, along with platinum bridal jewelry. Calle Fortaleza 200 (at the corner of Calle La Cruz). ✆ **787/723-1989.**

Emerald Isles   This jewelry boutique in the Old Town is smaller than other entities that specialize in colored gemstones, but because of its much lower overhead, its prices can sometimes be more reasonable. It specializes in Colombian emeralds, set into silver or gold settings already, or waiting for you to select one. But as long as you're in the shop, look also at the unusual inventories of contemporary reproductions of pre-Columbian jewelry, some of it gold-plated and richly enameled. Many of these pieces sell for around $50 each, and some of them are genuinely intriguing. Calle Fortaleza 105. ✆ **787/977-3769.**

Joyería Riviera   This emporium of 18-karat gold and diamonds adjacent to Plaza de Armas has an impeccable reputation. Its owner, Julio Abislaiman, stocks his store from such diamond centers as Antwerp, Tel Aviv, and New York. This is the major distributor of Rolex watches on Puerto Rico. Prices in the store range from $250 into the tens of thousands of dollars—at these prices, it's a good thing you can get "whatever you want," according to the owner. Calle Fortaleza 257. ✆ **787/725-4000.**

A Dying Art: Old Lace

Another Puerto Rican craft has undergone a big revival just as it seemed that it would disappear forever: lace. Originating in Spain, *mundillos* (tatted fabrics) are the product of a type of bobbin lace making. This 5-century-old craft exists today only in Puerto Rico and Spain.

The first lace made in Puerto Rico was called *torchon* (beggar's lace). Early examples of beggar's lace were considered of inferior quality, but artisans today have transformed this fabric into a delicate art form, eagerly sought by collectors. Lace bands called *entrados* have two straight borders, whereas the other traditional style, *puntilla,* has both a straight and a scalloped border.

The best outlet in San Juan for lace is **Linen House** (p. 187).

Reinhold Jewelers   This is one of Puerto Rico's top shops featuring work by local and world-renowned jewelry designers. Its main location, and the adjacent David Yurman design boutique, spreads across two locations at the ground floor of Plaza Las América inside one of its main entrances, and it's beautiful gazing through the long windows at the dazzling creations inside. There's also a location at El San Juan Hotel Gallery. This store's presence makes it necessary for the serious jewelry connoisseur to travel outside Plaza Las Américas. Plaza Las Américas 24A, 24B, Hato Rey. © 787/554-0528. Other location at El San Juan Hotel Gallery, Isla Verde. © 787/796-2521.

LACE & LINENS

Linen House   This unpretentious store specializes in table linens, bed linens, and lace and has the island's best selection. Some of the most delicate pieces are expensive, but most are moderate in price. Inventories include embroidered shower curtains that sell for around $35 each, and lace doilies, bun warmers, place mats, and tablecloths that seamstresses took weeks to complete. Some astonishingly lovely items are available for as little as $30. The aluminum/pewter serving dishes have beautiful Spanish-colonial designs. Prices here are sometimes 40% lower than those on the North American mainland. Calle Fortaleza 250, 104. © 787/721-4219 or 787/725-6233.

LEATHER & EQUESTRIAN ACCESSORIES

Coach   Here you can find fine leather goods, from belts to bags to purses. This outlet sells discontinued products so you can find some real bargains. Calle Cristo 150. © 787/722-6830.

Dooney & Bourke Factory Store   Leather lovers will also want to pass through here, especially for the buttery smooth women's handbags. It's right nearby, and it too has factory outlet prices, which means occasional bargains. Calle Cristo 200, Old San Juan. © 787/289-0075.

Lalin Leather Shop   Although it lies in an out-of-the-way suburb (Puerto Nuevo), about 2 miles (3.2km) south of San Juan, this is the best and most comprehensive cowboy and equestrian outfitter in Puerto Rico, probably in the entire Caribbean. Here you'll find all manner of boots, cowboy hats, and accessories. More important, however, is the wide array of saddles and bridles, some from Colombia, some from Puerto Rico, priced from a cost-conscious $159 to as much as $3,100. Even the highest-priced items cost a lot less than their U.S. mainland equivalents, so if you happen to have a horse or pony on the U.S. mainland, a visit here might be worth your while.

If you decide to make the rather inconvenient pilgrimage, you won't be alone. Regular clients come from as far away as Iceland, the Bahamas, and New York. Everything can be shipped. Av. Piñero 1617, Puerto Nuevo. (✆ 787/781-5305. No bus.

MALLS

Belz Factory Outlet World   The largest mall of its kind in Puerto Rico, and the Caribbean as well, opened in 2001 in Canóvanas, east of San Juan en route to El Yunque. Totally enclosed and air-conditioned, it re-creates the experience of strolling through the streets of Old San Juan, sans the traffic and heat. Five interconnected buildings comprise the mall, with dozens of stores from Nike to Gap, from Dockers to Levi's to Maidenform, from Samsonite to Guess, and from Papaya to Geoffrey Beene. State Rd. #3 18400, Barrio Pueblo, Canóvanas. (✆ 787/256-7040. No bus.

Plaza Las Américas   The island's first big mall and still the largest in the Caribbean, Plaza, as it is known by locals, is a world unto itself. Even by U.S. standards, it's a remarkable place with top-name retailers, full-service restaurants, a Cineplex, two food courts, a bowling alley and disco, plus spa and hair stylists. Retail outlets include Macy's, Armani Exchange, Banana Republic, and Guess, as well as high-quality designer boutiques, with over 300 stores in all. There is also a U.S. Post Office, branches of all major island banks, and a full medical and office center. There are often shows and special events—from boat and racecar exhibits to fashion shows and concerts—taking place along its hallways. There's action from morning to night, and it's a quick trip from any San Juan hotel. Av. FD Roosevelt 525, Hato Rey. (✆ 787/767-5202. Bus: B21.

MARKETS

Plaza del Mercado de Santurce   If you'd like an old-fashioned Puerto Rican market, something likely to be found in a small South American country, visit this offbeat curiosity. In a West Indian structure, the central market is filled with "botanicas" hawking everything from medicinal herbs to Puerto Rican bay rum. Here is your best chance to pick up some patchouli roots. What are they used for? In religious observances and to kill unruly cockroaches. Some little cantinas here offer very typical Puerto Rican dishes, including roast pork, and you can also order the best mango banana shakes on the island. The seafood and *criollo* restaurants are some of the best in the city, at affordable prices. Calle Dos Hermanos at Calle Capitol, Santurce. (✆ 787/723-8022. Bus: B5.

4 San Juan After Dark

San Juan nightlife comes in all varieties. From the vibrant performing-arts scene to street-level salsa and the casinos, discos, and bars, there's plenty of entertainment available almost any evening.

As in a Spanish city, nightlife begins very late, especially on Friday and Saturday nights. Hang out until the late, late afternoon on the beach, have dinner around 8pm (9 would be even more fashionable), and then the night is yours. The true party animal will rock until the broad daylight. Many bars and nightclubs are open until 2am during the week, and 4 am on weekends. Many clubs and some bars are closed on Mondays and Tuesdays.

¡Qué Pasa!, the official visitor's guide to Puerto Rico, lists cultural events, including music, dance, theater, film, and art exhibits. It's distributed free by the tourist office. The English-language newspaper *San Juan Star* publishes a weekend guide to entertainment every Thursday that gives a pretty complete guide to entertainment throughout

the whole week. Spanish newspapers *El Vocero, El Nuevo Día,* and *Primera Hora* also have concert and cultural listings published on Fridays.

THE PERFORMING ARTS

Centro de Bellas Artes   In the heart of Santurce, the Performing Arts Center is a 6-minute taxi ride from most of the Condado hotels. It contains the Festival Hall, Drama Hall, and the Experimental Theater. Some of the events here will be of interest only to Spanish speakers; others attract an international audience. Av. Ponce de León 22. (**C**) **787/724-4747,** or 787/725-7334 for the ticket agent. Tickets $40–$200; 50% discounts for seniors. Bus: 1.

Teatro Tapía   Standing across from Plaza de Colón and built about 1832, this is one of the oldest theaters in the Western Hemisphere (see "Historic Sights," earlier in this chapter). Productions, some musical, are staged throughout the year and include drama, dances, and cultural events. You'll have to call the box office (Mon–Fri 9am–6pm) for specific information. Av. Fortaleza at Plaza Colón. (**C**) **787/721-0180.** Tickets $20–$30, depending on the show. Bus: B8 or B21.

THE CLUB & MUSIC SCENE

Club Brava   This club is part of the reason the El San Juan has a reputation as the city hotel with the best nightlife. The young and privileged, local celebs, and urbane visitors mix it up on the club's dance floor to a mix of house, reggaeton, and Latin music styles. The nightclub is designed in the form of a circle, with a central dance floor and a wraparound balcony, where onlookers and voyeurs—a 25- to 45-year-old age group—can observe the activities on the floor below. As one patron put it, "Here's where gringos can shake their bon-bons with San Juan's old guard." There's also a stage for special shows and events. Equipped with one of the best sound systems in the Caribbean, its location within the most exciting hotel in San Juan allows guests the chance to visit the hotel's bars, its intricately decorated lobby, and its casino en route. Open Thursday through Saturday from 10pm until 3am. In El San Juan Hotel & Casino, Av. Isla Verde 6063, Isla Verde. (**C**) **787/791-2781.** Cover $15, free for guests of El San Juan Hotel. Bus: A5.

Club Lazer   This Old San Juan Club has been hopping for nearly two decades through various transformations. A huge cavernous place in the middle of town, there's salsa and other tropical music Friday nights and reggaeton Saturdays. Sundays, ladies night, are particularly jamming. The club opens at 10pm Wednesday and Friday through Sunday and attracts a large local crowd as well as regular customers who work on the cruise ship lines, and young people from throughout the world. Calle Cruz 251, Old San Juan. (**C**) **787/722-7581.**

Lupi's Mexican Grill & Sports Cantina   You can hear some of the best Spanish rock at this Mexican pub and restaurant. It is currently a hot spot, with typical South of the Border decoration and such familiar dishes as fajitas, nachos, and burritos. A wide range of people of all ages are attracted to the place, although after 10pm patrons in their 20s and 30s predominate. Live rock groups perform after 11pm. In addition to the nightly rock bands, Caribbean music is also played on Friday and karaoke on Sunday. There are also plenty of televisions throughout for sporting events. The Mexican food and pub fare is pretty good too. There are both Isla Verde and Old San Juan locations. Isla Verde: Av. Isla Verde, Km. 187. (**C**) **787/253-1664.** Old San Juan: Recinto Sur 313. (**C**) **787/722-1874.**

Music While You Munch

Several restaurants in Old San Juan, and elsewhere throughout the city, have live music on certain days of the week. Knowing the schedule could determine where you eat dinner, since starting your night off with great island music and food is the best way to do it. If it's Friday, you might consider **Amadeus** (p. 190) when it has live music for its weekly Bohemio nights. **The Parrot Club** has live Latin jazz and salsa Tuesdays and Sundays, while **Sonne,** which has a Latin-music DJ all week, hosts tropical music sensations like Tanya Rivera on Saturday nights. **Carli Café Concierto** (p. 134) has live jazz nightly at 9pm, while **Barrachina Restaurant** (p. 186) has a live flamenco music and dance show nightly. **La Playita** in Isla Verde hosts weekend troubadours, while Condado's **Yerba Buena** (Av. Ashford 1350, Condado; ℰ 787/721-7500) has Cuban salsa Friday nights, bohemian music Saturday nights, and great Cuban food in a nice setting.

Nuyorican Café   When the Rolling Stones played the new Coliseum during their last world tour, Mick Jagger and Keith Richards came straight here to listen to the salsa. There's live music here every night, with Latin jazz and reggae also complementing the salsa and Cuban music played on stage. There are also theatrical performances, art exhibits, and a damn good kitchen (the pizza is one of the island's best). Recent performers have included the top names in Puerto Rican music, including Pedro Guerra, Roy Brown, Alfredo Naranjo, Cultura Profética, and salsa greats Bobbie Valentín, Ray Santiago, Polito Huerta, Luis Marín, Jerry Medina, and Tito Allen. The cafe also hosts special week-long musical festivals and has put on long-running performance art and theatrical programs, usually earlier in the evening before the bands get going. The Polito Huerta house band on Saturday nights plays smoking salsa, and Tuesday nights are Latin jazz. Rock lovers should head here Monday nights for some very fine rock *en español.* A guesthouse with charming, affordable rooms has opened on top of the cafe if you don't mind the music. Pizzas are served to 1am, at least; bar until at least 3am. 312 Calle San Francisco 312 (entrance down the alley), Old San Juan. ℰ 787/977-1276 or 366-5074.

Rumba   This club has a full bar up front, a huge back room with a stage for live bands, and a huge dance floor. It's so photogenically hip that it was selected as the site for the filming of many of the crowd scenes within *Dirty Dancing: Havana Nights.* Set immediately adjacent to the also-recommended restaurant, Barú, with which it's not associated, it's known as another great venue for live music, with excellent salsa, Latin jazz, and other tropical music. There's a great crowd here, of different styles ranging from college kids to well-dressed gray beards who remember the music back in its 1970s heyday. The common denominator is the love of the music and dance. Open Tuesday to Sunday 9pm to 4am. Calle San Sebastián 152, Old San Juan. ℰ 787/725-4407.

THE BAR SCENE

Unless otherwise stated, there is no cover charge at the following bars.

Amadeus Bistro Bar   This location has great food like at the Old San Juan location, and there's live music here nightly along with the inventive Puerto Rican nouvelle cuisine. There are Latin jazz and Spanish ballads Tuesdays through Fridays with

The Birth of the Piña Colada

When actress Joan Crawford tasted the piña colada at what was then the Beachcombers Bar in the **Caribe Hilton,** Calle Los Rosales (© 787/721-0303), she claimed it was "better than slapping Bette Davis in the face."

This famous drink is the creation of bartender Ramon "Monchito" Marrero, now long gone, who was hired by the Hilton in 1954. He spent 3 months mixing, tasting, and discarding hundreds of combinations until he felt he had the right blend. Thus, the frothy piña colada was born. It's been estimated that some 100 million of them have been sipped around the world since that fateful time.

Monchito never patented his formula and didn't mind sharing it with the world. Still served at the Hilton, here is his not-so-secret recipe:

2 ounces light rum
1 ounce coconut cream
1 ounce heavy cream
6 ounces fresh pineapple
½ cup crushed ice
Pineapple wedge and maraschino cherry for garnish

Pour rum, coconut cream, cream, and pineapple juice in blender. Add ice. Blend for 15 seconds. Pour into a 12-ounce glass. Add garnishes.

presentations beginning at 6pm. Near the financial district, federal court and other important office buildings, the place caters to the local professional crowd. Av. Chardón 350. Hato Rey. © 787/641-7450. No bus.

The Brick House　A pub open to the wee hours serving good old "gringo Rican" cuisine. There's a big-screen television for sports events (even if it's poker) and great grub like super hot wings, nachos, wraps, burgers, and salads. The friendly Randall Butts is your proprietor and host. Anything slathered in sauce and barbecued here is great. The barbecue sauces are great. Calle Bori 496, Río Piedras. © 787/281-8466. No bus.

El Batey　Graffiti and business cards cover the walls of this dive bar with a great jukebox and a view of the procession up and down Calle Cristo during weekend nights. Drawings of the legends of this storied watering hole are hung in its main room. There's always somebody to talk to at the bar, which draws an eccentric local crowd and independent-minded visitors. Patrons play chess and backgammon as well. The jukebox has great classic and psychedelic rock, some great Sinatra, and some priceless jazz standards by the likes of Duke Ellington and Charlie Parker. Calle Cristo 101. © 787/725-1787. No bus.

El Patio de Sam　Except for the juicy burgers, we're not so keen on the food served here anymore (and neither are our readers), but we still like to visit Old Town's best-known watering hole, one of the most popular late-night joints with a good selection of beers. Live entertainment is presented here Monday to Saturday. This is a fun joint—that is, if you dine somewhere else before coming here. Open daily noon to 1am. Calle San Sebastian 102. © 787/723-1149. Bus: Old Town Trolley.

Ficus Café   This modern, open-air cafe has caught on fast as a favorite with *sanjuaneros*. It's a fabulous spot, with the illuminated Convention Center looming behind it and a huge fountain in front performing an unending dance of liquid and light as if this were the better future to which Puerto Rico is headed.

The haute tropical ambience is also at work in the tapas and entrees of chef Luis Álvarez Príncipe. The drinks taste great washing down grilled shark bites, Caribbean hummus, lobster dumplings, cinnamon chicken croquettes with mango Cole slaw, and sausages in wine with focaccia toast. The cafe is open Thursday through Saturday 5 to 11pm. There are special activities: Saturday nights have been dedicated to jazz and tapas, while Thursdays local liquor companies hold happy hours and sponsor DJs or other special activities. At the Puerto Rico Convention Bureau, 100 Convention Blvd. ⟨ 787/ 641-7722.

La Sombrilla Rosa   A nice neighborhood bar with daily happy hours, a relaxed atmosphere with friendly staff and patrons, and good music. Weekdays, until 3pm, it serves great *comida criolla* at prices ranging from $5.50 to $8. Basic stuff like steak and onions and grilled chicken, everything with rice and pink beans and *tostones*. Open from 9:30am to 3pm for lunch, then from 7pm to at least 3am nightly. Calle San Sebastián 154. ⟨ 787/725-5656. Bus: Old Town Trolley.

Maria's   Forget the tacky decorations. This is the town's most enduring bar, a favorite local hangout and a prime target for Old City visitors seeking Mexican food and sangria. The atmosphere is fun, and the tropical drinks include piña coladas and frosts made of banana, orange, and strawberry, as well as the Puerto Rican beer Medalla. Open daily 10:30am to 3am (closes at 4am Fri–Sat). Calle del Cristo 204. ⟨ 787/721-1678. Bus: Old Town Trolley.

Palm Court Lobby   This is the most beautiful bar on the island—perhaps in the entire Caribbean. Most of the patrons are hotel guests, but well-heeled locals make up at least a quarter of the business at this fashionable rendezvous. Set in an oval wrapped around a sunken bar area, amid marble and burnished mahogany, it offers a view of one of the world's largest chandeliers. After 7pm on Monday through Saturday, live music, often salsa and merengue, emanates from an adjoining room (El Chico Bar). Watch the models strut by, the honeymoon couple, or the table of high rollers from New York having a drink before trying their luck again. This is still the place to be seen in the city. Open daily 6pm to 3am. In El San Juan Hotel & Casino, Av. Isla Verde 6063, Isla Verde. ⟨ 787/791-1000. Bus: A5.

Raven Room   Set on the upper floor of an antique building near the cruise-ship docks, this is the most trendy, most appealing, and most hip bar in San Juan. Because there's no area that's specifically designated inside as a dance floor, it defines itself as a "lounge." By that, owner Jancy Rodriguez defines his "living room" as a labyrinth of artfully minimalist rooms with comfortable seating, a changing array of dramatic oil

---

Moments   **Romantic Sunsets**

There is no better place on a Sunday night from 5:30 to 7pm to watch the sun set over Old San Juan than at Paseo de la Princesa. In this evocative colonial setting, you can hear local trios serenade you as the sun goes down. After such a romantic interlude, the night is yours. Of course, you should take along a lover.

La Rumba Party Cruise

The trouble with most nightlife venues in San Juan is that the real parties in conventional nightclubs begin at hours so impossibly late that the average visitor will tend to be deep asleep by the time the first dancers begin to rock 'n' roll. So if you love to salsa and merengue, but if you maintain relatively conservative ideas about your bedtime, consider the *La Rumba Party Cruise* as a viable option. It all takes place aboard a neon-lit two-level minicruiser that's moored most of the time to a point near Old San Juan's cruise pier no. 1 (Plaza Darsenas). Schedules vary according to business, but cruises tend to last 120 minutes each, and depart every Friday and Saturday at 10:30pm, 12:30am, and 2:30am; and every Sunday at 7:30, 9:30, and 11:30pm. And if you show up about an hour prior to a scheduled departure, you can fit in up to an extra hour's worth of shaking your booty to Latino music as the boat sits in port, music blaring, waiting for other clients. Cruises cost $15 per person (tax included), with children's rates $7.50 and seniors $11. There's a cash bar on board selling beer for between $4 and $6 each, depending on the brand. There's a sightseeing benefit to the experience as well: En route, as it chugs out to sea, participants garner sea-fronting views of both of San Juan's 18th-century forts and the coastline of Isla Verde. For reservations and more information, call ℰ **787/375-5211.**

---

paintings *(olio)* on loan from the art gallery (Canvas) downstairs, and a mixture of bright lights and shadow that makes anyone look years younger. Tucked into an alcove, there's a sushi bar to alleviate those ultra-late-night-hunger pangs, and onyx bartops that are lit from beneath to create zebra-striped but tawny-colored patterns. Music emphasizes trance and house music that's either very loud or so loud that it's almost unbearable, but if you can overlook that (rather silly) quirk, you can have a lot of fun at this place. Although the place opens, at least theoretically, at 10pm, it doesn't begin to jump till after midnight. Open nightly until at least 2am. Recinto Sur 305. ℰ **787/977-1083.** Bus: Old Town Trolley.

Wet Bar   This chic drinking spot operates out of San Juan's finest boutique hotel, the Water Club. This is the best bar for watching the sun set over San Juan. Lying on the 11th floor, it features jazz music and the Caribbean's only rooftop fireplace for those nippy nights in winter when you want to drink outside. The sensuous decor here includes striped zebra-wood stools, futons, pillowy sofas, and hand-carved side tables. The walls feature Indonesian carved teak panels. It overlooks the brilliant Isla Verde coastline and its palm-fringed beachfront below. Latin rhythms mix with R&B standards and world rhythms. You can order sushi under the stars or some other delicacies from a limited menu. It's a beautiful place, with trendy martinis and plush comforts. Thursday through Saturday the Wet Bar is open 7pm to 1am. In the San Juan Water & Beach Club, Calle José M. Tartak 2. ℰ **787/728-3666.** Bus: A5.

Zabó   Among San Juan's young, restless, and unattached, this place is more famous for its bar than its restaurant. The bar is divided into two separate spaces, the more popular being a cottage-like outbuilding on the grounds of a turn-of-the-20th-century villa. There's lots of charm here, with the attractive crowd, stiff drinks such as

Barhopping

More than any other place in the Caribbean, San Juan has a nightlife that successfully combines New York hip with Latino zest and the music of the Spanish Tropics.

A good place to start your night is the bright and enchanting **El Picoteo** in the El Convento Hotel, Calle del Cristo 100 (𝄐 **787/723-9020**). Get warmed up with some tapas and a fine sangria as you sit at one of the tables on a terrace overlooking Cristo Street and the hotel's interior courtyard. It's a good hangout for late-night dialogues. At the bar inside, you can often hear live jazz. Older locals mingle with hotel guests, the patronage mainly in the post-35 age group.

Afterwards, head for a pair of holes in the wall across the street from the El Convento Hotel. **El Batey,** Calle del Cristo 101 (no phone), and **Don Pablo,** Calle del Cristo 103 (no phone), are battered, side-by-side hangouts with a clientele of locals, expatriates, and occasional visitors. (In the 1980s, a Hollywood director selected these spots as the set for a Central American drug den, much to the amusement of the regular clientele.) Whereas El Batey's music remains firmly grounded in the rock-'n'-roll classics of the 1970s, with a scattering of Elvis Presley and Frank Sinatra hits, Don Pablo prides itself on cutting-edge music that's continually analyzed by the counterculture aficionados who hang out here. El Batey is open daily from 2pm to 6am; Don Pablo, daily from 8pm to 4am.

You'll next want to head up the hill to **San Sebastián Street,** a place where Puerto Ricans have been partying for years. There is a line of restaurants and bars, running from Calle Cristo along this street down to Calle

Cosmopolitans and martinis, and live music on a select few Wednesday and Thursday nights from 8 to 11:45pm. Some nights, depending on the operating hours of the restaurant, the bar crowd moves into the restaurant's entrance vestibule, a cozy spot for mingling. Open Tuesday through Wednesday 6 to 10pm; Thursday 6 to 11pm; Friday through Saturday 7 to 11pm. Calle Candina 14 (entrance is via an alleyway on Av. Ashford). 𝄐 **787/725-9494.** Bus: 21.

HOT NIGHTS IN GAY SAN JUAN

Straight folks are generally welcome in each of these gay venues, and many local couples show up for the hot music and dancing. Local straight boys who show up to cause trouble are generally ushered out quickly. Unless otherwise stated, there is no cover.

Beach Bar   This is the site of a hugely popular Sunday afternoon gathering, which gets really crowded beginning around 4pm and stretches into the wee hours. There's an open-air bar protected from rain by a sloping rooftop and a space atop the seawall with a panoramic view of the Condado beachfront. Open daily 11am to 1am or later. On the ground floor of the Atlantic Beach Hotel, Calle Vendig 1. 𝄐 **787/721-6900.** Bus: B21.

Cups   Set in a Latino tavern, this place is valued as the only place in San Juan that caters almost exclusively to lesbians. Men of any sexual persuasion aren't particularly

Cruz. On weekend evenings, the area is packed with fashionable crowds out for fun. **Nono's** (San Sebastion 100 at the corner of Cristo; ℰ 787/579-5851), is a great spot to watch the action out on Plaza San José. **El Patio del Sam** (p. 139) has been a favorite watering hole for locals and tourists since the 1950s. **Candela** (100 Calle San Sebastián; ℰ 787/977-4305) is a late night avant-garde club that plays eclectic lounge music until the earlier morning hours. There are often festivals of experimental music and art held here. Any of the bars along this strip is worth a look; many have pool tables and jukeboxes with great selections of classic salsa. A must-stop, however, is **Rumba** (ℰ 787/977-4305; San Sebastián 152), where you will find live salsa and other tropical music. Your final stop will likely be **Aqui Se Puede** (corner of San Justo, 50 Calle San Justo; ℰ 787/579-5851), which has great music, either live or on the jukebox, plus frequent special events like performances and art shows.

If you need sustenance after all that drinking, head to **Tantra**, Calle Fortaleza 356 (ℰ 787/977-8141), which has the best late-night menu in town, as well as a creative martini menu, including versions with mango, passion fruit, and a personal favorite, a version with cinnamon and clove. Live belly dancers amuse the crowd on Friday and Saturday nights, and any night of the week you can rent, for $20, a Mogul-style hookah pipe for every member of your dining table if the idea of playing pasha for a night appeals to you.

welcome. The scene reminds many lesbians of a tropical version of one of the bars they left behind at home. Entertainment such as live music or cabaret is presented Wednesday at 9pm and Friday at 10pm. Open Wednesday through Saturday 7pm to 4am. Calle San Mateo 1708, Santurce. ℰ 787/268-3570. Bus: B21.

Junior's Bar   Lying on a secluded and poorly lit street in Santurce, about a 5-block walk from the more famous gay mecca Krash Klub (see below), Junior's Bar seems little known to most visitors. It's mainly a place where resident gays go to hang out, talk to each other, and order drinks. Most of the music comes from the jukebox. Drag queens (Sat–Sun) and male strippers (Mon–Fri) are standard features. There is no cover, but you are required to fulfill a two-drink minimum. Daily 8pm to 5am. Av. 613 (off Av. Ponce de León), Santurce. ℰ 787/723-9477. Bus: B21.

Krash Klub   Formerly Eros, this two-level nightclub is still the city's biggest gay club. Patterned after the dance emporiums of New York, but on a smaller scale, the club has cutting-edge music and bathrooms with creative decor. Regrettably, only 1 night a week (Wed) is devoted to Latino music; on other nights, the music is equivalent to what you'd find in the gay discos of either Los Angeles or New York City. Open Wednesday to Sunday 10pm to 3am or 5am. Av. Ponce de León 1257, Santurce. ℰ 787/722-1131. Cover $5. Bus: 1.

Tia Maria's Liquor Store   This is not a liquor store, but a bar that caters to both locals and visitors. As one habitué reports: "During the day, all the local boys claim they're straight. But stick around until after midnight." The place has a very welcoming and unpretentious attitude, attracting both men and women. Don't come here for entertainment, but to hang out with the locals. Open Monday to Thursday and Sunday 11am to midnight; Friday to Saturday 10am to 2am. Av. José de Diego 326 (near the corner of Av. Ponce de León), Santurce. ✆ 787/724-4011. Bus: B1.

CASINOS

Many visitors come to Puerto Rico on package deals and stay at one of the posh hotels at the Condado or Isla Verde just to gamble.

Nearly all the large hotels in San Juan/Condado/Isla Verde offer casinos, and there are other large casinos at some of the bigger resorts outside the metropolitan area. The atmosphere in the casinos is casual, but still you shouldn't show up in bathing suits or shorts. Most of the casinos open around noon and close at 2, 3, or 4am. Guest patrons must be at least 18 years old to enter.

The casino generating all the excitement today is the 18,500-square-foot (1,719-sq.-m) **Ritz-Carlton Casino,** Avenue of Governors, Isla Verde (✆ 787/253-1700), the largest casino in Puerto Rico. It combines the elegant decor of the 1940s with tropical fabrics and patterns. This is one of the plushest and most exclusive entertainment complexes in the Caribbean. You almost expect to see Joan Crawford—beautifully frocked, of course—arrive on the arm of Clark Gable. It features traditional games such as blackjack, roulette, baccarat, craps, and slot machines.

One of the splashiest of San Juan's casinos is at the **Old San Juan Hotel & Casino,** Calle Brumbaugh 100 (✆ 787/721-5100), where five-card stud competes with some 240 slot machines and roulette tables. You can also try your luck at the **El San Juan Hotel & Casino** (one of the most grand), Av. Isla Verde 6063 (✆ 787/791-1000), or the **Condado Plaza Hotel & Casino,** Av. Ashford 999 (✆ 787/721-1000). You do not have to flash passports or pay any admission fees.

COCKFIGHTS

A brutal sport not to everyone's taste, cockfights are legal in Puerto Rico. The most authentic are in Salinas, a town on the southern coast with a southwestern ethos, which has *galleras,* or rings, for cockfighting. But you don't have to go all the way there to see a match. About three fights per week take place at the **Coliseo Gallistico,** Av. Isla Verde 6600, Av. Isla Verde, esquina Los Gobernadores. Call ✆ 787/791-6005 for the schedule and to order tickets, which cost $10, $12, $20, or $35, depending on the seat. The best time to attend cockfights is from January to May, as more fights are scheduled at that time. Hours are Tuesday or Thursday 4 to 10pm and Saturday 2 to 9pm.

9

Near San Juan

Within easy reach of San Juan's cosmopolitan bustle are superb attractions and natural wonders. With San Juan as your base, you can explore the island by day and return in time for a final dip before dinner and an evening on the town.

In fact, travelers looking to have an extended vacation in Puerto Rico may consider cutting back on hotel expenses by renting a furnished condo on one of San Juan's beaches or a high-ceilinged historic rooftop apartment in the Old City. San Juan, with its historic sites, gorgeous beaches, and vibrant cultural activities and nightlife can easily keep you occupied for two weeks or more. But the lure of a long-term rental in the city increases exponentially when you realize how many beautiful places there are to see and how many great things there are to do within a leisurely day trip from the city.

Conversely, travelers looking for the ultimate Caribbean vacation experience, but who also appreciate San Juan's cosmopolitan charms, will find some of Puerto Rico's best resorts within an hour's drive of San Juan. In Río Grande, there's the Río Mar Beach Resort and Spa, a Wyndham Grand Resort, and the Gran Mélia Golf Resort & Villas.

To the west, there are two vacation and golf clubs operating out of the grand old facilities of the former Hyatt resorts on a breathtaking oceanfront coconut plantation. There's a limited number of villas and vacation homes available for now, but plans are underway to renovate the former Cerromar and reopen with an upscale luxury hotel operator. And Dorado has many other lodging options, such as the Embassy Suites Dorado Del Mar Beach & Golf Resort. Its stunning setting and facilities (including a Chi Chi Rodríguez Golf Course) live up to its resort billing.

Also, road improvements have cut the travel time from San Juan to other destinations and resorts covered in subsequent chapters. For example, you can get from San Juan to Fajardo and its mammoth El Conquistador Resort & Golden Door Spa in 45 minutes. Even the sprawling Palmas del Mar vacation community, with hotels, luxury villas, and vacation homes, approaches the one-hour day trip test. While it's halfway down Puerto Rico's East Coast, it's accessible through two major highways. And Ponce is now a 90 minute drive, making it possible to visit the city in the morning, hit the beach in Guánica for three hours, and return to San Juan in the early evening.

Many of Puerto Rico's must-see sites lie much closer to San Juan, however. A bit more than an hour west of San Juan is the world's largest radar/radio-telescope, **Arecibo Observatory.** After touring this awesome facility, you can travel west to nearby **Río Camuy Cave Park,** for a good look at marvels below ground. Here you can plunge deep into the subterranean beauty of a spectacular cave system carved over eons by one of the world's largest underground rivers. The caves are part of a wider natural wonderland known as Karst Country, which you can also further explore, as well as an adjacent section of the central mountains laced with beautiful lakes.

Just 35 miles (56km) east of San Juan is El Yunque National Forest, the only tropical rainforest in the U.S. National Park System. Named by the Spanish for its anvil-shaped peak, **El Yunque** receives more than 100 billion gallons of rainfall annually. If you have time for only one side trip, this is the one to take. Waterfalls, wild orchids, giant ferns, towering tabonuco trees, and sierra palms make El Yunque a photographer's and hiker's paradise. Pick up a map and choose from dozens of trails graded by difficulty, including El Yunque's most challenging—the 6-mile (9.7km) El Toro Trail to the peak. The best one is probably the hike to La Mina Falls, a 45-minute walk through plush jungle, with interpretative nature signs explaining the foliage along the way. The trail ends at a beautiful spot where waterfalls crash into a wondrous natural pool in the mountain stream below. At El Yunque is El Portal Tropical Center, with 10,000 square feet (929 sq. m) of exhibit space, plazas, and patios. This facility greatly expands the recreational and educational programs available to visitors. La Coca Falls and an observation tower are just off Route 191.

Visitors can combine a morning trip to El Yunque with an afternoon of swimming and sunning on tranquil **Luquillo**

Beach. Soft white sand, shaded by coconut palms and the blue sea, makes this Puerto Rico's best and best-known beach. Plan on having lunch—sampling local delicacies at a group of food kiosks right beside the public beach.

Fajardo, and its beautiful Caribbean coast, is about 15 minutes farther east. As noted previously, sailing and snorkeling trips off Fajardo are an easy day trip from San Juan through one of the luxury catamaran outfits that include transportation to and from San Juan area hotels (see chapter 8). Or you could visit undeveloped stretches of Fajardo beachfront, around **Las Cabezas de San Juan** nature reserve and **Seven Seas public beach** on your own (see chapter 12).

Many visitors overlook trips to San Juan suburbs in the capital's backyard. Bayamón has a great science park and zoo, while Guyanabo has an interesting sports museum and Caguas a botanical and cultural garden.

Central mountain towns like Cayey and Aibonito are also accessible by day trips from the capital. Having a lunch of roast pork and other Puerto Rican delicacies and breathing in the clean mountain air is reason enough for a drive from the capital. A favorite spot is **Guavate,** a 45-minute drive south, where open-air barbecue restaurants are lined along a country road with a mountain stream of the Carite Forest as a backdrop.

1 El Yunque ⭐⭐⭐

25 miles (40km) E of San Juan

The El Yunque rainforest, a 45-minute drive east of San Juan, is a major attraction in Puerto Rico. The El Yunque National Forest is the only tropical forest in the U.S. National Forest Service system. The 28,000-acre (11,331-hectare) preserve was given its status by President Theodore Roosevelt. Today the virgin forest remains much as it was in 1493, when Columbus first sighted Puerto Rico.

GETTING THERE

From San Juan, take Route 26 or the Baldorioty de Castro Expressway East to Carolina, where you will pick up Route 66 or the Roberto Sánchez Vilella Expressway. The $1.50 toll road will take you farther along Route 3, putting you in Canóvanas.

Attractions Near San Juan

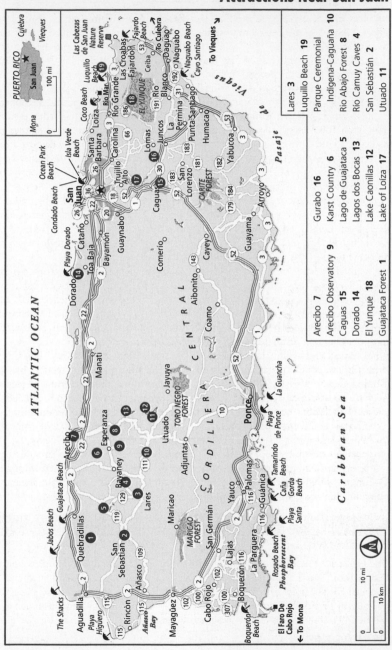

Arecibo **7**
Arecibo Observatory **9**
Caguas **15**
Dorado **14**
El Yunque **18**
Guajataca Forest **1**

Gurabo **16**
Karst Country **6**
Lago de Guajataca **5**
Lagos dos Bocas **13**
Lake Caonillas **12**
Lake of Loíza **17**

Lares **3**
Luquillo Beach **19**
Parque Ceremonial
Indígena-Caguaña **10**
Río Abajo Forest **8**
Río Camuy Caves **4**
San Sebastián **2**
Utuado **11**

Go right, east, on Route 3, which you follow east to the intersection of Route 191, a two-lane highway that heads south into the forest. Take 191 for 3 miles (4.8km), going through the village of Palmer. As the road rises, you will have entered the Caribbean National Forest. You can stop in at the El Portal Tropical Forest Center to pick up information (see below).

VISITOR INFORMATION

El Portal Tropical Forest Center, Route 191, Rio Grande (© 787/888-1880), an $18-million exhibition and information center, has 10,000 square feet (929 sq. m) of exhibition space. Three pavilions offer exhibits and bilingual displays. The actor Jimmy Smits narrates a documentary called "Understanding the Forest." The center is open daily from 9am to 5pm; it charges an admission of $3 for adults and $1.50 for children under 12.

El Yunque is the most popular spot in Puerto Rico for hiking; for a description of our favorite trails, see "Hiking Trails" below. Hikers will find useful information at any of the park's visitor information centers or at the **El Yunque Catalina Field Office,** near the village of Palmer, beside the main highway at the forest's northern edge (© 787/888-1880). The staff can provide material about hiking routes, and, with 10 days' notice, help you plan overnight tours in the forest. If you reserve in advance, the staff will also arrange for you to take part in 2-hour group tours. These tours are conducted Saturday to Monday every hour on the hour from 10:30am to 3:30pm; they cost $5 for adults and $3 for children under 12.

EXPLORING EL YUNQUE

Encompassing four distinct forest types, El Yunque is home to 240 species of tropical trees, flowers, and wildlife. More than 20 kinds of orchids and 50 varieties of ferns share this diverse habitat with millions of tiny tree frogs, whose distinctive cry of *coquí* (pronounced "ko-*kee*") has given them their name. Tropical birds include the lively, greenish blue, red-fronted Puerto Rican parrot, once nearly extinct and now making a comeback. Other rare animals include the Puerto Rican boa, which grows to 7 feet (2.1m). (It is highly unlikely that you will encounter a boa. The few people who have are still shouting about it.)

El Yunque is the best of Puerto Rico's 20 forest preserves. The forest is situated high above sea level, with El Toro its highest peak. You can be fairly sure you'll be showered upon during your visit, since more than 100 billion gallons of rain fall here annually. However, the showers are brief and there are many shelters. On a quickie tour, many visitors reserve only a half-day for El Yunque. But we think it's unique and deserves at least a daylong outing.

HIKING TRAILS   The best hiking trails in El Yunque have been carefully marked by the forest rangers. Our favorite, which takes 2 hours for the round-trip jaunt, is called **La Mina & Big Tree Trail,** and it is actually two trails combined. The La Mina Trail is paved and signposted. It begins at the picnic center adjacent to the visitor center and runs parallel to La Mina River. It is named for gold once discovered on the site. At La Mina Falls, there is a great waterfall and natural pool where you should take a dip. The mountain stream seems freezing at first, but becomes absolutely refreshing nearly instantaneously. Beyond the falls, the Big Tree Trail begins (also signposted). It winds a route through the towering trees of Tabonuco Forest until it approaches Route 191. Along the trail you might spot such native birds as the Puerto Rican woodpecker, the tanager, the screech owl, and the bullfinch.

Those with more time might opt for the **El Yunque Trail,** which takes 4 hours round-trip to traverse. This trail—signposted from El Caimitillo Picnic Grounds—takes you on a steep, winding path. Along the way you pass natural forests of sierra palm and *palo colorado* before descending into the dwarf forest of Mount Britton, which is often shrouded in clouds. Your major goal, at least for panoramic views, will be the lookout peaks of Roca Marcas, Yunque Rock, and Los Picachos. On a bright, clear day, you can see all the way to the eastern shores of the Atlantic.

DRIVING THROUGH EL YUNQUE   If you're not a hiker but you appreciate rainforests, you can still enjoy El Yunque. You can drive through the forest on Route 191, which is a tarmac road. This trail goes from the main highway of Route 3, penetrating deep into El Yunque. You can see ferns that grow some 120 feet (37m) tall, and at any minute you expect a hungry dinosaur to peek between the fronds, looking for a snack. You're also treated to lookout towers offering panoramic views, waterfalls, picnic areas, and even a restaurant.

WHERE TO STAY

Ceiba Country Inn *(Finds)*   If you're looking for an escape from the hustle and bustle of everyday life, this is the place for you. This small, well-maintained bed-and-breakfast is located on the easternmost part of Puerto Rico (you must rent a car to reach this little haven in the mountains). El Yunque is only 15 miles (24km) away, and San Juan is 40 miles (64km) to the west. The rooms are on the bottom floor of a large, old family home, and each has a private shower-only bathroom. They are decorated in a tropical motif with flowered murals on the walls, painted by a local artist. For a quiet evening cocktail, you might want to visit the small lounge on the second floor.

Road no. 977 Km 1.2 (P.O. Box 1067), Ceiba, PR 00735. ℭ **888/560-2816** or 787/885-0471. Fax 787/885-0471. 9 units (shower only). $85 double. Rate includes breakfast. AE, DISC, MC, V. Free parking. **Amenities:** Bar (guests only); patio for outdoor entertainment. *In room:* A/C, fridge, ceiling fan.

2 Luquillo Beach *(★(★(★*

31 miles (50km) E of San Juan

Luquillo Beach is the island's best and most popular public stretch of sand. From here, you can easily explore El Yunque rainforest (see above). "Luquillo" is a Spanish adaptation of *Yukiyu,* the god believed by the Taínos to inhabit El Yunque.

GETTING THERE

If you are driving, follow the above directions to Canovánas and continue on Route 3 east into Río Grande. The entrance to El Yunque is on the right, and just beyond is the left turn to the Wyndham. The Gran Melía Puerto Rico is also off Highway 3.

A hotel limousine (ℭ **787/888-6000**) from the San Juan airport costs $225 per carload to the Wyndham Río Mar Beach Resort and Spa. A taxi costs approximately $70. Hotel buses make trips to and from the San Juan airport, based on the arrival times of incoming flights; the cost is $28 per person, each way, for transport to El Conquistador; $25 per person, each way, to the Wyndham.

HITTING THE BEACH

Luquillo Beach *(★(★(★,* Puerto Rico's finest beach, is palm-dotted and crescent-shaped, opening onto a lagoon with calm waters and a wide, sandy bank. It's very crowded on weekends but much better during the week. There are lockers, tent sites, showers, picnic tables, and food stands that sell a sampling of the island's *frituras* (fried fare), especially cod fritters and tacos. The beach is open from 8:30am to 5pm, Wednesday through Sunday, plus holidays.

You can also snorkel and skin-dive (see below) among the living reefs with lots of tropical fish. Offshore are coral formations and spectacular sea life—eels, octopuses, stingrays, tarpon, big puffer fish, turtles, nurse sharks, and squid, among other sea creatures.

GREAT GOLF

One of Puerto Rico's newest golf courses is also among the very best. Tom Kite and Bruce Besse designed two 18-hole courses for the **Trump International Golf Club Puerto Rico,** 100 Clubhouse Dr., Río Grande 00745 (© 787/657-2000), adjacent to the well-recommended Gran Melia Puerto Rico (see below). You face a spectacular vista of fairways, lakes, and the Atlantic beyond. Four 9-hole loops fan out from the Caribbean's largest clubhouse. Each paspalum-grass course is imbued with its own character, including elevation changes. In the backdrop El Yunque's peaks stare at you. The Palms is a sprawling layout skirting wetlands, with the most difficult par 3 and the longest (571 yards/522m) par 5. Winter fees are $160 per 18 holes or $140 after noon. Fees include golf carts. The Paradise Bay Grill overlooks the ocean and serves up serves freshly caught lobster and succulent steaks, and the locker rooms feature massages and Jacuzzis. Donald Trump announced a $600-million investment with a local partner to construct luxury vacation villas and make other improvements when he bought it in 2008.

The **Wyndham Río Mar Beach Resort** (see below) has two world-class courses located at this resort, stretching out in the shadow of El Yunque rain forest along a dazzling stretch of coast. The entire 6,782 yards (6,201m) of Tom and George Fazio's Ocean Course has seaside panoramas and breezes, and fat iguanas scampering through the lush grounds. The other course, a 6,945-yard (6,351m) design by golf pro Greg Norman, follows the flow of the Mameyes River through mountain and coastal vistas. Greens fees are $165 for guests, $200 for non-resident walk-ons. Another nice option in town is the **Bahia Beach Plantation Resort and Golf Club** (Rte. 187 Km 4.2; © 787/857-5800), with greens fees weekdays at $225 and weekends at $275. For years it was a favorite of local golfers, but Robert Trent Jones, Jr., renovated the course with a breathtaking new design that was inaugurated in April 2008. He spent 3 years working on the 7,014-yard (6,414m) course, sprawling across some 480 acres (194 hectares) of lush beachfront, running from the tip of Loiza River to the mouth of the Espíritu Santo River. Much of the course overlooks a verdant green valley of El Yunque rainforest. The new course is part of the new luxury Saint Regis resort being developed on the beautiful site with a planned opening in winter 2009. Clusters of beachfront luxury villas, with the aim of less environmental impact on the coastal area, are planned. The new course completes a Puerto Rico trifecta for the Jones family. Dad Trent Jones, Sr., built the legendary Dorado Beach East golf course and brother Rees Jones completed Palmas del Mar's Flamboyán course in 1999.

SCUBA DIVING & SNORKELING

The best people to take you diving are at the **Dive Center** at the Wyndham Rio Mar Beach Resort (© 787/888-6000). This is one of the largest dive centers in Puerto Rico, a PADI five-star facility with two custom-designed boats that usually take no more than six to ten divers. Snorkeling and skin diving costs $75 for a half-day. The center also offers a full-day snorkeling trip, including lunch and drinks, for $95 per person. Boat tours are available daily from 9am to 4pm. For scuba divers, a two-tank dive costs $135 to $185.

WHERE TO STAY

Gran Melia Puerto Rico ✿✿✿ *Kids*   Checking into this pocket of posh on the Miquillo de Rio Grande peninsula is the best reason for heading east of San Juan. An all-suite luxury resort, it has set new standards for comfort, convenience, and amenities along the Atlantic northeastern shoreline. Set amidst gardens of 40 acres (16 hectares), it opens onto the white sands of the mile-long (1.6km) shoreline of Coco Beach. From watersports to two 18-hole golf courses, the resort has everything on-site, including whirlpool baths and massage tables. Spa treatments revitalize and rejuvenate.

You can also wander the globe in the widely varied restaurants, ranging from Italian to Southeast Asian. Naturally, the chefs also prepare locally caught seafood imbued with Creole flavor. One restaurant serves only Caribbean and Puerto Rican cuisine, whereas another offers its take on contemporary California. Yet another serves teppanyaki dinners with an adjoining sushi bar.

Melía ditched the original all-inclusive concept and reopened emphasizing the resort's luxury, golf, spa, and other top-flight amenities. Royal Service entitles guests to continental breakfast, evening drinks and hors d'oeuvres, use of a private lounge, and other benefits. Bedrooms and suites are spacious and furnished luxuriously. The signature suites are divided among 20 elegant two-story bungalows. Rich mahogany pieces and elegant fabrics are used throughout. If you can afford it, opt for a Royal Service Suite; some even have a private Jacuzzi facing the Atlantic. The marble bathrooms are sumptuous.

There's a lot to do here. The world-class golf courses are adjacent to the property at the **Trump International Golf Club Puerto Rico,** there's a full-service spa, a slew of watersports possibilities, and a Kids Club that will keep your young ones happy and busy. The staff is great at organizing water polo and beach volleyball games, and you can take salsa and merengue dancing lessons by the pool. It's a big reason why this resort is a cut above some competitors, and why you will have so much fun here. We're still talking about our stunning come-from-behind beach volleyball victory nearly a year later.

Coco Beach Blvd. 1000, Rio Grande, PR 00745. © **866/436-3542** or 787/809-1770. Fax 787/809-1785. www.puerto ricoparadisus.com. 582 units. Winter $610–$700 suite for 2, $760–$910 Royal Service Suite; off season $264–$314 suite for 2, $344–$424 Royal Service Suite. AE, DISC, MC, V. **Amenities:** 6 restaurants; 3 bars; 2 outdoor pools; 2 golf courses; 3 lit tennis courts; fitness center; gym; spa; sauna; kids' clubs; business center; 24-hr. room service; babysitting; laundry service/dry cleaning; nonsmoking rooms; casino; medical services; rooms for those w/limited mobility. *In room:* A/C, TV, dataport, kitchenette, minibar, beverage maker, hair dryer, iron, safe.

The Río Mar Beach Resort & Spa, A Wyndham Grand Resort ✿   This is a
great spot to have fun in the sun and relax, but if you're expecting roaring nightlife or a cultural experience, stay elsewhere. The resort lies between the El Yunque rainforest and the Atlantic coastline. One of its championship golf courses, designed by George and Tom Fazio, crisscrosses the dramatic coastline, while the other, by Greg Norman, winds through lush tropical forest. Watersports offerings include sailing, snorkeling, scuba, parasailing, windsurfing, kite boarding, and others. There are also other sports activities like volleyball and water polo, and lots to do for children, including the Iguana Club for kids and a game room. There's a kids' pool next to the adult pool, which are both right near the beach. And you can actually fulfill a Caribbean dream

and go horseback riding through the rainforest and along the beach. (We highly recommend this.)

Landscaping includes several artificial lakes situated amid tropical gardens. Guest rooms either overlook the palm-lined Atlantic or the green mountains of the rainforest. The style is Spanish hacienda with nods to the surrounding jungle; unusual art and sculpture alternate with dark woods, deep colors, rounded archways, big windows, and tile floors. In the bedrooms, muted earth tones and natural woods add to the ambience. Bedrooms are spacious, with balconies or terraces, and good mattresses, plus tub/shower combinations in the large bathrooms.

The resort has ample meeting space, and the number of conventions held here is cause for complaint for some visitors. There's not much going on at night except the lobby bar and the hotel's 6,500-square-foot (604-sq.-m) casino. The restaurants include Italian, Latin American, Oriental, and steak and seafood for fine dining choices and three different cafes. We like especially Palío, but it's on the expensive side, which is the case with most of the resort restaurants.

Río Mar Blvd. 6000, Rio Grande, PR 00745. ℂ 877/636-0636 or 787/888-6000. Fax 787/888-6600. www.wyndham riomar.com. 600 units. Winter $359–$509 double; off season $189–$339 double; year-round from $695 suite. Children ages 5–17 staying in parent's room $85, including meals and activities; free for 4 and under. AE, DC, DISC, MC, V. 19 miles east of Luís Muñoz Marín International Airport, with entrance off Puerto Rico Hwy. 3. **Amenities:** 8 restaurants; 4 bars; outdoor pool; 13 tennis courts; health club and spa; deep-sea fishing; sailing; children's programs; 24-hr. room service; laundry; dry cleaning; nonsmoking rooms; casino; horseback riding nearby; rooms for those w/limited mobility. In room: A/C, TV, high-speed Internet access, fridge, coffee and beverage maker, hair dryer, iron, safe.

WHERE TO DINE

Brass Cactus (Finds AMERICAN/REGIONAL   On a service road adjacent to Route 3 at the western edge of Luquillo, within a boxy-looking concrete building that's in need of repair, is one of the town's most popular bar/restaurants. Permeated with a raunchy, no-holds-barred spirit, this amiable spot has thrived since the early 1990s, when it was established by an Illinois-born bartender who outfitted the interior with gringo memorabilia. It's a great American-style pub, where you can hear rock 'n' roll or catch a game on television. Menu items include king crab salad; tricolor tortellini laced with chicken and shrimp; several kinds of sandwiches, burgers, and wraps; and platters of churrasco, T-bone steaks, chicken with tequila sauce, barbecued pork, and fried mahimahi. A second location has opened in Canóvanas along Highway 3 that has a children's area where they can play video games or do other activities, leaving you to eat in peace. We love the barbecue here, especially the ribs in the Jack Daniels sauce. Portions are large.

In the Condominio Complejo Turistico, Rte. 3, Marginal. ℂ 787/889-5735. Another location at Rte. 3, Plaza Noreste Centro Comercial, Loíza. ℂ 787/256-0595. Reservations not necessary. Sandwiches $8–$11; main courses $8–$26. MC, V. Sun–Thurs 11am–11pm; Fri–Sat 11am–midnight.

Palío ℛ ITALIAN   This richly decorated restaurant is the premier dining outlet of the region's largest and splashiest hotel. A certain attachment to culinary tradition doesn't preclude a modern approach to the cookery. Dishes we've sampled have a superbly aromatic flavor and are beautifully presented and served. The sophisticated menu includes potato and sage gnocchi; rack of American lamb; fresh Maine lobster; center-cut veal chops stuffed with fresh mozzarella, tomatoes, and avocado and served with grappa-laced mashed potatoes; and baby free-range chicken, spit-roasted and served with rosemary jus.

In the Wyndham Rio Mar Beach Resort and Golf Club. © **787/888-6000**. Reservations recommended. Main courses $22–$52. AE, DC, MC, V. Daily 6am–11pm.

Sandy's Seafood Restaurant & Steak House (★ *Value* SEAFOOD/STEAKS/ PUERTO RICAN   The concrete-and-plate-glass facade is less obtrusive than that of other restaurants in town, and the cramped, Formica-clad interior is far from stylish. Nonetheless, Sandy's is one of the most famous restaurants in northeastern Puerto Rico, thanks to the wide array of luminaries—U.S. and Puerto Rican political figures, mainstream journalists, beauty-pageant winners, and assorted slumming rich—who travel from as far away as San Juan to dine here. Set about a block from the main square of the seaside resort of Luquillo, it was founded in 1984 by Miguel Angel, aka Sandy.

Platters, especially the daily specials, are huge—so copious, in fact, that they're discussed with fervor by competitors and clients alike. The best examples include fresh shellfish, served on the half-shell; *asopaos;* four kinds of steak; five different preparations of chicken, including a tasty version with garlic sauce; four kinds of gumbos; paellas; a dozen preparations of lobster; and even jalapeño peppers stuffed with shrimp or lobster.

Calle Fernandez García 276. © **787/889-5765**. Reservations recommended. Main courses $8–$25; lunch special Mon–Fri 11am–2:30pm $5. AE, MC, V. Wed–Mon 11am to between 9:30 and 11pm, depending on business.

3 Dorado ★

18 miles (29km) W of San Juan

Dorado—the name itself evokes a kind of magic—is a small town with some big resorts, a world of storied luxury hotels and villas unfolding along Puerto Rico's north shore west of San Juan. For decades, the Hyatt Cerromar and Dorado Beach formed the epicenter of this world, storied resorts housed in classic quarters with world-class facilities along a stunning coastal stretch of rolling palm groves and white-sand beaches. Currently, vacation and golf clubs are operated on the former site, and there are plans to renovate the old resort buildings and reopen as a luxury resort.

The site was originally purchased in 1905 by Dr. Alfred T. Livingston, a Jamestown, New York, physician, who developed it as a 1,000-acre (405-hectare) grapefruit-and-coconut plantation. Dr. Livingston's daughter, Clara, widely known in aviation circles as a friend of Amelia Earhart, owned and operated the plantation after her father's death. It was she who built the airstrip here. In 1955, Clara Livingston sold her father's 1,700-acre (688-hectare) Hacienda Sardinera to the Rockefeller family. Her former house, now called Su Casa, which served as a golf clubhouse in the '70s and restaurant from 1982 to 2006, remains on the property. On May 31, 2006, 48 years after Laurence Rockefeller officially opened the hotel, the resorts that had made Dorado synonymous with upscale tourism closed their doors. It brought an end to a legendary resort—with a list of clients including former presidents John F. Kennedy, Dwight Eisenhower, Gerald Ford, and George H. Bush, as well as athletic greats Joe Namath, Mickey Mantle, and Joe DiMaggio, and actresses Joan Crawford and Ava Gardner.

GETTING THERE

If you're driving from San Juan, take Expressway 22 west. Take Exit 22-A to get on Route 165 north to Dorado. Alternately, you can take the meandering coastal route along Highway 2 west to Route 693 north to Dorado (trip time: 40 min.). You'll pass a couple interesting beaches and coastal lookouts, as well as a fine spots to eat.

HITTING THE BEACHES

If you take this later route, you'll want to detour down Route 870 in the Palo Seco area of Toa Alta. This narrow road runs through the middle of a narrow peninsula famous for the restaurants serving seafood and Puerto Rican cuisine running along it. At the end of the road is the **Parque Nacional Isla de Cabra** (Rte. 870, Toa Baja; © 787/384-0542; Wed–Sun and holidays 8:30am–5pm, parking $3), a fascinating spit of land at the mouth of San Juan Bay that has an incredible view of the Old City. The water here is not great for swimming, but there are play areas and green picnic areas with great views. There are also small restaurants and bars, everywhere a great coastal view and the whole area with great breezes. The area was a former leper colony built by the Spanish and then was a shooting range and training area for many decades for police. There is a small fort within the park called **El Cañuelo** that was built to protect the entrance of the Bayamón River and back up the much larger El Morro across the bay, by providing crossfire to invading ships. This is a favorite picnic area for Sundays and a good spot to ride a bike or fly a kite.

There are also a few fine bathing beaches along this route before getting to Dorado. The best is probably **Cerro Gordo** public beach (Rte. 690, Vega Alta; © 787/883-2730), along with the **Manuel "Nolo" Morales** public beach along Dorado's "Costa del Oro," or "Gold Coast" (© 787/796-2830). Both charge $3 per car parking fee and keep the same hours as other public beaches and parks, Wednesday through Sunday and holidays, 8:30am to 5pm.

WHERE TO STAY

Dorado's lodging options were severely limited when the two Hyatt properties shut their doors, but staying at the former Hyatt resort is still possible, and the Embassy Suites property is a unique, all-suites resort with great facilities.

Dorado Beach Resort & Club   With 72 holes, Dorado has the highest concentration of golf on the island. The legendary Dorado Beach and Cerromar hotels run by Hyatt are now gone, but the four courses and other facilities—spectacular tennis, pool, and beaches—live on, and resort villa rentals are available. Of the courses, Dorado East is the favorite. Designed by Robert Trent Jones, Sr., it was the site of the Senior PGA Tournament of Champions throughout the 1990s. True tennis buffs head here, too. The Dorado courts are the best on the island. The current accommodations are available in cottages hugging a beautiful ocean grove, with palm streets and a white-sand beach with a protected swimming area. They are bright and cheerful, opening right out to the beachfront, and are fairly spacious, including the bathrooms. The terraces overlook the beach.

Fine dining has always been an integral part of this resort's appeal, with a fabulous dining room overlooking the surf and resort chefs who regularly won big awards. Two of the finer restaurants, Hacienda del Sol and Zafra, have remained open. When we visited, the resort was offering golf stay and play rates for 2 nights, 2 games at: Single $670 per person, double $505 per person, triple $450 per person, and quadruple $425 per person. For 3 nights, 3 games: Single $845, Double $595, Triple $510, and Quadruple $475.

100 Dorado Beach Drive, Ste. 1, Dorado, PR 00646. © 787/796-1234 [main], 787/626-1001 [front desk], or 787/626-1040 [reservations]. Fax 787/278-1993. www.doradobeachclubs.com. 36 units available in the Su Casa cottages

Tips World-Class Golf at the Former Hyatt Dorado

The Hyatt Dorado Beach and Cerromar closed their doors in May 2006, but luckily their world-class golf courses and country club are still open and there are a limited number of vacation rentals available. (See below.) The former **Dorado Beach resort's professional golf courses** ★★, designed by Robert Trent Jones, Sr., match the finest anywhere. They are now operated by the **Dorado Beach Resort & Club**. The two original courses, known as East and West, were carved out of a jungle and offer tight fairways bordered by trees and forests, with lots of ocean holes. The somewhat newer and less noted North and South courses, now called the Plantation Club, feature wide fairways with well-bunkered greens and an assortment of water traps and tricky wind factors. Each is a par-72 course (call ✆ **787/796-8961** or 787/626-1006, the Dorado Beach Pro Shop, for tee times). The longest is the South course, at 7,047 yards (6,444m). Fees for all courses hover around $160 for non-residents. Golf carts are included for all courses, and the two pro shops have both a bar and snack-style restaurant. Both are open daily from 7am until dusk. There are plenty of opportunities for a post-game meal in Dorado afterwards, but none better than the two upscale restaurants right near the golf course that have remained open: Hacienda del Sol and Zafra (call ✆ **787/796-8999** for either). *Tip:* Ask about rates for game play that starts after 1:30pm, which is sometimes marked down significantly.

on a gorgeous beachfront. Year-round $229–$249 double. AE, DC, DISC, MC, V. **Amenities:** 3 restaurants and bars; 2 outdoor pools; 4 18-hole championship golf courses; 10 tennis courts; spa; nonsmoking rooms. *In room:* A/C, cable TV, dataport, wireless Internet, minibar, coffeemaker, hair dryer, iron, safe, free local calls, pullout sofa.

Embassy Suites Dorado del Mar Beach & Golf Resort ★   This beachfront property in Dorado lies less than 2 miles (3.2km) from the center of Dorado and within easy access from the San Juan airport. It is the only all-suite resort in Puerto Rico, and it has been a success since its opening in 2001. The property offers two-room suites with balconies and 38 two-bedroom condos.

The suites are spread over seven floors, each spacious and furnished in a Caribbean tropical motif, with artwork and one king-size bed or two double beds. Most of them have ocean views of the water. Each condo has a living room, kitchen, whirlpool, and balcony.

Although the accommodations are suites or condos, one bedroom in a condo can be rented as a double room (the rest of the condo is shut off). Likewise, it's also possible for two people to rent one bedroom in a condo, with the living room and kitchen facilities available (the other bedroom is closed off). Because condos contain two bedrooms, most of them are rented to parties of four.

The hotel attracts many families because of its very spacious accommodations. It also attracts golfers because of its Chi Chi Rodriguez signature par-72, 18-hole golf course set against a panoramic backdrop of mountains and ocean.

Dorado del Mar Blvd. 210, Dorado, PR 00646. ✆ **787/796-6125.** Fax 787/796-6145. www.embassysuitesdorado. com. 212 units. Year-round $160–$250 suite; $260–$485 1-bedroom villa; $360–$560 2-bedroom villa. AE, DC, DISC,

MC, V. **Amenities:** 2 restaurants; bar and grill; pool; golf; tennis court; limited room service; massage; laundry service; dry cleaning; rooms for those w/limited mobility. *In room:* A/C, TV, dataport, kitchenette, wet bar, hair dryer, iron, safe.

Hacienda del Mar: A Hyatt Vacation Club Resort

A set of condos adjacent to the former Hyatt Cerromar is still available for vacationers, and visitors can use the golf, tennis, and pool facilities now run by the neighboring **Dorado Beach Resort & Club.** The famous river pool is closed, but there's still the Olympic swimming pool and children's pool. The resort also has the Spa Del Sol, which gives massage and yoga. This is the closet you'll get to the former Cerromar property until it reopens. There are studio, 1-bedroom, and 2-bedroom apartments. The 2-bedrooms have master suites with king-size beds and adjoining baths, a guest suite with queen bed and sofa bed, and a full kitchen and living area with sofa bed. The 1-bedrooms lack the guest suites, while the studios lack the guest suites and living area and have kitchenettes instead of full kitchens. The restaurant **Bohio Beach Bar & Grill** serves basic burgers, sandwiches, and salads, and it has a full service bar. There's also a nightclub and bar called the **Ocean Blue Cocktail Bar.**

301 Hwy. 693, Dorado. © **787/796-3000.** Fax 787/796-3610. www.hyatthaciendadelmar.hyatt.com. 270 units. $255 studio; $325 1-bedroom; $425 2-bedroom. AE, DISC, MC, V. Free parking. **Amenities:** Restaurant/bar; pool and beach services; room service. *In room:* Cable TV/DVD, Internet, full kitchen, safe, stereo.

WHERE TO DINE

El Vigia *Finds* PUERTO RICAN   En route to Dorado from San Juan, stop by this down-to-earth restaurant with a great ocean view. It's the first restaurant on the main road into Isla de Cabras. This unpretentious place serves great seafood and Puerto Rican cuisine. On nice days you can eat on a wooden deck with the waves crashing against the rocks below. There are about 50 different items—plenty of seafood, steaks, and Puerto Rican food—on the menu. You can't go wrong with the *mofongo* stuffed with stewed conch or shrimp, or the mixed seafood Puerto Rican stew, *asopao.* There's also a delicious surf and turf, with a filet mignon and lobster tail. We loved the red snapper Creole style, which is in a light, sweet tomato sauce. There are plenty of non-seafood dishes, a mix of Puerto Rican and American fare. The house sangria is tasty and has a kick.

Calle Principal, Entrance Isla de Cabras. © **787/788-5000.** Main courses $11–$40. AE, MC, V. Daily 11am–10pm.

Hacienda del Sol Restaurant LATIN AMERICAN   The restaurant at the Dorado Beach Clubhouse, overlooking Sardinera Bay and the 18th hole of the East Course, serves expertly prepared Latin and Continental meals but also has some surprisingly successful fusion experiments on the menu. If you eat lunch, have the Asiatico, the chicken pot stickers with ponzu sauce and oriental cucumber slaw, or the Into the Island Salad, which incorporates Puerto Rican farmer cheese, roasted peppers, and plantain crisps with mixed greens. Everything we've tried has been good, but we can't say enough about the tamarind glazed pork chops and the grilled salmon with Puerto Rican guava barbecue sauce.

Dorado Beach Resort & Club, 100 Dorado Beach Drive, Suite 1, Dorado. © **787/796-8999** or 787/626-1012. Main courses $20–$38. AE, MC, V. Daily 11:30am–4pm; Wed–Sun 6:30–9:30pm.

Zafra Restaurant NEW WORLD CUISINE   The main dining room and veranda overlook the lush valley surrounding the Plantation Clubhouse and the mountains looming in the distance over its surrounding greens. We love the remake of the Caribbean obsession with the North Atlantic codfish by serving it saltimboca style, with prosciutto, sage, and red and yellow tomato chimchuri, as well as the classic prime rib with horseradish au jus. For lunch, you won't do better than its version of Puerto Rican barbecued chicken or a grilled tilefish in a mango-lime mojito.

Dorado Beach Resort & Club, 100 Dorado Beach Drive, Ste. 1, Dorado. ✆ 787/626-1025. Main courses $24–$39. AE, MC, V. Daily 11:30am–4pm; Fri–Sat 6:30–9:30pm; bar menu available from 11am—7pm Sun–Thurs.

4 Arecibo & Camuy ⭐

68 to 77 miles (109–124km) W of San Juan

GETTING THERE

Arecibo Observatory lies a 1¼-hour drive west of San Juan, outside the town of Arecibo. From San Juan head west along four-lane Route 22 until you reach the town of Arecibo. At Arecibo, head south on Route 10; the 20-mile (32km) drive south on this four-lane highway is almost as interesting as the observatory itself. From Route 10, take exit 75-B and follow the signposts along a roller-coaster journey on narrow two-lane roads. First you will go right on Route 652 and take a left on Route 651. Proceed straight through the intersection of Route 651 and Route 635, and then turn left at the cemetery onto Route 625, which will lead you to the entrance of the observatory.

On the same day you visit the Arecibo Observatory, you can also visit the Río Camuy Cave Park. The caves also lie south of the town of Arecibo. Follow Route 129 southwest from Arecibo to the entrance of the caves, which are at Km 18.9 along the route, north of the town of Lares. Like the observatory, the caves lie approximately 1½ hours west of San Juan.

EXPLORING THE AREA

Dubbed "an ear to heaven," **Observatorio de Arecibo** ⭐ (✆ 787/878-2612; www. naic.edu) contains the world's largest and most sensitive radar/radio-telescope. The telescope features a 20-acre (8-hectare) dish, or radio mirror, set in an ancient sinkhole. It's 1,000 feet (305m) in diameter and 167 feet (51m) deep, and it allows scientists to monitor natural radio emissions from distant galaxies, pulsars, and quasars, and to examine the ionosphere, the planets, and the moon using powerful radar signals. Used by scientists as part of the Search for Extraterrestrial Intelligence (SETI), this is the same site featured in the movie *Contact* with Jodie Foster. This research effort speculates that advanced civilizations elsewhere in the universe might also communicate via radio waves. The 10-year, $100-million search for life in space was launched on October 12, 1992, the 500-year anniversary of the New World's discovery by Columbus.

Unusually lush vegetation flourishes under the giant dish, including ferns, wild orchids, and begonias. Assorted creatures like mongooses, lizards, and dragonflies have also taken refuge there. Suspended in an outlandish fashion above the dish is a 600-ton (544,311kg) platform that resembles a space station.

This is not a site where you'll be launched into a *Star Wars* journey through the universe. You are allowed to walk around the platform, taking in views of this gigantic dish. At the Angel Ramos Foundation Visitor Center, you are treated to interactive exhibitions on the various planetary systems and introduced to the mystery of meteors and educated about intriguing weather phenomena.

Tours are available at the observatory Wednesday through Friday from noon to 4pm, Saturday and Sunday from 9am to 4pm. Normal hours are Wednesday through

am to 4pm, but during a summer session (June 1–July 31) and a winter ses-
15–Jan 15) the observatory is open to visitors every day. The cost is $5 for
for seniors and children. There's a souvenir shop on the grounds. Plan to
spend about 1½ hours at the observatory.

Parque de las Cavernas del Río Camuy (Río Camuy Caves) ★★★ (© 787/898-
3100) contains the third-largest underground river in the world. It runs through a
network of caves, canyons, and sinkholes that have been cut through the island's limestone base over the course of millions of years. Known to the pre-Columbian Taíno
peoples, the caves came to the attention of speleologists in the 1950s; they were led to
the site by local boys already familiar with some of the entrances to the system. The
caves were opened to the public in 1986. Visitors should allow about 2 hours for the
total experience.

Visitors first see a short film about the caves and then descend into the caverns in
open-air trolleys. The trip takes you through a 200-foot-deep (61m) sinkhole and a
chasm where tropical trees, ferns, and flowers flourish, along with birds and butterflies. The trolley then goes to the entrance of Clara Cave of Epalme, one of 16 caves
in the Camuy caves network, where visitors begin a 45-minute walk, viewing the
majestic series of rooms rich in stalagmites, stalactites, and huge natural "sculptures"
formed over the centuries.

Tres Pueblos Sinkhole, located on the boundaries of the Camuy, Hatillo, and Lares
municipalities, measures 65 feet (20m) in diameter, with a depth of 400 feet (122m)—
room enough to fit all of El Morro Fortress in San Juan. In Tres Pueblos, visitors can
walk along two platforms—one on the Lares side, facing the town of Camuy, and the
other on the Hatillo side, overlooking Tres Pueblos Cave and the Río Camuy.

The caves are open Wednesday through Sunday from 8am to 3pm. Tickets cost $12
for adults, $7 for children 4 to 12, and $5 for seniors. Parking is $2. For more infor-
mation, phone the park.

Back down in Arecibo, a fun and interesting stop, especially if you are traveling with
children, is the **Arecibo Lighthouse & Historic Park** (Hwy. 655, El Muelle, Barrio
Islote, Arecibo; © 787/880-7540; www.arecibolighthouse.com). Housed in a lighthouse built by the Spanish in 1898, this "cultural theme park" takes visitors on a history of Puerto Rico. But it's a very tactile tour, where you can actually walk through
many of the exhibits. It really hits kids; it hit the kid in us. That's how we were riv-
eted by the slave quarters, thrilled with the mammoth pirate ship, and excited and
scared at the same time upon entering the pirate's cave, with its alligators and sharks.
Tickets are $9 adults, $7 children and seniors. The park is open 9am to 6pm weekdays and holidays and 10am to 7pm weekends.

WHERE TO DINE

If you want to eat before heading back to the city, Arecibo is a good place, with several
fine restaurants. The hands-down best, however, is the nearby **Salitre Mesón Costero**
(Rte. 681 km 3.8, Barrio Islote, Arecibo; © 787/816-2020). You can taste the salt of
the sea in the breeze blowing through this charming oceanfront restaurant's terrace
dining area and in the smacking fresh seafood served here. The dining room has big
windows overlooking the coast and there's also a comfortable bar. This is a great place
to watch the sunset. We love the house specialty, a kind of *criolla* version of the classic Spanish seafood paella, called *mamposteado de mariscos,* with mussels; shrimp; and
freshly caught fish, octopus, or calamari. Its seafood-stuffed *mofongo* platters and the

whole red snapper with *tostones* are hard to beat, but the mahimahi in parcha sauce came close.

5 Karst Country ★★

One of the most interesting areas of Puerto Rico to explore is the large **Karst Country,** south of Arecibo. One of the world's strangest rock formations, karst is formed by the process of water sinking into limestone. As time goes by, larger and larger basins are eroded, forming sinkholes. *Mogotes* (karstic hillocks) are peaks of earth where the land didn't sink into the erosion pits. The Karst Country lies along the island's north coast, directly northeast of Mayagüez in the foothills between Quebradillas and Manatí. The region is filled with an extensive network of caves. One sinkhole contains the 20-acre (8-hectare) dish of the world's largest radio/radar telescope at the Arecibo Observatory (see above).

South of the Karst Country looms the massive central mountain region and Utuado at the heart of the massive Cordillera Central mountain range, which rides the island's back from east to west like an elevated spine.

The Karst Country area was deforested in the late 1940s; alluvial valleys and sinkholes were then used for pastures, shifting cultivation, and coffee plantations. In this region, most of the coffee sites were abandoned in the 1960s, and today most of these sites are covered with secondary forests. The recovery of these forests has been very rapid because of a close seed source—trees left on the steep slopes—and the presence of large populations of dispersers, mainly bats.

GETTING THERE   The only way to explore the Karst Country, which is easy to reach from San Juan, is by car. Leave San Juan on the four-lane highway, Route 22, until you come to the town of Arecibo, a 1½-hour drive, depending on traffic. Once at Arecibo, take Route 10 south, in the direction of Utuado.

If you'd like a specific goal for exploring in the Karst Country, visit the Arecibo Observatory and the Río Camuy Caves, previewed above. However, you can also spend a day driving at random, exploring lakes and forests at your leisure. If you decide to go this route, make the commercial town of **Arecibo** your base. Although not of tourist interest itself, it is the capital of the Karst Country and the starting point from which you can drive south along many interesting and winding roads.

From Arecibo you can take Route 10 south in the direction of Utuado (see "Central Mountains," below), which serves as the southern border to Karst Country. Along the way you'll pass **Lagos dos Bocas** ★, one of the most beautiful lakes of the Karst Country. This is a reservoir adjacent to the Río Abajo Forest (see below). Lagos dos Bocas, which lies 12 miles (19km) south of Arecibo, is in the mountains of Cordillera Central. Along with a nearby lake, **Lake Caonillas,** it is the main source of water for the North Coast Superaqueduct, which provides water for north coast towns stretching from Arecibo to San Juan.

Tips Get a Good Map

Arm yourself with the most detailed map you can find at one of the bookstores in San Juan. The free maps dispensed by the tourist office are not sufficiently detailed and do not show the tiny secondary roads you'll need to traverse for a motor tour of the Karst Country.

Take time out at Lagos dos Bocas to ride one of the free government-operated **launches** ⚘ that traverse the lake. Established as a taxi service for residents of the area, these launches can be used by sightseers as well. The launches leave from a dock along Route 123 on the west side of the lake, with departures scheduled every hour unless the weather is bad. It's a 30-minute ride across the lake to the other main dock. On weekends, modest wooden restaurants around the lake open to serve visitors, and the launch makes stops at them. Most have tasty snacks, fried turnovers and the like, and cold drinks. We recommend Rancho Marina for a typical Puerto Rican lunch in the country. The launch will take you back to your car, and then you can continue your journey.

You can head back down to Arecibo, and then take the expressway back to San Juan.

6 Central Mountains ⚘

Utuado marks the southern border of Karst Country. It's a municipality at the dead center of the island that sprawls across the spine of the Cordillera Central mountain range. To experience the island's central mountains, continue driving up into the mountains above Lago Dos Bocas. After about 20 minutes you'll reach the **Casa Grande Mountain Retreat** (see below), which is open from 5 to 8:30pm weekdays and 3 to 8:30pm on weekends, a guesthouse and a restaurant that serves upscale *comida criolla*–inspired dishes with vegetarian options. Café Casa Grande spills from a dining room and patio to a veranda overlooking a lush mountain valley. But you may want to spend the night if you dine too late. The property is reached via curving country roads, which can be tough to handle at night.

This is Utuado, a good base in the Cordillera Central massif overlooking the heartland of karst. Utuado is a stronghold of *jíbaro* ("country folk") culture, reflecting the mountain life of the island as few other settlements do.

Just south of here you'll hook up again with Route 111 going west to Lares. You'll almost immediately come to **Parque Ceremonial Indígena Caguaña (Indian Ceremonial Park at Caguaña).** The site is signposted and need not take up more than 30 minutes of your time. Built by the Taíno Indians some 1,000 years ago, the site was used for both recreation and worship, and it is encircled by mountains near the Tanama River. You can still see the outlines of the ancient *bateyes* (ball courts), which are bordered by carved stone monoliths decorated with petroglyphs (see "Life After Death: Taíno Burial & Ceremonial Sites," below). The best-known petroglyph is the much-photographed *Mujer de Caguaña,* squatting in the position of an earth-mother fertility symbol. There is a small and very minor museum of Indian artifacts and skeletons on-site. Charging no admission, the site is open daily from 8am to 4pm. For more information, call © **787/894-7300.**

From Lares, take Route 129 south to return to Arecibo, a good spot for a meal before taking the Expressway back to San Juan (p. 209).

WHERE TO STAY

Casa Grande Mountain Retreat   This parador, situated on 107 lush and steeply inclined acres (43 hectares) of a former coffee plantation in the Caonillas Barrios district, about 1½ hours from San Juan, originated in the 19th century as a hacienda.

Life After Death: Taíno Burial & Ceremonial Sites

The **Taíno Indians** who lived in Puerto Rico before Europeans came here were ruled by *caciques,* or chiefs, who controlled their own villages and several others nearby. The Taínos believed in life after death, which led them to take extreme care in burying their dead. Personal belongings of the deceased were placed in the tomb with the newly dead, and bodies were carefully arranged in a squatting position. Near Ponce, visitors can see the oldest known Indian burial ground in the Antilles, the **Tibes Indian Ceremonial Center** (p. 220).

Even at the time of the arrival of Columbus and the conquistadores who followed, the Taínos were threatened by the warlike and cannibalistic Carib Indians coming up from the south. But though they feared the Caribs, they learned to fear the conquistadores even more. Within 50 years of the Spanish colonization, the Taíno culture had virtually disappeared, the Indians annihilated through either massacres or European diseases.

But Taíno blood and remnants of their culture live on. The Indians married with Spaniards and Africans, and their physical characteristics—straight hair, copper-colored skin, and prominent cheekbones—can still be seen in some Puerto Ricans today. Many Taíno words became part of the Spanish language that's spoken on the island even today. Hammocks, the weaving of baskets, and the use of gourds as eating receptacles are part of the heritage left by these ill-fated tribes.

Still standing near Utuado, a small mountain town, **Parque Ceremonial Indígena-Caguaña (Indian Ceremonial Park at Caguaña),** Rte. 111 Km 12.3 (© 787/894-7325), was built by the Taínos for recreation and worship some 800 years ago. Stone monoliths, some etched with petroglyphs, rim several of the 10 *bateyes* (playing fields) used for a ceremonial game that some historians believe was a forerunner to soccer. The monoliths and petroglyphs, as well as the *dujos* (ceremonial chairs), are extant examples of the Taínos' skill in carving wood and stone.

Archaeologists have dated this site to approximately 2 centuries before Europe's discovery of the New World. It is believed that the Taíno chief Guarionex gathered his subjects on this site to celebrate rituals and practice sports. Set on a 13-acre (5.3-hectare) field surrounded by trees, some 14 vertical monoliths with colorful petroglyphs are arranged around a central sacrificial stone monument. The ball complex also includes a museum, which is open daily from 8:30am to 4pm; admission is $2, free for children under 2.

There is also a gallery called Herencia Indígena, where you can purchase Taíno relics at reasonable prices, including the sought-after *Cemis* (Taíno idols) and figures of the famous little frog, the *coquí.* The Taínos are long gone, and much that was here is gone, too. This site is of special interest to those with academic pursuits, but of only passing interest to the lay visitor.

Thanks to Steve Weingarten, a retired lawyer from New York City, the isolated compound functions today as a simple, eco-sensitive hotel. The cement-sided core of the original hacienda is on view in the lobby and in the likable eatery, Jungle Jane's Restaurant, which serves an array of well-prepared international and Puerto Rican Creole-style dishes. Nonguests can eat here daily from 7:30am to 9:30pm.

Accommodations lie within five wood-sided cottages (four units to a cottage, some of them duplex) scattered throughout the surrounding acreage. Each unit has deliberately simple, spartan-looking decor with exposed wood, airy verandas, a balcony, hammock, view of the mountains, and a small bathroom with shower. None has TV, phone, or air-conditioning—as such, they're popular with urbanites who want to get back to nature, and some come here to brush up on yoga and meditation skills. A nature trail is carved out of the surrounding forest. Under separate management, a riding stable offers horseback riding a short distance away.

P.O. Box 1499, Utuado, PR 00641. (C) **888/343-2272** or 787/894-3900. Fax 787/894-3900. www.hotelcasagrande. com. 20 units. Year-round $80–$90 double. AE, DISC, MC, V. From Arecibo, take Rte. 10 south to Utuado, then head east on Rte. 111 to Rte. 140; head north on Rte. 140 to Rte. 612 for ¼-mile/.4km. **Amenities:** Restaurant; bar; pool. *In room:* Ceiling fan, no phone.

THE SOUTHERN ROUTE TO THE MOUNTAINS

A much easier way to the central mountains from San Juan, however, is to head south along the Luis A. Ferré Expressway, Highway 52, to **Cayey** and even farther up to **Aibonito.** You can take an afternoon drive and have dinner as the sun sets in the mountains; from some vantage points, the view goes all the way to the coast.

In fact, this path is well worn by *sanjuaneros* heading south with mountain air and food on their mind. Their first stop is usually **Guavate.** Take the exit for Route 184, which winds through rolling farmland and farther up along a mountain stream flowing through the lush **Carite State Forest.** In addition to the eateries, the sector is famous for local arts and crafts and plants and flowers that are sold from stands along the roadway. While the area began gaining fame years ago for a cluster of restaurants outside the natural reserve's main entrance, the string of *lechoneras* has now extended along the entire route from the Expressway. Indeed, **Los Amigos,** at the Expressway exit, is for those who want to dive in to the genuine experience, and make a quick escape. (On Sunday afternoons, especially around Christmas season, traffic is often clogged along the country road.) It has among the best food we've had here, and though utterly unscenic (like a restaurant converted from a gas station) it draws a lively crowd from early on. A merengue band was getting the party started right when we last stopped in around 2pm on a Sunday, when patrons were already burning up the dance floor in between the cafeteria and the food stands in front of the open-air fire pits where whole pigs, chickens, and turkeys were being slowly roasted Puerto Rican style.

The best restaurants, however, have a certain rustic charm in addition to their utilitarian nature. Some look like wooden tropical chalets with blooming flowers, while others are set in front of a stream gushing through a lush mountainside. Our favorites include **La Casa del Guanime** (Rte. 184 Km 27.8; (C) **787/744-3921**), **El Rancho Original** (Rte. 184 Km 27.5; (C) **787/747-7296**), **Los Pinos** (Rte. 184 Km 27.7; (C) **787/286-1917**), and **El Mojito** (Rte. 184 Km 32.9 (C) **787/738-8888**). The truth is, however, that we have been rarely disappointed in any of the restaurants we visited.

Most have live music on weekend afternoons, so whether your taste runs from salsa to merengue to local *jíbaro* country music or to something more contemporary may play a big role in your choice. Also, the road carves through a lush forest and a string of restaurants along its right-hand side is set in front of the mountain stream; several have dining rooms overlooking the stream and in the quieter ones its gurgling is the only music you'll hear.

The atmosphere is important, but the main thing about Guavate is the food: roast pork and chicken, fried rice and pigeon peas, boiled root vegetables soaked in oil and spices, blood sausage. This is traditional Puerto Rican mountain food, but the level of the cooking keeps getting better every time we return. The roast turkey (yes, they keep it juicy) is a healthy alternative to the pig; it has recently been showing up *escabeche* style, drenched in olive oil, garlic and onions, roasted peppers and herbs—absolutely delicious.

Just south of Guavaté is the northern entrance to the **Carite Forest Reserve** ⚓, a 6,000-acre (2,428-hectare) reserve that spreads from Cayey to neighboring Caguas and San Lorenzo, and all the way down to Patillas and Guayama on the south coast. The forest ranges from heights of 820 to 2,963 feet (250m–903m) above sea level, and from several peaks you can see clear down to the south coast and Ponce. The forest, with frequent rain and high humidity, is covered with Caribbean pine and has several ponds and streams. Some of the forest's most interesting sites are near the northern entrance by Guavate. On one peak is Nuestra Madre, a Catholic spiritual meditation center that permits visitors to stroll the grounds. The large natural pond, called Charco Azul, is a favorite spot for a swim. It is surrounded by a picnic area and campground. There are over 50 species of birds in the forest.

Guavate is just the start of Cayey, which is a beautiful town through which to take a drive. Another mountain road with fine restaurants is found in its **Jájome** sector. All of these are open Thursday through Sunday for lunch and dinner. This is probably a better choice for visitors wanting a more refined dining experience than the raucous pig roast that is Guavaté. To get here, take the main exit to Cayey, turn left on Route 1, and then exit on to Route 15 on the left and follow signs to the community. From some spots you can see all the way down to the south coast. Two of these are the **Jájome Terrace** (Rte. 15 Km 18.6, Cayey; ☎ **787/738-4016**) and the **Sand and the Sea Inn** (Rte. 715, Cayey; ☎ **787/738-9086**).

Farther up into the mountains is **Aibonito,** a pretty town overlooking the island's gorgeous green valleys. From Route 15, take the exit to Route 14 and follow signs for Aibonito. A good time to visit is during the annual Fiesta de las Flores at the end of June and beginning of July, a festival stretching across two weeks where local growers present some of the most beautiful flowers grown on the island, including locally grown orchids. There are various gardening seminars and official shows, but the event is much more than flowers. Like most Puerto Rican parties, count on a lot of great food and live music too. This mountain town, with its cool, crisp air, is worth a trip any time of the year, however. **La Piedra Restaurant** (Rte. 7718 Km 0.8; ☎ **787/ 735-1034**) has been luring diners from San Juan for decades with its gourmet, inventive local cuisine using locally grown ingredients. It has one of the best views around. Other local favorites are **El Rincón Familiar** (Rte. 14 Km 48.8; ☎ **787/735-7425**) and **Tío Pepe Restaurant** (Rte. 723 Km 0.3; ☎ **787/735-9615**).

10

Ponce & the Southwest

For those who want to see a less urban side of Puerto Rico, head south to Ponce and the breathtaking southwest, with great beaches, dramatic coastal bluffs, and green flatlands unfolding across the horizon to the foothills of the Cordillera Central mountain range.

Ponce is a great center for sightseeing, and you can take a side trip to the rare bonsai-like Guánica State Forest; visit Puerto Rico's second-oldest city and site of the oldest church in the New World, San Germán; and venture north through the island's central mountains to the lush Toro Negro rainforest. Both nature reserves are hits with hikers and birdwatchers.

Founded in 1692, Ponce is Puerto Rico's second-largest city, and its historic sectors have been beautifully restored. San Germán and Ponce are home to some of the finest historic architecture in the hemisphere.

Ponce also attracts beach lovers. No, there's no real beach in town, but to the west are the coastal towns of Guánica, La Parguera, and Boquerón, where the best swimming beaches on the island are located. The southwest is where Puerto Ricans go for holidays by the sea. This is the real Puerto Rico; it hasn't been taken over by high-rise resorts and posh restaurants.

Puerto Rico's west coast mimics the U.S. southwest; cacti pop up from sunbaked rock crevices, while cattle graze in the rolling Lajas Valley in the shadow of the majestic central mountains. Comparisons have also been made between the peninsula of Cabo Rojo here and Baja, California. All across the region, a beautiful western sunset settles over its charming beach towns, with their white sands and aquamarine waters, bringing very much to mind the best of the California coastline.

1 Ponce ★★

75 miles (121km) SW of San Juan

"The Pearl of the South," Ponce was named after Loíza Ponce de León, great-grandson of Juan Ponce de León. Founded in 1692, Ponce is today Puerto Rico's principal shipping port on the Caribbean. The city is well kept and attractive, with an air of being stuck in the past, like a provincial Mediterranean town. On weekday afternoons, men dressed in starched *guayaberas* and hats play dominoes while uniformed school girls run along the large walkways.

Its historic district underwent a $440-million restoration for 1992's 500th anniversary celebration of Christopher Columbus's voyage to the New World, and improvements have continued. The streets are lit with gas lamps and lined with neoclassical buildings, just as they were a century ago. Horse-drawn carriages clop by, and strollers walk along sidewalks edged with pink marble. Ponce now recalls the turn of the 20th century, when it rivaled San Juan as a wealthy business and cultural center.

Sitting in its sun-bleached plaza on a sunny afternoon, visitors may be struck by Ponce's heat, and the nearly always-dry weather conditions. Threats of rain are most often held at bay by the central mountains; you can see the potential humidity condensing into a violet haze over them in the distance as the late afternoon finally begins to fade.

ESSENTIALS

GETTING THERE   Flying from San Juan to Ponce five times a day, **Cape Air** (© **800/352-0714;** www.flycapeair.com), a small regional carrier, offers flights for $154 round-trip. Flight time is 25 minutes.

If you're driving, take Las Américas Expressway south to the Luis A. Ferré Expressway Highway 52, then continue south. Once you pass over the central mountain range and reach the south coast, you will continue west until Ponce. The trip takes about 1½ hours.

GETTING AROUND   The town's inner core is small enough that everything can be visited on foot. Taxis provide the second-best alternative.

VISITOR INFORMATION   Maps and information can be found at the **tourist office,** Paseo del Sur Plaza, Suite 3 (© **787/841-8044**). It's open daily 8am to 4:30pm.

SEEING THE SIGHTS
ATTRACTIONS IN PONCE

Most visitors go to Ponce to see the city's renovated historic section, which beautifully restored much of the city's whimsical architectural style. While the city dates back to 1692, its unique "Ponce Creole" architecture, mixing Spanish colonial, neoclassical, Caribbean, and contemporary influences, was mostly created from the 1850s through the 1930s. The style is marked by the use of wide balconies, distinctive masonry work, and touches like plaster garlands, punched tin ceilings, and stained glass panels, while other architectural motifs are present within specific geographic areas of the city, such as common grill work or building size. The style takes European concepts, but adapts them to the city's tropical climate by using pastel colors on building facades and adding high ceilings that help keep houses cool.

The city's unique architecture was created during the years of Ponce's heyday, in the 19th century, when it trumped San Juan as the island's most important city and rose as a regional trading power. Cut off from San Juan because of geographic barriers, Ponce's trade brought foreign influences and style that also impacted its architecture, as well as its wider culture, including music and cuisine.

City residences, which initially were a basic colonial style, became more intricate as the city's fortunes and its foreign influences began rising. First, ornate neoclassical and then art nouveau touches were incorporated, and interiors were adorned with mosaic tile floors, jalousies, stained glass panels, and detailed moldings and cornices. Interior balconies, often with a wall of tiny windows that allows sunlight into the patio, are also used. Calle Reina Isabel, one of the city's major residential streets, is a virtual textbook of the Ponceño style, ranging from interpretations of European neoclassical to Spanish colonial. The neoclassical style here often incorporates balconies, as befits the warm climate, and an extensive use of pink marble. The "Ponce Creole" style, a term for Spanish colonial, includes both exterior and interior balconies. The interior balconies have a wall of tiny windows that allows sunlight into the patio.

There are more than 1,000 historic buildings in Ponce, and the vast majority has been restored. Many are on streets radiating from the stately **Plaza Las Delicias**

(Plaza of Delights). On calles Isabel, Reina, Pabellones, and Lolita Tizol, electrical and telephone wires have been buried, replica 19th-century gas lamps have been installed, and sidewalks have been trimmed with the distinctive locally quarried pink marble. Paseo Atocha is a main shopping street that is now a delightful pedestrian mall with a lively street festival on the third Sunday of every month. Paseo Arias, or Callejon del Amor (Lover's Alley), is a charming pedestrian passage between two 1920s bank buildings, Banco Popular and Banco Santander, on Plaza Las Delicias, where outdoor cafe tables invite lingering. Two monumental bronze lions by Spanish sculptor Victor Ochoa guard the entrance to the old section of the city.

In addition to the attractions listed below, the **weekday marketplace,** open Monday through Friday from 8am to 5pm, at calles Atocha and Castillo, is colorful. Perhaps you'll want to simply sit in the plaza, watching the Ponceños at one of their favorite pastimes—strolling about town.

Casa de la Masacre de Ponce

This small museum is a memorial to one of the bloodiest chapters of political violence in Puerto Rican history—the Ponce Massacre. Police killed 19 people and wounded 100 during a Nationalist Party march in the city on Palm Sunday, March 21, 1937, after shots rang out. Party members had planned a march to protest the imprisonment of their leader Pedro Albizu Campos, but authorities cancelled their permit under pressure from American colonial governor Blanton Winship. The shooting occurred when protesters met up with a police blockade. Both protesters and bystanders were among the dead, which included a woman and a 7-year-old girl. The remnants of the Nationalist Party still mark the occasion with a ceremony here each year, and it is an important date for independence supporters. The museum is located at the site of the tragedy in a restored shoemaker's shop that used to be a meeting place for Nationalist Party members. The museum also documents other episodes of the political persecution of island *independentistas,* including the infamous *carpetas,* the secret dossiers that a police intelligence unit, with the backing of U.S. government officials, kept on independence supporters over the course of decades. The museum is a concise review of the political repression of independence supporters and will prove illuminating for many visitors.

At callea Aurora and Marina Plaza Las Delicias. © 787/844-9722. Free admission. Daily 8am–noon.

Cathedral of Our Lady of Guadalupe

In 1660 a rustic chapel was built on this spot on the western edge of the Plaza Las Delicias, and since then fires and earthquakes have razed the church repeatedly. In 1919 a team of priests collected funds from local parishioners to construct the Doric- and Gothic-inspired building that stands here today. Designed by architects Francisco Porrato Doría and Francisco Trublard in 1931, and featuring a pipe organ installed in 1934, it remains an important place for prayer for many. The cathedral, named after a famous holy shrine in Mexico, is the best-known church in southern Puerto Rico.

At calles Concordia and Union. © 787/842-0134. Free admission. Mon–Fri 6am–12:30pm; Sat–Sun 6am–noon and 3–8pm.

El Museo Castillo Serralles ⊀

Two miles (3.2km) north of the center of town is the largest and most imposing building in Ponce, constructed high on El Vigía Hill (see below) during the 1930s by the Serrallés family, owners of a local rum distillery. One of the architectural gems of Puerto Rico, it is the best evidence of the wealth produced by the turn-of-the-20th-century sugar boom. Guides will escort you through the Spanish Revival house with Moorish and Andalusian details. Highlights include panoramic courtyards, a baronial dining room, a small cafe and souvenir shop, and a series of photographs showing the tons of earth that were brought in for the construction of the terraced gardens, a beautiful place to sit outside the castle that overlooks the city.

El Vigía 17. © 787/259-1774. Admission $9 adults, $4.50 seniors, $4 children and students. (Admission includes all attractions on El Vigía Hill.) Tues–Sun 9:30am–5pm. Free trolley leaving from Plaza Las Delicias de Ponce. Take Ruta Norte (northern route) 9am–9pm everyday.

El Vigía Hill   The city's tallest geologic feature, El Vigía Hill (300 ft./91m) dominates Ponce's northern skyline. Its base and steep slopes are covered with a maze of 19th- and early-20th-century development. In addition to the castle, as soon as you reach the summit, you'll see the soaring Cruz del Vigía (Virgin's Cross). Built in 1984 of reinforced concrete to replace a 19th-century wooden cross in poor repair, this modern 100-foot (30m) structure bears lateral arms measuring 70 feet (21m) long and an observation tower (accessible by elevator), from which you can see all of the natural beauty surrounding Ponce. The cross commemorates Vigía Hill's colonial role as a deterrent to contraband smuggling. In 1801, on orders from Spain, a garrison was established atop the hill to detect any ships that might try to unload their cargoes tax-free along Puerto Rico's southern coastline. Make sure to take a break in the beautifully tranquil Japanese garden, with bonsai plantings and dry areas, and elevated bridges running between ponds and streams; it's a perfect spot for a break.

At the north end of Ponce. Free trolley from Plaza Las Delicia.

Museo de Arte de Ponce 😊😊😊   The museum is closed while undergoing extensive renovations but is set to reopen better than ever in 2010. In the meantime, the museum is holding exhibitions at an annex it opened in San Juan's Plaza Las Américas, and it is lending some of its best pieces out to traveling shows at fine arts institutions throughout the world.

Donated to the people of Puerto Rico by the late Luís A. Ferré, the former governor who founded the pro-statehood New Progressive Party, this museum has the finest collection of European and Latin American art in the Caribbean. The building itself was designed by Edward Durell Stone (who also designed the John F. Kennedy Center for the Performing Arts in Washington, D.C.) and has been called the "Parthenon of the Caribbean." Its collection represents the principal schools of American and European art of the past 5 centuries. Among the nearly 400 works on display are exceptional pre-Raphaelite and Italian baroque paintings. Visitors will also see artworks by other European masters, as well as Puerto Rican and Latin American paintings, graphics, and sculptures. On display are some of the best works of the two "old masters" of Puerto Rico, Francisco Oller and José Campéche. The museum also contains a representative collection of the works of the old masters of Europe, including Gainsborough, Velázquez, Rubens, and Van Dyck. The museum is best known for its pre-Raphaelite and baroque paintings and sculpture—not only from Spain, but from Italy and France as well.

Av. de Las Américas 23–25. © 787/848-0505. www.museoarteponce.org. CLOSED UNTIL 2010. Follow Calle Concordia from Plaza Las Delicias 1½ miles/2.4km south to Av. de Las Américas.

Museum of the History of Ponce (Casa Salazar)   Opened in the Casa Salazar in 1992, this museum traces the history of the city from the time of the Taíno peoples to the present. Interactive displays help visitors orient themselves and locate other attractions. The museum has a conservation laboratory, library, souvenir-and-gift shop, cafeteria, and conference facilities.

Casa Salazar ranks close to the top of Ponce's architectural treasures. Built in 1911, it combines neoclassical and Moorish details, while displaying much that is typical of the Ponce decorative style: stained-glass windows, mosaics, pressed-tin ceilings, fixed jalousies, wood or iron columns, porch balconies, interior patios, and the use of doors as windows.

Calle Reina Isabel 51–53 (at Calle Mayor). ⓒ 787/844-7071. Free admission. Tues–Sun 9am–5pm.

Museum of Puerto Rican Music   This museum showcases the development of Puerto Rican music, with displays of Indian, Spanish, and African musical instruments that were played in the romantic danza, the favorite music of 19th-century Puerto Rican society, as well as the more African-inspired *bomba* and *plena* styles. Also on view are memorabilia of composers and performers. It is housed in one of the city's most beautiful private residences designed by Alfredo Wiechers and dating from the turn of the 20th century.

Calle Isabel 50. ⓒ 787/848-7016. Free admission. Wed–Sun 8:30am–4:30pm.

Parque de Bombas   Constructed in 1882 as the centerpiece of a 12-day agricultural fair intended to promote the civic charms of Ponce, this building was designated a year later as the island's first permanent headquarters for a volunteer firefighting brigade. It has an unusual appearance—it's painted black, red, green, and yellow. A tourist-information kiosk is situated inside the building (see "Visitor Information," above).

Plaza Las Delicias. ⓒ 787/284-3338. Free admission. Daily 8am–5pm.

Teatro la Perla   This theater, built in the neoclassical style in 1864, remains one of the most visible symbols of the economic prosperity of Ponce during the mid–19th century. Designed by Juan Bertoli, an Italian-born resident of Puerto Rico who studied in Europe, it was destroyed by an earthquake in 1918, and rebuilt in 1940 according to the original plans; it reopened to the public in 1941. It is noted for acoustics so clear that microphones are unnecessary. The theater is the largest and most historic in the Spanish-speaking Caribbean. Everything from plays to concerts to beauty pageants takes place here.

At calles Mayor and Christina. ⓒ 787/843-4322. Prices and hours vary.

NEARBY ATTRACTIONS

Hacienda Buena Vista   Built in 1833, this hacienda preserves an old way of life, with its whirring water wheels and artifacts of 19th-century farm production. Once it was one of the most successful plantations on Puerto Rico, producing coffee, corn, and citrus. It was a working coffee plantation until the 1950s, and 86 of the original 500 acres (35 of 202 hectares) are still part of the estate. The rooms of the hacienda have been furnished with authentic pieces from the 1850s.

Rte. 123, Barrio Magüeyes Km 16.8. ⓒ 787/722-5882 (weekdays), 787/284-7020 (weekends). Tours $7 adults, $4 children and seniors. Reservations required. 2-hr. tours Wed–Sun at 8:30am, 10:30am, 1:30pm, and 3:30pm (in English only at 1:30pm). A 30-min. drive north of Ponce, in the small town of Barrio Magüeyes, between Ponce and Adjuntas.

Tibes Indian Ceremonial Center   Bordered by the Río Portuguéz and excavated in 1975, this is the oldest cemetery in the Antilles. It contains some 186 skeletons, dating from A.D. 300, as well as pre-Taíno plazas from A.D. 700. The site also includes a re-created Taíno village, seven rectangular ball courts, and two dance grounds. The arrangement of stone points on the dance grounds, in line with the solstices and equinoxes, suggests a pre-Columbian Stonehenge. Here you'll also find a museum, an exhibition hall that presents a documentary about Tibes, a cafeteria, and a souvenir shop.

Rte. 503, Tibes, at Km 2.2. ✆ **787/840-2255.** Admission $3 adults, $2 children. Guided tours in English and Spanish are conducted through the grounds. Tues–Sun 9am–4pm. 2 miles/3.2km north of Ponce.

WALKING TOUR   PONCE

Start:	East side of Plaza Las Delicias
Finish:	North side of Plaza Las Delicias
Time:	90 minutes, excluding coffee breaks, museum visits, and shopping stops

The downtown revitalization of Ponce has required more money and generated more publicity than that of any other city in Puerto Rico except Old San Juan. Your tour of this Caribbean showplace begins on the eastern edge of the town's main square, the Plaza Las Delicias (also known as Plaza Muñoz Rivera). Within the symmetrical borders of this main square, you'll see the red-and-black-striped clapboard facade of the town's most frequently photographed building. (Red and black, incidentally, are the colors of the city's flag.)

As you begin the tour, note the Victorian gingerbread and the deliberately garish colors of the:

❶ Parque de Bombas (Old Municipal Fire House)

This building housed the fire department before it moved into more modern quarters in another part of the city. You can still see a handful of bright red fire engines parked inside.

On the plaza's opposite side, adjacent to Calle Concordia/Calle Union, is the:

❷ Cathedral of Our Lady of Guadalupe

When you visit, there will almost certainly be parishioners at prayer inside this, the best-known church in southern Puerto Rico. Its alabaster altars were commissioned by an ex-governor of Puerto Rico in the late 1960s in Burgos, Spain.

As you leave the cathedral, notice the many impeccably clipped trees ringing the perimeter of the plaza. Identified as Indian laurels, they were planted between 1906 and 1908 and are one of the botanical triumphs of Ponce. Clipped manually into topiary forms and carefully groomed by a master gardener, they are well worth a second or third glance. The elaborate iron lampposts nearby date from 1916.

Across Calle Concordia from the main entrance to the cathedral is one of Ponce's most famous houses, at the western border of the Plaza Las Delicias:

❸ Casa Armstrong-Poventud

This paneled and ornately crafted building was once the home of a wealthy Scottish-born banker. The Poventud family moved in after the Armstrongs. Today, it's a cultural center, and it's open Monday through Friday from 8am to noon and 1 to 4:30pm. Admission is free.

Turn right upon exiting Casa Armstrong-Poventud and walk southward beneath the Indian laurels. On the square's southern edge, you'll see one of the most historic buildings of Ponce, restored to reflect its original function during Spanish colonial days:

❹ Casa Alcaldía (City Hall)

Standing on the site of an 18th-century monastery, this building was erected in 1840 as a general assembly, and then it served as the civic jail until 1905. Speeches

Walking Tour: Ponce

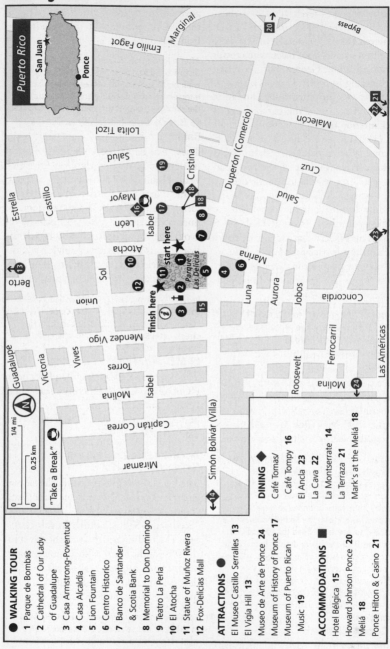

Puerto Rico
San Juan
Ponce

N
1/4 mi
0.25 km

"Take a Break"

WALKING TOUR

1 Parque de Bombas
2 Cathedral of Our Lady of Guadalupe
3 Casa Armstrong-Poventud
4 Casa Alcaldía
5 Lion Fountain
6 Centro Histórico
7 Banco de Santander & Scotia Bank
8 Memorial to Don Domingo
9 Teatro La Perla
10 El Atocha
11 Statue of Muñoz Rivera
12 Fox-Delicias Mall

ATTRACTIONS ●
El Museo Castillo Serralles 13
El Vigía Hill 13
Museo de Arte de Ponce 24
Museum of History of Ponce 17
Museum of Puerto Rican Music 19

ACCOMMODATIONS ■
Hotel Bélgica 15
Howard Johnson Ponce 20
Meliá 18
Ponce Hilton & Casino 21

DINING ◆
Café Tomas/Café Tompy 16
El Ancla 23
La Cava 22
La Montserrate 14
La Terraza 21
Mark's at the Meliá 18

by Theodore Roosevelt (in 1906), Herbert Hoover (in 1931), and Franklin D. Roosevelt (in 1934) were delivered from its central second-floor balcony to crowds assembled below. George Bush (I) visited the building in 1987. The clock set into the tower was imported from London in 1877, and a tour of the baronial street-level interior reveals a memorial plaque dedicated to the fallen American dead (Second Wisconsin Regiment) during the Spanish-American War. A few paces farther, you'll see a galleried courtyard that formerly served as prisoners' cells. The building's main courtyard was used for public executions. In City Hall, other plaques make clear that the city of Ponce was named not after Juan Ponce de León, but rather after de León's great-grandson, Loíza Ponce de León, one of the town's early civic leaders.

Across from the entrance to City Hall (in Plaza Las Delicias), you'll see one of the most beautiful fountains of Puerto Rico, the:

5 Lion Fountain (Puente de los Léones)

Crafted from marble and bronze, the Lion Fountain was modeled after a famous fountain in Barcelona, Spain. It was made for the 1939 New York World's Fair and later purchased by the mayor of Ponce.

Continue your walk along the southern edge of the square. Note the way the plaza has "chopped corners" (broadly rounded 45-degree corners rather than 90-degree perpendicular corners). They were designed this way for increased visibility by the Spanish armies as a deterrent to civil unrest and the contraband trade that flourished here during their regime. Ponce is said to have the only large square on Puerto Rico designed with such a feature.

When you reach the corner of Calle Marina and Calle Duperón (Comercio), head south (to your right) for 1 block until you come to the landmark:

6 Centro Histórico

Originally built in 1922, this landmark served as the town's casino until it was closed in the mid-1960s. Today it houses government agencies and is not open to the public, although it can be admired from the outside.

After admiring the facade of the Centro Histórico, backtrack along Calle Marina (that is, walk north again) until you again come to the intersection with Calle Duperón (Comercio). On the far right (east) of this intersection loom the:

7 Banco de Santander & Scotia Bank

These two banks are both adorned with intricate stained-glass windows, Art Nouveau detailing, and dozens of unusual architectural features. The alleyway separating the two banks, Callejon Amor, is lined with African tulip trees planted to evoke the romantic spirit of a couple in love. This is also the site of public concerts that are held every Sunday between 8 and 9pm by classical orchestras or dance bands.

Proceed eastward along Calle Cristina. Behind you, you should see the red-and-black-sided fire station at Plaza Las Delicias. At the next cross street, Calle Mayor, diagonal to where you're standing, you'll see the:

8 Memorial to Don Domingo

This statue is dedicated to Don Domingo ("Cocolia") Cruz, longtime leader of Ponce's municipal band and one of the best-known musicians from Ponce. He died in 1934.

Turn left on Calle Mayor and admire:

9 Teatro La Perla

The neoclassical facade of this, the largest and most historic theater in the Caribbean, is graced by six classical columns (see "Seeing the Sights," earlier in this chapter). Depending on the time of day and the season, the lobby of this theater might be open for a quick look at the interior decoration. In late afternoons, it's also quite possible to hear rehearsals.

Continue walking northward along Calle Mayor to the first intersection (Calle Isabel). To your right stands a Moorish-inspired building known as the Casa Salazar (Salazar House), which accommodates a branch of the Puerto Rican Museum of History.

TAKE A BREAK
Stop for an ice cream or drink at **King's Ice Cream** (📞 787/843-8520), right across the street from the Parque de Bombas on the city's main square. This institution has been scooping up delicious ice cream for decades. Another option is a drink or sandwich at the **Café Tomas/Café Tompy,** Calle Isabel at Calle Mayor (📞 787/840-1965). Divided into less formal and more formal sections, it is open daily from 7am to midnight. For more information, see "Where to Dine," below.

Walk westward along Calle Isabel until you reach the edge of the previously explored Plaza Las Delicias. From the square's northeastern corner stretches:

⑩ El Atocha

El Atocha is the city's main shopping street. Stroll along its broad borders, noting the Spanish-inspired turn-of-the-20th-century architecture, the cast-iron benches, and the many police guards who ensure the street's tranquillity.

After your shopping, return to the Plaza Las Delicias and walk westward along its northern edge. Note that within the confines of the square is the:

⑪ Statue of Luis Muñoz Rivera

This statue is a memorial to Muñoz Rivera (1859–1916), one of Puerto Rico's best-known politicians. He helped Puerto Ricans become U.S. citizens after a career of political lobbying. The bronze piece was completed in 1923.

Proceeding west along the edge of the square, note the:

⑫ Fox-Delicias Hotel

Originally built in 1931 as a movie theater, this is now a hotel and adjacent outdoor food court. Its pink walls are excellent examples of Art Deco architecture in Puerto Rico. In crumbling disrepair, the theater was transformed into a disco during the 1960s. In 1989 the government of Spain earmarked funds for the restoration of this building to its original celluloid glamour. The cafes make this place a good stop for refreshment at the end of your stroll.

After a break, you can walk out and cross Calle Isabel, heading south. You will once again be at Plaza Las Delicias.

BEACHES & OUTDOOR ACTIVITIES

Ponce is a city—not a beach resort—and should be visited mainly for its sights. There are no beaches within the city, but an offshore cay ringed with white sand and aquamarine waters filled with marine life is a ferry ride from the city.

About 30 minutes to the west, however, are some of Puerto Rico's best beaches. They ring the coast from Guánica through Cabo Rojo.

Because the northern shore of Puerto Rico fronts the often-turbulent Atlantic, many snorkelers prefer the more tranquil southern coast, especially the waters off the coast of **La Parguera.** Throughout the southwest coast, water lovers can go snorkeling right off the beach, and it isn't necessary to take a boat trip. Waters here are not polluted, and visibility is usually good, unless there are heavy winds and choppy seas.

La Guancha is a sprawling boardwalk around Ponce's bayside harbor area near the Ponce Hilton. A free trolley called **Chu Chu Tren,** because it is a model train, provides free transportation from downtown Ponce from 9am to 9:30pm. The trip goes through the historic sector. Several eateries are located here, and it is the scene of free concerts and other events at night. There's no beach, but during weekend afternoons children and their families come here to fly kites or ride bicycles. Hundreds of yachts and pleasure craft tie up here, which is also home to the Ponce Yacht Club. La Guancha is a relatively wholesome version of Coney Island, with a strong Hispanic accent and vague hints of New England. On hot weekends, the place is mobbed with thousands of families who listen to merengue and salsa. Lining the boardwalk are at least a dozen emporiums purveying beer, party-colored drinks, high-calorie snacks, and souvenirs. There is also a lookout tower here, which is worth a climb.

A ferry runs from La Guancha to **Caja de Muertos,** or **Coffin Island,** an uninhabited cay that's covered with mangrove swamps and ringed with worthwhile beaches. It's some of the best snorkeling in the southwest. A 125-passenger ferry run by **Island Venture** (© **787/842-8546** or 787/866-7827) provides transportation daily to and from the island. Roundtrip fare is $15 for adults, and $10 for children. Other private outfits will take passengers to the island, with some providing snorkeling equipment and even lunch to guests. There are hiking trails, gazebos and basic bathrooms but no running water. The island has an old lighthouse and a nice beach.

The city owns two **tennis complexes,** one at Poly Deportivos, with nine hard courts, and another at Rambla, with six courts. Both are open from 9am to 10pm daily and are lighted for night play. You can play for free, but you must call to make a reservation. For information, including directions on how to get there, call the city **Sports and Recreation Department** at © **787/840-4400.**

One of the south coast's finest and newest courses is the **Costa Caribe Golf & Country Club** 🏌️🏌️ (© **787/848-1000** or 787/812-2650), on the site of the Ponce Hilton & Casino (see below). This 27-hole course charges from $85 ($75 for guests) to play 18 holes. The beautifully landscaped holes—with commanding views of the ocean and mountain—are laid out in former sugar-cane fields. The no. 12 hole, one of the most dramatic, calls for a 188-yard carry over water from the back tees. Trade winds add to the challenge. The three 9s can be played in 18-hole combinations, as conceived by golf architect Bruce Besse. The greens are undulating and moderate in speed, averaging 6,000 square feet (557 sq. m). Golf carts are included in the greens fees, and both gas and electric carts are available.

Another course, **Club Deportivo del Oeste,** Hwy. 102 Km 15.4, Barrio Jogudas, Cabo Rojo (© **787/851-8880** or 787/254-3748), lies 30 miles (48km) west of Ponce. This course is an 18-holer, open daily from 7am to 5pm. Greens fees are $35 during the week and $40 on the weekend.

SHOPPING

If you feel a yen for shopping in Ponce, there are many shops in the renovated downtown area that have local arts and crafts. **The Atochoa Pedestrian Mall** (© **787/841-8044**) runs along Calle Cristina just off the city's central **Plaza Las Delicias.** It's been one of Ponce's main shopping areas for decades.

The best outlet for souvenirs and artisans' work is **El Palacio del Coquí Inc.,** Calle Marina 9227 (© **787/812-0216**), whose name means "palace of the tree frog." This is the place to buy the colorful *veijantese* masks (viewed as collectors' items) that are used at carnival time. Ask the owner to explain the significance of these masks.

Utopía, Calle Isabel 78 (© **787/848-8742**), conveniently located in Plaza Las Delicias, has the most imaginative and interesting selection of gift items and handicrafts in Ponce. Prominently displayed are *vegigantes,* brightly painted carnival masks inspired by carnival rituals and crafted from papier-mâché. In Ponce, where many of these masks are made, they sell at bargain prices of between $5 and $500, depending on their size. Other items include cigars, pottery, clothing, and jewelry; gifts imported from Indonesia, the Philippines, and Mexico; and rums from throughout the Caribbean. Julio and Carmen Aguilar are the helpful and enthusiastic owners, who hail from Ecuador and Puerto Rico, respectively.

WHERE TO STAY
EXPENSIVE

Hilton Ponce Golf & Casino Resort 🏿🏿 On an 80-acre (32-hectare) tract of land on the coast, this is the most glamorous hotel in southern Puerto Rico. At the western end of Avenida Santiago de los Caballeros, it's about a 15-minute drive from the center of Ponce. Designed like a miniature village, with turquoise-blue roofs, white walls, and lots of tropical plants, ornamental waterfalls, and gardens, it welcomes both conventioneers and individual travelers. The main pool behind the hotel is spacious and stretches like a wave through towering palms and gardens. The 28-hole golf course is the best in the area, and there's another set of pools by its clubhouse. The small beach is pretty, but it does not compare with those to the west. There's a large playground for kids and two children's pools. A trolley shuttles guests around the property, and the city government **Chu Chu Tren** provides transportation to downtown Ponce and the nearby La Guancha boardwalk area.

Accommodations contain tropically inspired furnishings, ceiling fans, and terraces or balconies. All the rooms are medium to spacious, with adequate desk and storage space, tasteful fabrics, good upholstery, and fine linens. The ground-floor rooms are the most expensive. Each is equipped with a generous tiled bathroom with a tub/shower combination.

The food is the most sophisticated and refined on the south coast of Puerto Rico. All the waiters seem to have an extensive knowledge of the menu and will guide you through some exotic dishes—of course, you'll find familiar fare, too.

Av. Caribe 1150 (P.O. Box 7419), Ponce, PR 00716. © 800/HILTONS (445-8667) or 787/259-7676. Fax 787/259-7674. www.hilton.com. 153 units. High season $279–$419; off season $152–$269 double; $400 suite. AE, DC, DISC, MC, V. Valet parking $10; self-parking $4.50. **Amenities:** 2 restaurants; 2 bars; pool ringed w/gardens; 2 tennis courts; golf course; fitness center; bike rentals; playground; children's program; business center; room service (7am–midnight); babysitting; laundry service; dry cleaning; casino; nightclub; rooms for those w/limited mobility. *In room:* A/C, TV, high-speed Internet access, minibar, coffeemaker, hair dryer, iron, safe.

MODERATE

Howard Johnson Ponce *Kids* This hotel, a 15-minute drive east of Ponce, has modest bedrooms. They are conservative and comfortable, equipped with contemporary furnishings. Each unit has a small tiled bathroom with tub/shower combination. The prices appeal to families. The hotel is set on a hill overlooking the coast right near a string of popular coastal seafood restaurants. Unless you have kids, who will enjoy the pool, you are probably better off staying in town.

Turpo Industrial Park 103, Mercedita, Ponce, PR 00715. © 787/841-1000. Fax 787/841-2560. www.hojo.com. 120 units. Year-round $116–$155 double; $170 suite. AE, DC, DISC, MC, V. Free parking. East of Ponce on Hwy. 52, opposite the Interamerican University. **Amenities:** Restaurant; bar/disco; pool; children's wading pool; gym; whirlpool; limited room service; laundry service; dry cleaning; rooms for those w/limited mobility. *In room:* A/C, TV, coffeemaker, hair dryer, iron, safe.

Meliá A city hotel with southern hospitality, the Meliá, which has no connection with the international hotel chain, attracts businesspeople. The location is a few steps away from the Cathedral of Our Lady of Guadalupe and from the Parque de Bombas (the red-and-black firehouse). Although the more expensive Hilton long ago outclassed this old and somewhat tattered hotel, many people who can afford more upscale accommodations still prefer to stay here for its old-time atmosphere. The lobby floor and all stairs are covered with Spanish tiles of Moorish design. The desk clerks speak English. The small rooms are comfortably furnished and pleasant enough, and most have a balcony facing either busy Calle Cristina or the old plaza. Bathrooms are tiny, each with a shower stall. Breakfast is served on a rooftop terrace with a good view of Ponce, and Mark's at the Meliá thrives under separate management (see "Where to Dine," below). You can park your car in the lot nearby.

Calle Cristina 2, Ponce, PR 00731. (2) **800/448-8355** or 787/842-0260. Fax 787/841-3602. www.hotelmeliapr.com. 73 units (shower only). Year-round $105–$115 double; $130 suite. Rates include continental breakfast. AE, MC, V. Parking $3. **Amenities:** Restaurant; bar; outdoor pool; limited room service; rooms for those w/limited mobility. *In room:* A/C, TV, free high-speed Internet, hair dryer, iron, safe.

INEXPENSIVE

Hotel Bélgica   This hotel was recently spiffed up, but accommodations remain basic. Still, this Spanish colonial mansion from around 1911 has cathedral ceilings, and some rooms have double doors opening up onto balconies. You might find this cost-conscious spot wonderful or horrible, depending on your point of view and room assignment. The most appealing accommodations are nos. 8, 9, and 10; these rooms are spacious and have balconies that hang over Calle Villa, a few steps from Plaza Las Delicias. Each unit has a small, tiled, shower-only bathroom. No restaurants are here, but this is downtown, right off the plaza, with many restaurants nearby.

Calle Villa 122 (at Calle Union/Concordia), Ponce, PR 00731. (2) **787/844-3255.** Fax 787/844-3255. www.hotel belgica.com. 20 units (shower only). Year-round $65–$75 double. MC, V. *In room:* A/C, TV, no phone.

WHERE TO DINE
EXPENSIVE

La Cava 𝒢𝒢 INTERNATIONAL   This hive of venerable rooms within a 19th-century coffee plantation is the most appealing and elaborate restaurant in Ponce. There's a well-trained staff, old-fashioned charm, well-prepared cuisine, and a champagne bar where the bubbly sells for around $8 a glass. Menu items change every 6 weeks, but might include duck foie gras with toasted brioche, Parma ham with mango, cold poached scallops with mustard sauce, a fricassee of lobster and mushrooms in a pastry shell, and grilled lamb sausage with mustard sauce on a bed of couscous. Dessert could be a black-and-white soufflé or a trio of tropical sorbets.

In the Ponce Hilton, Av. Caribe 1150. (2) **787/259-7676.** Reservations recommended. Main courses $26–$35. AE, DC, DISC, MC, V. Mon–Sat 6:30–10:30pm.

Mark's at the Meliá 𝒢𝒢𝒢 INTERNATIONAL   Mark French (isn't that a great name for a chef?) makes international haute cuisine with a Puerto Rican flair at this landmark eatery. You'd think he'd been entertaining the celebs in San Juan instead of cooking at what is somewhat of a Caribbean backwater. French was hailed as "Chef of the Caribbean 2000" in Fort Lauderdale. With his constantly changing menus and his insistence that everything be fresh, he's still a winner. You'll fall in love with this guy when you taste his tamarind barbecued lamb with yucca mojo. Go on to sample the grilled lobster with tomato-and-chive salad or the freshly made sausage with pumpkin, cilantro, and chicken. All over Puerto Rico you get fried green plantains, but here they come topped with sour cream and a dollop of caviar. The corn-crusted red snapper with yucca purée and tempura jumbo shrimp with Asian salad are incredible. The desserts are spectacular, notably the vanilla flan layered with rum sponge cake and topped with a caramelized banana, as well as the award-winning bread pudding soufflé with coconut vanilla sauce.

In the Meliá Hotel, Calle Cristina. (2) **787/284-6275.** Reservations recommended. Main courses $16–$30. AE, MC, V. Tues–Sat noon–3pm and 6–10:30pm; Sun noon–5 pm.

MODERATE

El Ancla ⚘ PUERTO RICAN/SEAFOOD   This is one of Ponce's best restaurants, with a lovely, informal location 2 miles (3.2km) south of the city center, in the Playa del Ponce sector overlooking the Caribbean Sea. Look out at the water from the dining room and enjoy the culinary delights from the sea. Menu items are prepared with real Puerto Rican zest and flavor. A favorite here is red snapper stuffed with lobster and shrimp, served either with fried plantains or mashed potatoes. Other specialties are filet of salmon in caper sauce, and a seafood medley of lobster, shrimp, octopus, and conch. Most of the dishes are reasonably priced, especially the chicken and conch. Lobster tops the price scale. The side orders, including crabmeat rice and yucca in garlic, are delectable.

Av. Hostos Final, Playa Ponce. ℂ 787/840-2450. Main courses $13–$36. AE, DC, MC, V. Sun–Thurs 11am–10pm; Fri–Sat 11am–11pm.

La Montserrate PUERTO RICAN/SEAFOOD   This is one of a string of seaside restaurants specializing in Puerto Rican cuisines and seafood lined along the beautiful coastline about 4 miles (6.4km) west of the town center. This restaurant draws a loyal following from the surrounding neighborhood. A culinary institution in Ponce since it was established 20 years ago, it occupies a large, airy, modern building divided into two different dining areas. The first of these is slightly more formal than the other. Most visitors head for the less formal, large room in back, where windows on three sides encompass a view of some offshore islands. Specialties, concocted from the catch of the day, might include octopus salad, several different kinds of *asopao*, a whole red snapper in Creole sauce, or a selection of steaks and grills. Nothing is innovative, but the cuisine is typical of the south of Puerto Rico, and it's a family favorite. The fish dishes are better than the meat selections.

Sector Las Cucharas, Rte. 2. ℂ 787/841-2740. Main courses $12–$26. AE, DISC, MC, V. Daily 11am–10pm.

La Terraza ⚘ INTERNATIONAL   This big and sunny restaurant has a dramatic view. Two-story walls of windows sweep the eye out over the greenery of the hotel's garden. Lunchtimes focus on a well-stocked buffet that dominates rooms off to the side of the eating area. At nighttime, except for a sprawling soup-and-salad bar (access to which is included in the price of any main course), the buffet is eliminated in favor of a la carte dining that's choreographed by a carefully trained staff. There are different themed menus every day. Menu items change but are likely to include grilled grouper with either lemon butter or *criolla* sauce; T-bone steaks with béarnaise, red-wine, or mushroom sauce; a succulent chateaubriand that's prepared for two diners at a time; and lobster that's available several different ways.

In the Ponce Hilton, Av. Caribe 1150. ℂ 787/259-7676. Breakfast $5–$19; lunch buffet $22; dinner main courses $24–$36. AE, DC, DISC, MC, V. Daily 6:30–10:30am, 12:30–4:30pm, and 6:30–10:30pm.

INEXPENSIVE

Café Tomas/Café Tompy *Value* PUERTO RICAN   The more visible and busier section of this establishment functions as a simple cafe for neighbors and local merchants. At plastic tables often flooded with sunlight from the big windows, you can order coffee, sandwiches, or cold beer, perhaps while relaxing after a walking tour of the city.

The family-run restaurant part of this establishment is more formal. The discreet entrance is adjacent to the cafe on Calle Isabel. Here, amid a decor reminiscent of a

Spanish *tasca* (tapas bar), you can enjoy such simply prepared dishes as salted filet of beef, beefsteak with onions, four kinds of *asopao,* buttered eggs, octopus salads, and yucca croquettes.

Calle Isabel 56, at Calle Mayor. © **787/840-1965.** Breakfast $2–$4; main courses lunch and dinner $5–$8. AE, MC, V. Restaurant daily 11:30am–midnight; cafe daily 7am–midnight.

2 The Southwest Coast

The southwest corner of the island is where the locals go to kick back and chill out. The area is a favored vacation spot for San Juan and Ponce residents, as well as a weekend getaway destination. In fact, for many travelers the area will be too crowded during Easter week and the month of July, the height of the Puerto Rico tourism season. Here are some of Puerto Rico's great beaches, notably the beaches of **Guánica** and **Boquerón Beach** 🏖🏖, and a lot of mom-and-pop operations that offer nightly rentals and good seafood dinners.

Southern Puerto Rico is increasingly gaining a reputation among **scuba divers,** although the outfitters are a bit lean here and not as well organized or plentiful as in the Cayman Islands. The attraction is the continental shelf that drops off a few miles off the southern coast. Within this watery range is a towering wall that is some 20 miles (32km) long and filled with one of the best assortments of marine life in the West Indies. Diving is possible from the town of La Parguera in the west all the way to Ponce in the east. The wall drops from 60 to 120 feet (18–37m) before it "vanishes" into 1,500 feet (457m) of sea. With a visibility of around 100 feet (30m), divers experience the beautiful formations of some of Puerto Rico's most dramatic coral gardens.

Bird-watchers should head to the **Guánica State Forest,** which is the sanctuary that has the greatest number of birds on the island. For beachcombers, there are many hidden places, such as Gilligan's Island off the coast of the little village of Guánica. For snorkelers, there are miles of coral reefs, awash with tropical fish, coral, and marine life. The Cabo Rojo lighthouse, south of Boquerón, offers views of the rocky coastline and a panoramic sweep of the Caribbean.

GUANICA

Guánica, on the Caribbean Sea, lies 73 miles (118km) southwest of San Juan and 21 miles (34km) west of the city of Ponce. The Guánica Dry Forest and adjacent area is a UNESCO-designated world biosphere reserve. The rare bonsai-like forest is home to more than 100 species of migratory and resident birds, the largest number in Puerto Rico. The beach at Guánica is pristine, and the crystal-clear water is ideal for swimming, snorkeling, and diving. Directly offshore is the famed Gilligan's Island, plus six of Puerto Rico's best sites for night or day dives. The area was once known for its leaping bullfrogs. The Spanish conquerors virtually wiped out this species. But the bullfrogs have come back and live in the rolling, scrub-covered hills that surround the 18-acre (7.3-hectare) site of the Copamarina Beach Resort, the area's major hotel (see below.)

Guánica is adjacent to the unique Dry Forest and experiences very little rainfall. Nearby mountains get an annual rainfall of 15 feet (4.6m), but Guánica receives only about 15 inches (38 cm). This is the world's largest dry coastal forest region. The upper hills are ideal for hiking. Guánica was once the haunt of the Taíno Indians, and it was the place where Ponce de León first explored Puerto Rico in 1508. One of his descendants later founded the nearby city of Ponce in 1692.

It is also the site of the landing of the Americans in 1898 during the Spanish-American war that began Puerto Rico's century-long relationship with the United States. You reach the harbor by taking the main exit to Guánica from Route 116 to Avenida 25 de Julio. A large rock monument on the town's *malecón,* or harbor, commemorates the landing. The Williams family, descendants of a doctor who arrived with the troops and settled here after marrying a local girl, still live in one of the historic wooden homes along the waterfront. The area has lots of seafood restaurants and bars, as well as snack vendors along a bayside promenade. It is festive on weekend evenings.

HIKING & BIRD-WATCHING IN GUANICA STATE FOREST

Heading directly west from Ponce, along Route 2, you reach **Guánica State Forest** (© 787/821-5706), a setting that evokes Arizona or New Mexico. Here you will find the best-preserved subtropical ecosystem on the planet. UNESCO has named Guánica a World Biosphere Reserve. Some 750 plants and tree species grow in the area.

The Cordillera Central cuts off the rain coming in from the heavily showered northeast, making this a dry region of cacti and bedrock, a perfect film location for old-fashioned western movies. It's also ideal country for birders. Some 50% of all of the island's terrestrial bird species can be seen in this dry and dusty forest. You might even spot the Puerto Rican emerald-breasted hummingbird. A number of migratory birds often stop here. The most serious ornithologists seek out the Puerto Rican nightjar, a local bird that was believed to be extinct. Now it's estimated that there are nearly a thousand of them.

To reach the forest, take Route 334 northeast of Guánica, to the heart of the forest. There's a ranger station here that will give you information about hiking trails. The booklet provided by the ranger station outlines 36 miles (58km) of trails through the four forest types. The most interesting is the mile-long (1.6km) **Cueva Trail,** which gives you the most scenic look at the various types of vegetation. You might even encounter the endangered bufo lemur toad, once declared extinct but found to still be jumping in this area.

SCUBA DIVING, SNORKELING & OTHER OUTDOOR PURSUITS

The best dive operation in Guánica is **Sea Venture Dive Copamarina** (© 787/821-0505, ext. 729), part of the **Copamarina Beach Resort.** Copamarina has a long pier where fishing is permitted, and a 42-foot (13m) Pro Jet dive boat. Guánica is one of the Caribbean's best areas for day and night dives. A two-tank dive costs $119, with full diving equipment. You can also rent snorkeling gear or take a ride to one of the islands nearby. It's good to reserve in advance to assure the dive master is working that day.

Whale-watching excursions can be arranged from January to March at the hotel's tour desk, which also offers ecotours, kayaking, deep-sea fishing, and sunset sails. Horseback riding and sunset biking are also available.

At one of the local beaches, **Playa Santa,** west of town, **Pino's Boat & Water Fun** (© **787/821-6864** or 787/484-8083) will rent you a paddle boat or kayak at prices ranging from $13 to $22 hourly. A banana-boat ride costs $7.50 per person, while water scooters cost $45 for a half-hour.

One of the most visited sites is **Gilligan's Island,** a series of mangrove and sand cays near the Caña Gorda peninsula. Part of the dry forest reserve, it is set aside for recreational use. A small ferry departs from in front of Restaurant San Jacinto, just past

Copamarina Beach Resort, every hour daily from 10am to 5pm, weather permitting; round-trip costs $6. **Ballena Beach** is farther down Route 333, in the coastal border of the Dry Forest. This is a beautiful beach, with huge palm trees and golden sand. During winter storms, surfers flock here for rare, tubular waves.

WHERE TO STAY

Copamarina Beach Resort 👍👍 *Value*   In the 1950s, Copamarina was the private vacation retreat of the de Castro family, Puerto Rican cement barons. In 1991 it was enlarged and upgraded by talented entrepreneurs. Today, charming, low-key, and discreetly elegant, it stands head and shoulders above everything else along Puerto Rico's western coast, except for the regal Horned Dorset Primavera (its strongest competitor). Situated beside a public beach (the best in the area), amid a landscaped palm grove, the resort is airy and relaxing. A favorite destination of *sanjuaneros,* it also draws a well-heeled crowd of clients from Europe and North America, who know good value when they see it.

The accommodations are in one- and two-story wings that radiate from the resort's central core, as well as a set of villas. The attractively decorated units have tile floors, lots of exposed wood, and louvered doors with screens that open onto large verandas or terraces. Everything is airy and comfortable. Bathrooms are larger than you might expect, and up-to-date, some with shower, others with tub.

The resort houses two restaurants, one of which reigns as one of the finest in western Puerto Rico: Alexandra is a destination for clients from as far away as San Juan (see "Where to Dine," below). Less formal, and staffed with a hardworking crowd of young people, is Las Palmas, which is set in the open air beneath a canopy.

The dive facilities here are the best and most varied in western Puerto Rico, attracting divers of all levels of expertise. The array of watersports and sports activities is incredible, and tours can be gotten here to anywhere on the island, including next door at the Guánica Dry Forest reserve. The hotel also offers guests all-inclusive options. We recommend renting a car and trying some of the local restaurants in Guánica and other coastal villages you will visit while staying here.

Rte. 333 Km 6.5, Caña Gorda (P.O. Box 805), Guánica, PR 00653. (*C*) **888/881-6233** or 787/821-0505. Fax 787/821-0070. www.copamarina.com. 106 units. High season $235–$285 double; low season $190–$240 double; year round $350–$450 suite, $800–$1,000 villa. AE, DC, MC, V. From Ponce, drive west along Rte. 2 to Rte. 116 and go south to Rte. 333, then head east. **Amenities:** 2 restaurants; bar; 2 outdoor pools; tennis courts; health club; limited room service; babysitting; laundry service; dry cleaning; rooms for those w/limited mobility. *In room:* A/C, TV, dataport, fridge, coffeemaker, hair dryer, safe.

Mary Lee's by the Sea 👍 *Finds*   Owned and operated by Michigan-born Mary Lee Alvarez, a former resident of Cuba and a self-described "compulsive decorator," this is an informal collection of cottages, seafront houses, and apartments, located 4 miles (6.4km) east of Guánica. Five California-style houses are subdivided into eight living units, each suitable for one to three couples. Rooms are whimsically decorated in an airy, somewhat bohemian way, with a sense of 1960s comfort and a sometimes soothing sense of clutter. Each unit has a small, tiled bathroom with a tub. The entire compound, which grew in an artfully erratic way, is landscaped with flowering shrubs, trees, and vines. Overall, the ambience is kind and low-key.

There aren't any formally organized activities here, but the hotel sits next to sandy beaches and a handful of uninhabited offshore cays. The management maintains rental boats with motors, two waterside sun decks, and several kayaks for the benefit of active guests. Hikers and bird-watchers can go north to the Guánica State Forest.

Don't come here looking for nighttime activities or enforced conviviality. The place is quiet, secluded, and appropriate for low-key vacationers looking for privacy. There isn't a bar or restaurant here, but each unit has a modern kitchen and an outdoor barbecue pit. The rooms are serviced weekly, although guests can arrange daily maid service for an extra fee.

Rte. 333 Km 6.7 (P.O. Box 394), Guánica, PR 00653. ℂ 787/821-3600. Fax 787/821-0744. www.maryleesbythesea. com. 11 units. Year-round $80–$120 double; $100–$140 studio and 1-bedroom apt; $160–$200 2-bedroom apt; $250 3-bedroom house. MC, V. From Ponce, take Rte. 2. When you reach Rte. 116, head south toward Guánica. The hotel is signposted from the road. **Amenities:** Laundry service. *In room:* A/C, kitchen, coffeemaker, iron, safe, no phone.

Parador Guánica 1929   This charming property lies on one of the island's prettiest roads, enveloped by a canopy of trees as it winds along Ensenada Bay and a line of plantation homes atop a hill overlooking it. Guánica's Ensenada sector was once the site of one of the largest sugar mills in the Caribbean, but it's been a bit of a ghost town since it shut down in the 1980s. Shadows of its former opulence can be glimpsed in the sun-baked decaying structures throughout the area, as well as the few restored buildings, such as this immaculate hotel. A classic Spanish-style plantation home, with a wide, wrap-around veranda on each of its two levels, its rooms have subdued tropical decor and are comfortable and well equipped. Breakfast is served on the downstairs side veranda overlooking the large pool area, with sun chairs on its surrounding deck. The food at the on-site restaurant is only okay. Prices at area restaurants are extremely competitive.

Rte. 3116 Km 2.5, Av. Los Veteranos, Ensenada, Guánica 00767. ℂ 787/821-0099 or 787/842-0260. Fax 787/841- 3602. www.tropicalinnspr.com. 21 units. Year-round $102 double. Rates include continental breakfast. AE, MC, V. **Amenities:** Coin laundry facility. *In room:* A/C, satellite TV, high-speed Internet, kitchen, coffeemaker, hair dryer, iron, safe.

WHERE TO DINE

Alexandra ✛ INTERNATIONAL   This is a genuinely excellent restaurant with a kitchen team turning out delectable dishes that include fried red snapper with Creole sauce, filet of mahimahi with pigeon peas, garlic shrimp with local rice, and beef parmigiana with red-wine sauce. The interior is air-conditioned but tropical in its feel, providing a welcome dose of relaxed glamour.

In the Copamarina Beach Resort, Rte. 333 Km 6.5, Caña Gorda (P.O. Box 805), Guánica. ℂ 787/821-0505. Reservations recommended. Main courses $18–$36. AE, DC, DISC, MC, V. Sun–Thurs 6–10:30pm; Fri–Sat 6–11pm.

The Blue Marlin SEAFOOD   The most established restaurant on Guánica's famous harbor, this is still the best place for local seafood. Housed in a rambling plantation style structure overlooking the pretty bay, there is a large but relaxed quiet dining area, with some tables on balconies overlooking the harbor, serving excellent local meals, with an accent on freshly caught seafood. We love everything from the Caribbean lobster ceviche salad to the *mofongo* stuffed with mixed seafood (conch, octopus, shrimp, and red snapper) in a light tomato sauce. But culinary landlubbers can find satisfaction here with budget priced *comida criolla*. Even the pork chops are tasty. There's an adjacent bar area with a jukebox playing all sorts of local hits—from reggaeton to classic salsa—and televisions tuned to sports or music videos. The long rectangular bar not only overlooks the harbor-side drive, but also one of its sides is actually on the street. Tasty snacks like seafood turnovers and fried fish fritters are available as well as more substantial menu items. There's even a more informal outdoor terrace area with cafeteria-style booths perfect for families who want a quick snack after the beach.

55 Calle Esperanza Idrach, Malecón de Guánica (at the end of Calle 25 de Julío), Guánica. © 787/821-5858. Reservations recommended. Main courses $9.50–$23. MC, V. Thurs–Mon 11am–1am.

Taíno's Seafood & Steak House SEAFOOD/ECLECTIC   This new restaurant on Guánica's pretty harbor-side drive is another good choice, with a menu a bit more international than you'd normally find here. Fat steaks and fresh fish are the specialty, but we even loved the spaghetti marinara. The basics—churrasco and red snapper—rule here.

69 Calle Esperanza Idrach, Malecón de Guánica (at the end of Calle 25 de Julío), Guánica. © 787/821-7171. Reservations recommended. Main courses $9–$27. MC, V. Sun–Sat 11am–1am.

LA PARGUERA ⚓

This charming fishing village lies 78 miles (126km) southwest of San Juan and 26 miles (42km) west of Ponce, just south of San Germán. From San Germán, take Route 320 directly south and follow the signposts. Note that this route changes its name several times along the way, becoming Route 101, 116, 315, 305, and then 304 before reaching La Parguera—even though it's all the same highway.

The name of the village comes from *pargos,* meaning snapper. Its main attraction, other than its beaches and diving, is **Phosphorescent Bay,** which contains millions of luminescent dinoflagellates (microscopic plankton). A disturbance causes them to light up the dark waters. For dramatic effect, they are best seen on a moonless night. Boats leave for a troll around the bay nightly from 7:30pm to 12:30am from La Parguera pier, depending on demand. The trip costs $7.50 per person.

Offshore are some 12 to 15 reefs with a variety of depths. The Beril reef goes down to 60 feet (18m), then drops to 2,000 feet (610m). This wall is famous among divers, and visibility ranges from 100 to 120 feet (30–37m). These reefs also provide some of the best snorkeling possibilities in Puerto Rico. Marine life is both abundant and diverse, including big morays, sea turtles, barracudas, nurse sharks, and manatees. **Paradise Scuba Center,** Hotel Casa Blanca Building, at La Parguera (© 787/899-7611), offers the best diving and snorkeling. A two-tank dive costs $150; a 3-hour snorkeling jaunt goes for $35 per person. Full equipment can be rented.

WHERE TO STAY

La Jamaka   Set on a low but breezy hillside, a 10-minute hike from the town's congested center, this is a tasteful vacation compound in a verdant setting of bougainvillea and flowering shrubs. Guests here are pulled into the gregarious life of the establishment simply by the warmth of the owners, Elsie Cintrón and Carlos Rosado. La Jamaka has a small swimming pool, a communal kitchen, and a garden-style setting for relaxation. Bedrooms are small—almost to the point of being a bit claustrophobic—but they're well-maintained and filled in midsummer with vacationers from other parts of Puerto Rico. Each unit has a small, tiled, shower-only bathroom.

Colinas de la Parguera, P.O. Box 303, Lajas, La Parguera, PR 00667. ©/fax 787/899-6162. 9 units (shower only). Year-round $110 double. MC, V. From La Parguera, head north on Rte. 304 until you reach the junction with Rte. 116. Continue north on 116 until you see the sign for the resort. **Amenities:** Restaurant; bar; outdoor pool; limited room service. *In room:* A/C, TV, no phone.

Parador Posada Porlamar   Developed by the Pancorbo family in 1967 as one of the first full-service hotels in town, this parador evokes life in a simple fishing village. A horseshoe-shaped compound that overlooks a narrow channel flanked by mangroves, it conducts an ongoing business with dive enthusiasts, thanks to its on-site

Finds **Puerto Rico's Secret Beaches**

Some of Puerto Rico's most beautiful and isolated beaches lie on the island's southwestern coast, on the Caribbean Sea, far from major highways. Stretching between Ponce in the east and Cabo Rojo on Puerto Rico's extreme southwestern tip, these beaches flank some of the least densely populated parts of the island. And because the boundaries between them are relatively fluid, only a local resident (or perhaps a professional geographer) could say for sure where one ends and the other begins.

If you consider yourself an aficionado of isolated beaches, it's worth renting a car and striking out for these remote locales. Drive westward from Ponce along Highway 2, branching south along Route 116 to **Guánica**, the self-anointed gateway and capital of this string of "secret beaches."

By far the most accessible and appealing beach is **Caña Gorda** ⟨*⟩. Set about a quarter-mile (.4km) south of Guánica, at the edge of a legally protected marsh that's known for its rich bird life and thick reeds, Caña Gorda is a sprawling expanse of pale beige sand that's dotted with picnic areas and a beach refreshment stand/bar, showers, bathrooms and other facilities. Just beyond the public beach is the well-recommended hotel, the **Copamarina Beach Resort** (ⓒ 787/821-0505); see p. 231. You can check in for a night or two of sun-flooded R&R. Even if you're not staying at the hotel, consider dropping in for a *cuba libre*, a margarita, or a meal.

Farther along is **Ballena Beach,** which stretches for a mile or more along a deserted beachfront, protected by rocky bluffs and a grove of towering palm trees. There are several other smaller beaches as Route 333 cuts farther into the dry forest and ends at an undeveloped parking area, adjacent to a foundation built right on the coast, with the sandy **Tamarindo Beach** beyond

---

scuba shop. Bedrooms are plain and neat but don't invite lingering. Some have balconies, minibars, and small sitting rooms, and each has a small, tiled, shower-only bathroom. All are nonsmoking. The social center here is a patio overlooking the channel. The restaurants and bars of La Parguera are within a short walk of this centrally located place. On the premises is a rather formal restaurant, La Pared. Specialties include seafood in Creole sauce, lamb chops in Dijon mustard, and sautéed shrimp in soursop-flavored butter sauce.

Rte. 304 (P.O. Box 3113), La Parguera, Lajas, PR 00667. ⓒ **787/899-4343.** Fax 787/899-5558. www.parguera puertorico.com. 40 units (shower only). Winter $117–$145 double; off season $80–$119 double. AE, DISC, MC, V. Drive west along Rte. 2 until you reach the junction of Rte. 116; then head south along Rte. 116 and Rte. 304. **Amenities:** Restaurant; bar; pool; rooms for those w/limited mobility. *In room:* A/C, TV, minibar, coffeemaker, hair dryer, safe.

Parador Villa Parguera *(Kids* Although the water in the nearby bay is too muddy for swimming, guests can enjoy a view of the harbor and take a dip in the swimming pool. Situated on the southwestern shore of Puerto Rico, this parador is favored by *sanjuaneros* for weekend escapes. It's also known for its seafood dinners (the fish are not caught in the bay), comfortable and uncomplicated bedrooms, and location next it. Hills surround the area, covered by the dwarfed pines at the outskirts of the reserve.

Another beautiful beach in town is **Playa Santa,** which also lies off Route 116 (the exit to Rte. 325 is signposted). The white-sand beach has incredibly tranquil salty water, and there is a string of eateries serving snacks and cold drinks around a harbor beside it. **La Jungla** and **Manglillo** are two other beautiful, undeveloped beaches bordering here, with great snorkeling because of coral reefs just offshore and interesting mangrove canals. The road to Playa Santa first cuts through a section of undeveloped dry forest before ending at the beach town. An unmarked dirt road on the left-hand side leads to another breathtakingly beautiful sand beach.

In the very southwest sector of Puerto Rico are some relatively hidden and very secluded beaches, although getting to them is a bit difficult along some potholed roads. Head west on Route 101, cutting south at the junction with Route 301, which will carry you to one of the most westerly beaches in Puerto Rico, Playa Sucia. The beach opens onto **Bahia Sucia** ✮, whose name rather unappetizingly translates as "Dirty Bay." Actually it isn't dirty; it's a lovely spot. Hikers willing to walk a while will also be rewarded for their efforts from the Boquerón public beach and over the bluffs bordering it.

All these beaches might be hard to reach, but persevere and you'll be met with warm water and long, uncrowded stretches of sand, where towering king palms and salt-tolerant sea grapes provide an idyllic tropical backdrop for sun and surf. Keep in mind that most of the beaches mentioned here have virtually no services or public utilities. Pack what you'll need for the day—food, water, sunscreen, and so forth.

to the bay's famous phosphorescent waters. Each unit has either a balcony or a terrace. Bathrooms are rather cramped but well maintained, and each has either a shower or a tub. This place is more gregarious and convivial, and usually more fun, than the Porlamar, a few steps away.

The spacious, air-conditioned restaurant, where the occasionally slow service might remind you of Spain in a bygone era, offers traditional favorites, such as filet of fish stuffed with lobster and shrimp. Nonguests are welcome here, and there's a play area for children. Because the inn is popular with local vacationers, there are frequent specials, such as a $395 weekend (Fri–Sun) special for two that includes welcome drinks, breakfasts, dinners, flowers, and dancing, along with a free show.

There's a dock right outside the restaurant where boats tie up, which is convenient because the thing to do here is to hire a boat and explore the beautiful shallow coast replete with reefs and tropical sea life.

Main St. 304 (P.O. Box 3400), Carretera 304 Km 303, La Parguera, Lajas, PR 00667. ℂ **787/899-7777.** Fax 787/899-6040. www.villaparguera.net. 74 units (all with either shower or tub). Year round $107–$165 double. 2 children 9 or under stay free in parent's room. AE, DC, DISC, MC, V. Drive west along Rte. 2 until you reach the junction with Rte. 116; then head south along Rte. 116 and Rte. 304. **Amenities:** Restaurant; bar; pool; babysitting; rooms for those w/limited mobility. *In room:* A/C, TV.

WHERE TO DINE

Besides the following recommendation, **La Jamaka** also serves excellent cuisine, as does the more formal dining quarters at **Parador Villa Parguera** (see "Where to Stay," above).

La Casita SEAFOOD   This is the town's most consistently reliable and popular restaurant. It's flourished here since the 1960s, in a simple wooden building. Inside, lots of varnished pine acts as a decorative foil for platters of local and imported fish and shellfish. Filets of fish can be served in any of seven different styles; lobster comes in five. Even the Puerto Rican starchy staple of *mofongo* comes in versions stuffed with crab, octopus, shrimp, lobster, and assorted shellfish. Begin with fish chowder, a dozen cheese balls, or fish croquettes. End with coconut-flavored flan. Don't expect grand service or decor, but rather a setting where food is the focus.

Calle Principal 304. (*C*) 787/899-1681. Reservations not necessary. All main courses $8. AE, MC, V. Tues–Sun 11am–10:30pm. Closed 2 weeks in Sept.

BOQUERON

Lying 85 miles (137km) southwest of San Juan and 33 miles (53km) west of Ponce is the little beach town of Boquerón. It is just south of Cabo Rojo, west of the historic city of San Germán, and near the western edge of the Boquerón Forest Preserve.

What puts sleepy Boquerón on the tourist map is its lovely public beach, one of the island's finest for swimming. It is also known for the shellfish found offshore. The beach has facilities, including lockers and changing places, plus kiosks that rent watersports equipment. Parking costs $2. On weekends the resort tends to be crowded with families driving down from San Juan.

The outfitter that offers the best scuba diving and snorkeling in the area is **Mona Aquatics,** on Calle José de Diego, directly west of the heart of town (*C* **787/851-2185**) near the town marina and Hotel Boquemar. It offers several dive packages (a two-tank dive starts at $105 per person), including trips to Desecheo and Mona Island some 50 miles (81km) out to sea, a sanctuary known for its spectacular dive opportunities. The company also rents snorkeling gear and, if enough people are interested, conducts boat tours of the Bahía de Boquerón.

From Boquerón you can head directly south to **El Faro de Cabo Rojo** at the island's southernmost corner. The century-old Cabo Rojo Lighthouse lies on Route 301, along a spit of land between Bahía Sucia and Bahía Salinas. Looking down from the lighthouse, you'll see a 2,000-foot (610m) drop along jagged limestone cliffs. The lighthouse dates from 1881, when it was constructed under Spanish rule. The famous pirate Roberto Cofresi used to terrorize the coast along here in the 19th century and was said to have hidden out in a cave nearby.

WHERE TO STAY

Bahia Salinas Beach Resort & Spa *(★ Finds*   You live close to nature here. Nature lovers and bird-watchers are drawn to this intimate inn in Cabo Rojo in the far southwestern corner of Puerto Rico. At the tip of the western coast, the sanctuary is bordered by a mangrove reserve, bird sanctuaries, and salt flats in the undeveloped coastal region near the Cabo Rojo Lighthouse. Salt mineral waters, similar to those of the Dead Sea, supply water for the on-site Jacuzzi and for treatments at its Cuni Spa,

A Wildlife Refuge for Bird Fanciers

The area around Cabo Rojo, the **Refugio Nacional Cabo Rojo (Red Cape National Refuge;** ✆ 787/851-7297) attracts serious bird-watchers to its government-protected sector. The refuge, run by the U.S. Fish & Wildlife Service, is on Route 301 at Km 5.1, 1 mile (1.6km) north of the turnoff to El Combate. At the entrance to the refuge is a visitor center. The only time you can visit the refuge is from 7:30am to 4pm Monday to Friday; admission is free. Migratory birds, especially ducks and herons but also several species of songbirds, inhabit this refuge. Birders have reported seeing at least 130 species. Trails for bird-watchers have been cut through the reserve. The best time to observe the birds is during the winter months, when they have fled from their cold homelands in the north.

which gives a full range of beauty and relaxation treatments. There is ample opportunity for jogging and hiking in the natural surroundings as well as all sorts of watersports. It is near many white-sand beaches, including the town's large public beach. Both restaurants—the fine-dining **Agua al Cuello Bistro** and **Balahoo's Bar & Grill**—are excellent. The Bistro features local music on Saturday nights. There is also a conference room and business center. Fresh seafood is a specialty. The bedrooms are midsize to large, and are furnished in the so-called "hacienda" Puerto Rican style, which means wooden colonial-style furniture and four-poster beds. The place is well run and maintained.

Rd. 301 Km 11.5, Sector El Faro, Cabo Rojo, PR 00622. ✆ 787/254-1212. Fax 787/254-1215. www.bahiasalina.com. 22 units. Year-round $193–$205 double. Children 11 and under stay free in parent's room. AE, MC, V. **Amenities:** Restaurant; bar; 2 outdoor pools; high-speed Internet access; room service (noon–9pm); rooms for those w/limited mobility. *In room:* A/C, TV.

Cofresi Beach Hotel   Set on the town's main road across from one of the area's best dive shops, this is a choice for clients who can live without maid service and other resort-oriented amenities—there is no full-time reception or concierge staff. The apartments here have kitchens with cutlery, plates, and cooking equipment, durable furniture, and comfortable beds; each has a small, tiled bathroom with a tub and shower. It's about as laissez-faire as they come.

Calle Muñoz Rivera 57, P.O. Box 1209, Boquerón, PR 00622. ✆ 787/254-3000. Fax 787/254-1048. www.cofresi beach.com. 12 units. Year-round $129 1-bedroom; $165 2-bedroom; $219 3-bedroom. Frequent specials offer rates as low as $90 nightly. AE, MC, V. **Amenities:** Pool. *In room:* A/C, TV, kitchenette, coffeemaker, hair dryer, iron.

Parador Boquemar   This family favorite lies right at the heart of town by Boquerón Beach. A recent renovation has spruced up the common areas and guest rooms, which gives them a more tropical feel, but the hotel still lacks character. Despite the small units here, Puerto Rican families like this place a lot, causing readers to complain that children sometimes run up and down the corridors. Rooms are simple but comfortable and clean. This is not the place to stay if you are going for ambience, but it is a good deal at a great location. Kids will enjoy the pool. Stay here only if you plan to spend most of your time outside the hotel. The hotel's restaurant, **Las Cascadas,** has good food, but again the atmosphere leaves much to be desired (see "Where to Dine," below).

Carretera 101, Poblado de Boquerón, Cabo Rojo, PR 00622. ⓒ 787/851-2158. Fax 787/851-7600. www.boquemar. com. 75 units (shower only). Year-round $95–$115 double; $120 junior suite. AE, DC, MC, V. **Amenities:** Restaurant; bar; outside pool; babysitting; rooms for those w/limited mobility. *In room:* A/C, TV, small fridge.

WHERE TO DINE

Boquerón has great roadside food stands. You can get everything from fresh oysters to hand-rolled burritos from vendors set up along the beach village's main drag. Open air bars and restaurants also sell turnovers stuffed with fresh fish, lobster, or conch, as well as seafood ceviche salad in plastic cups.

Galloway's ⓖ CREOLE/CONTINENTAL   This is our favorite restaurant in Boquerón, right near the center of town but set back along the water. Sit in the back dining room that is on a dock over Boquerón Bay. It's a great spot for a fresh seafood meal as you watch one of those perfect western sunsets. This is a casual spot, but the food is first rate. Being right on the water, we can't help but take our seafood straight up—such as a whole fried red snapper and boiled Caribbean lobster. While much of the menu is typical of the area, specializing in local cuisine and seafood, you'll also find great pasta dishes and pub fare like burgers and nachos. The bar near the entrance is a good spot to mix with locals and ex-pats and pick up tips on area activities. On weekends, there's often live music.

12 Calle José de Diego, Poblado de Boquerón, Cabo Rojo. ⓒ 787/254-3302. Reservations not necessary. Main courses $8–$26. AE, MC, V. Thurs–Tues noon–midnight; closed Wed.

Las Cascadas CREOLE/CONTINENTAL   One of the best restaurants in the area, this popular bar and restaurant is a *meson gastronómico,* a Puerto Rico Tourism Company program that sponsors local restaurants it deems of sufficient quality to cater to tourists. Inside Parador Boquemar, it boasts a waterfall in its interior. The day begins early here. The chef's breakfast specialty is an omelet Cascada, with ham, tomatoes, onions, peppers, and cheese. At dinner many Creole recipes appear, such as *mofongo relleno* (stuffed mashed plantains); the plantains can be stuffed with lobster, shrimp, octopus, or conch.

The meats, such as filet mignon, are imported but tasty. Lobster can be served with five different sauces. Other specialties of the chef include chicken breast stuffed with lobster or shrimp. The tastiest appetizers are fish and cheese balls.

In the Parador Boquemar, Carretera 101, Poblado de Boquerón, Cabo Rojo. ⓒ 787/851-2158. Reservations not necessary. Breakfast $5–$10; main courses $13–$27. AE, MC, V. Daily 7:30–11:30am; Thurs–Tues 6–10pm.

Roberto's Fish Net PUERTO RICAN   This is one of two restaurants, both named "Roberto," on the same sleepy street in the center of Boquerón. Both belong to Roberto Aviles and offer roughly equivalent versions of the same food. We prefer this spot to **Roberto's Restaurant Villa Playera** (ⓒ 787/254-3163). However, the Villa Playera is still a good choice, particularly on Monday and Tuesday, when the Fish Net is closed. Within the Fish Net's simple environment, a cross between a luncheonette and a bar, you can order tender beefsteaks, well-flavored chicken breasts, or fresh fish, any of which comes with rice and beans. More unusual are the *pilones,* a combination of mashed plantains flavored with your choice of shrimp, conch, or octopus, usually served with salsa, that come in tall wooden cups with old-fashioned mortars.

Calle José de Diego s/n (without number). ⓒ 787/851-6009. Reservations not necessary. Main courses $5–$23. AE, DISC, MC, V. Wed–Sun 11am–10pm.

3 San Germán (★(★

104 miles (167km) SW of San Juan, 34 miles (55km) W of Ponce

Only an hour's drive from Ponce and right near the beaches of the southwest coast, and just over 2 hours from San Juan, San Germán, Puerto Rico's second-oldest town, is a little museum piece. It was founded in 1512 and destroyed by the French in 1528. Rebuilt in 1570, it was named after Germain de Foix, the second wife of King Ferdinand of Spain. Once the rival of San Juan, San Germán harbored many pirates who pillaged the ships that sailed off the nearby coastline. Indeed, many of today's residents are descended from the smugglers, poets, priests, and politicians who once lived here.

The pirates and sugar plantations are long gone, but the city retains colorful reminders of its Spanish colonial past. Flowers brighten some of the patios here as they do in Seville. Also, as in a small Spanish town, many of the inhabitants stroll through the historic zone in the early evening. Nicknamed *Ciudad de las Lomas* (City of the Hills), San Germán boasts verdant scenery that provides a pleasant backdrop to a variety of architectural styles—Spanish colonial (1850s), *criolla* (1880s), neoclassical (1910s), Art Deco (1930s), and international (1960s)—depicted in the gracious old-world buildings lining the streets. So significant are these buildings that San Germán is included in the National Register of Historic Places.

The city's 249 historical treasures are within easy walking distance of one another. Regrettably, you must view most of them from the outside. If some of them are actually open, count yourself fortunate, as they have no phones, keep no regular hours, and are staffed by volunteers who rarely show up. Also, be aware that the signage for the historic buildings can be confusing, and many of the streets in the old town tend to run one-way. Most of the city's architectural treasures lie uphill from the congested main thoroughfare (Calle Luna). We usually try to park on the town's main street (Carretera 102, which changes its name within the borders of San Germán to Calle Luna), and then proceed on foot through the city's commercial core before reaching the architectural highlights described below.

One of the most noteworthy churches in Puerto Rico is **Iglesia Porta Coeli (Gate of Heaven)** (★ ((*C*) **787/892-0160**), which sits atop a knoll at the eastern end of a cobble-covered square, the Parque de Santo Domingo. Dating from 1606 and built in a style inspired by the Romanesque architecture of northern Spain, this is the oldest church in the New World. Restored by the Institute of Puerto Rican Culture, and sheathed in a layer of salmon-colored stucco, it contains a museum of religious art with a collection of ancient *santos,* the carved figures of saints that have long been a major part of Puerto Rican folk art. Look for the 17th-century portrait of St. Nicholas de Bari, the French Santa Claus. Inside, the original palm-wood ceiling and tough ausobo-wood beams draw the eye upward. Other treasures include early choral books from Santo Domingo, a primitive carving of Jesus, and 19th-century Señora de la Monserrate Black Madonna and Child statues. Admission is $3 for adults, $2 for seniors and children over 12, free for children under 12. The church is open Wednesday through Sunday from 8:30am to noon and 1 to 4:30pm.

Less than 100 feet (30m) downhill from Iglesia Porta Coeli, at the bottom of the steps that lead from its front door down to the plaza below, is the **Casa Morales** (also known as the **Tomás Vivoni House,** after its architect), San Germán's most photographed and widely recognized house. Designed in the Edwardian style, with wraparound porches, elaborate gables, and elements that might remind you of a Swiss chalet, it was built in 1913, reflecting the region's turn-of-the-20th-century agrarian prosperity. (Note that it is a private residence and can be admired only from the outside.)

The long and narrow, gently sloping plaza that prefaces Iglesia Porta Coeli is the Parque de Santo Domingo, one of San Germán's two main plazas. Street signs also identify the plaza as the Calle Ruiz Belvis. Originally a marketplace, the plaza is paved with red and black cobblestones, and it's bordered with cast-iron benches and portrait busts of prominent figures in the town's history. This plaza merges gracefully with a second plaza, which street signs and maps identify as the Plaza Francisco Mariano Quiñones, the Calle José Julian Acosta, and the Plaza Principal. Separating the two plazas is the unused (and closed to the public) **Viejo Alcaldía (Old Town Hall).** Built late in the 19th century, it's awaiting a new vision, perhaps as a museum or public building.

San Germán's most impressive church—and the most monumental building in the region—is **San Germán de Auxerre** (© **787/892-1027**), which rises majestically above the western end of the Plaza Francisco Mariano Quiñones. Designed in the Spanish baroque style, it was built in 1573 in the form of a simple chapel with a low-slung thatch roof. Its present grandeur is the result of at least five subsequent enlargements and renovations. Much of what you see today is the result of a rebuilding in 1688 and a restoration in 1737 that followed a disastrous earthquake. Inside are three naves, 10 altars, three chapels, and a belfry that was rebuilt in 1939, following an earthquake in 1918. The central chandelier, made from rock crystal and imported from Barcelona in 1866, is the largest in the Caribbean. The pride of the church is the *trompe l'oeil* ceiling, which was elaborately restored in 1993. A series of stained-glass windows with contemporary designs was inserted during a 1999 restoration. The church can be visited daily from 8 to 11am and 1 to 3pm.

A few lesser sights are located near the town's two main squares. **Farmacia Martin,** a modern pharmacy, is incongruously set within the shell of a graceful but battered Art Deco building at the edge of the Parque Santo Domingo (Calle Ruiz Belvis 22; © **787/892-1122**). A cluster of battered and dilapidated clapboard-sided houses line the southern side of the Calle Dr. Ueve, which rambles downhill from its origin at the base of the Iglesia Porta Coeli. The most important house is no. 66, the **Casa Acosta y Fores.** Also noteworthy is **Casa Juán Perichi,** a substantial-looking structure at the corner of Calle Dr. Ueve and Parque Santo Domingo, nearly adjacent to the Iglesia Porta Coeli. Both houses were built around 1917, of traditional wood construction, and are viewed as fine examples of Puerto Rican adaptations of Victorian architecture. Regrettably, both are seriously dilapidated, although that might change as San Germán continues the slow course of its historic renovations.

To the side of the Auxerre church is the modern, cement-sided **Public Library,** Calle José Julia Acosta, where you might be tempted to duck into the air-conditioned interior for a glance through the stacks and periodical collection. It's open Monday through Thursday from 8am to 8:30pm, Friday from 8am to 6pm, and Saturday from 8am to 1pm and 2 to 4:30pm. Behind the Auxerre church is at least one masonry-fronted town house whose design might remind you of southern Spain (Andalusia), especially when the flowers in the window boxes add splashes of color.

WHERE TO STAY & DINE

Parador El Oasis   Although it's not state of the art, this hotel has a hardworking staff and Spanish colonial charm. As an anchor in this quaint old town, far removed from the beaches, it's a fine place to stay. A three-story building constructed around a pool and patio area, the hotel originated in the late 1700s as a privately owned mansion. With its mint-green walls and white wicker furniture, some of the grace remains. Guest rooms were fixed up during 2008 and the restaurant is closed for renovation as we go to press. The older rooms, positioned close to the lobby, are more charming, while modern rooms, located in the back, are more spacious. Three of the units have private balconies, and all units have small shower-only bathrooms. The in-house restaurant has served *comida criolla*.

Calle Luna 72, San Germán, PR 00683. © 787/892-1175. Fax 787/892-4546. paradoroasis@prtc.net. 52 units (shower only). Year-round $90 double. Children 12 and under stay free in parent's room. Extra person $10. AE, DC, MC, V. Free parking. **Amenities:** Restaurant; bar; outdoor pool; limited room service; 1 room for those w/limited mobility. *In room:* A/C, TV, hair dryer.

Tapas Café 🔍 *Finds*   This charming restaurant is our favorite spot in the historic district of San Germán, an oasis of sophistication in the provincial countryside. The interior dining room, with mosaic tiles and blue stars on the ceiling, offers a cool respite from the heat. Portions are sizeable. The seafood paella is loaded with prawns, mussels, and lobster, and the beef medallions in blue cheese did not disappoint. Other menu items range from Spanish sausage sautéed in wine sauce to the classic soup *caldo gallego* to fried fish fritters.

50 Calle Dr. Santiago Veve, San Germán. © 787/264-0610. Reservations not necessary. Tapas $2–$15. AE, MC, V. Thurs–Fri 4:30–11pm; Sat 11am–11pm; Sun 11am–9pm.

Villa Del Rey 🔍 *Finds*   This is the best place to stay in historic San Germán, although you'll have to drive 15 minutes west to a good beach. The fine country inn is completely modernized and attractively furnished, mostly with picture windows. You're offered a choice of midsize-to-spacious and well-furnished accommodations—single, doubles, or suites. Both the doubles and suites are suitable for families with two children under 12 years old. Each unit comes with a private bathroom with tub and shower. Light meals can be prepared in the suites, each equipped with kitchenette. Guests meet fellow guests at La Veranda, sheltered but in the open air, featuring three meals a day, with a focus on regional dishes.

Rte. 361 Cain Alto Ward Km 0.8, San Germán. © 787/642-2627. Fax 787/264-1579. www.villadelrey.net. 19 units. Year-round $85–$95 double; $110–$120 suite. $10 per child in parent's room. MC, V. **Amenities:** Restaurant; bar; outdoor pool; business center. *In room:* A/C, TV.

4 Coamo

Legend has it that the hot springs in this town, located inland on the south coast about a 2-hour drive from San Juan, were the Fountain of Youth sought by Ponce de León. It is believed that the Taíno peoples, during pre-Columbian times, held rituals and pilgrimages here as they sought health and well-being. Between 1847 and 1958, the site was a center for rest and relaxation for Puerto Ricans and others, some on their honeymoons, others in search of the curative powers of the geothermal springs, which lie about a 5-minute walk from **Parador Baños de Coamo.** Nonguests can come here to use the baths, but the experience is hardly special today. The baths are in poor condition.

WHERE TO STAY & DINE

Parador Baños de Coamo   The spa at Baños de Coamo features this parador, offering hospitality in traditional Puerto-Rican style. The Baños has welcomed many notable visitors over the years, including Franklin D. Roosevelt, Frank Lloyd Wright, Alexander Graham Bell, and Thomas Edison, who came here to swim in the on-site hot springs, said to be the most curative in the world. Since those days and since those long-departed visitors, the spa world is now state-of-the-art in many places, including San Juan and some nearby resorts. Such is not the case here; maintenance is poor, and the bathrooms show signs of aging. The parador has one regular pool and one pool fed by the hot springs. (If you just want to take a dip, it's $5 for adults, $3 for children.)

The buildings range from a lattice-adorned two-story motel unit with wooden verandas to a Spanish colonial pink stucco building, which houses the restaurant. The bedrooms draw a mixed reaction from visitors, so ask to see your prospective room before deciding to stay here. Many of the often-dark rooms are not well maintained, and the bathrooms seem more appropriate for a campsite. Mildew is also evident. The cuisine is both Creole and international, and the coffee Baños-style is a special treat. There's a nice simple bar by the pool.

P.O. Box 1867, Coamo, PR 00769. (℃ **787/825-2186.** Fax 787/825-4739. 48 units. Year-round $93 double. AE, DC, DISC, MC, V. From Rte. 1, turn onto Rte. 153 at Santa Isabel; then turn left onto Rte. 546 and drive west 1 mile/1.6km. **Amenities:** Restaurant; bar; 2 pools; laundry service; coin-op laundry; dry cleaning; 1 room for those w/limited mobility. *In room:* A/C, TV, iron.

5 The Southern Mountains

The mountain towns surrounding the gorgeous Toro Negro Forest Reserve straddle Puerto Rico's highest peaks that run along the center of the island. The area is included here because it is most accessible from the south, from Ponce and surrounding towns. The mountain towns include Villalba, Orocovis, Adjuntas, and Jayuya, as well as parts of Utuado, Coamo, and Juana Díaz. Even from Ponce, the best route to this region is to head east first along the coastal Highway 2 to neighboring Juana Díaz. Then take Route 149 north through town and into the lush mountains of Villalba. Continue straight until the intersection of Route 143 west to get to **Toro Negro Forest Reserve** (there's an entrance at Km 32.4).

TORO NEGRO FOREST RESERVE *✸✸✸* & LAKE GUINEO *✸*

North of Ponce, **Toro Negro Forest Reserve***✸✸✸* (℃ **787/867-3040**) lies along the Cordillera Central, the cloud-shrouded, lush central mountain chain that spans Puerto Rico's spine from the southeast town of Yabucoa all the way to outside Mayagüez on the west coast. This 7,000-acre (2,833-hectare) park, ideal for hikers, straddles the highest peak of the Cordillera Central at the very heart of Puerto Rico, quite near the midway point between east and west coasts. A forest of lush trees, the reserve also contains the headwaters of several main rivers and lakes, and has several crashing waterfalls. The reserve lies between Villalba and Jayuya, Adjuntas and Orocovis.

The lowest temperatures recorded on the island—some 40°F (4°C)—were measured at **Lake Guineo** ⚔, the island's highest lake, which lies within the reserve. The best trail to take here is a short, paved, and wickedly steep path on the north side of Route 143, going up to the south side of **Cerro de Punta,** which at 4,390 feet (1,338m) is the highest peak on Puerto Rico. Allow about half an hour for an ascent. Once at the top, you'll be rewarded with Puerto Rico's grandest view, sweeping across the lush interior from the Atlantic to the Caribbean coasts. Other mountains in the reserve also offer hiking possibilities. The reserve spans several distinct types, including a sierra palm forest, which in places forms a complete canopy from the sun, and a mountainous cloud forest, with dwarfed, but vibrantly green plants and trees.

The main entrance to the forest is at the Doña Juana recreational area, which has a swimming pool filled with cold water from the mountain streams, a picnic area, and a rustic campground. An adjacent restaurant serves up Puerto Rican barbecued chicken and pork and other local delicacies. Many hiking trails originate from this area. One of the best is a 2-mile (3.2km) trek to an observation post and the impressive 200-foot (61m) Doña Juana Falls.

Jayuya lies north of the reserve, but to access it, you must return east along Route 143 to Route 149, and take that north, farther into the central mountains to Route 144, which you'll take back west to access the town. This is a beautiful area, filled with old coffee estates and lush mountain forest. The local parador is a country inn built on the grounds of an old coffee plantation (**Parador Hacienda Gripiñas;** see below), which is one of the best places to stay in Puerto Rico's interior. There's also a fine restaurant on the grounds. Built by a Spanish coffee baron more than 150 years ago, the restored plantation home is surrounded by gardens and coffee fields.

Jayuya is also known for the relics found here from Puerto Rico's Taíno past. Off Route 144 is La Piedra Escrita, the Written Rock, a huge boulder beside a stream, with Taíno petroglyphs carved into the stone. It's a wonderful picnic spot. Jayuya also hosts an annual Indigenous Festival in November, which combines native crafts with music and food. The **Cemi Museum,** Rte. 144 Km 9.3 (© **787/828-1241**), in town has a collection of Taíno pottery and cemís, amulets sacred to the island's indigenous peoples. The adjacent **Casa Museo Canales,** Rte. 144 Km 9.4 (© **787/828-1241**), is a restored 19th-century coffee plantation home with interesting exhibits. Both museums charge $1 for adults and 50¢ for children and are open from 9am to 3pm every day.

WHERE TO STAY & DINE
Hacienda Gripiñas   This restored plantation home is set amidst 20 acres of coffee fields and nature. It's a charming respite from the 21st century. Take a walk in the cool mountain countryside, then stake out a hammock or rocking chair on the porch or one of the many balconies and relax awhile. First built in 1853 by coffee baron and Spanish nobleman Eusebio Pérez del Castillo, the former plantation home was turned into an inn in 1975 but retains the elegance and grandeur of its past. A wide porch wraps around this restored plantation home, and there are gorgeous gardens and coffee fields surrounding it. There are also reading rooms and common areas in which to lounge. The sweet song of chanting *couquís,* ubiquitous small Puerto Rican tree frogs, fills the air. There are also an excellent restaurant on the premises and a pool. A small trail from here leads to the summit of Cerro Punta, Puerto Rico's highest peak. There

are frequent specials with meals included that make sense for visitors because of the parador's isolation. If you are looking for solitude, go during the week, and you will likely have the place to yourself and a few other guests and save a few bucks on your tab.

Rte. 527 Km 2.5, Jayuya PR 00664. ⓒ 787/828-1717. Fax 787/828-1718. www.haciendagripinas.com. 48 units. Year-round weekdays $75 double; weekends $91 double. AE, MC, V. **Amenities:** Restaurant; bar; 2 pools; game room; library. *In room:* A/C, TV, iron.

11

Mayagüez & the Northwest

Mayagüez lies in the middle of Puerto Rico's west coast, a major fun in the sun zone, but it lacks its own quality beach.

Yet Puerto Rico's third largest city is close enough to several world-class beaches to make it worth a stay. And it can offer guests dueling visions of the Caribbean vacation.

To the north, along the northwest coast that stems from Rincón to Isabella, lie the Caribbean's best surfing beaches, which compare favorably to those of California when conditions are right. These are the beaches we'll focus on in this chapter. And to the south are equally attractive beaches with among the calmest waters in the Caribbean, offering excellent snorkeling, scuba and sailing opportunities (see chapter 10).

The city is not as renowned for its historic sites, architecture, and attractions as San Juan or Ponce, but it has all three.

Mayagüez is also close to the western mountains, especially Maricao, perhaps the prettiest of the mountain towns in Puerto Rico. You can stay here in a renovated coffee plantation house, or just have lunch on its charming veranda. Or rent a cabin at the Monte del Estado national park, or just spend the day in its swimming pool fed by mountain streams.

Throughout the calm southwestern coastal villages and the northwest beach towns, there are a few top-level properties, several modestly priced and attractive hotels and guesthouses, and a few noteworthy paradores, privately operated country inns approved by the Puerto Rico Tourism Company that choose to participate in its joint promotion program.

This western part of Puerto Rico contains the greatest concentration of paradores, which are both along the coast and in the cool mountainous interior of the west, a wonderful escape from pollution and traffic on a hot day.

One of the biggest adventure jaunts in Puerto Rico, a trip to Mona Island, can also be explored from the coast near Mayagüez.

1 Mayagüez ⭐

98 miles (158km) W of San Juan, 15 miles (24km) S of Aguadilla

Approaching from the north, where Highway 2 swoops down along beautiful coastal overpasses, it's easy to dismiss Mayagüez at first glimpse as a rather drab commercial port city, but the so-called "Sultan of the West" warms to visitors who give it a chance to show off its charms.

Although it's a commercial city, Mayagüez is a convenient stopover for those exploring the west coast. And it has its own charms.

If you want a big-wave beach with dramatic coastal cliffs, you can head north to Rincón, Aguadilla, and Isabella (see Rincón, later in this chapter). And if you want white sand and palms, with tranquil aquamarine water, head south to Cabo Rojo, Lajas, and Guánica (see chapter 10).

One of our favorite hotels is in the city, the **Mayagüez Resort & Casino,** which is nice enough to warrant a stay here. Mayagüez makes a good base from which to explore the whole west coast with a rental car, a good idea for first-time visitors wanting to experience several different destinations. That's especially so if you want the luxury of a first-class resort at night and don't want to keep switching rooms every night.

Once you start poking around Mayagüez, the city will begin to win you over. A unique architectural style was forged here after successive renovations following a string of disasters that struck the city.

A great fire in 1841 ripped through the city, destroying large parts of its downtown area. A 1918 earthquake striking offshore along the Puerto Rico Trench knocked down buildings and unleashed a tsunami that sent 20-foot waves crashing over Mayagüez.

The rebuilding efforts afterwards were a conglomeration of styles popular at the time of the reconstructions, with the last great wave taking place in the 1930s.

Mayagüez is a port whose elegance and charm reached its zenith during the mercantile and agricultural prosperity of the 19th century.

Although the town itself dates from the mid–18th century, the area around it has figured in European history since the time of Christopher Columbus, who landed nearby in 1493. Today, in the gracious plaza at the town's center, a bronze statue of Columbus stands atop a metallic globe of the world.

Famed for the size and depth of its **harbor** (the second largest on the island, after San Juan's harbor), Mayagüez was built to control the **Mona Passage,** a route essential to the Spanish Empire when Puerto Rico and the nearby Dominican Republic were vital trade and defensive jewels in the Spanish crown. Today this waterway is notorious for the destructiveness of its currents, the ferocity of its sharks, and the thousands of boat people who arrive illegally from either Haiti or the Dominican Republic, both on the island of Hispaniola.

Queen Isabel II of Spain recognized Mayagüez's status as a town in 1836. Her son, Alfonso XII, granted it a city charter in 1877. Permanently isolated from the major commercial developments of San Juan, Mayagüez, like Ponce, has always retained its own distinct identity.

Today, the town has been hit by the closure of its tuna packing industry (which once packed 60% of the tuna consumed in the United States) and its manufacturing plants, victims to low-cost jobs elsewhere.

But the town has a future in tourism and some of the life science and high-tech manufacturing springing up around the fine University of Puerto Rico Mayagüez

---

Fun Fact **A History of Honeymooning**

Mayagüez is the target of a peculiarly romantic 16th-century legend. It is said that local farmers often kidnapped young Spanish sailors who had stopped at Mayagüez for provisions en route to South America. There was a scarcity of eligible bachelors in Mayagüez, and the farmers kidnapped the young sailors in hopes of providing their daughters with husbands and their farms with overseers. However, it's anyone's guess whether this was good or bad luck.

Some tradition-minded Puerto Rican couples still come here on their honeymoons. But for most visitors, Mayagüez would rank low as a honeymoon retreat.

Mayagüez

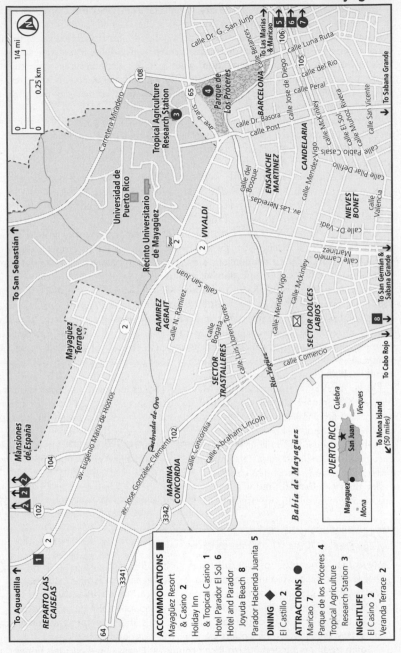

To Aguadilla

REPARTO LAS CAISEAS

To San Sebastián

Mansiones de España

104

102

Mayagüez Terrace

av. Eugenio María de Hostos

Universidad de Puerto Rico

Recinto Universitario de Mayagüez

Carretera Miradero

108

65

ave. París

Tropical Agriculture Research Station

Parque de Los Próceres

calle Dr. G. San Jurjo

calle Betances

BARCELONA

To Las Marías & Maricao

106

105

calle José de Diego

calle Luna Ruta

calle del Río

calle Peral

To Sabana Grande

calle Dr. Basora

calle Post

ENSANCHE MARTINEZ

CANDELARIA

calle del Bosque

calle Mendez-Vigo

calle Pablo Casals

calle Pilar Defillo

calle El Sol

calle Muñoz Rivera

calle San Vicente

NIEVES BONET

calle Valencia

av. Las Nereidas

calle Dr. Vadi

calle Carmelo Martínez

To San Germán & Sabana Grande

VIVALDI

Spur 2

2

calle San Juan

calle Mendez Vigo

calle McKinley

SECTOR DOLCES LABIOS

To Cabo Rojo

RAMIREZ AGRAIT

calle N. Ramírez

Calle Bogatá

calle Luis Lloréns Torres

SECTOR TRASTALLERES

Río Yagüez

calle Comercio

2

MARINA CONCORDIA

Quebrada de Oro

av. José González Clemente

calle Concordia

calle Abraham Lincoln

102

3342

3341

64

Bahía de Mayagüez

PUERTO RICO

Culebra

Vieques

★ San Juan

Mayagüez

Mona

To Mona Island (50 miles)

ACCOMMODATIONS ■
Mayagüez Resort & Casino **2**
Holiday Inn & Tropical Casino **1**
Hotel Parador El Sol **6**
Hotel and Parador Joyuda Beach **8**
Parador Hacienda Juanita **5**

DINING ◆
El Castillo **2**

ATTRACTIONS ●
Maricao **7**
Parque de los Próceres **4**
Tropical Agriculture Research Station **3**

NIGHTLIFE ▲
El Casino **2**
Veranda Terrace **2**

1/4 mi

0.25 km

247

Campus, which specializes in engineering and the sciences. The university community adds much to the city's cultural life.

Today, the city is getting ready to host the 2010 Caribbean and Central American Games, with a slew of new construction projects, including new sports facilities, underway. Some $400 million is being invested.

ESSENTIALS

GETTING THERE   Cape Air (© 800/352-0714; www.flycapeair.com) flies from San Juan to Mayagüez twice daily (flying time: 40 min.). Round-trip passage is $132 per person.

If you rent a car at the San Juan airport and want to drive to Mayagüez, it's fastest and most efficient to take the northern route that combines sections of the newly widened Route 22 with the older Route 2. Estimated driving time for a local resident is about 90 minutes, although newcomers usually take about 30 minutes longer. The southern route, which combines the modern Route 52 with transit across the outskirts of historic Ponce, and final access into Mayagüez via the southern section of Route 2, requires a total of about 3 hours and affords some worthwhile scenery across the island's mountainous interior.

GETTING AROUND   Taxis meet arriving planes. If you take one, negotiate the fare with the driver first because cabs are unmetered here.

There are branches of **Avis** (© 787/832-0406), **Budget** (© 787/832-4570), and **Hertz** (© 787/832-3314) at the Mayagüez airport.

VISITOR INFORMATION   The **Mayagüez Municipal Tourism Development Office** (© 787/832-5882) can help orient visitors. In Aguadilla, there is also a **Puerto Rico Tourism Company** office (© 787/890-3315). If you're starting out in San Juan, you can inquire there before you set out (see "Visitor Information" under "Orientation" in chapter 5).

EXPLORING THE AREA
MAYAGÜEZ ATTRACTIONS

The area surrounding the city's elegant central Plaza Colón is among the prettiest in the city, with several restored historic buildings. A bronze monument of Christopher Columbus atop a globe surrounded by 16 female statues dominates the plaza, which is also marked by mosaic tiled walkways and gurgling fountains, blooming tropical gardens, and squat leafy trees.

The neo-Corinthian **Mayagüez City Hall** and the **Nuestra Señora de la Candelaria,** which has gone through several incarnations since the first building went up in 1780, are noteworthy buildings right off the plaza.

Make sure to stroll down nearby **Calle McKinley,** home to the fabulous, recently restored **Yaguez Theater.** The neoclassical jewel served as both an opera and a silent movie house and is still in active use today. Originally inaugurated in 1909, a fire destroyed the structure in 1919, but it was rebuilt. The city's smashing Art Deco post office is also located here.

Mayagüez's historic waterfront district, with a restored 1920s Custom House and rows of neat warehouses, is also worth a look. The century-old **University of Puerto Rico Mayagüez Campus** is also beautiful.

To soak in the magical sunsets of the Puerto Rican west coast, either head to the hills surrounding the city or try a room with a view on the waterfront.

Juan A. Rivero Zoo   This 14-acre (5.7-hectare) zoo recently underwent a $14-million renovation. The African safari exhibit has lions, elephants, zebras, and rhinos, and jaguars are part of a Caribbean exhibit. There's also a butterfly and lizard exhibit and gorgeous grounds. The birdhouse has this fantastic elevated walkway where you look down on colorful tropical birds like parrots. There are also eagles, hawks, and owls. You can see the entire zoo in 2 hours.

Rte. 108, Barrio Miradero, Mayagüez Union. ✆ 787/834-8110. Admission $6 adults, $4 ages 11–17, $2 ages 5–10, free age 4 and under. Wed–Sun and holidays 8:30am–5pm.

The Tropical Agricultural Research Station   This is not a botanical garden but a working research facility of the U.S. Department of Agriculture. It's located on Route 65, between Post Street and Route 108, adjacent to the University of Puerto Rico at Mayagüez campus and across the street from the **Parque de los Próceres (Patriots' Park).** At the administration office, ask for a free map of the tropical gardens, which have one of the largest collections of tropical plant species intended for practical use, including cacao, fruit trees, spices, timbers, and ornamentals. There are lots of trees and a wide variety of plants. A hacienda-style building houses the visitor's office. The area is divided into fruit trees, a palm plantation, a bamboo forest, and a botanical garden. There are labs, greenhouses, and other research facilities throughout the area.

2200 Av. Pedro Albizu Campos. ✆ 787/831-3435. Free admission. Mon–Fri 9am–5pm.

BEACHES & WATERSPORTS

Nearly the entire west coast has great beaches except for Mayagüez, but beach lovers might consider staying here if they want to explore several different beaches. That's because the city perhaps alone puts visitors in such easy reach of the tranquil Caribbean waters to its south, or the rough surfing paradise to its north.

Trips to either area, which can be combined with, say, a day of sailing and snorkeling or windsurfing lessons, can be arranged through either of the large hotels. Or refer to the destination location either below (for the north) or chapter 10 for the south.

WHERE TO STAY

Holiday Inn & Tropical Casino   This six-story hotel competes with the Mayagüez Resort & Casino, though we like the latter better. The Holiday Inn is well maintained, contemporary, and comfortable. It has a marble-floored, high-ceilinged lobby, an outdoor pool with a waterside bar, and a big casino, but its lawn simply isn't as dramatically landscaped as the Mayagüez resort's surrounding acreage. Bedrooms here are comfortably but functionally outfitted in motel style; they've recently been refurbished. Each unit is equipped with a tiled bathroom with a tub/shower combination. The restaurant serves Puerto Rican and International cuisine.

2701 Rte. 2 Km 149.9, Mayagüez, PR 00680-6328. ✆ 800/465-4329 or 787/833-1100. Fax 787/833-1300. www.hidpr.com. 142 units. Year-round $109–$149 double; $167–$185 suite. AE, DC, DISC, MC, V. Amenities: Restaurant; 2 bars; outdoor pool; gym; business center; limited room service; laundry service; casino; rooms for those w/limited mobility. In room: A/C, TV, dataport, coffeemaker, hair dryer, iron, safe.

Howard Johnson Downtown Mayagüez   This converted monastery is a charming historic hotel right near Plaza Colón. With its wide tiled walkways wrapped around an interior courtyard and Spanish colonial furnishings, this hotel is at home in the city's prettiest neighborhood. The construction allows the breeze in and affords nice vistas of historic Mayagüez. A pool is located in one courtyard. But the hotel is outfitted with high-speed Internet and other modern amenities. There's no restaurant on premises but there are several nearby, including the delectable Ricomini Café across the street, where you'll have your free continental breakfast. It can get noisy on weekends.

Calle Mendez Vigo Este 57, Mayagüez, PR 00680. © **787/832-9191.** Fax 787/832-9122. www.hojo.com. 35 units. Year-round $85–$125 double; $140 suite. Rates include continental breakfast at neighboring bakery. AE, MC, V. $4 parking. **Amenities:** Pool; 1 room for those w/limited mobility. *In room:* A/C, TV, fridge, hair dryer, some have Internet access.

Mayagüez Resort & Casino ⋆ This is the largest and best general hotel resort in western Puerto Rico, appealing equally to business travelers and vacationers. Set atop a hill, it benefits from a country-club format spread of 20 acres (8 hectares) of tropical landscaping with trees and gardens. The landscaped grounds have been designated an adjunct to the nearby Tropical Agriculture Research Station. Five species of palm trees, eight kinds of bougainvillea, and numerous species of rare flora are set adjacent to the institute's collection of tropical plants, which range from a pink torch ginger to a Sri Lankan cinnamon tree. The river pool is also set among palms and boulders. There is high-speed Internet access throughout the property.

The hotel's well-designed bedrooms open onto views of the swimming pool, and many units have private balconies. Guest rooms tend to be small, but they have good beds. The restored bathrooms are well equipped with makeup mirrors, scales, and tub/shower combinations.

For details about El Castillo, the hotel's restaurant, see "Where to Dine," below. The hotel is the major entertainment center of Mayagüez. Its casino has free admission and is open 24 hours a day. You can also drink and dance at the Victoria Lounge.

Rte. 104 Km 0.3 (P.O. Box 3781), Mayagüez, PR 00680. © **888/689-3030** or 787/832-3030. Fax 787/265-3020. www.mayaguezresort.com. 140 units. Year-round $189–$259 double; $335 suite. AE, DC, DISC, MC, V. Parking $4.50. **Amenities:** 2 restaurants; 3 bars; Olympic-size pool; children's pool; 3 tennis courts; small fitness room; Jacuzzi; steam room; playground; 24-hr. room service; massage; babysitting; laundry service; casino; rooms for those w/limited mobility. *In room:* A/C, TV, high-speed Internet, minibar, coffeemaker, iron.

WHERE TO DINE

El Castillo INTERNATIONAL/PUERTO RICAN   This is one of the best large-scale dining rooms in western Puerto Rico, as well as the main restaurant for the largest hotel and casino in the area. The food has real flavor and flair, unlike the typical bland hotel fare so often dished up. Known for its generous lunch buffets, El Castillo serves only a la carte items at dinner, including seafood stew served on a bed of linguine with marinara sauce, grilled salmon with a mango-flavored Grand Marnier sauce, and filets of sea bass with a cilantro, white-wine, and butter sauce. Steak and lobster are served on the same platter, if you want it.

In the Mayagüez Resort & Casino, Rte. 104 Km 0.3. © **787/832-3030.** Breakfast buffet $13; Mon–Fri lunch buffet $16; Sun brunch buffet $27; main courses $14–$36. AE, MC, V. Daily 6:30am–midnight.

MAYAGÜEZ AFTER DARK

El Casino   At the completely remodeled casino at the Mayagüez Resort & Casino, with the adjoining Player's Bar, you can try your luck at blackjack, dice, slot machines, roulette, and minibaccarat. Open 24 hours. At the Mayagüez Resort & Casino, Rte. 104. © **787/832-3030,** ext. 3301.

Veranda Terrace   On a large and airy covered terrace that opens to a view of a manicured tropical garden, this is a relaxing and soothing place for a cocktail. The

Mona Island: The Galápagos of Puerto Rico

Off Mayagüez, the unique **Isla Mona** 🐢🐢🐢 teems with giant iguanas, three species of endangered sea turtles, red-footed boobies, and countless other seabirds. It features a tabletop plateau with mangrove forests and cacti, giving way to dramatic 200-foot-high (61m) limestone cliffs that rise above the water and encircle much of Mona.

A bean-shaped pristine island with no development at all, Mona is a destination for the hardy pilgrim who seeks the road less traveled. It lies in the middle of the Mona Passage, about halfway between Puerto Rico and the Dominican Republic. A pup tent, backpack, and hiking boots will do fine if you plan to forego the comforts of civilization and immerse yourself in nature. Snorkelers, spelunkers, biologists, and eco-tourists find much to fascinate them in Mona's wildlife, mangrove forests, coral reefs, and complex honeycomb, which is the largest marine-originated cave in the world. There are also miles of secluded white-sand beaches and palm trees.

Uninhabited today, Mona was for centuries the scene of considerable human activity. The pre-Columbian Taíno Indians were the first to establish themselves here. Later, pirates used it as a base for their raids, followed by guano miners, who removed the rich crop fertilizer from Mona's caves. Columbus landed in Mona during his 1494 voyage, and Ponce de León spent several days here en route to becoming governor of Puerto Rico in 1508. The notorious pirate Captain Kidd used Mona as a temporary hide-out.

Mona can be reached by organized tour from Mayagüez. Camping is available at $10 per night. Everything needed, including water, must be brought in, and everything, including garbage, must be taken out. For more information, call the **Puerto Rico Department of Natural and Environmental Resources** at (℡) **787/999-2200**.

The Puerto Rico government invested $1.7 million on a new visitor's center on Mona, which includes living quarters for researchers and park rangers.

To reach the island, contact **Adventures Tourmarine**, Rte. 102 Km 14.1, Playa Joyuda, Cabo Rojo ((℡) **787/375-2625**). Captain Elick Hernández operates boat charters to Mona with a minimum of 10 passengers, each paying $135 for a round-trip day adventure. **Acampa Nature Adventures** (Av. Piñero 1221, San Juan; (℡) **787/706-0659**) runs a 4-day, 3-night trip to Mona, which includes all equipment, meals, and guides. The trips are run in groups with a 10-person limit. Price depends on how many people are in the group.

Warning: The passage over is extremely rough, and many passengers prone to seasickness take Dramamine the night before the boat ride. There is no bottled water on the island, so bring your own. Also bring food, mosquito repellent, and even toilet paper. Alcoholic drinks are forbidden. While Mona's uninhabited landscape and surrounding turquoise water are beautiful, this can also be a dangerous, unforgiving place. In 2001, a Boy Scout got lost and died from hypothermia; in 2005, a psychologist suffered the same fate.

bartenders specialize in rum-based concoctions that go well with the hibiscus-scented air. Open daily 11am to 1am. In the Mayagüez Resort & Casino, Rte. 104. © **787/831-7575.**

2 Rincón

100 miles (161km) W of San Juan, 6 miles (9.7km) N of Mayagüez

North of Mayagüez lies the resort town of Rincón, the first of a string of beach destinations you'll encounter as you head north, but not the closest, as the town lies at the western end of a piece of land jutting off the coast.

We've always lost our bearings a bit driving to Rincón, but it's probably as it should be. You drive a jumble of circuitous country roads over La Cadena Hills to reach the town, the center of which eludes most visitors, who head to the guesthouses and hotels along the coast. Rincón sits on a flattened peninsula of land jutting off Puerto Rico's western coast, so there's water surrounding it on three sides, which has another confusing effect.

Rincón is no longer a sleepy coastal village attracting surfers and bohemian travelers. They, of course, are still coming, but a building boom has brought a wave of new condo, hotel, and luxury vacation residence projects, which has attracted more and more visitors here over the last decade. In fact the town is beginning to worry about the pace of development and its effect on the beautiful natural resources here.

There's still a lot of space to get lost in, though, with the surrounding hills on one side, and water on the town's other three borders. The town dates from the 16th century when a landowner allowed poor families to set down roots on his land. It was a sleepy agricultural town for centuries afterwards. It eventually gained fame as the Caribbean's best surfing spot, a fact reinforced by its hosting the World Surfing Championship in 1968. It remains the surfing capital of the Caribbean, a center for expatriot North Americans and a tourist magnet.

With over a dozen beaches in town, great surfing, sailing, and snorkeling, and an ever better nightlife and cultural scene, it's not hard to see why. It continues evolving as a destination, reinforcing the fact it's one of the best stops to make in Puerto Rico.

There was a time when non-surfers visited Rincón for only one reason: the Horned Dorset Primavera Hotel, not only one of the finest hotels in Puerto Rico, but one of the best in the entire Caribbean. Now there are several reasons for them to come.

SURFING & OTHER OUTDOOR PURSUITS

There are 8 miles (13km) of beachfront in Rincón, and each little spot seems to have its own name: **Maria's, Indicator, Domes, The Point, Steps-Tres Palmas, Dog Man's.** The reasons behind the names are also varied. One stems from the hulk of an abandoned nuclear power plant just off the beach, another for an old man who lived nearby.

Part of the town's appeal is that it has both rough surfing beaches and tranquil Caribbean coastal areas. Along the north side of Rincón, the Atlantic coast gets large, powerful waves, while other beaches are tranquil, perfect for snorkeling. Yet many beaches provide both, depending on the time of year.

During winter, uninterrupted swells from the North Atlantic form perfect waves, averaging 5 to 6 feet (1.5–1.8m) in height, with rideable rollers sometimes reaching 15 to 20 feet (4.6–6.1m). In 2008, a rare winter storm created 25-foot to 30-foot (7.6–9.1m) waves here that had local surfers musing whether it was the biggest surf ever here. On the southern side of Rincón, the ocean is calm, and long, wide sand beaches unfold with swaying palm trees along them.

Western Puerto Rico & the Northwest Coast

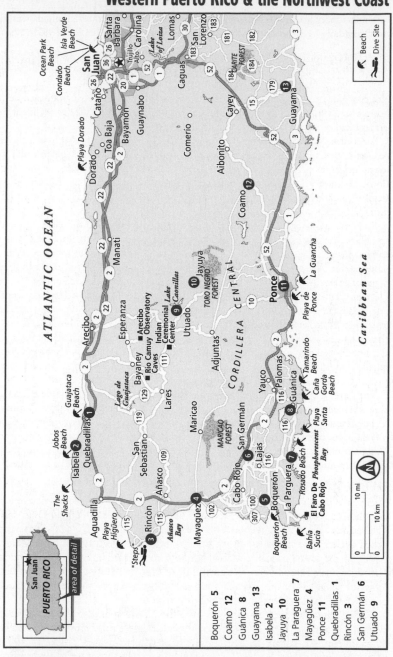

Boquerón	5	
Coamo	12	
Guánica	8	
Guayama	13	
Isabela	2	
Jayuya	10	
La Parguera	7	
Mayagüez	4	
Ponce	11	
Quebradillas	1	
Rincón	3	
San Germán	6	
Utuado	9	

The best surfing beaches include **Las Maria's, Spanish Wall,** and **Domes** near the town lighthouse on the north side. **Córcega** is probably the best of the Caribbean beaches.

Some beaches, meanwhile, can show different faces at different times of the year. For instance, **Steps,** which is also named **Tres Palmas,** is a great surfing beach in winter, but in summer is calm and one of the best spots for snorkeling. It was recently named a natural marine reserve.

Visitors need to proceed with caution during winter when venturing into the surf off Rincón, which can be particularly strong, with powerful riptides and undertows that routinely cause drownings. This should not stop visitors from coming here, however. The town has beaches with both tranquil and strong surf. Just proceed with caution and ask locals about surf conditions.

Windsurfing, and increasingly kite-boarding, is also extremely popular here, with **Sandy Beach** a favored site because it does not have the rocks found on the ocean floor that some of the other beaches in the area have. Also, from December to February it gets almost constant winds every day. Windsurfers wait on the terrace of Tamboo Tavern (see "Where to Dine," later in this chapter) for the right wind conditions before hitting the beach.

Excellent scuba, snorkeling, parasailing, and sailing are also available in Rincón, making it one of the most active of Caribbean destinations.

Endangered humpback whales winter here, attracting a growing number of whale-watchers from December to March. The lighthouse at El Faro Park is a great place to spot these mammoth mammals.

Rincón remains a mecca for surfing aficionados, but it's also a great place to learn the sport. **The Rincón Surf School** (P.O. Box 1333, Rincón; ⓒ **787/823-0610**) offers beginners lessons or can teach surfers how to improve their performance. One lesson costs $95, and there are also 2-day ($180), 3-day ($260), and 5-day ($390) packages. A private 2-hour lesson is $150, $75 each for two people. The school also arranges surf vacation packages in conjunction with the Casa Verde Guesthouse. **Puntas Surf School** (P.O. Box 4319, HC-01 Calle Vista del Mar; ⓒ **787/823-3618** or 207/251-1154) is another great option. It's run by Melissa Taylor and Bill Woodward, whose love of the sport is infectious, and they say they can teach would-be surfers of any age, from 5 to 105. Private lessons cost $40 per hour, $60 for 2 hours. Group rates and package deals are also available. A professional photographer takes photos of lessons for sale.

There are many surfing outfitters in town, and one of the most established is the **West Coast Surf Shop,** Muñoz Rivera 2E, Rincón (ⓒ **787/823-3935**), open daily 9am to 6pm. The shop rents surfing equipment and gives lessons. The **Hot Wavz Surf Shop,** Maria's Beach (ⓒ **787/823-3942**), also rents long boards, as well as boogie boards. Prices for board rentals start at around $25 daily. Snorkeling gear can also be rented at these shops.

Good snorkeling can be found just off the beach. When conditions are right, **Tres Palmas–Steps** is a great spot. Scuba divers and snorkeling enthusiasts will also want to head out to **Desecheo Island,** the large mass of land seen offshore from Rincón looking west. A quick half-hour boat trip, the small island is a nature reserve with great coral formations and large reef fish. Visibility is 100 feet plus (30m) and average water temperature is between 80° and 86°F (27°–30°C).

A good scuba outfitter is **Taíno Divers,** Black Eagle Marina at Rincón (ⓒ **787/823-6429**), which offers local boat charters along with scuba and snorkeling trips.

The Desecheo day trip departs at 8am and returns at 2pm. Snorkeling costs $75 while a 2-tank dive is $109. Prices include gourmet sandwiches and drinks. The outfit also runs half-day fishing charters for $725 and whale-watching expeditions and sunset cruises for $35.

Makaira Fishing Charters (P.O. Box 257, Rincón; © 787/823-4391 or 787/299-7374) offers fishing charters from a no-frills, tournament-rigged, 35-foot 2006 Contender that fits six comfortably. Half-day rates are $575 and full-day $850. **Moondog Charters** (© 787/823-3059) also runs fishing excursions and dive charters aboard a 32-foot Albermarle Express Sport Fisherman.

Katarina Sail Charters (© 787/823-SAIL [7245]) gives daily sailing trips aboard a 32-foot catamaran. The day sail (from around 10:20am–2:30pm) consists of some fine cruising, a stop for a swim and snorkel, and then lunch. It costs $60, $30 for children under 12. The sunset sail leaves at 4:30 and returns after sunset about 2 hours later. Watching the western sunset while sailing and listening to great music is wonderful, with rum punch, beer, and non-alcoholic drinks.

The most visible and sought-after whale-watching panorama in Rincón is **Parque El Faro de Rincón (Rincón Lighthouse Park),** which lies on El Faro Point peninsula at the extreme western tip of town. Within its fenced-in perimeter are pavilions that sell souvenirs and snack items, rows of binoculars offering 25¢ views, and a stately looking lighthouse built in 1921. The park is at its most popular from December to March for whale-watching and in January and February for surfer gazing. The park is locked every evening between midnight and 7am. Otherwise, you're free to promenade with the locals any time you like.

The park's snack bar is called **Restaurant El Faro,** Barrio Puntas, Carretera 413 Km 3.3 (no phone), which serves basic Puerto Rican fare and burgers. Best for a drink or ice cream. When is it open? The owner told us, "I open whenever I want to. If I don't want to, I stay home."

WHERE TO STAY
VERY EXPENSIVE
Horned Dorset Primavera *ฅฅฅ*   This is the most sophisticated hotel on Puerto Rico and one of the most exclusive and elegant small properties anywhere in the Caribbean. Set on 8 acres (3.2 hectares), it opens onto a secluded semiprivate beach, and it was built on the massive breakwaters and seawalls erected by a local railroad many years ago. The hacienda evokes an aristocratic Spanish villa, with wicker armchairs, hand-painted tiles, ceiling fans, seaside terraces, and cascades of flowers. Accommodations are in a series of suites that ramble amid lush gardens. The decor is tasteful, with four-poster beds and brass-footed tubs (with showers) in marble-sheathed bathrooms. Rooms are spacious and luxurious, with Persian rugs over tile floors, queen-size sofa beds in the sitting areas, and fine linens and tasteful fabrics on the elegant beds.

The eight-suite Casa Escondida villa, set at the edge of the property, adjacent to the sea, is decorated with an accent on teakwood and marble. Some of the units have private plunge pools; others offer private verandas or sun decks. Each contains high-quality reproductions of colonial furniture by Baker.

The hotel's restaurant, also called Horned Dorset Primavera, is one of the finest on Puerto Rico (see "Where to Dine," below). Rates do not include meals. The Modified American Plan, or MAP (breakfast and dinner), is available at the price of $200 per night per couple.

Apartado 1132, Rincón, PR 00677. ℂ 800/633-1857 or 787/823-4030. Fax 787/823-5580. www.horneddorset.com. 55 units. Winter $496–$1,070 double, $1,385 ocean suite; holidays $696–$1,270 double, $1,385 ocean suite; summer $260–$670 double, $800 ocean suite. AE, MC, V. Children 11 and under not accepted. **Amenities:** 2 restaurants; bar; 3 outdoor pools (1 infinity); fitness center; kayaking (free); limited room service; massage; laundry service; library. *In room:* A/C, hair dryer, safe.

EXPENSIVE

Rincón Beach Resort   Everybody from Romantic lovebirds to hipsters in logo T-shirts to families with young children check into this secluded hideaway. At this beachfront resort, an open-air deck stretches along the coastline at the end of an "infinity pool." It's perhaps the most welcoming place along the western coastline. The staff can help you arrange everything from watersports to golf. Guests meet fellow guests in the lobby bar, and later enjoy a savory Caribbean cuisine in Brasas Restaurant, with its open-air terrace. You're given a choice of oceanview or poolside-view units, and can also rent well-furnished one- and two-bedroom apartments. The decor is tropical throughout, with vibrant colors.

Rte. 115 Km 5.8, Añasco, PR 00610. ℂ 866/598-0009 or 787/589-9000. Fax 787/589-9040. www.rinconbeach.com. 118 units. Winter $240–$280 double, $355 junior suite, $459 1-bedroom suite, $650 2-bedroom suite; off season $205–$245 double, $315 junior suite, $405 1-bedroom suite, $570 2-bedroom suite. Rates include continental breakfast. AE, DISC, MC, V. **Amenities:** Restaurant; grill; 3 bars; outdoor pool; gym; babysitting; laundry service; nonsmoking rooms; rooms for those w/limited mobility. *In room:* A/C, TV, Internet access, kitchenettes in suites, fridge, hair dryer, iron, safe.

MODERATE

Casa Isleña Inn ⓧ *Finds*   "Island House" is created from a simple oceanfront former home right on the beach. Behind its gates, away from the water, is a private and tranquil world that offers a series of medium-size and comfortably furnished bedrooms decorated in bright Caribbean colors and designs. Each room has a neatly maintained shower-only bathroom. A natural tidal pool formed by a reef is an 8-minute stroll from the inn. At the tidal pool and from the inn's terraces guests can enjoy views of Aguadilla Bay and Mona Passage. In winter, while standing on the terraces, you can often watch the migration of humpback whales. There is a large Olympic-size swimming pool surrounded by a nice sun deck with lounge chairs. This area overlooks the adjacent beach. The inn is built in a Spanish style, with several balconies and a tiled veranda where breakfast is served. The fine tapas restaurant operates Wednesday through Sunday afternoons and evenings.

Barrio Puntas Carretera Interior 413 Km 4, Rincón, PR 00677. ℂ 888/289-7750 or 787/823-1525. Fax 787/823-1530. www.casa-islena.com. 9 units (shower only). Year-round $115–$165 double. Extra person $15. MC, V. **Amenities:** Tapas restaurant and bar; 1 room for those w/limited mobility. *In room:* A/C, TV, no phone.

Lemontree Waterfront Suites ⓧ *Finds*   Right on a good, sandy beach, these spacious apartments with kitchenettes are for those who don't want to limit themselves to hotel rooms and meals. With the sound of the surf just outside your private back porch, these well-furnished seaside units can provide a home away from home, with everything from ceiling fans to air-conditioning, from paperback libraries to custom woodworking details. The suites have been refreshed recently with new furnishings and tropical colors. The property is well maintained. Families enjoy the three-bedroom, two-bathroom oceanfront suite called "Papaya;" "Mango" and "Pineapple" are ideal for two persons. Each unit contains a midsize shower-only bathroom. The least expensive units, "Banana" and "Coconut," are studio units for those who want a kitchen but don't require a living room. Spa treatments are available as well as scuba-diving lessons. The cottages lie a 10-minute drive west of Rincón.

Rte. 4290 (P.O. Box 3200), Rincón, PR 00677. © **888/418-8733** or 787/823-6452. Fax 787/823-5821. www.lemon treepr.com. 6 units (shower only). Year-round $165–$195 double, $265 quad, $295 for 6. AE, MC, V. *In room:* A/C, TV, kitchenette, coffeemaker.

Tres Sirenas Beach Inn ⚝ *Finds*   This B&B opens onto Sandy Bottom Beach, giving you a chance to live in a certain tropical elegant style. It's casual but oh, so tasteful. A boutique hotel, the complex is sometimes rented as a private oceanfront villa to a dozen or so guests (high season $870 per night; low season $780.) Otherwise you have a choice of two spacious and elegantly furnished bedrooms or else two apartments, all with a certain old–Puerto Rican charm. The pool studio would be ideal for families, as it accommodates two adults and two children, and features a private balcony. Apartments sleep four and come with a loft and full kitchen. Innkeepers Lisa and Harry are wonderful hosts, "attentive" but never "intrusive," and breakfast is delicious.

Sea Beach Dr. 26, Rincón, PR 00677. © **787/823-0558**. www.tressirenas.com. 4 units. Winter $175 double, $220 studio for 4, $300 apt; off season $160 double, $200 studio for 4, $285 apt. AE, DC, MC, V. **Amenities:** Outdoor pool; hot tub; limited room service; laundry service; nonsmoking rooms, Wi-Fi Internet throughout property. *In room:* A/C, TV, kitchenette, minibar, beverage maker, hair dryer, iron.

INEXPENSIVE
Beside the Pointe Guesthouse   This tiny guesthouse sits on a lovely spot on the beach and has a popular tavern and restaurant and shop on the grounds. With only a handful of rooms though, this is probably not for everyone. We recommend the more expensive oceanfront double and the oceanview suites on the upper deck, which are removed enough from the public areas to maintain a sense of privacy. The view is also beautiful, and there's a great sun deck.

Carretera 413 Km 4 Sandy Beach, Rincón. © **888/823-8550**. Fax 787/823-8550. www.besidethepointe.com. 21 units. High season $120–$140 double, $170 oceanfront double, $185–$210 suites; low season $80–$120 double, $140 oceanfront double, $165–$190 suites. AE, MC, V. **Amenities:** Restaurant; bar; Wi-Fi Internet service in lobby; gift shop w/local crafts. *In room:* A/C, TV, kitchenette (suites), fridge.

The Lazy Parrot   Set within an unlikely inland neighborhood, this place is nonetheless one of the best spots in Rincón to stay. It's one of the only hotels on Route 413, the so-called "road to happiness" because it's the main road to town from the rest of Puerto Rico. "Value" rooms are located on the first floor. They are clean, well-organized, and comfortable, if not overly large. They have no view, but each has either a deck, patio, or balcony, and attractive decor of light, natural colors. The upstairs "panoramic" rooms have a view to the pretty Cadena Hills and the coast and overlook the pool area. These are also larger and have upgraded facilities like flatscreen TVs. Definitely pay the extra cost for an upstairs room if privacy is important to you. The other rooms are close to the lobby, pool, and restaurant. Smilin' Joes is one of the best eateries in Rincón, while the Rum Shack serves light fare and drinks poolside, and can be a lot of fun at night. This is one of the better-managed properties in town. Though its inland location is a drawback, you should have a car rental to explore several of the area's beaches anyway, and the pool area is quite nice.

Rd. 413 Km 4.1, Barrio Puntas, Rincón, PR 00677. © **800/294-1752** or 787/823-5654. Fax 787/823-0224. www.lazy parrot.com. 21 units. Year-round $125 double value rooms; $165 double panoramic rooms. The smallest room goes for $99 single or double. Rates include continental breakfast. AE, DISC, MC, V. **Amenities:** 2 restaurants; bar; pool; limited room service; babysitting; Wi-Fi Internet service in lobby; gift shop w/local crafts. *In room:* A/C, TV, fridge.

Parador Villa Antonio *(Kids)*   Ilia and Hector Ruíz offer apartments by the sea in this privately owned and run parador. The beach outside is nice, but the local authorities don't keep it as clean as they ought to. Surfing and fishing can be enjoyed just outside your front door, and you can bring your catch right into your cottage and prepare a fresh seafood dinner in your own kitchenette (there's no restaurant). This is a popular destination with families from Puerto Rico, who crowd in on the weekends to occupy the motel-like rooms with balconies or terraces. Furnishings are well used but offer reasonable comfort, and the shower-only bathrooms are small. It's a great spot for kids with a video and game room, playground and other activities.

Rte. 115 Km 12.3 (P.O. Box 68), Rincón, PR 00677. ✆ 787/823-2645. Fax 787/823-3380. www.villa-antonio.com. 61 units (shower only). $115–$145 studio (up to 2 people); $155–$170 2-bedroom apt (holds up to 4 people); $140 junior suite; $150 suite. AE, DISC, MC, V. **Amenities:** 2 pools; 2 tennis courts; playground; babysitting; laundry service; rooms for those w/limited mobility. *In room:* A/C, TV, coffeemaker, iron, safe.

Villa Cofresi *(Kids)*   About a mile (1.6km) south of Rincón's center, this is a clean, family-run hotel with a view of the beach. Thanks to the three adult children of the Caro family, the place is better managed than many of its competitors. Bedrooms are comfortable and airy, with well-chosen furniture that might remind you of something in southern Florida. Each unit has a white-tile floor and a small bathroom with a tub and shower. Most rooms have two double beds; some have two twin beds. All are nonsmoking. The two units that tend to be reserved out long in advance are nos. 47 and 55, which have windows opening directly onto the sea.

The in-house restaurant, La Ana de Cofresi, is named after the ship that was captained by the region's most famous 18th-century pirate, Roberto Cofresi. Hand-painted murals highlight some of his adventures. Open Monday through Friday from 5 to 10pm and Saturday and Sunday from noon to 10pm, it charges $8 to $30 for well-prepared main courses that are likely to include fish consommé, four kinds of *mofongo*, breaded scampi served either with Creole sauce or garlic, and very good steaks, including a 12-ounce New York sirloin.

Rd. 115 Km 12.0, Rincón, PR 00677. ✆ 787/823-2450. Fax 787/823-1770. www.villacofresi.com. 80 units. Winter $135–$155 double, $160 suite; off season $115–$135 double, $160 suite. AE, DC, MC, V. **Amenities:** Restaurant; bar; outdoor pool; room service; rooms for those w/limited mobility. *In room:* A/C, TV, fridge, hair dryer, iron.

WHERE TO DINE
VERY EXPENSIVE

Horned Dorset Primavera *(★★)* FRENCH/CARIBBEAN   This is the finest restaurant in western Puerto Rico—so romantic that people sometimes come from San Juan just for an intimate dinner. A masonry staircase sweeps from the garden to the second floor, where soaring ceilings and an atmosphere similar to that in a private villa awaits you.

The menu, which changes virtually every night based on the inspiration of the chef, might include chilled parsnip soup, a fricassee of wahoo with wild mushrooms, grilled loin of beef with peppercorns, and medallions of lobster in an orange-flavored beurre-blanc sauce. The grilled breast of duckling with bay leaves and raspberry sauce is also delectable. Mahimahi is grilled and served with ginger-cream sauce on a bed of braised Chinese cabbage. It's delicious.

In the Horned Dorset Primavera Hotel, Apartado 1132. ✆ 787/823-4030. Reservations recommended. Fixed-price dinner $68 for 5 dishes, $92 for 8 dishes. AE, MC, V. Daily 7–9:30pm.

EXPENSIVE

Smiling Joe's ✆ CARRIBBEAN ASIAN FUSION   With an inventive menu and beautiful but laid-back setting, this is one of Rincón's best restaurants. Worldwide flavors are brought together for optimal impact, and diners sit in an open-air terrace with panoramic views or a tropical garden. The restaurant's takes on such local classics as churrasco and red snapper are a delicious mix of Puerto Rican *sabor*, down-island flavorings, and Asian herbs, and we love the way it kicks up classic Jamaican jerk with a bit of tamarind and mango salsa and then targets grilled mahimahi rather than chicken. But the plates that really wowed us were the pork tenderloin, filled with chorizo–red pepper stuffing and glazed in guava and rum, and the almond crusted chicken with a goat cheese–veggie filling. We got off to a roaring start with the spicy red coconut curry mussels and the tempura pepper stuffed with lobster risotto.

Rd. 413 Km 4.1, Barrio Puntas, Rincón, PR 00677. ✆ 787/823-0101. AE, DISC, MC, V. Reservations not necessary. Main courses $19–$33 dinner only. Daily 5:30–10pm.

MODERATE

The Rum Shack ASIAN AMERICAN   The pool bar and cafe at the Lazy Parrot has much better food than you'd expect, and it draws an eclectic mix of customers into the evening. Typical bar food is given an Asian flare, and sushi is served Wednesday through Sunday from 6 to 10pm. The house burger goes upscale with caramelized onions; there are also tasty and unique chicken wraps, mahimahi tacos, and a panini of Mediterranean veggies. The bar is a good place to pick up travel tips and meet other visitors and resident ex-pats.

Rd. 413 Km 4.1, Barrio Puntas, Rincón, PR 00677. ✆ 787/823-0101. AE, DISC, MC, V. Reservations not necessary. Sandwiches, salads, etc. $6–$12. Daily 11am–11pm.

Tamboo Tavern and Seaside Grill Restaurant   AMERICAN-CARIBBEAN This tavern and restaurant at Beside the Pointe Guesthouse on Sandy Beach is the favored hangout for the young and beautiful beach crowd and surfing enthusiasts from the island and across the planet. It's a great place to eat, offering good food and a beautiful setting, no matter who you are. Beachfront dining does not get realer than this. Tables are stretched along a deck running along the beach sands and palm trees. It's basic steaks, ribs, and lots of seafood, but it's well prepared and tastes extra great while you're breathing in the sea and the salt. The mahimahi in caper sauce and grilled Caribbean lobster are both recommended, and you might want to start out with a platter of Puerto Rican appetizers. Burgers, wraps, and salads are also available for lunch and dinner.

Carretera 413 Km 4, Sandy Beach, Rincón. ✆ 888/823-8550 or 787/823-8550. Reservations not accepted. Main courses $16–$26 dinner; lunch items $6–$10. MC, V. Bar daily noon–2am; restaurant Thurs–Tues noon–9:30pm.

INEXPENSIVE

Panaderia/Cafeteria Calvache AMERICAN/PUERTO RICAN   The food-service area of this place occupies one end of a store otherwise devoted to the sale of rum, baked goods, and hardware. But it's so friendly and the counter setting is so appropriate for the food (bacon and eggs, spaghetti with sausage, and such local fare as rice with seafood) that we wanted to add it to our listings. In the evening, the staff offers only sandwiches, no hot food. You'll find this Formica-clad heaven about 1½ miles (2.4km) south of the center of Rincón.

Rte. 115 Km 9. © 787/823-6658. Reservations not necessary. Breakfast and sandwiches $2–$6; fixed-price lunch $4–$7. MC, V. Daily 4am–10pm.

A NEARBY PLACE TO STAY & DINE IN AGUADA

J. B. Hidden Village Hotel 🐾   Named using the initials of its owners (Julio Bonilla, his wife, Jinnie, and their son, Julio, Jr.), this is a well-maintained and isolated hotel launched in 1990. Half-a-mile (.8km) east of Aguada, on a side street that runs off Route 4414, it's nestled in a valley between three forested hillsides, almost invisible from the road. The hotel is a quiet and simple refuge to vacationers who enjoy exploring the area's many beaches. There are two restaurants on the premises (one with a view of a neighboring ravine). Each comfortable bedroom offers views of the pool and has a small tiled bathroom with tub/shower combination. Nice place but not near any beach.

Carretera 2, Intersection 4416, Km 1, Punta Nueve, Barrio Piedras Blancas, Sector Villarrubia, Aguada, PR 00602. © 787/868-8686. Fax 787/868-8701. 42 units. Year-round $72–$120 double; $125 suite. AE, MC, V. **Amenities:** Restaurant; bar; 2 outdoor pools; rooms for those w/limited mobility. *In room:* A/C, TV, no phone.

RINCON AFTER DARK

Join the surfers for a "sundowner" at **Calypso's Tropical Bar,** Maria's Beach (© 787/ 823-1626), which lies on the road to the lighthouse. Locals gather to watch the sunset in the outdoor courtyard. Happy-hour specials are daily 5 to 7pm. Live music takes place Friday and Saturday nights, and the bar is open daily from 11am until the last customer leaves (usually long after midnight). The Calypso Café has grilled seafood and pub fare. If you decide to eat something here, go for the grilled seafood, with main courses costing from $4 to $12.

One of the best *simpático* bars is **Rock Bottom,** adjoining Casa Verde Guest House along Sandy Beach Road (© 787/823-3756). It serves burgers and other stateside food. The upstairs surfer bar is decorated with dozens of graffitized surf boards and has a tree house feel to it. Great piña coladas and daily drink specials. The bar is open until midnight, at least. Wednesdays are acoustic jam nights, and Sundays are dedicated to movies and surf videos.

A young crowd gathers at **Tamboo Tavern** (© 787/823-8550), another surfer's bar in a tropical dream location right on Sandy Beach. The action percolates throughout the day, and really takes off as the sun begins to set. Watch it from the terrace or sit at the bar inside tapping your feet to rock *en español* and progressive American music. There's live music most weekend nights. The **Rum Shack** (© 787/823-0101) is a good place to rub shoulders with local ex-pats and a diverse group of travelers. Don't miss the full-moon party or reggae nights if one is occurring while you are in town. There's also a weekly movie night.

3 Aguadilla & the Northwest

Aguadilla is the biggest town on Puerto Rico's northwest corner, which is filled with great beaches and other natural blessings for an active vacation experience. And it makes a good base from which to explore the area, with lots of hotels, restaurants, good infrastructure, a fairly large mall, and lots of attractions, like a water park and golf course.

Several airlines now run direct flights to the town's **Rafael Hernández Airport,** especially during the high season. It's the island's second international airport after Luis Muñoz Marín in San Juan. So visitors who want to spend their whole vacation in the west don't have to go through San Juan. Puerto Rico's best surfing spots run from Rincón south of here, around the northwest corner to Isabela and points east along the north coast.

The region also is near major attractions like the **Arecibo Observatory** and the **Río Camuy Cave Park** (see chapter 9). In addition to its coast, there are mountain forests and lakes nearby (see below).

ESSENTIALS
GETTING THERE & GETTING AROUND   Both JetBlue and Continental have non-stop flights from East Coast destinations, particularly from New York and Florida, direct to the **Rafael Hernández Airport** (Antigua Base Ramey, Hangar 405, Aguadilla; © 787/891-2226). Many other flights offer connections from San Juan onto Aguadilla.

There are branches of **Avis** (© 787/890-3311), **Budget** (© 787/890-1110), and **Hertz** (© 787/833-3170) at the Aguadilla airport.

If you're driving from San Juan, travel west on Highway 22, then Route 2 (trip time: 2 hr.).

VISITOR INFORMATION   There is a Puerto Rico Tourism Company office in Aguadilla for the whole northwest region, from Mayagüez in the south through Isabela on the north coast (© 787/890-3315).

WATERSPORTS & OTHER OUTDOOR PURSUITS
While Rincón has wider name recognition, Aguadilla and Isabela have equally good surf spots. In fact, the Puerto Rican Pipeline is actually composed of beaches in the three towns. **Gas Chambers, Crash Boat,** and **Wilderness** rule in Aguadilla, while the preferred spots in **Isabela** include **Jobos** and **Middles.** The best time to surf is from November through March, but summer storms can also kick up the surf. In the summer season, however, when the waves diminish, these northwest beaches double as perfect spots for windsurfing and snorkeling, with calm waters filled with coral reefs and marine life. The towns are quite close together, and the string of beaches through both really forms a single destination.

Crash Boat is popular; vendors sell street food from stands by its parking lot while a local restaurant serves freshly caught seafood (brightly colored wooden fishing boats are often parked on the beach). One half of the beach is protected, with the aquamarine water kissing the white sand, while the other side faces the open water and is much rougher. **Shacks** draw both snorkelers and scuba divers, who converge on one section of the large beach filled with reefs and coral caverns that teem with rainbow-hued fish. It's also the best spot in the area for kite-boarding and windsurfing.

The **Isabela** coastline is also beautiful. In some places dirt roads still weave between cliffs and white beaches, set off by dramatic rock formations and submerged coral reefs that send surf crashing skyward. This is an area of salt-water wells and blowholes, through which dramatic eruptions of saltwater spew from submerged sea caves. Several are found in the area known as **La Princesa,** and **Jobos** beach is home to one of the most famous saltwater wells, **El Pozo de Jacinto.**

Jobos is a large beach with a famed surf break at its western end, but kids can frolic along more protected areas along this mammoth shore. There are also guesthouses and restaurants here, and on summer and holiday weekends it's got a party atmosphere. The **Ocean Front Hotel and Restaurant** (© 787/872-3339), right at the beach, is a good spot for a drink and seafood. **Montones Beach** has rock outcroppings and reefs that make a beguiling seascape and also protect the water from the raging surf in this area. You won't find the restaurants and bars here that you will in Jobos, but you can find your own secluded spot on the beach.

Steep cliffs drop in flat jagged lines to the rough surf along the rugged Atlantic coastline of **Quebradillas. Guajataca Beach,** named after a powerful Taíno Indian chief. It is a great spot, but think twice about swimming here. The currents are extremely powerful and dangerous, and while surfers love it, casual swimmers should proceed with caution. The white sand is as smooth as silk though, so it's a great spot for sunbathing and watching the surfers risking all and loving every minute of it. It's a great spot for seashell collecting. The beach is also called **El Tunel** because there's a large abandoned railroad tunnel carved out of a mountain at the entrance to the beach. It was once part of a railroad that ran all around the Puerto Rico coast that was built to haul sugar cane. There is a parking area here and a no-frills, open-air restaurant and bar. It's a nice shady spot, a cool respite from the sun-bleached beach.

Aquatica Dive, Bike and Surf Adventures (Rte. 110 Km 10, outside gate 5 of Rafael Hernández Airport, Aguadilla; ✆ **787/890-6071**) is a full-service dive and surf shop, but it also rents equipment and gives lessons in scuba and surfing. The outfit also runs mountain-bike excursions to the Guajataca Forest. Prices depend on season and group size, but surf lessons cost from $45 to $65 for 1½ hours, and a 2-tank scuba dive is from $60 to $85. Bicycle tours cost between $45 and $65 per person and last up to 3 hours. Surf and scuba equipment rentals run from $20 to $45 per day, while bicycles are $25 per day.

The Hang Loose Surf Shop (Rte. 4466 Km 1.2, Playa Jobos, Isabela; ✆ **787/872-2490;** Tues–Sun 10am–5pm) is well stocked with equipment. It gives surf lessons ($55 per hour private lesson) and rents boards for $25 daily. The shop is owned by Werner Vega, a great big-wave rider, who is one of Puerto Rico's premier board shapers.

The Northwest has more going for it than its beaches, however. That's especially so with **Aguadilla,** which has converted many of the old facilities of the former Ramey Air Force Base and put them to good public use (such as developing an international airport on a portion of it). **Punta Borinquén Golf Club,** Route 107 (✆ **787/890-2987**), 2 miles (3.2km) north of Aquadilla's center, across the highway from the city's airport, was originally built by the U.S. government as part of Ramey Air Force Base. Today, it is a public 18-hole golf course, open daily from 7am to 7pm. Greens fees are a bargain at $20 per round; a golf cart that can carry two passengers rents for $30 for 18 holes. A set of clubs can be rented for $15. The clubhouse has a bar and a simple restaurant. It's also a nice course with coastal views. **Parque Aquatica Las Cascadas** (Hwy. 2 Km 126.5, Aguadilla; ✆ **787/819-0950** or 787/819-1030) is a water park run by the municipality that the kids will love. There are giant slides and tubes and the Río Loco rapids pool. A big drawback is that it is only open in the summer, from May through September (10am–5pm weekdays, 10am–6pm weekends). Tickets are $16 for adults and $14 for kids (ages 4–12) plus a $5 tube-rental fee.

You probably did not come to Puerto Rico to go ice skating, but you can do it at the **Aguadilla Ice Skating Rink** (Hwy. 442; ✆ **787/819-5555,** ext. 221). This is another city-run facility open from 9:30am to 11pm. It's popular with kids and is a training facility for island figure skaters. Cost is $10 an hour during the day and $13 in the evening (including skates).

Isabela enjoys a reputation for horse breeding. This activity is centered around Arenales, south of the town, where a number of horse stables are located.

WHERE TO STAY & DINE

Marriott Courtyard Aguadilla *Kids*   The whole family will love this hotel with pool, aquatics playground, and spacious guest rooms near some of the prettiest beaches on the island, and right around attractions like the Camuy Caves, Arecibo Observatory, local water park, and ice-skating rink. Beautiful beaches ring the coast here from Isabela to the east and Rincón to the west. It's built on the old Ramey Air Force Base near a coastal suburb. Great location and facilities make a good base to explore the northwest.

West Parade/Belt Road Antigua Base Ramey, Aguadilla, PR 00603. © 800/321-2211 or 787/658-8000. Fax 787/658-8020. www.marriott.com. 152 units. Year-round $169–$199 double. AE, MC, V. **Amenities:** 2 restaurants; 2 bars; 2 pools; fitness center; business services; beauty shop; room service; babysitting; dry cleaning; Wi-Fi Internet. *In room:* A/C, TV, Internet access, coffeemaker, iron.

Parador El Guajataca *Kids*   You'll find this place on a rolling hillside reaching down to a surf-beaten beach along the north coast. Stay here for the stunning natural setting and don't expect too much. The hotel was recently spruced up but remains standard. Each room has its own entrance and private balcony opening onto the turbulent Atlantic. Bathrooms are functional, each with a tub.

Served in a glassed-in dining room where all the windows face the sea, the cuisine is also basic Creole international fare. Sometimes, there is live music on weekends.

There are two swimming pools (one for adults, another for children), plus a playground for children.

Rte. 2 Km 103.8 (P.O. Box 1558), Quebradillas, PR 00678. © 800/965-3065 or 787/895-3070. Fax 787/895-3589. www.elguajataca.com. 38 units. Year-round $119 double. AE, MC, V. From Quebradillas, continue northwest on Rte. 2 for 1 mile/1.6km; the parador is signposted. Hotel advertises specials as low as $82. **Amenities:** Restaurant; bar; 2 pools; limited room service; laundry service; coin-op laundry; dry cleaning. *In room:* A/C, TV, coffeemaker, iron.

Parador Vistamar   In the Guajataca area, this parador, one of the largest in Puerto Rico, sits like a sentinel surveying the scene from high atop a mountain overlooking greenery and a seascape. There are gardens and intricate paths carved into the side of the mountain, where you can stroll while enjoying the fragrance of the tropical flowers. Or you might choose to search for the calcified fossils that abound on the carved mountainside. For a unique experience, visitors can try their hand at freshwater fishing just down the hill from the hotel (bring your own gear). Flocks of rare tropical birds are frequently seen in the nearby mangroves.

Bedrooms (all nonsmoking) are comfortably furnished in a rather bland motel style. Bathrooms with either shower or tub are functional, but without much decorative zest. There's a dining room with an ocean view where you can have a typical Puerto Rican dinner or choose from the international menu.

A short drive from the hotel will bring you to the Punta Borinquén Golf Course. Tennis courts are just down the hill from the inn itself. Sightseeing trips to the nearby Arecibo Observatory (p. 209)—the largest radar/radio-telescope in the world—and to Monte Calvario (a replica of Mount Calvary) are available. Another popular visit is to the plaza in the town of Quebradillas.

Rte. 113N 6205, Quebradillas, PR 00678. © 787/895-2065. Fax 787/895-2294. www.paradorvistamar.com. 55 units (each with either shower or tub). Year-round $76–$125 double. Up to 2 children 11 and under stay free in parent's room. AE, DISC, MC, V. At Quebradillas, head northwest on Rte. 2, then go left at the junction with Rte. 113 and continue for a mile/1.6km. **Amenities:** Restaurant; bar; pool; limited room service; rooms for those w/limited mobility. *In room:* A/C, TV, coffeemaker (in some).

Villas del Mar Hau 🐾 *(Kids)*   Opening onto a long, secluded beach, this family-friendly parador complex is peppered with typical Puerto Rican country cottages in vivid Caribbean pastels with Victorian wood trim. The location is midway between the west coast cities of Arecibo in the east and Aguadilla in the west, right outside the smaller town of Isabela. Under the shelter of Causuarina pine trees, most guests spend their days lying on Playa Montones. The huge tidal "wading" pool is ideal for children. The place is unpretentious but not completely back-to-nature, as the beachfront cottages are well furnished and equipped, each with a balcony and with capacities for two to six guests. Some have ceiling fans, others have air-conditioning, and all units are equipped with small, tiled, shower-only bathrooms. Since 1960 the Hau family has run this little beach inn. The on-site restaurant is well known in the area for its creative menu featuring fresh fish, shellfish, and meats.

Carretera 4466 Km 8.3, Playa Montones, Isabela, PR 00662. © **787/830-8315.** Fax 787/830-4988. 42 units (shower only). High season $110–$160 double, $185–$260 cottage; low season $90–$140 double, $175–$200 cottage. AE, MC, V. From the center of Isabella, take Rte. 466 toward Aguadilla. **Amenities:** Restaurant; bar; barbecue area; pool w/snack bar; tennis; beach toy rental; photocopy and fax; convenience store; babysitting; laundry service; horseback riding. *In room:* A/C, TV (in most rooms), kitchenette, coffeemaker.

Villa Montana Beach Resort 🐾 *(Finds)*   This breathtaking property is set on a 35-acre (14-hectare) beachfront plot. The rooms and villas are spread across Caribbean-style plantation buildings with large verandas and balconies. The buildings have cathedral ceilings, peaked tin roofs, and interior courtyards. The facades use muted pastel colors, and rooms are beautifully decorated with a subdued tropical aesthetic and have large terra-cotta tile. There are two beautiful pools and a 3-mile (4.8km) beach, where every watersport you can imagine is possible to practice. You can also hike through tropical forests, ride horses, go biking, or use the climbing wall on the property. There's a health club, spa, and sports facilities like basketball courts. Both restaurants, Eclipse and O, have quality food but are on the expensive side. The grounds are lush and beautiful, and there are numerous tropical birds. This is a place to kick way back.

Carretera 4466 Km 1.9, Barrio Bajuras, Isabela, PR 00662. © **888/780-9195** or 787/872-9554 Fax 787/872-9553. 60 units. $200–$400 double, $400–$600 villas. AE, MC, V. **Amenities:** 2 restaurants; bar; 2 pools; tennis court; basketball court; volleyball court; climbing wall; spa; watersports rentals; business center; store; babysitting; laundry service; horseback riding. *In room:* A/C, TV, kitchenette (in villas), ceiling fans.

4 The Western Mountains

The west is also a good area to head up into the mountains, and Maricao, west of Mayagüez, is one of the prettiest of Puerto Rico's mountain towns. You can reach Maricao from Mayagüez, but you'll have to take a number of routes heading east. First take Route 106 east to Route 119, which you will turn right on. Take this until the community of Las Vegas, then turn left on Route 357 toward Maricao, which you will reach when you intersect with Route 105. The scenery is beautiful, but the roads are narrow and the going is slow. It's quicker to head south along Highway 2 until Sabana Grande, then take Highway 120 directly to Maricao.

One of the nicest spots is the **Monte del Estado National Park** (Rte. 120 Km 13.2; © **787/873-5632**), a picnic area and campground in the Maricao Forest, with wonderful pools fed by mountain streams. The stone observation tower, at 2,600 feet (792m) above sea level, provides a panoramic view across the green mountains up to the coastal plains, and you can see clear out to Mona Island. Nearly 50 species of birds live in this forest, including the Lesser Antillean pewee and the scaly naped pigeon. Nature watchers will delight to know that there are some 280 tree species in this reserve, 38 of which are found only here. The area has about 18 rivers and creeks running through the forest.

Marciao is coffee country, and there are several plantations and historic plantation houses in the town. **Parador Hacienda Juanita** is a beautiful inn and restaurant in a restored former coffee plantation house that was built in 1836.

Nearby is **Lares,** which has a lovely central plaza with shady trees and scattered tropical gardens. It's called La Plaza de la Revolucíon, named after one of the few nationalist uprisings in Puerto Rican history. In 1863, El Grito de Lares took place when hundreds of Puerto Rican patriots seized the town from the Spanish on September 28, 1868. While a republic of Puerto Rico was declared, the Spanish quickly resumed control. Today, thousands of independence supporters come here to commemorate the event each year on its September 28 anniversary. Surrounded by mountains and green valleys, it is one of the island's prettiest towns, though it lacks hotels and attractions for tourists.

From Isabela, you can visit **Lago de Guajataca** and the **Guajataca Forest Reserve,** which are located in the mountains south of town.

Before heading into **Bosque Estatal de Guajataca (Guajataca Forest)** &&, you can stop in at the **Dept. de Recursos Naturales Oficina**, Rte. 446 Km 9, Barrio Llanadas (© **787/872-1045** or 787/999-2000), which is open daily 7am to 3:30pm. The office has a stock of detailed hiking routes through the forest reserve. Guajataca Forest sprawls across nearly 2,400 acres (971 hectares) of forestland, rising and falling at various elevations, ranging from 500 to 1,000 feet (152–305m) or more.

The woodland in the forest is punctuated by mogotes and covered with 25 miles (40km) of hiking trails. It is also home to the endangered Puerto Rico boa (you are unlikely to encounter one) and is the habitat of nearly 50 different species of birds. The highlight of the forest is the *Cueva del Viento,* the "Cave of the Wind." The hiking trails have been well marked by park rangers.

Reaching the lake from the forest can be difficult. Take Route 446 south until Route 119. The **Lago de Guajataca** &, one of the most majestic bodies of water on Puerto Rico, is our favorite lake for some R&R on the island. It is both a 4-mile-long (6.4km) body of water and a wildlife refuge. For a scenic look at the lake, drive along its north shore which is a haven for island freshwater anglers. You can go fishing here, but you have to bring your own equipment. The most sought-after fish is *tucunare,* with which the lake is stocked. At the dam here, you can gaze upon an evocative "lost valley" of conical peaks.

WHERE TO STAY & DINE
Parador Hacienda Juanita &   Named after one of its long-ago owners, a matriarch named Juanita, this pink stucco building dates from 1836, when it was a coffee plantation. Situated 2 miles (3.2km) west of the village of Maricao, beside Route 105 heading to Mayagüez, it has a long veranda and a living room furnished with a large-screen TV and decorated with antique tools and artifacts of the coffee industry. Relatively isolated, it's surrounded by only a few neighboring buildings and the jungle. Situated on 24 acres (9.7 hectares) of plantation, the parador is a beautiful spot to hike around. It has a fine restaurant, and both breakfast and dinner are included with the room. There's a swimming pool, billiards table, and ping-pong table on the premises. Its restaurant, **La Casona de Juanita,** serves tasty, hearty Puerto Rican fare. The best

spot to dine is on the veranda overlooking the verdant grounds. The bedrooms are simple and rural, with ceiling fans, rocking chairs, and rustic furniture, plus small tub-and-shower bathrooms. All are nonsmoking. None of the rooms has air-conditioning (ceiling fans suffice in the cool temperatures of this high-altitude place). It sits at 1,600 feet (488m) above sea level.

Rte. 105 Km 23.5 (HC01 Box 8200), Maricao, PR 00606. (© 787/838-2550. Fax 787/838-2551. www.hacienda juanita.com. 21 units. $125 double. Rate includes breakfast and dinner. Children 11 and under stay free in parent's room. AE, MC, V. Free parking. **Amenities:** Restaurant; bar; pool; tennis; 1 room for those w/limited mobility. *In room:* TV, Internet access, ceiling fan, no phone.

12

Eastern Puerto Rico

The northeast corner of the island, only about 45 minutes from San Juan, contains the island's major attractions, El Yunque rainforest, two of the world's rare bioluminescent bays whose waters glow at night, and several great beaches, including Luquillo Beach (see chapter 9). There are a variety of landscapes, ranging from miles of forest to palm groves and beachside settlements. Here you will find one of the best resorts on the island, El Conquistador Resort and Country Club, which literally sits on the northeast corner of Puerto Rico, where the Atlantic Ocean and the Caribbean Sea meet.

This is the site of Fajardo, a preeminent sailor's haven, where you can catch ferries to the nearby island municipalities of Vieques and Culebra (see chapter 13). The east coast city is actually part of a hub of islands, weaving through the neighboring Spanish Virgin Islands, and on to the U.S. and British Virgin Islands. Not for nothing, as there's at least seven

marinas in town, which also has its share of gorgeous beaches, snorkeling spots, and untamed forest.

Farther down the east coast is the **Palmas del Mar,** an ever-growing resort and upscale vacation home community on a wildly gorgeous beachfront. There's a hotel and another on the way, and visitors can also rent private vacation homes and villas throughout the resort, which has marinas, golf, tennis, stores, restaurants, and bars. There are several pools and a great beach, with all watersports activities available. Palmas also has its own school and post office.

The coast has small fishing towns, rural farmland, and quaint historic plazas surrounded by beautiful Spanish colonial architecture.

The southeast corner of Puerto Rico is still relatively undiscovered, despite the beauty of its untarnished coastline and traditional towns.

1 Fajardo

35 miles (56km) E of San Juan

A huge submerged coral reef off Fajardo's coast protects its southeastern waters, which are also blessed by trade winds—adding up to sailors' delight. The Caribbean waters here are run through with coral and marine life, from barracudas and nurse sharks to shimmering schools of tropical fish—a diving and snorkeling paradise.

There are dozens of small islands off the coast of this eastern town, making the beauty of its waters all the more accessible. Fajardo itself has untrammeled beaches, surrounded by wilderness, with great snorkeling and scuba opportunities right offshore. It also has a bioluminescent bay and other natural wonders. We also love the unvarnished town center, with atmospheric bars and *cafetíns* serving up tasty Creole cooking at bargain prices.

To the Lighthouse: Exploring Las Cabezas de San Juan Nature Reserve

Las Cabezas de San Juan Nature Reserve is better known as El Faro, or "The Lighthouse." Located in the northeastern corner of the island, it is one of the most beautiful and important areas in Puerto Rico. Here you'll find seven ecological systems and a restored 19th-century Spanish colonial lighthouse. From the lighthouse observation deck, majestic views extend to islands as far off as St. Thomas in the U.S. Virgin Islands.

Surrounded on three sides by the Atlantic Ocean, the 316-acre (128-hectare) site encompasses forestland, mangroves, lagoons, beaches, cliffs, offshore cays, and coral reefs. Boardwalk trails wind through the fascinating topography. Ospreys, sea turtles, and an occasional manatee are seen from the windswept promontories and rocky beach.

The nature reserve is open Wednesday through Sunday. Reservations are required; for reservations during the week, call ℰ **787/722-5882,** and 787/860-2560 for reservations on weekends (weekend reservations must be made on the day of your visit). Admission is $7 for adults, $4 for children under 13, and $2.50 for seniors. Guided 2½-hour tours are conducted at 9:30am, 10am, 10:30am, and 2pm (in English at 2pm).

Laguna Grande, within the reserve, is one of the world's best bioluminescent bays, along with one on the neighboring island of Vieques. The presence of multitudes of tiny organisms, called dinoflagellates, in the protected bay is responsible for the nocturnal glow of its waters. They feed off the red mangroves surrounding the water. Kayaking through the bay at night should be on your bucket list. We highly recommend **Las Tortugas Adventures,** P.O. Box 1637, Canóvanas 00729 (ℰ **787/636-8356** or 787/809-0253; http://kayak-pr.com). Gary Horne is one of the most experienced guides in Puerto Rico; he's a certified dive master and Coast Guard veteran. There are two nightly tours of the bay at 6pm and 8pm Monday through Saturday, which cost $45 per person—or daytime kayak and snorkel adventures for $65, which we highly recommend as well. Another option is a kayak adventure through the Río Espirtu Santo, a beautiful river through El Yunque rainforest.

There are at least seven marinas in town, and with reason. Fajardo is the first of a string of ports extending to Vieques and Culebra, the U.S. and British Virgin Islands, and the Windward island chain, the pleasure boating capital of the Caribbean.

Las Croabas, a village within the municipality, is the site of the El Conquistador Resort and Golden Door Spa. El Conquistador was the leader in luxury resorts in the Caribbean from the 1960s through the late 1970s. Celebrities Elaine May, Jack Gilford, Celeste Holm (with her husband and two poodles), Elaine Stritch (and her dog), Amy Vanderbilt, Jack Palance, Burt Bacharach, Angie Dickinson, Omar Shariff, Marc Connelly, Maureen O'Sullivan, and Xavier Cugat attended its grand inaugural festivities in 1968. Later, its circular casino, in black and stainless steel, appeared in the James Bond movie *Goldfinger.* The original hotel closed in 1980, but it was reborn in 1993 as the distinctive $250-million El Conquistador we have today.

Eastern Puerto Rico

El Yunque	1
Fajardo	5
Humacao	2
Las Cabezas de San Juan Nature Reserve	7
Las Croabas	6
Luquillo Beach	8
Naguabo	4
Palmas del Mar	3

The resort sprawls across a dramatic cliff and down along a harbor area, overlooking the coast with an infinite view of water stretching out from all sides. The back terraces and circular casino share the view, as do the leveled infinity pools stretching across the bluff.

The buildings are wrought with Mediterranean motifs, from blooming Spanish courtyards to elegant neoclassical facades and fountains. A tramway takes guests down to sea level and the resort marina, and a ferry takes guests to the resort's beach on an offshore island.

Las Croabas is a charming fishing village, with boats tied up at harbor and open-air seafood restaurants. Many are clustered along Route 987 at the entrances of the Seven Seas public beach and Las Cabezas de San Juan Nature Reserve, over 300 acres (121 hectares) of dry forest, virgin coast, and mangrove swamp. It also borders the exquisite biobay, with glowing nocturnal waters. The restored 19th-century lighthouse still functions.

GETTING THERE

El Conquistador staff members greet all guests at the San Juan airport and transport them to the resort. Guests can take a taxi or a hotel shuttle to the resort ($68, for hotel guests only). The cost of a taxi from the San Juan airport is about $60.

If you're driving from San Juan, head east along the new Route 66 Corridor Noreste highway and then Route 3 toward Fajardo. At the intersection, cut northeast on Route 195 and continue to the intersection with Route 987, at which point you turn north.

OUTDOOR ACTIVITIES

In addition to the lovely beach and the many recreational facilities that are part of the El Conquistador (p. 271), there are other notable places to play in the vicinity.

Some of the best snorkeling in Puerto Rico is in and around Fajardo. Its public beach, **Playa Seven Seas,** is an attractive and sheltered strip of sand. The beach lies on the southwestern shoreline of Las Cabezas peninsula and is crowded on weekends. For even better snorkeling, walk to the western end of this beach and along a dirt path cutting though a wooded mount. After about a half-mile (.8km), you'll come to another path heading to **Playa Escondido (Hidden Beach),** a small white-sand cover with coral reefs in aquamarine waters right off this beach. If you continue straight for another mile, you will come to the gorgeous **El Convento Beach,** stretching out along the miles-long undeveloped coastline between Fajardo and Luquillo.

The area has managed to ward off development despite the building craze taking place across much of the rest of Puerto Rico, with only a few unmarked dirt roads providing access, and paths like the one from Seven Seas.

The area is a nesting ground for endangered sea turtles, and its waters team with reefs and fish. A small forest runs along much of the beach, and behind it stands the imposing El Yunque rainforest, looming over the white sand beach and pristine blue waters. About a mile down the beach is the governor's official beach house, El Convento, a rustic wooden cottage. Just beyond the cottage is a great spot to snorkel. The water plunges steeply just offshore, and it is pocked with large reefs, which draw even large fish to the brink of the beach.

Environmentalists have pushed to protect this area from development, while developers want to build two large resorts. Legislation to name a nature reserve here failed to win legislative approval, but the governor signed a less binding executive order doing so, which would only permit low-impact tourism in the area.

TENNIS   The seven Har-Tru courts at the **El Conquistador** 𝕉𝕉 are among the best tennis courts in Puerto Rico, rivaling those at Palmas del Mar. The staff at the pro shop is extremely helpful to beginning players. Courts are the least crowed during the hottest part of the day, around the lunch hour. If you're a single traveler to the resort and in search of a player, the pro shop will try to match you up with a player of equal skill.

WATERSPORTS   Several operators offer day sailing trips (10am–3pm) from Fajardo marinas, which include sailing, snorkeling, swimming, and a stop at one of the island beaches, where lunch is usually served. It's the easiest way to really experience the Caribbean marine world while in Puerto Rico. Prices, including lunch and equipment, start from $69 per person. The trips are aboard luxury catamarans, with plush seating, a sound system, and other comforts, like a bar. Captains know the best spots, where reefs attract schools of feeding fish, depending on conditions. These are among the most gin-clear and tranquil waters in Puerto Rico. They are teeming with wildlife, including several species of fish such as grouper, but also lobster, moray eels, and sea turtles. Among the local operators are **Traveler Sailing Catamaran** (© 787/853-2821), **East Island Excursions** (© 787/860-3434), and **Catamaran Spread Eagle** (© 787/887-8821). **Erin Go Bragh Charters** (© 787/860-4401) offers similar day trips aboard a 50-foot sailing ketch.

For scuba divers, **La Casa del Mar** (© 787/863-1000) is one good option operating out of El Conquistador. You can go for ocean dives on the outfitter's boats; a two-tank dive goes for $150, including equipment. A PADI snorkel program, at $65 per person, is also available. **Sea Ventures Dive Center** (Rte. 3 Km 51.4, Puerto del Rey; © 787/863-3483) has a $95 offer for a two-tank dive.

Fajardo's seven marinas are proof that it is a sailor's paradise. The most renowned is the **Puerto del Rey Marina** (Rte. 3 Km 51.4; © 787/860-1000 or 787/801-3010). The swankiest marina in Fajardo, it's a beautiful 1,100-slip facility south of town, the largest in the Caribbean. It's like a city unto itself with restaurants, bars, and a host of other services. **Villa Marina Yacht Harbour** (Rte. 987 Km 1.3; © 787/863-5131 or 787/863-5011) is the other main marina in town, and is the shortest ride to the offshore cays and isolated white-sand beaches on the mainland. Charters operate out of both. There's a private 35-slip marina at the lowest level of the El Conquistador (© 787/863-1000).

WHERE TO STAY
VERY EXPENSIVE
El Conquistador Resort & Golden Door Spa 🏖️🏖️ *Kids*   El Conquistador is a destination unto itself. Its array of facilities sits on 500 acres (202 hectares) of forested hills sloping down to the sea. Accommodations are divided into five separate sections united by their Mediterranean architecture and lush landscaping. Most lie several hundred feet above the sea. At the same altitude, a bit off to the side, is a replica of an Andalusian hamlet, Las Casitas Village, which seems straight out of the south of Spain. These pricey units, each with a full kitchen, form a self-contained enclave.

A short walk downhill takes you to a circular cluster of tastefully modern accommodations, Las Olas Village. And at sea level, adjacent to an armada of pleasure craft bobbing at anchor, is La Marina Village, whose balconies seem to hang directly over the water. The accommodations are outfitted with comfortable furniture, tropical colors, and robes. All the far-flung elements of the resort are connected by serpentine, landscaped walkways, and by a railroad-style funicular that makes frequent trips up and down the hillside.

One of the most comprehensive spas in the Caribbean, the Golden Door maintains a branch in this resort. The hotel is sole owner of a "fantasy island" (Palomino Island), with caverns; nature trails; horseback riding; and watersports such as scuba diving, windsurfing, and snorkeling. Free private ferries at frequent intervals connect the island, which is about a half-mile (.8km) offshore, to the main hotel. There's also a 25-slip marina. The hotel operates an excellently run children's club with activities planned daily. The resort has opened up a water park that's a hit with the kids (and the young at heart) with water slides, a lazy river, and a large pool. It's on the harbor level, right by the water, below the pool's main deck.

Av. Conquistador 1000, Las Croabas, Fajardo, PR 00738. © 866/317-8932 or 787/863-1000. Fax 787/863-6500. www.elconresort.com. 918 units. Winter $299–$558 double, $499–$2,000 Las Casitas Village suites; off season $179–$399 double, $350–$1,700 Las Casitas suites. MAP (breakfast and dinner) packages are available. Children ages 16 and under stay free in parent's room. AE, DC, DISC, MC, V. Self-parking $16 per day; valet parking $21. **Amenities:** 12 restaurants; 8 bars; nightclub; 7 pools; golf course; 7 Har-Tru tennis courts; health club; spa; 35-slip marina; dive shop; fishing; sailing; children's programs; tour desk; business center; limited room service; massage; laundry service; dry cleaning; nonsmoking rooms; casino; rooms for those w/limited mobility. *In room:* A/C, TV, mini-bar, fridge, coffeemaker, hair dryer, iron, safe.

MODERATE

The Fajardo Inn 🏷️ *(Finds*   A good base for those visiting El Yunque, this inn is ideal for those who are seeking a location in the east and don't want to pay the prices charged at the El Conquistador (above). Lying on a hilltop overlooking the port of Fajardo, this parador evokes a Mediterranean villa with its balustrades and grand staircases. The midsize bedrooms, most of which open onto good views, are spotless, and each has a small shower-only bathroom. The inn and its pool are handsomely landscaped. The on-site Star Fish restaurant specializes in Creole and Continental cuisine, especially fresh fish, with indoor and outdoor dining. The Blue Iguana Mexican Grill & Bar is a casual pub with good food. Coco's Park is a new pool area with activities like a beach pool, slide, Jacuzzi, tennis, basketball, and miniature golf. It's separated from the rest of the hotel so as not to disturb the relative tranquillity of the rest of the grounds.

Parcela Beltrán 52, Fajardo, PR 00740. ☎ **787/860-6000.** Fax 787/860-5063. www.fajardoinn.com. 105 units (shower only). Year-round $100–$132 double; $150–$300 suite. AE, DISC, MC, V. A 15-min. walk east of the center of Fajardo. **Amenities:** 2 restaurants; 2 bars; pool; snorkeling and diving arranged; limited room service; 1 room for those w/limited mobility. *In room:* A/C, TV, hair dryer, iron.

WHERE TO DINE
EXPENSIVE

Blossoms 🏷️ CHINESE/JAPANESE   Blossoms boasts some of the freshest seafood in eastern Puerto Rico. Sizzling delights are prepared on teppanyaki tables, and there's a zesty selection of Hunan and Szechuan specialties. On the teppanyaki menu, you can choose dishes ranging from chicken to shrimp, from filet mignon to lobster. Sushi bar selections range from eel and squid to salmon roe and giant clams.

In the El Conquistador Resort. ☎ **787/863-1000.** Reservations recommended. Main courses $18–$49. AE, DC, DISC, MC, V. Daily 6–11:30pm.

Otello's 🏷️ NORTHERN ITALIAN   Here you can dine by candlelight either indoors or out. The decor is neo-Palladian. You might begin with one of the soups, perhaps pasta fagioli, or select one of the zesty Italian appetizers, such as an excellently prepared clams Posillipo. Pastas can be ordered as a half portion for an appetizer or as a main dish, and they include homemade gnocchi and fettuccine with shrimp. The

---

Top Caribbean Spa: The Golden Door

Perched atop a stunning 300-foot (91m) bluff overlooking the Caribbean Sea and the Atlantic Ocean, the **Golden Door** 🏷️🏷️, in Las Casitas Village complex at the Wyndham El Conquistador Hotel (☎ **787/863-1000**), is the most sophisticated, well-managed, and comprehensive spa in the Caribbean, and it is one of the finest in the world. One of only three branches of a spa founded in Escondido, California, and today administered by the Wyndham group, it's devoted to the relaxation and healing of body, soul, and mind. Spa rituals are taken seriously; New Age mysticism is gracefully dispensed within a postmodern setting that's a cross between a Swiss clinic, a state-of-the-art health club, and a Buddhist monastery.

Spa treatments begin at $160 for 80 minutes. The spa is open daily from 6:30am to 8:30pm. American Express, MasterCard, and Visa are accepted.

chef is known for his superb veal dishes. A selection of poultry and vegetarian food is offered nightly, along with several shrimp and fish dishes. The salmon filet in champagne sauce has beautiful accents, as does the veal chop in an aromatic herb sauce.

Rte. 987, Km 3.4, in the El Conquistador Resort. (*) **787/863-1000.** Reservations required in winter, recommended off season. Main courses $26–$43. AE, DC, DISC, MC, V. Daily 6–10:30pm.

Stingray Café 🐟🐟 CARIBBEAN FUSION   We loved this resort's harbor-side restaurant, with a deliciously crafted seafood menu and views of the Caribbean and Palomino Island. The modern decor is inconsequential compared to the view and the Latin, down-island, and Asian-infused Continental classics. Flavors float in the air with the smell of the sea—saffron clams and chorizo and the cilantro conch chowder, seared tuna in a szechuan au poivre and the lemon sole filet lobster beurre blanc. But the filet mignon in roasted bacon shallot sauce and the pistachio-crusted veal medallions also command attention. Fruit sorbets are the dessert specialty. Really, it's all about the food and the view.

In the El Conquistador Resort. (*) **787/863-1000.** Reservations recommended. Main courses $29–$50. AE, DISC, MC, V. Daily 6–10:30pm.

2 Palmas del Mar

46 miles (74km) SE of San Juan

Halfway down the east coast, south from Fajardo, lies the resort and luxury residential community of Palmas del Mar in the municipality of Humacao. Here you'll find one of the most action-packed sports programs in the Caribbean, offering golf, tennis, scuba diving, sailing, deep-sea fishing, and horseback riding. Palmas del Mar's location is one of its greatest assets. The pleasing Caribbean trade winds steadily blow across this section of the island, stabilizing the weather and making Palmas del Mar ideal for many outdoor sports.

If you travel south from Fajardo, you can drive through the picturesque coastal fishing town of Naguabo, whose small harbor is fronted by numerous casual, open-air seafood restaurants, serving tasty, economically priced seafood and other local specialties. The 1917 revival mansion Castillo Villa del Mar, now a National Historic Monument, is at the harbor's southern end.

But the quickest way to get here from San Juan is to head south to along Highway 52 and then east Highway 30 to Humacao.

Palmas del Mar sprawls across 2,700 acres (1,092 hectares) of beautifully landscaped coast, a self-contained resort and residential community with several different luxury neighborhoods, ranging from Mediterranean-style villas to modern marina town houses.

It's a town unto itself: with a school, hospital and post office, several restaurants, shops, and other facilities that any town center would have. There's one existing hotel and two luxury properties under construction, and several of the residences are available for rent through a vacation club or real estate office.

There are negotiations ongoing for two new resorts (reportedly a $312-million Mandarin Oriental and a $300-million Regent) that should improve the luxury enclave's hotel offerings, which is just what Palmas needs. We find the existing Four Points hotel resort level, but pretty ordinary beyond that; a few more hotels will improve all the offerings. Until a few more hotels come on line, most guests will probably prefer staying at El Conquistador (p. 271) or one of the Río Grande resorts, the

Río Mar or Gran Melía, despite the charms of Palmas del Mar, which appear to be ever on the rise. If you are after a short-term rental of a condo or town house, then Palmas is more likely your place. A beach club, marina, and tennis club add to its resort appeal.

GETTING THERE

Humacao Regional Airport is 3 miles (4.8km) from the northern boundary of Palmas del Mar. It accommodates private planes; no regularly scheduled airline currently serves the Humacao airport. Palmas del Mar Resort will arrange minivan or bus transport from Humacao to the San Juan airport. Two persons can book the van for $40. If five or more passengers book the van, the cost is only $20 per person. The bus can accommodate up to 10 passengers. At night the price goes up to $45 per person for two. That is lowered to $22 per person if five or more share the ride. For reservations, call © **787/285-4323.** Call the resort if you want to be met at the airport.

If you're driving from San Juan, take Highway 52 south to Caguas, then take Highway 30 east to Humacao. Follow the signs from there to Palmas del Mar. A van ride to San Juan is $90 for the first three passengers, and $25 per person for four or more.

BEACHES & OUTDOOR ACTIVITIES

BEACHES   Palmas del Mar Resort has 3 exceptional miles (4.8km) of white sand beaches (all open to the public). Nonguests must park at the hotel parking ($2 per hour), and there are showers and bathrooms near the beach. The waters here can get rough in winter but are generally calm, and there's a watersports center and marina. (see "Scuba Diving & Snorkeling," below).

FISHING   Some of the best year-round fishing in the Caribbean is found in the waters just off Palmas del Mar. **Capt. Bill Burleson,** based in Humacao (© **787/850-7442**), operates charters on his customized, 46-foot sport-fisherman, *Karolette*, which is electronically equipped for successful fishing. Burleson prefers to take fishing groups to Grappler Banks, 18 nautical miles (33m) away, which lie in the migratory paths of wahoo, tuna, and marlin. A maximum of six people are taken out, costing $800 for 4½ hours, $960 for 6 hours, or $1,280 for 8 hours. Burleson also offers snorkeling charter expeditions starting at $640 for up to 6 persons.

GOLF   Few other real-estate developments in the Caribbean devote as much attention and publicity to their golf facilities as the **Palmas del Mar Country Club** *୧୧* (© **787/285-2256**). Today, both the older course, the Gary Player–designed Palm course, and the newer course, the Reese Jones–designed Flamboyant course, have pars of 72 and layouts of around 2,250 yards (2,057m) each. Crack golfers consider holes 11 to 15 of the Palm course among the toughest five successive holes in the Caribbean. The pro shop that services both courses is open daily from 6:30am to 6pm. To play the course costs $85 for guests of Villas at Palmas of Four Points by Sheraton or $100 for nonguests.

HIKING   Palmas del Mar's land is an attraction in its own right. Here you'll find more than 6 miles (9.7km) of Caribbean ocean frontage—3½ miles (5.6km) of sandy beach amid rocky cliffs and promontories. Large tracts of the 2,700-acre (1,092-hectare) property have harbored sugar and coconut plantations over the years, and a wet tropical forest preserve with giant ferns, orchids, and hanging vines covers about 70 acres (28 hectares) near the resort's geographic center.

SCUBA DIVING & SNORKELING   Some of the best dives in Puerto Rico are right off the eastern coast. Two dozen dive sites south of Fajardo are within a 5-mile (8km) radius offshore. See "The Best Scuba Diving" section in chapter 1.

Set adjacent to a collection of boutiques, bars, and restaurants at the edge of Palmas del Mar's harbor, **Palmas Dive Center** ⟨𝒻⟩, Anchors Village, 110 Harbor Dr. (ℂ **787/863-3483**), owns a 44-foot-long dive boat with a 16-foot (4.9m) beam to make it stable in rough seas. They offer both morning and afternoon sessions of two-tank dives (for experienced and certified divers only), priced at $99 each. Half-day snorkeling trips, priced at $60 per participant and departing for both morning and afternoon sessions, go whenever there's demand to the fauna-rich reefs that encircle Monkey Island, an offshore uninhabited cay.

TENNIS   The **Tennis Center at Palmas del Mar** ⟨𝒻𝒻⟩ (ℂ **787/852-6000,** ext. 51), the largest in Puerto Rico, features 13 hard courts, two Omni courts, and four clay courts, open to resort guests and nonguests. Fees for guests are $20 per hour during the day and $25 per hour at night. Fees for nonguests are $25 per hour during the day and $33 per hour at night. Within the resort's tennis compound is a **fitness center,** which has the best-equipped gym in the region; it's open Monday to Friday 6am to 9pm, and Saturday and Sunday 6am to 8pm.

WHERE TO STAY

It's still possible to rent either a studio or villa from the **Villas at Palmas del Mar,** 295 Palmas Inn Way, Suite 6, Carretera no. 3 Km 86.4, Candelero, Humacao, PR 00791 (ℂ **800/468-3331;** fax 787/852-0927). Some 40 studios and villas are available. Renting year-round for $245 to $340, studios come with one bedroom, a kitchenette, and full bathroom. Air-conditioning and cable TV are available. Villas rent year-round for $290 to $595, come with anywhere from one to three bedrooms, and have full kitchens and dining rooms. On the grounds are six pools, two golf courses, 20 tennis courts, a fitness center, and a dive shop. Fishing, bike or car rentals, babysitting, and horseback riding can be arranged.

Four Points by Sheraton Palmas del Mar Resort ⟨𝒻⟩   This long-dormant property came alive again in the spring of 2006, reincarnated by Sheraton. Completely restored and imbued with a post-millennium update, the resort offers bedrooms that are spacious and handsomely furnished. The junior suites are especially comfortable and inviting. A plethora of on-site activities may keep you from ever leaving the premises: Championship golf courses, a country club, a casino and pool bar, along with an "infinity pool," are just some of the offerings.

Furnishings are tasteful and exceedingly comfortable, typical of Sheraton's deluxe hotels. Available extras include private balconies, luxury bathrooms, and work desks. The hotel also offers business services for commercial travelers, plus a special pool for kids. The hotel restaurant offers a varied international menu (some dine here every night), and you'll also find a wine and cigar bar.

Candelero Dr. 170, Humacao, PR 00791. ℂ 787/850-6000. Fax 787/850-6001. www.starwoodhotels.com. 107 units. Year-round $160–$240 double; winter $355 suite; off season $270 suite. AE, MC, V. Self-parking $12; valet parking $15. **Amenities:** Restaurant; 2 bars; outdoor pool; kids' pool; golf; tennis; fitness center; scuba diving; business services; 24-hr. room service; laundry service; dry cleaning; nonsmoking rooms; casino; rooms for those w/limited mobility. In room: A/C, TV, dataport, fridge, beverage maker, hair dryer, iron, safe.

WHERE TO DINE

Thanks to the kitchens that are built into virtually every unit in Palmas del Mar, many guests prepare at least some of their meals "at home." This is made relatively feasible thanks to the on-site general store at the Palmanova Plaza, which sells everything from fresh lettuce and sundries to liquor and cigarettes.

> ### Finds Where the Locals Go for Soul Food
>
> To escape the confines of the resort for the evening, drive over to a local dive, **Trulio's Sea Food** (© 787/850-1840), just off Route 3 on Calle Isidro Andreu in the hamlet of Punta Santiago. This is strictly no-frills. Though very low in cost, the food is top-notch and even memorable, especially the fried plantain filled with sea conch. The shrimp in garlic sauce will have you asking for more, and you can also order perfectly baked lobster in garlic sauce. Also try the grilled whole red snapper in garlic and onions. You get the point now: Garlic is king here. Puerto Ricans rave about the chef's dessert specialty, which is pound cake soaked in sweet milk. It tastes better than it sounds and is like soul food to the locals because it's just like Mom used to make.

Blue Hawaii CHINESE   This is the best Chinese restaurant in the region. It combines Polynesian themes (similar to a toned-down Trader Vic's) with an Americanized version of Chinese food that's flavorful and well suited to Puerto Rico's hot, steamy climate. Menu items include lobster with garlic-flavored cheese sauce; blackened salmon or steaks reminiscent of styles in New Orleans; and a superb house version of honey chicken. You'll find the place within the dignified courtyard of the resort's shopping center, with tables for alfresco dining. Your host is Tommy Lo, former chef aboard the now-defunct ocean liner SS *United States*.

La Brochette, in the Palmanova Shopping Center. © 787/285-6644. Reservations recommended. Main courses $13–$39. AE, MC, V. Daily noon–10:30pm.

Chez Daniel ★ FRENCH   It's French, and it's the favorite of the folks who tie up their yachts at the adjacent pier. Normandy-born Daniel Vasse, the owner, along with his French Catalonian wife, Lucette, maintain a dining room that is the most appealing in Palmas del Mar. Chez Daniel shows a faithful allegiance to the tenets of classical French cuisine, placing emphasis on such dishes as bouillabaisse, onion soup, and snails as well as lobster and chicken dishes. For dessert, consider a soufflé au Cointreau.

Marina de Palmas del Mar. © 787/850-3838. Reservations required. Main courses $23–$36 at dinner; $8–$19 at lunch; $42 Sun brunch (includes 1st drink). AE, DISC, MC, V. Wed–Mon 6:30–10pm; Fri–Sun noon–3pm. Closed June.

3 The Southeast

More and more visitors are discovering the bewitching allure of Puerto Rico's wild and wooly southeast coast, with deep sand beaches, powerful waves, and cliffs cutting across the landscape straight down to the coast. There are still empty beaches with lighthouses, but now there are more restaurants and lodging options than just a few years ago.

In Yabucoa, you can also catch the start of the Panoramic Route, a tangle of narrow country roads crisscrossing Puerto Rico's mountainous interior from the east to west coasts (see chapter 4). And if there is one thing that these mountains roads have in common, it's that there's not a straight line to be found amongst them.

Off Route 3, Route 901 climbs steep oceanfront cliffs, cutting back and forth in switchbacks that afford outstanding views of the Caribbean and the islands in the distance. The road again descends into Maunabo, a sleepy coastal village that despite its charms remains off the beaten path for most visitors to Puerto Rico. At Punta Tuna, there is a beautiful lighthouse built in 1892 and a nice public beach beside it, with restaurants, bathroom facilities, and an outdoor picnic area. The wide sand beach here is among the nicest in the region. Elsewhere in town, the beaches are mostly deserted, used more by fishermen than beachgoers. The sand is heavier, darker, and deeper than elsewhere in Puerto Rico, and the currents can be strong. The beaches, protected by palm trees and bluffs, are beautiful, however.

Beyond Maunabo, the main coastal road Route 3 travels through the pretty town of Patillas and then Arroyo, the site of a public beach and government-run vacation center, and then onto Guayma, a once important sugar town that has some beautiful Spanish colonial architecture. Time stands still at its downtown plaza, with beautifully restored buildings and a provincial air. From here, Route 3 hooks up with Highway 52, the quickest way over the mountains and back into San Juan (about a 45-min. drive).

WHERE TO STAY & DINE
MODERATE
Hotel Parador Palmas de Lucía ★ *(Finds*   In the southeastern corner of Puerto Rico, where accommodations are scarce, this parador is a knockout discovery. It lies at the eastern end of Ruta Panorámica, a network of scenic, winding roads along which you can take in some of the finest views in the Caribbean before coming to rest at Palmas de Luca, just steps from the pleasant sands of Playa Lucía. This is one of the newest hotels in eastern Puerto Rico, filling a vast gap in accommodations in this remote part of the island. The López family is your host, and their complex combines colonial styling with tropical decoration. Each midsize bedroom is well furnished and has a pool-view balcony and an efficiently organized, tiled, shower-only bathroom. The López family, under its Tropical Inns Puerto Rico company, also runs two nearby small hotels we also recommend, **Parador Costa del Mar** in Yabucoa and **Mauna Caribe** in nearby Maunabo. All are clean, well managed, and surprisingly affordable for what you get.

Palmas de Lucía, routes 901 and 9911, Camino Nuevo, Yabucoa, PR 00767. (© **787/893-4423.** Fax 787/893-0291. www.palmasdelucia.com. 34 units (shower only). Year-round $102 double. AE, MC, V. From Humacao, take Rte. 53 south to Yabucoa, to the end of the hwy., where you connect with Rte. 901 to Maunabo. After a 2-min. drive, turn left at the signposted Carretera 9911, which leads to Playa Lucía. **Amenities:** Restaurant; bar; pool; basketball court. *In room:* A/C, TV.

El Nuevo Horizonte *(Finds* PUERTO RICAN/SEAFOOD   With the best view in southeast Puerto Rico and great food, this restaurant in the coastal hills of Yabucoa is probably our favorite of the typical Puerto Rican eateries on the island. Seafood is the star here. The house special is the paella rey, or king paella, prepared to moist perfection and loaded with lobster, clams, shrimp, and mussels. The stuffed *mofongo* with seafood is among the island's best, and the restaurant has a great stuffed lobster dish as well. While the restaurant is simple, the view is outstanding. The dining room is perched on a cliff overlooking the Caribbean, and you can see clear out to Vieques and the other islands. The restaurant has an outdoor deck that serves drinks and food in a more informal environment.

Rte. 901 Km. 8.8, Yabucoa. (© **787/893-5492.** Reservations not necessary. Main courses $12–$45. AE, MC, V. Thurs–Sat 11am–9pm; Sun 11am–8pm.

13

Vieques & Culebra

Long the best-kept secret of local travelers and a few in-the-know visitors from the East Coast, Puerto Rico's island municipalities Vieques and Culebra are finally getting their due.

The towns remain blissfully undeveloped (without a fast food restaurant or traffic light between them) and both still retain the air of Puerto Rico back in the 1950s.

You will find sandy beaches and breathtaking coastal waters, as well as low prices. Vieques has a bit more action than Culebra, but both are places to kick back and relax.

Now known as the Spanish Virgin Islands, the two islands have created a buzz with their unspoiled beaches and stylish inns. When you spot Sandra Bernhard on the beach, you know the times are changin'.

Vieques, which has more tourist facilities than Culebra, lies 7 miles (11km) off the eastern coast of the Puerto Rican "mainland." It is visited mainly for its 40-odd white-sand beaches. Vieques was occupied at various times by the French and the British before Puerto Rico acquired it in 1854. The ruins of many sugar and pineapple plantations testify to its once-flourishing agricultural economy.

The U.S. military took control of two-thirds of the island's 26,000 acres (10,522 hectares) in 1941. The area was used for military training with live-fire maneuvers. After massive protests, the U.S. announced in 2003 that it was shutting down its Roosevelt Roads Naval Station, the site of the Atlantic Fleet Weapons Training Facility.

Culebra, 18 miles (29km) east of the Puerto Rican "mainland" and 14 miles (23km) west of St. Thomas in the U.S. Virgin Islands, is surrounded by coral reefs and edged with nearly deserted, powdery, white-sand beaches. Much of the island has been designated a wildlife refuge by the U.S. Fish and Wildlife Service.

1 Vieques (*

41 miles (66km) E of San Juan, 7 miles (11km) SE of Fajardo

About 7 miles (11km) east of the big island of Puerto Rico lies Vieques (Bee-*ay*-kase), an island about twice as large as New York's Manhattan, with about 9,300 inhabitants and some 40 palm-lined white-sand beaches.

From World War II until 2003, about two-thirds of the 21-mile-long (34km) island was controlled by U.S. military forces. Much of the government-owned land is now leased for cattle grazing.

Unlike the U.S. military, the Spanish conquistadores didn't think much of Vieques. They came here in the 16th century but didn't stay long, reporting that the island and neighboring bits of land held no gold and were, therefore, *las islas inútiles* (the useless islands). The name Vieques comes from the native Amerindian word *bieques* meaning "small island."

Vieques & Culebra

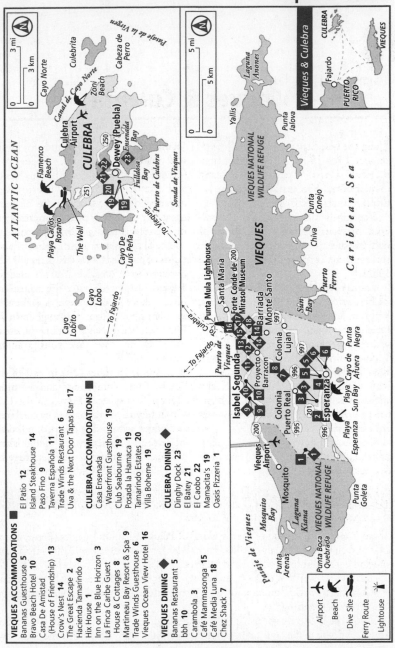

VIEQUES ACCOMMODATIONS ■
Bananas Guesthouse **5**
Bravo Beach Hotel **10**
Casa De Amistad
(House of Friendship) **13**
Crow's Nest **14**
The Great Escape **2**
Hacienda Tamarindo **4**
Hix House **1**
Inn on the Blue Horizon **3**
La Finca Caribe Guest
House & Cottages **8**
Martineau Bay Resort & Spa **9**
Trade Winds Guesthouse **6**
Vieques Ocean View Hotel **16**

VIEQUES DINING ◆
Bananas Restaurant **5**
bbh **10**
Carambola **3**
Café Mammasonga **15**
Café Media Luna **18**
Chez Shack **7**

El Patio **12**
Island Steakhouse **14**
Paso Fino **9**
Taverna Española **11**
Trade Winds Restaurant **6**
Uva & the Next Door Tapas Bar **17**

CULEBRA ACCOMMODATIONS ■
Casa Ensenada
Waterfront Guesthouse **19**
Club Seabourne **19**
Posada la Hamaca **19**
Tamarindo Estates **20**
Villa Boheme **19**

CULEBRA DINING ◆
Dinghy Dock **23**
El Batey **21**
El Caobo **22**
Mamacita's **19**
Oasis Pizzeria **1**

279

The Spaniards later changed their minds and founded the main town, **Isabel Segunda,** on the northern shore. Construction on the last Spanish fort built in the New World began here around 1843, during the reign of Queen Isabella II, for whom the town was named. The fort, never completed, is not of any special interest. The island's fishermen and farmers conduct much of their business here. The **Punta Mula lighthouse,** north of Isabel Segunda, provides panoramic views of the land and sea.

On the south coast, **Esperanza,** once a center for the island's sugar-cane industry and now a pretty little fishing village, lies near **Sun Bay (Sombe) public beach** ⚓. Sun Bay, a government-run, panoramic crescent of sand, is the beach to visit if you have only 1 day to spend on the island. The fenced area has picnic tables, a bathhouse, and a parking lot. A resort, marina, and other facilities add to the allure of the many scalloped stretches of sandy waterfront.

ESSENTIALS

GETTING THERE   Unless you're on a budget, skip the ferry and fly to Vieques, especially if your time is limited. The money you'll save will buy you another day on one of its beautiful beaches, a bargain for the $100 tops airfare. Flights to Vieques leave from Isla Grande Airport near the heart of San Juan as well as the main Luis Muñoz Marín International Airport near Isla Verde. Your best hassle-free option is Isla Grande.

Vieques Air Link (© **888/901-9247** or 787/741-8331) has the most flights and the best prices. It operates three daily flights from LMM International as well as six flights from the smaller and more convenient Isla Grande Airport. The VAL flight from Isla Grande, about $98 round-trip, is the most reliable and convenient travel option to Vieques. It's about half the rate from LMM International, which is $180. **Isla Nena** (© **787/741-8331**) is an on-demand airline that flies to Vieques from the Luis Muñoz Marín International Airport outside Isla Verde (round-trip at $180 is no bargain, however.) **M&N Aviation** (© **787/791-7008**) is another option and has some of the best aircraft servicing the island.

The **Puerto Rico Port Authority** operates two **ferries** a day to Vieques from the eastern port of Fajardo; the trip takes about an hour. The round-trip fare is $4.50 for adults, $2 for children. Tickets for the morning ferry that leaves Saturday and Sunday sell out quickly, so you should be in line at the ticket window in Fajardo before 8am (it opens at 6:30am) to be certain of a seat on the 9am boat. Otherwise, you'll have to wait until the 1 or 3pm ferry. For more information about these sea links, call © **800/ 981-2005,** or 787/863-0705 (Fajardo), or 787/741-4761 (Vieques). Ferries leave Fajardo for Vieques at 9:30am, 1pm, 4:30pm, and 8pm during the week and at 9am, 3pm, and 6pm on weekends and holidays.

GETTING AROUND   Public cabs or vans called *públicos* transport people around the island. To fully experience Vieques, however, you should rent a jeep, so that you can fully explore it. The mountainous interior, more than a dozen beaches, and the nature reserves on former military bases absolutely require it. To do this, contact **Island Car Rental** (© 787/741-1666), in the hamlet of Florida, about a 12-minute ride southwest of Isabel Segunda, 5 minutes from the airport. The office is next door to the Crow's Nest hotel (p. 285). The cost of the local vehicles begins at $51 per day, plus another $12 for collision-damage-waiver insurance. American Express, Master-Card, and Visa cards are accepted. We also recommend **Marcos Car Rental** (© 787/ 741-1388).

You can also rent a Jeep Wrangler or Cherokee from **Martineau Car Rental,** Rte. 200 Km 3.2 (© **787/741-0078**), with prices also starting out at $50 a day. The rental outlet is the closest to the airport, right outside the Martineau Bay resort. But all the rental agencies will meet you at the airport or ferry if you prearrange a rental (which we recommend).

Aficionados of Vieques praise the island for its wide profusion of sandy beaches. Since the pullout of the U.S. Navy, some of the sites that were formerly off-limits have been made accessible to hikers, cyclists, bird-watchers, beachcombers, and other members of the public.

The best beaches are **Red Beach (Bahia Corcha), Blue Beach (Bahia de la Chiva),** and **Playa Plata.** To reach these, take the tarmac-covered road that juts eastward from a point near the southern third of Route 997. Entrance to this part of the island, formerly occupied by the navy, will be identified as **Refugio Nacional de Vida Silvestre de Vieques,** with warnings near its entrance that camping and littering are not allowed. Drive for about a mile (1.6km) along this road, turning right at the sign pointing to Red Beach (Bahia Corcha). En route, you'll have one of the few opportunities in the world to gun your rented car along the battered tarmac of what used to be a landing strip (a very long one) for the navy. Pretend, if you like, however briefly, that you're on a test track for the Indianapolis 500, exercising, naturally, all due caution.

Continue driving to the crescent-shaped, wide-open-to-view expanses of Red Beach, where about a dozen metal-roofed gazebos, many atop cement slabs and accented with picnic tables, provide shelter from the sun, and where "Job Jonnies" (that is, portable chemical toilets) are available. Red Beach, which has picnic tables, is the most family-friendly beach on the island.

At **Blue Beach** the sands are less wide than those of Red Beach. At Blue Beach mangrove and scrub trees grow close to the water's edge. This beach attracts romantic couples or escapists who fantasize they'll happen across a porno shoot. Devotees appreciate the broken sightlines between the bathing spaces, the labyrinth of narrow, rutted dirt roads leading to the individual bathing sites, and the sense of genteel isolation from other sunbathers.

There are signs, within the park, to minor beaches, **Playa Caracas, Caya Melones,** and even **Playuela,** but the access roads are blocked off by the Park Service.

We like the myriad coves, one of which is **Playa Chiva,** that pepper the coastline between Blue Beach and the end of the line, Playa Plata, which is as far as a conventional visitor can travel within the park. They're secluded from view, and you'll get the distinct feeling that some of the sunbathers might be making love behind the seagrapes, scrub trees, and palmettos.

The most visible public-works project on Vieques is **Sun Bay Beach.** Its entrance lies off the southern stretch of Route 997. You'll recognize it by a metal sign announcing *Balneario Público Sun Bay.* Just beyond this sign, you'll see a park dotted with trees, an absurdly large number of parking spaces (which no one uses), and a formal entryway to the park, which virtually everybody ignores. (It evokes a public housing project—anonymous and unused and unloved.) Locals, as a means of getting closer to the water and the sands, drive along the access road stretching to the left. It parallels a ¾-mile (1.2km) stretch of tree-dotted beachfront, and they park wherever they find a spot that appeals to them. If you continue to drive past the very last parking spot along Sun Bay Beach, a rutted and winding and very hilly road will lead, after a right-hand fork, to **Media Luna Beach** and **Navio Beach,** both pleasant and isolated. A left-hand fork leads to the muddy and rutted parking lot that services Mosquito Bay (or, Phosphorescent Bay).

Playa Esperanza is one of the most frequented beaches on Vieques. It's best for snorkeling, not for beaching it. The beach opens onto the little fishing village of Esperanza on the south coast.

DIVING & OTHER OUTDOOR PURSUITS

The small scale of Vieques, and the fact that virtually everyone on the island is either related to or linked in some way to everybody else, creates a situation whereby many of the island's watersports outfitters are in constant communication with one another. Therefore, **Blue Caribe Kayaks,** Calle Flamboyan 149 (El Malecón; ☏ 787/741-2522), has evolved into a kind of clearinghouse for the island's watersports outfitters. Consequently, if you're interested in kayaking, snorkeling, water-skiing, scuba-diving, fishing, or swimming in the nighttime waters of Vieques's luminescent bays, the staff here can funnel your request to an appropriate, and competitively priced, outfitter. Through them, you'll gain access to, and information about, any of the following activities:

Renting a Kayak: The cost is $10 an hour, $25 for 4 hours (a half-day), and $45 for a full day.

Renting snorkeling equipment: Fins, a mask, and a snorkel rent for $12 for a 24-hour period.

Guided snorkeling tours in a kayak are available from the harborfront of Esperanza to a sizable island offshore. You can take a kayak at the cost of $35 per person, including guide, to Cayo de Afuera. Snorkelers seek out the island for its gin-clear waters, revealing a stunning collection of antler coral. On some days you can see nurse sharks swim by, and you might even spot the increasingly elusive manatee. Some visitors swim to the island, but that takes a lot of stamina.

A 3- to 4-hour spin-casting fishing tour from a kayak, wherein you'll fish for barracuda, grouper, or other reef fish, using segments of squid or octopus as bait costs $50 per person. Tours last from around 3pm to sundown daily.

A well-rehearsed outfit that's good at leading newcomers into the island's most savage landscapes is **Vieques Adventure Company** (no physical address; ☏ 787/692-9162; www.bikevieques.com). Gary Lowe and members of his staff lead mountain bikers on half-day ($75 per person) and full-day ($105 per person) tours of obscure trails that are noteworthy for their panoramas and technical difficulties. Use of a mountain bike, usually an aluminum-framed, 28-speed, state-of-the-art model, is included in the price. You can rent one of these bikes, without the services of a trail guide, for $25 per day. The company also rents sea kayaks ($45 daily). Anglers will want to try a kayak fly-fishing tour at a price of $150 for a half day, a truly unique experience.

If you want to go diving, the best scuba operator is **Nancy's Charters** (149 Calle Flamboyan, Vieques; ☏ 787/741-2390).

THE LUMINOUS WATERS OF PHOSPHORESCENT BAY ⚘

One of the major attractions on the island is **Mosquito Bay** ⚘, also called **Phosphorescent Bay,** with its glowing waters produced by tiny bioluminescent organisms. These organisms dart away from boats, leaving eerie blue-white trails of phosphorescence. The *Vieques Times* wrote: "By any name the bay can be a magical, psychedelic experience and few places in the world can even come close to the intensity of concentration of the dinoflagellates called pyrodiniums (whirling fire). They are tiny (⅟₅₀₀-in./.13cm) swimming creatures that light up like fireflies when disturbed but nowhere are there so many fireflies. Here a gallon of bay water may contain almost three-quarters of a million." The ideal time to tour is on a cloudy, moonless night. If the moon is shining on a cloudless night, you can save your money as you'll see almost nothing. Some boats go, full moon or not. You should wear a bathing suit because it's possible to swim in these glowing waters.

Island Adventures (© 787/741-0720) operates trips in Phosphorescent Bay aboard *Luminosa*. These trips are not offered around the time of the full moon. The charge is $30, and most jaunts last about 2 hours. A similar tour on a kayak that also costs $30 is offered by **Blue Caribe Kayak** (call © 787/741-2522 for details).

SEEING THE SIGHTS

Fort Conde de Mirasol Museum, Barriada Fuerte at Magnolia 471 (© 787/741-1717), is the major man-made attraction on the island. In the 1840s, Count Mirasol convinced the Spanish government to build a defensive fortress here. Today the carefully restored fort houses a museum of art and history celebrating the story of Vieques. There are Indian relics, displays of the Spanish conquest, and old flags of the Danes, British, and French. The French sugar-cane planters and their African slaves are depicted, and there's even a bust of the great liberator Simón Bolívar, who once visited Puerto Rico. A unique collection of maps shows how the world's cartographers envisioned Vieques. The museum and fort are open Wednesday to Sunday 8:30am to 4:20pm. Admission is $2, or free for ages 11 and under.

WHERE TO STAY
EXPENSIVE

Bravo Beach Hotel 🏖🏖 In a secluded residential area, this boutique hotel with its Frette linens and Philippe Starck designs comes as a surprise—and a pleasant one. Most of the bedrooms are within only 30 feet (9.1m) of the Atlantic with a good white sandy beach. Units open onto a private terrace facing the sea. It's the little things that count here: an honor bar poolside, those Aveda bath products in the bathroom, or the box lunch the staff will pack for you to take to the beach. Rooms are decorated in a minimalist style, effectively using lots of white, draped plantation-era beds, and wicker furnishings. On-site is a two-bedroom cottage, a vision in white, accented by bamboo and mahogany pieces. You can even check your e-mail poolside, or else enjoy Caribbean-inspired tapas served outdoors.

North Shore Rd. 1, Vieques, PR 00765. © 787/741-1128. www.bravobeachhotel.com. 12 units. Year-round $190–$275 double, $300 suites, $550 villas. AE, DC, MC, V. **Amenities:** Restaurant; bar; 2 outdoor pools; nonsmoking rooms. *In room:* A/C, TV, minibar, beverage maker, hair dryer.

Hix House 🏖 *(Finds* No one leaves Hix House without a strong opinion about its value as an eco-sensitive experiment. Angular and avant-garde, and minimalist to the point of looking almost barren, it's one of the most iconoclastic and most admired pieces of eco-sensitive architecture in the Caribbean. It is set on 12 acres (4.9 hectares) of land, formerly used for the cultivation of sugar cane, on a scrub- and tree-covered landscape on a hillside in the center of the island. The inn consists of four separate buildings, designed, respectively, with triangular, circular, or rectangular floor plans. Each of them was created by the celebrated Toronto-based architect John Hix (a "climate and design architect"), who has won awards for the designing of low-maintenance houses in chilly Canada. None of the units has window screens or air-conditioning, and each is—in an aggressive kind of eco-sensitivity that might remind you of a postmodern concrete bunker—outfitted with mosquito netting, low-wattage lighting (brighter lights attract mosquitoes), and virtually indestructible furniture that's crafted either from poured and polished concrete or pressure-treated lumber. And other than yoga classes, conducted 3 mornings a week from 10:30am till noon, there's virtually nothing to do other than the entertainment you create yourself.

Rooms come with refrigerators that are stocked with milk, orange juice, eggs, cereal, freshly baked bread, and fruit. None has a bathtub, and showers are artfully rustic affairs set within open-air concrete alcoves.

Rte. 995 Km 1.5, Vieques, PR 14902. (✆ 787/741-2302. Fax 787/741-2797. www.hixislandhouse.com. 13 units. Winter $255–$310 double; off season $195–$255 double. AE, MC, V. **Amenities:** Outdoor pool. *In room:* Open-air showers, ceiling fans.

Inn on the Blue Horizon ☆☆   Set on the island's southern coastal road, less than a mile (1.6km) west of Esperanza, this is the most charming hotel on Vieques, and it's the one that has repeatedly earned the highest accolades from the international press. In winter, it reigns as the most hip and stylish gathering place in Vieques for the low-key rendezvous of North America's fashion photographers and supermodels. Its centerpiece is an airy seafront house, built in a Mediterranean style in 1975, whose soaring living area opens onto a view of the blue horizon.

In the mid-1990s, the site was transformed into an inn by hotel and restaurant entrepreneur James Weis, a refugee from the New York fashion world. It is now run by the same folks behind the successful At Wind Chimes Inn in San Juan. Three of the bedrooms are in the main house; a half-dozen others are in a trio of bungalows, each of which contains two spacious and comfortable units, each with a private balcony and sea view. Airy and clean, they're outfitted with early-19th-century North American antiques and eclectic art from a variety of artists. Two units contain tubs, and the rest are equipped with showers.

Symmetrically positioned arbors are covered with cascades of bougainvillea, with a pool and lawns that slope gracefully down to cliffs at the edge of the sea. The sea adjacent to the hotel has a rocky coastline, but the staff will direct you to the dozens of fine local beaches. The inn's restaurant, Carambola (see "Where to Dine," below), serves the best food on Vieques. There is a great bar with a gorgeous view that serves food throughout the day. The hotel also has a new cliff side with a bar and dining area, and the best views in town.

Rte. 996 (P.O. Box 1556) Km 4.3, Vieques, PR 00765. (✆ **787/741-3318.** Fax 787/741-0522. www.innontheblue horizon.com. 10 units (some with shower only). Winter $160–$375 double; off season $130–$260 double. AE, MC, V. Closed Sept–Oct. **Amenities:** Restaurant; cafe/bar; outdoor pool; tennis; gym. *In room:* A/C, coffeemaker, hair dryer, no phone.

MODERATE

Hacienda Tamarindo ☆   Established in the late 1990s on the site of an expanded nightclub, less than a mile (1.6km) west of Esperanza, this inn has lots of flair, style, and pizzazz. Vermont-born owners Burr and Linda Vail transformed a thick-walled, rather unimaginative-looking concrete building into a replica of a Spanish colonial hacienda, thanks to Linda's skills as a decorator. The inn was built around a massive 200-year-old tamarind tree, whose branches rise majestically through the hotel's atrium. Its production of fruit (Feb–Mar) is heralded with much excitement. Rooms are stylish, tiled, and spacious. Each contains an eclectic mishmash of art and dark-wood antiques, some of which were brought from Vermont. Bathrooms are modern,

clean, and well designed; some contain a tub, others a shower. Although the inn is set about ⅛ mile (.2km) from the sea, there's access to a beach via a footpath, and there's a pool. The restaurant and cafe at the Inn on the Blue Horizon lie within a 5-minute walk. No children under 12 in the off season, under 16 in season.

Rte. 996 Km 4.5, Barrio Puerto Real (P.O. Box 1569), Vieques, PR 00765. ✆ 787/741-0420. Fax 787/741-3215. www.haciendatamarindo.com. 17 units (some with shower only, some with tub only). Winter $185–$210 double, $325 suite; off season $135–$200 double, $275 suite. Rates include full breakfast. AE, MC, V. **Amenities:** Bar; pool; Wi-Fi Internet and computer for guests; beach towels and cooler. *In room:* A/C, hair dryer, iron, no phone.

INEXPENSIVE

Bananas Guesthouse   On the island's south shore, on the main tourist strip of Esperanza and best known for its bar and restaurant (see "Where to Dine," below), this guesthouse has eight simple rooms. Each has a ceiling fan; and some rooms are air-conditioned and have screened-in porches. We urge you to consider one of the air-conditioned rooms rather than those without, as a means of cutting down on heat and noise from the outside. Each unit has a bathroom with a tub. The units are unadorned cubicles with little architectural interest; they provide shelter and calm and a basic level of comfort. The ambience is convivial, the staff friendly and accommodating. The best room is the $100 unit with air-conditioning and deck.

Barrio Esperanza (P.O. Box 1300), Vieques, PR 00765. ✆ 787/741-8700. Fax 787/741-0790. www.bananasguest house.com. 8 units. Year-round $65–$100 double. AE, MC, V. **Amenities:** Restaurant/bar. *In room:* A/C (in 4 units), ceiling fans, no phone.

Casa de Amistad (House of Friendship)   Until it was radically renovated in 2002 by a likable former resident of Wisconsin and Minnesota, Owen Smith, this boxy-looking, two-story cement building functioned as a battered and run-down boarding-house that focused on cheap mattresses and cheap but bountiful meals for itinerant workers. Today, in far better-maintained premises, something of the same spirit still prevails, albeit in cleaner, more hip, and more convivial circumstances. Owen is a very hands-on manager, who, from the premises of a cottage in back, is always available for advice, counseling, or humor. There's the sense, on the building's ground floor, of something akin to a bohemian commune, thanks to the owner's friendly sense of informality, a tucked-away bar in one corner, a communal kitchen where residents are invited to prepare their own meals, a tiny "lending library" stocked with dog-eared paperback books, and a gift shop where some of Owen's artwork is on sale. Bedrooms are angular, tawny-colored units that evoke a summer beach hotel in Provincetown, Massachusetts, or Fire Island, New York: breezy and airy enclaves with simple but comfortable furniture and a sense of well-intentioned *laissez-faire*. Although any hotel on the island will genuinely welcome gay and lesbian clients, this is the guesthouse that does so the most visibly, attracting a clientele that, at least in high season, is about 50% gay. The establishment's social center is within a cement-walled courtyard, around a very small, L-shaped swimming pool sheathed in cerulean-blue tiles.

Calle Benitez Castaño 27, Vieques, PR 00765. ✆ 787/741-3758. www.casadeamistad.com. 7 units. Year-round $70–$80 double; $90 suite. MC, V. **Amenities:** Small outdoor pool; courtyard garden/sun terrace; rooftop sun deck; communal kitchen; TV room; small gift boutique. *In room:* A/C, small unstocked fridge, fan.

Crow's Nest   Set high on 5 acres (2 hectares) of forested hillside, about 1½ miles (2.4km) west/southwest of Isabel Segunda, this inn enjoys a cozy, responsive setting that's favored by many repeat guests. It's one of our favorite places to stay, maybe because it's the closest thing you will get to the old Casa Française, even if it's not too

A New Day for Vieques Wildlife Refuge

On May 1, 2003, the U.S. Navy transferred 15,500 acres (6,273 hectares)—often the best beachfront property—to the U.S. Fish & Wildlife Service, which added them to the **Vieques National Wildlife Refuge** ✹✹✹. This is now the largest landmass of its kind in the Caribbean. Refuge lands lie on both the eastern and western ends of Vieques. In 2001, 3,100 acres (1,255 hectares) on the western end were already turned over to the refuge. These tracts of virgin landscape contain several ecologically distinct habitats, including the island's best white sandy beaches along with upland forests and mangrove wetlands, the latter the habitat of some endangered species such as the sea turtle, the manatee, and the brown pelican. Binocular-bearing bird-watchers also flock to the site. The coastal area of the refuge is characterized by coral reef and sea-grass beds. Within the refuge the best beaches are Red Beach and Blue Beach, both open to the public. The refuge is open to the public and also contains a **Visitor Center at Vieques Office Park,** Rd. 200 Km 0.4 (② **787/741-2138**). The refuge is open 7 days a week during daylight hours (naturally, closings are earlier in winter because of the shorter days).

---

close geographically). Each of the units has some kind of cooking facilities. Rooms are more upscale-looking than those at either Bananas (which is very basic) or Trade Winds, but they're less elegant and charming than those at Inn on the Blue Horizon. Each unit has a neatly tiled, shower-only bathroom. Like most of the other hotels on the island, this one requires a car ride of around 10 minutes for access to the nearest worthwhile beach. There's a wonderful pool area out back, and the grounds are lovely.

Rte. 201 Km 1.6, Barrio Florida, Box 1521, Vieques, PR 00765. ② **787/741-0033.** Fax 787/741-1294. www.crows nestvieques.com. 17 units (shower only). Winter $135 double, $267 suite; off season $109 double, $218 suite. AE, MC, V. **Amenities:** Bar; pool; Wi-Fi Internet. *In room:* A/C, kitchen, coffeemaker, iron, microwave.

The Great Escape ✹ *(Finds* This is the newest bed-and-breakfast on Vieques, and judging by the high-quality furniture, the large size, and the attentive maintenance of the place, one of the most appealing. It occupies a pair of blue-and-white concrete houses, set on the crest of a hill, in a rural neighborhood just north of Esperanza. Your hostess is Danuta Schwartzwald, a Polish émigré who selected Vieques as a place to live after years of self-imposed exile in Switzerland. You might feel just a wee bit isolated here, located as it is behind metal gates, at the end of a long, uphill, and rutted road from Route 201. But the size and solid, surprisingly upscale furnishings—including some mahogany, four-poster beds; tiled floors; upscale bathrooms; and the sense of calm that reigns over the place, might eventually persuade you that, indeed, this is a desirable, although uneventful, place to stay. No meals are served other than breakfast, but the staff and managers of this place will offer advice about nearby venues. Danuta now rents out her own house as well for $400 nightly.

Barrio La Llave, directly off Rte. 201, 2 miles (3.2km) northwest of Esperanza, Vieques, PR 14501. ② **787/741-2927.** www.enchanted-isle.com/greatescape. 11 units. Nov–July $125 double; Aug–Oct $115 double; $200 1-bedroom apts in any season (3-day minimum rental required for all apts). AE, DISC, MC, V. **Amenities:** Pool; bar. *In room:* Ceiling fan.

La Finca Caribe Guest House & Cottages This bare-bones, eco-sensitive establishment caters to budget-conscious travelers and youthful adventurers. *Finca* means "rustic estate" in Spanish. The centerpiece of the property is a guesthouse with a spacious porch, outfitted with hammocks and swinging chairs. An admirably maintained garden wraps itself around the scattered components of the compound. The rustic-looking outbuildings include a bathhouse, a communal kitchen, and two self-contained cottages suitable for up to three ("The Casita") or four ("The Cabana") occupants. Both cottages have private decks and kitchens. There's a nonchlorinated pool on the premises (it stays clean through frequent recirculation of water from a mountain stream) and a crew of entrepreneurs that takes clients on bike tours to obscure parts of Vieques (see "Beaches, Diving & Other Outdoor Pursuits," later in this chapter). La Finca is situated on a forested hillside 3 miles (5km) from Sun Bay.

Rte. 995 Km 1.2 (P.O. Box 1332), Vieques, PR 00765. (C) 787/741-0495. Fax 787/741-3584. www.lafinca.com. 6 units (none with bathroom), 2 cottages. Winter $80 double, $735–$1,295 1-week cottage rental for 2–4 occupants; off season $65 double, $550–$1,085 1-week cottage rental for 2–4 occupants. MC, V. Closed Sept. **Amenities:** Pool; communal kitchen. *In room:* Kitchen (in cottages).

Trade Winds Guesthouse   Along the shore on the south side of the island, in the fishing village of Esperanza, this oceanside guesthouse offers 11 units, 4 of which are air-conditioned and have terraces; some others have terraces and ceiling fans. Bedrooms are white-walled and durable, with absolutely no imagination in terms of decor; the units (all nonsmoking) might remind you of a barracks. They're almost equivalent to the rooms at Bananas, a few buildings away, but they're just a bit better. Each unit has a small, tiled, shower-only bathroom. Because of their low rates, they're usually booked solid, often with divers from the United States or residents of the Puerto Rican mainland who want low rates. This place is well known for its hospitable ambience and its open-air restaurant overlooking the ocean (see "Where to Dine," below).

Calle Flamboyan 107, Barrio Esperanza (P.O. Box 1012), Vieques, PR 00765. (C) 787/741-8666. Fax 787/741-2964. www.enchanted-isle.com/tradewinds. 11 units (shower only). Winter $80–$90 double; off season $60–$70 double. AE, MC, V. **Amenities:** Restaurant; bar; laundry service; dry cleaning. *In room:* A/C (in 4 units), fan (in some), no phone.

Vieques Ocean View Hotel   Situated in the heart of Isabel Segunda, directly on the coast and a block from the wharf where the ferry lands, this three-story building is one of the tallest on Vieques. Built in the early 1980s, it offers simple rooms with uncomplicated furniture and balconies overlooking either the sea or the town. Most of the rooms are air-conditioned, and each has a small shower-only bathroom. The hotel restaurant serves Chinese and Creole food daily from 11am to 11pm.

Calle Plinio Peterson 57, Isabel Segunda (P.O. Box 124), Vieques, PR 00765. (C) 787/741-3696. Fax 787/741-1793. 35 units (shower only). Year-round $90 double. AE, MC, V. **Amenities:** Restaurant; bar; pool. *In room:* A/C, TV, no phone.

WHERE TO DINE
EXPENSIVE

Café Media Luna (★) (*Finds*) ASIAN/CARIBBEAN/INTERNATIONAL   This laidback joint grew out of a dumpy building in Isabel Segunda. Today it's a charming little eatery, created by Ricardo Betancourt, a photographer turned restaurateur, and his wife, Monica, born in Bombay. There are now three separate areas to eat, a charming dining room, lounge, or rooftop terrace. The kitchen turns out a terrific medley of international dishes, with Italian and Caribbean flavors. It's good and healthy. The appetizers are freshly made concoctions, based on the best shopping on any given day. We like to arrive here with a party, order several appetizers, and share the goodies. The fresh fish and well-flavored meats round out the main dishes. Ask what is good on any given day; the staff gives good advice. Depending on road conditions, allow 15 to 20 minutes when driving from Esperanza.

Calle Antonio G. Mellado 351, Isabel Segunda. ℂ 787/741-2594. Reservations required. Main courses $24–$27; tasting menu $60–$70. AE, MC, V. May–Aug Thurs–Sun 7–10pm; Oct–Apr Wed–Sun 7–10pm. Closed Sept.

Carambola ℛℛ INTERNATIONAL   In the premises of the Inn on the Blue Horizon (see "Where to Stay," above), this restaurant serves the best food on Vieques. Also on-site is a bar that a team of journalists declared as one of their favorites in the world, so consider starting your evening with a drink or two in the octagonal Blue Moon Bar. Meals are served within the inn's main building or beneath an awning on a seafront terrace lined with plants. We loved the pork loin in rum chutney and the lamb chop bathed in herbs and grilled. There is a daily stuffed *mofongo* special. Expect a crowd of fashion-industry folk, temporarily absent from New York and Los Angeles, and local residents, all mixing in ways that are gregarious, stylish, and usually a lot of fun.

In the Inn on the Blue Horizon, Rte. 996 Km 4.3. ℂ 787/741-3318. Reservations required. Main courses $24–$33. AE, MC, V. 1 mile (1.6km) west of Esperanza. Wed–Sun 6–10pm. Closed Sept–Oct.

Island Steak House INTERNATIONAL   Set in the cool and breezy highlands of Vieques, on a verdant hillside with sweeping views of the island's interior, this restaurant is perched within a gracefully proportioned open-sided building that gives the impression of something midway between a simplified gazebo and a treehouse. It's prefaced with a bar, where the once-a-week happy hour (Tues evenings 5–7pm) is an island-wide event, thanks partly to an ongoing roster of free hors d'oeuvres. Menu items include up to four different kinds of steak, lamb chops, chicken breasts stuffed with goat cheese and cherry tomatoes, jumbo fried shrimp, and Vieques lobster basted with a sauce made from spiced rum and butter. Burgers are also an option.

In the Crow's Nest hotel. Rte. 201 Km 1.6, Barrio Florida. ℂ 787/741-0033. Reservations recommended. Burgers $8–$9; main courses $17–$39. AE, MC, V. Fri–Tues 6–9:30pm. Bar stays open till midnight.

INEXPENSIVE

Bananas Restaurant INTERNATIONAL   This is an informal and unpretentious restaurant that falls midway between a burger-and-salad joint and a steakhouse, depending on the kind of food you select. Associated with a simple, also-recommended guesthouse, it's positioned on a narrow veranda, astride the sleepy, seafront boulevard of Esperanza's main drag, behind a screen of verdant plants. There's a definite link here with the Old Town of Key West, Florida, thanks to the establishment's recent acquisition by Glenn Curry (descendant of a family that was prominent there in the late 19th c.) and his Philadelphia-born wife, Wynne. Together, they run a down-to-earth, but not particularly whimsical, establishment with a busy bar trade. Expect a menu that includes Caesar salads, served with or without a garnish of grilled or jerk-marinated chicken; grilled pork chops; grilled fish; steaks; baby back ribs; pizzas; and sandwiches that include BLTs, burgers, and chicken-breast sandwiches. Expect slow service.

Calle Flamboyan (El Malecón), in Esperanza. ℂ 787/741-8700. Reservations not necessary. Salads and sandwiches $5–$11; main courses $15–$17. MC, V. Daily noon–10pm.

bbh ℛℛ CARIBBEAN/INTERNATIONAL   This is Vieques at its most idyllic. A flawless reception and service are backed up by the island's most imaginative cuisine, which shows the range of Executive Chef Christopher Ellis. The restaurant also offers the largest wine selection on island, the bottles stacked in a walk-in wine-tasting cooler. Tapas by the sea are a special feature of the menu. Our party dug into the Jamaican jerk chicken lettuce wraps with mango, tomato, and herbed sour cream or the seared ahi tuna with a soba noodle salad. Also memorable were those grilled portobello mushrooms with blue cheese and a side of creamy polenta. Roasted beef tenderloin came with a garlic root mash, and other specials included a grilled pork medallion with pineapple relish.

In the Bravo Beach Hotel, North Shore Rd. 1. ℂ 787/741-1128. Reservations recommended at dinner. Main courses $7–$18. AE, DC, MC, V. Wed–Sat 11am–3pm and 6–11pm; Sun 11:30 am–2:30 pm.

Chez Shack INTERNATIONAL   Chez Shack wins, almost without competition, as the most bohemian and countercultural restaurant on Vieques. The setting is exactly what the name implies—a battered wood-sided utility building that evolved from a virtual ruin after it was acquired by a grizzled and outspoken entrepreneur, Hugh Duffy, who was instrumental in the career of the Mamas and the Papas. This group, when still getting its act together, worked at Duffy's Love Shack in St. Thomas, where Mama Cass was said to have been the world's worst waitress. Today, replete with naughty anecdotes that are among the most valuable currency-in-trade on the island, the site is defined as a local monument. Chez Shack opens for business on summer nights even when other restaurants are closed. Menu items include tried-and-true favorites, many of which attract repeat diners who memorized the menu long ago. Examples include baked crab, seafood cocktail, steaks, fish filets, and barbecued ribs. You'll find the place near the edge of the highway, within the closest thing on Vieques to a tropical rainforest. The best time to go is for Monday barbecue nights, with great food and a live band playing reggae music.

Hwy. 995 (Airport Rd.), north of Esperanza. ℂ 787/741-2175. Reservations recommended. Main courses $18–$22. MC, V. Mon–Fri 6–10pm. Closed Sept–Oct.

El Patio PUERTO RICAN   This is a simple, uncomplicated, and completely unpretentious Hispanic luncheonette that manages to feed impressive numbers of local residents every day at breakfast and lunch, often with lots of banter about island personalities and politics. It lies beside the western terminus of the road (Rte. 200) that leads eastward from the rest of Vieques into the island's biggest settlement, Isabel Segunda. Expect a cramped and somewhat dusty street-side patio and a Formica-sheathed interior that includes a TV set that drones on throughout the morning and afternoon. But as a breakfast or lunch stopover that's cheap, filling, friendly, and intensely local, we recommend it highly. Gui Sanchez (who was born in Vieques) and Noemi (his wife, who originally came from the Puerto Rico "mainland"), plus extended members of their family, are your hosts. Breakfasts focus on a predictable array of eggs and bacon. Lunches and (early) suppers might include marinated octopus or seafood salads or shrimp, served either buttered, battered, or fried with garlic. There's also *asopao de mariscos* (shellfish stew, with rice); steaks; meat patties served "Parmesan" style with tomato sauce and cheese; and, when it's available, cold lobster with mayonnaise.

Calle Antonio G. Mellado 340 (Rte. 200, in Isabel Segunda). ℂ 787/741-6381. Reservations not accepted. Breakfast platters $1.50–$6; main courses $6–$20. MC, V. Mon–Fri 6:30am–6pm.

Taverna Española SPANISH/PUERTO RICAN   This is the restaurant that every local resident talks about in almost reverential terms. Part of that has to do with the quirky eccentricities of the steely willed matriarch who owns it, and part of it has to do with the sense of bounty and good flavors that emerge in an endless procession of steaming platters from the cramped kitchens. Don't expect anything fancy. There's something that hints at this boxy-looking place's decidedly unglamorous origins as a warehouse, despite a recent cosmetic overlay. Staff members can become hysterical under pressure, and food is sometimes slung rather than served. But despite that, the place remains a popular staple on the dining scene of Isabel Segunda, thanks to dishes that include breaded shrimp; *pastellitos* (stuffed dumplings) with chicken or beef; *chorizos* (spicy Spanish sausages); fried fish in *mojo* (Creole) sauce; and shellfish stew (*asopao de mariscos*).

Calle Carlos Libron, Isabel Segunda. ⓒ 787/741-1175. Reservations recommended on weekends. Main courses $12–$15. AE, MC, V. Daily 5–11pm.

Trade Winds Restaurant STEAK/SEAFOOD   This restaurant is often recommended by hotel owners across the island and therefore manages to feed the residents of a large cross section of island hotels. It lies beside the oceanfront esplanade in the fishing village of Esperanza. A dining experience here often begins with a drink at the open-air Topside Bar. For dinner, the chef's specialties revolve around steak; fish; and lobster, which are often served with butter-flavored rum sauce. The best steak is an 8-ounce filet, cooked just right over the charbroiler and served with a baked potato and a house or Caesar salad; also available is herb-marinated pork loin with mashed potatoes. The fresh fish special varies and is usually a good item to order, as is the jumbo shrimp sautéed with garlic and lemon, or served with curry sauce. Black-bean soup is a good opener.

In Trade Winds Guesthouse, Calle Flamboyan, Barrio Esperanza. ⓒ 787/741-8666. Reservations recommended. Main courses $13–$28. AE, MC, V. Dec–May daily 8am–2pm and 6–9:30pm; June–Nov Fri–Sun 6–9:30pm.

SHOPPING

There aren't a lot of shopping possibilities on Vieques; however, you might want to visit **Siddhia Hutchinson Fine Art Studio & Gallery,** Calle 3, A15, Isabel Segunda (ⓒ 787/741-8780), located between the lighthouse and the ferry dock. Here you can purchase prints of local seascapes and landscapes, native flowers, fish, and birds. There are also lovely bowls, mugs, and platters for sale.

VIEQUES AFTER DARK

Al's Mar Azul   This is the most successful Anglo-Hispanic bar on Vieques, with a reputation that extends from the waterfront of Isabel Segunda to San Juan, New York City, and some of the capitals of Europe. That's a remarkable achievement for a raffish-looking, cement-built, open-sided bungalow that's perched on a low cliff above the sea, a short uphill walk from the piers where the ferryboats land from the "mainland" (Fajardo). Within a mostly blue environment of fish nets, wide-open views of the harbor, ceiling fans, and nautical memorabilia, within sightlines of a pool table, you'll find a setting that might have been inspired by beachfront venues in either Florida or Southern California. There's a brisk demand for rum punches, frozen piña coladas, and a "Key Lime Pie" that's made from sour mix, milk, and vanilla liqueur. Each is priced at between $4.50 and $5. Open Sunday through Thursday 11am to 1am, and Friday and Saturday 11am to 2:30am. On the Waterfront, adjacent to the ferryboat piers, in Isabel Segunda. ⓒ 787/741-3400.

Bar Plaza   If you travel enough in the Spanish-speaking Caribbean, you'll occasionally stumble across the kind of old-fashioned bar that Hemingway used to celebrate.

Macho, unpretentious, and nostalgic, with a history going back to the 1940s, and murals that advertise products from now-defunct companies, it virtually drips with a sense of frozen time. High-ceilinged, shadowy, and cool, even on the hottest day, it might be a direct transplant from colonial Havana or Madrid during the Spanish Civil War. There's a pool table in the corner, an old-fashioned cement trough that functions as the men's urinal, and a staff and stoic regular patrons that indeed show their age. No food of any kind is served—only drinks. Beer costs about $3.50. Open daily 9am to 9pm. Plaza del Recreo, in Isabel Segunda. ℂ **787/741-2176.**

2 Culebra ⟨★

52 miles (84km) E of San Juan, 18 miles (29km) E of Fajardo

A tranquil, inviting little island, Culebra lies in a mini-archipelago of 24 chunks of land, rocks, and cays, 18 miles (29km) east of Puerto Rico's main island and halfway to St. Thomas, U.S. Virgin Islands. It's just 7 miles (11km) long and 3 miles (5km) wide and has only 2,000 residents. The landscape is dotted with everything from scrub and cacti to poincianas, frangipanis, and coconut palms.

Today vacationers and boaters can explore the island's beauties, both on land and underwater. Culebra's white-sand beaches (especially Flamenco Beach), its clear waters, and its long coral reefs invite swimmers, snorkelers, and scuba divers.

Culebra, in what was once called the Spanish Virgin Islands, was settled as a Spanish colony in 1886, but like Puerto Rico and Vieques, it became part of the United States after the Spanish-American War in 1898. In fact, Culebra's only town, a fishing village called **Dewey,** was named for Admiral George Dewey, a U.S. hero of that war, although the locals defiantly call it **Puebla.**

Both illustrious and notorious characters visited Culebra in the past. It is believed that Columbus spotted the island on his second voyage to the New World in 1493. When the Spanish started colonizing Puerto Rico, many of the Taíno Indians fled to Culebra as a last refuge. It wasn't many decades later that the swashbuckling Sir Henry Morgan and other notorious pirates used Culebra as a hide-out. The island supposedly still shelters their buried loot.

From 1909 to 1975, the U.S. Navy used Culebra as a gunnery range and as a practice bomb site in World War II. Today the four tracts of the **Culebra Wildlife Refuge,** plus 23 other offshore islands, are managed by the U.S. Fish and Wildlife Service. The refuge is one of the most important turtle-nesting sites in the Caribbean, and it also houses large seabird colonies, notably terns and boobies.

Culebrita, a mile-long (1.6km) coral-isle satellite of Culebra, has a hilltop light-house and crescent beaches.

ESSENTIALS
GETTING THERE   **Vieques Air-Link** (ℂ **787/741-8331**) flies to Culebra twice a day from San Juan's Isla Grande Airport. Round-trip is $105. We recommend flying as you will spend the day traveling to get to the island otherwise.

The **Puerto Rico Port Authority** operates one or two **ferries** per day (depending on the day of the week) from the mainland port of Fajardo to Culebra; the trip takes about an hour. The round-trip fare is $4.50 for adults, $2.25 for children 3 to 12 (free for 2 and under). For reservations, call ℂ **800/981-2005,** or 787/742-3161, or 787/ 863-0705 (Fajardo).

GETTING AROUND   With no public transportation, the only way to get to Culebra's beaches is by bike or rental car.

There are a number of little **car-rental** agencies on the island, although they seem to open and close when the spirit moves them. **Carlos Jeep Rental,** Parcela 2, Barriada Clark, Dewey (© 787/742-3514), lies a 3-minute ride from the airport. The outfitter rents Jeeps for $45 to $79 per day. If you give them notice, they will meet you at the airport. When you drop off your rental, the staff will also drive you back to the airport. Charging exactly the same prices is another reliable operator, **Coral Reef,** Carretera Pedro Marquez 3, Dewey (© 787/742-0055). A final option for vehicles is **Willie's Jeep Rental,** Calle Escudero, Barriada Clark, Dewey (© 787/742-3537), lying a 5-minute walk from the airport. Vehicles here begin at $45 per day.

Bike riding is a popular means of getting around the island's hills, dirt trails, and bad roads. You can rent mountain bikes at **Dick and Cathy** (© 787/742-0062) for $15 for 24 hours. To rent from them, call them, and one of them will come by your hotel with your bike.

BEACHES, DIVING & OTHER OUTDOOR PURSUITS

The island's most popular and best beach is **Flamenco Beach** ⚓, a mile-long (1.6km) horseshoe-shaped cove on the northwestern edge. It's popular partly because of its nearness to Dewey, partly because of its soft sands. If you find Flamenco too crowded, all you need do is walk over the hill to **Playa Carlos Rosario** ⚓. The sands here aren't quite as good as those at Flamenco, but the snorkeling is even better in these clear waters. A barrier reef protects this beach, so you are almost guaranteed tranquil waters. Snorkelers can also walk south from Playa Carlos Rosario for ¼ mile (.4km) to a place called **"The Wall"** ⚓. There are 40-foot (12m) drop-offs into the water where you are likely to see schools of fish gliding by.

The isolated **Zoni Beach** is a 1-mile (1.6km) strip of sand flanked by large boulders and scrub. Located on the island's northeastern edge, about 7 miles (11km) from Dewey (Puebla), it's one of the most beautiful beaches on the island. Snorkelers, but not scuba divers, find it particularly intriguing; despite the surf that makes underwater visibility a bit murky during rough weather.

Known for its beautiful corals, unspoiled underwater vistas, and absence of other divers, Culebra is what the Caribbean used to be before crowds of divers began exploring the sea. At least 50 dive sites, all around the island, are worthwhile. **Culebra Divers,** Calle Escobar 138 (© 787/742-0803), offers a resort course for novice divers, including training in a sheltered cove and a tank dive in 15 to 20 feet (4.6–6.1m) of water ($95). Full PADI certification costs $550 and requires 4 days of participation in both classroom and ocean experience. Certified divers pay $95 for a two-tank open-water dive. The outfitter provides all the equipment you need for any of the dive experiences. It's rare that more than six divers go out in one of these boats on any day.

Kayak trips are offered by **Jim Petersen's Oceans Safaris,** Calle Escudero 189, Dewey (© 787/379-1973). Kayaks for can be rented for $60 per day the first day, $40 afterwards, and Jim will tell you the best spots to enjoy this sport. He also offers a full-day tour for $105, taking you to such remote islets as Isla Culebrita or Cayo Luis Peña.

WHERE TO STAY

If you operate happily within a rented villa, preparing your own meals, consider making a call to **Culebra Island Realty** (© 787/742-0052; www.culebraislandrealty.com).

Jim Galasso, the rental agent, knows what's happening with most of the island's rental villas and can probably come up with something that's appropriate for your needs.

MODERATE
Club Seabourne
About an 8-minute drive from the center of town, this concrete-and-wood structure is set in a garden of crotons and palms, at the mouth of one of the island's best harbors, Ensenada Bay. It offers scattered villas and four rooms inside the clubhouse. Each unit has a small, tiled, shower-only bathroom.

Overlooking Fulladosa Bay, the club's dining room serves some of the best food on Culebra, with fresh lobster, shrimp, snapper, grouper, and conch, as well as steaks. The hotel also has a patio bar with a nightly happy hour, plus one of two pools on the island. Dive packages and day sails can be arranged at the office.

Fulladosa Rd. (P.O. Box 357), Culebra, PR 00775. (☎) 787/742-3169. Fax 787/742-0210. www.clubseabourne.com. 12 units (shower only). Winter $189–$219 villa; off season $165–$195 double. Rates include continental breakfast. AE, MC, V. From Dewey (Puebla), follow Fulladosa Rd. along the south side of the bay for 1½ miles (2.4km). **Amenities:** Restaurant; bar; pool; 1 room for those w/limited mobility. *In room:* A/C, fridge, safe, no phone.

Tamarindo Estates ✦ (Finds)
On 60 lush acres (24 hectares) beside a private bay, this is a small, intimate Puerto Rican beachfront resort of kitchen-equipped cottages. Living here is like occupying your second home, with laid-back island living. There is a simple, even pristine, aura here, but comfort nonetheless with panoramic views from the roofed verandas. Each unit has either one or two bedrooms, and when *Travel + Leisure* staffers visited, they named this property one of the 20 great and affordable gateways in the Caribbean. The mecca of this nicely secluded place is a swimming pool with an ocean view and a roofed deck. There is easy access to shoreline snorkeling in gin-clear waters. The resort lies a 10-minute drive from town, and all cottages are screened and have ceiling fans. Each cottage has a shower-only bathroom. Housekeeping is not provided.

Tamarindo Beach Rd., Culebra, PR 00775. (☎) **787/742-3343.** Fax 787/742-3342. www.tamarindoestates.com. 12 cottages (shower only). Winter $190 double, $335 quad; off season $140 double, $240 quad. AE, MC, V. **Amenities:** Pool; beach house. *In room:* A/C, TV, kitchen, coffeemaker.

INEXPENSIVE
Casa Ensenada Waterfront Guesthouse
This is a laid-back, tropical-looking house with relatively humble but clean and comfortable bedrooms. Many guests begin their day by taking a kayak over to the Dinghy Dock restaurant (see "Where to Dine," below) for breakfast and later return to sunbathe on the patio. In the evening, guests gather again on the patio for drinks and for barbecue—the catch of the day on the grill. Each unit is midsize and has a tiled, shower-only bathroom. All are nonsmoking. You can rent the Pequeño unit, which sleeps two in a double bed, or the Grande unit for four (two in a king-size bed in the master bedroom and two on a double futon in the living room). The on-site Estudio unit sleeps four, in twin beds and a double futon.

Calle Escudero 142, Dewey, Culebra, PR 00775. (☎) **866/210-0704** or 787/742-3559. Fax 787/742-0278. www. casaensenada.com. 3 units (shower only). Winter $125–$175; spring and summer $100–$150; fall $85–$115. MC, V. **Amenities:** Kayaking; scuba diving; snorkeling; bikes; laundry service; library. *In room:* A/C, kitchenette, coffeemaker.

Posada la Hamaca (Value)
This was one of Culebra's original guesthouses, lying in town next to the Dewey Bridge. Although much competition has opened to challenge it, this place is still going strong. The rooms are housed in a modest island home. Although simply furnished, each of the accommodations is well maintained and tidily

kept, each with a private bathroom with shower. Beach towels, coolers, and free ice are provided for beach outings. You'll also find an exterior shower to wash sand off your body before you enter. Room no. 8 is the coziest nest and is often rented by honeymooners. Some units are large enough to accommodate four guests, making them suitable for families. One apartment is spacious enough to accommodate 8 to 12 guests.

Calle Castalar 68, Culebra, PR 00775. © 787/742-3516. www.posada.com. 10 units. Year-round $97 double; $117 studio; $134–$190 apt. MC, V. **Amenities:** Wi-Fi Internet. *In room:* A/C, TV, kitchenette (in some), beverage maker (in some).

Villa Boheme   This modest guesthouse opens onto views of Ensenada Bay, and its hosts invite you to explore their little island in kayaks or bikes. Out back is a great terrace with hammocks that invite you to lead the life of leisure. The best units are a trio of large efficiencies; they are better equipped than the other units here. Each of another three rooms has a small kitchen with a large refrigerator. Occupants of the rest of the rooms share a fully equipped modern kitchen that is located in the patio area. Beds range from twins to king-size. Room nos. 2 and 12 can house up to six guests comfortably.

Calle Fulladosa 368, Dewey, Culebra, PR 00775. ©/fax **787/742-3508.** www.villaboheme.com. 11 units. Year-round $107–$152 double. $16 per extra person. AE, MC, V. **Amenities:** Communal kitchen; cable TV. *In room:* A/C, kitchen (in some), fridge (in some), no phone.

WHERE TO DINE
MODERATE
Dinghy Dock AMERICAN/CARIBBEAN/PUERTO RICAN   For the best preview of laid-back tropical Culebra, head here. The hangout lies on the banks of Ensenada Honda, just south of the Dewey drawbridge, and it has a dock where dinghies and other boats anchor. Come here for the bar or the restaurant—or perhaps both—and meet the locals along with visiting boaters from the Puerto Rican mainland. We like to come here to enjoy margaritas or Puerto Rico's own Medalla beer and watch the sunsets. You can visit three times a day if you wish: tropical fruit-flavored waffles for breakfast, freshly grilled tuna for lunch, and a lobster and rice dish for dinner.

Punta del Soldado Rd., outside Dewey. © **787/742-0233.** Reservations not necessary. Breakfast $5–$10; main courses $5.25–$15 lunch, $14–$30 dinner. AE, MC, V. Daily 8am–11am, 11:30am–2:30pm, and 6–9pm.

INEXPENSIVE
El Batey DELI   Across from the harbor and cooled by its breezes, this large, clean establishment maintains a full bar and prepares an array of deli-style sandwiches. They'll hand you a cold beer when the afternoon sun is out, and the pool tables make the place lively, especially on weekends, when many locals come here. Disco reigns on Friday and Saturday nights. Weekdays, it's much calmer.

Parque de Pelota 250, Carretera. © **787/742-3828.** Sandwiches $3–$5. No credit cards. Wed–Sun noon–midnight (till 2am Fri–Sat).

Mamacita's ⊛ PUERTO RICAN   It is highly likely that this dive will become your hangout during your stay on Culebra. You can even room here, but it's noisy at night, especially on Saturday when the conga drummers rattle the joint. The island food is good and affordable, enough so to attract expats, locals, and visitors.

Lunch fare is simple, mostly rice and beans type fare, but at night the menu improves considerably, especially if you opt for the locally caught and perfectly grilled seafood. The steaks, although imported, are also a good choice if you've got a large appetite. The house drink special is an Iguana Colada. After you've consumed it, you can always ask what's in it.

If you like to stay up late, you can ask to rent one of the simply furnished bedrooms, 10 in all, each with a private bathroom with shower. Rooms are colorfully decorated, the older units with murals. Two are suites with kitchenettes, but our favorite is the Crow's Nest on the top floor, opening onto a panoramic view. Rates are $95 double, or $105 to $135 suite.

Calle Castelar 64–66. (C) **787/742-0090.** Reservations not required. Lunch main dishes $6.50–$10; dinner main dishes $12–$22. MC, V. Daily 8am–2:30pm and 6–9pm. Bar Mon–Thurs and Sun 8am–10pm; Fri–Sat 8am–11pm.

Heather's Pizzeria PIZZA   This is the best place to go for pizza on the island. With its funky decor, it is a popular hangout for local expatriates. In addition to those piping-hot pies, the kitchen also turns out an array of freshly made salads, pastas, and well-stuffed sandwiches. The food here is quite good.

Calle Marques 14, Dewey. (C) **787/742-3175.** Reservations not necessary. Pizzas, sandwiches, and platters $9–$25. No credit cards. Daily 6–11pm. Closed first 2 weeks of Oct.

Appendix: Fast Facts, Toll-Free Numbers & Websites

1 Fast Facts: Puerto Rico

AREA CODE The telephone area code for Puerto Rico is **787.** For calls on the island, the area code is not used.

BANKS All major U.S. banks have branches on Puerto Rico; their hours are 8am to 4pm Monday through Friday and 8:30am to noon on Saturday.

BUSINESS HOURS Regular business hours are Monday through Friday from 8am to 5pm. Shopping hours vary considerably. Regular shopping hours are Monday through Thursday and Saturday from 9am to 6pm. On Friday, stores have a long day: 9am to 9pm. Many stores also open on Sunday from 11am to 5pm.

CAMERA & FILM It's important to protect your camera not only from theft but also from saltwater and sand; furthermore, your camera can become overheated and any film it contains can be ruined if left in the sun or locked in the trunk of a car. For camera supplies, see p. 106.

CURRENCY The U.S. dollar is used throughout Puerto Rico. See "Money" in chapter 3 for more.

DRUGS A branch of the Federal Narcotics Strike Force is permanently stationed on Puerto Rico, where illegal drugs and narcotics are a problem. Convictions for possession of marijuana can bring severe penalties, ranging from 2 to 10 years in prison for a first offense. Possession of hard drugs, such as cocaine or heroin, can lead to 15 years or more in prison.

DRUGSTORES It's a good idea to carry enough prescription medications with you to last the duration of your stay. If you're going into the hinterlands, take along the medicines you'll need. If you need any additional medications, you'll find many drugstores in San Juan and other leading cities. One of the most centrally located pharmacies in Old San Juan is the **Puerto Rican Drug Co.,** Calle San Francisco 157 (© 787/725-2202); it's open daily from 7:30am to 9:30pm.

ELECTRICITY The electricity is 110 volts AC, as it is in the continental United States and Canada.

EMBASSIES & CONSULATES Because Puerto Rico is part of the United States, there is no U.S. embassy or consulate. Instead, there are branches of all the principal U.S. federal agencies. Foreign governments have no embassies here, since Puerto Rico is part of the United States. A number of governments, however, have honorary consulates on the island. There are no special provisions or agencies catering to British travel needs in Puerto Rico, nor are there agencies serving citizens of Australia or New Zealand. Canada does have a consulate in San Juan (© 787/759-6629).

EMERGENCIES In an emergency, dial © **911.** Or call the local police (© 787/726-7020), fire department (© 787/725-3444), or medical emergency line (© 787/754-2550).

GAMBLING In addition to **casino gambling** at major Puerto Rico resorts, the island also has a **lottery,** for which tickets can be purchased at hundreds of kiosks, stores, and shops around the island. The major casino gambling on the island includes Caribbean stud poker, blackjack, roulette, and craps, along with thousands of slot machines. Under Puerto Rican law, alcoholic beverages cannot be served in a casino.

HEALTHCARE Medical-care facilities, including excellent hospitals and clinics, in Puerto Rico are on par with those in the United States. Hotels can arrange for a doctor in case of an emergency. Most major U.S. health insurance plans are recognized here, but it's advisable to check with your carrier or insurance agent before your trip, because medical attention is very expensive. See "Health & Safety" in chapter 3.

HOSPITALS In a medical emergency, call © **911. Ashford Presbyterian Community Hospital,** Av. Ashford 1451, San Juan (© **787/721-2160**), maintains 24-hour emergency service. Service is also provided at **Clinica Las Americas,** Franklin Delano Roosevelt Ave. 400, Hato Rey (© **787/765-1919**), and at **Puerto Rico Medical Center,** Av. Americo Miranda, Río Piedras (© **787/777-3535**).

INTERNET ACCESS Public access to the Internet is available at some large-scale resorts; the staff often provides access from their own computers. Another place to try is **Cybernet Cafe,** Av. Ashford Condado 1128 (© **787/724-4033**), which is open Monday to Thursday from 9am to 11pm, Friday and Saturday from 9am to midnight, and Sunday from 10am to 10pm. It charges $3 for 20 minutes, $5 for 35 minutes, $7 for 50 minutes, and $9 for 65 minutes. A second location with the same hours and pricing is in Isla Verde at Av. Isla Verde 5980 (© **787/728-4195**).

LANGUAGE English is understood at the big resorts and in most of San Juan. Out in the island, Spanish is still *numero uno.*

LIQUOR LAWS You must be 18 years of age to purchase liquor in stores or buy drinks in hotels, bars, and restaurants.

LOST & FOUND Be sure to tell all of your credit card companies the minute you discover your wallet has been lost or stolen, and file a report at the nearest police precinct. Your credit card company or insurer may require a police report number or record of the loss. Most credit card companies have an emergency toll-free number to call if your card is lost or stolen; they may be able to wire you a cash advance immediately or deliver an emergency credit card in a day or two. Visa's U.S. emergency number is © **800/ 847-2911** or 410/581-9994. American Express cardholders and traveler's check holders should call © **800/221-7282.** MasterCard holders should call © **800/ 307-7309** or 636/722-7111. For other credit cards, call the toll-free number directory at © **800/555-1212.**

If you need emergency cash over the weekend when all banks and American Express offices are closed, you can have money wired to you via **Western Union** (© **800/325-6000;** www.westernunion. com). **Travelers Express/MoneyGram** is the largest company in the U.S. for money orders. You can transfer funds either online or by phone in about 10 minutes (© **800/ MONEYGRAM;** www.moneygram.com).

Identity theft and fraud are potential complications of losing your wallet, especially if you've lost your driver's license along with your cash and credit cards. Notify the major credit-reporting bureaus immediately; placing a fraud alert on your records may protect you against liability for criminal activity. The three major U.S. credit-reporting agencies are **Equifax** (© **800/766-0008;** www.equifax. com), **Experian** (© **888/397-3742;** www. experian.com), and **TransUnion** (© **800/ 680-7289;** www.transunion.com). Finally, if you've lost all forms of photo ID, call your airline and explain the situation;

they might allow you to board the plane if you have a copy of your passport or birth certificate and a copy of the police report you've filed.

MARRIAGE REQUIREMENTS There are no residency requirements for getting married in Puerto Rico. You need parental consent if either of you is under 18. Blood tests are required, although a test conducted in your home country within 10 days of the ceremony will suffice. A doctor must sign the license after an examination of the bride and groom. For complete details, contact the **Commonwealth of Puerto Rico Health Department,** Demographic Register, Franklin Delano Roosevelt Ave., Hato Rey (P.O. Box 11854), San Juan, PR 00910 (© **787/728-7980**).

NEWSPAPERS & MAGAZINES THE SAN JUAN STAR, a daily English-language newspaper, has been called the "*International Herald Tribune* of the Caribbean." It concentrates extensively on news from the United States. You can also pick up copies of *USA Today* at most news kiosks. If you read Spanish, you might enjoy *El Nuevo Día,* the most popular local tabloid. Few significant magazines are published on Puerto Rico, but *Time* and *Newsweek* are available at most newsstands.

PETS To bring your pet in, you must produce a health certificate from a U.S. mainland veterinarian and show proof of vaccination against rabies. Very few hotels allow animals, so check in advance. One exception is Isla Verde's Water Club.

POSTAL SERVICES Because the U.S. Postal Service is responsible for handling mail on Puerto Rico, the regulations and tariffs are the same as on the mainland United States. Stamps can be purchased at any post office, all of which are open Monday through Friday from 8am to 5pm. Saturday hours are from 8am to noon (closed Sun). As on the mainland, you can purchase stamps at vending machines in airports, stores, and hotels. First-class letters to addresses within Puerto Rico, the United States, and its territories cost 42¢. Letters and postcards to Canada both cost 72¢ for the first half-ounce. Letters and postcards to other countries cost up to 94¢ for the first half-ounce.

SAFETY Crime exists here as it does everywhere. Use common sense and take precautions. Theft and occasional muggings do occur on the Condado and Isla Verde beaches at night, so you might want to confine your moonlit beach nights to the fenced-in and guarded areas around some of the major hotels. The countryside of Puerto Rico is safer than San Juan, but caution is always in order. Avoid narrow country roads and isolated beaches, night or day.

SMOKING Stringent antismoking regulations have been passed banning smoking in all public areas including restaurants, bars, casinos, and hotel rooms. Enforcement, however, is less strict than other areas in the United States. Smoking is even banned at outdoor cafes that are serviced by waiters or waitresses.

TAXES All hotel rooms in Puerto Rico are subject to a tax, which is not included in the rates given in this book. At casino hotels, the tax is 11%; at noncasino hotels, it's 9%. At country inns you pay a 7% tax. Most hotels also add a 10% service charge. If they don't, you're expected to tip for services rendered. When you're booking a room, it's always best to inquire about these added charges. There is now a 7% sales tax on a broad range of goods and services. There is no airport departure tax.

TELEPHONE & FAX Coin-operated phones can be found throughout the island, with a particularly dense concentration in San Juan. Most phone booths contain printed instructions for dialing, but basically, after depositing your coins, dial the number at the sound of the dial tone. Local calls are 75¢.

If you're calling long distance within Puerto Rico or to the U.S. mainland, add a 1 before the numbers. If you're placing a call to foreign countries, preface the number with 011. For these calls, an operator (or a recorded voice) will tell you how much money to deposit, although you'll probably find it more practical to use a calling card issued by such long-distance carriers as Sprint, AT&T, or MCI. Most Puerto Ricans buy phone cards for sale in most drugstores and gift shops on the island. Public phones that allow credit cards such as American Express, Visa, or MasterCard to be inserted or "swiped" through a magnetic slot are rare on the island. Most of these are located at the San Juan airport.

Most hotels can send a telex or fax for you and bill the costs to your room, and in some cases, they'll even send a fax for a nonguest if you agree to pay a charge. Barring that, several agencies in San Juan will send a fax anywhere you want for a fee. Many are associated with print shops/ photocopy stands.

Major cellular operators, such as AT&T, Suncom, and Mexican wireless giant Claro, operate on the island, and most national plans include Puerto Rico within their U.S. national roaming or overall minute plans.

Inexpensive cell phones, which come with prepaid calling cards, are widely available in tourist areas, shopping malls, drug stores and gas stations. Ditto for low priced accessories like chargers and cases, and the whole island is dotted with electronics and computer shops, such as Radio Shack, Best Buy, and Circuit City.

TIME Puerto Rico is on Atlantic Standard Time, which is 1 hour later than Eastern Standard Time. Puerto Rico does not go on daylight saving time, however, so the time here is the same year-round.

TIPPING Tipping is expected here, so hand over the money as you would on the U.S. mainland. That usually means 15% in restaurants, 10% in bars, and 10% to 15% for taxi drivers, hairdressers, and other services, depending on the quality of the service rendered. Tip a porter, either at the airport or at your hotel, $1 per bag. The U.S. government imposes income tax on waitstaff and other service-industry workers whose income is tip-based according to the gross receipts of their employers; therefore, if you don't tip them, those workers could end up paying tax anyway.

WEIGHTS & MEASURES There's a mixed bag of measurements in Puerto Rico. Because of its Spanish tradition, most weights (meat and poultry) and measures (gasoline and road distances) are metric. But because of the U.S. presence, speed limits appear in miles per hour and liquids such as beer are sold by the ounce.

2 Toll-Free Numbers & Websites

MAJOR U.S. AIRLINES
(*flies internationally as well)

Alaska Airlines/Horizon Air
© 800/252-7522
www.alaskaair.com

American Airlines*
© 800/433-7300 (in U.S. and Canada)
© 020/7365-0777 (in U.K.)
www.aa.com

Cape Air
© 800/352-0714
www.flycapeair.com

Collins Aviation
© 305/743-4222
www.flyparadiseair.com

Continental Airlines*
℗ 800/523-3273 (in U.S. or Canada)
℗ 084/5607-6760 (in U.K.)
www.continental.com

Delta Air Lines*
℗ 800/221-1212 (in U.S. or Canada)
℗ 084/5600-0950 (in U.K.)
www.delta.com

Frontier Airlines
℗ 800/432-1359
www.frontierairlines.com

Hawaiian Airlines*
℗ 800/367-5320 (in U.S. and Canada)
www.hawaiianair.com

JetBlue Airways
℗ 800/538-2583 (in U.S.)
℗ 080/1365-2525 (in U.K. or Canada)
www.jetblue.com

Midwest Airlines
℗ 800/452-2022
www.midwestairlines.com

Nantucket Airlines
℗ 800/635-8787
www.nantucketairlines.com

North American Airlines*
℗ 800/371-6297
www.flynaa.com

Northwest Airlines
℗ 800/225-2525 (in U.S.)
℗ 870/0507-4074 (in U.K.)
www.flynaa.com

PenAir (The Spirit of Alaska)
℗ 800/448-4226 (in U.S.)
www.penair.com

United Airlines*
℗ 800/864-8331 (in U.S. and Canada)
℗ 084/5844-4777 (in U.K.)
www.united.com

US Airways*
℗ 800/428-4322 (in U.S. and Canada)
℗ 084/5600-3300 (in U.K.)
www.usairways.com

Virgin America*
℗ 877/359-8474
www.virginamerica.com

MAJOR INTERNATIONAL AIRLINES

Air France
℗ 800/237-2747 (in U.S.)
℗ 800/375-8723 (in U.S. and Canada)
℗ 087/0142-4343 (in U.K.)
www.airfrance.com

Air New Zealand
℗ 800/262-1234 (in U.S.)
℗ 800/663-5494 (in Canada)
℗ 0800/028-4149 (in U.K.)
www.airnewzealand.com

Alitalia
℗ 800/223-5730 (in U.S.)
℗ 800/361-8336 (in Canada)
℗ 087/0608-6003 (in U.K.)
www.alitalia.com

British Airways
℗ 800/247-9297 (in U.S. and Canada)
℗ 087/0850-9850 (in U.K.)
www.british-airways.com

Caribbean Airlines (formerly BWIA)
℗ 800/920-4225 (in U.S. and Canada)
℗ 084/5362 4225 (in U.K.)
www.caribbean-airlines.com

Cubana
℗ 888/667-1222 (in Canada)
℗ 020/7538-5933 (in U.K.)
www.cubana.cu

Iberia Airlines
℗ 800/722-4642 (in U.S. and Canada)
℗ 087/0609-0500 (in U.K.)
www.iberia.com

Japan Airlines
℗ 012/025-5931 (international)
www.jal.co.jp

Korean Air
℗ 800/438-5000 (in U.S. and Canada)
℗ 0800/413-000 (in U.K.)
www.koreanair.com

Lan Airlines
℡ 866/435-9526 (in U.S.)
℡ 305/670-9999 (in other countries)
www.lan.com

Lufthansa
℡ 800/399-5838 (in U.S.)
℡ 800/563-5954 (in Canada)
℡ 087/0837-7747 (in U.K.)
www.lufthansa.com

Philippine Airlines
℡ 800/I-Fly-Pal (800/435-9725; in U.S. and Canada)
℡ 632/855-8888 (in Philippines)
www.philippineairlines.com

Quantas Airways
℡ 800/227-4500 (in U.S.)
℡ 084/5774-7767 (in U.K. or Canada)
℡ 13 13 13 (in Australia)
www.quantas.com

South African Airways
℡ 271/1978-5313 (international)
℡ 0861 FLYSAA (086/135-9122; in South Africa)
www.flysaa.com

Swiss Air
℡ 877/359-7947 (in U.S. and Canada)
℡ 084/5601-0956 (in U.K.)
www.swiss.com

TACA
℡ 800/535-8780 (in U.S.)
℡ 800/722-TACA (8222; in Canada)
℡ 087/0241-0340 (in U.K.)
℡ 503/2267-8222 (in El Salvador)

CAR RENTAL AGENCIES

Alamo
℡ 800/GO-ALAMO (800/462-5266)
www.alamo.com

Avis
℡ 800/331-1212 (in U.S. and Canada)
℡ 084/4581-8181 (in U.K.)
www.avis.com

Budget
℡ 800/527-0700 (in U.S.)
℡ 087/0156-5656 (in U.K.)
℡ 800/268-8900 (in Canada)
www.budget.com

Dollar
℡ 800/800-4000 (in U.S.)
℡ 800/848-8268 (in Canada)
℡ 080/8234-7524 (in U.K.)
www.dollar.com

Hertz
℡ 800/645-3131
℡ 800/654-3001 (for international reservations)
www.hertz.com

National
℡ 800/CAR-RENT (800/227-7368)
www.nationalcar.com

Payless
℡ 800/PAYLESS (800/729-5377)
www.paylesscarrental.com

Thrifty
℡ 800/367-2277
℡ 918/669-2168 (international)
www.thrifty.com

MAJOR HOTEL & MOTEL CHAINS

Best Western International
℡ 800/780-7234 (in U.S. and Canada)
℡ 0800/393-130 (in U.K.)
www.bestwestern.com

Clarion Hotels
℡ 800/CLARION or 877/424-6423 (in U.S. and Canada)
℡ 0800/444-444 (in U.K.)
www.choicehotels.com

Comfort Inns
✆ 800/228-5150
✆ 0800/444-444 (in U.K.)
www.choicehotels.com

Courtyard by Marriott
✆ 888/236-2427 (in U.S.)
✆ 0800/221-222 (in U.K.)
www.marriott.com/courtyard

Crowne Plaza Hotels
✆ 888/303-1746
www.ichotelsgroup.com/crowneplaza

DoubleTree Hotels
✆ 800/222-TREE (800/222-8733; in U.S. and Canada)
✆ 087/0590-9090 (in U.K.)
www.doubletree.com

Four Seasons
✆ 800/819-5053 (in U.S. and Canada)
✆ 0800/6488-6488 (in U.K.)
www.fourseasons.com

Hampton Inn
✆ 800/HAMPTON (800/426-4766)
www.hamptoninn.com

Hilton Hotels
✆ 800/HILTONS (800/445-8667; in U.S. and Canada)
✆ 087/0590-9090 (in U.K.)
www.hilton.com

Holiday Inn
✆ 800/315-2621 (in U.S. and Canada)
✆ 0800/405-060 (in U.K.)
www.holidayinn.com

Hyatt
✆ 888/591-1234 (in U.S. and Canada)
✆ 084/5888-1234 (in U.K.)
www.hyatt.com

InterContinental Hotels & Resorts
✆ 800/424-6835 (in U.S. and Canada)
✆ 0800/1800-1800 (in U.K.)
www.ichotelsgroup.com

Marriott
✆ 877/236-2427 (in U.S. and Canada)
✆ 0800/221-222 (in U.K.)
www.marriott.com

Quality
✆ 877/424-6423 (in U.S. and Canada)
✆ 0800/444-444 (in U.K.)
www.QualityInn.ChoiceHotels.com

Radisson Hotels & Resorts
✆ 888/201-1718 (in U.S. and Canada)
✆ 0800/374-411 (in U.K.)
www.radisson.com

Ramada Worldwide
✆ 888/2-RAMADA (888/272-6232; in U.S. and Canada)
✆ 080/8100-0783 (in U.K.)
www.ramada.com

Residence Inn by Marriott
✆ 800/331-3131
✆ 800/221-222 (in U.K.)
www.marriott.com/residenceinn

Westin Hotels & Resorts
✆ 800-937-8461 (in U.S. and Canada)
✆ 0800/3259-5959 (in U.K.)
www.starwoodhotels.com/westin

Index

See also Accommodations and Restaurant indexes, below.

GENERAL INDEX

AAA Island Tours (San Juan), 71, 169
AARP, 67
Above and Beyond Tours, 66
Acampa Nature Adventures, 251
Access-Able Travel Source, 65
Access America, 62
Accessible Journeys, 65
Accommodations. *See also* Accommodations Index
  Aguadilla and the northwest, 263–264
  best, 12–15
  best beaches at, 6
  Boquerón, 236–238
  Coamo, 242
  Culebra, 292–294
  Dorado, 206–208
  Fajardo, 271–272
  Guánica, 231–232
  La Parguera, 233–236
  Mayagüez, 249–250
  near El Yunque, 201
  Palmas del Mar, 275
  Ponce, 226–227
  Rincón, 255–258
  Río Grande, 203–204
  San Germán, 241
  San Juan, 1, 108–129
  southeast Puerto Rico, 277
  tips on, 74–77
  Vieques, 283–287
  the western mountains, 265–266
  what's new in, 1–2
Active vacations, 5, 54–62
Adobo, 39
Adventures Tourmarine, 251
Aguadilla, 79, 260–264
Aguadilla Ice Skating Rink, 262
Aibonito, 214, 215
Aibonito Flower Festival, 52–53

AirAmbulanceCard.com, 65–66
Air Canada, 68
Air travel, 96–99
Albizu Campos, Pedro, 31–32
Alcaldía (City Hall; San Juan), 165
Al's Mar Azul (Vieques), 290
Alto Grande coffee, 184
Amadeus Bistro Bar (San Juan), 190–191
Ambassador Tours, 72
American Airlines, 67
American Airlines Vacations, 70
American Express
  San Juan, 105
  traveler's checks, 48
American Foundation for the Blind (AFB), 65
Amerindians, 22, 24, 25. *See also* Taíno Indians
Apartment rentals, San Juan, 113
Aqui Se Puede (San Juan), 195
Arecibo, 79, 209–211
Arecibo Lighthouse & Historic Park, 210
Arecibo Observatory, 209–210
Art galleries, San Juan, 168, 180
Asopao, 40
Atlantic San Juan Tours, 72
ATMs (automated teller machines), 47
Atochoa Pedestrian Mall (Ponce), 225
Aventuras Tierra Adentro, 59

Bacardi Artisans' Fair (San Juan), 54
Bacardi Distillery (Cataño), 171
Backstage Partners, 72
Bahia Beach Plantation Resort and Golf Club (Río Grande), 202
Bahia Corcha (Red Beach), 281

Bahia de la Chiva (Blue Beach), 281
Bahia Sucia, 235
Ballena Beach, 231, 234
Banco de Santander (Ponce), 223
Bared & Sons (San Juan), 184
Bar Plaza (Vieques), 290–291
Barrachina (San Juan), 186
Barrachina Restaurant (San Juan), 190
Baseball, 53
Beaches, 34. *See also specific beaches*
  Aguadilla and Isabela, 261–262
  best, 4–6
    hotel beaches, 6–7
  Culebra, 292
  Dorado, 206
  Mayagüez, 249
  Palmas del Mar, 274
  Rincón, 252, 254
  San Juan, 172–173
  southwestern coast, 234–235
  warning, 55
Belz Factory Outlet World (San Juan), 188
Ben & Jerry's Café Galería Puerto Rico (San Juan), 170
Benítez Fishing Charters, 173
Berwind Country Club (Loiza), 174
Biking
  San Juan, 105, 173
  Vieques, 282
Bird-watching
  Culebra, 291
  El Yunque, 200
  Guánica State Forest, 229
  Monte del Estado National Park, 264–265
  Refugio Nacional Cabo Rojo, 237
  Vieques, 286
Bligh, Capt. William, 41

Blue Beach (Bahia de la Chiva), 281

Boating and sailing, 54–56
Fajardo, 270

Boat tours and cruises
Lagos dos Bocas, 212
San Juan, 173
La Rumba Party Cruise, 193

Books, recommended, 44

Boquerón, 82, 236–238

Boquerón Beach, 5

Bosque Estatal de Guajataca (Guajataca Forest), 35, 56, 262, 265

Bóveda (San Juan), 113, 184

The Brick House (San Juan), 191

British Airways, 68

Business hours, 296

Butterfly People (San Juan), 180

Cabo Rojo, 82

Cabo Rojo Lighthouse, 236

Caja de Muertos, 225

Calendar of events, 51–54

Calle McKinley (Mayagüez), 248

Calypso's Tropical Bar (Rincón), 260

Camarero Racetrack (Canovanas), 174

Cambalache State Forest, 35, 56

Camping, 56–57

Caña Gorda (near Guánica), 5, 234

Candela (San Juan), 195

Cangrejos Yacht Club (San Juan), 55, 173

Caonillas, Lake, 211

Cape Air, 68

Capilla de Cristo (San Juan), 160–161

Captain's Duck Tours (San Juan), 170

Caribbean National Forest, 59

Caribbean-On-Line, 45

Caribbean Outfitters, 174

Caribe Aquatic Adventures (San Juan), 174–175

Caribe Hilton (San Juan), Beachcombers Bar in, 191

Carib Hilton (San Juan), Olas Spa at, 178

Carite State Forest, 56, 59, 214, 215

Carli Café Concierto (San Juan), 190

Carnival Cruise Lines, 73

Carnival masks, San Juan, 181, 182

Carnival Ponceño (Ponce), 51

Carolina Public Beach (San Juan), 4–5

Car rentals, 68–69

Car travel and scenic drives, 68–70
El Yunque, 201
La Ruta Panorámica, 93–95

Casa Acosta y Fores (San Germán), 240

Casa Alcaldía (City Hall; Ponce), 221, 223

Casa Armstrong-Poventud (Ponce), 221

Casa Bacardi Visitor Center (Cataño), 171

Casa Blanca (San Juan), 165

Casa de la Masacre de Ponce, 218

Casa Galesa (San Juan), 183

Casa Juán Perichi (San Germán), 240

Casals, Pablo, Museo de Pablo Casals (San Juan), 164

Casals Festival (San Juan), 51–52

Casa Morales (San Germán), 239–240

Casa Museo Canales (Jayuya), 243

Casa Salazar (Museum of the History of Ponce; Ponce), 219–220

Casinos, 296–297
Mayagüez, 250
San Juan, 196

Castillo de San Felipe del Morro (El Morro; San Juan), 158, 160

Castillo Fishing Charters, 173–174

Castillo Sightseeing Tours & Travel Services (San Juan), 169

Catedral de San Juan, 161

Cathedral of Our Lady of Guadalupe (Ponce), 218, 221

Cayey, 214

Cayo Santiago, 83

Celebrity Cruises, 73

Cellphones, 299

Cemi Museum (Jayuya), 243

Centers for Disease Control and Prevention, 64

Central Mountains (Cordillera Central), 212–215, 230

Centro de Bellas Artes (San Juan), 189

Centro Histórico (Ponce), 223

Cerro de Punta, 243

Cerro Gordo (near Dorado), 206

Children's Museum (San Juan), 171

Chu Chu Tren (Ponce), 224

The Cigar House (San Juan), 182

CIRCO (San Juan), 169, 176

City Hall (Alcaldía; San Juan), 165

City Hall (Casa Alcaldía; Ponce), 221, 223

City walls (San Juan), 164

Climate, 49

Club Brava (San Juan), 189

Club Deportivo del Oeste (Cabo Rojo), 225

Club Lazer (San Juan), 189

Club Nautico de Boquerón, 55

Club Nautico de La Parguera, 55

Club Nautico de San Juan, 55, 173

Coach (San Juan), 187

Coamo, 82–83, 241–242

Cockfights, 18
San Juan, 196

Coffee, 42–43
San Juan, 183–184

Coffee Harvest Festival (Maricao), 51

Coffin Island, 225

Coliseo Gallistico (San Juan), 18, 196

Columbus, Christopher, 24–25

Columbus Day, 53

Comida criolla, 39

Condado (San Juan), 101
accommodations, 116–121
restaurants, 144–148

Condado Beach, 172, 175

Condado Plaza Hotel & Casino (San Juan), 196
Plaza Spa at, 178

Continental Airlines, 68

Continental Airlines Vacations, 71

Copamarina Beach Resort (Guánica), 230

Córcega Beach, 254

Cordillera Central, 212–215, 230

Corné Port-Royal Chocolatier (San Juan), 183

Costa Caribe Golf & Country Club, golf course at, 225

Costa Cruise Lines, 73
Costazul (San Juan), 182
Crash Boat Beach, 261
Credit cards, 48
Crime, 22
Cruise-ship travelers, 72–74
Cruises of Distinction, 72
Cruises One, 72
Cruises Only, 72
Cuadragésimo Cuarto Torneo
  de Pesca Interclub del
  Caribe, 53
Cuatro Estaciones (San Juan),
  136
Cueva Trail, 230
Cuisine, 39–42, 156
Culebra, 18, 36, 83, 291–295
Culebra Wildlife Refuge, 291
Culebrita, 291
Currency and currency
  exchange, 47–48
Customs regulations, 46–47

Deep-sea fishing. See Fishing
Delta Airlines, 67
Delta Vacations, 70
Desecheo Island, 254
Dewey (Puebla), 291
Disabilities, travelers with,
  65–66
Dive Center (Wyndham Río Mar
  Beach Resort), 202–203
The Divers Alert Network
  (DAN), 63
DMR Designs (San Juan), 184
Domes Beach, 254
Don Collin's Cigars (San Juan),
  182
Don Pablo (San Juan), 194
Dooney & Bourke Factory Store
  (San Juan), 187
Dorado, 205–209
  brief description of, 79–80
Dorado Beach Resort & Club
  golf courses at, 174, 207
  spa and pool at, 208
Drinks, 42–44
Driving rules, 69
Drugs, 22, 296
Drugstores, 296

Easter, 52
Eastern Puerto Rico, 267–277
Economy of Puerto Rico, 20–22
Eduardo Barquet (San Juan),
  186

El Alcazar (San Juan), 179–180
El Arsenal (San Juan), 165
El Atocha (Ponce), 224
El Batey (San Juan), 191, 194
El Cañuelo (Dorado), 206
El Casino (Mayagüez), 250
El Convento Beach, 270
Electricity, 296
El Escambrón public beach
  (San Juan), 172
El Faro (Las Cabezas de San
  Juan Nature Reserve), 268
El Faro de Cabo Rojo, 236
El Gigante Marathon
  (Adjuntas), 53
El Morro (San Juan), 158, 160
El Morro Fortress (San Juan),
  170
El Morro Trail (San Juan), 160
El Museo Castillo Serralles
  (Ponce), 218–219
El Palacio del Coquí Inc.
  (Ponce), 225
El Patio de Sam (San Juan),
  191, 195
El Picoteo (San Juan), 194
El Portal Tropical Forest Center
  (Río Grande), 200
El Pozo de Jacinto, 261
El San Juan Hotel & Casino
  (San Juan), 178, 196
El Tunel, 262
El Vigía Hill (Ponce), 219
El Yunque, 198–201
  exploring, 200–201
  traveling to, 198, 200
  visitor information, 200
El Yunque Catalina Field Office
  (near Palmer), 200
El Yunque National Forest, 10,
  11, 35, 57, 59, 80–81
El Yunque Trail, 201
Emancipation Day, 52
Emerald Isles (San Juan), 186
Emergencies, 296
Entry requirements, 45–46
Escorted general-interest
  tours, 72
Esperanza, 280
Espiritismo (spiritualism), 39

Fajardo, 198, 267–273
  brief description of, 81
  marinas, 55
Families with children
  best beach for, 4
  best resorts, 12

San Juan
  accommodations, 127
  restaurants, 154
  sights and attractions,
    170–171
  suggested itinerary, 91–93
Farmacia Martin (San Germán),
  240
Felisa Rincón de Gautier
  Museum (San Juan), 161
Festival La Casita, 54
Festival of Puerto Rican Music
  (San Juan), 53
Festivals and special events,
  51–54
Ficus Café (San Juan), 192
Fishing, 57–58
  Palmas del Mar, 274
  Rincón, 255
  San Juan, 173
  Vieques, 282
Flamenco Beach, 292
Flying Wheels Travel, 65
Fort Conde de Mirasol Museum
  (Vieques), 283
Fort San Cristóbal (San Juan),
  160
Fox-Delicias Hotel (Ponce), 224

Galaxy Lanes (San Juan),
  170–171
Galería Botello (San Juan), 180
Galería Exodo (San Juan), 180
Galería Nacional (San Juan),
  168
Galería Sánchez (San Juan),
  180–181
Galería San Juan, 181
Gas Chambers Beach, 261
Gasoline, 69
Gays and lesbians, 66
Gifts and handicrafts, San Juan,
  184–186
Gilligan's Island, 230–231
Golden Age Passport, 67
Golden Door (Fajardo), 272
Golf, 58–59
  Aguadilla, 262
  best, 9–10
  Luquillo Beach/Río Grande
    area, 202
  Palmas del Mar, 274
  Ponce environs, 225
  San Juan, 174
Good Friday, 52
Grand Circle Travel, 67
Guajataca Beach, 262

Guajataca Lake, 265
Guajataca State Forest, 35, 56, 262, 265
Guánica, 229–234
Guánica State Forest, 10, 59, 229
Guavate, 198, 214
Guesthouses, 75–76
Guineo, Lake, 243

Hacienda Buena Vista (near Ponce), 220
Haitian Gallery (San Juan), 181
Hartford Holidays Travel, 72
Hatillo Masks Festival, 54
Hato Rey (San Juan), 102
Healthcare, 297
Health concerns, 63–64
Health insurance, 62–63
Hecho a Mano (San Juan), 183
Hideaways Aficionado, 77
High season, 49
Hiking, 59
    best, 10–11
    El Yunque, 200–201
    Palmas del Mar, 274
History of Puerto Rico, 22–34
    American rule, 30–32
    Amerindians, 22, 24
    books about, 44
    the Dutch, 26
    the English, 25–26
    Spanish rule, 24–30
Holidays, 51
Honeymoon resorts, best, 12–13
Horse racing, San Juan, 174
Hospitals, 297
Hot Dog Cycling (San Juan), 173
Hotels. See also Accommodations Index
    Aguadilla and the northwest, 263–264
    best, 12–15
    best beaches at, 6
    Boquerón, 236–238
    Coamo, 242
    Culebra, 292–294
    Dorado, 206–208
    Fajardo, 271–272
    Guánica, 231–232
    La Parguera, 233–236
    Mayagüez, 249–250
    near El Yunque, 201
    Palmas del Mar, 275
    Ponce, 226–227

Rincón, 255–258
Río Grande, 203–204
San Germán, 241
San Juan, 1, 108–129
southeast Puerto Rico, 277
tips on, 74–77
Vieques, 283–287
the western mountains, 265–266
what's new in, 1–2
Hot Wavz Surf Shop (Rincón), 254
Humacao, 83
Humacao Regional Airport (near Palmas del Mar), 274
Hurricane season, 49

ICan, 66
Iglesia Porta Coeli (San Germán), 239
Iguana Water Sports (Río Grande), 56
Indian Ceremonial Park at Caguaña, 212, 213
Insurance, car-rental, 69
International Association for Medical Assistance to Travelers (IAMAT), 63–64
International Billfish Tournament (San Juan), 53
International Fitness (San Juan), 178
International Gay & Lesbian Travel Association (IGLTA), 66
International Society of Travel Medicine, 64
Internet access, 297
Isabela, 261, 262, 264
Isabel Segunda, 280
Isla de Mona Wildlife Refuge, 57
Isla Mona, 10–11, 18, 36, 83, 251
Isla Verde (San Juan), 101–102
    accommodations, 124–129
    public beach, 172, 173
    restaurants, 152–156
Isla Verde Tennis Club (San Juan), 178–179
Itineraries, suggested, 83–95

Jájome, 215
Jardín Botánico (San Juan), 167
Jayuya, 243
Jayuya Indian Festival, 53
Jet-Blue, 68

Jewelry, San Juan, 186
Jobos Beach, 261
José de Diego Day, 52
Joyería Riviera (San Juan), 186
Juan A. Rivero Zoo (Mayagüez), 249
Juan Ponce de León Museum (San Juan), 165
Junior's Bar (San Juan), 195
Just-A-Vacation, 71

Karst Country, 35, 211–212
Katarina Sail Charters (Rincón), 255
Kayaking
    Culebra, 292
    Vieques, 282
Kelly Cruises, 72
King's Ice Cream (Ponce), 224
Krash Klub (San Juan), 195

La Calle (San Juan), 181, 182
La Casa del Libro (San Juan), 165
Lace, 187
La Fortaleza (San Juan), 165
Lago de Guajataca, 265
Lago Lucchetti Wildlife Refuge, 57
Lagos dos Bocas, 211, 212
La Guancha (Ponce), 224
Laguna Grande, 268
La Jungla Beach, 235
Lalin Leather Shop (San Juan), 187–188
La Mina & Big Tree Trail, 200
Languages, 38
La Parguera, 82, 224, 233–236
La Playita (San Juan), 190
La Raza Day, 53
Lares, 265
La Rumba Party Cruise (San Juan), 193
La Ruta Panorámica, 93–95
Las Cabezas de San Juan Nature Reserve (El Faro), 11–12, 81, 268
Las Croabas, 268, 269
Las Mañanitas (Ponce), 54
Las Maria's Beach, 254
La Sombrilla Rosa (San Juan), 192
Las Tortugas Adventures, 268
La Tertulia (San Juan), 181
Legends of Puerto Rico, 72
LeLoLai VIP Program, 71

LIAT, 68
Liberty Travel, 71
Librería Cronopios (San Juan), 181
Lighting of the Town of Bethlehem (San Juan), 54
Linen House (San Juan), 187
Lion Fountain (Ponce), 223
Liquor laws, 297
Loíza Aldea, 22, 182
Loíza Carnival, 53
Lost and found, 297–298
Lost-luggage insurance, 63
Luis A. Ferré Performing Arts Center, 52
Luis Muñoz Marín Foundation (San Juan), 161–162
Luis Muñoz Marín International Airport (San Juan), 96
Luis Muñoz Marín Park (San Juan), 167, 170
Luis Muñoz Rivera Park (San Juan), 167
Lupi's Mexican Grill & Sports Cantina (San Juan), 189
Luquillo Beach, 4, 198, 201–205

Malls, San Juan, 188
Manglillo Beach, 235
Manuel "Nolo" Morales beach, 206
MAPR at Plaza (San Juan), 169
Maria's (San Juan), 192
Maricao State Forest, 59, 95, 264
Marinas, 55
Markets
    Ponce, 218
    San Juan, 188
Marriage requirements, 298
Marshalls (San Juan), 184
Masks, San Juan, 181, 182
Mayagüez, 82, 245–252
Mayagüez City Hall, 248
MEDEX International, 63
Media Luna Beach, 281
MedicAlert Identification Tag, 63
Medical insurance, 62–63
Memorial to Don Domingo (Ponce), 223
Mesones gastronómicos, 71
Middles Beach ., 261
Miramar (San Juan), 100–101
    accommodations, 121–122
    restaurants, 148–149

Mofongo, 40–41
Mona Aquatics (Boquerón), 236
Mona Island, 10–11, 18, 36, 83, 251
Mona Passage, 246
Money matters, 47–49
Monte del Estado National Park, 264–265
Monte Guilarte State Forest, 56
Montones Beach, 261–262
Mosquito Bay (Phosphorescent Bay), 18, 233, 282–283
Mosquitoes, 64
Moss-Rehab, 65
Mountains, 34–35
Mrs. and Miss Boutique (San Juan), 183
Mujer de Caguaña, 212
Muñoz Marín, Luís, 32
Muñoz Rivera, Luis, Statue of (Ponce), 224
Museo de Arte (San Juan), 176
Museo de Arte Contemporáneo (San Juan), 169
Museo de Arte de Ponce, 169, 219
Museo de Arte de Puerto Rico (San Juan), 162, 169
Museo de Arte e Historia de San Juan, 163
Museo de las Américas (San Juan), 163–164
Museo del Niño (San Juan), 171
Museo de Pablo Casals (San Juan), 164
Museo Nuestras Raíces Africanas (San Juan), 165–166
Museum of History, Anthropology & Art (San Juan), 168
Museum of Puerto Rican Music (Ponce), 220
Museum of the History of Ponce (Casa Salazar; Ponce), 219–220
Music, 37–38
    Museum of Puerto Rican Music (Ponce), 220

National Plantain Festival, 53
Navio Beach, 281
Noches de galería (San Juan), 168
Nono Maldonado (San Juan), 183

Nono's (San Juan), 195
The north coast, 79–80
Northeast Puerto Rico, 80–81
Northwest Puerto Rico, 260–264
    brief description of, 79
Now, Voyager, 66
Nuestra Señora de la Candelaria (Mayagüez), 248
Nuyorican Café (San Juan), 190

Obra Galería Alegría (San Juan), 181
Observatorio de Arecibo, 209–210
Ocean Park (San Juan), 101
    accommodations, 122–124
    beach, 4, 172–173
    restaurants, 149–151
    restaurants near, 152
Ocean Sports (San Juan), 175
Off season, 50–51
Old San Juan, 100
    accommodations, 109–114
    restaurants, 133–142
Old San Juan Hotel & Casino (San Juan), 196
Old Town Hall (San Germán), 240
Olé (San Juan), 184–185
Olivia Cruises & Resorts, 66

Package deals, 70–71
Palmas del Mar, 83, 267, 273–276
Palm Court Lobby (San Juan), 192
Paradise Scuba Center (La Parguera), 233
Paradores, 71, 76
Parque Acuático Las Cascadas (Aguadilla), 262
Parque Barbosa (San Juan), 174
Parque Central Municipio de San Juan, 168
Parque Ceremonial Indígena Caguaña, 212, 213
Parque de Bombas (Ponce), 220, 221
Parque de las Cavernas del Río Camuy, 210
Parque de los Próceres (Mayagüez), 249
Parque El Faro de Rincón, 255
Parque Lineal Marti Coli (San Juan), 177

Parque Nacional Isla de Cabra (Dorado), 206
Parrot Club (San Juan), 176
The Parrot Club (San Juan), 190
Paseo de la Princesa (San Juan), 167, 192
Patron Saint Festivals, 54
Petroglyphs, 185, 212, 213, 243
Pets, 298
Phosphorescent Bay (Mosquito Bay), 18, 233, 282–283
Piña colada, 191
Pine Grove Beach, 4
Pino's Boat & Water Fun, 56, 230
Planning your trip, 45–77
    accommodations tips, 74–77
    active vacation planner, 54–62
    for cruise-ship travelers, 72–74
    customs regulations, 46–47
    entry requirements, 45–46
    escorted general-interest tours, 72
    getting around, 68–70
    health and safety, 63–65
    insurance, 62–63
    money matters, 47–49
    package deals and group tours, 70–71
    traveling to Puerto Rico, 67–68
    visitor information, 45
    when to go, 49–51
Playa Carlos Rosario, 292
Playa Chiva, 281
Playa Esperanza, 282
Playa Plata, 281
Playa Santa (Guánica), 5, 56, 230, 235
Playa Seven Seas, 270
Plaza de Colón (San Juan), 166
Plaza de Las Armas (San Juan), 166–167
Plaza del Mercado de Santurce, 188
Plaza del Quinto Centenario (San Juan), 166
Plaza de Mercado de Santurce (San Juan), 177
Plaza Las Américas (San Juan), 169, 179, 188
Plaza Las Delicias (Ponce), 217–218, 225
Plazuela de la Rogativa (San Juan), 164

Polo Ralph Lauren Factory Store (San Juan), 183
Ponce, 216–229
    accommodations, 226–227
    beaches and outdoor activities, 224–225
    brief description of, 82
    restaurants, 227–229
    shopping, 225
    sights and attractions, 217–224
    traveling to, 217
    visitor information, 217
    walking tour, 221–224
Ponce de León, Juan, 23, 25, 229
Ponce Yacht & Fishing Club, 55
Popular culture, 37–38
Population of Puerto Rico, 37
Porta Coeli (San Germán), 239
Postal services, 298
Prehistoric era, 22, 24
Princess Cruises, 73
Public Library (San Germán), 240
Públicos, 70
Puebla (Dewey), 291
Puente de los Léones (Ponce), 223
Puerta de Tierra (San Juan), 100
    accommodations, 114–116
    restaurants, 142–144
Puerto Chico, 55
Puerto del Rey Marina, 55, 271
Puerto Real, 55
Puerto Rican Arts & Crafts (San Juan), 185–186
Puerto Rican Danza Week (San Juan), 52
Puerto Rico Convention Center (San Juan), 176
Puerto Rico Discovery Day, 53
Puerto Rico Miguel José Miguel Agrelot Coliseum (San Juan), 176
Puerto Rico Symphonic Orchestra, 52
Puerto Rico Tourism Company, 76
Puerto Rico Tours, 72
Punta Las Marías (San Juan), 101, 173
Punta Mula lighthouse, 280
Puntas Surf School, 254

Quebradillas, 262
Quincentennial Plaza (San Juan), 166

Radisson Seven Seas Cruises, 73–74
Raven Room (San Juan), 192–193
Red Beach (Bahia Corcha), 281
Reggaeton, 37
Regions in brief, 78–83
Reinhold Jewelers (San Juan), 187
Religions, 38–39
Restaurants. See also Restaurant Index
    Arecibo, 210–211
    best, 16–17
    Boquerón, 238
    central mountains, 214–215
    Culebra, 294–295
    Dorado, 208–209
    Fajardo, 272–273
    Guánica, 232–233
    La Parguera, 236
    Luquillo Beach/Río Grande area, 204–205
    Mayagüez, 250
    Palmas del Mar, 275–276
    Ponce, 227–229
    Rincón, 258–260
    San Germán, 241
    San Juan, 130–157
    Vieques, 287–290
Rico Suntours (San Juan), 169
Rincón, 79, 252–260
Rincón Lighthouse Park, 255
The Rincón Surf School, 254
Río Abajo State Forest, 56, 211
Río Bayamón Golf Course, 174
Río Camuy Caves, 11, 35–36, 79, 210
Río Grande, 201, 202
    accommodations, 203–204
Río Piedras (San Juan), 102
Ritz-Carlton Casino (San Juan), 196
Ritz-Carlton San Juan Hotel, Spa & Casino, spa at, 177
Rivera, Luis Muñoz, Birthday of, 53
Road food, 18–19
Road maps, 69–70
Rock Bottom (Rincón), 260
Royal Caribbean International, 74
Rum, 43, 171
Rumba (San Juan), 190, 195
Rum Shack (Rincón), 260
Running, San Juan, 174

S afety, 298
Safety concerns, 64–65
SAGA Holidays, 67
Sailing. *See* Boating and sailing
San Blas de Illescas Half Marathon (Coamo), 51
Sandflies, 64
Sandy Beach, 254
San Germán, 82, 239–241
San Germán de Auxerre, 240
San Juan, 96–196. *See also specific neighborhoods*
   accommodations, 1, 108–129
      apartment rentals, 113
      Condado, 116–121
      family-friendly, 127
      Isla Verde, 124–129
      Miramar, 121–122
      Old San Juan, 109–114
      Puerta de Tierra, 114–116
      reservations, 108–109
      Santurce and Ocean Park, 122–124
      taxes and service charges, 108
   arriving in, 96–99
   banks, 105
   beaches, 172–173
   brief description of, 78–79
   consulates, 106
   currency exchange, 106
   drugstores, 106
   emergencies, 106
   finding an address in, 100
   getting around by taxi, 102–105
   hospitals, 106
   Internet access, 106
   layout of, 99–100
   neighborhoods in brief, 100–102
   nightlife, 188–196
   parking, 98–99
   picnic fare and places, 151
   police, 106
   post office, 106
   restaurants, 1–2, 130–157
      best bets, 131–133
      Condado, 144–148
      Isla Verde, 152–156
      Miramar, 148–149
      near Ocean Park, 152
      Old San Juan, 133–142
      Puerta de Tierra, 142–144
      Santurce and Ocean Park, 149–151
   restrooms, 107
   safety, 107

shopping, 179–188
sights and attractions, 158–171
   for kids, 170–171
sightseeing tours, 168–170
sports and outdoor activities, 172–179
street maps, 100
suburbs of, 102
taxis, 97, 102–103
visitor information, 99
San Juan Bautista Day, 52
San Juan Bay Marina, 173
San Juan Cemetery, 164
San Juan Central Park, 174, 178
San Juan Gate, 164
San Juan National Historic Site, 158
San Juan Vacations, 113
San Juan Water Fun, 56
San Sebastián Street (San Juan), 194–195
San Sebastián Street Festival (San Juan), 51
Santos, 185, 239
Santurce (San Juan)
   accommodations, 122–124
   restaurants, 149–151
SATH (Society for Accessible Travel & Hospitality), 65
Scotia Bank (Ponce), 223
Scuba diving, 59–60
   best, 7–8
   Boquerón, 236
   Culebra, 292
   Fajardo, 271
   Guánica, 230
   La Parguera, 233
   Palmas del Mar, 274–275
   Río Grande, 202–203
   San Juan, 174–175
   the southwest coast, 229
   Vieques, 282
Seaborne Airlines, 68
Semana de la "Danza" Puerto-rriqueña (San Juan), 52
Senior travel, 66–67
Siddhia Hutchinson Fine Art Studio & Gallery (Vieques), 290
Sights and attractions, best, 15–16
Slavery, 25, 29–30
Smoking, 298
Snorkeling, 60–61
   Aguadilla and Isabela, 261
   best beaches for, 6, 8–9
   Boquerón, 236
   Fajardo, 270

   Guánica, 230
   La Parguera, 233
   Palmas del Mar, 274–275
   Rincón, 252, 254–255
   Río Grande, 202–203
   San Juan area, 175–176
   Vieques, 282
SoFo (San Juan), 176
Sofrito, 39
Sonne (San Juan), 190
Southeast Puerto Rico, 82–83, 276–277
The southern mountains, 242–244
The southwest coast, 81–82, 229–238
Spanish Wall, 254
Spas and fitness centers
   Fajardo, 272
   San Juan, 177–179
Special events and festivals, 51–54
Spicy Caribbee (San Juan), 183
Spiritualism (espiritsmo), 39
Statehood, 22, 32–33
Steps Beach (Tres Palmas Beach), 254
Sugar Harvest Festival (San Germán), 52
Sun Bay (Sombe) public beach, 280, 281
Sun exposure, 64
Sunshine Tours, 72, 169
Surfing, 61
   best beaches for, 5
   Rincón, 252, 254

T aíno Divers (Rincón), 254
Taíno Indians, 24, 26–27, 229, 251
   burial and ceremonial sites, 213
   petroglyphs, 185, 212, 213, 243
Tamarindo Beach, 234–235
Tamboo Tavern (Rincón), 260
Taxes, 298
Teatro la Perla (Ponce), 220, 223
Teatro Tapía (San Juan), 166, 189
Telephone, 298–299
Temperatures, average, 49
Tennis, 61
   best, 9, 10
   Fajardo, 270
   Palmas del Mar, 275
   Ponce, 225
   San Juan, 178

Three Kings Day, 51
Tia Maria's Liquor Store
  (San Juan), 196
Tibes Indian Ceremonial Center
  (near Ponce), 213, 220–221
Tienda del Instituto de Cultura
  Puertorriqueño (San Juan),
  186
Time Out Family Amusement
  Center (San Juan), 171
Time zone, 299
Tipping, 299
Tomás Vivoni House (San
  Germán), 239–240
Toro Negro Forest Reserve, 57,
  59, 85, 94, 242–243
Tourism industry, 21
Tourist information, 45
TourScan Inc., 71
Transportation, 68
Travel Assistance Interna-
  tional, 63
Traveler's checks, 48–49
Travelex Insurance Services, 62
Travel Guard International, 62
Traveling to Puerto Rico, 67–68
Travel insurance, 62–63
Travel Insured International, 62
Tren Urbano (San Juan), 104
Tres Palmas Beach (Steps
  Beach), 254
Trip-cancellation insurance, 62
The Tropical Agricultural
  Research Station
  (Mayagüez), 249
Truman, Harry S., 32
Trump International Golf Club
  Puerto Rico (Río Grande),
  golf courses at, 174, 202

Unemployment, 22
United States Tour Operators
  Association, 71
United Vacations, 71
University of Puerto Rico
  Mayagüez Campus, 248
US Airways, 68
US Airways Vacations, 70
Utopía (Ponce), 225
Utuado, 212

Vacations to Go, 72
Vacation Together, 71
Vaccinations, 46
Vaughn's Gifts & Crafts
  (San Juan), 186
Velauno (San Juan), 179

Veranda Terrace (Mayagüez),
  250, 252
VHR, Worldwide, 77
Vida Urbana (San Juan), 113
Viejo Alcaldía (San Germán),
  240
Vieques, 18, 36, 83, 278–291
  accommodations, 283–287
  getting around, 280–281
  nightlife, 290–291
  outdoor activities, 282–283
  restaurants, 287–290
  shopping, 290
  traveling to, 280
Vieques National Wildlife
  Refuge, 286
Villa Marina Yacht Harbour,
  55, 271
Villas and vacation homes,
  76–77
Visitor information, 45

Water, drinking, 64
Watersports, 56. See also
  specific sports
  Aguadilla and Isabela,
    261–262
  Fajardo, 270–271
  Mayagüez, 249
Weights and measures, 299
West Coast Surf Shop (Rincón),
  254
The western mountains,
  264–266
Wet Bar (San Juan), 193
Wet Boutique (San Juan), 183
Wheelchair accessibility, 65–66
White Christmas Festival
  (Old San Juan), 54
Wilderness Beach, 261
Window of the Sea Park
  (San Juan), 101
Windsurfing, 61–62
  best beaches for, 5
Windsurfing and kite surfing,
  San Juan, 179
Wyndham Río Mar Beach
  Resort and Spa
  golf courses at, 174, 202
  traveling to, 201

Xian Imports (San Juan), 186

Yaguez Theater (Mayagüez),
  248
Yerba Buena (San Juan), 190

Zabó (San Juan), 193–194
Zen Spa (San Juan), 178
Zoni Beach, 292

ACCOMMODATIONS
Acacia Seaside Inn (San Juan),
  119–120
Aleli by the Sea (San Juan),
  119–120
Atlantic Beach Hotel
  (San Juan), 120
Bahia Salinas Beach Resort &
  Spa (Boquerón), 236–237
Bananas Guesthouse (Vieques),
  285
Beside the Pointe Guesthouse
  (Rincón), 257
Best Western Hotel Pierre
  (San Juan), 118
Borinquen Beach Inn
  (San Juan), 129
Bravo Beach Hotel (Vieques),
  283
The Caleta Guesthouse
  (San Juan), 113
Caribe Hilton (San Juan), 114,
  116, 127
Casa de Amistad (Vieques), 285
Casa del Caribe (San Juan), 120
Casa Ensenada Waterfront
  Guesthouse (Culebra), 293
Casa Grande Mountain Retreat
  (Utuado), 212, 214
Casa Isleña Inn (Rincón), 256
Ceiba Country Inn, 201
Chateau Cervantes (San Juan),
  109
Club Seabourne (Culebra), 293
Cofresi Beach Hotel
  (Boquerón), 237
Comfort Inn (San Juan),
  118–119
Condado Plaza Hotel & Casino
  (San Juan), 116–117
Copamarina Beach Resort
  (Guánica), 231
The Coquí Inn (San Juan), 129
Courtyard by Marriott Isla
  Verde Beach Resort (San
  Juan), 127, 128
Crow's Nest (Vieques), 285–286
Da House (San Juan), 112
Dorado Beach Resort & Club,
  206–207
El Canario by the Lagoon Hotel
  (San Juan), 119
El Canario Inn (San Juan), 121

El Conquistador Resort & Golden Door Spa (Fajardo), 271

El Nuevo Horizonte (Yabucoa), 277

El San Juan Hotel & Casino, 124

Embassy Guest House Condado (San Juan), 121

Embassy Suites Dorado del Mar Beach & Golf Resort, 207–208

Embassy Suites Hotel & Casino (San Juan), 128

The Fajardo Inn (Fajardo), 272

Four Points by Sheraton Palmas del Mar Resort, 275

Gallery Inn at Galería San Juan, 110, 112

Gran Melia Puerto Rico (Río Grande), 203

The Great Escape (Vieques), 286

Hacienda del Mar: A Hyatt Vacation Club Resort (Dorado), 208

Hacienda Gripiñas (Coamo), 243–244

Hacienda Tamarindo (Vieques), 284–285

Hampton Inn (San Juan), 127, 128–129

Hilton Ponce Golf & Casino Resort, 226

Hix House (Vieques), 283–284

Holiday Inn & Tropical Casino (Mayagüez), 249

Holiday Inn Express (San Juan), 121

Horned Dorset Primavera (Rincón), 255–256

Hosteria del Mar (San Juan), 122–123

Hotel Bélgica, 227

Hotel El Convento (San Juan), 109–110

Hotel Milano (San Juan), 112

Hotel Parador Palmas de Lucía (Yabucoa), 277

Howard Johnson Downtown Mayagüez, 249–250

Howard Johnson Hotel (San Juan), 129

Howard Johnson Old San Juan Hotel Plaza de Armas, 112, 114

Howard Johnson Ponce, 226

Inn on the Blue Horizon (Vieques), 284

Inter-Continental San Juan Resort & Casino, 124, 126

La Concha: A Renaissance Resort (San Juan), 117

La Finca Caribe Guest House & Cottages (Vieques), 286–287

La Jamaka (La Parguera), 233

The Lazy Parrot (Rincón), 257

Lemontree Waterfront Suites (Rincón), 256–257

Marriott Courtyard Aguadilla, 263

Marriott Courtyard San Juan Miramar, 122

Mary Lee's by the Sea (near Guánica), 231–232

Mayagüez Resort & Casino, 246, 250

Meliá (Ponce), 226–227

Normandie Hotel (San Juan), 116

Número 1 Guest House (San Juan), 123

Oceana Hostal Playero (San Juan), 123

Parador Baños de Coamo, 241–242

Parador Boquemar (Boquerón), 237–238

Parador El Guajataca (Quebradillas), 263

Parador El Oasis (San Germán), 241

Parador Guánica 1929, 232

Parador Hacienda Juanita (Maricao), 265–266

Parador Posada Porlamar (La Parguera), 233–234

Parador Villa Antonio (Rincón), 258

Parador Villa Parguera (La Parguera), 234–236

Parador Vistamar (Quebradillas), 263

Posada la Hamaca (Culebra), 293–294

Radisson Ambassador Plaza Hotel & Casino (San Juan), 118

Rincón Beach Resort, 256

The Río Mar Beach Resort & Spa, A Wyndham Grand Resort (Río Grande), 203–204

Ritz-Carlton San Juan Spa & Casino, 126, 127

San Juan MarRiott Resort & Stellaris Casino, 117–118

Sheraton Old San Juan Hotel & Casino, 110

Tamarindo Estates (Culebra), 293

Trade Winds Guesthouse (Vieques), 287

Tres Palmas Inn (San Juan), 123–124

Tres Sirenas Beach Inn (Rincón), 257

Vieques Ocean View Hotel, 287

Villa Boheme (Culebra), 294

Villa Cofresi (Rincón), 258

Villa Del Rey (San Germán), 241

Villa Montana Beach Resort (Isabela), 264

Villas at Palmas del Mar, 275

Villas del Mar Hau (Isabela), 264

The Water Club (San Juan), 127

At Wind Chimes Inn (San Juan), 120, 127

RESTAURANTS

Ajili Mójili (San Juan), 145

Al Dente (San Juan), 136–137

Alexandra (Guánica), 232

The Algave Ranch (San Juan), 155

Amadeus (San Juan), 137

The Ambassador Grill (San Juan), 146

Aquaviva (San Juan), 133–134

Augusto's Cuisine (San Juan), 148

Bananas Restaurant (Vieques), 288

Barú (San Juan), 134

bbh (Vieques), 288–289

Bistro de Paris (San Juan), 149

Blossoms (Fajardo), 272

BLT Steak (San Juan), 153

Blue Hawaii (Palmas del Mar), 276

The Blue Marlin (Guánica), 232–233

Bodega Chic (San Juan), 137

Bodega Compostela (San Juan), 145

Brass Cactus (Luquillo), 204

Budatai (San Juan), 144

Burén (San Juan), 137

Café Berlin (San Juan), 138

Café del Angel (San Juan), 147

Café Media Luna (Vieques), 287–288

Café Puerto Rico (San Juan), 141

Café Tomas/Café Tompy (Ponce), 224
Caña (San Juan), 138–139
Carambola (Vieques), 288
Carli Café Concierto (San Juan), 134–135
Chayote (San Juan), 148–149
Che's (San Juan), 152
Chez Daniel (Palmas del Mar), 276
Chez Shack (Vieques), 289
Ciao Mediterranean Café (San Juan), 154, 155–156
Cielito Lindo (San Juan), 147
Danny's International Restaurant (San Juan), 147–148
Deliro (San Juan), 149
Dinghy Dock (Culebra), 294
Don Tello (San Juan), 150–151
Dragonfly (San Juan), 139
El Batey (Culebra), 294
El Castillo (Mayagüez), 250
El Hamburger (San Juan), 143–144
El Jibarito (San Juan), 138
El Mojito (Guavate), 214
El Patio (Vieques), 289
El Patio de Sam (San Juan), 139
El Picoteo (San Juan), 139
El Rancho Original (Guavate), 214
El Rincón Familiar (Aibonito), 215
El Vigia (Dorado), 208
Galloway's (Boquerón), 238
Great Taste (San Juan), 147
Hacienda del Sol Restaurant (Dorado), 208
Heather's Pizzeria (Culebra), 295
Horned Dorset Primavera (Rincón), 258
Il Perugino (San Juan), 134
Island Steak House (Vieques), 288
Jájome Terrace (Cayey), 215
J. B. Hidden Village Hotel (Aguada), 260

La Bombonera (San Juan), 142
La Casa del Guanime (Guavate), 214
La Casita (La Parguera), 236
La Casita Blanca (San Juan), 152
La Casona (San Juan), 150
La Casona de Juanita (Maricao), 265–266
La Cava (Ponce), 227
La Mallorquina (San Juan), 140
La Piccola Fontana (San Juan), 154
La Piedra Restaurant (Aibonito), 215
Las Cascadas (Boquerón), 238
Los Amigos (Guavate), 214
Los Pinos (Guavate), 214
Madrid-San Juan (San Juan), 143
MakaRios (San Juan), 140
Mamacita's (Culebra), 294–295
Mark's at the Meliá (Ponce), 227–229
Metropol (San Juan), 156
Morton's of Chicago (San Juan), 142–143
Niché (San Juan), 145–146
Old Harbor Brewery Steak and Lobster House (San Juan), 140–141
Ostra Cosa (San Juan), 141
Otello's (Fajardo), 272–273
Outback Steakhouse (San Juan), 155
Palio (Río Grande), 204–205
The Palm (San Juan), 153
Palmera (San Juan), 154
Palmeras (San Juan), 143
Pamela's (San Juan), 150
Panaderia/Cafeteria Calvache (Rincón), 259–260
Panadería España Repostería (San Juan), 156
Parrot Club (San Juan), 135
Patio del Nispero (San Juan), 142
Pikayo (San Juan), 150

Pinky's (San Juan), 151
Raíces (San Juan), 142
Ramiro's (San Juan), 144
Repostería Kassalta (San Juan), 151
Ristorante Tuscany (San Juan), 146
Roberto's Fish Net (Boquerón), 238
Roberto's Restaurant Villa Playera (Boquerón), 238
The Rum Shack (Rincón), 259
Ruth's Chris Steak House (San Juan), 153
Salitre Mesón Costero (Arecibo), 210–211
Sand and the Sea Inn (Cayey), 215
Sandy's Seafood Restaurant & Steak House (Río Grande), 205
Smiling Joe's (Rincón), 259
Sofia (San Juan), 135
Soleil Beach Club Piñones, 157
Stingray Café (Fajardo), 273
Taíno's Seafood & Steak House (Guánica), 233
Tamboo Tavern and Seaside Grill Restaurant (Rincón), 259
Tangerine (San Juan), 154
Tantra (San Juan), 141, 195
Tapas Café (San Germán), 241
Taverna Española (Vieques), 289–290
Tierra Santa Restaurant (San Juan), 152
Tío Pepe Restaurant (Aibonito), 215
Toro Salao (San Juan), 135–136
Trade Winds Restaurant (Vieques), 290
Trois Cent Onze (San Juan), 136
Trulio's Sea Food (Punta Santiago), 276
Via Appia (San Juan), 148
Yamato (San Juan), 154–155
Zabó (San Juan), 146
Zafra Restaurant (Dorado), 208–209